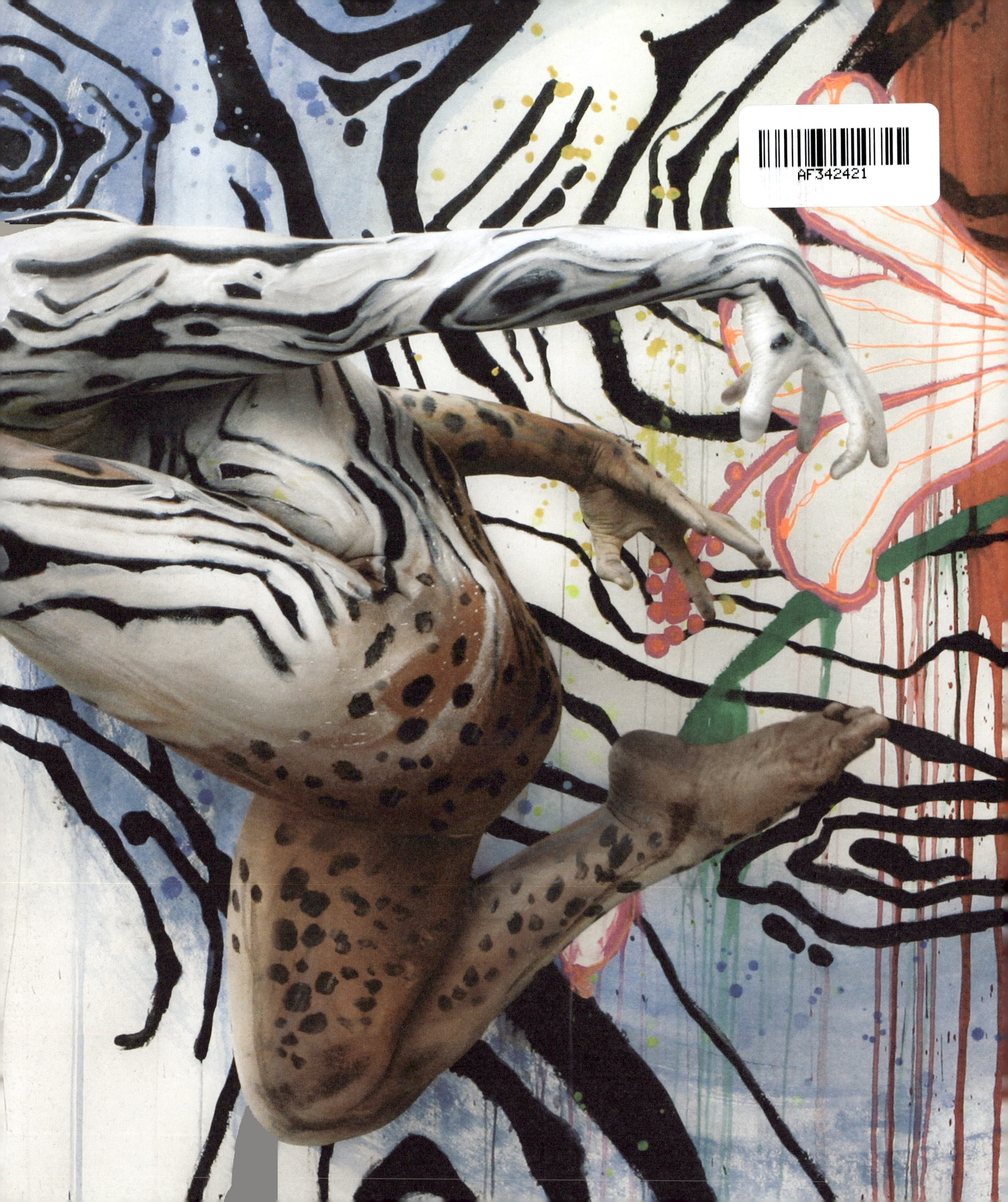
AF342421

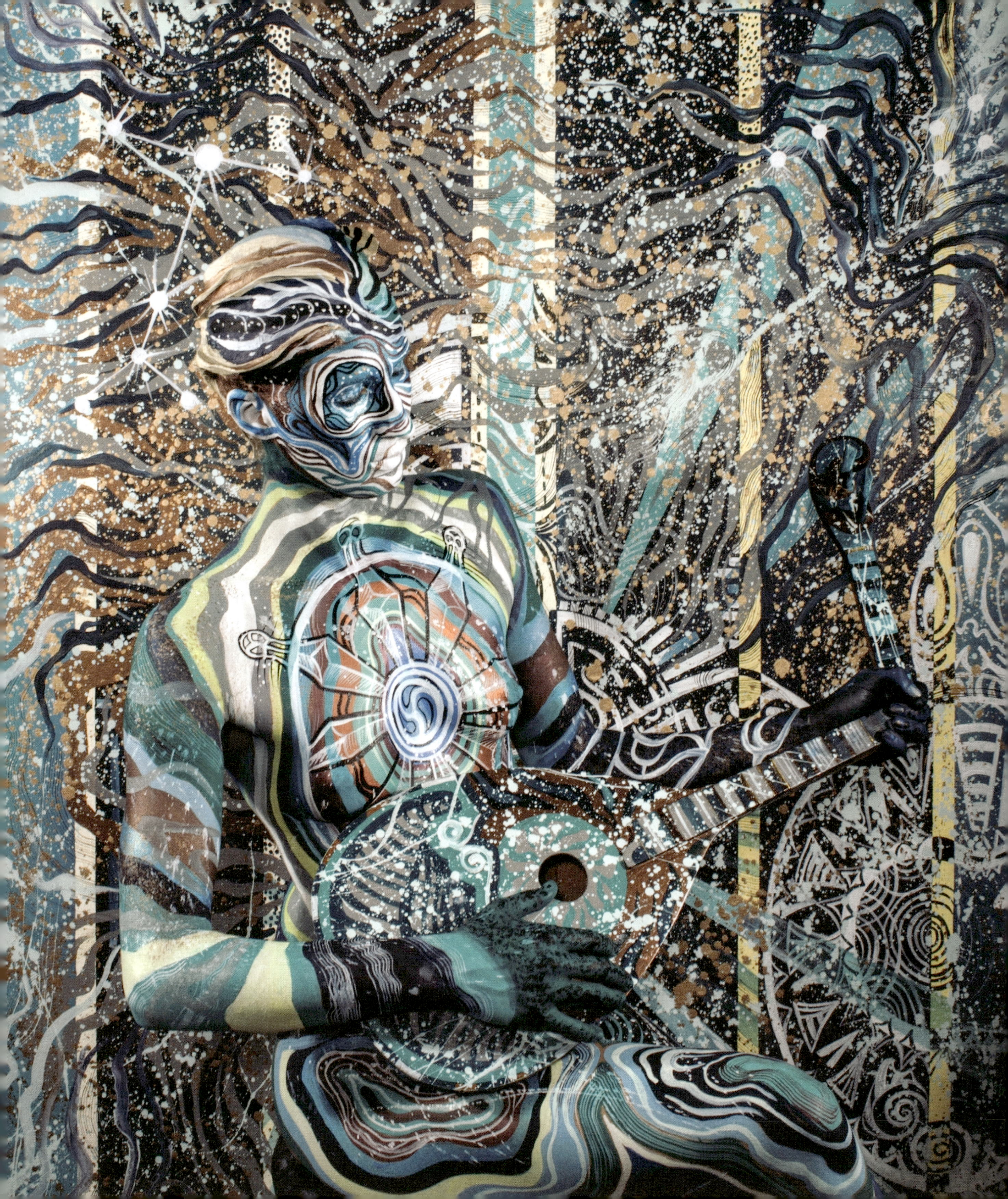

THE HUMAN CANVAS

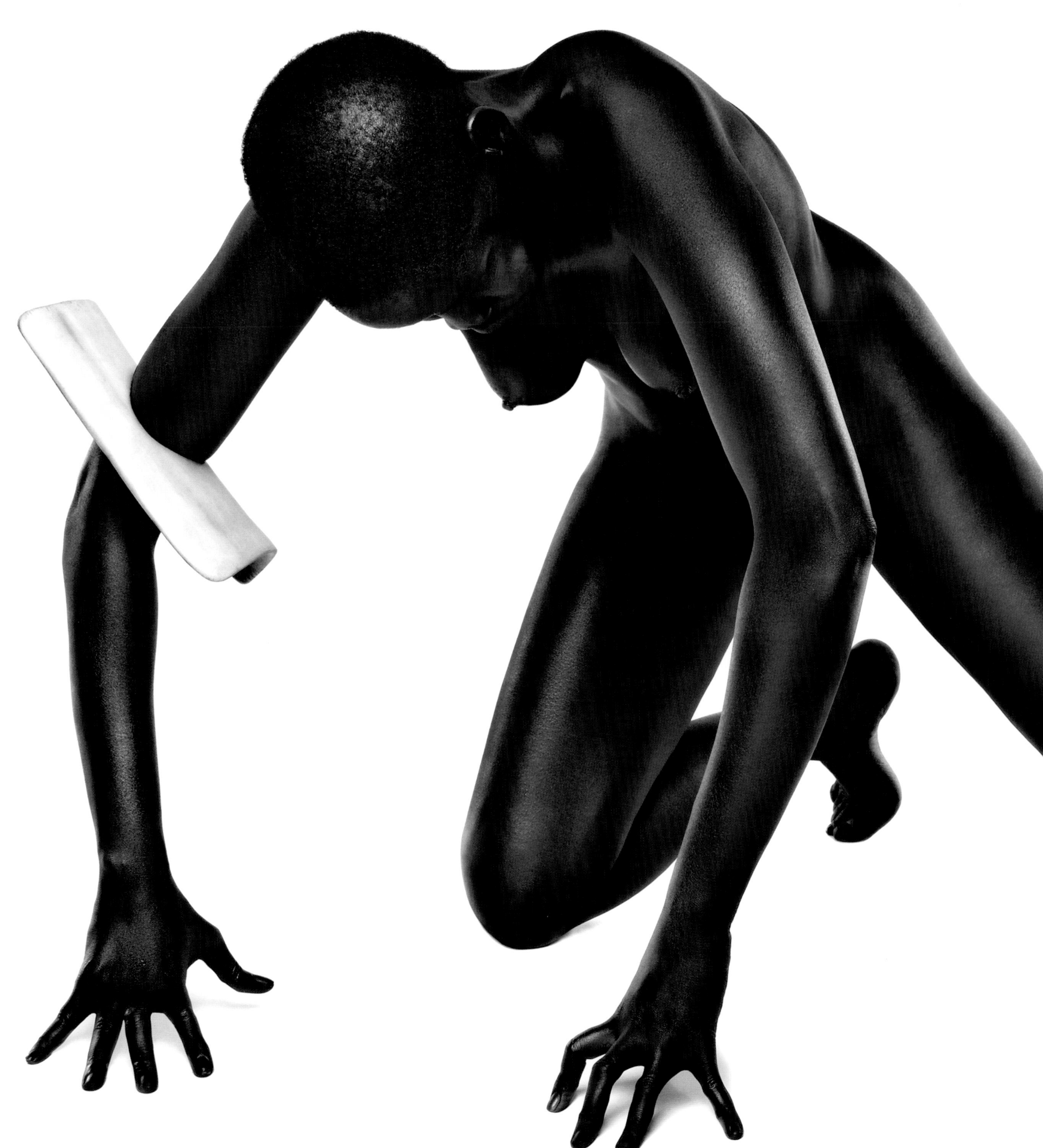

THE HUMAN CANVAS

THE WORLD'S BEST BODY PAINTINGS | KARALA B.

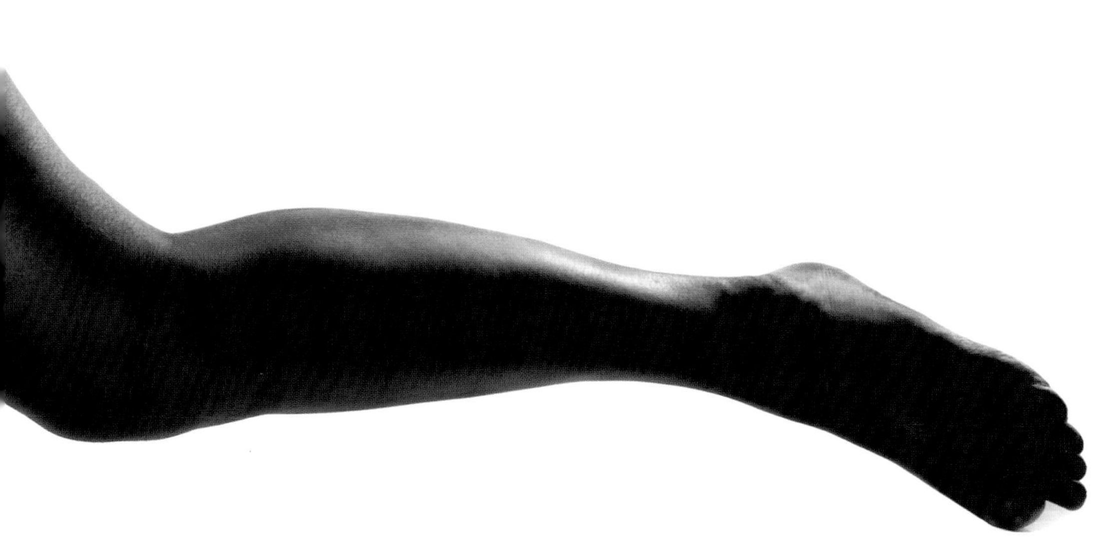

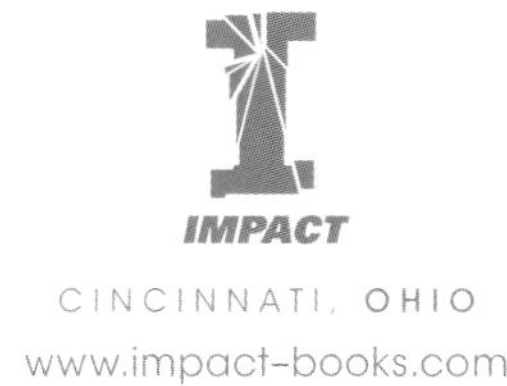

IMPACT

CINCINNATI, OHIO

www.impact-books.com

This book is dedicated to a very special artist, a man who is truly a champion at heart.

I first met Brian Wolfe and his twin brother, Nick, in Holland in November 2004 at a bodypainting event. I walked into a restaurant and heard roars of laughter coming from a large group of artists. Nick and Brian were spreading their joy.

Over the years I crossed paths with these two amazing men in countries around the world and observed the way they spread positive energy and thought, artistic ability and a love for art to the people around them. I was constantly impressed by their openness, honesty and joy. They were full of acceptance and patience. They were truly in a place of nonjudgment. Brian and Nick were enjoying a highly awarded arts career together as well as spreading their talent through teaching around the world.

In July 2012 I was sitting with artists in the week running up to the World Bodypainting Festival when Nick and Brian's absence was noticed. The news spread through the room like fire that Brian had been diagnosed with pancreatic cancer. There was such an outpouring of love for this man and a desire to do everything possible to help.

And so this book came into being. Through the great efforts of many artist friends and colleagues, a group of artists has come together to share what they do best in support of one of their own. Sadly, Brian passed away in October 2013, leaving behind a wife, daughter, brother and family as well as many friends around the world who were touched by his life. Proceeds from every sale of this book will go to Brian's dear wife.

With love and admiration,
KARALA B.

"Imagine a painter who can create an image from an idea in the fullness of color, design and expression, and then imagine this artist asking their canvas to sing, dance or scream."
—Karala B.

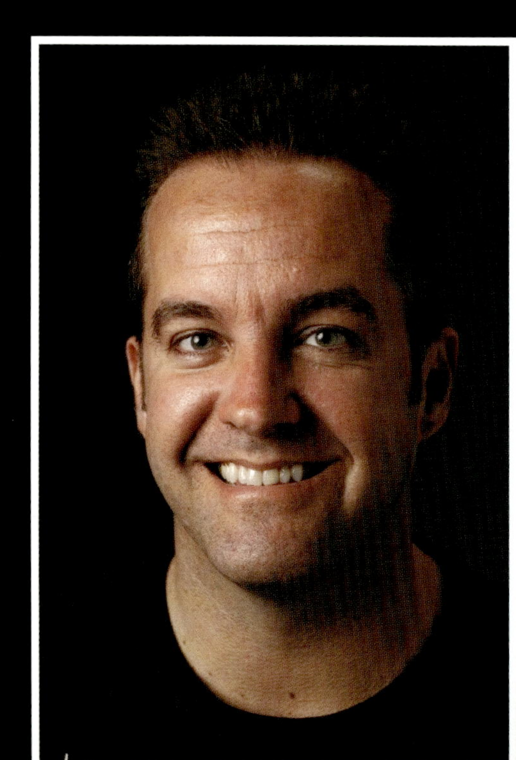

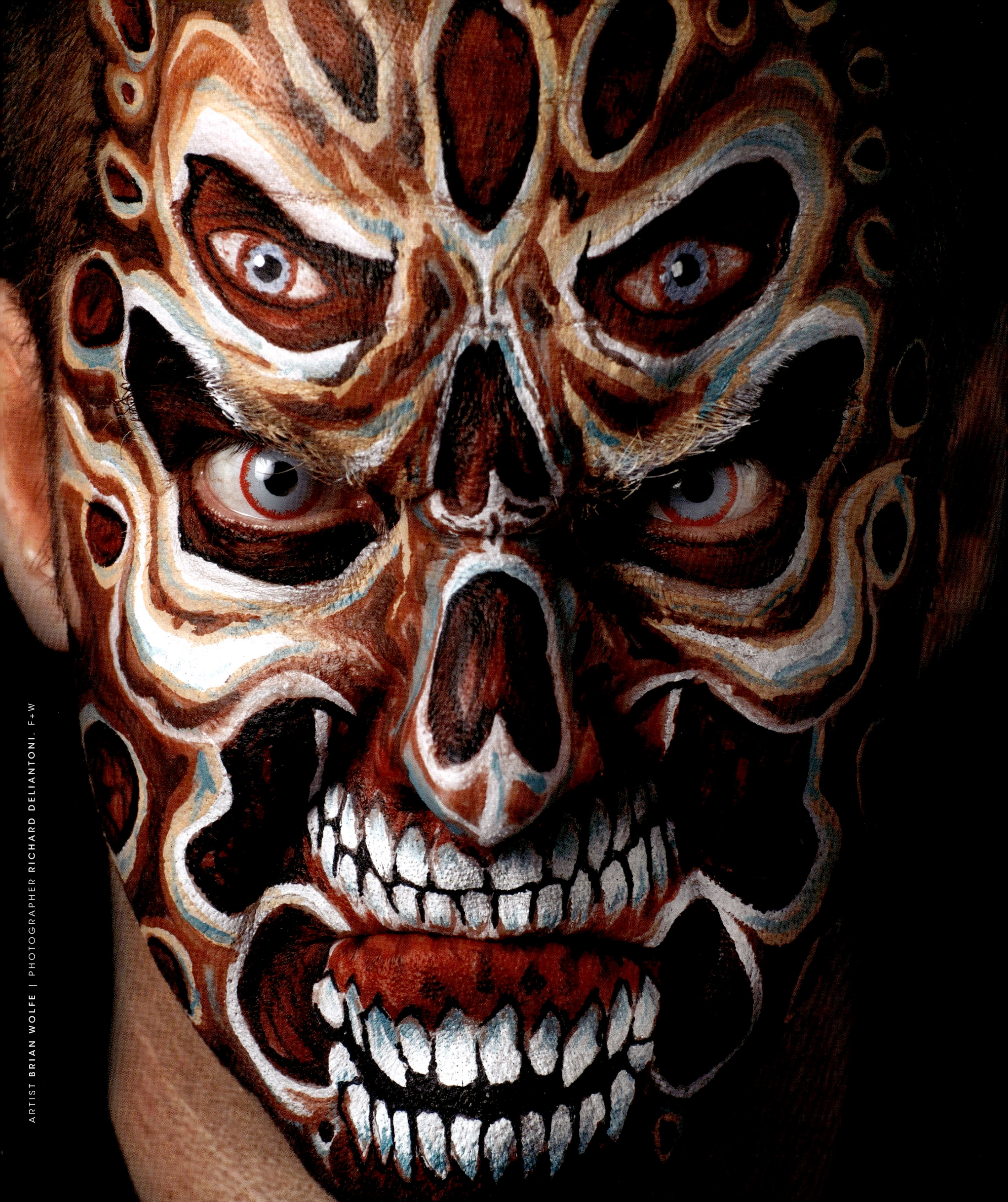
ARTIST BRIAN WOLFE | PHOTOGRAPHER RICHARD DELIANTONI. F+W

Contents

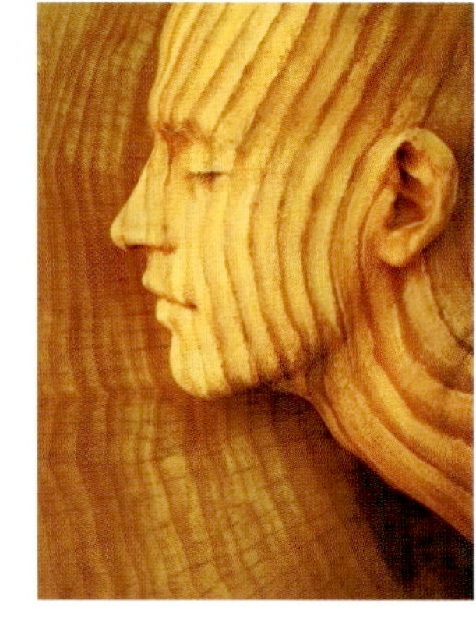

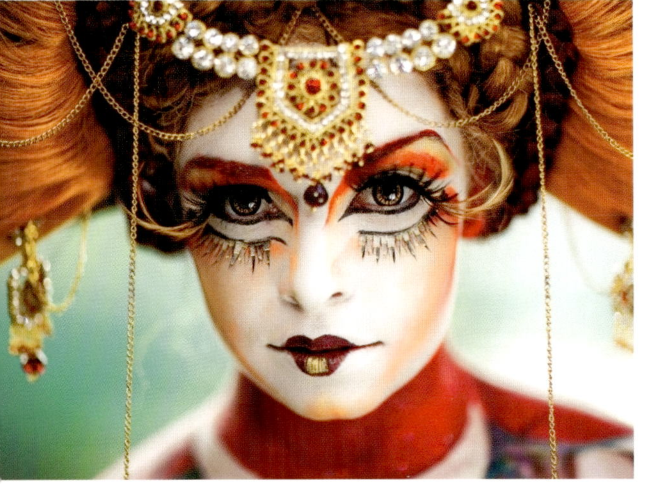

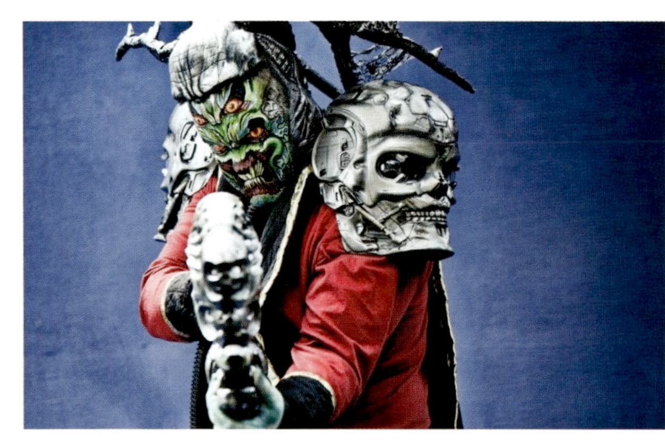

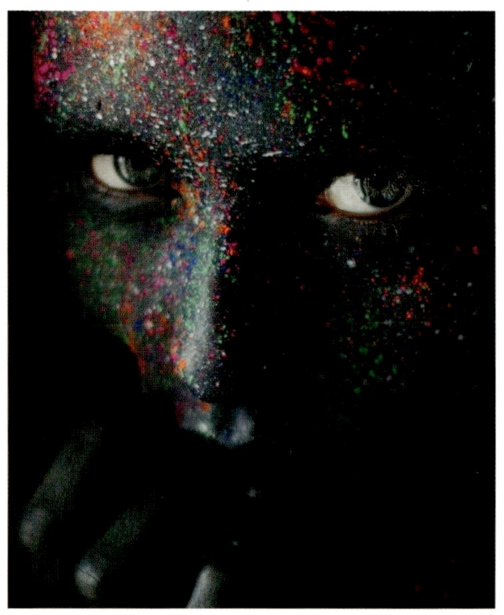

INTRODUCTION 8   WORLD BODYPAINTING FESTIVAL 10   ALEX HANSEN 48
BIRGIT MÖRTL 72   CAROLYN ROPER 82   CRAIG TRACY 86   EINAT DAN 100
JINNY (GENEVIÈVE HOULE) 140   JOHANNES STÖTTER 144   KARALA B. 150
NICK & BRIAN WOLFE 180   SCOTT FRAY & MADELYN GRECO 186

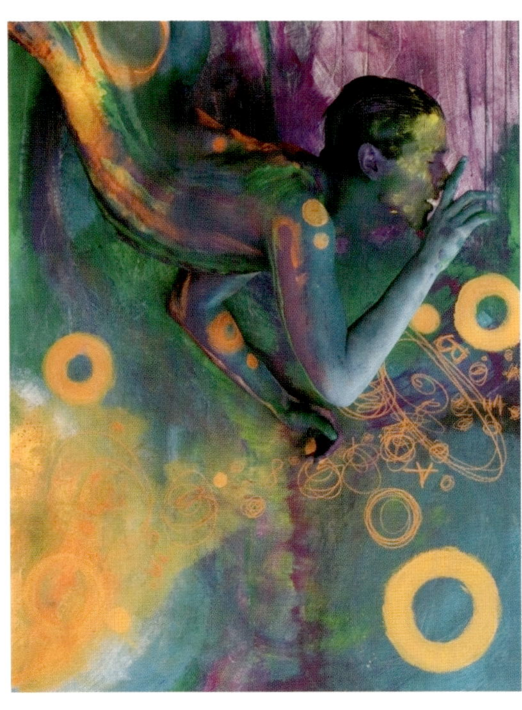

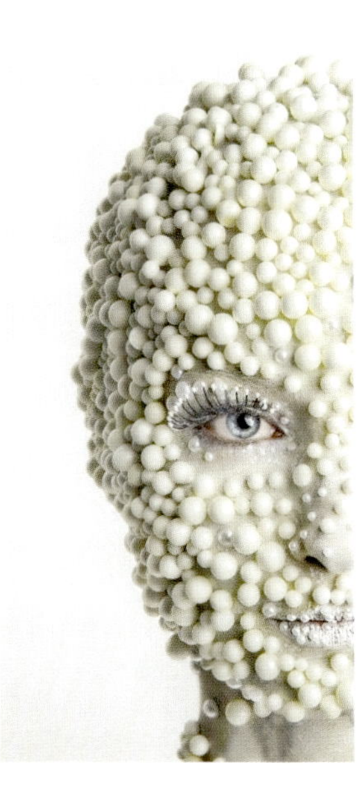

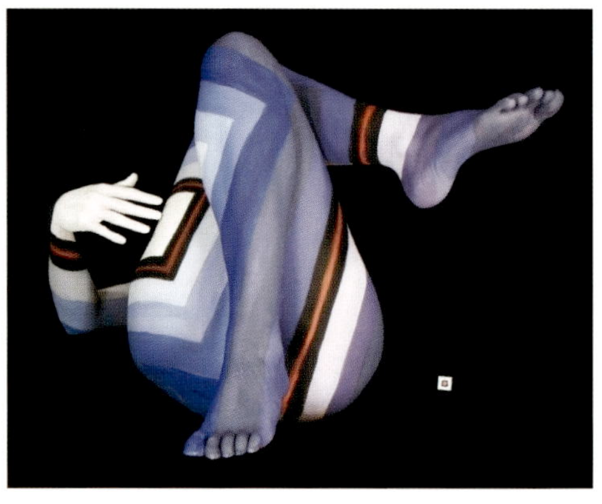

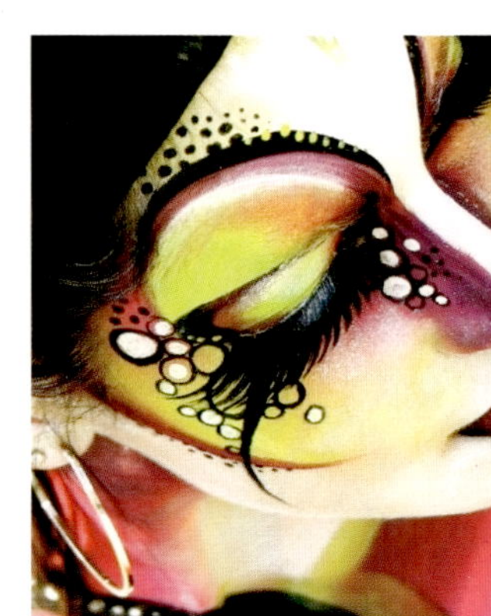

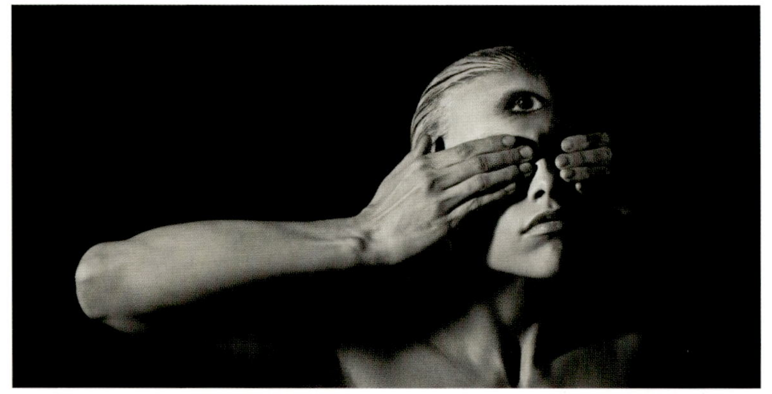

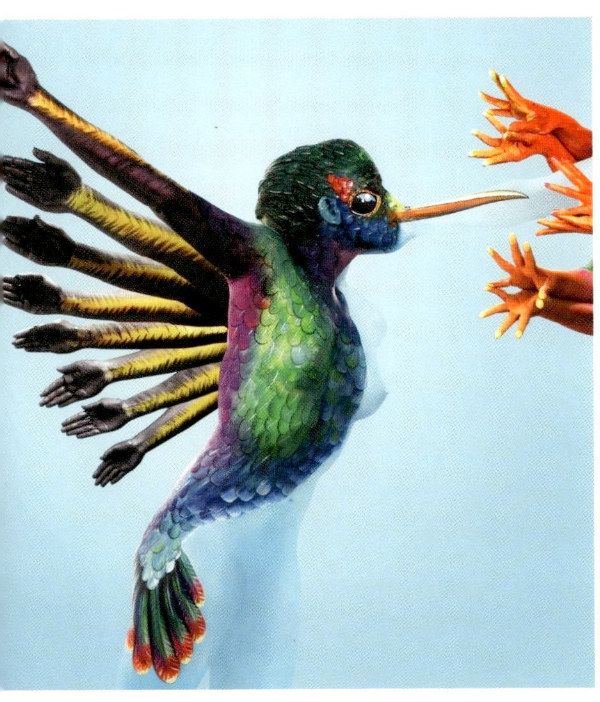
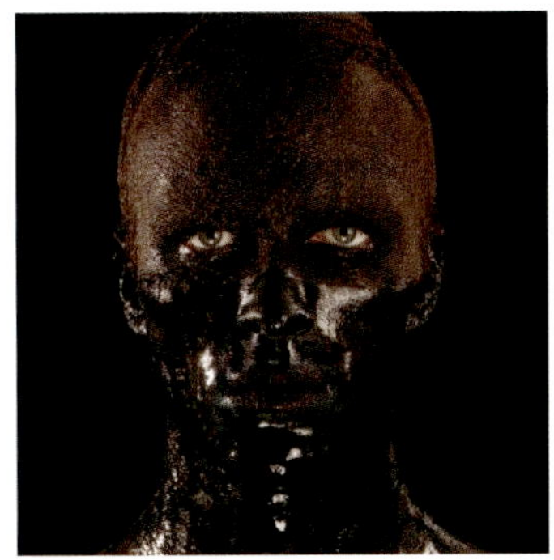
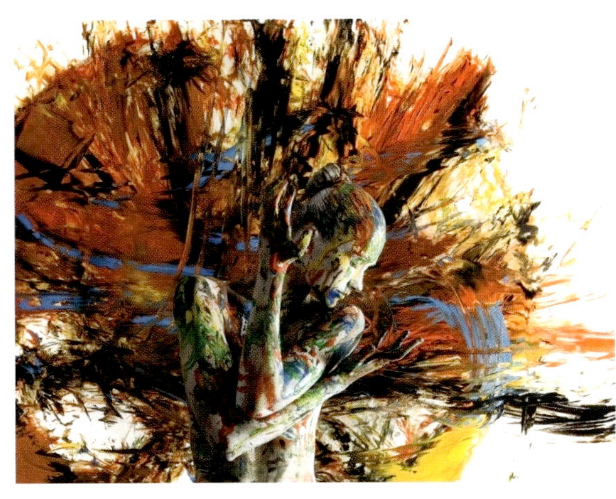
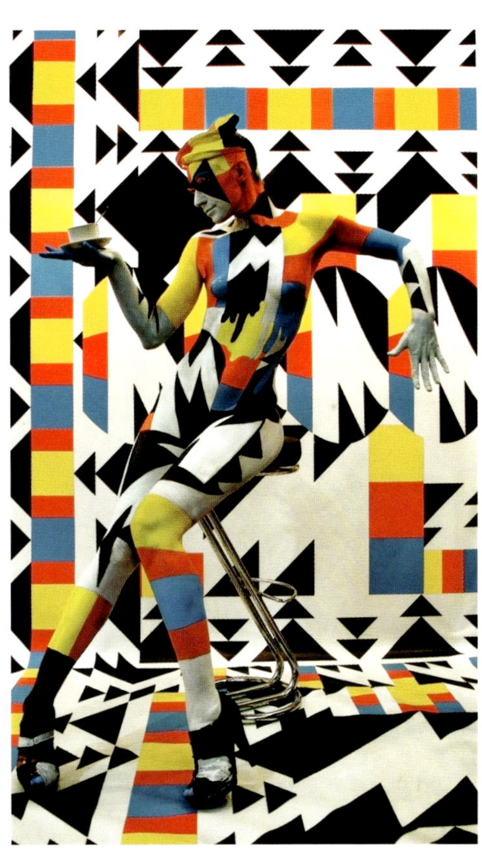

ART COLOR BALLET, DIRECTED BY AGNIESZKA GLINSKA 54   BELLA VOLEN 64
ELENA TAGLIAPIETRA 112   FILIPPO IOCO 118   HELEN DEMI 136
KAREN YIU 158   KATE DEAN 164   KRISTINA ELIZAROVA 168   MIKE SHANE 174
GALLERY 194   CONCLUSION 204   ABOUT THE AUTHOR 205   INDEX 206

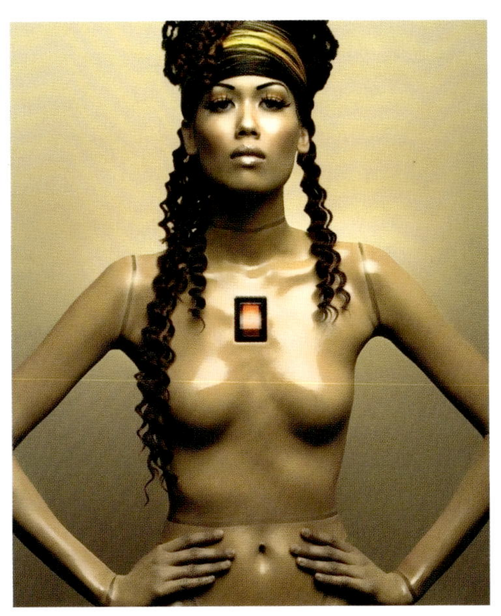
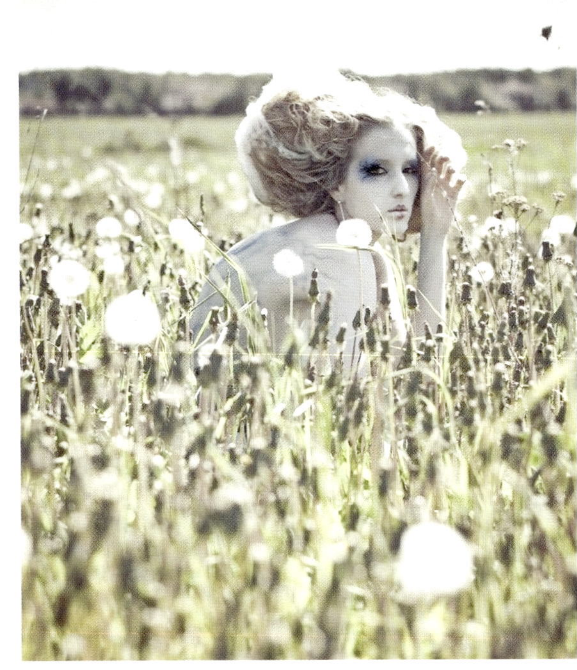
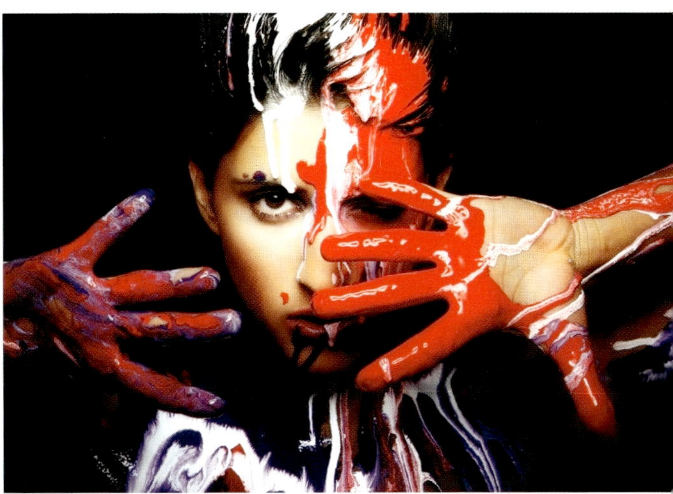
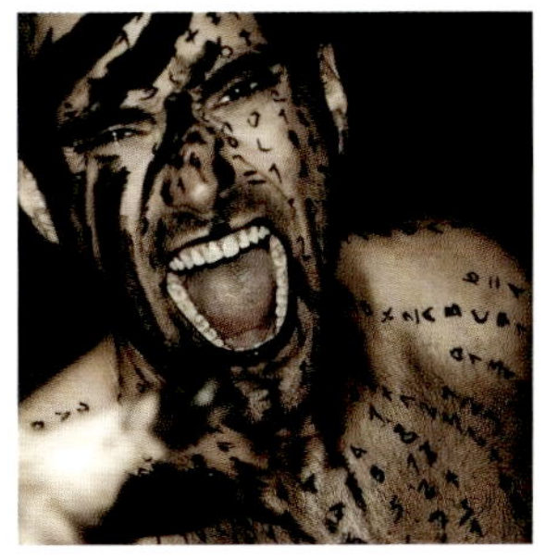

Introduction

Bodypainting has been used for tens of thousands of years in traditional cultures all over the world. Some of those cultures are still practicing their traditions today; some we know only through the records of history and the paintings on cave walls. Traditional cultures using body art demonstrate common links between history, spirituality and the body. Ceremonies are used in every culture to commemorate birth, death, weddings and coming of age. Covering the body with symbols and imagery increases the potency of ritual by clothing the skin in thoughts and emotions. Painting onto the body is a process of transformation and enlargement of the soul.

Many styles and uses for body art can be seen over this great expanse of time. The interesting fact is that it has been used on every continent around the world, and linking themes run through these styles of art. Humans have had a natural connection to creating art on our bodies, and it's no surprise that modern forms of art are reinterpreting the ancient practices and expressions.

The root of bodypainting today comes from those traditional civilizations. The modern-day culture of body art reaches around the world throughout many countries and industries. It is an art form that is as diverse in its uses as in its styles and techniques. Many artists are now using body art to return to a more spiritual connection with their way of life and are rediscovering how their expression can bring meaning to their lives. The bodypainting artist is not just an artist; they are a painter, a conceptualist, a choreographer, a director and a photographer.

Bodypainting has many uses in many different areas of work. A visual artist may move into bodypainting to give their art a life of its own. A performer may take up bodypainting to create an illusion around their character that is not possible with just makeup and costume. Fashion can be heightened when makeup moves into bodypaint, and the film industry can never have enough special effects in living color.

All of these are forms of expression. From the moment we become self-aware, we take action in the presentation of our being. We are human. We are a complex and brilliant concoction of thoughts, actions, dreams, fears and history. We use our presentation and expression as a tool. When we choose to analyze the culture we come from and the way this affects our personal presentation of self, we take control of the image we project to the outside world. Through our art and expression, we have an effect on the world we live in.

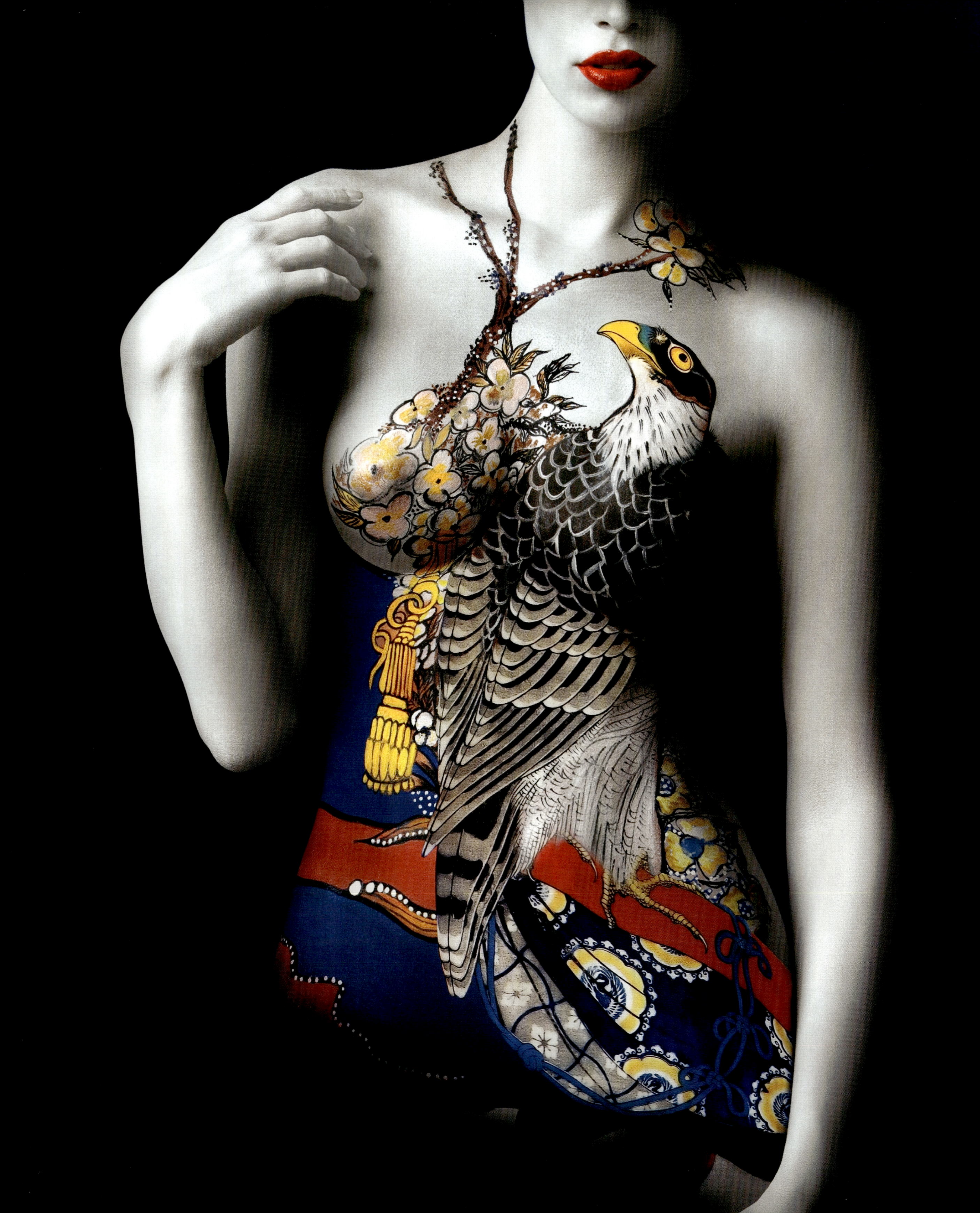

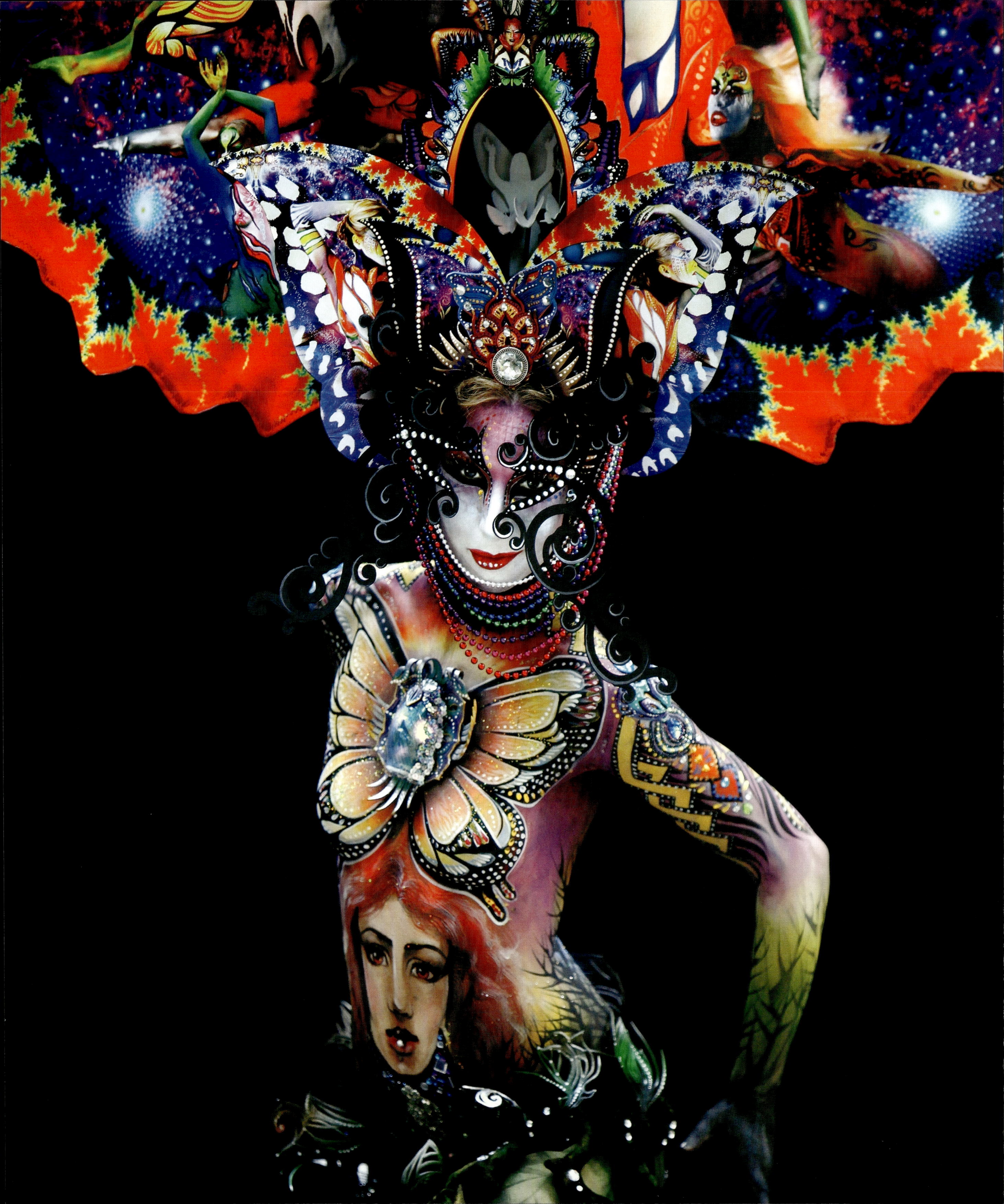

World Bodypainting Festival

WWW.BODYPAINTING-FESTIVAL.COM

One of the driving forces of the bodypainting world for the past two decades has been the World Bodypainting Festival in the south of Austria. This event hosts the World Bodypainting Championships and has distinguished and encouraged the different aspects of the art form.

The festival itself is such a melting pot of artistic talent that many artists count it as one of the forces behind the growth of their careers. Receiving hundreds of hours of broadcast time internationally each year, the World Bodypainting Festival has taken a little-known art form and carried it into the consciousness of everyday people on almost every continent.

For a week, thousands of artists, models, performers, photographers and film producers converge on a small town on a lake to take part in events, parties, shows and three days of competition at the highest level in a wide range of categories. This spectacle of the world's best special effects, bodypainting and costume artists performing on the main stage is accompanied by international music acts, a fashion show, photography and a range of live entertainment.

The World Bodypainting Association has grown parallel to the festival and supports artists in their careers. Association members travel the world lecturing on body art in schools and universities and at trade shows with the media. The association also works as an agency and has set up many amazing advertising and artistic collaborations between artists, companies, galleries and events.

It is hard to imagine the depth of experience available at an event such as this. More than a thousand artworks are created for competition and stage shows. These are photographed and filmed extensively by seven hundred photographers, and months of creative editing follow the event each year. Perhaps the most touching and personal experience of the World Bodypainting Festival is the feeling of becoming part of a massive artistic family with years of history, creativity and experience waiting to be shared.

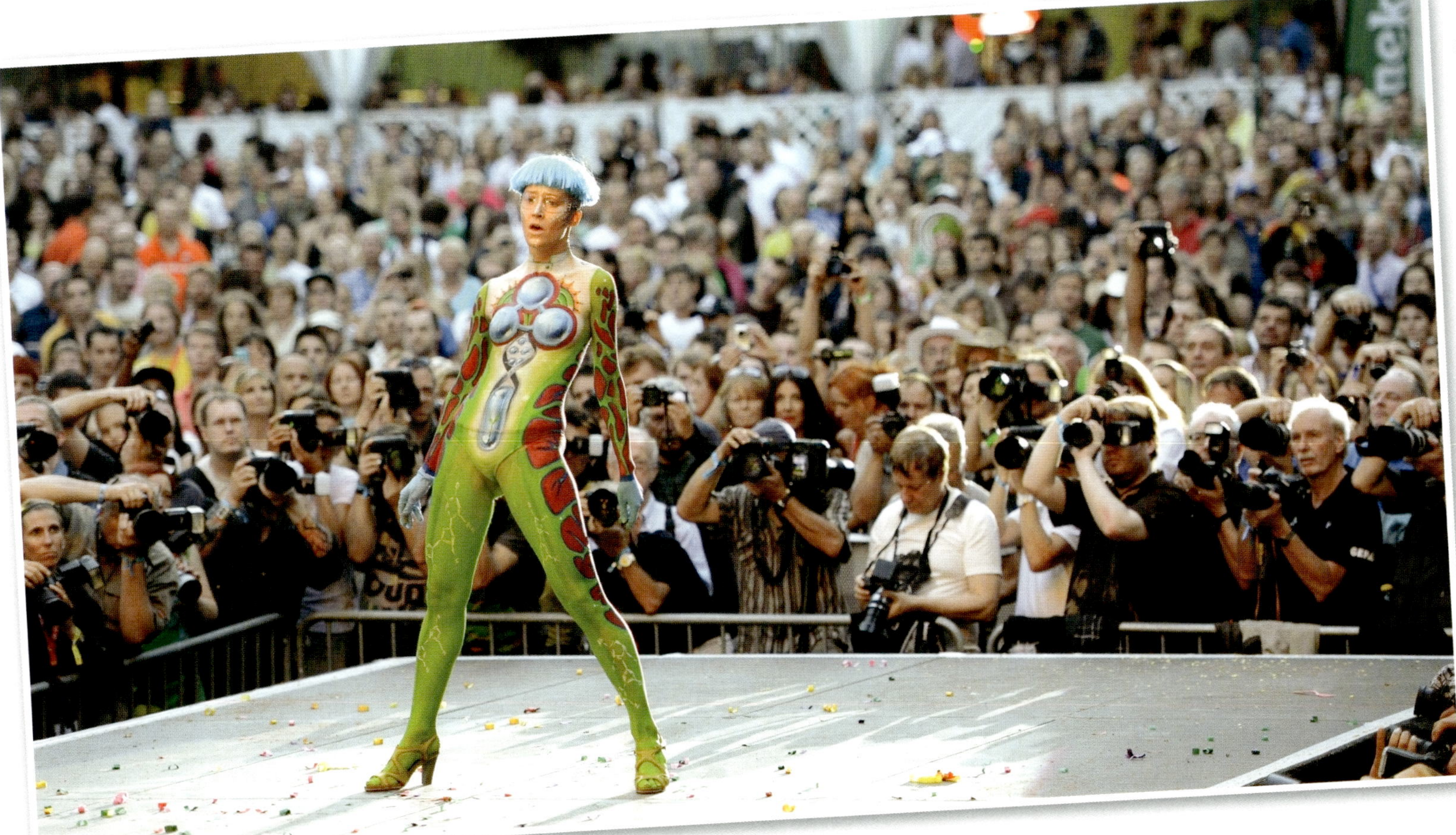

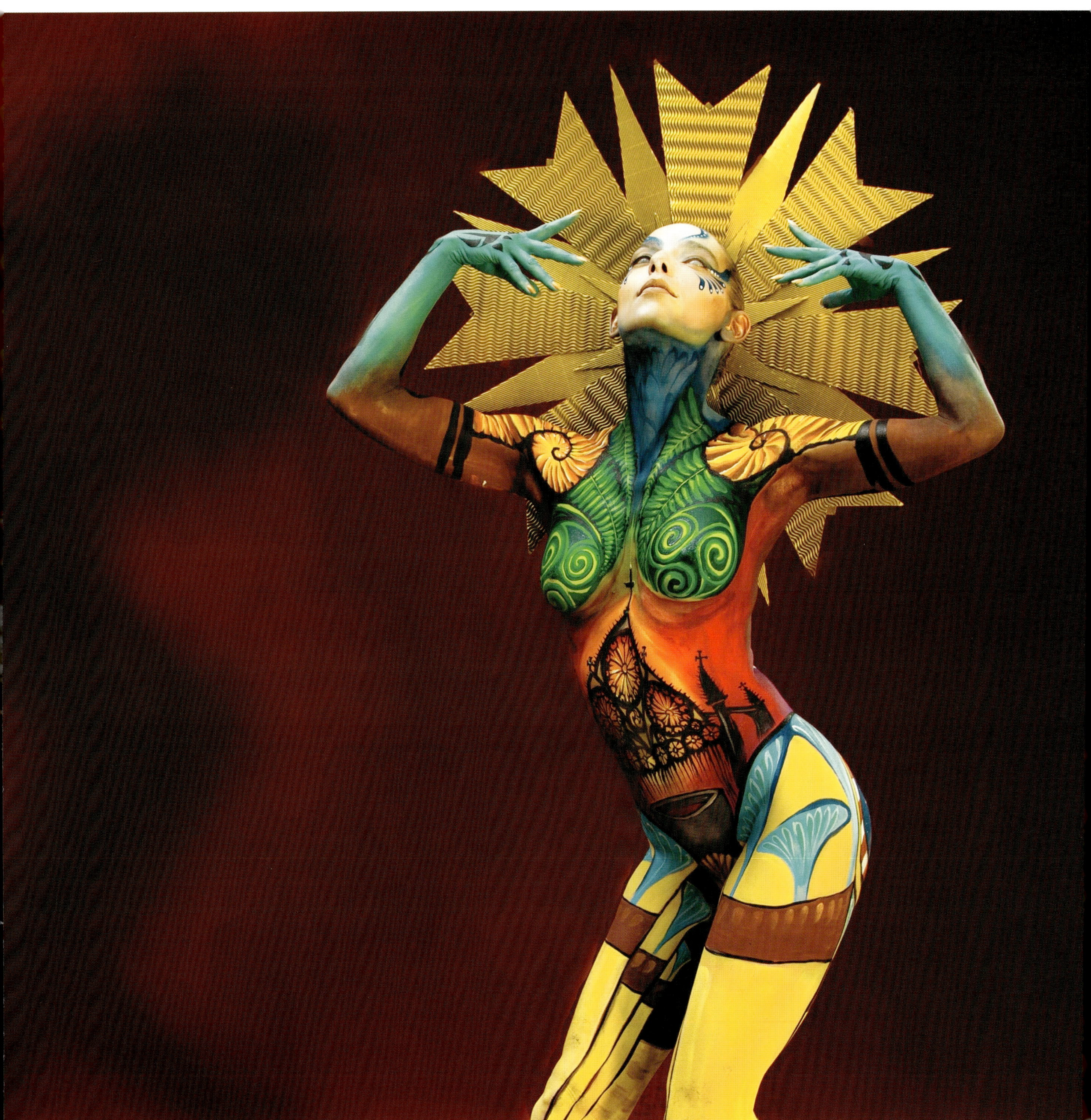

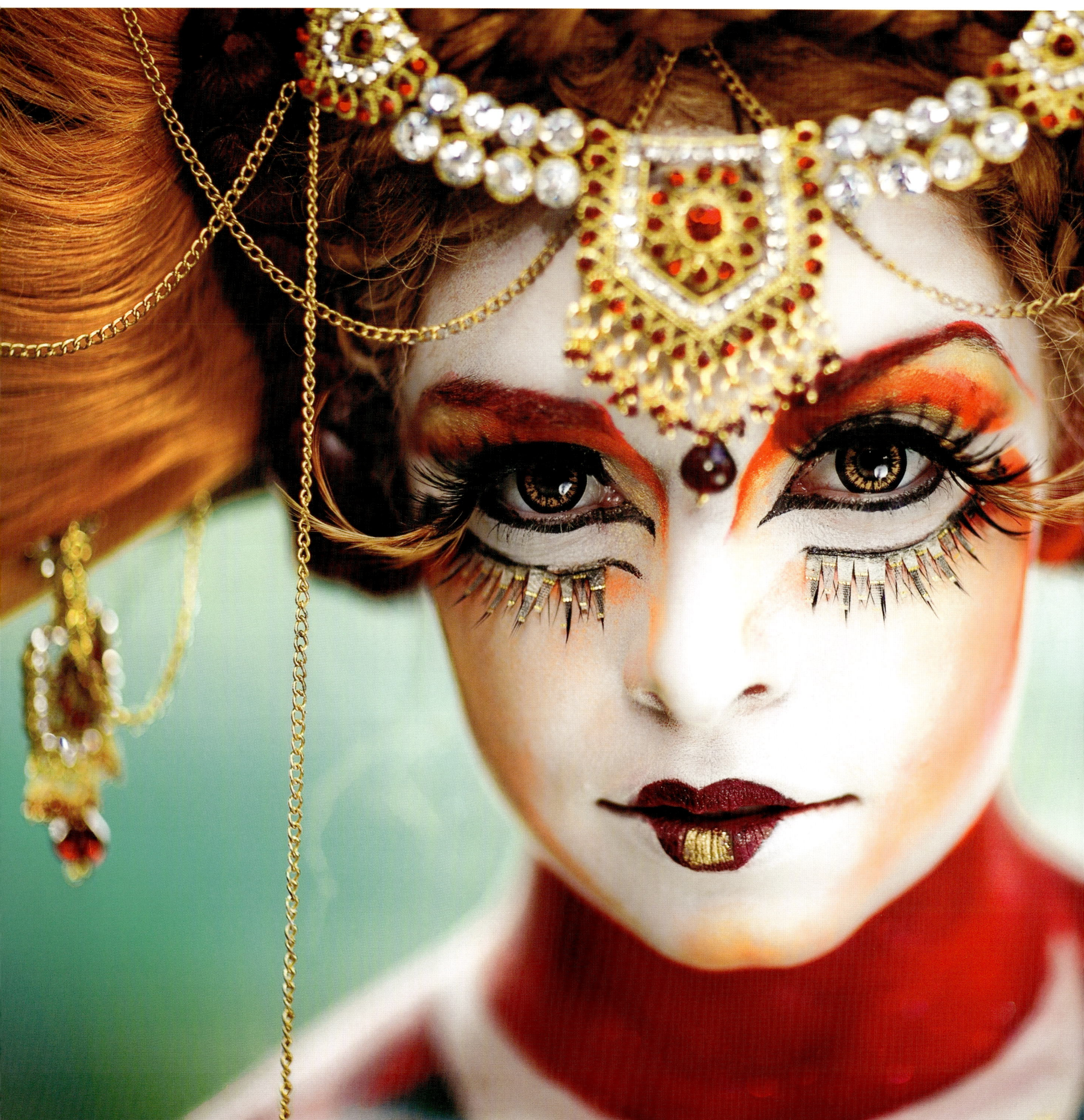

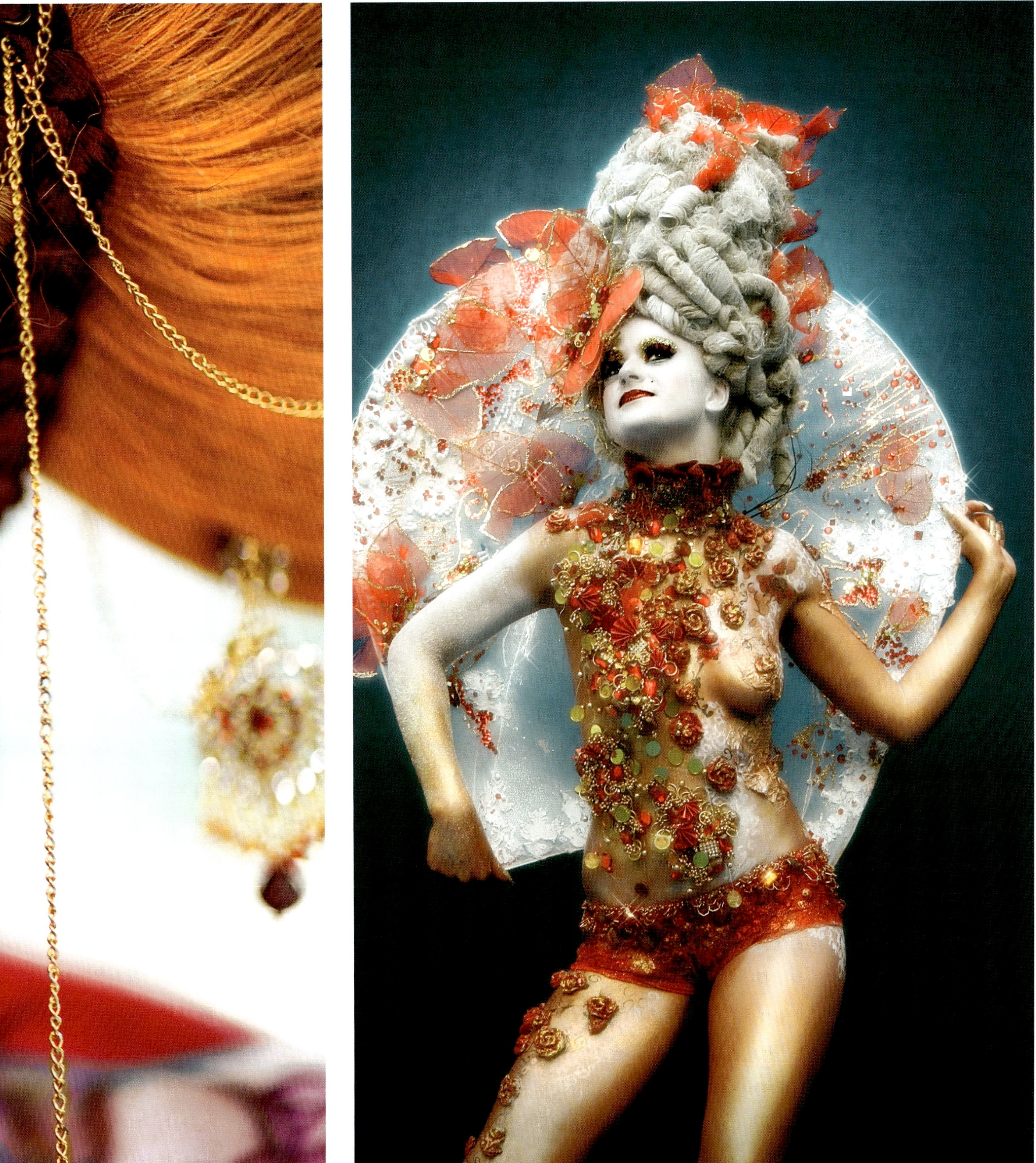

ARTIST SOPHIA BENOMAR | PHOTOGRAPHER TOBIAS SPRANGER (OPPOSITE)
ARTISTS INESE DEKSNE & LAUMA PURVENA | PHOTOGRAPHER GABRIELE STEINER

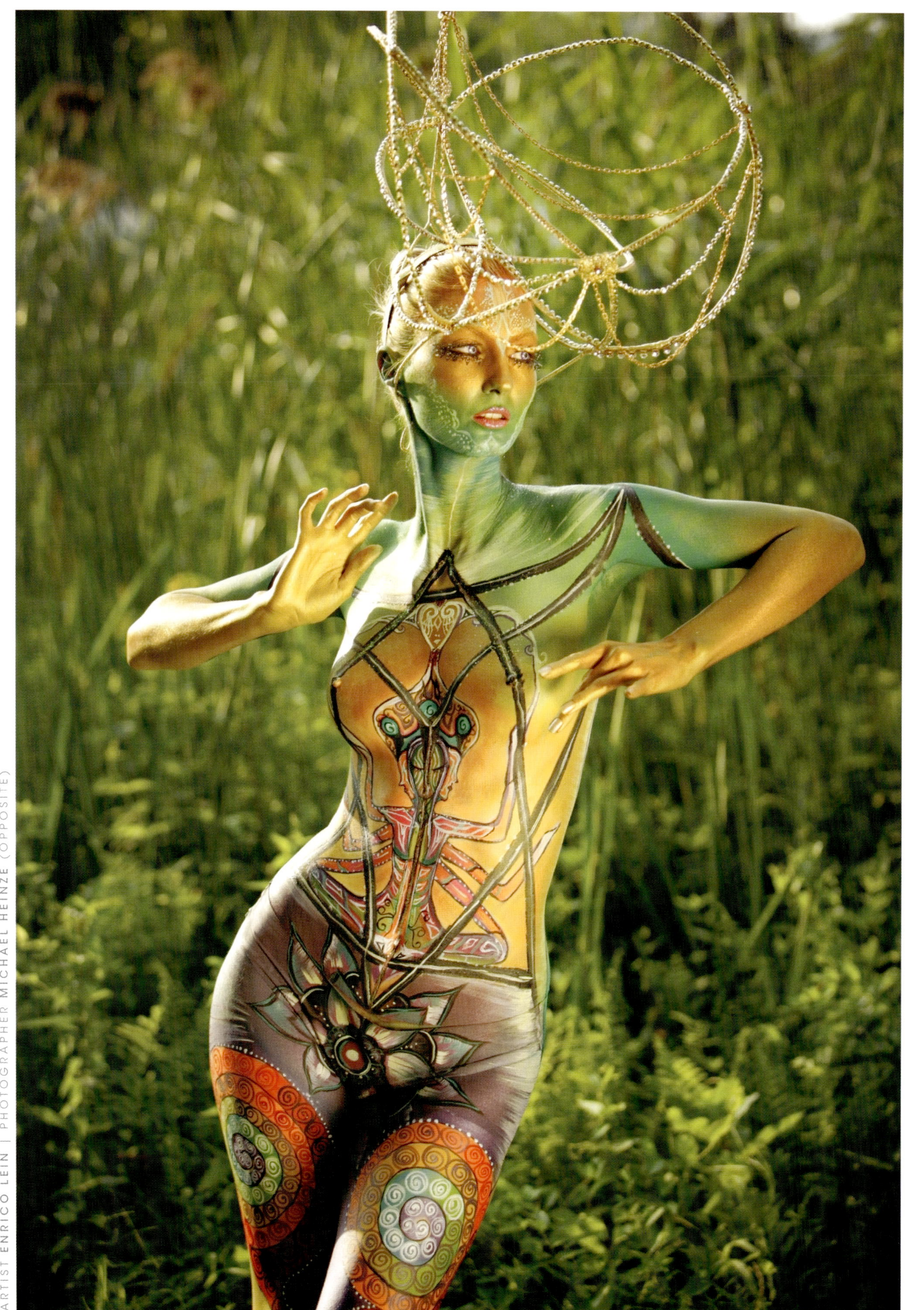

ARTIST EINAT DAN | PHOTOGRAPHER DMITRI MOISEEV
ARTIST ENRICO LEIN | PHOTOGRAPHER MICHAEL HEINZE (OPPOSITE)

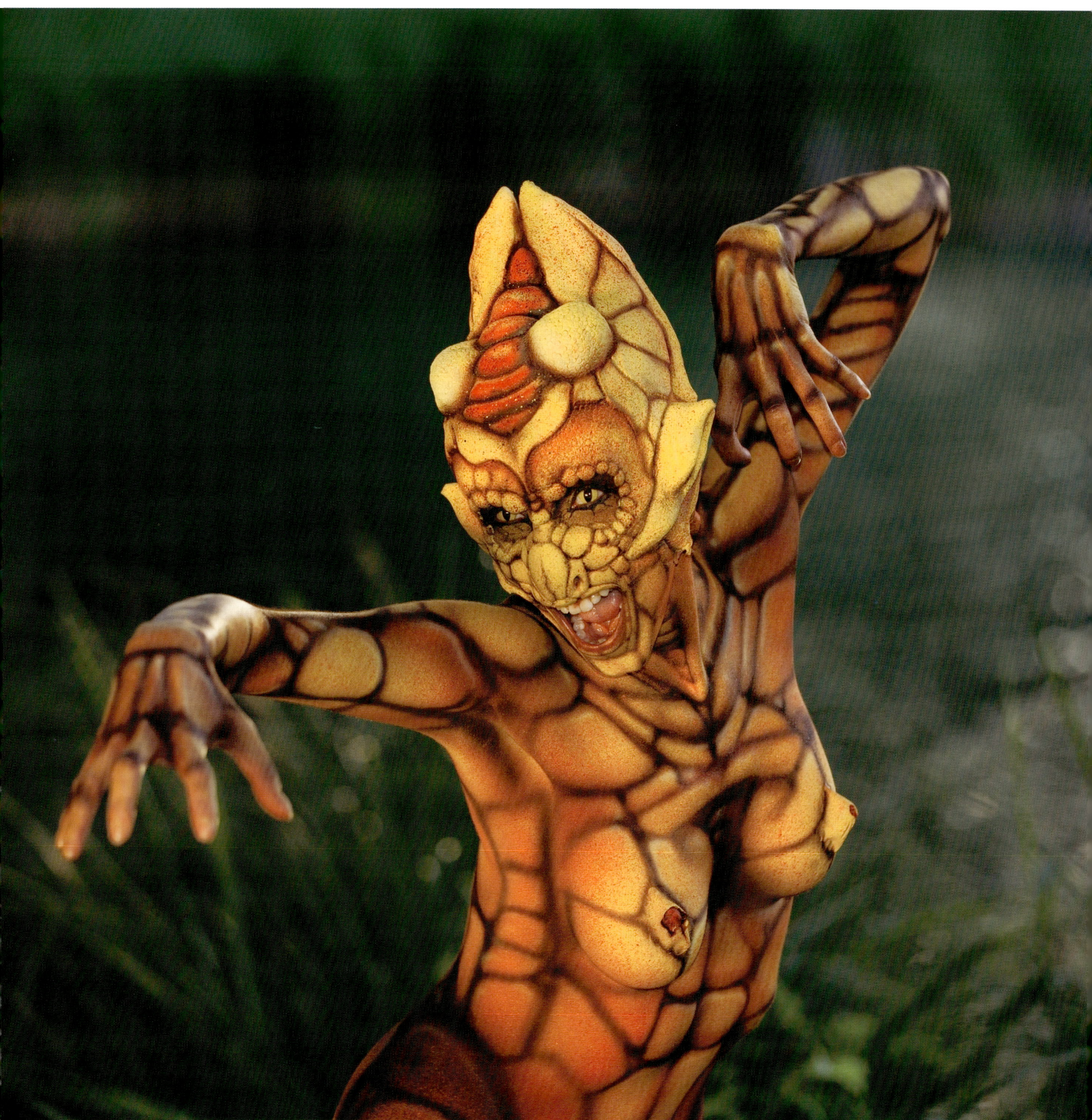

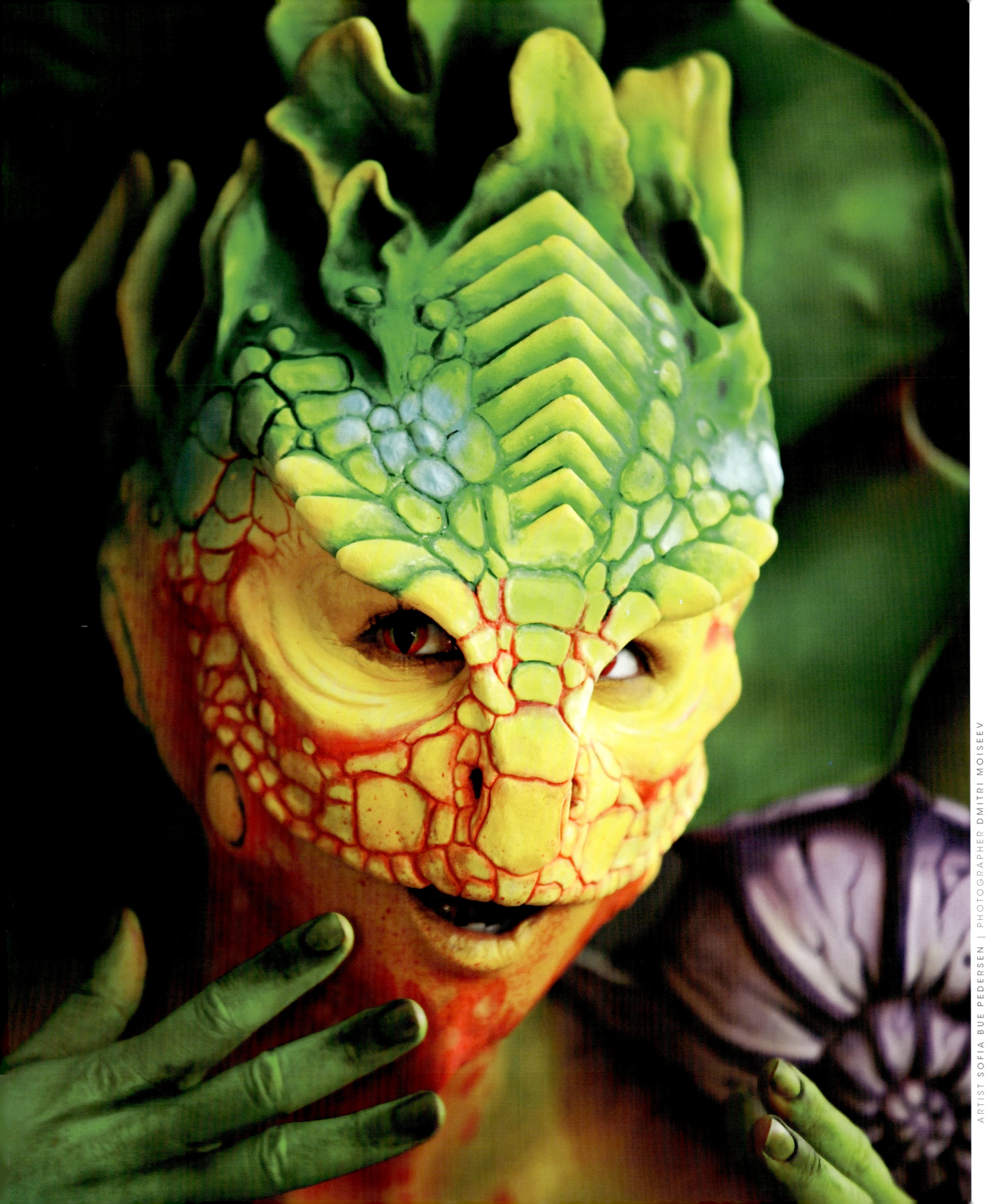

ARTIST SOFIA BUE PEDERSEN | PHOTOGRAPHER DMITRI MOISEEV

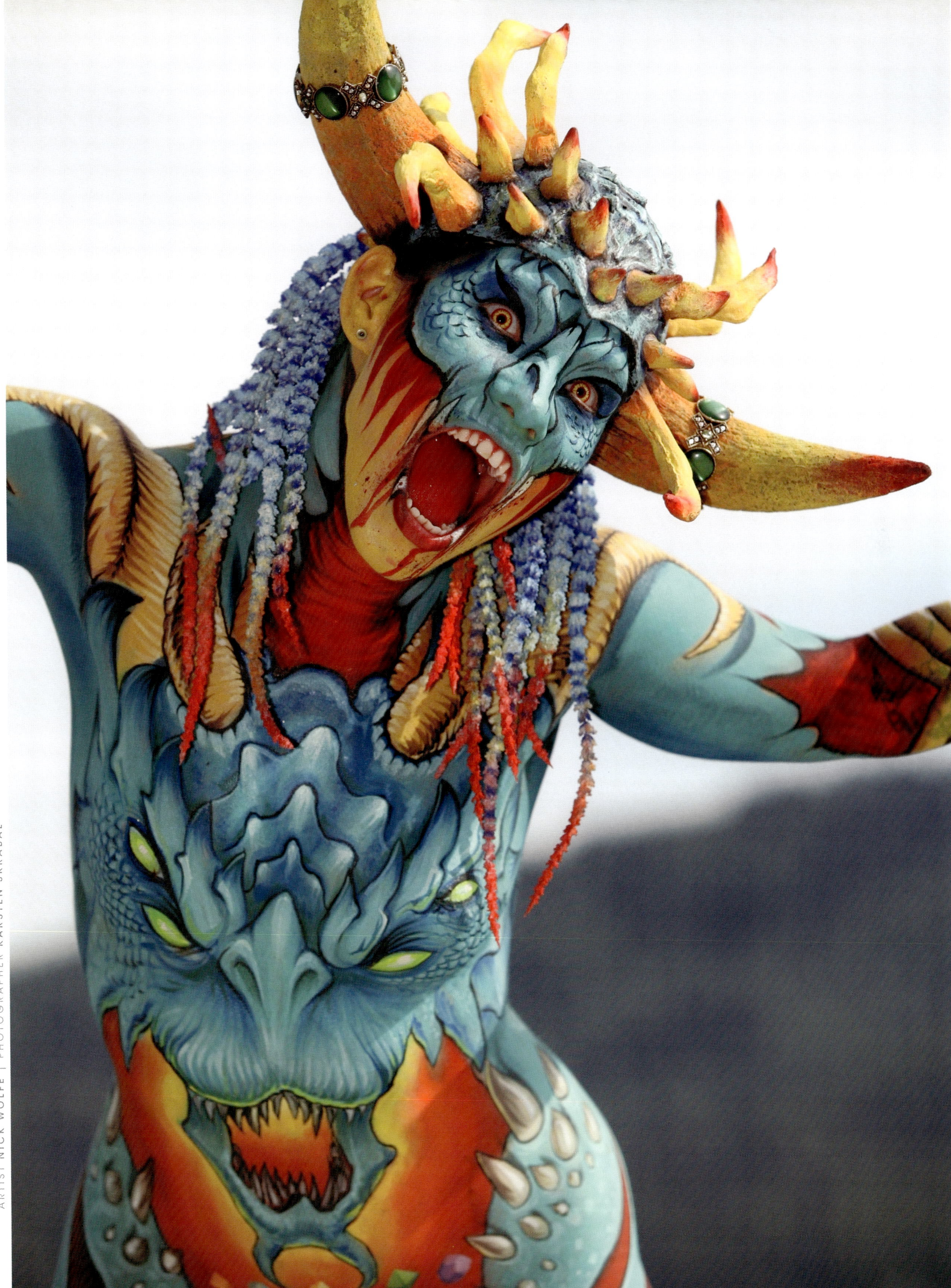

ARTIST NICK WOLFE | PHOTOGRAPHER KARSTEN SKRABAL

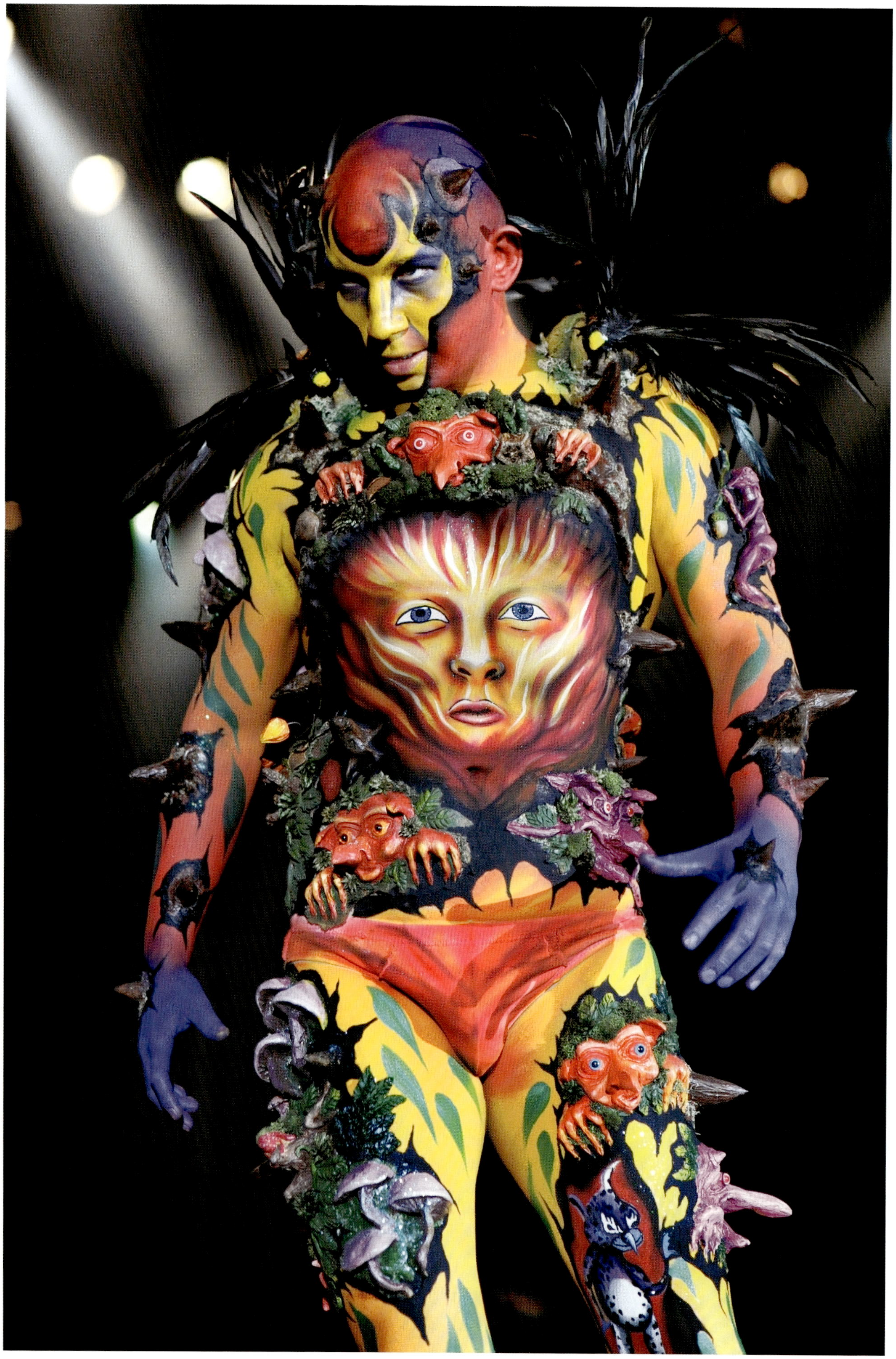

ARTIST CAROLYN ROPER | PHOTOGRAPHER MARKUS MAYER

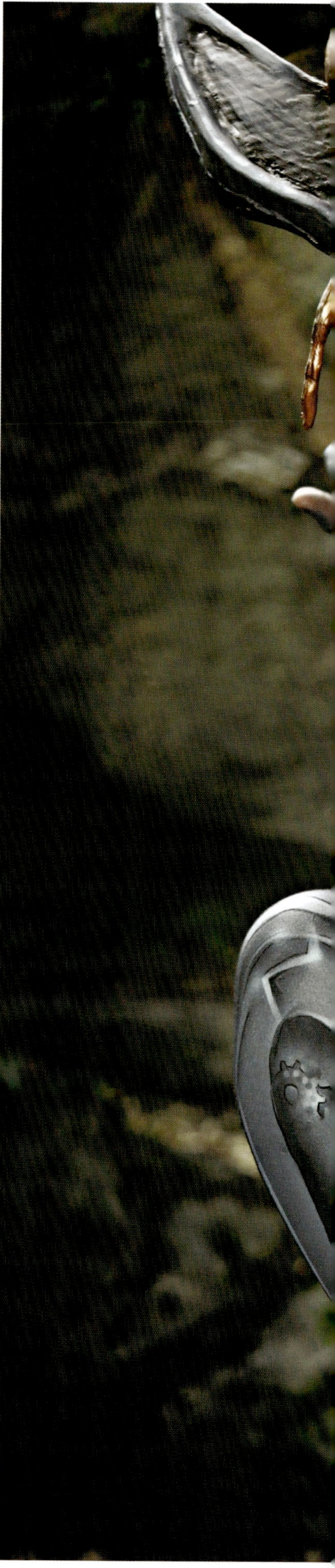

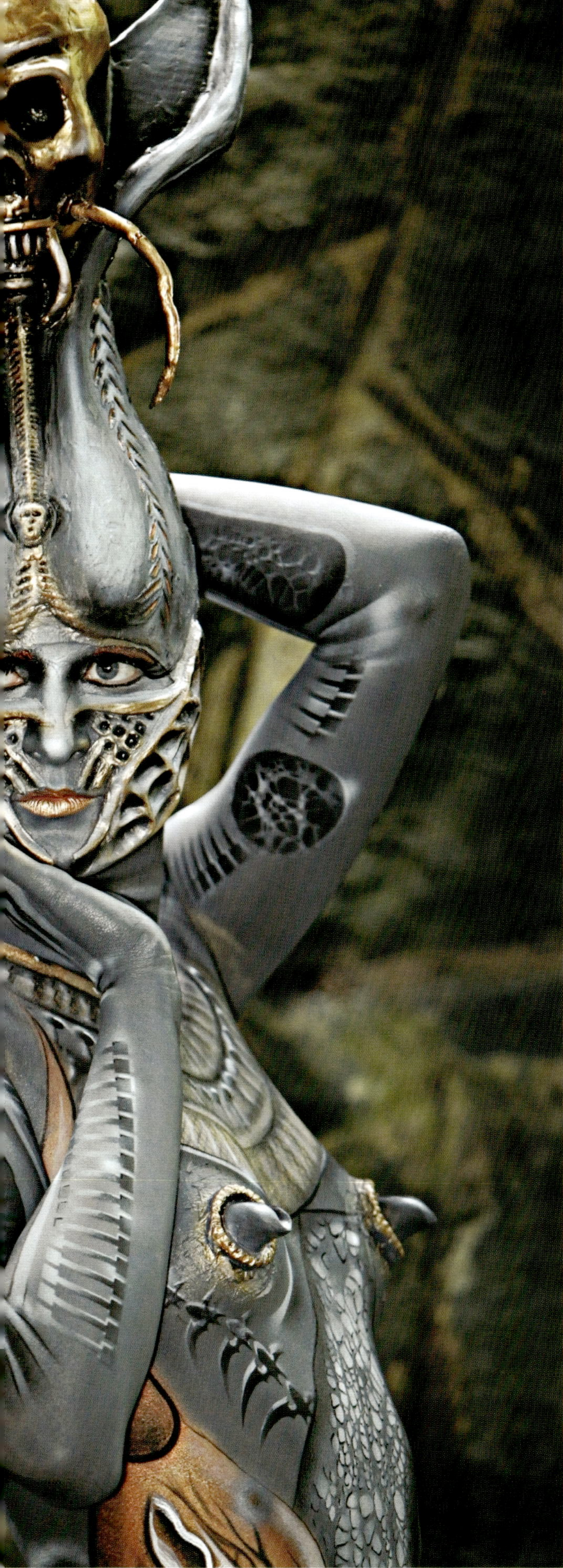

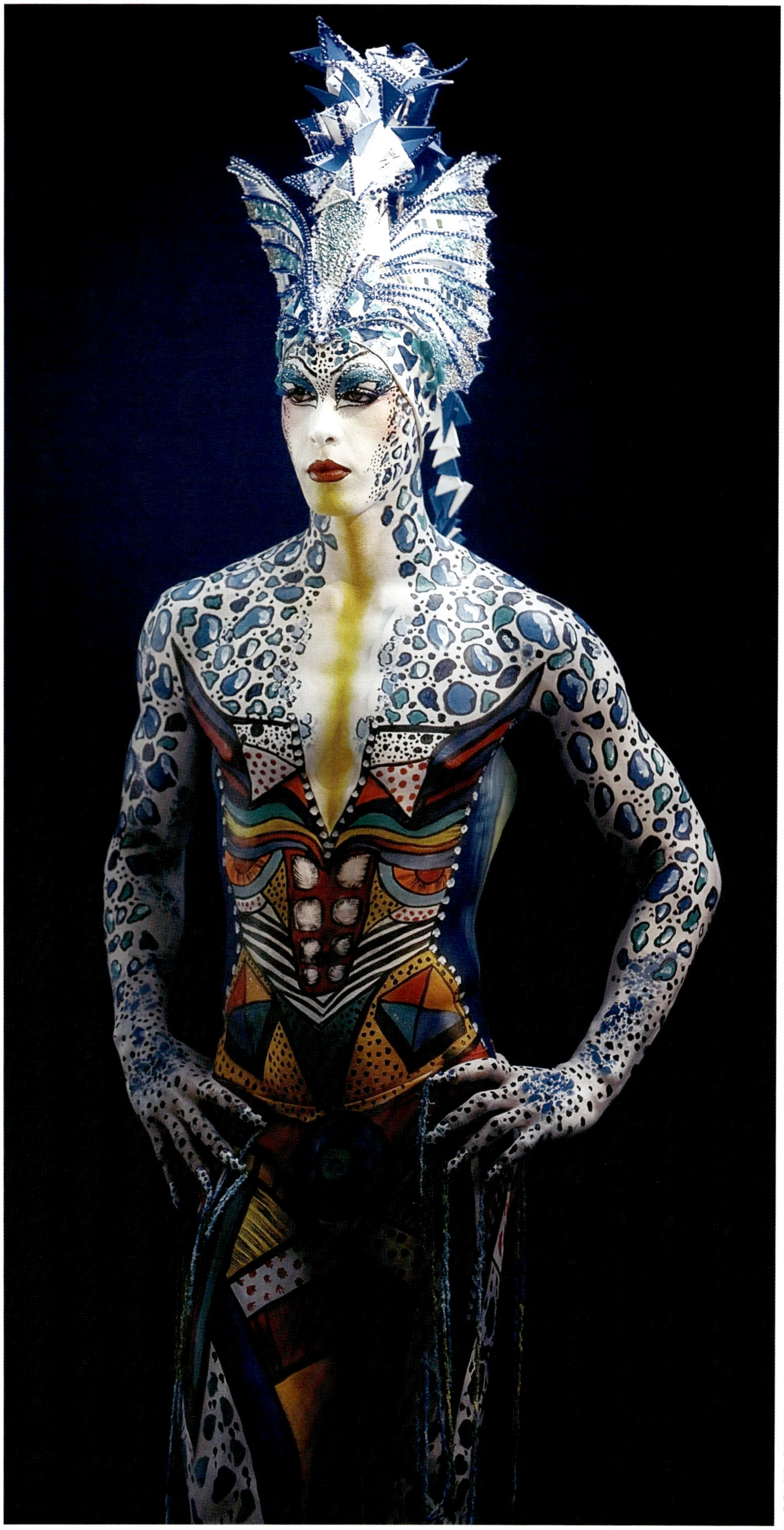

ARTIST FREDI SCHMID | PHOTOGRAPHER DMITRI MOISEEV (CENTER)
ARTIST EINAT DAN | PHOTOGRAPHER ANDREA PERIA

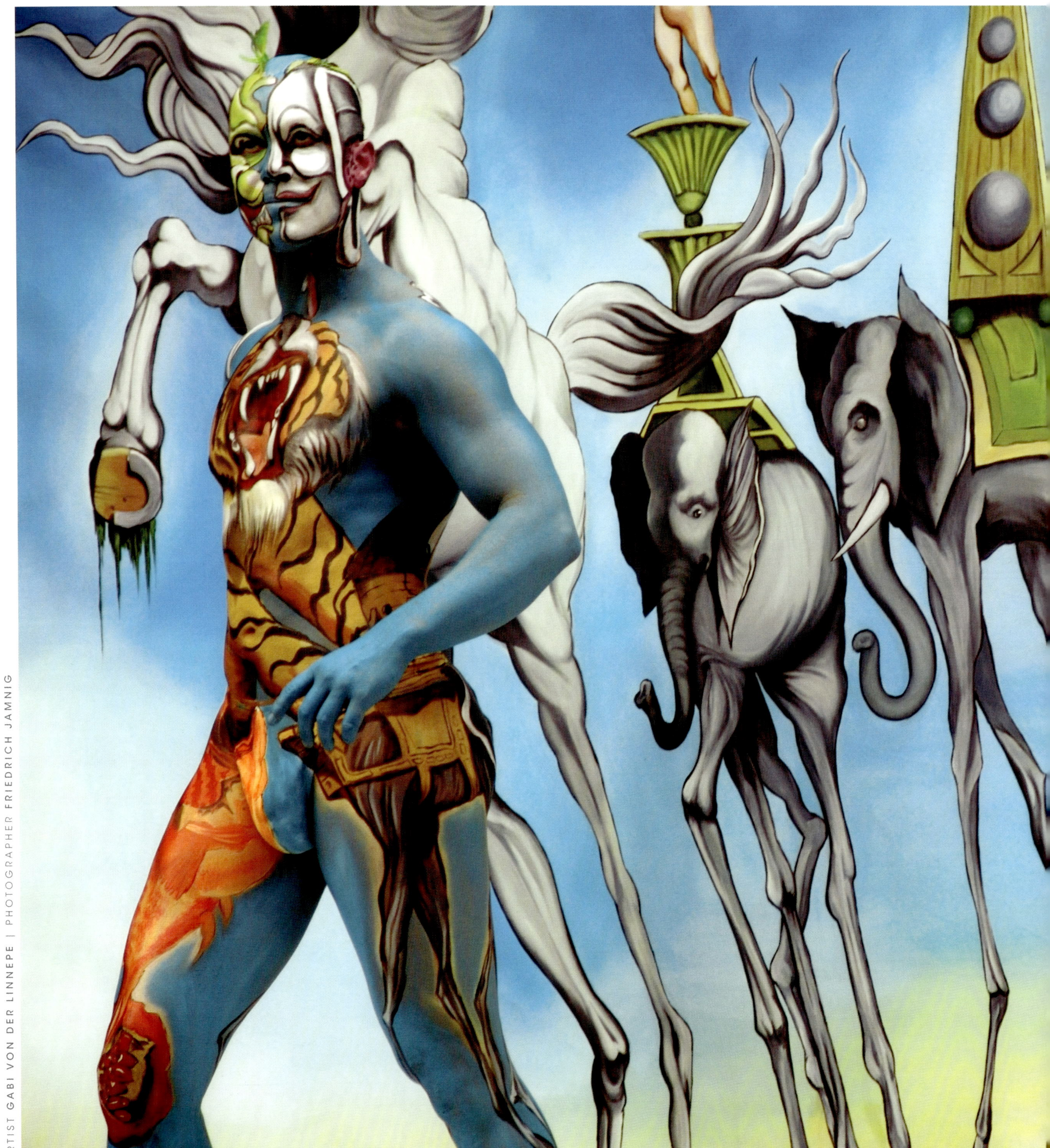

ARTIST GABI VON DER LINNEPE | PHOTOGRAPHER FRIEDRICH JAMNIG

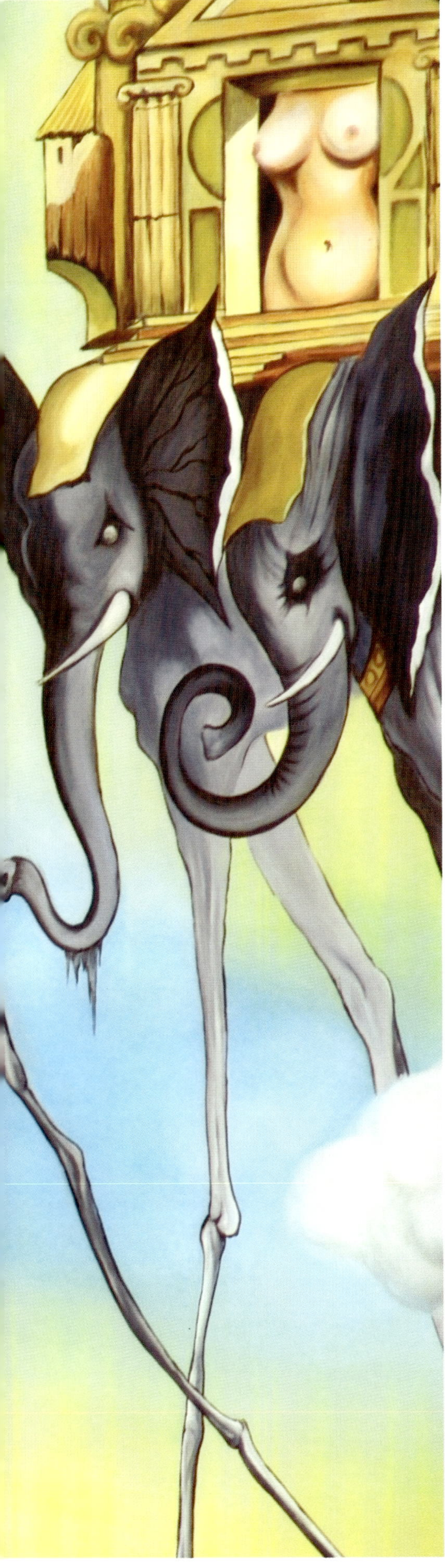

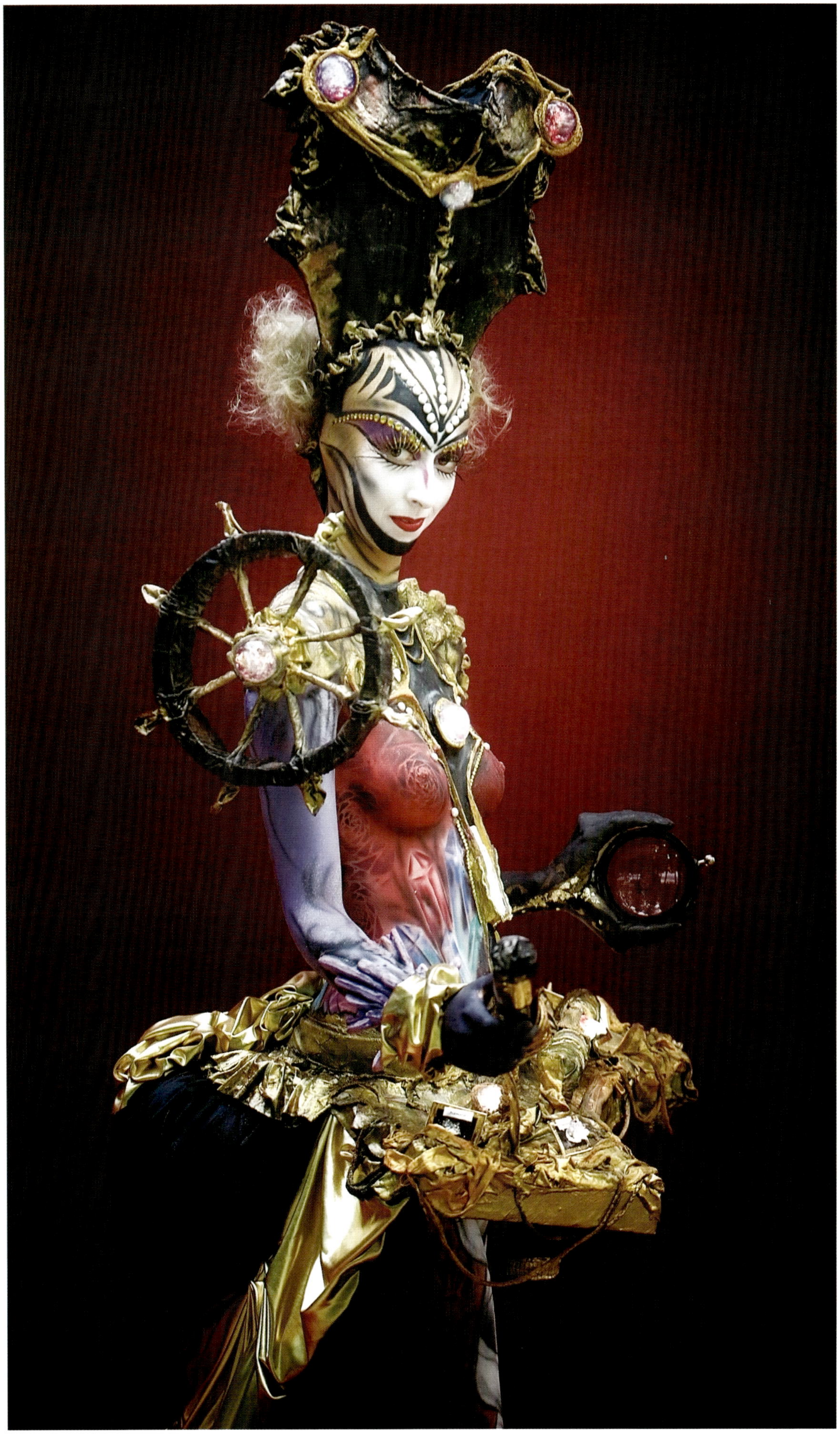

ARTIST GABRIELA HAJEK-RENNER | PHOTOGRAPHER ANDREA PERIA

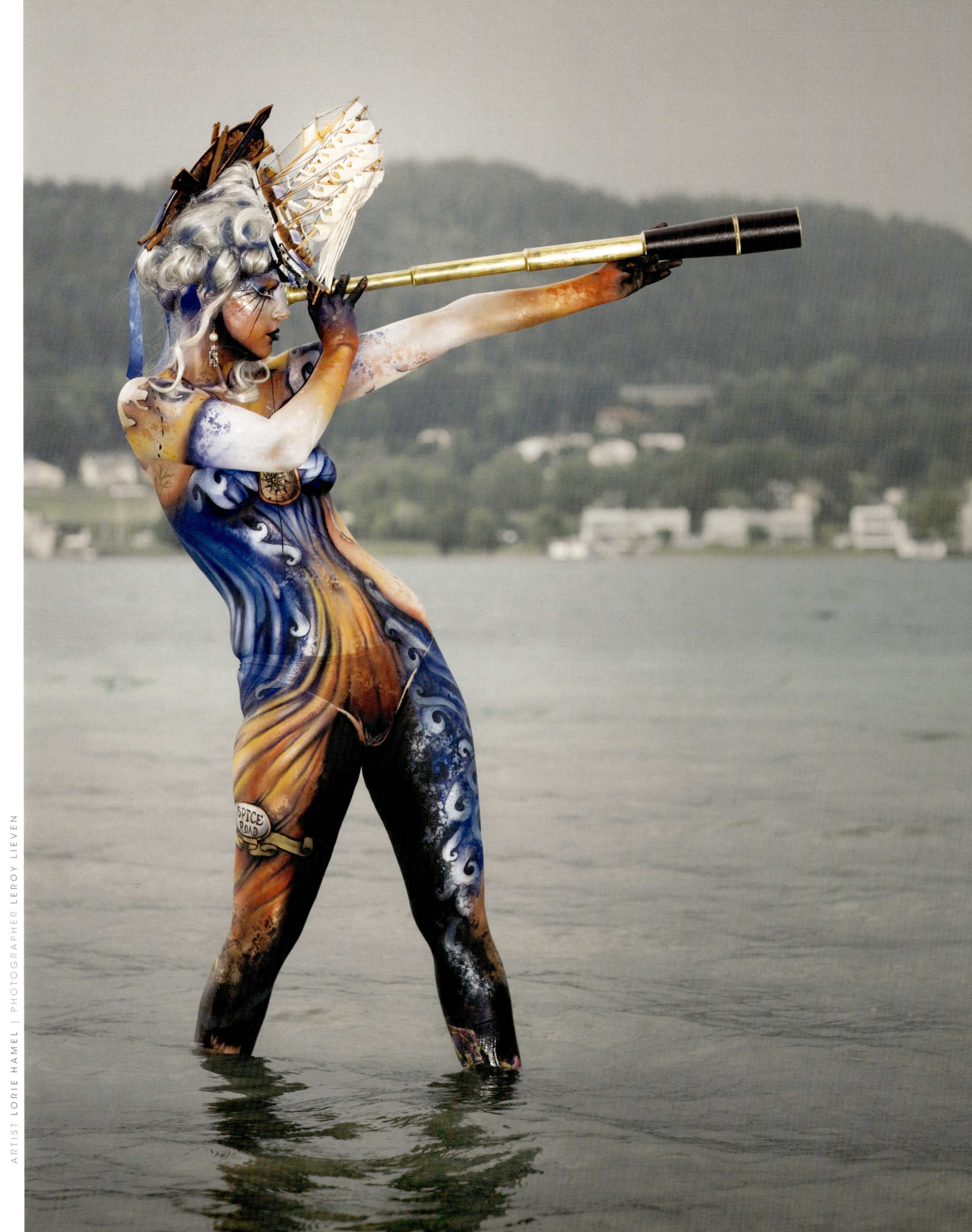

ARTIST LORIE HAMEL | PHOTOGRAPHER LEROY LIEVEN

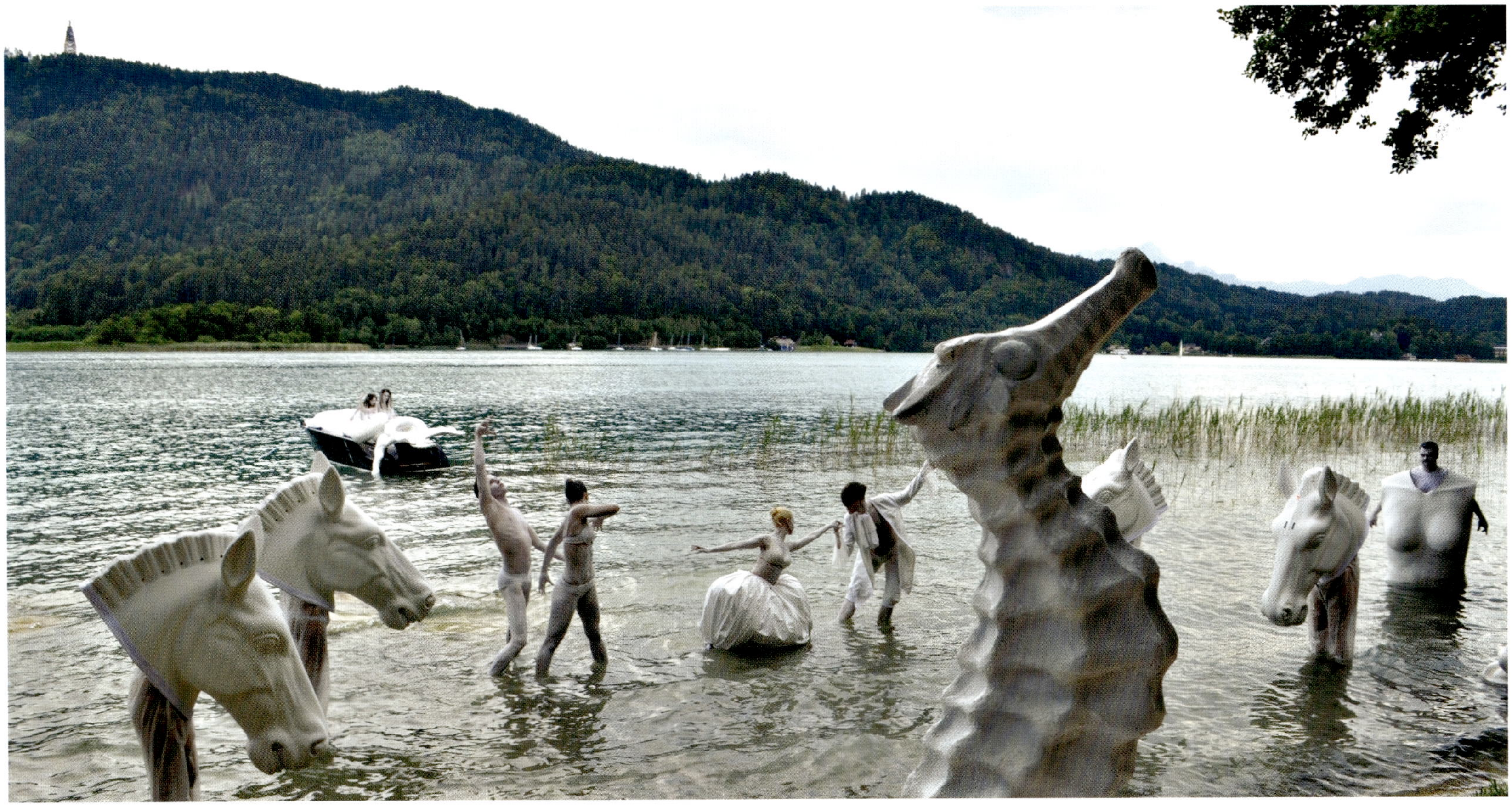

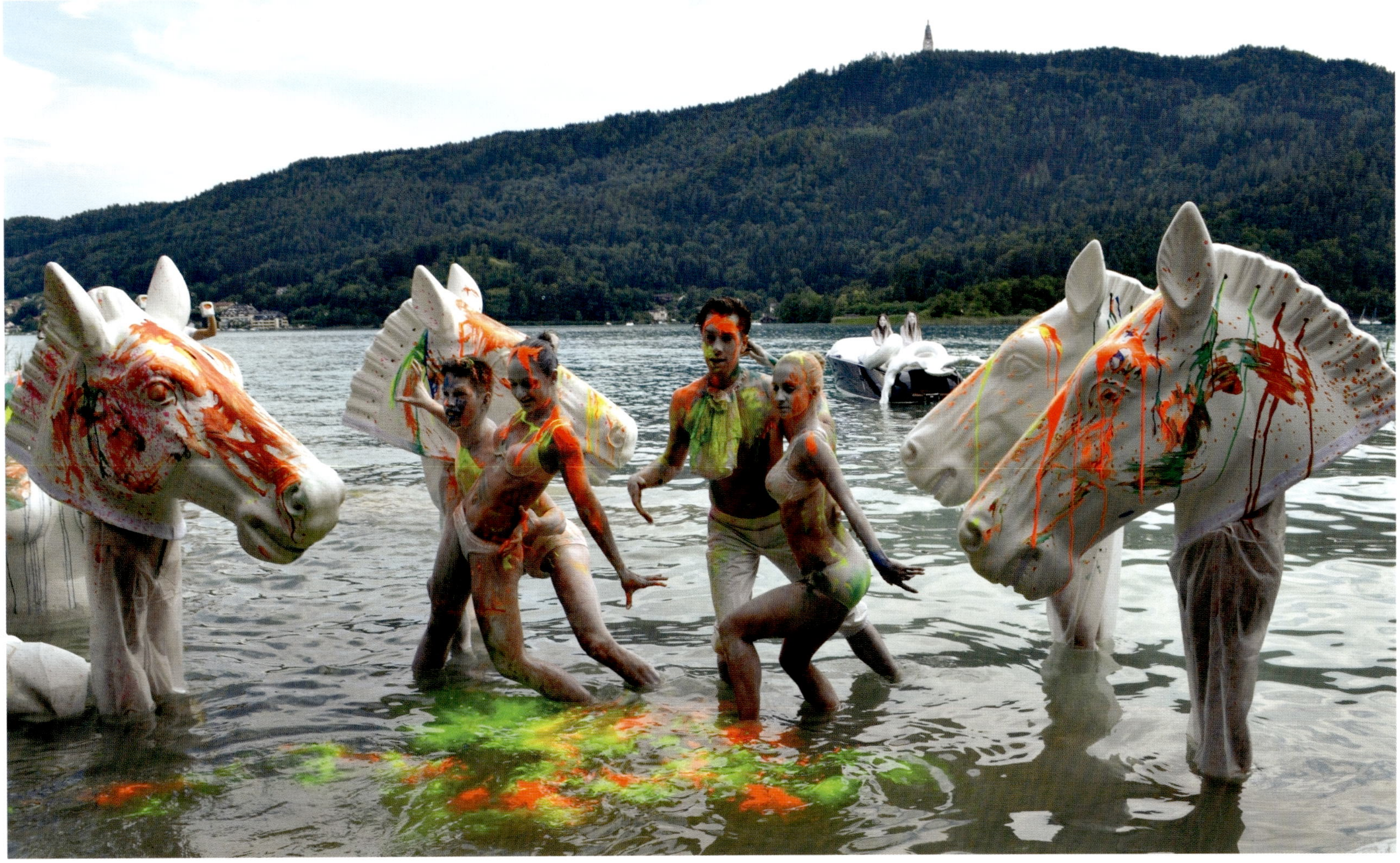

ARTIST BIRGIT MÖRTL | PHOTOGRAPHER MARTIN AIGNER

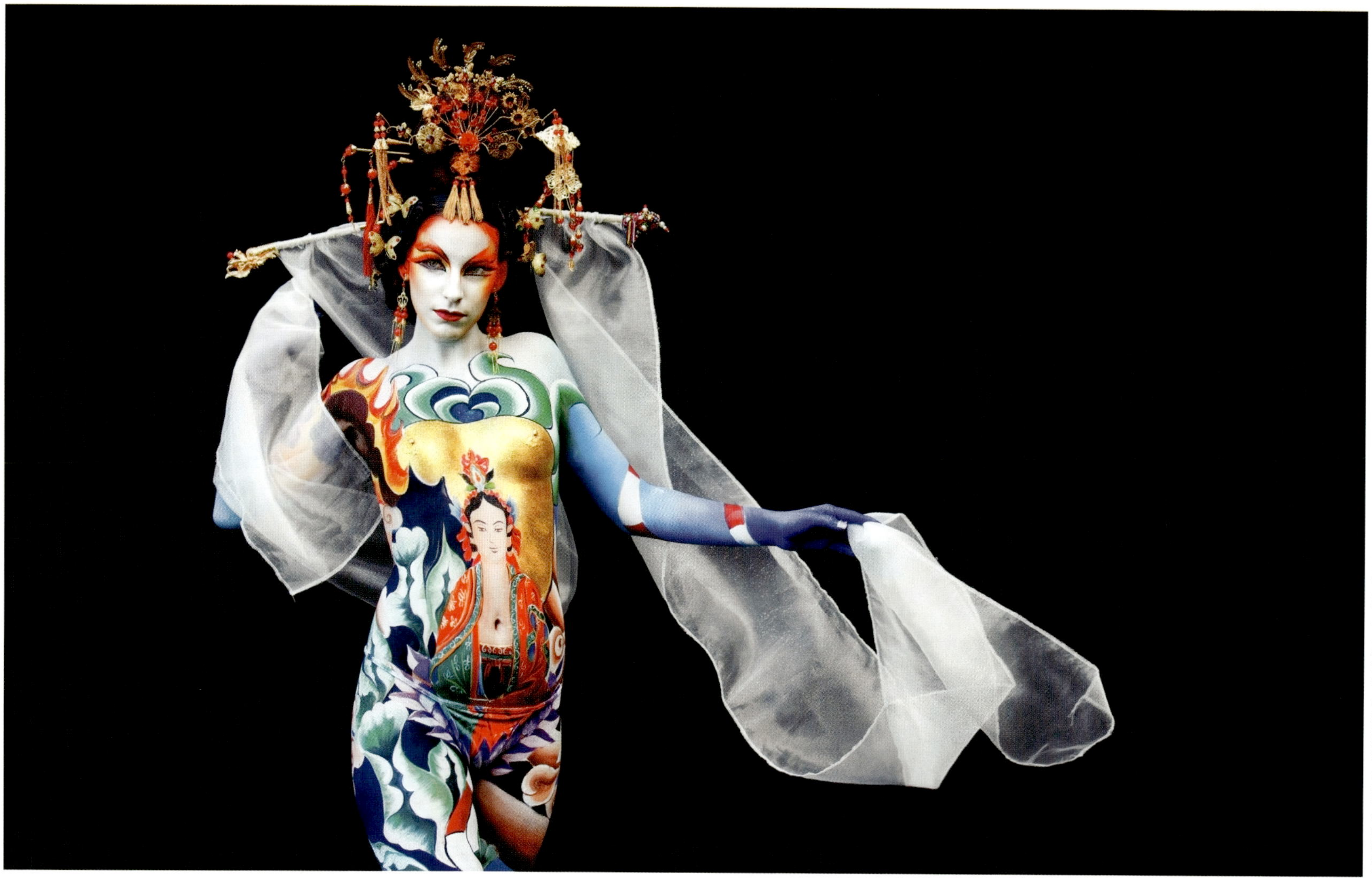

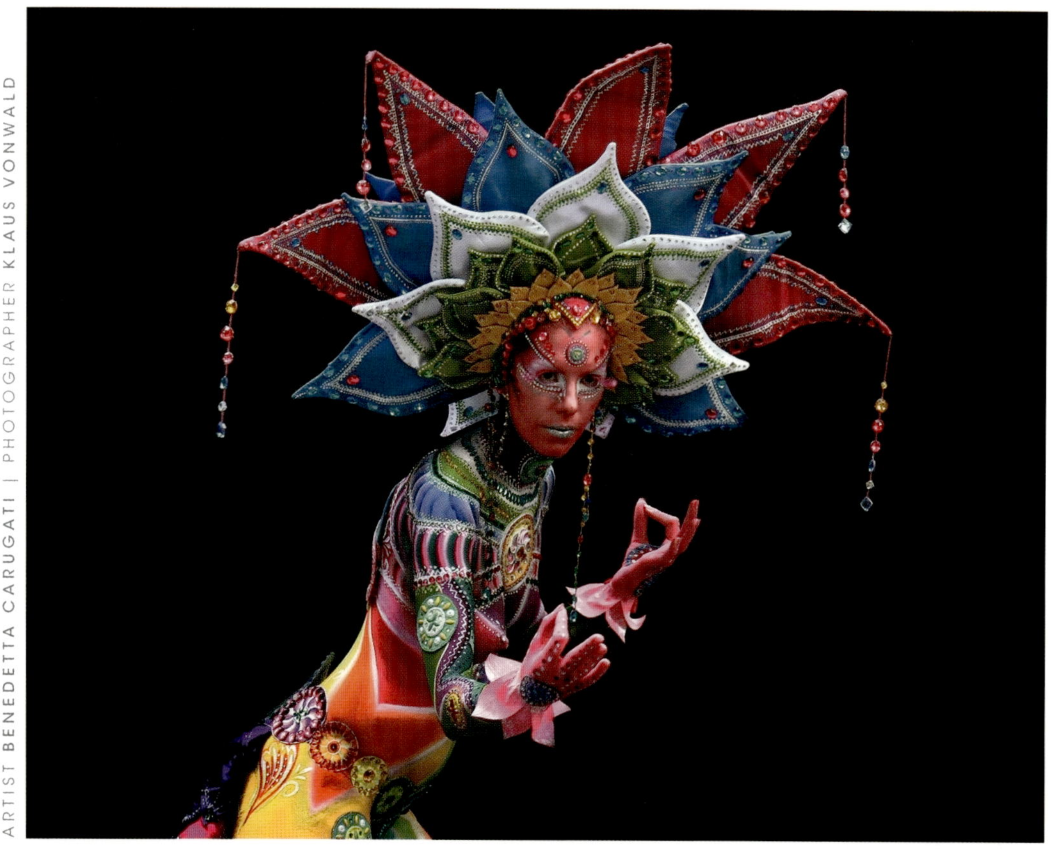

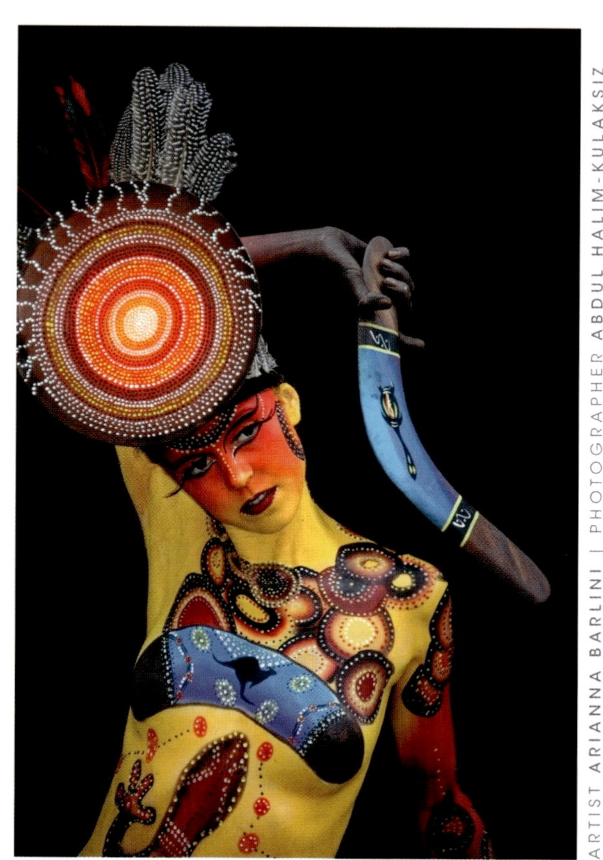

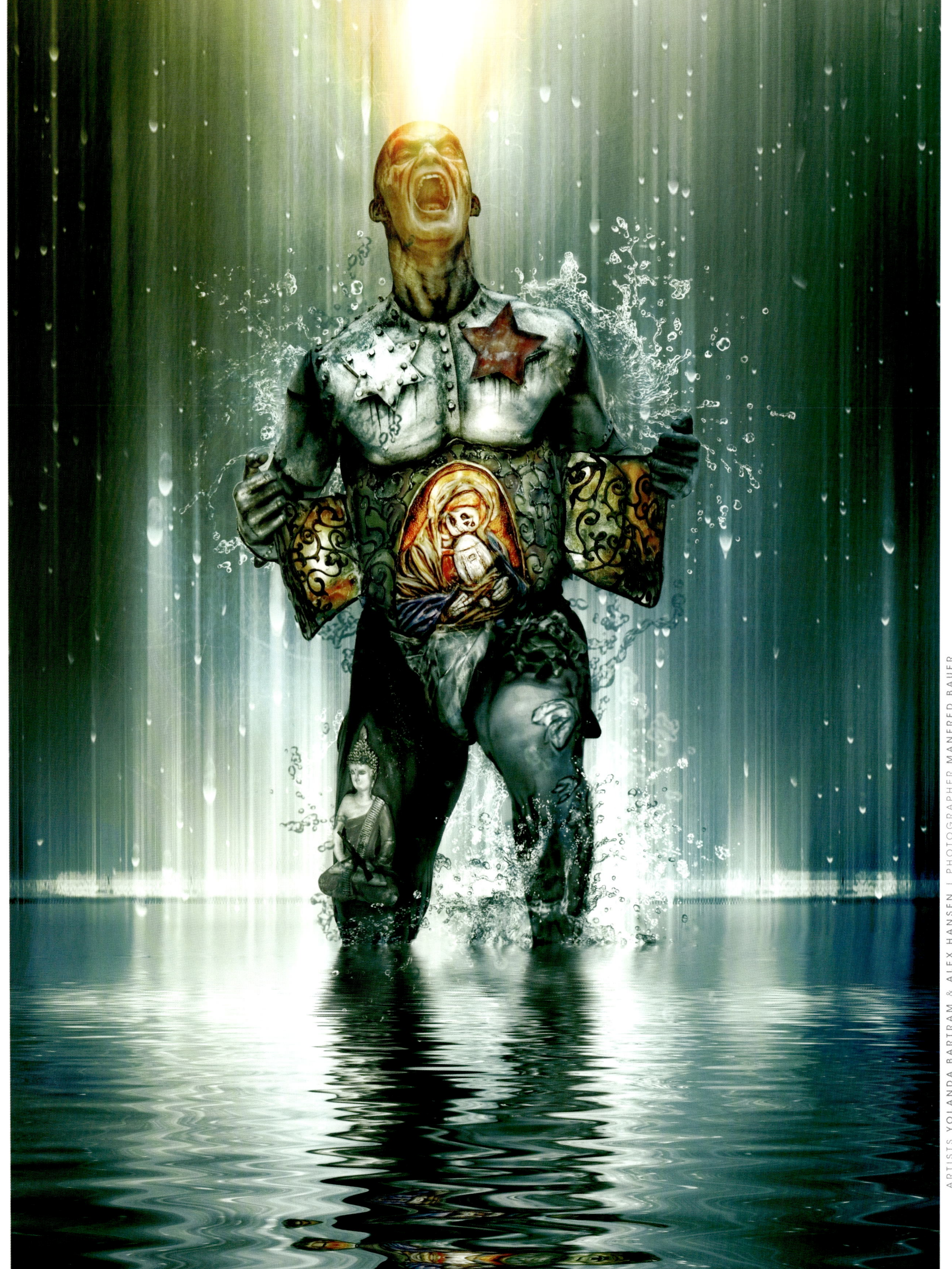

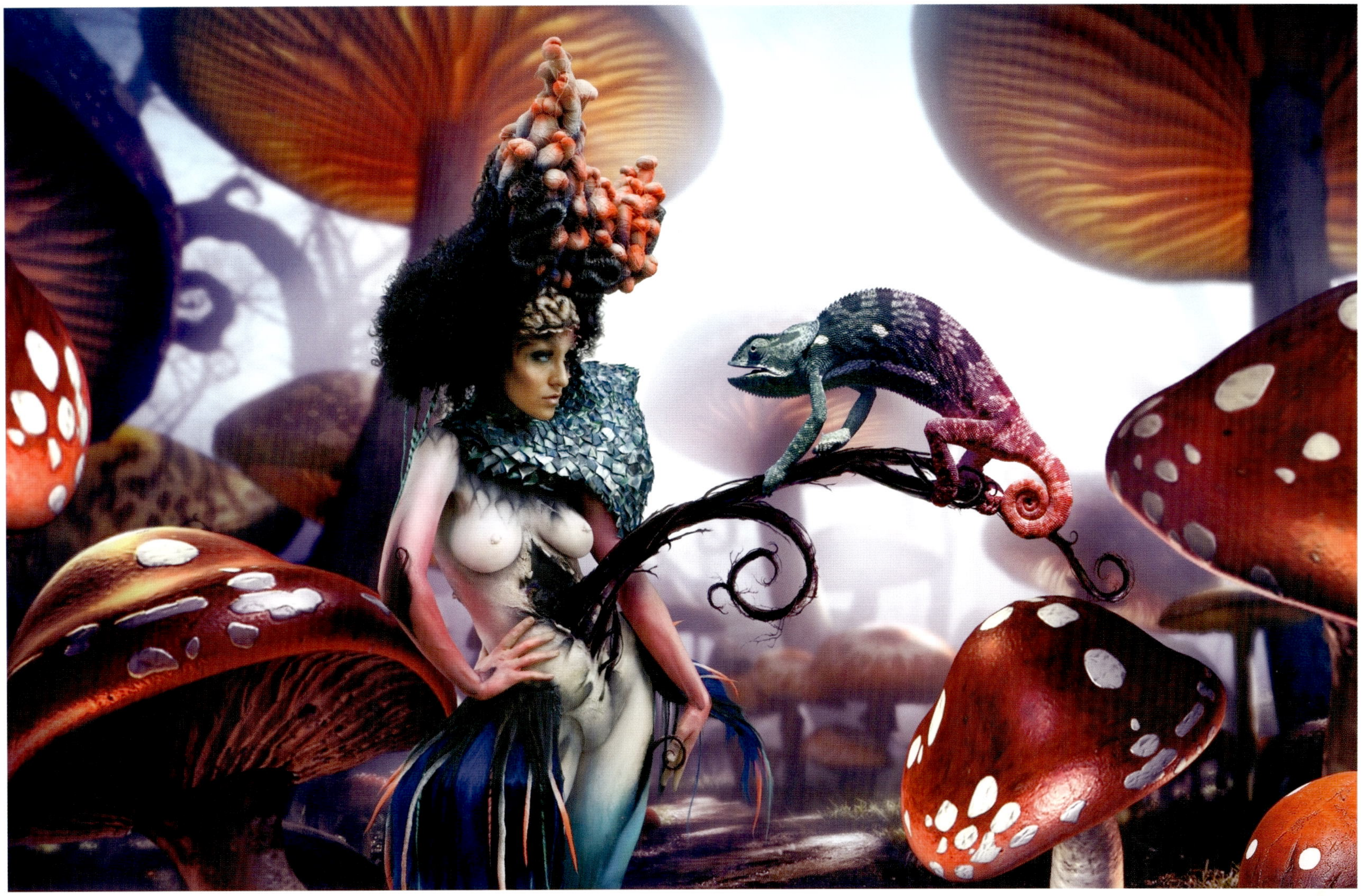

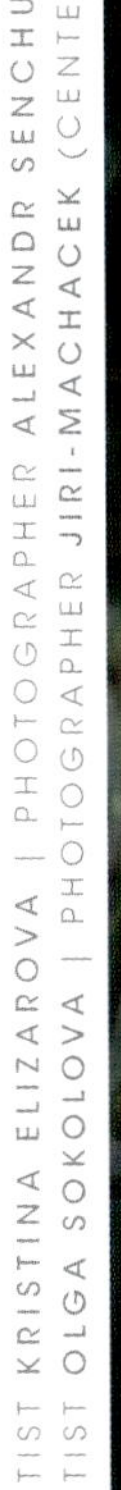

ARTIST KRISTINA ELIZAROVA | PHOTOGRAPHER ALEXANDR SENCHUK

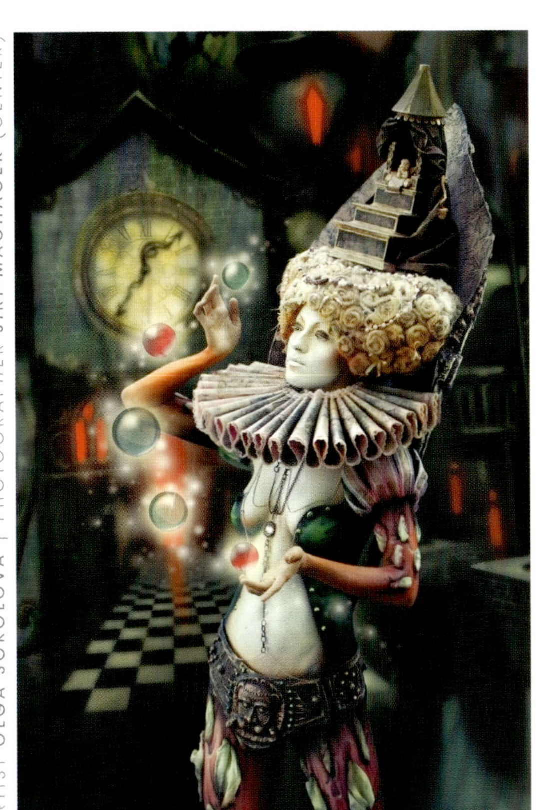

ARTIST KRISTINA ELIZAROVA | PHOTOGRAPHER ALEXANDR SENCHUK
ARTIST OLGA SOKOLOVA | PHOTOGRAPHER JIRI-MACHACEK (CENTER)

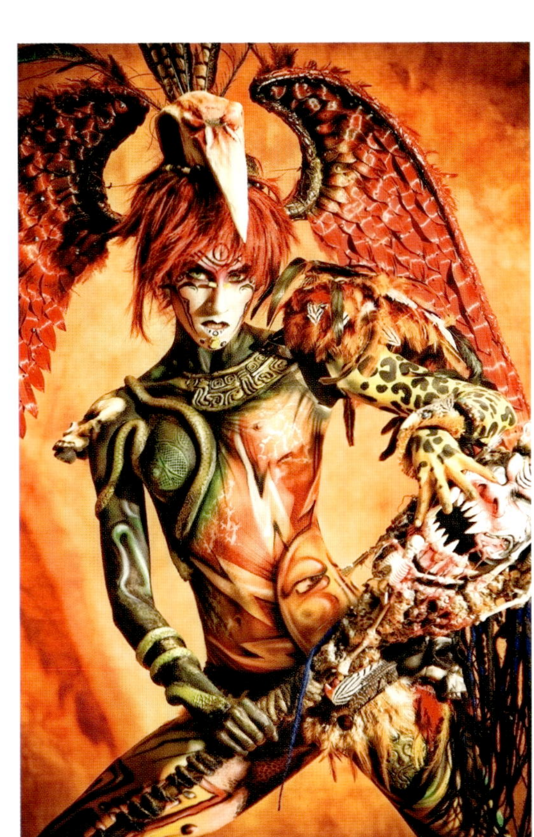

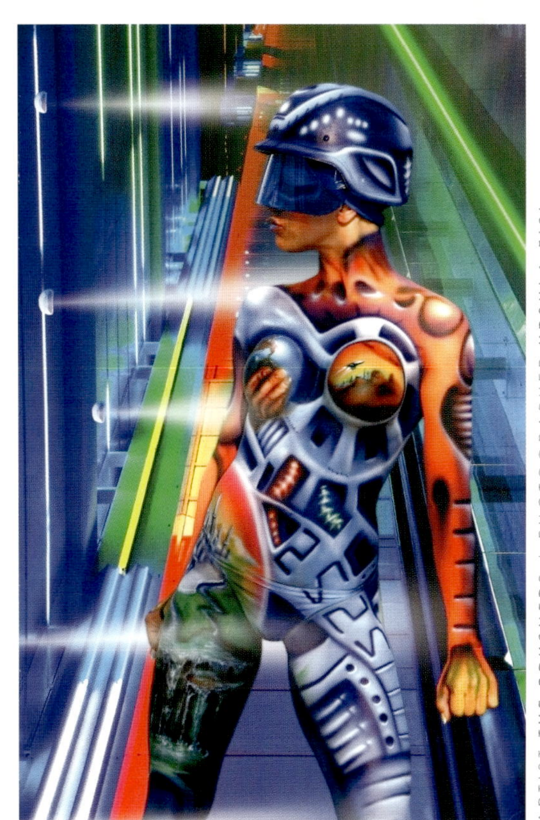

ARTIST THE BRUSHERS | PHOTOGRAPHER URSULA EISL

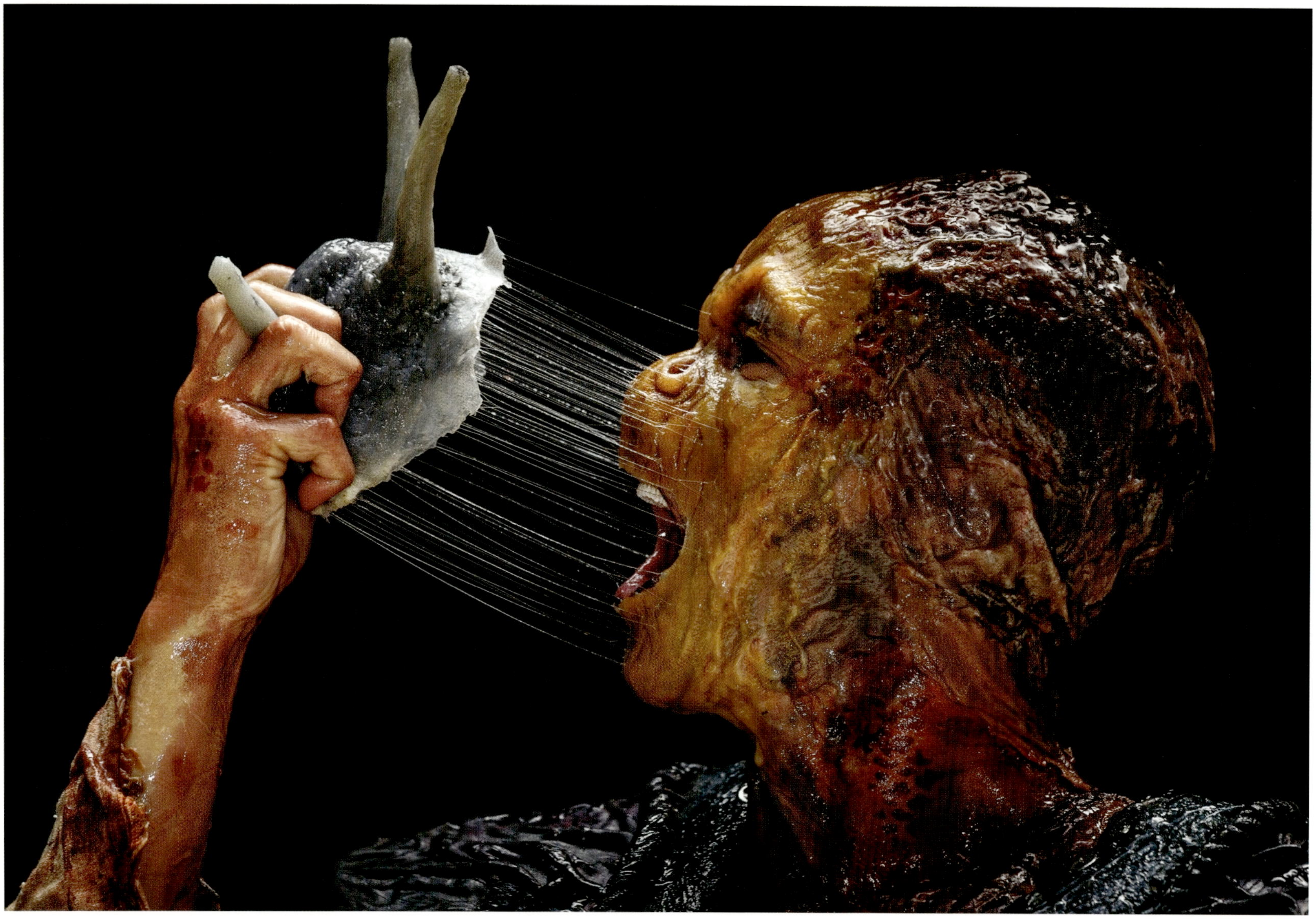

ARTIST JULIAN BARTRAM | PHOTOGRAPHER PETER ZIEGLER

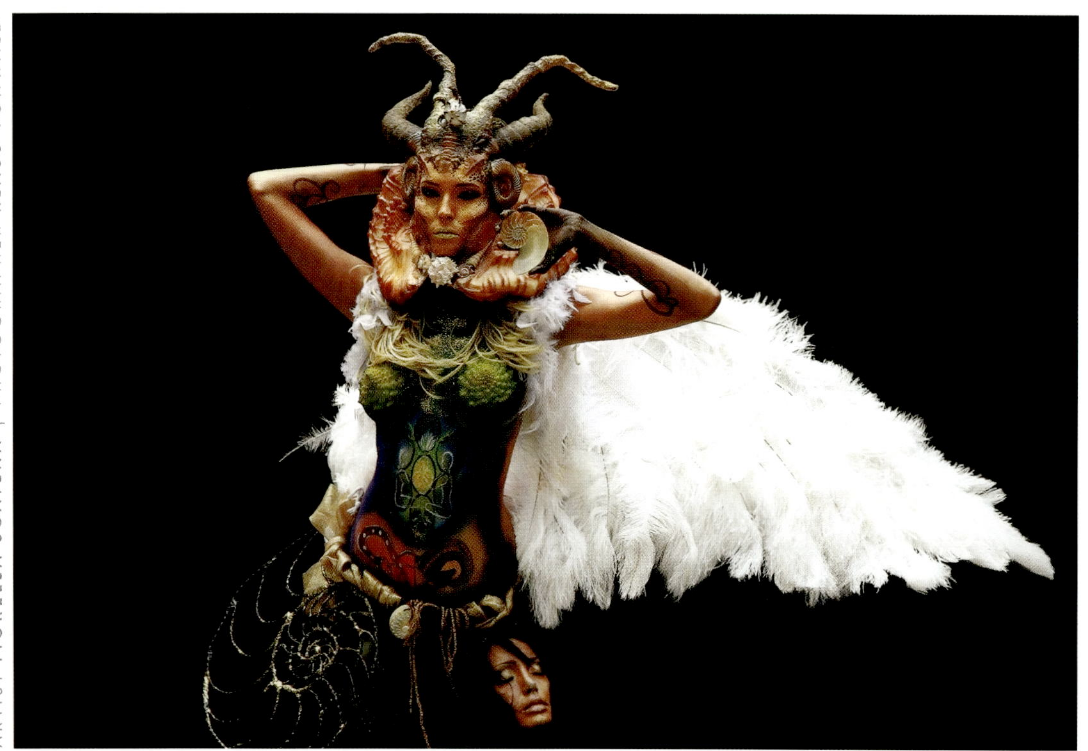

ARTIST FIORELLA SCATENA | PHOTOGRAPHER KLAUS VONWALD

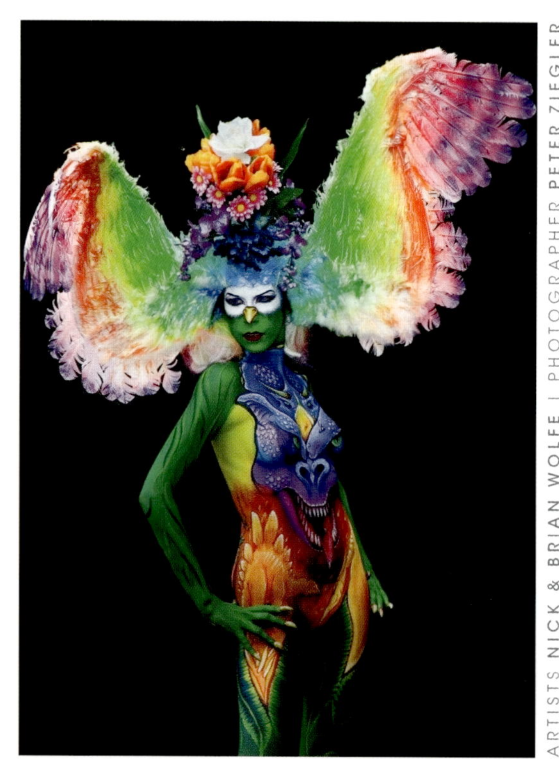

ARTISTS NICK & BRIAN WOLFE | PHOTOGRAPHER PETER ZIEGLER

ARTIST ANNE CAZE | PHOTOGRAPHER CARSTEN RENTZ

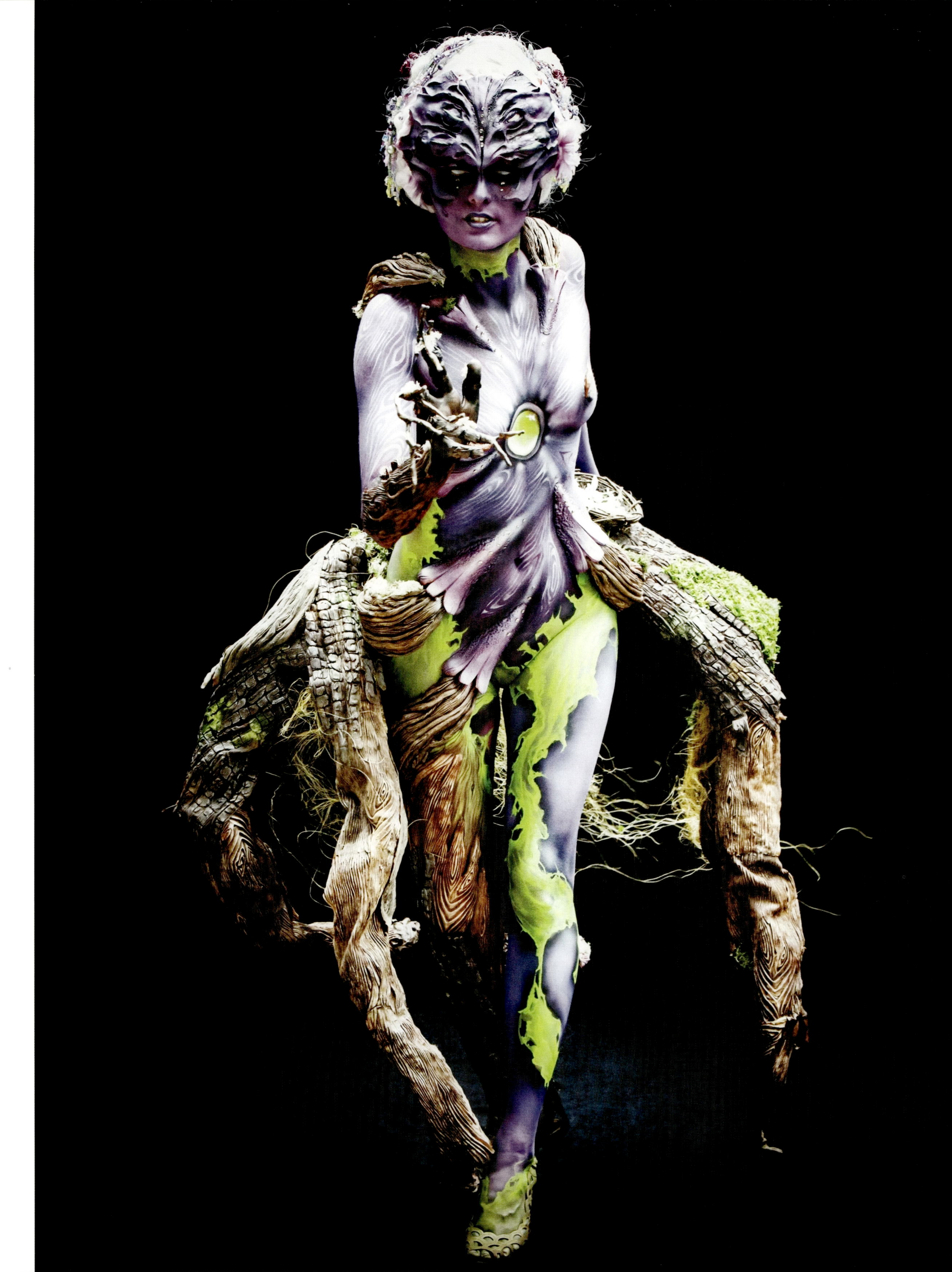
ARTIST HOUYAM HAJLAOUI | PHOTOGRAPHER PHILIPP SIMONIS

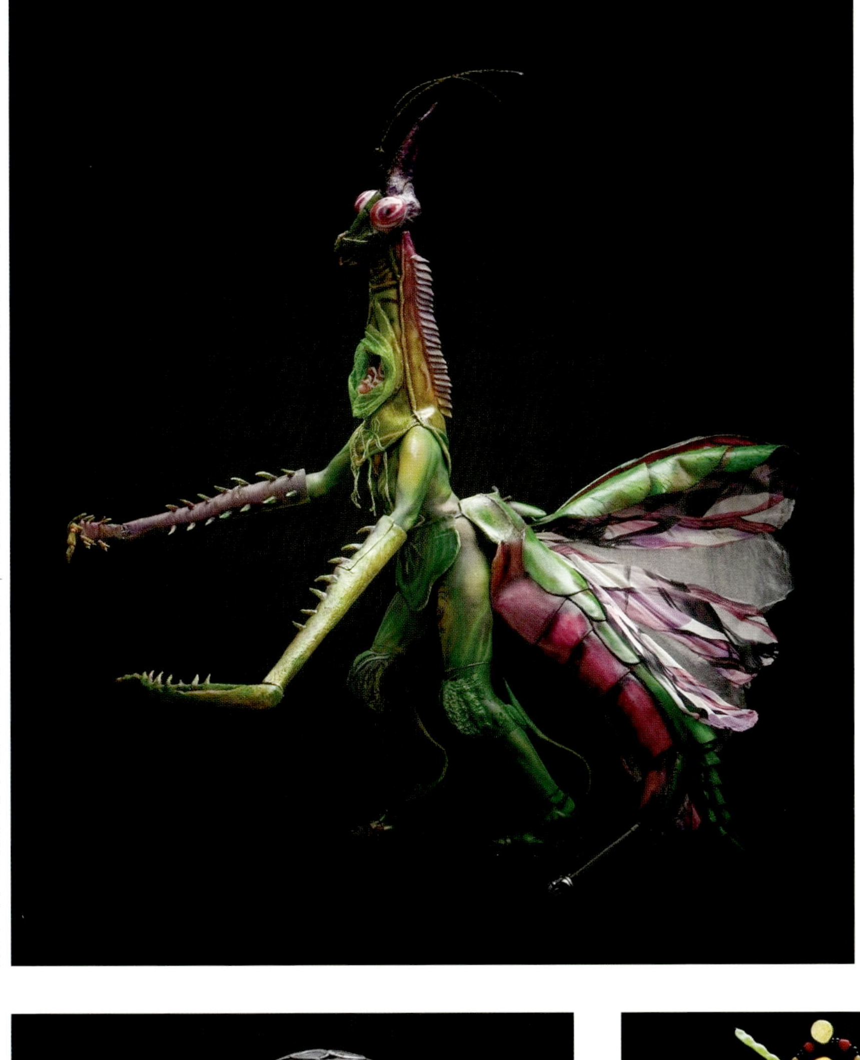

ARTIST RICHARD VAN DER LAAN | PHOTOGRAPHER ANDREA PERIA

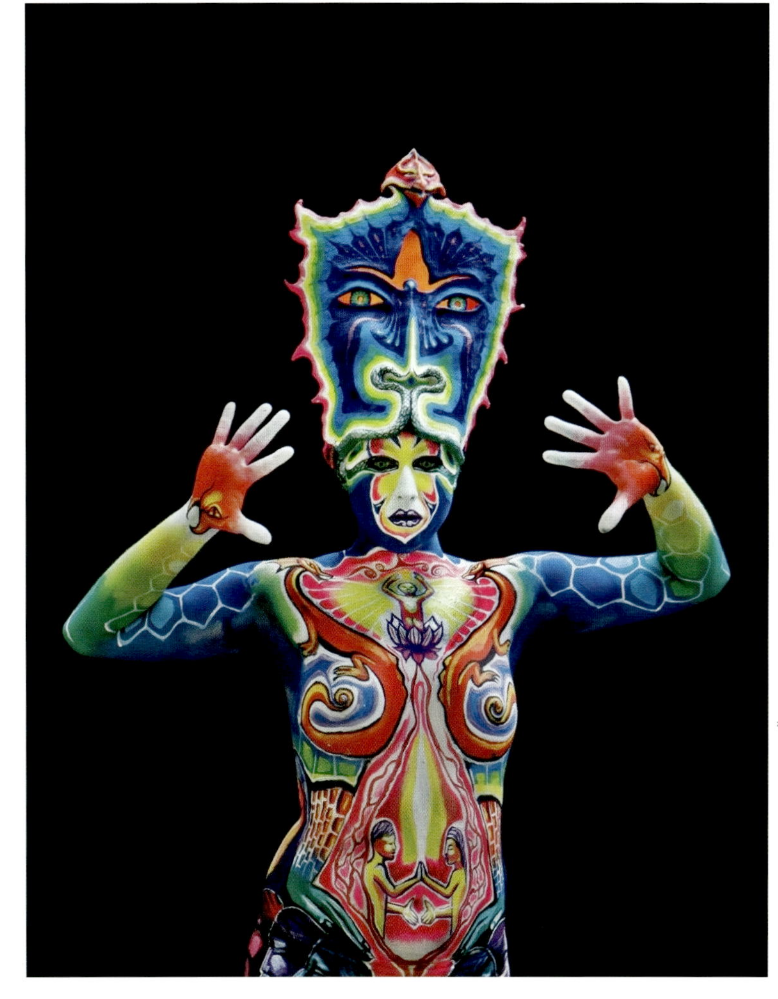

ARTIST JOHANNES STÖTTER | PHOTOGRAPHER TOBIAS OETZBRUGGER

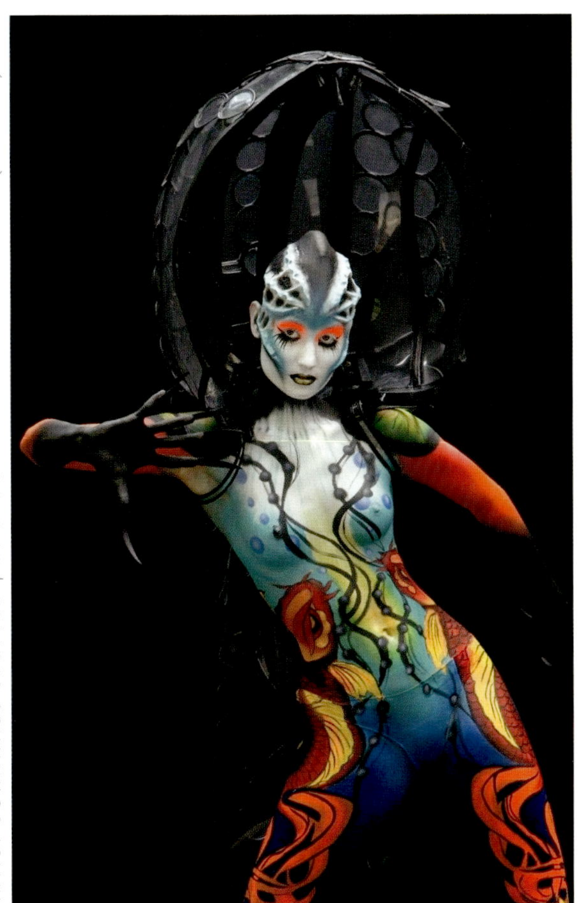

ARTIST EDINA VADÓCZ | PHOTOGRAPHER CLAUDIA HÖPFL
ARTIST JOHANNES STÖTTER | PHOTOGRAPHER EHUD MELAMED (CENTER)

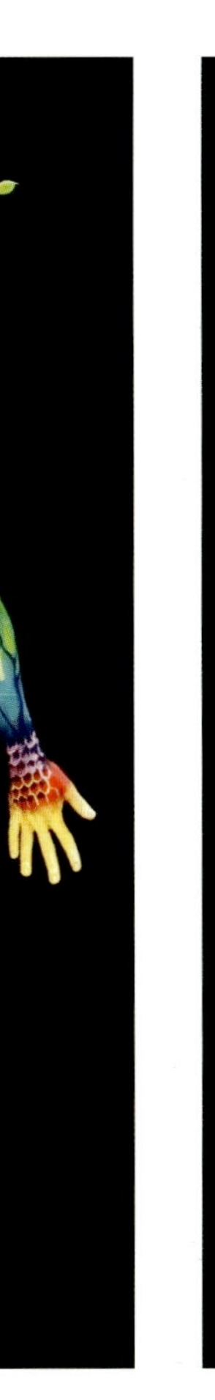

ARTISTS NICK HERRERA & ALEX HANSEN | PHOTOGRAPHER PETER ZIEGLER

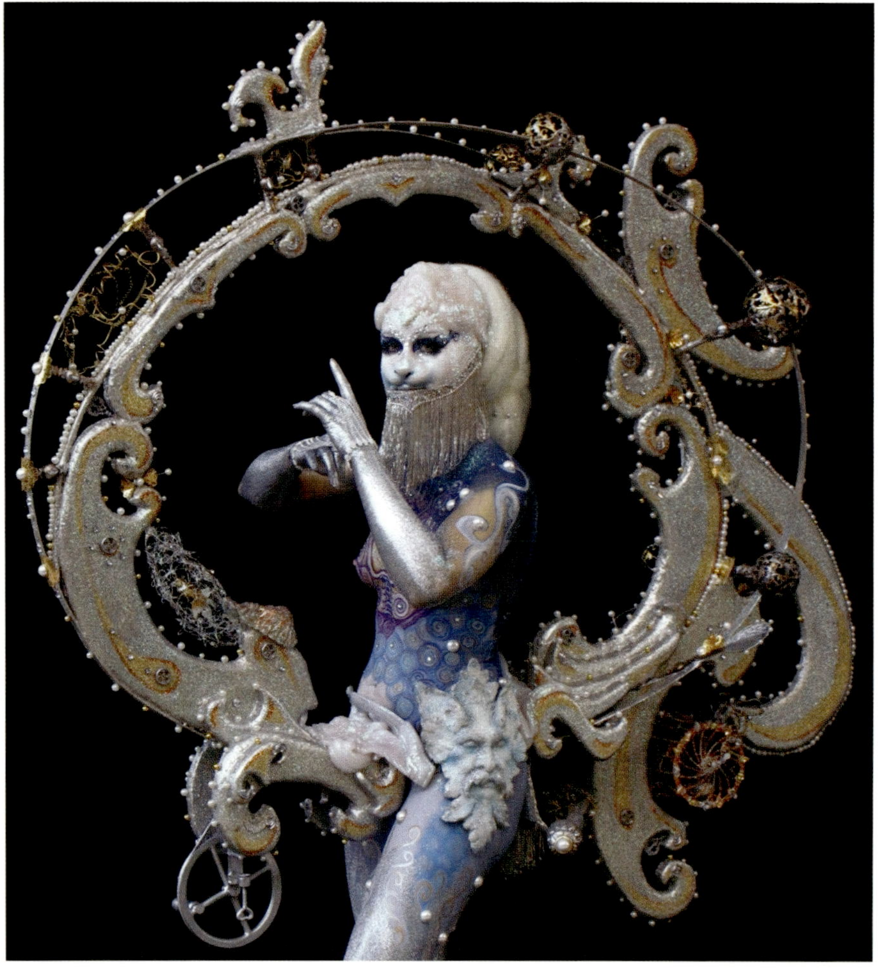

ARTIST BIRGIT MÖRTL | PHOTOGRAPHER HELMUT KURZ

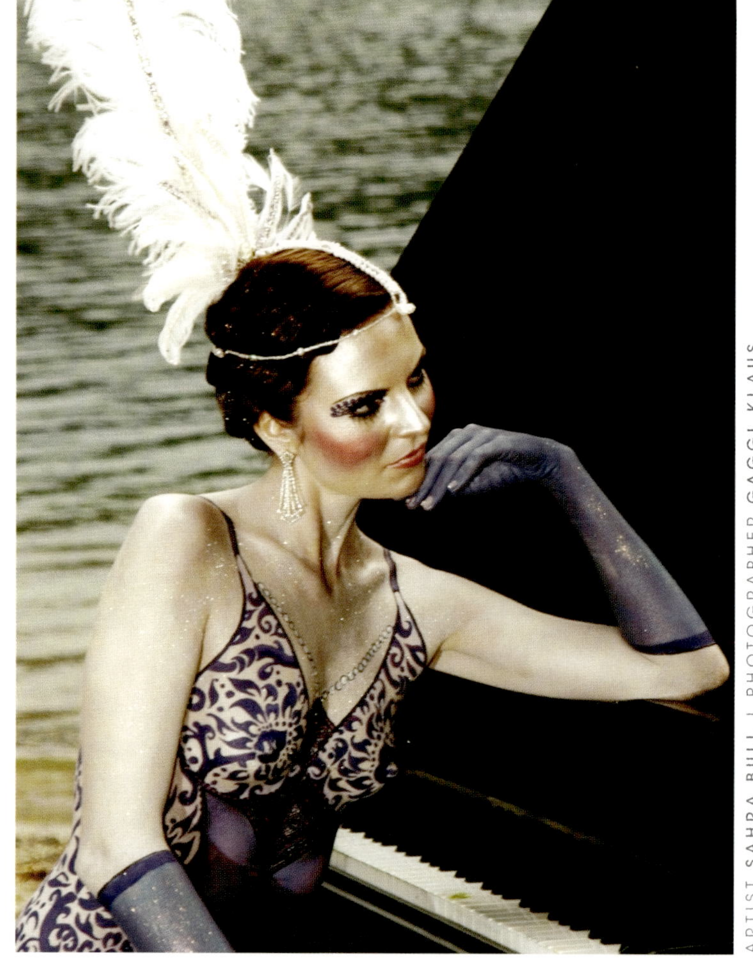

ARTIST SAHRA BULL | PHOTOGRAPHER GAGGL KLAUS

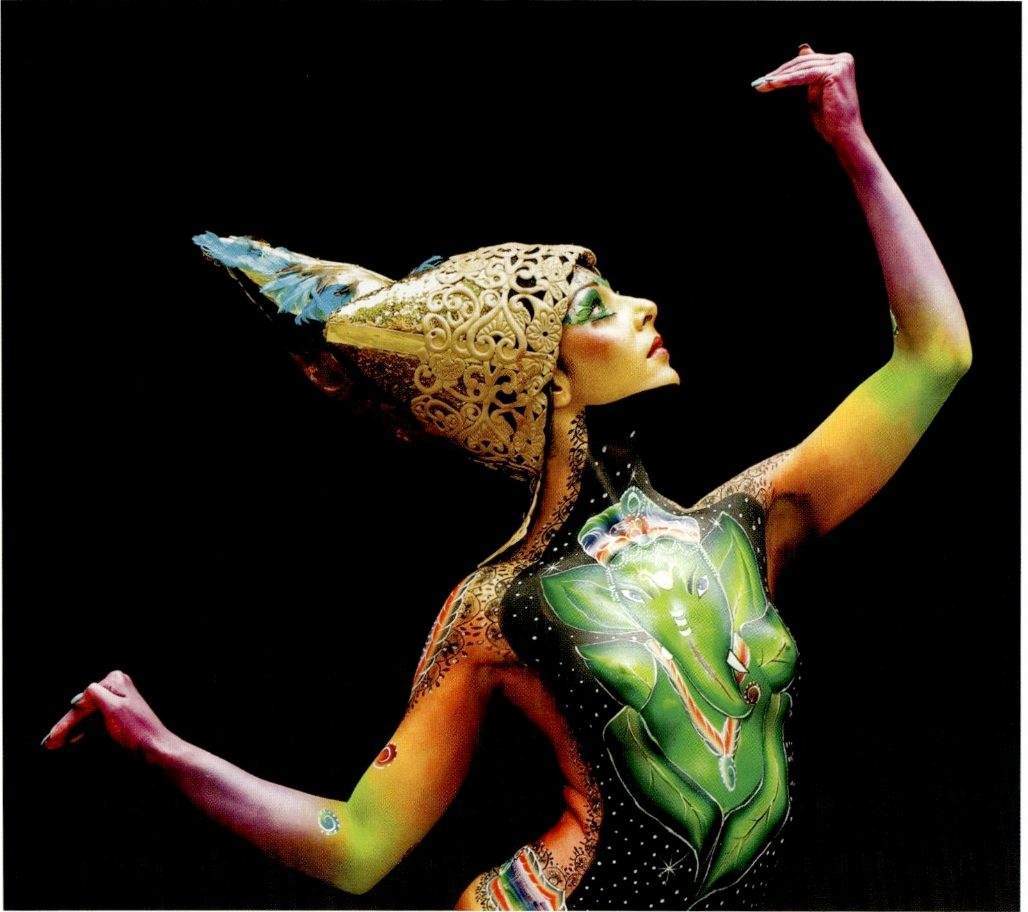

ARTIST EVA MOLNAR | PHOTOGRAPHER GIANANDREA UGGETTI

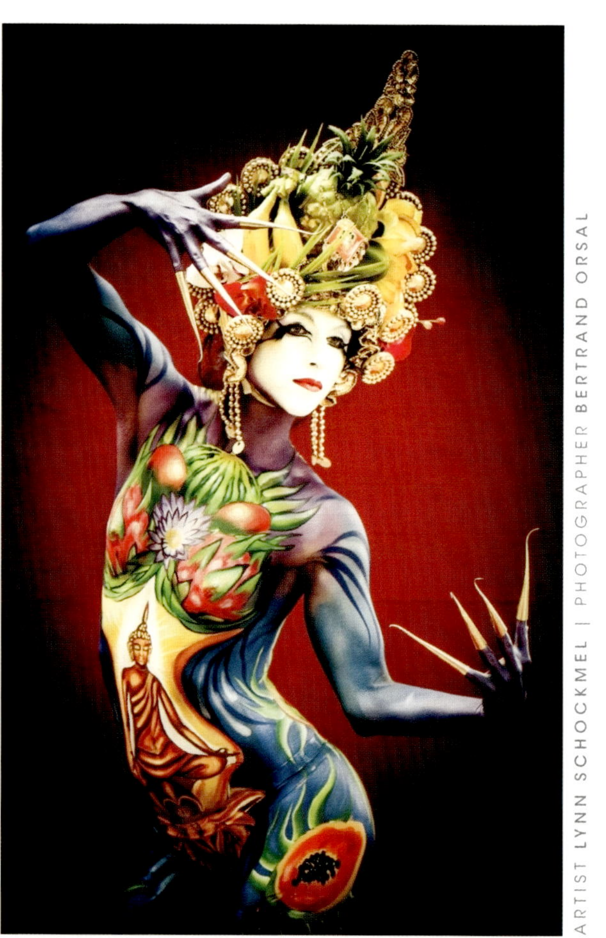

ARTIST LYNN SCHOCKMEL | PHOTOGRAPHER BERTRAND ORSAL

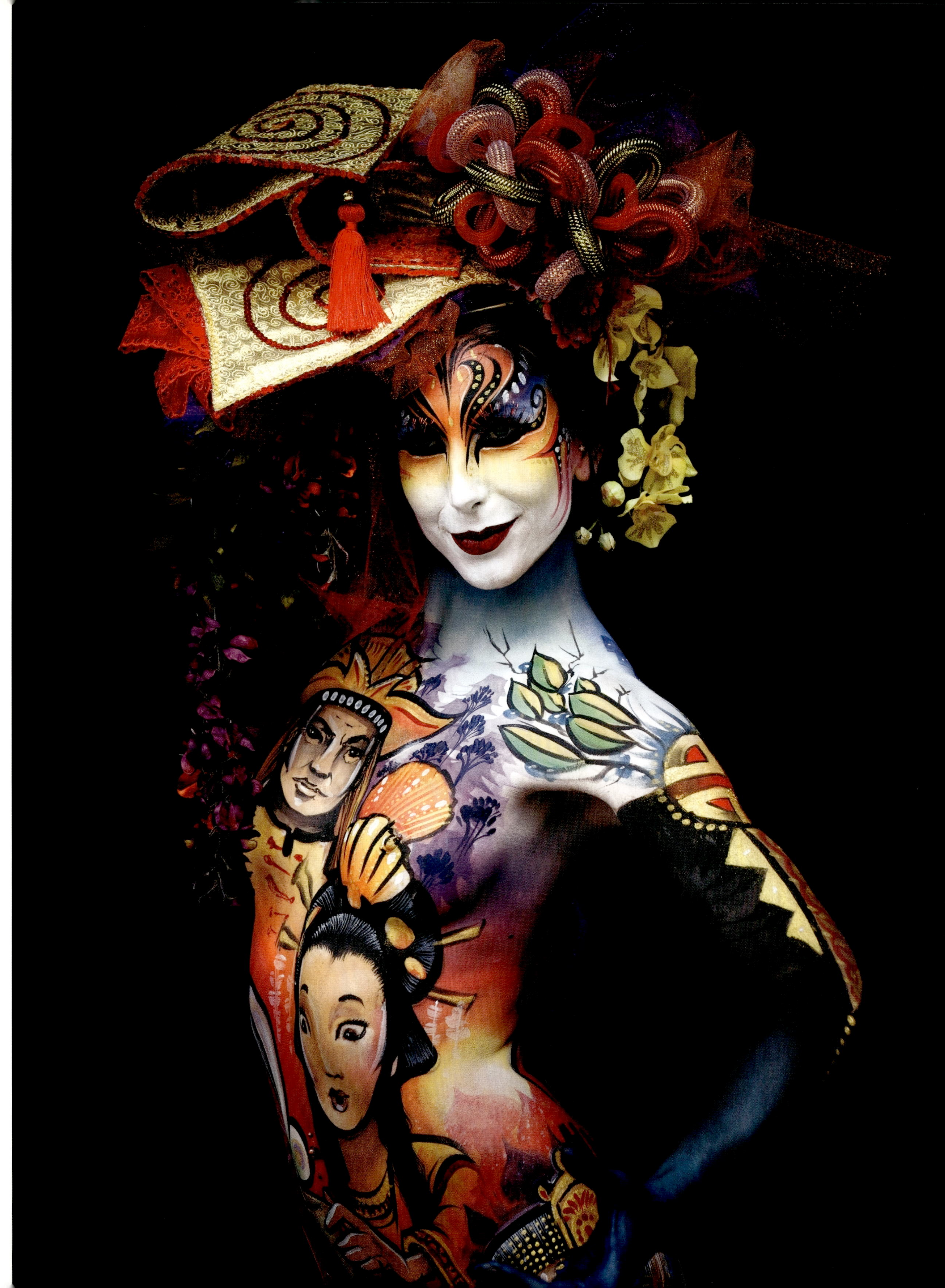

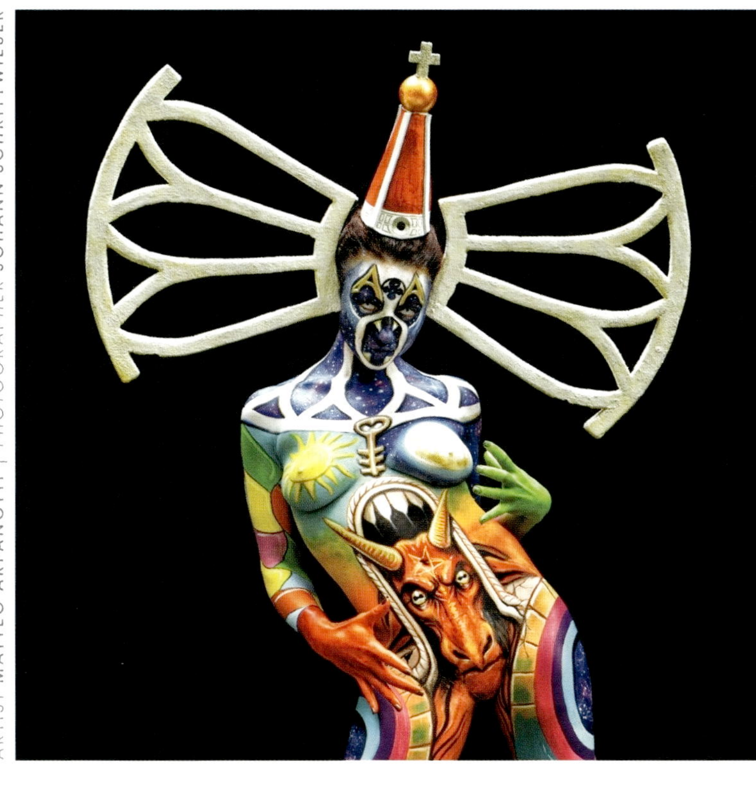

ARTIST MATTEO ARFANOTTI | PHOTOGRAPHER JOHANN SCHRITTWIESER

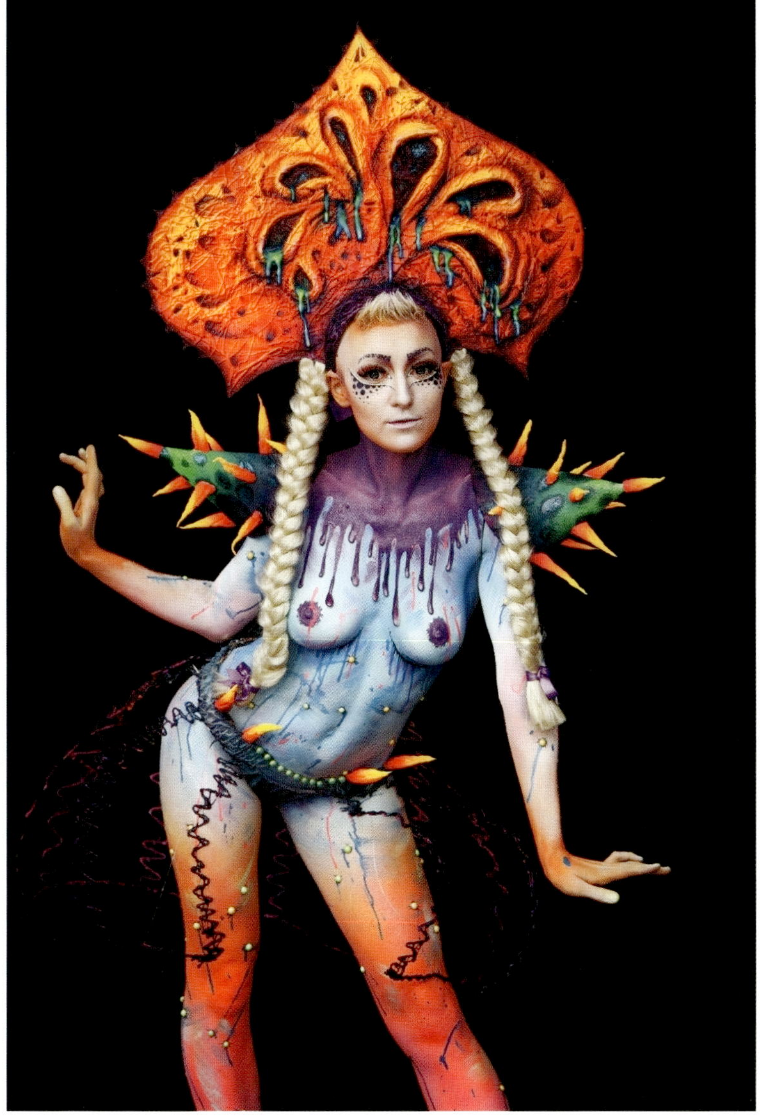

ARTIST KRISTINA ELIZAROVA | PHOTOGRAPHER PETER ZIEGLER

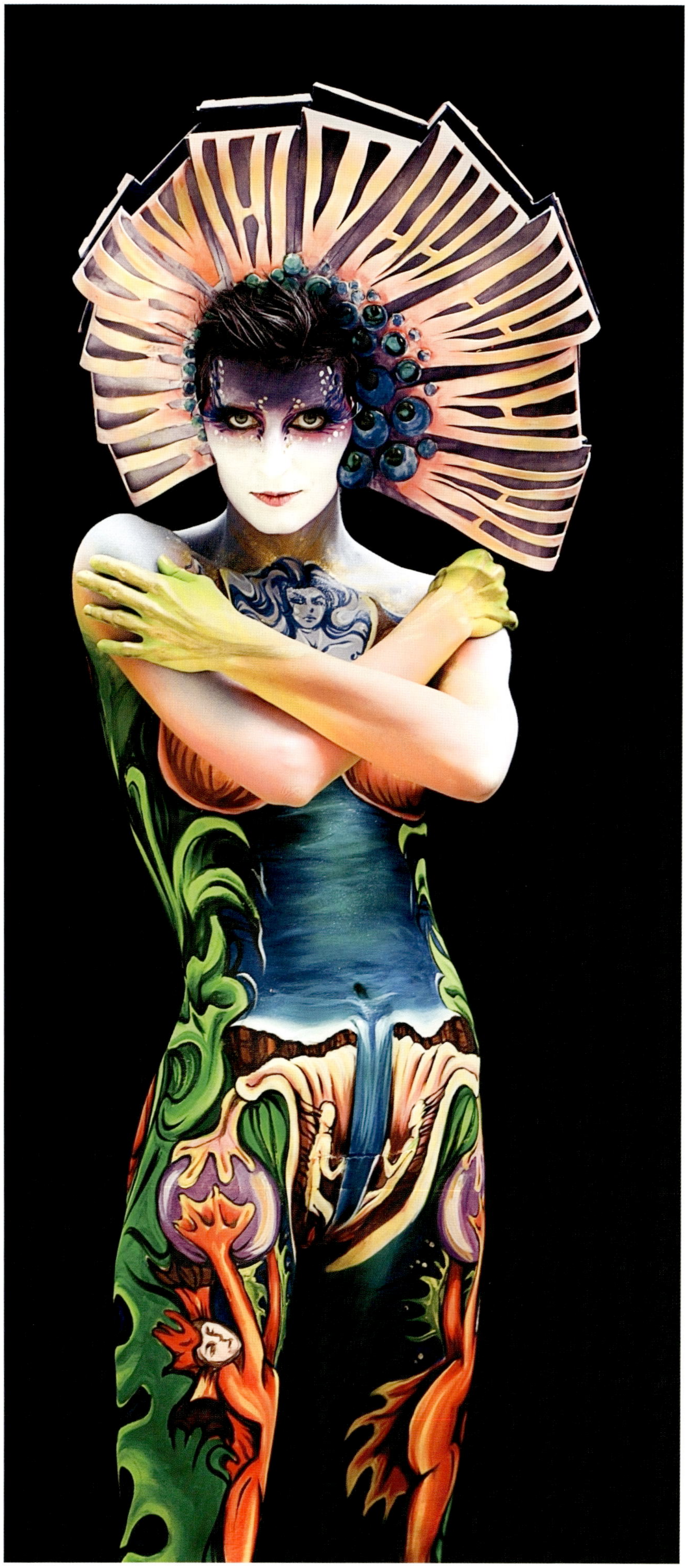

ARTIST MIN AH KIM | PHOTOGRAPHER GIANANDREA UGGETTI

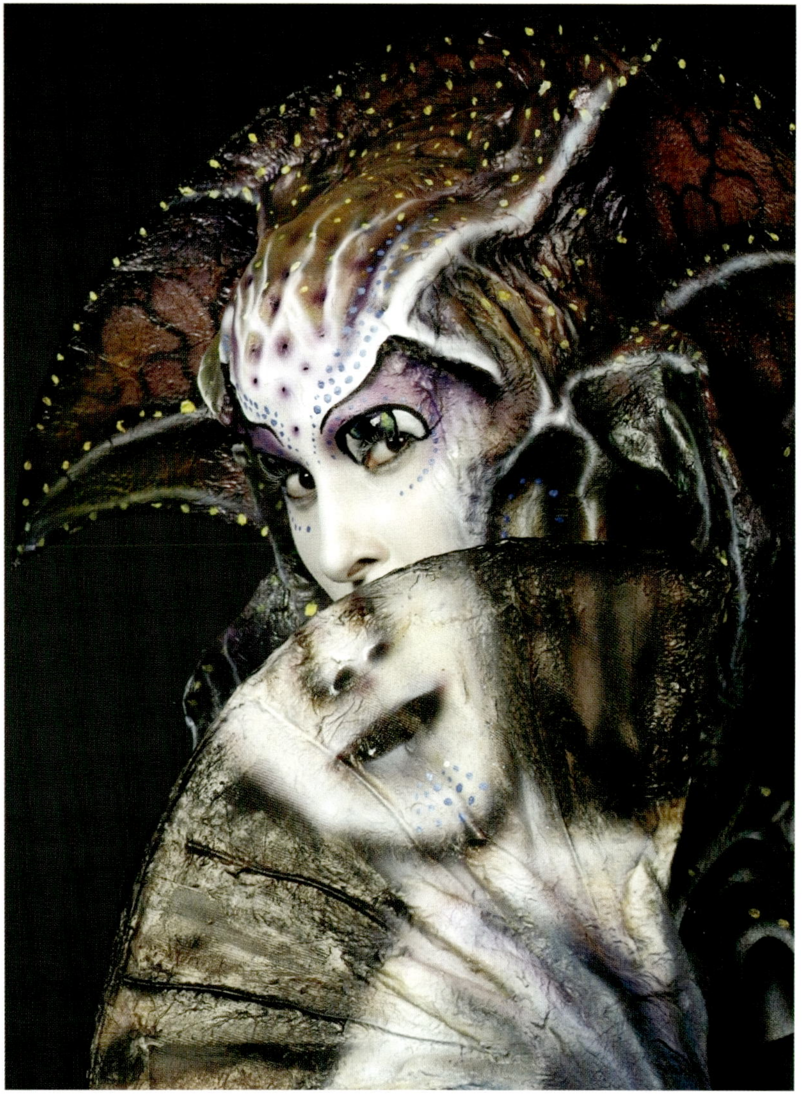

ARTIST PATRICK LEIS | PHOTOGRAPHER JOACHIM BERGAUER

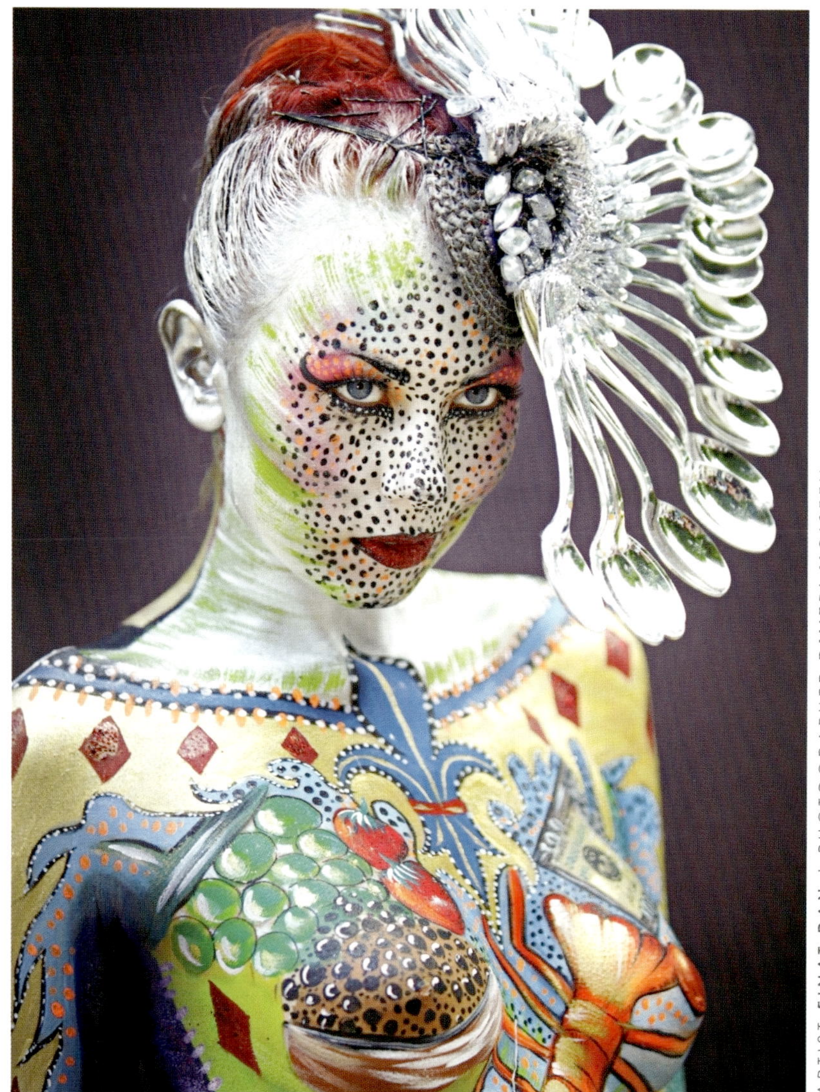

ARTIST EINAT DAN | PHOTOGRAPHER DMITRI MOISEEV

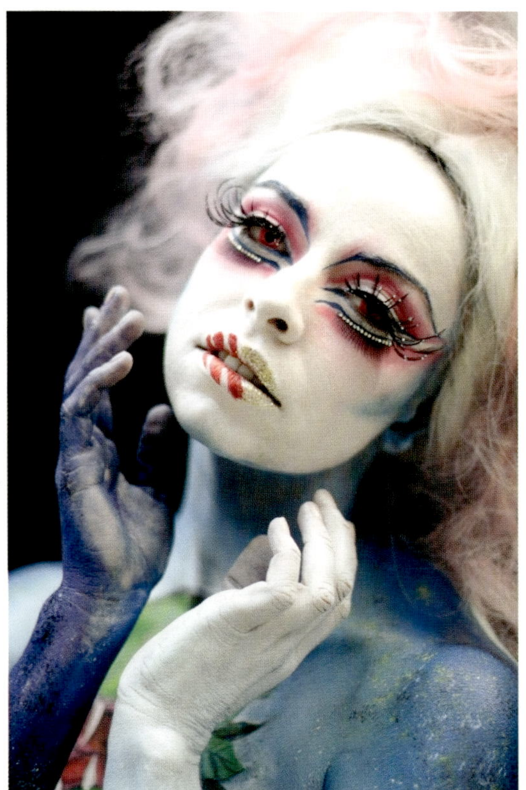

ARTIST SOPHIA BENOMAR | PHOTOGRAPHER MARTINEZ BASALO

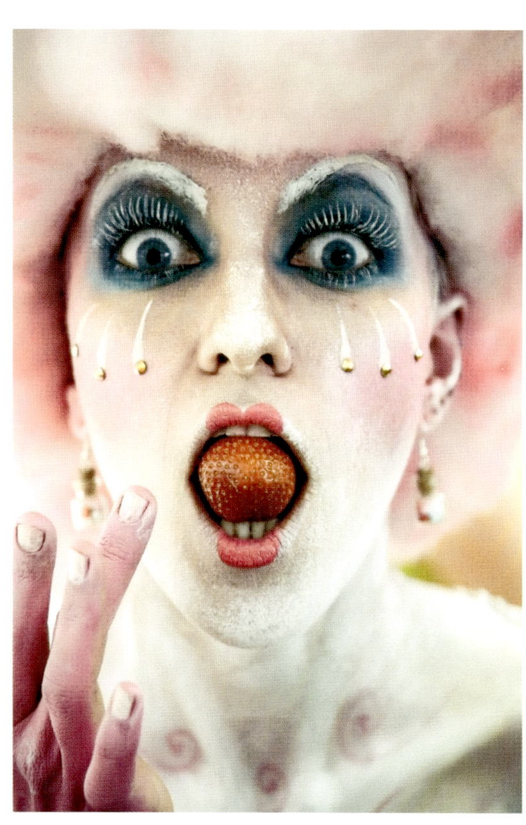

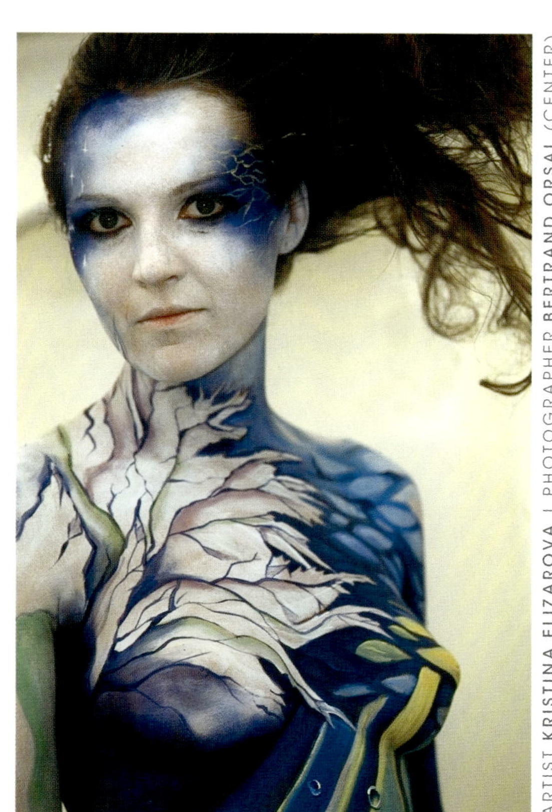

ARTIST KRISTINA ELIZAROVA | PHOTOGRAPHER BERTRAND ORSAL (CENTER)
ARTIST RAPHAELLE FIELDHOUSE | PHOTOGRAPHER PETER ZIEGLER

38

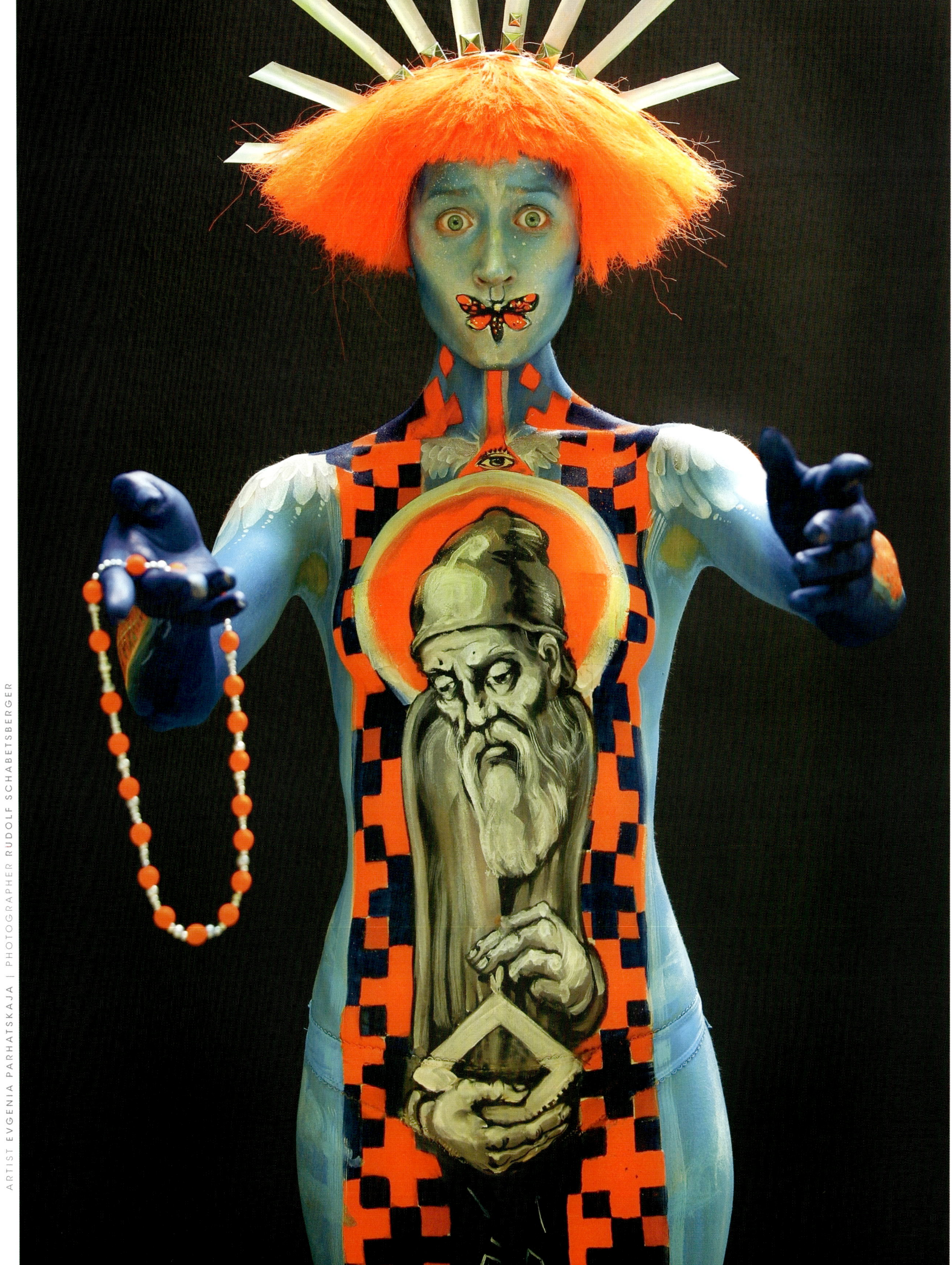
ARTIST EVGENIA PARHATSKAJA | PHOTOGRAPHER RUDOLF SCHABETSBERGER

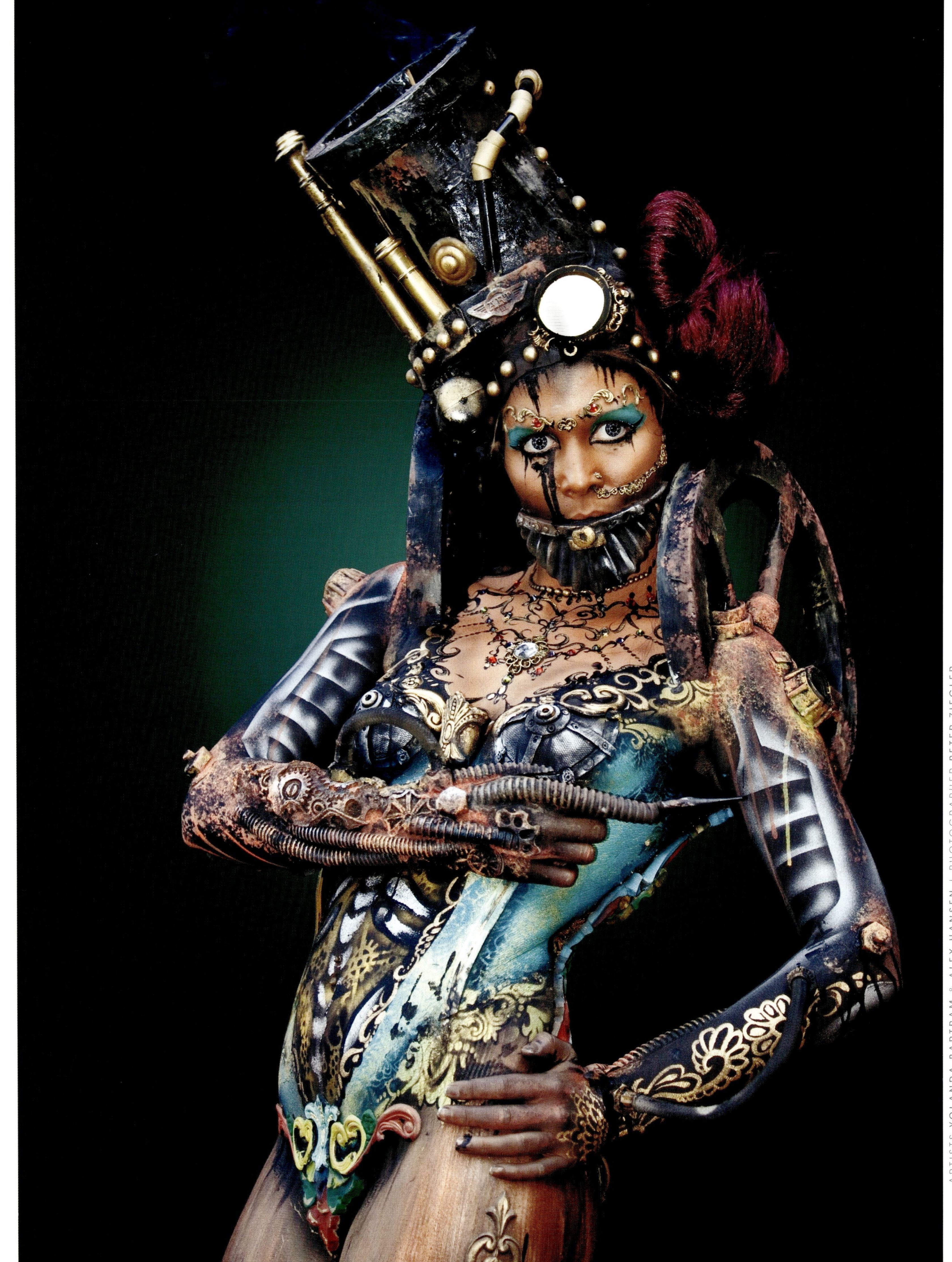

ARTISTS YOLANDA BARTRAM & ALEX HANSEN | PHOTOGRAPHER PETER ZIEGLER

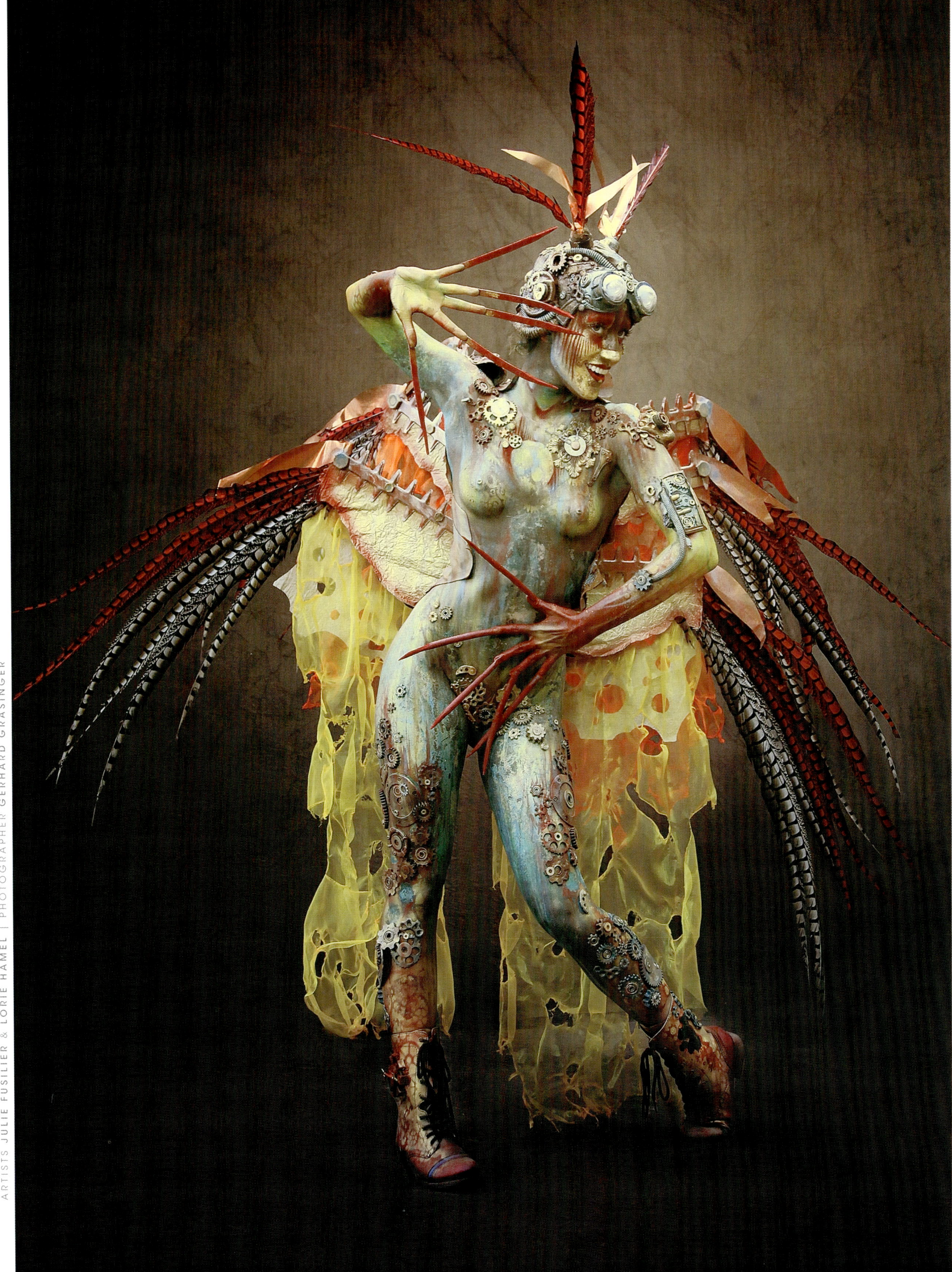

ARTISTS JULIE FUSILIER & LORIE HAMEL | PHOTOGRAPHER GERHARD GRASINGER

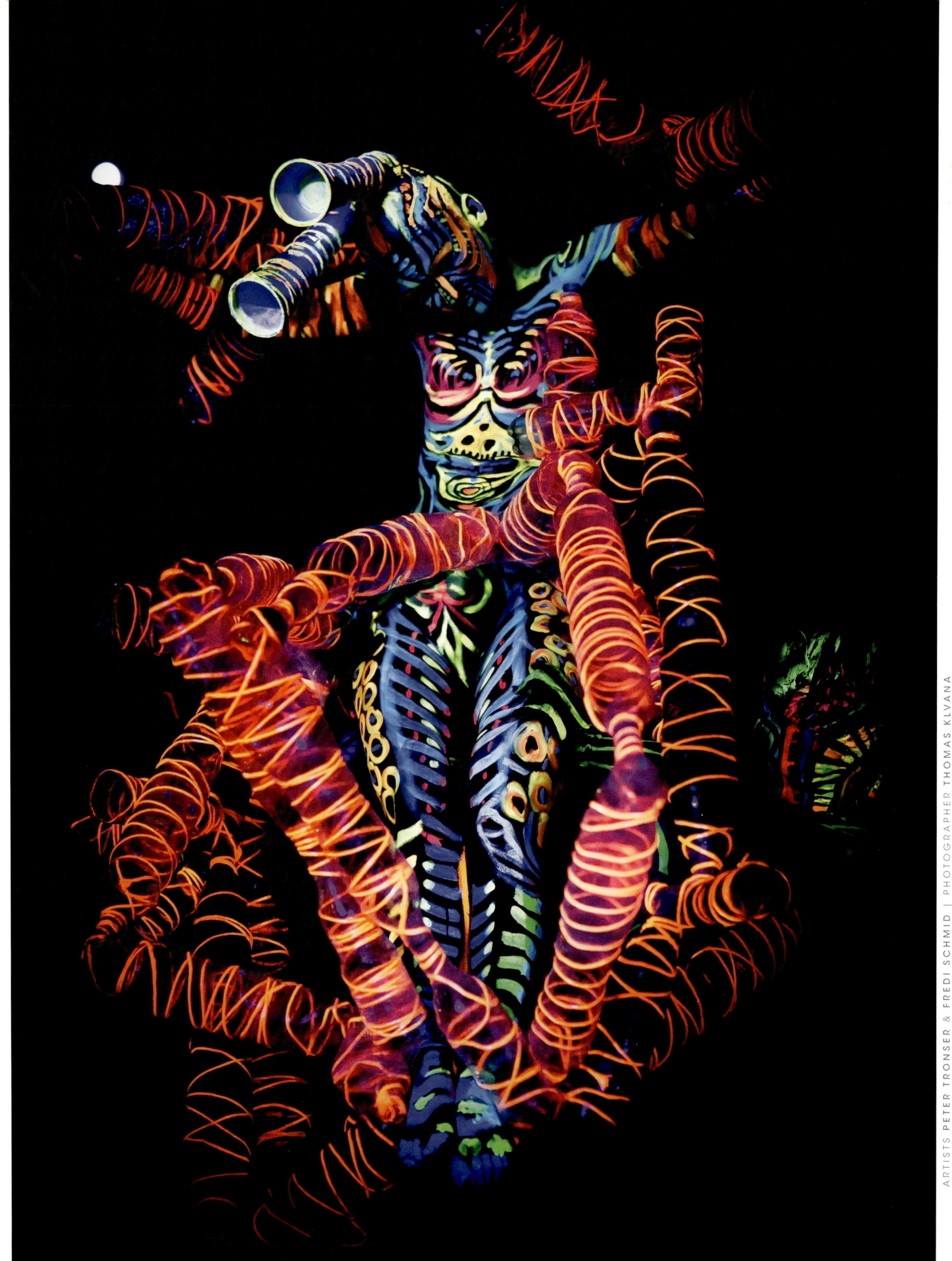

ARTISTS PETER TRONSER & FREDI SCHMID | PHOTOGRAPHER THOMAS KLVANA

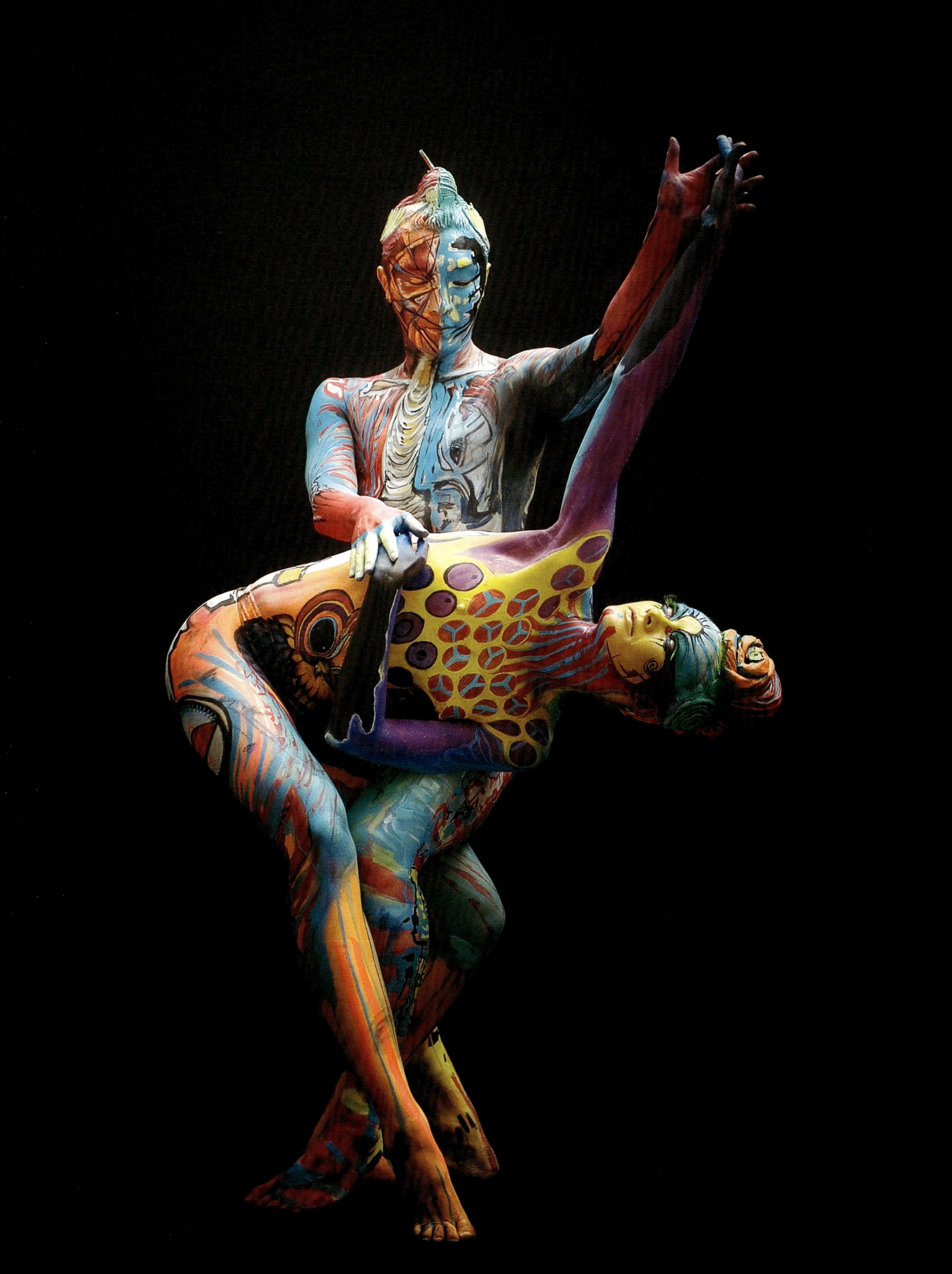

ARTIST AGNIESZKA GLINSKA | PHOTOGRAPHER ANDREA PERIA

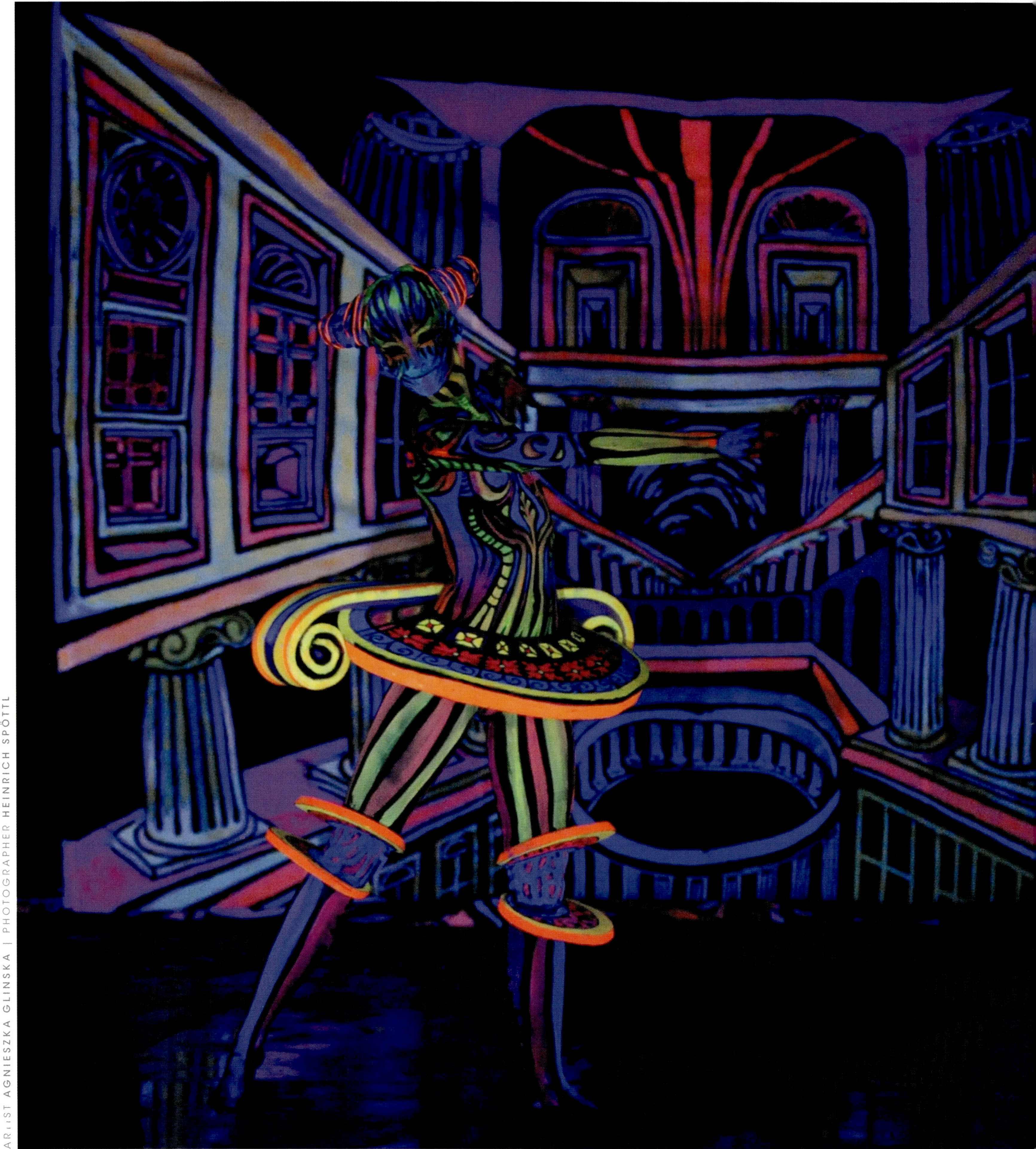

ARTIST AGNIESZKA GLINSKA | PHOTOGRAPHER HEINRICH SPÖTTL

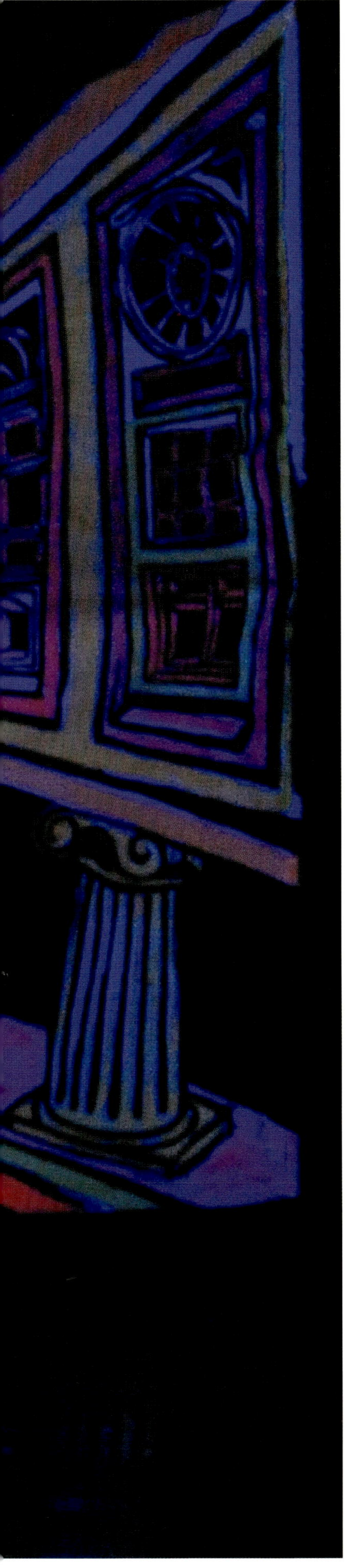

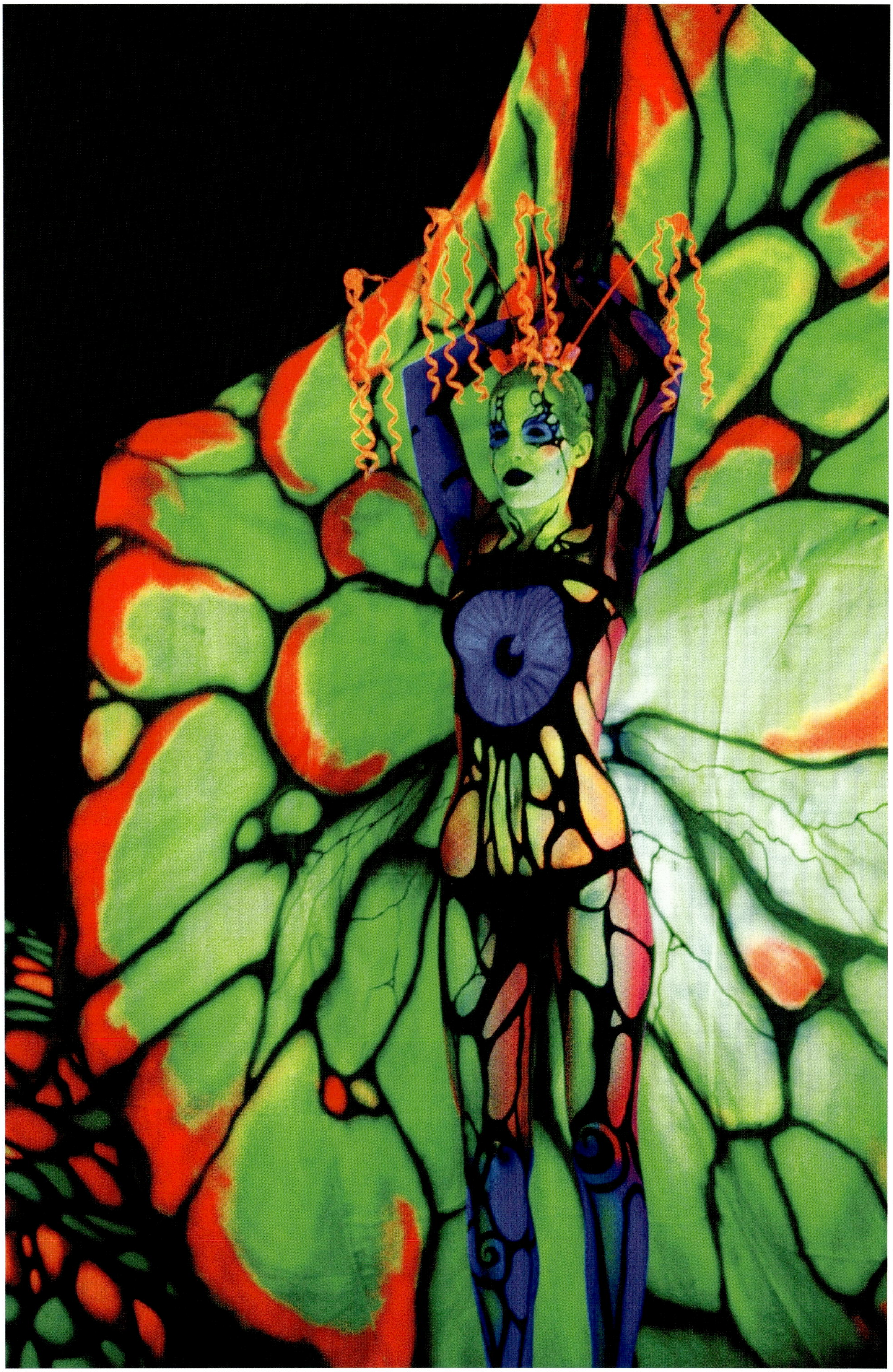

ARTIST AGNIESZKA GLINSKA | PHOTOGRAPHER ARNOLD BRUNNER

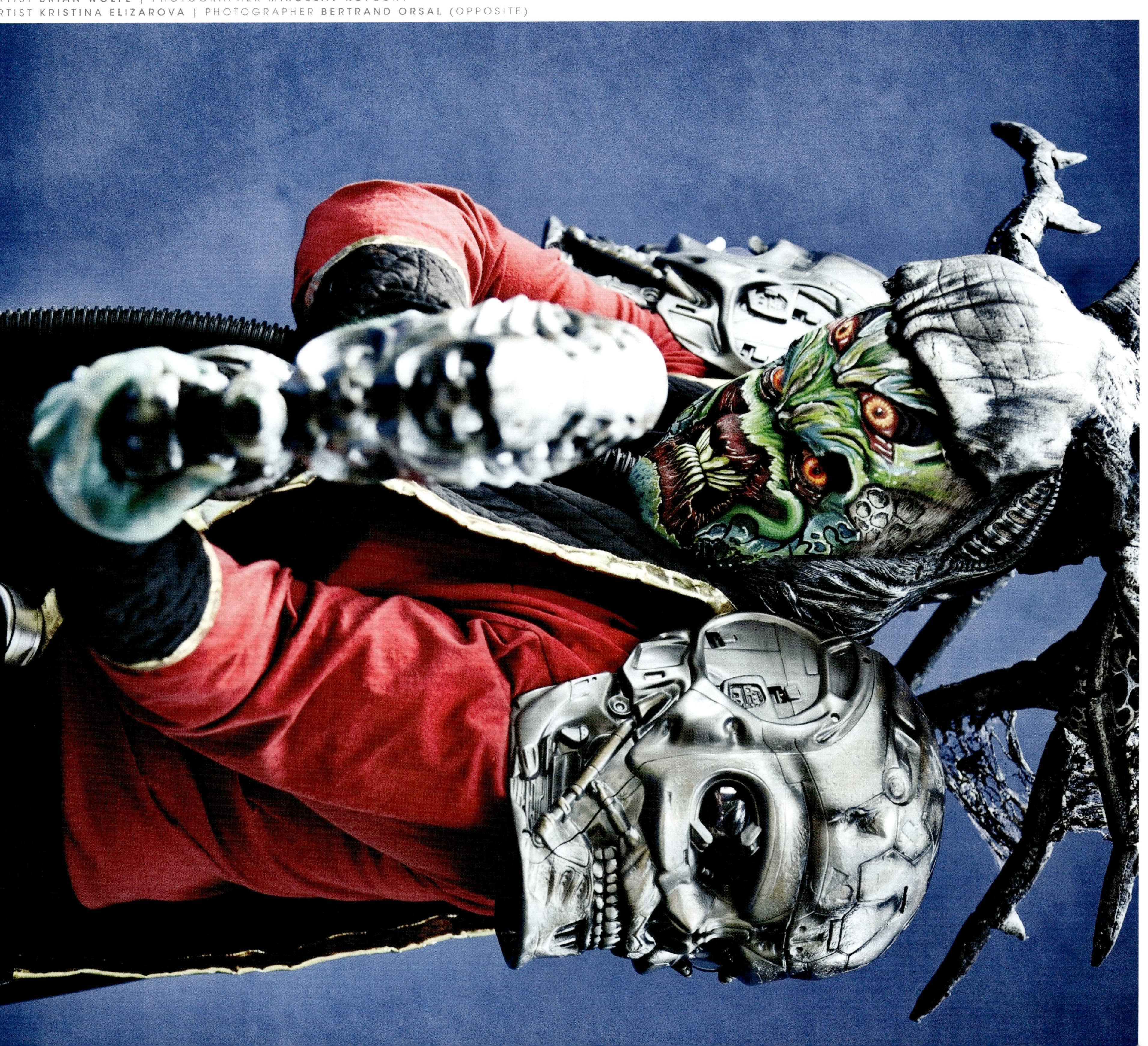

ARTIST BRIAN WOLFE | PHOTOGRAPHER MIROSLAV KOPECKY
ARTIST KRISTINA ELIZAROVA | PHOTOGRAPHER BERTRAND ORSAL (OPPOSITE)

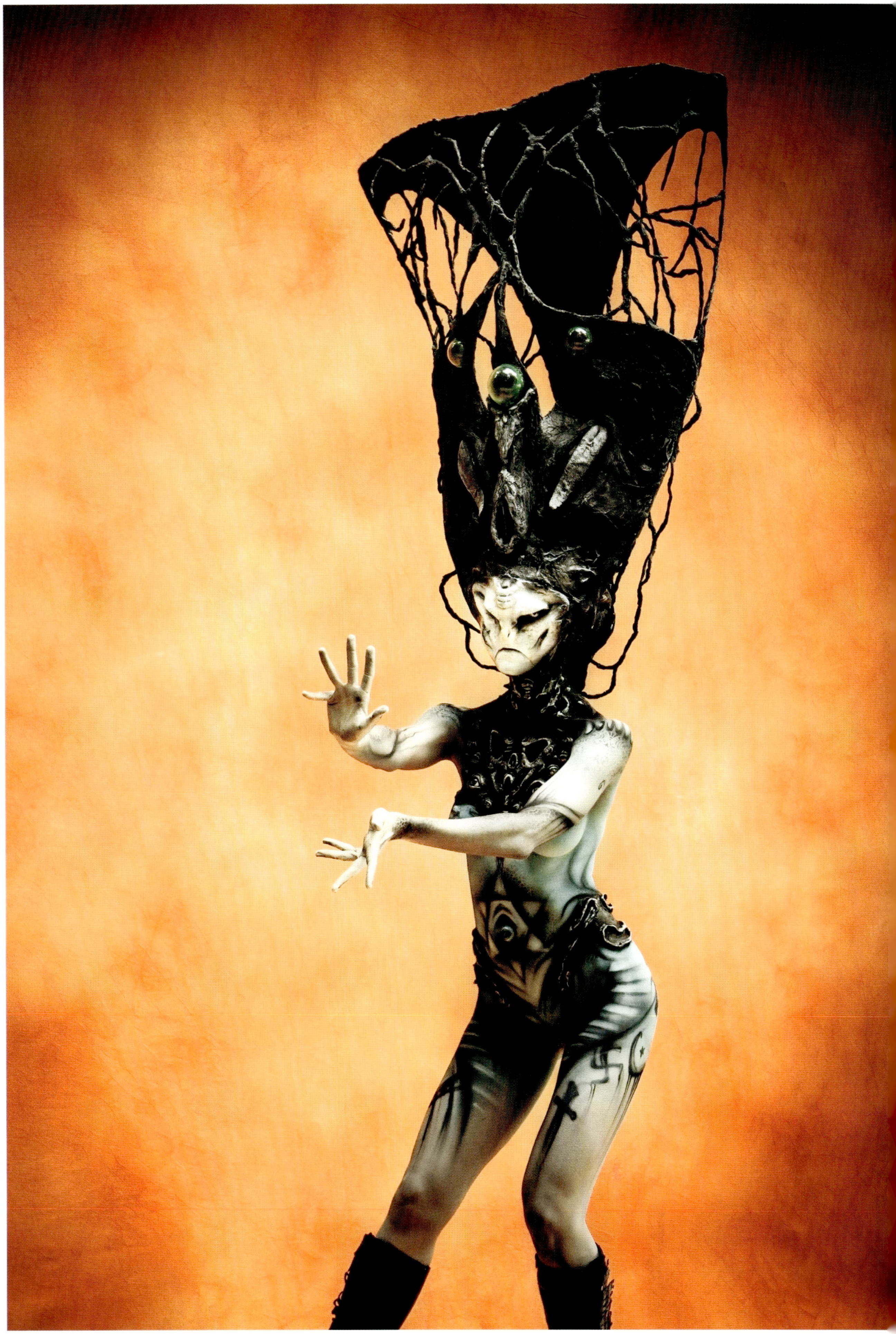

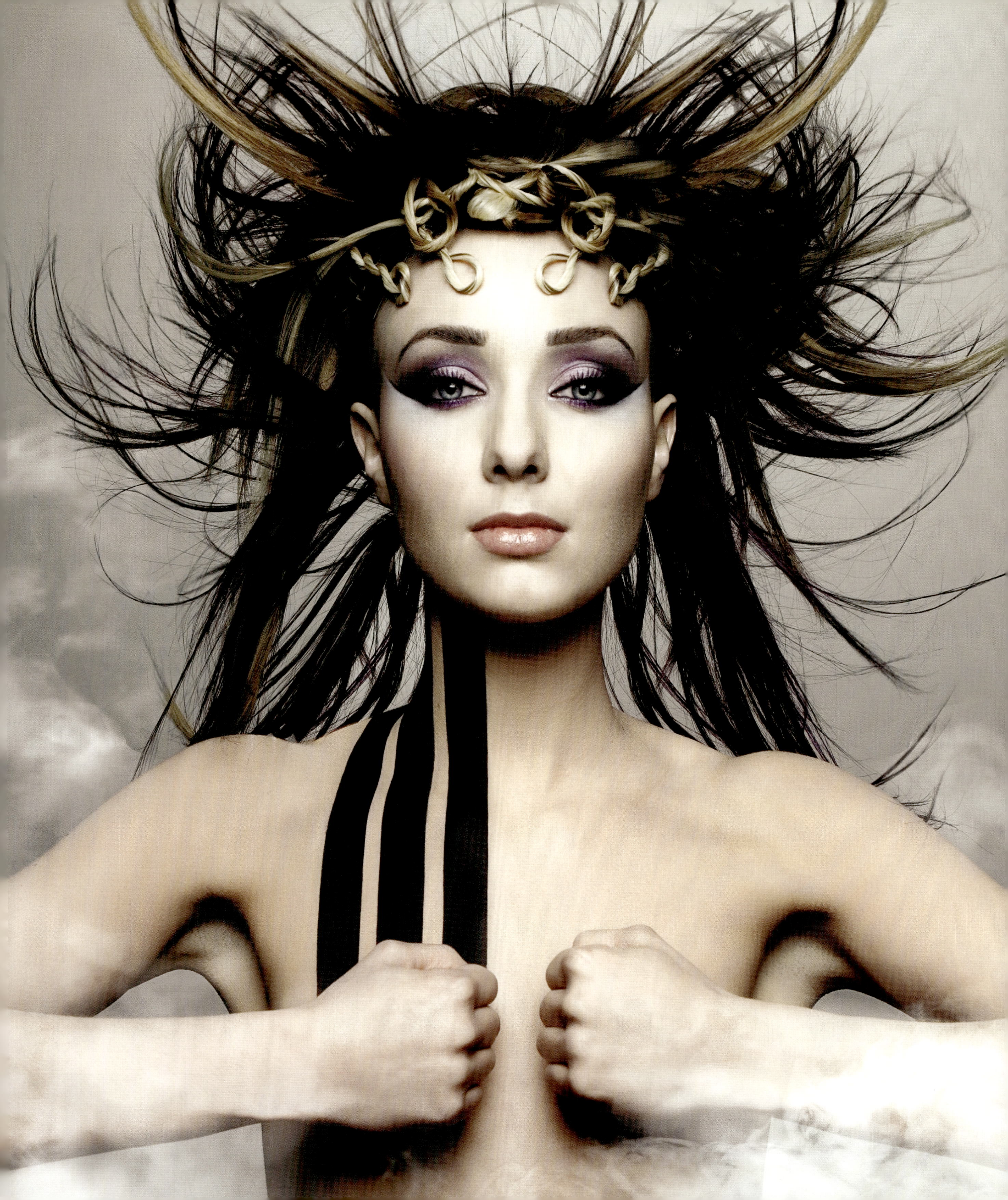

Alex Hansen

WWW.ALEXHANSEN-ART.COM

Alex Hansen is a known talent throughout the bodypainting industry and his airbrush bodypainting style has inspired many developing artists. Alex is a master airbrush and prosthetics teacher around the world. His creations often have a recognizable style and theme that mix the human form with mechanical shapes, producing an organic, robotic finish. Alex has won many national and international awards for his art.

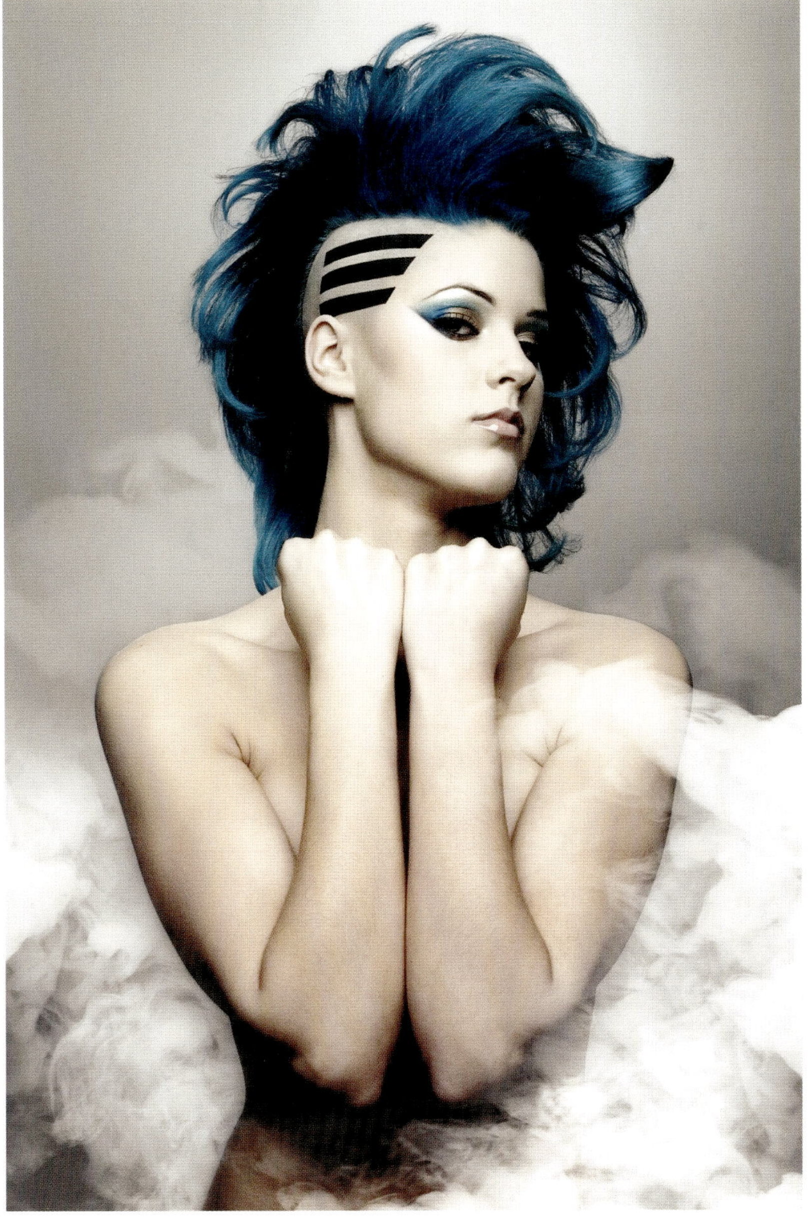

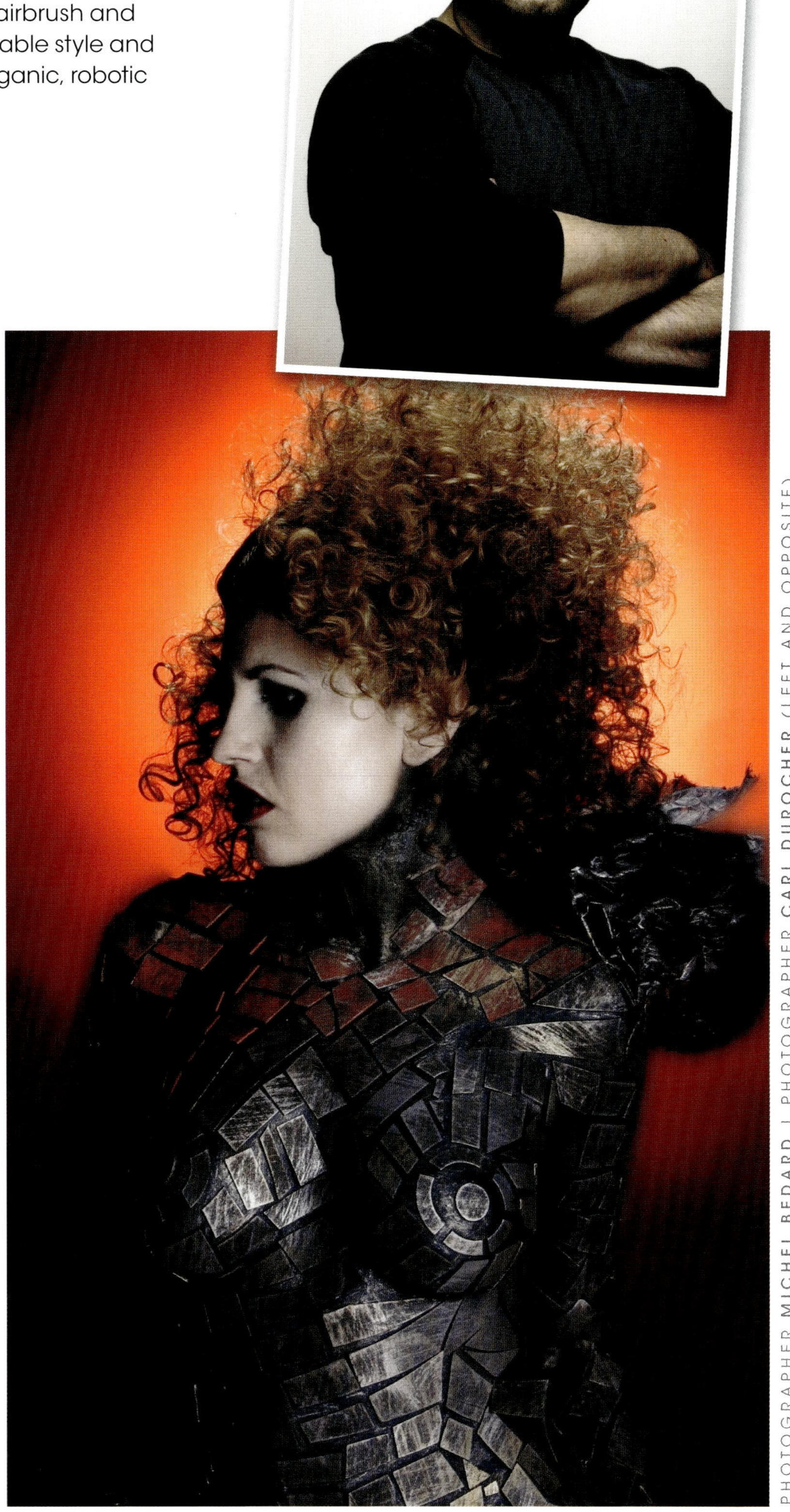

PHOTOGRAPHER MICHEL BEDARD | PHOTOGRAPHER CARL DUROCHER (LEFT AND OPPOSITE)

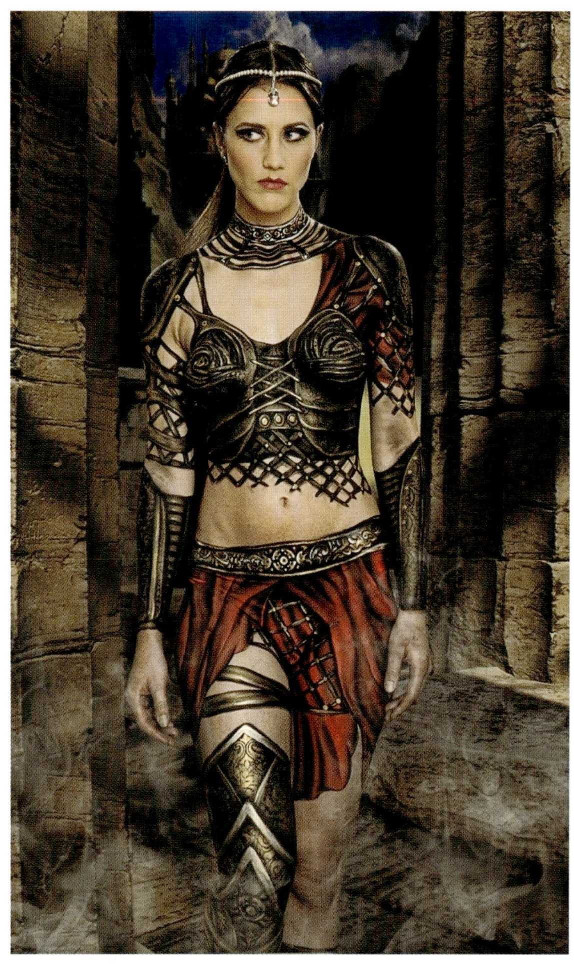

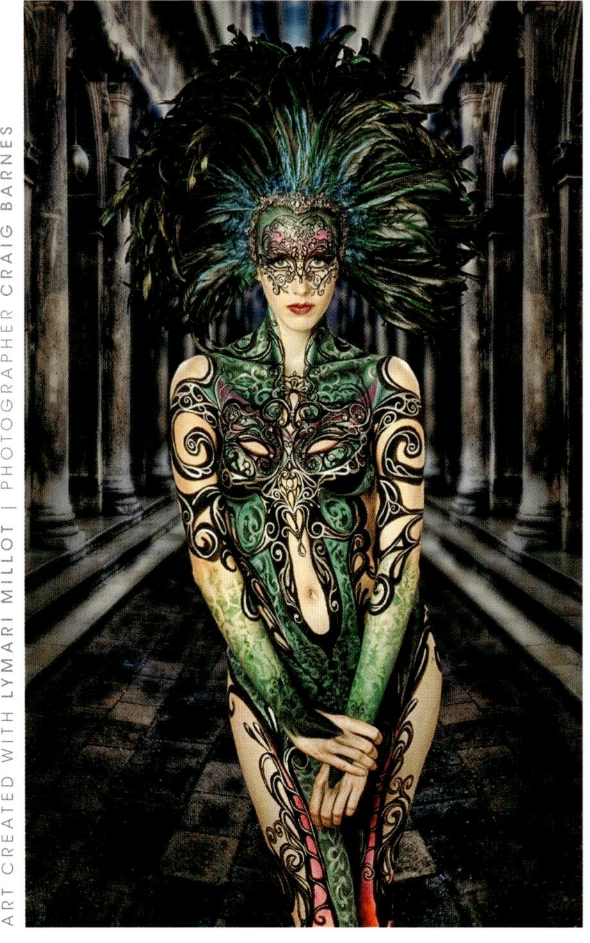

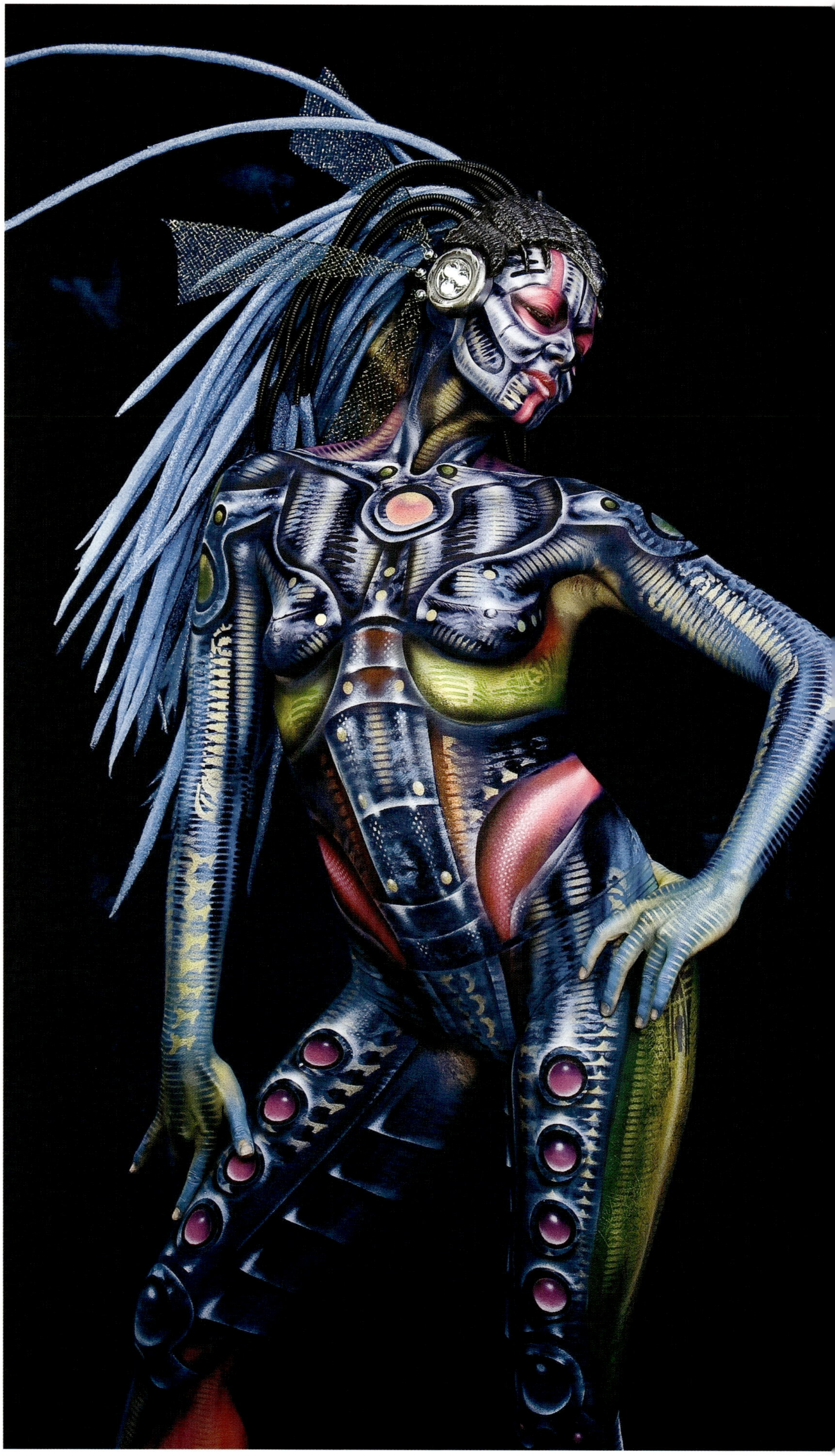

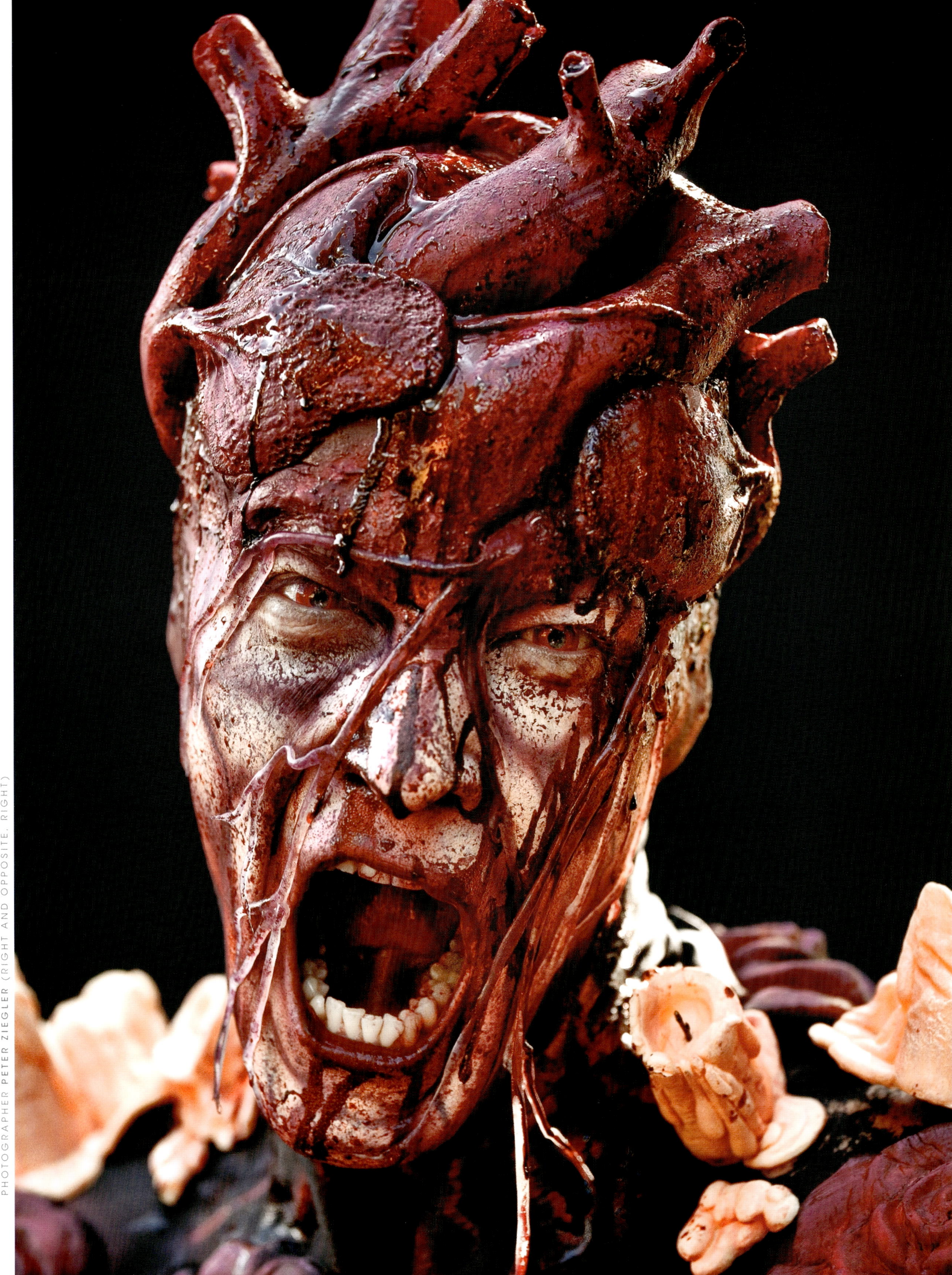

"I love to travel
the world, teach
and learn
from others,
and continue
producing
new art. I'm still
learning as I go.
I still have much
to learn, but I
see the world
differently than
most regular
people. I feel
that my art is
now respected
for what it is."

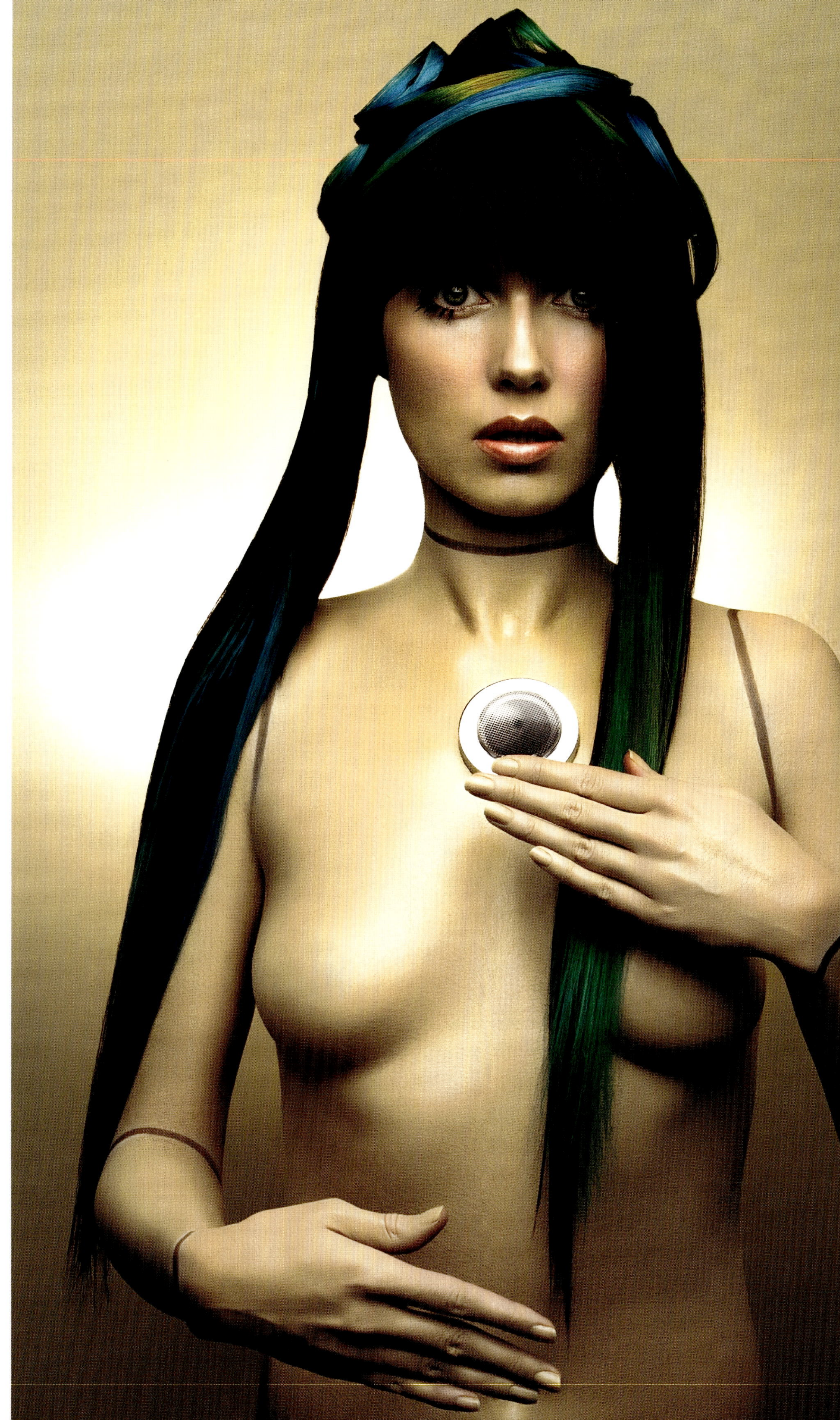

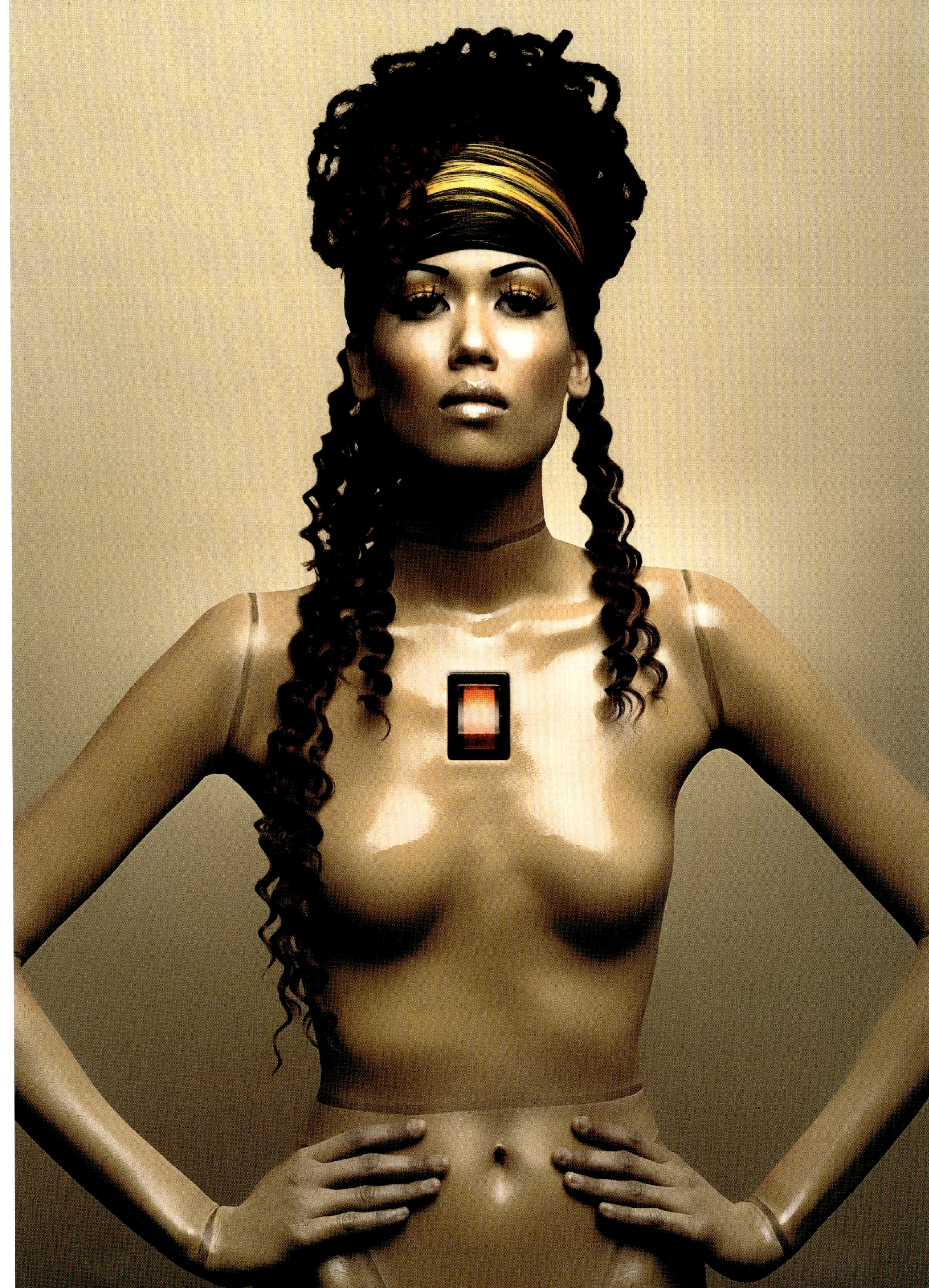

PHOTOGRAPHER CARL DUROCHER

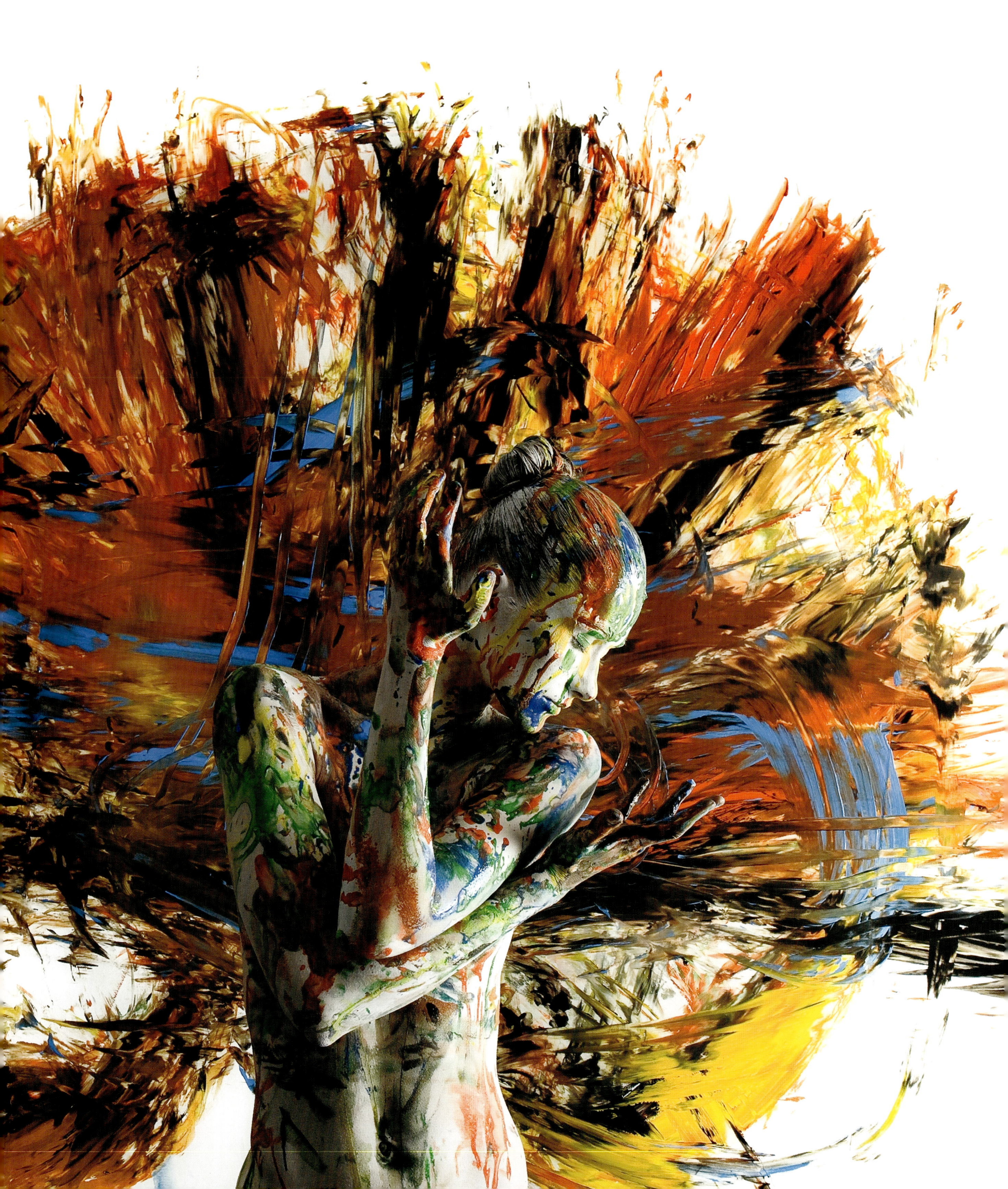

Art Color Ballet

The Art Color Ballet from Poland is a dynamic group of performing artists who have created some of the most amazing expressions in bodypainting. The group was established by artist and choreographer Agnieszka Glinska in 1998 with the idea to combine dance with the art of bodypainting. Over the following years, they have had a changing and growing company consisting of dancers, painters and acrobats working with artists and photographers to explore endless possibilities of living creation.

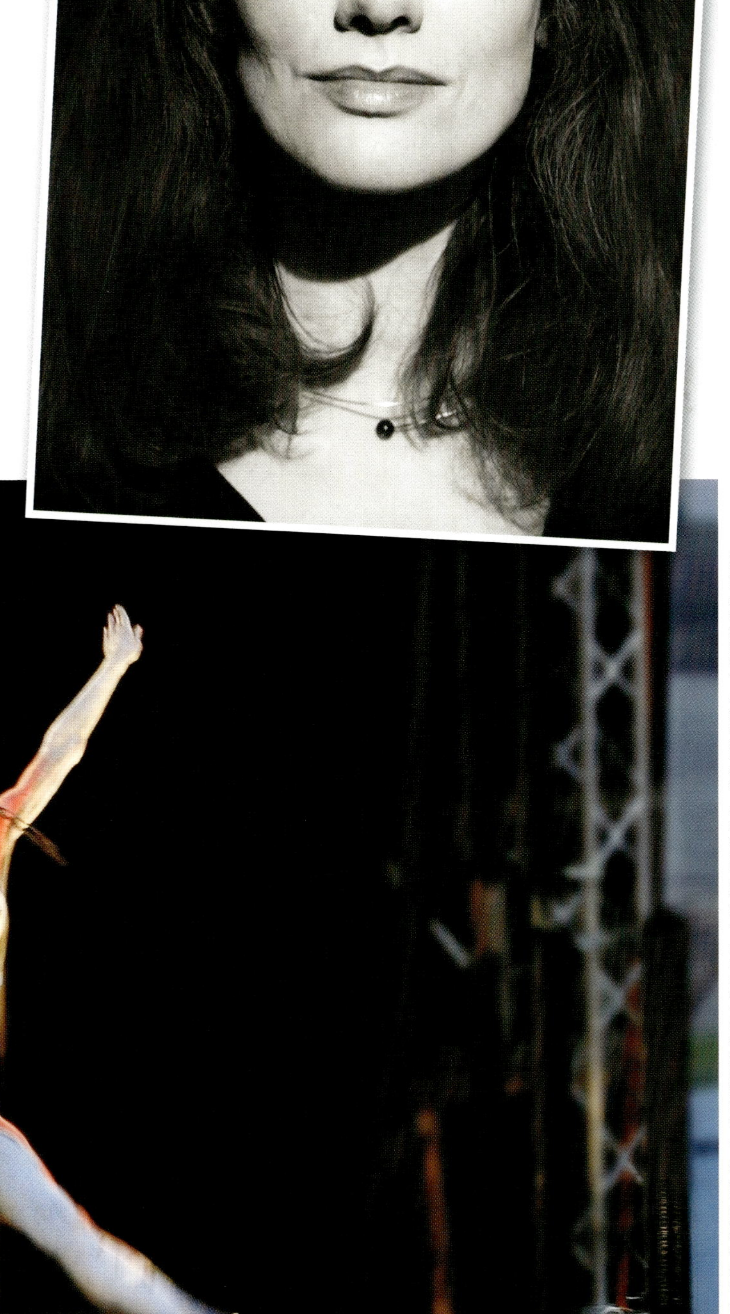

PHOTOGRAPHER ULF SCHERLING | PHOTOGRAPHER AGNIESZKA GLINSKA (OPPOSITE)

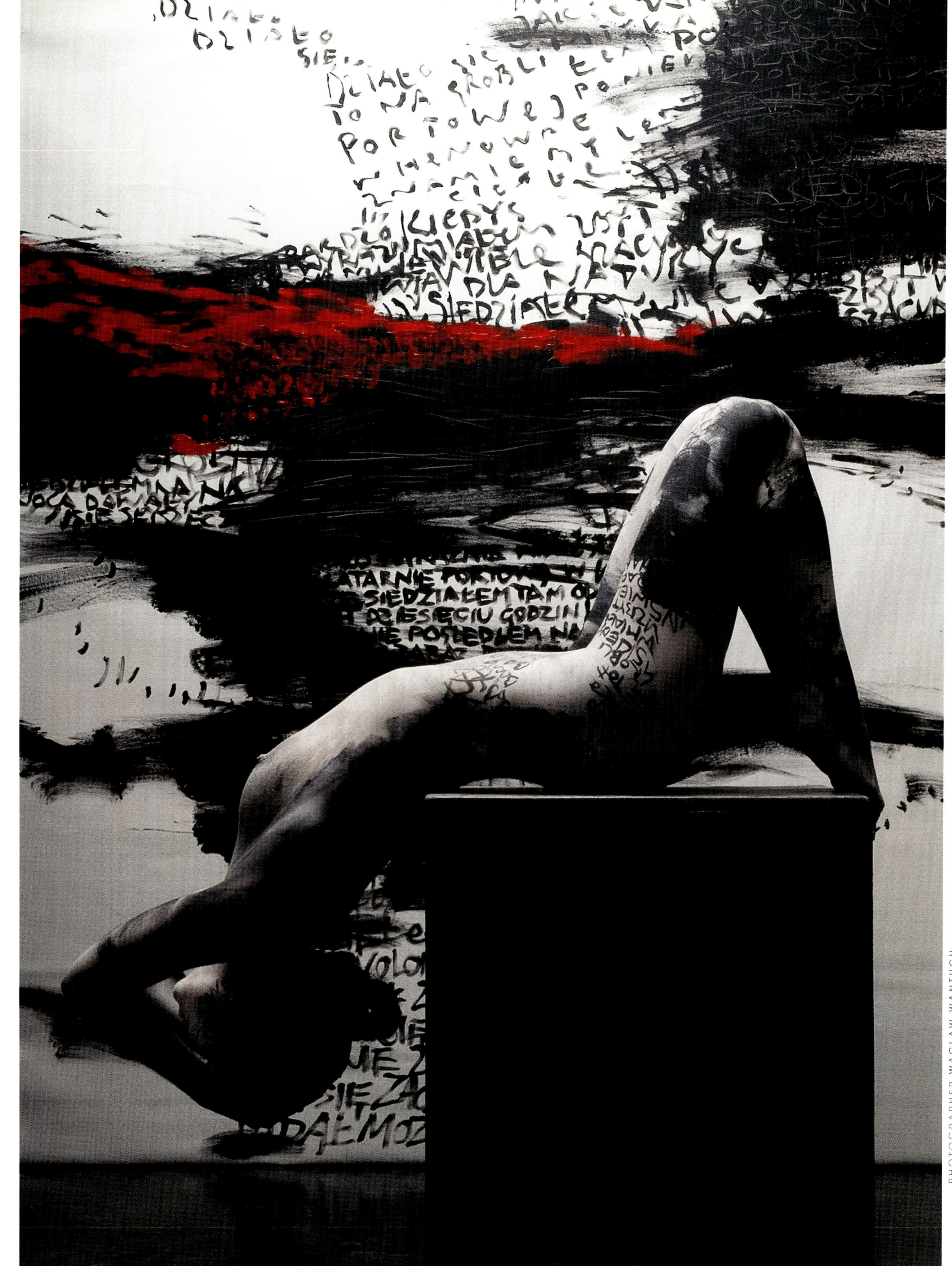

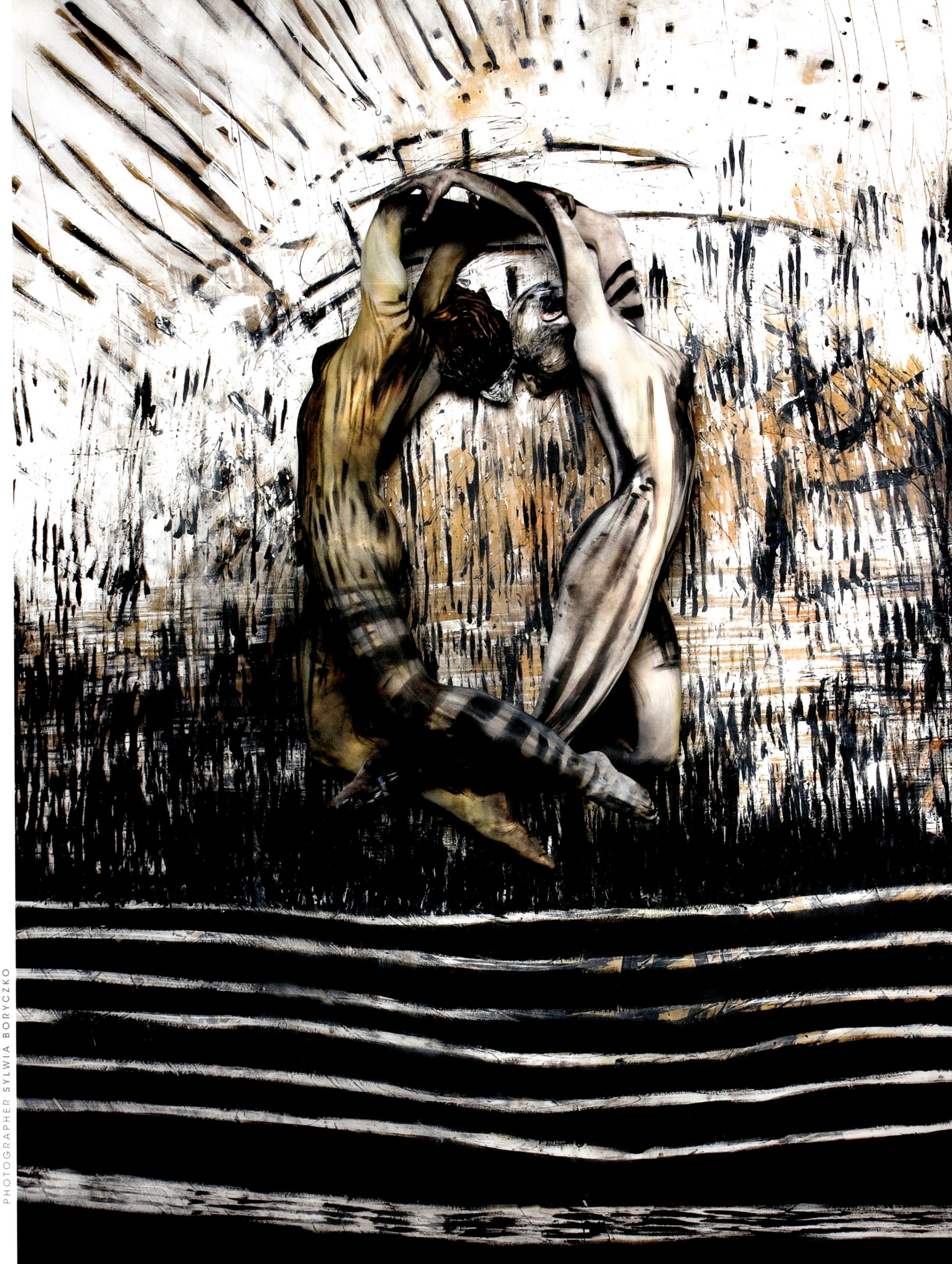

PHOTOGRAPHER SYLWIA BORYCZKO

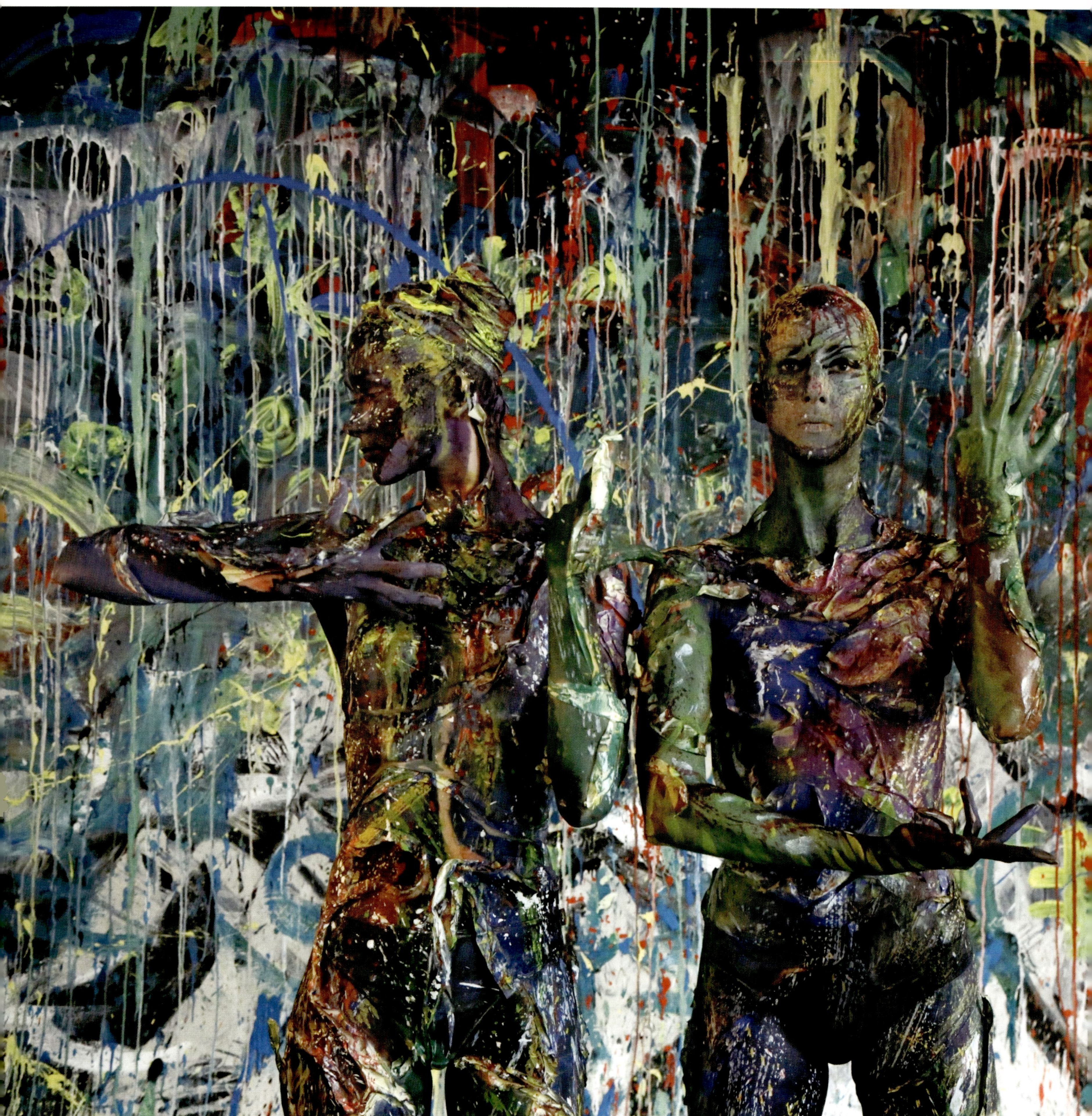

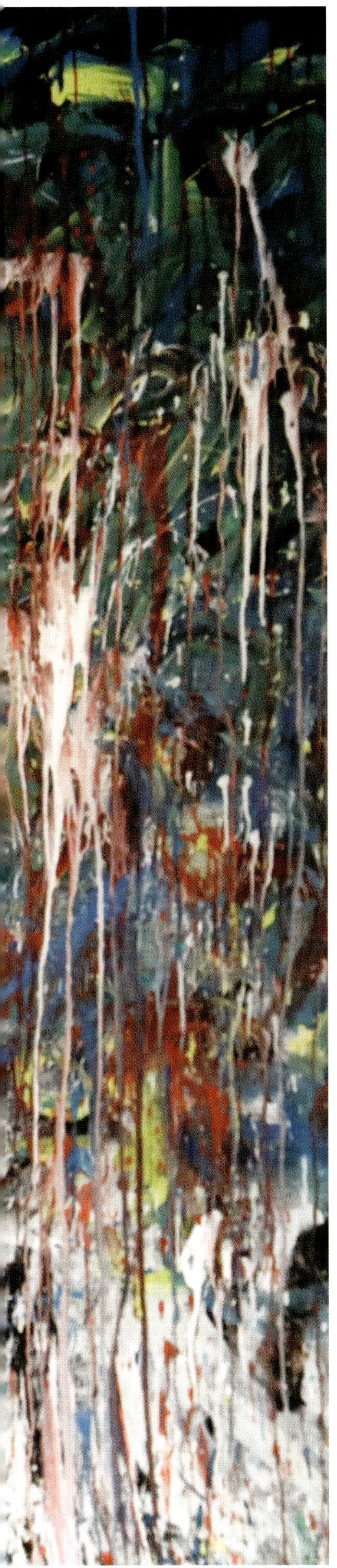

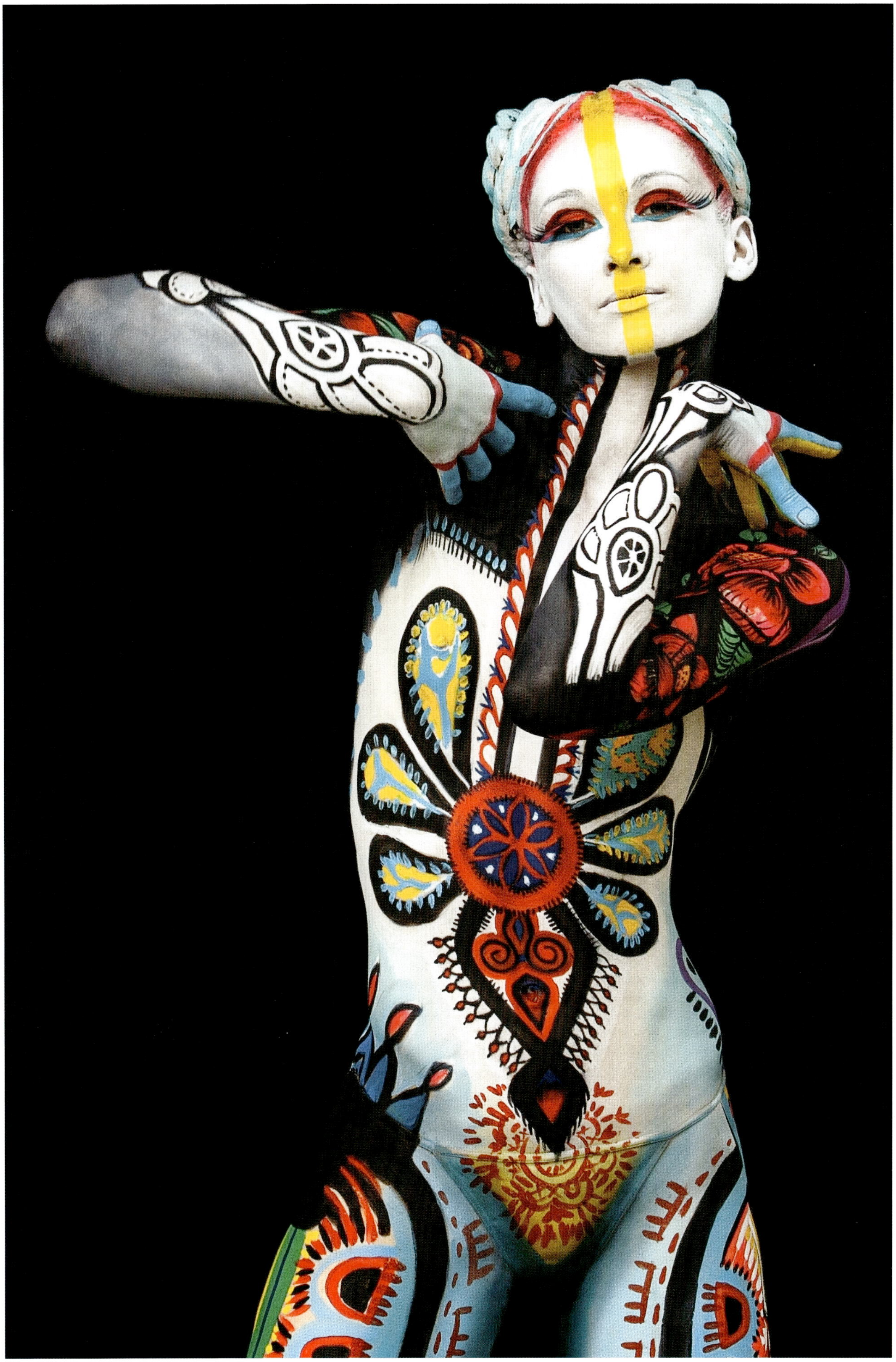

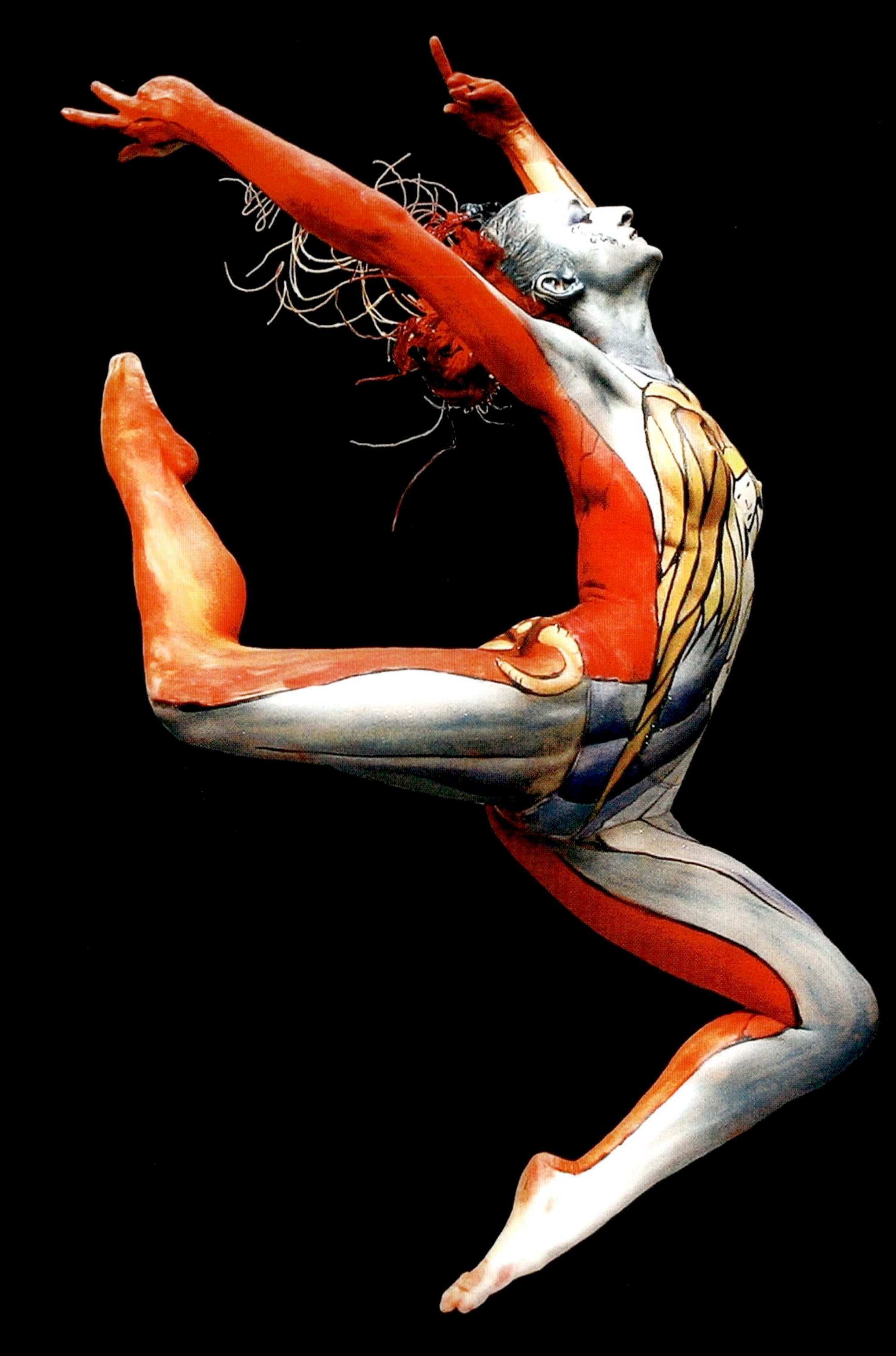

PHOTOGRAPHER MANFRED HALBWEISS

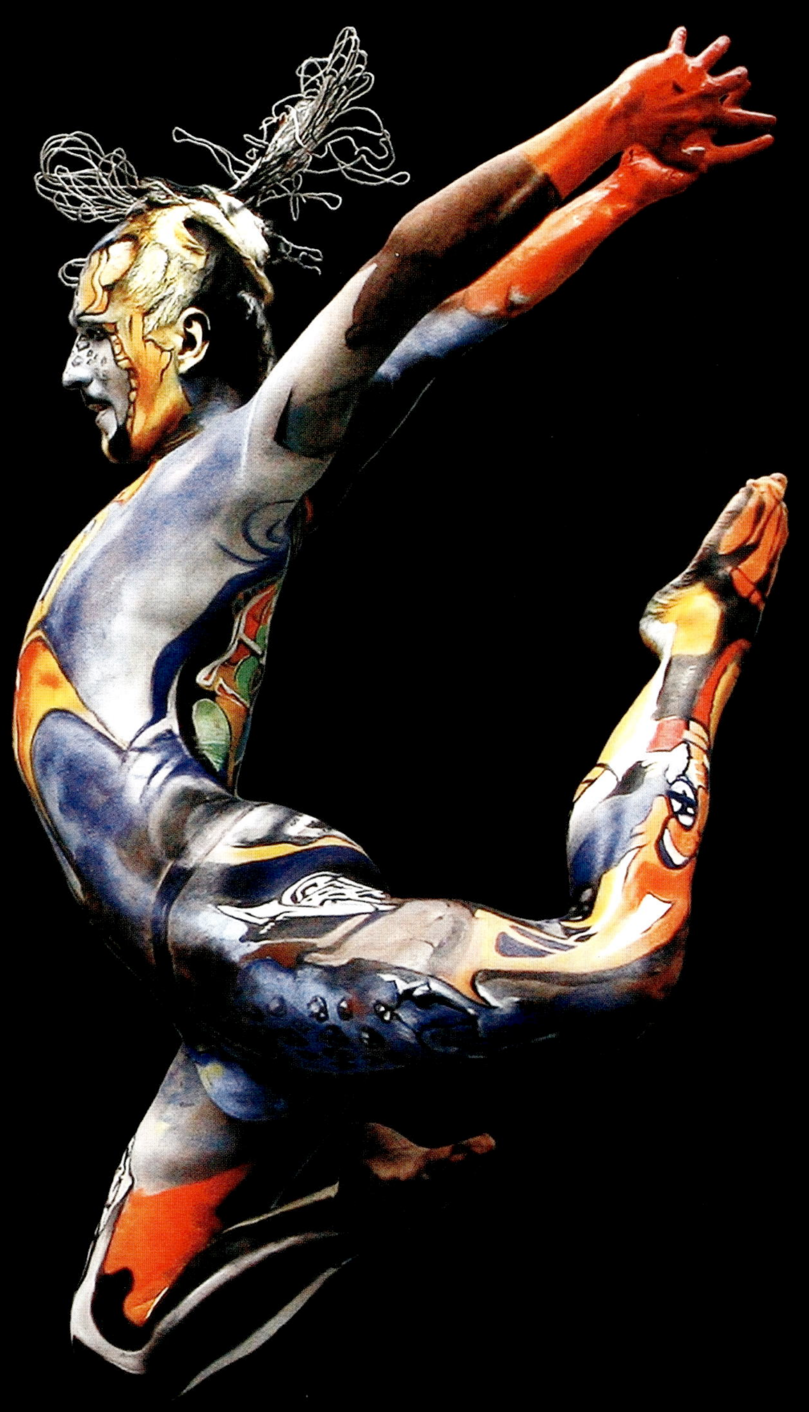

"With combinations of modern contemporary dance, classical, acrobatics, pantomime, Afro dance and new forms of expression developed by the group, we can get through to the audience on more levels. We can show them not only expression through dance but also tell them a story through lines, colors, shapes and images captured in designs painted on the dancers."

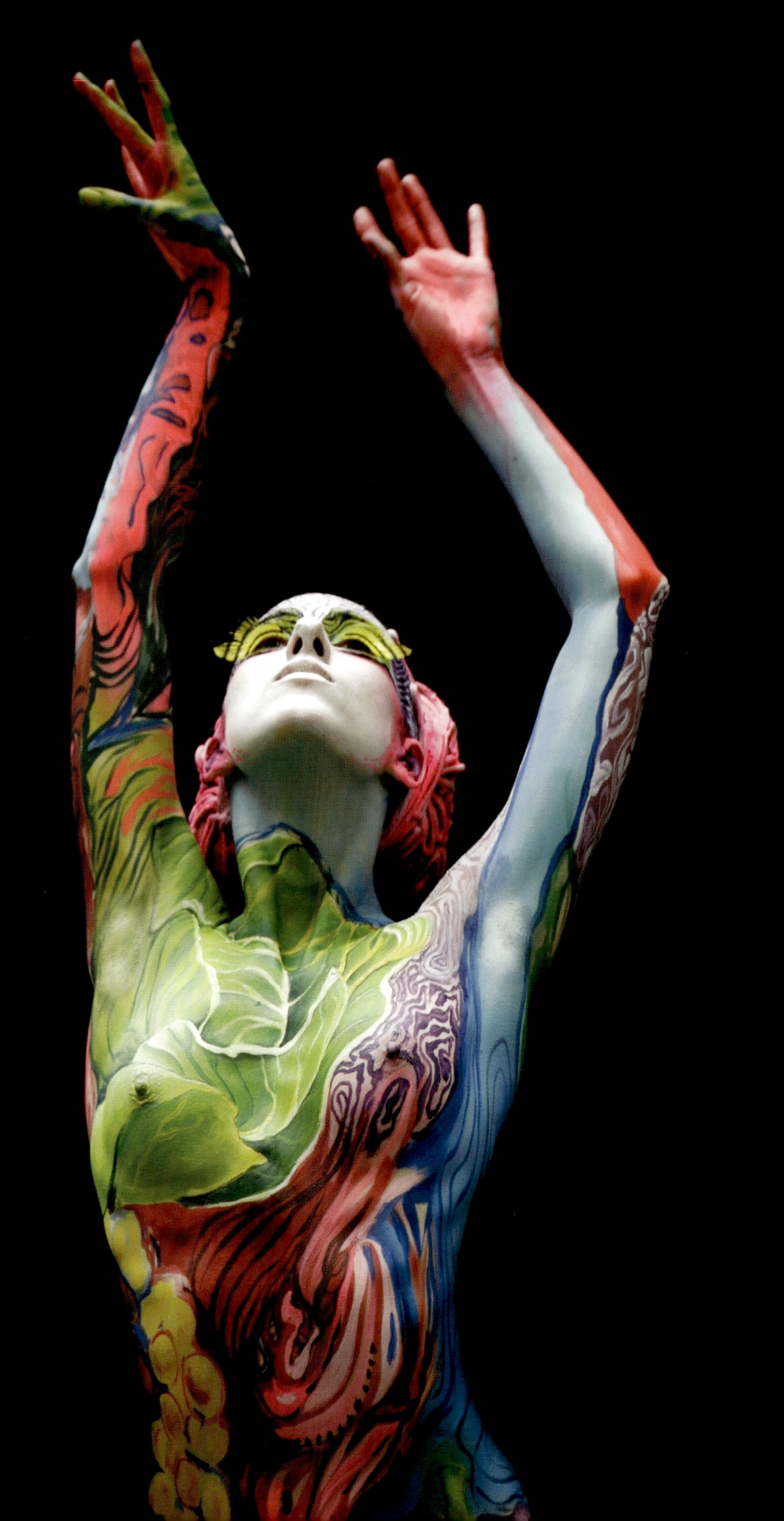

PHOTOGRAPHER AGNIESZKA GLINSKA

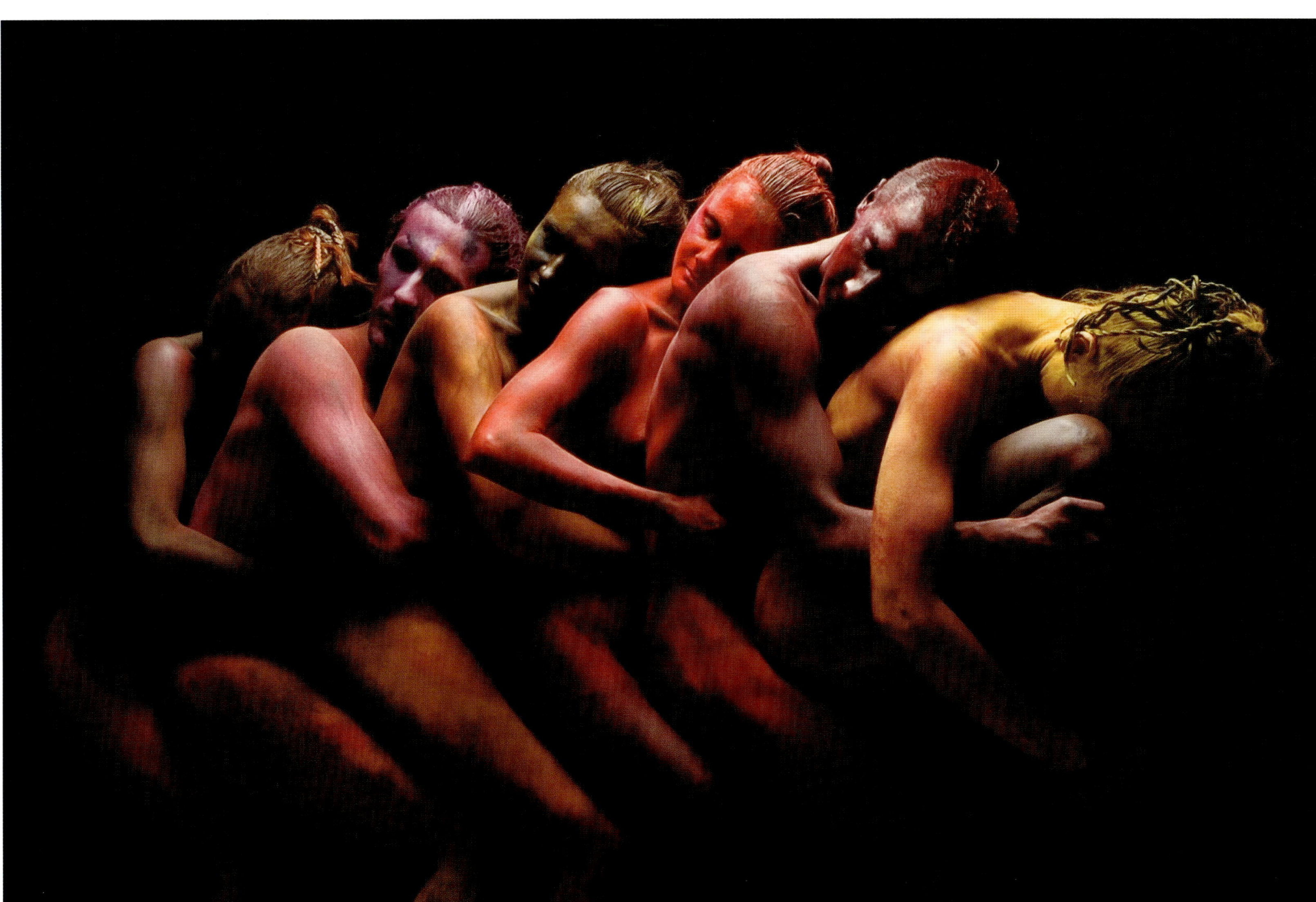

PHOTOGRAPHER OSWIN EDER

PHOTOGRAPHER WACLAW WANTUCH

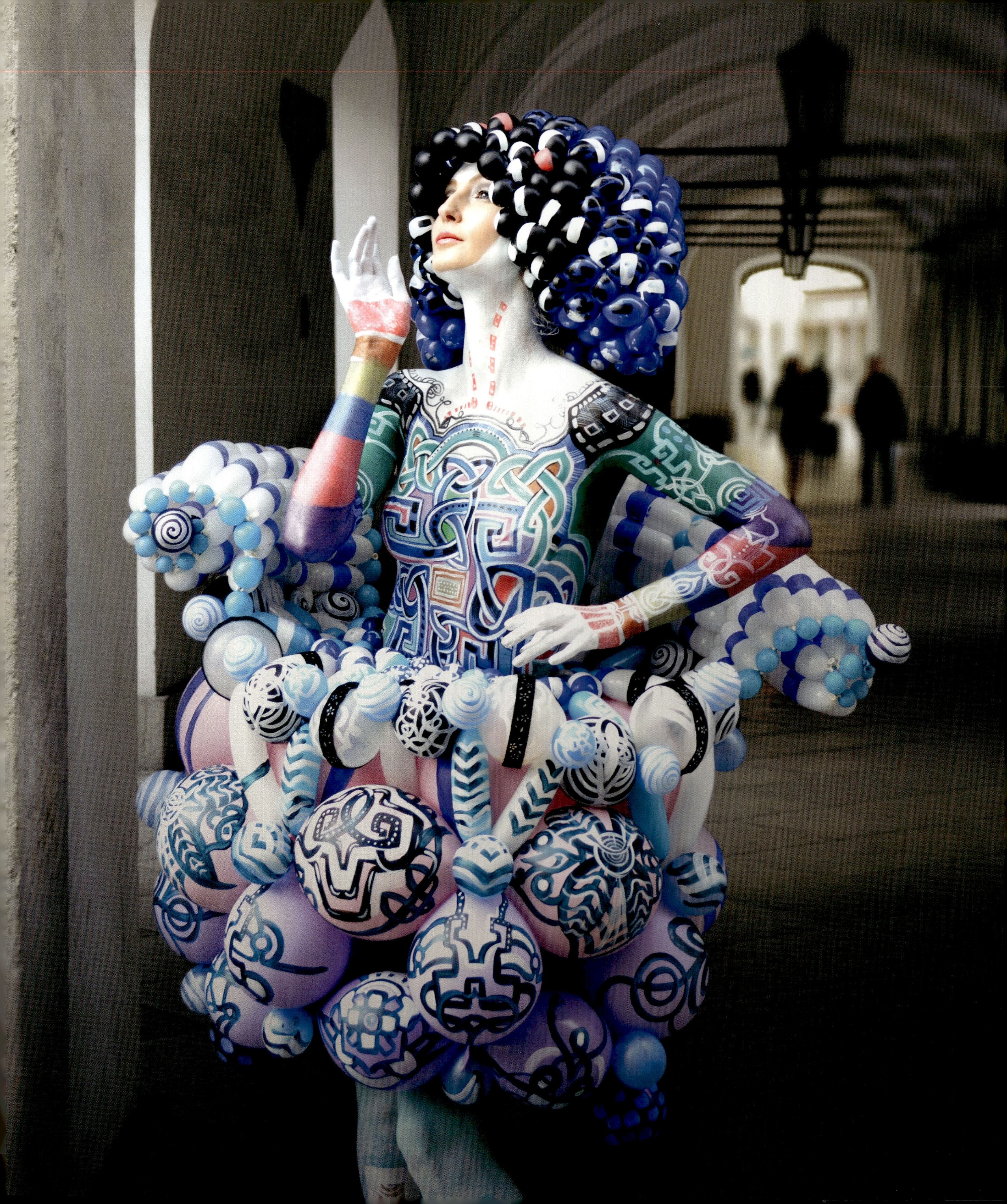

Bella Volen

Bella Volen is a professional fine artist with a master's degree in painting. She enjoys working with different media in the same way cooks use different flavors. Bella's focus is in canvas painting and the human transformations that are achieved through bodypainting. Her fine art and transformation skills fit perfectly in the advertising and fashion worlds. She also enjoys other art directions such as murals, performances, book illustrations, theater art and photography. In 2009, Bella created the paintloon concept, which combines balloon art, painting and bodypainting. It is a unique and new art form.

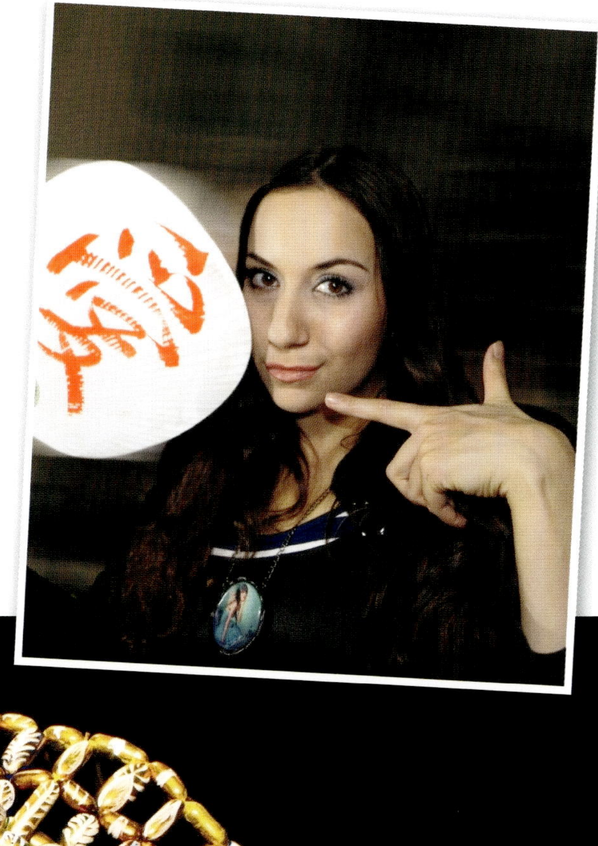

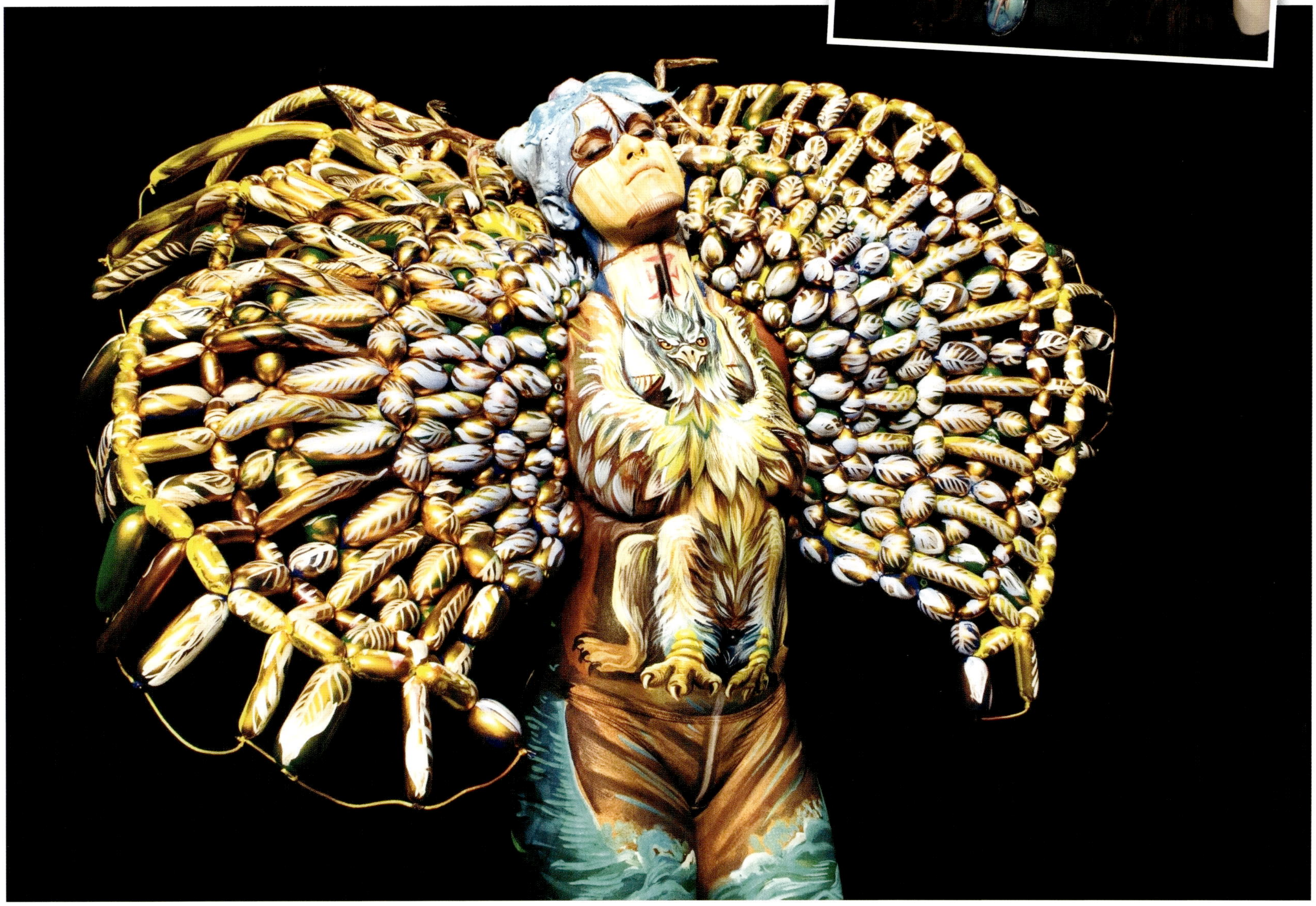

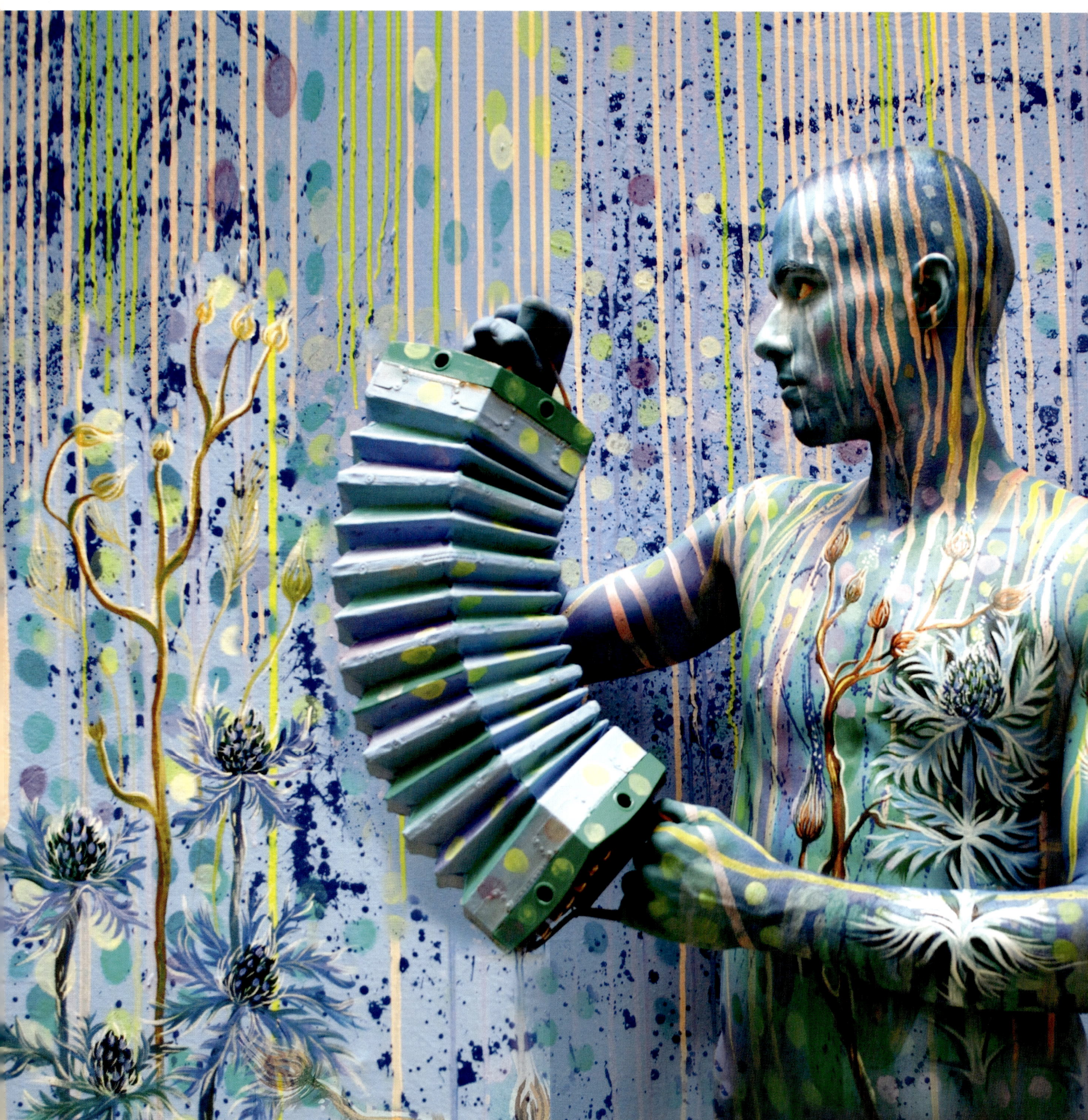

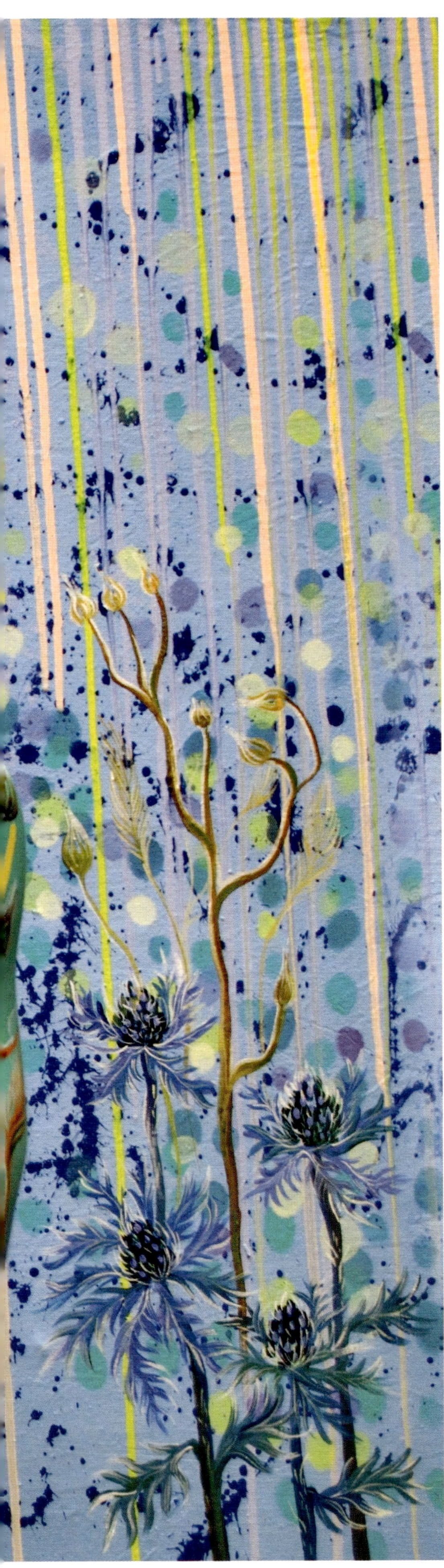

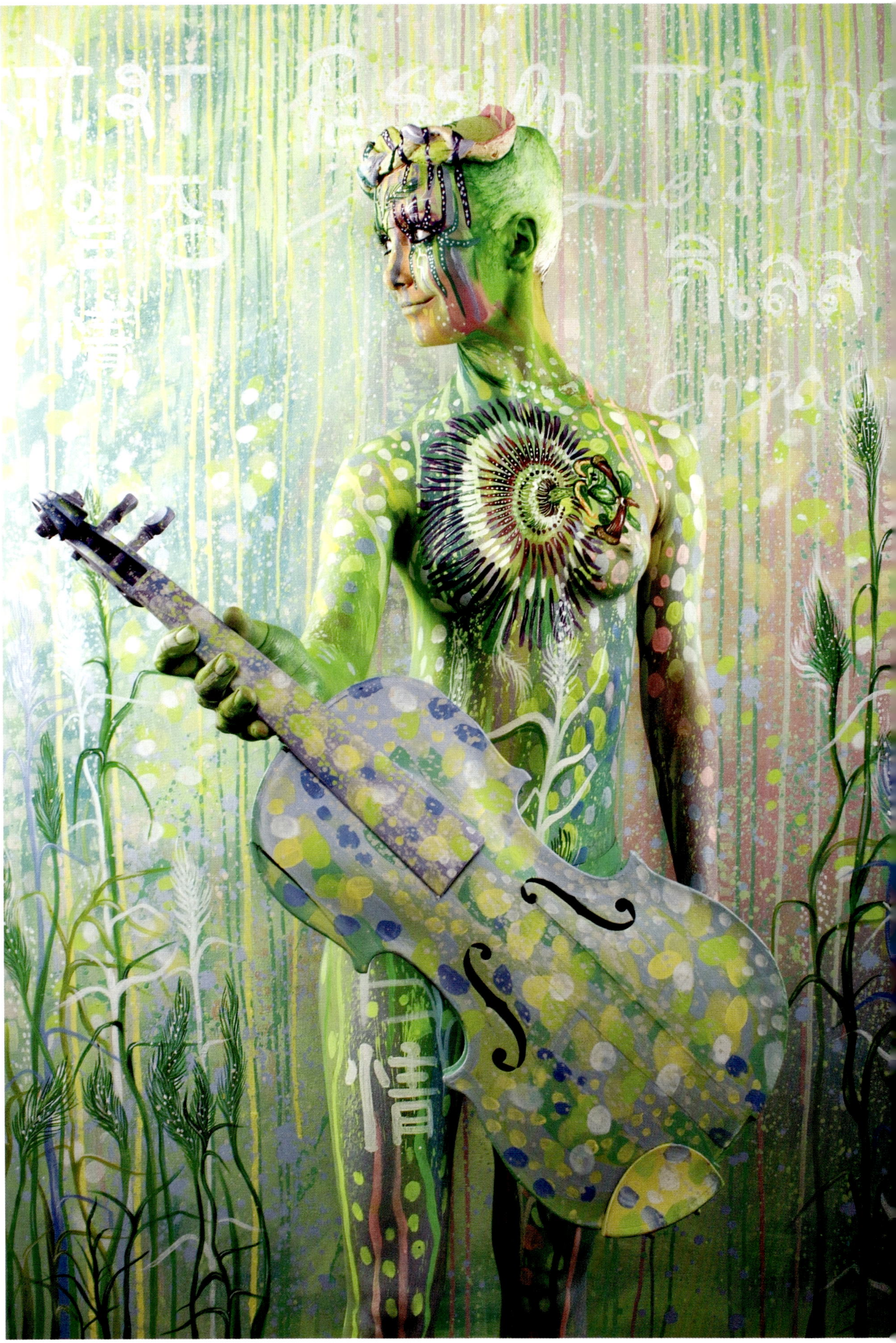

Passion Tattoo
情

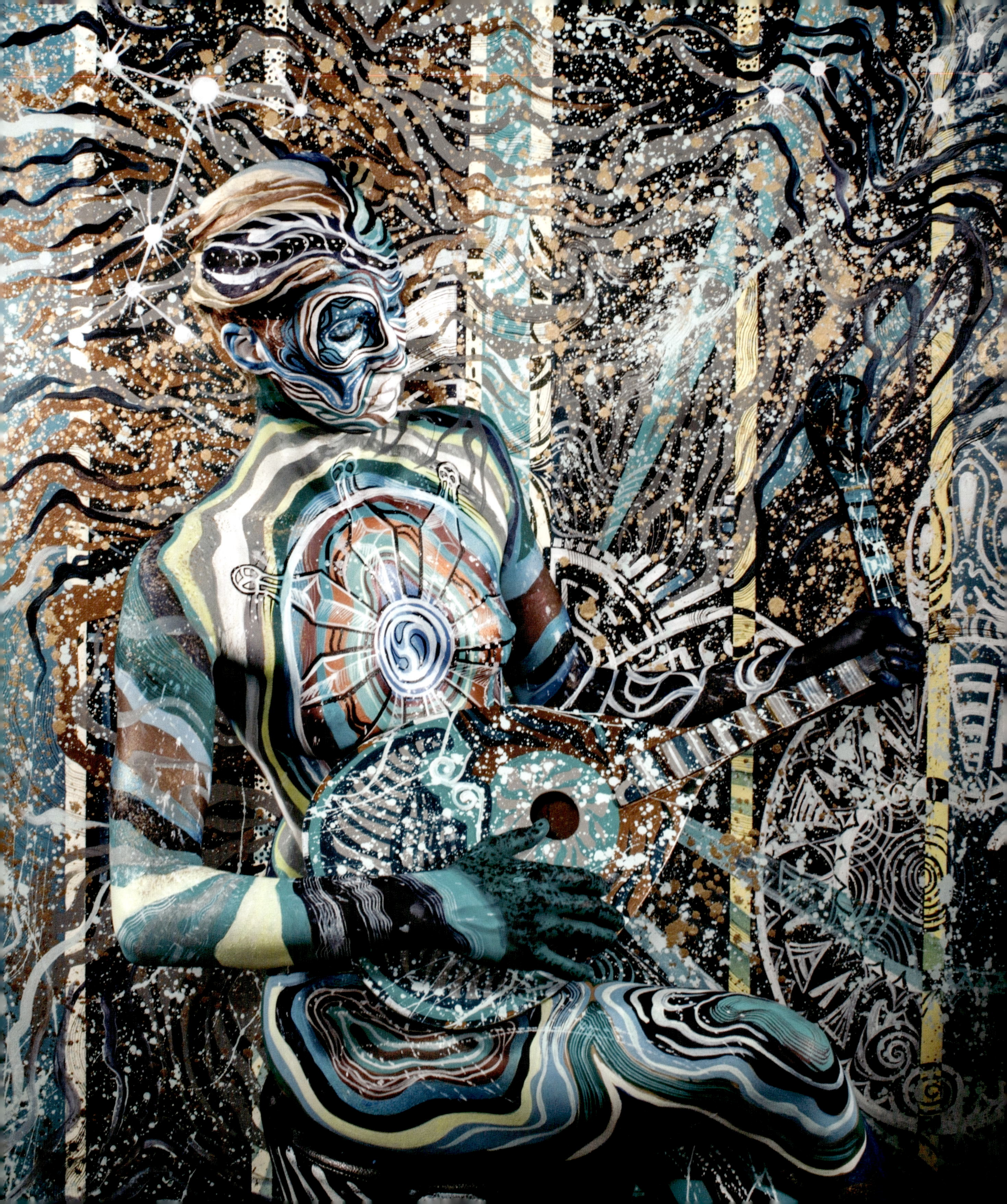

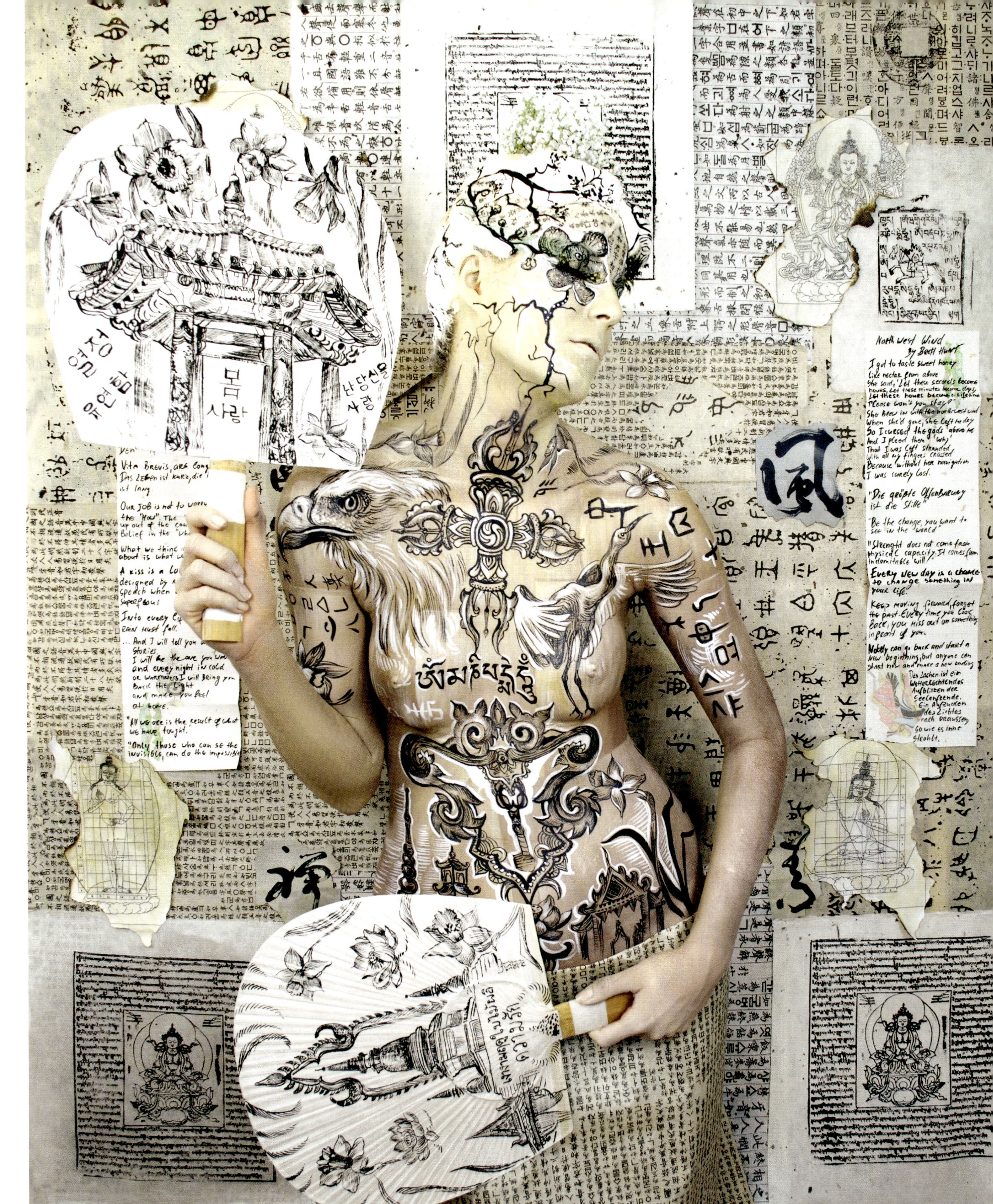
North West Wind
by Beth Hunt
I got to taste sweet honey
Like nectar from above
She said, 'Let these seconds become
hours, Let these minutes become days,
Let these hours become a Lifetime
Please won't you stay?
She blew in with the north-west wind
When she'd gone, she left no day
So I cursed the gods above me
And I pleed them 'why'
That I was left stranded,
With all my fingers crossed
Because without her navigation
I was surely lost.

"Die größte Offenbarung
ist die Stille"

"Be the change, you want to
see in the world"

"Strenght does not come from
physical capacity. It comes from
indomitable will."

Every new day is a chance
to change something in
your life.

Keep moving forward, forget
the past. Every time you look
Back, you miss out on something
in front of you.

Nobody can go back and start a
new beginning, but anyone can
start now and make a new ending
Des Lachen ist ein
Weiterleuchtendes
Aufblitzen der
Seelenfreude.
Ein Aufzucken
des Lichtes
nach Draussen
So wie es inne
Strahlt.
Vita Brevis, ars Long
Das Leben ist kurz, die
ist lang.

Our job is not to worry
the "How". The
up out of the con
Belief in the "Wh

What we think
about is what w

A kiss is a Lo
designed by
speach when
superflous

Into every li
Rain must fall.
...And I will tell you
stories.
I will be the one you w
and every night in cold
or warmness I will bring yon
back the light
and make you feel
at home.

"All we are is the result of what
we have teught.

"Only those who can see the
invisible, can do the impossible

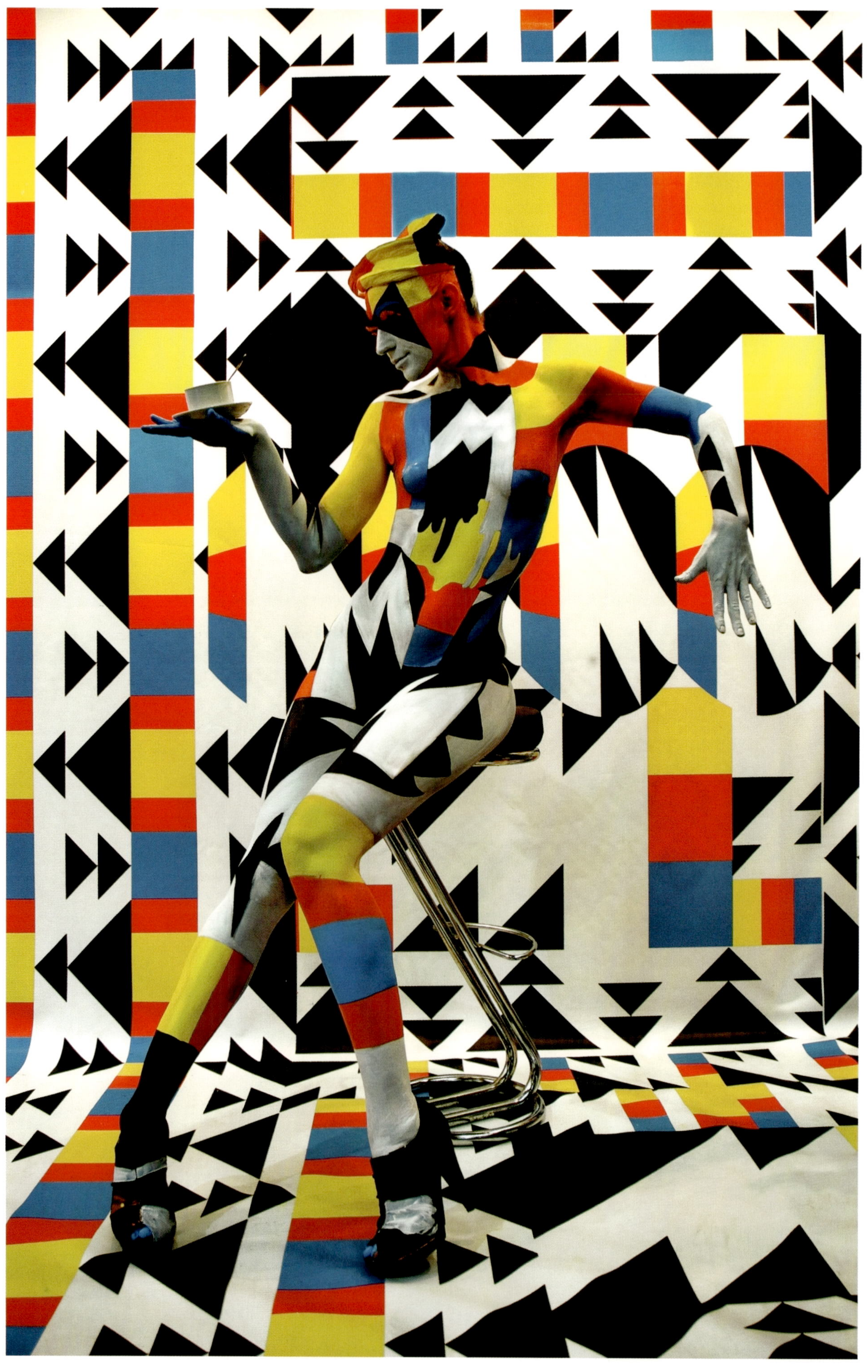

"I have three parts to me—Bella as an artist, woman and person. Only one of those is really female. The person and the artist are just thinking, feeling the energy river around the creating process. So, of course, those parts of me like androgynous art. If God, the creator, doesn't have a gender, then why should art, being a creation, have a gender?"

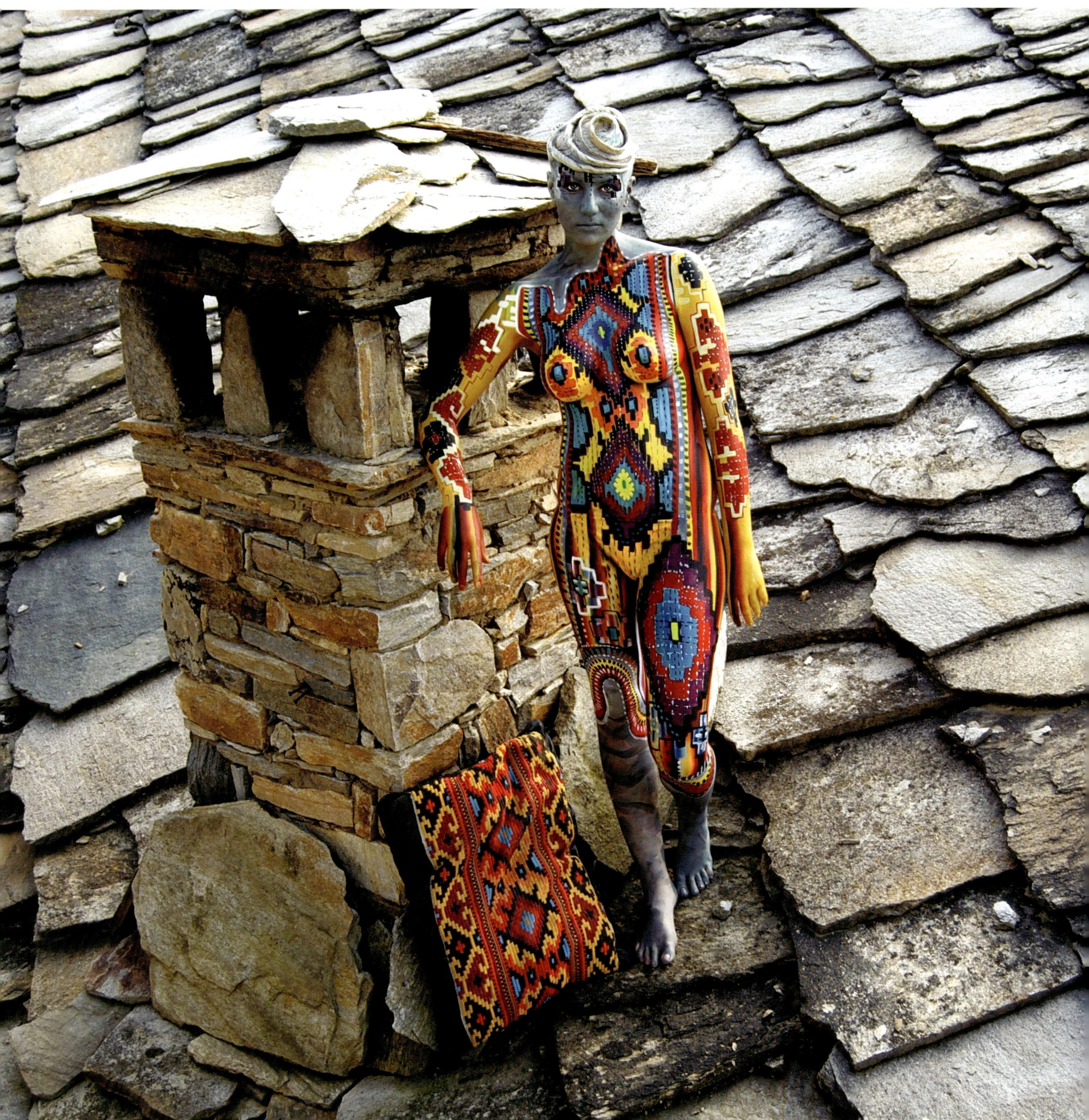

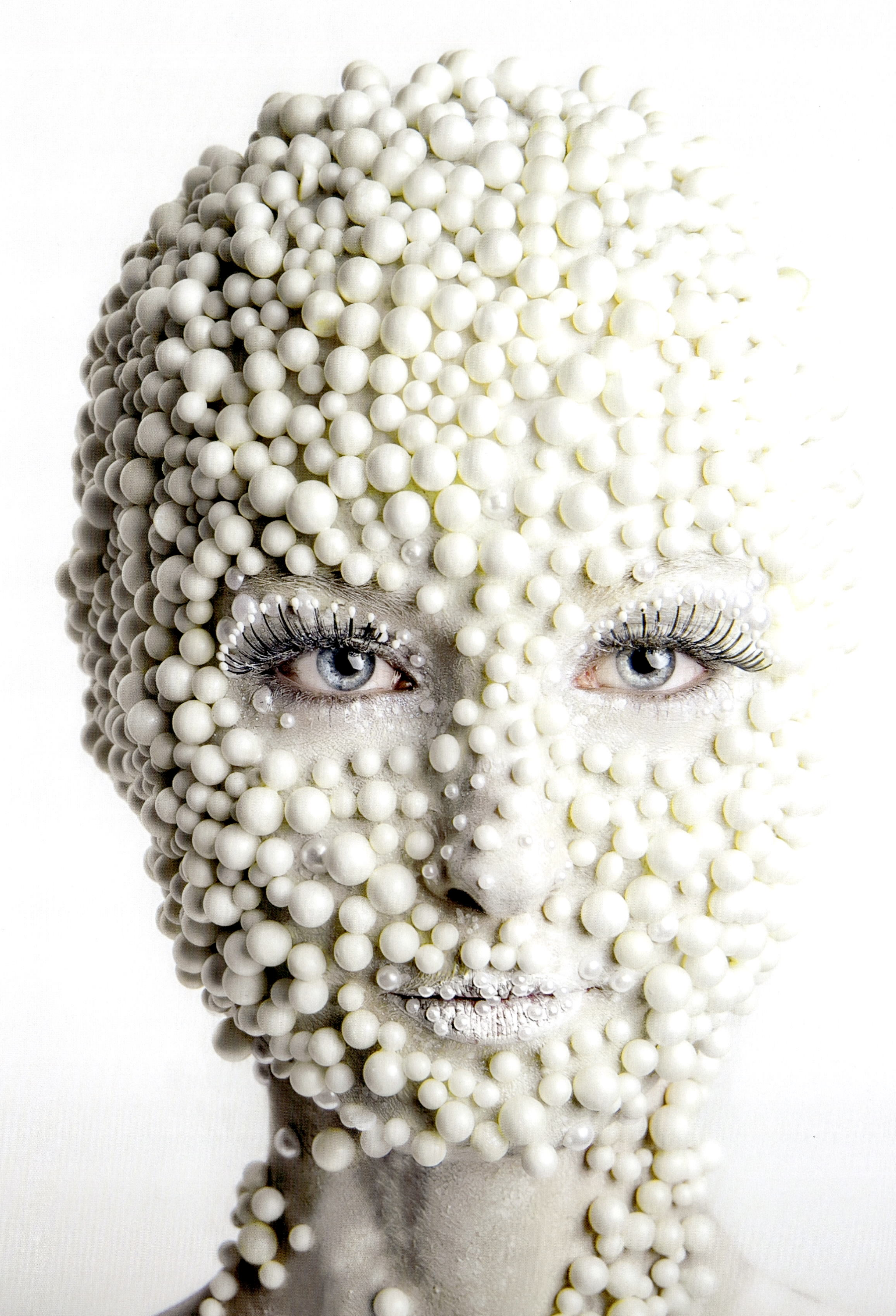

Birgit Mörtl

WWW.DESIGNFACTOR.AT

Birgit Mörtl is an internationally awarded bodypainter and fashion designer. She is most well-known for her years of work creating the costumes and body art for the Life Ball, which is Europe's largest charity event supporting people with HIV or AIDS. Birgit has collaborated on many magazine and advertising shoots and has been profiled as a leading designer in many articles and television programs. Mixing her costume design with her bodypainting abilities is what makes Birgit unique. She has won many awards in countries around the world, including becoming a two-time Special Effects World Champion in body art.

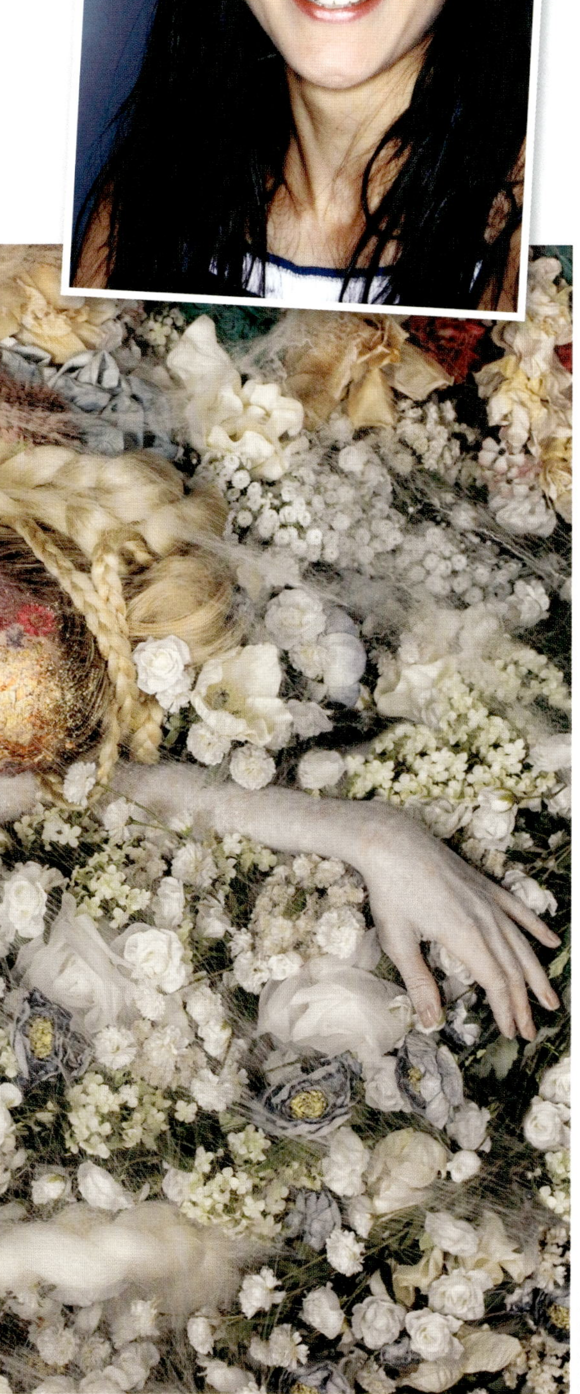

PHOTOGRAPHER MARTIN AIGNER

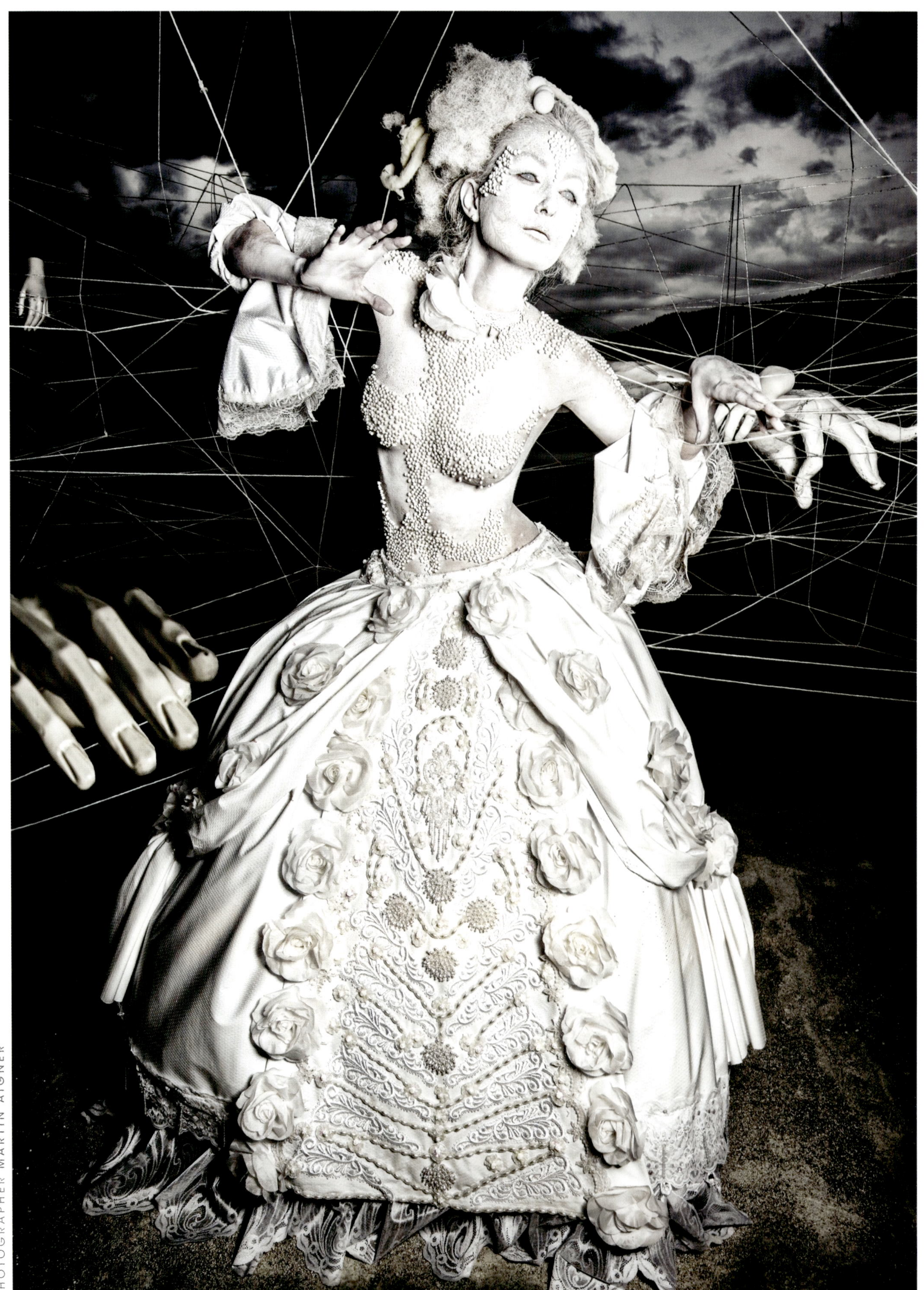

PHOTOGRAPHER MARTIN AIGNER

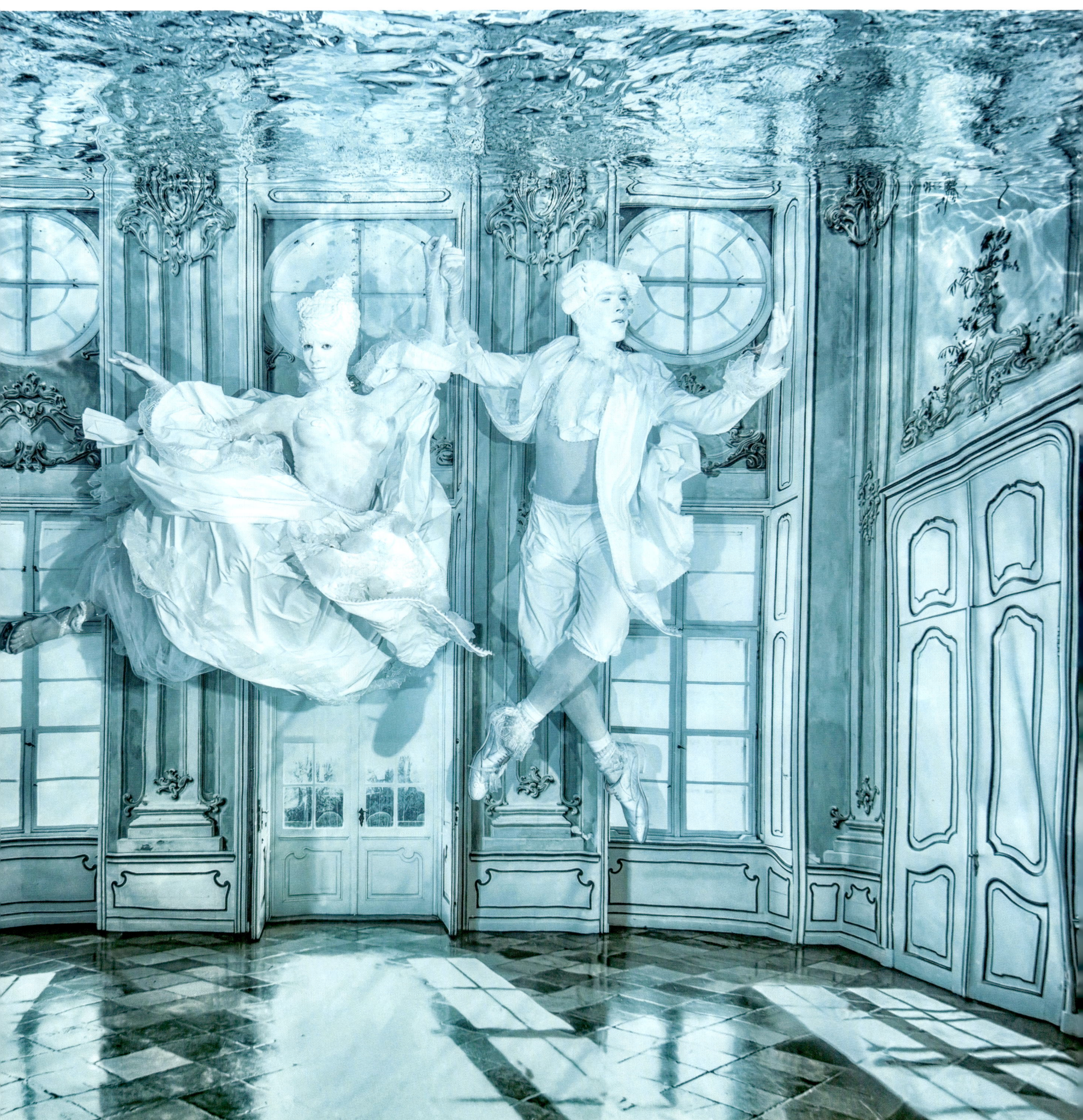

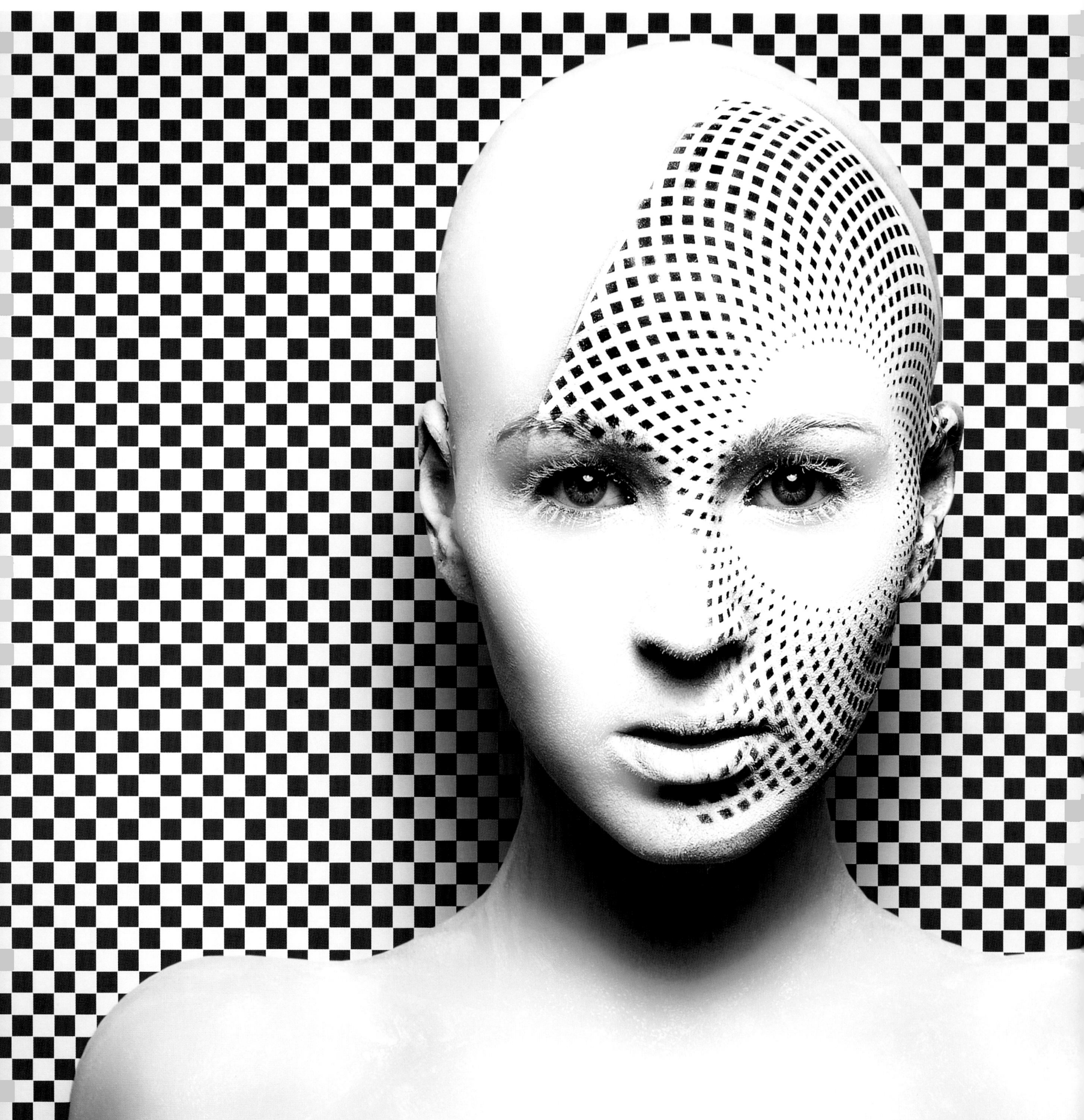

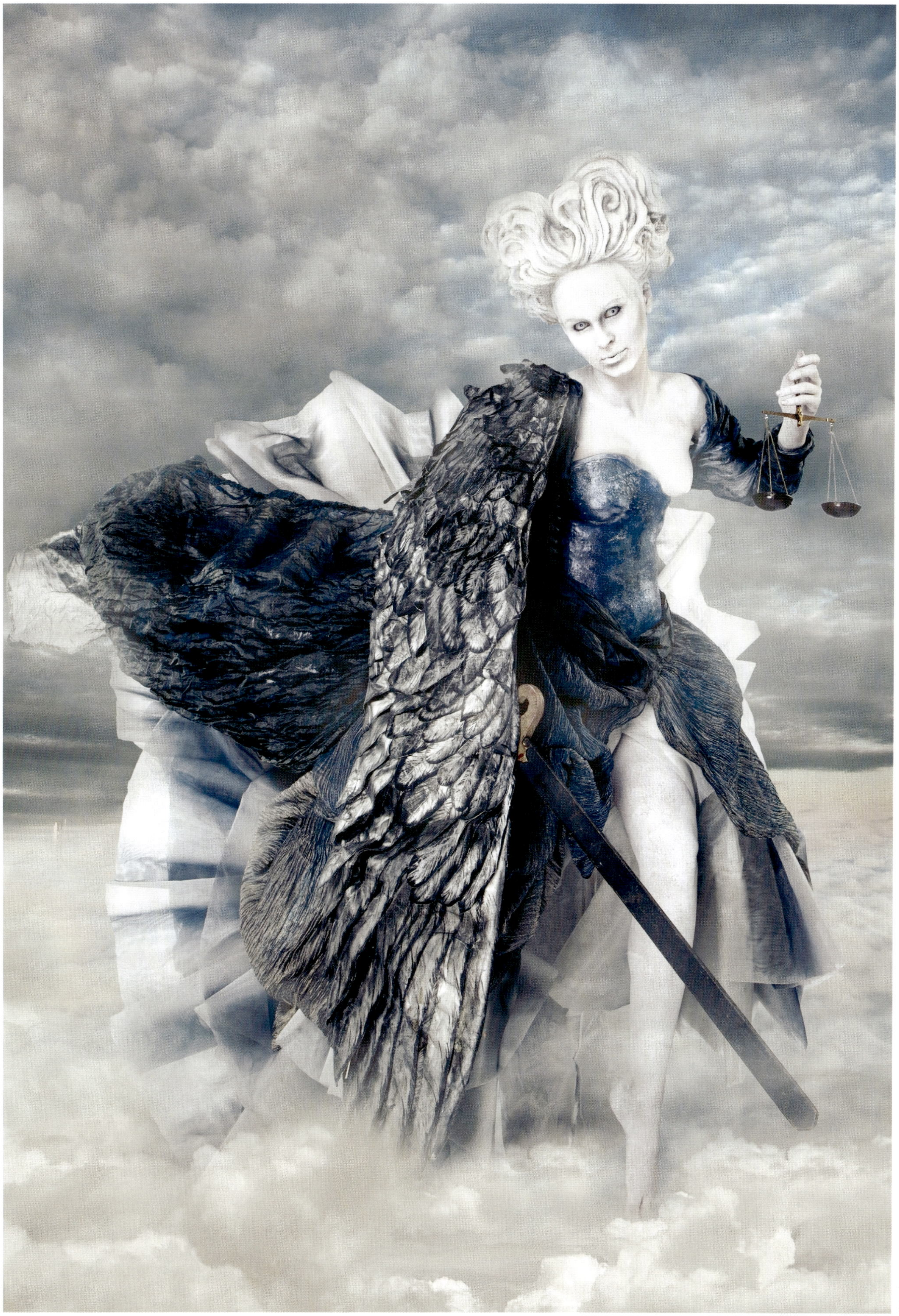

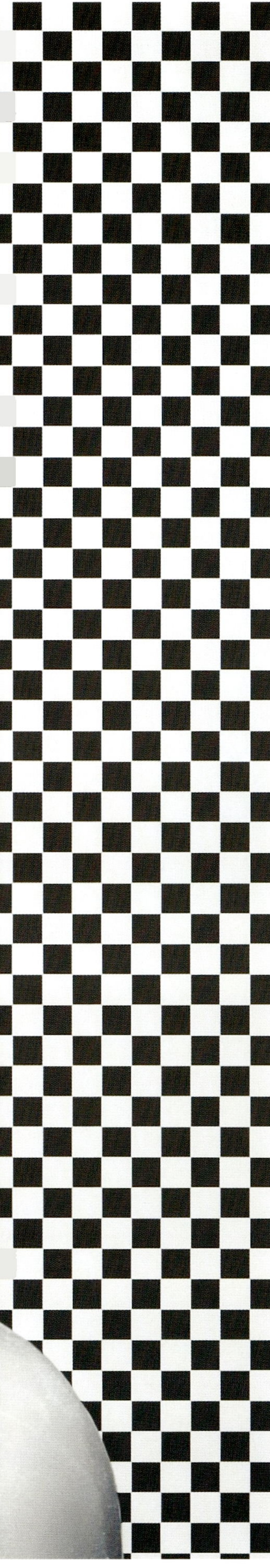

PHOTOGRAPHER MARKUS MORIANZ, LIFEBALL | PHOTOGRAPHER STEFAN DOKUPIL (OPPOSITE)

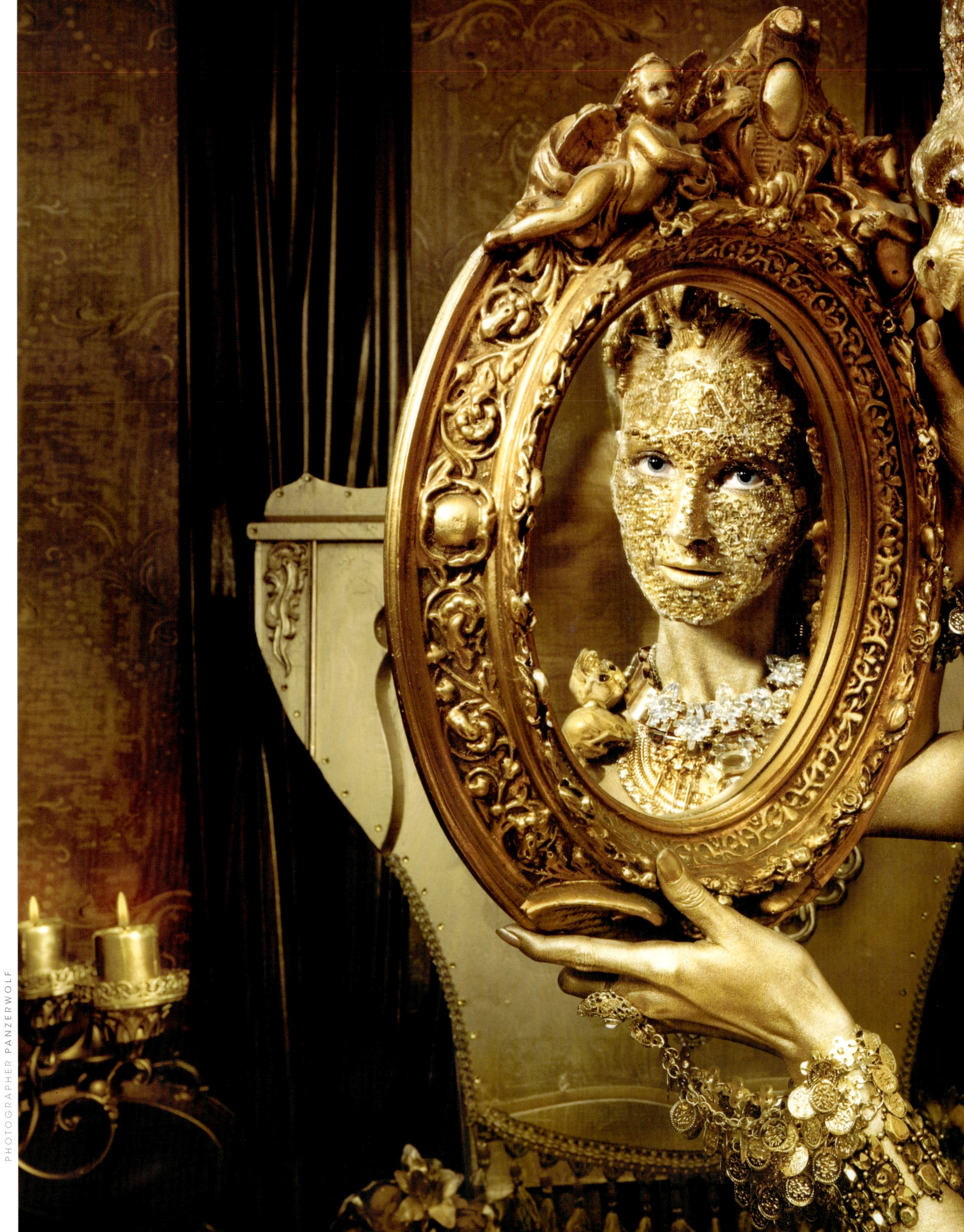
PHOTOGRAPHER PANZERWOLF

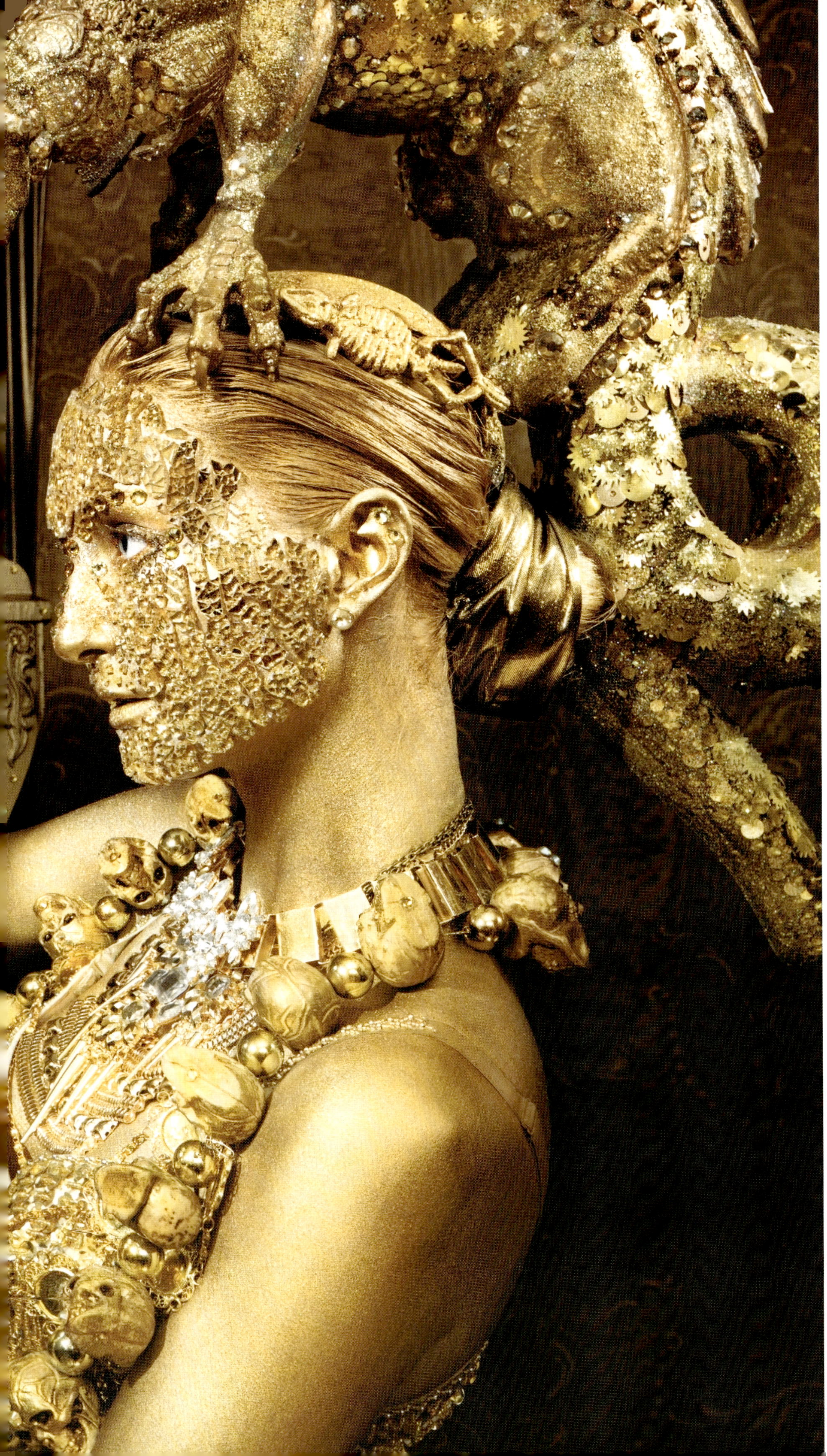

"I love to arrange a three-dimensional body with color and special effects to transform it and dive into a fantastic dream. My work then begins to live through the movements of the model. Effects can be obtained on the body that would never be possible on a flat canvas. I am dressing people, just like I do in my work as a costume maker. They do not feel naked. The model carries a dress manufactured by me, a breath-thin costume of color."

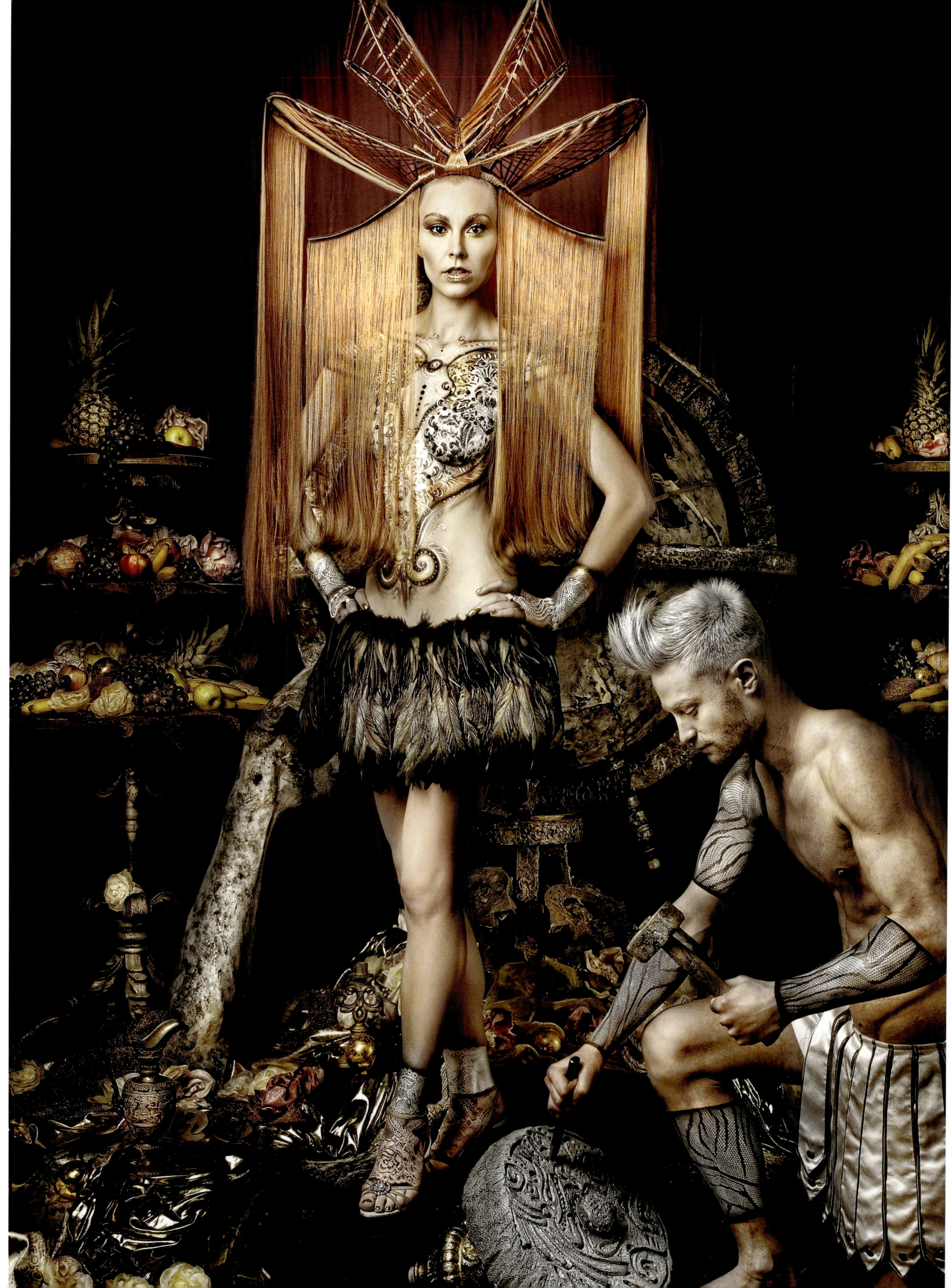
HAIRDRESSING AWARD ALEX LEPSCHI | PHOTOGRAPHER STEFAN DOKUPIL

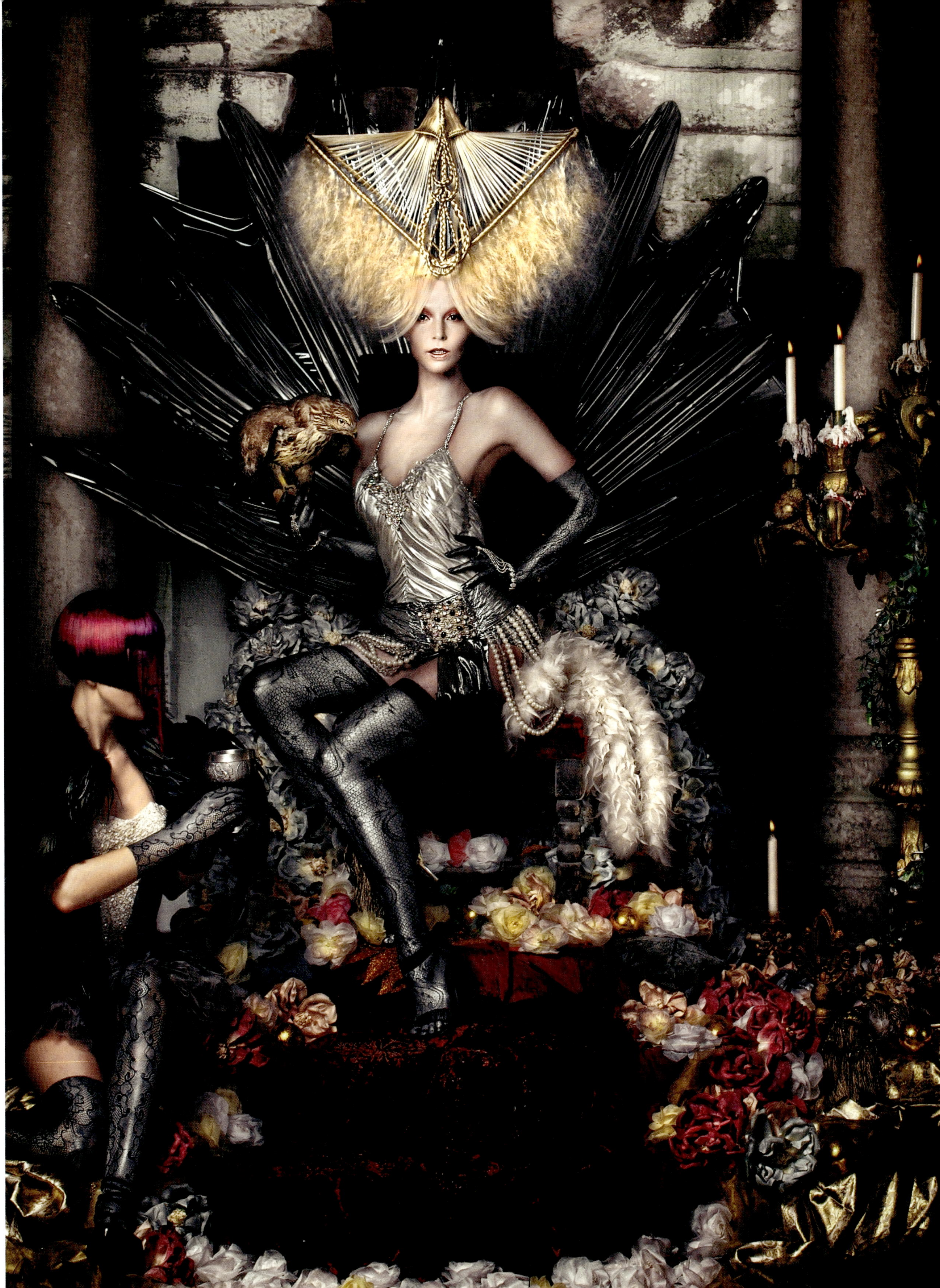

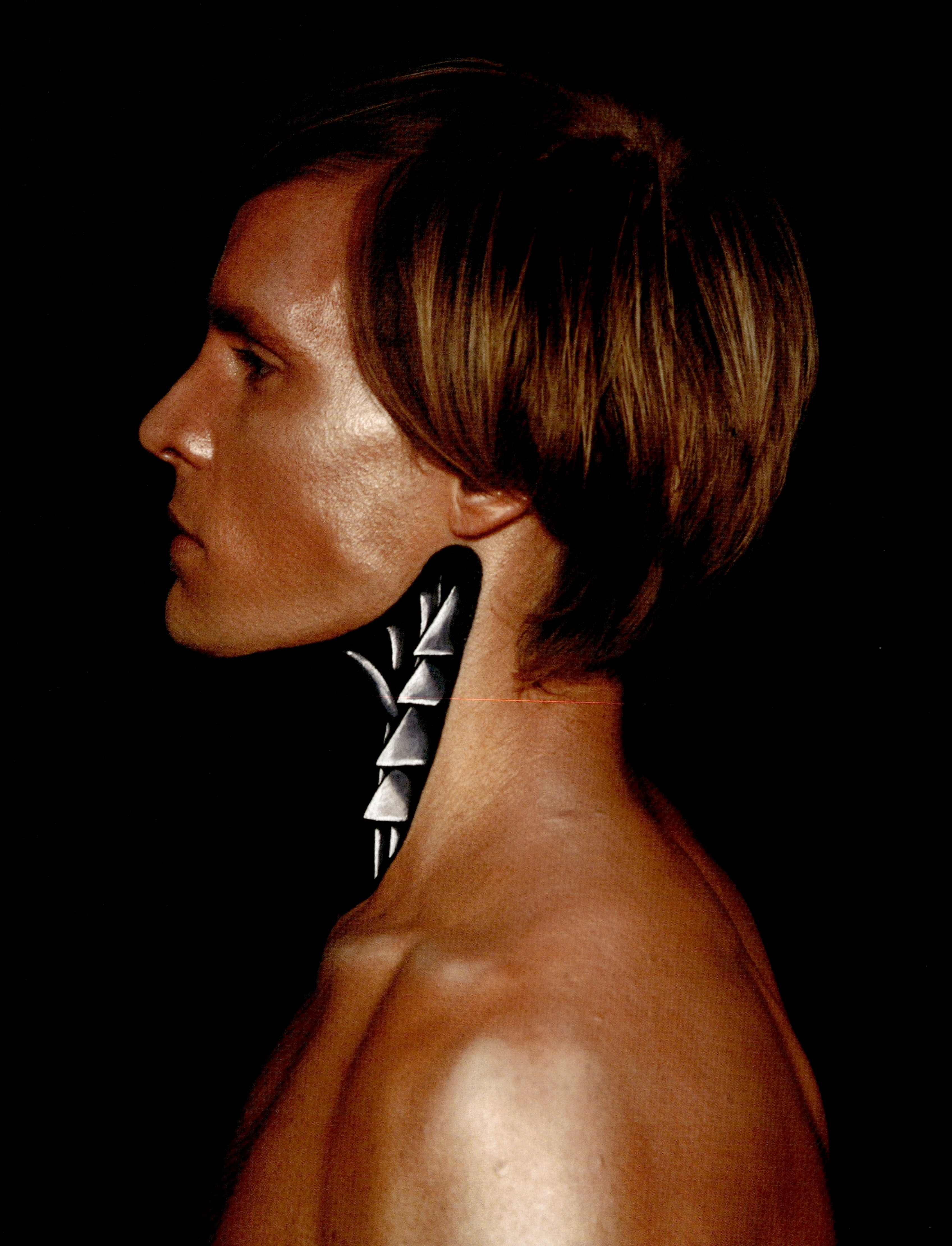

Carolyn Roper

With her amazing artistic talents, Carolyn Roper is now recognized as one of the world's leading body paint artists. Carolyn has won major industry awards and is a double World Bodypainting Champion. She first won the World Championship in the Brush & Sponge Category in 2007 with her good friend and fellow artist Carly Utting. Carolyn won again in 2009 when she took first place in the Special Effects Category with her assistant, Paula Southern.

Carolyn is based in London but regularly travels throughout the UK and internationally to undertake assignments. Her outstanding artwork is regularly featured in film, television advertisements, music videos, magazines and newspapers. Carolyn's art has also been on CD and book covers. Her makeup credits include *The X Factor* live shows.

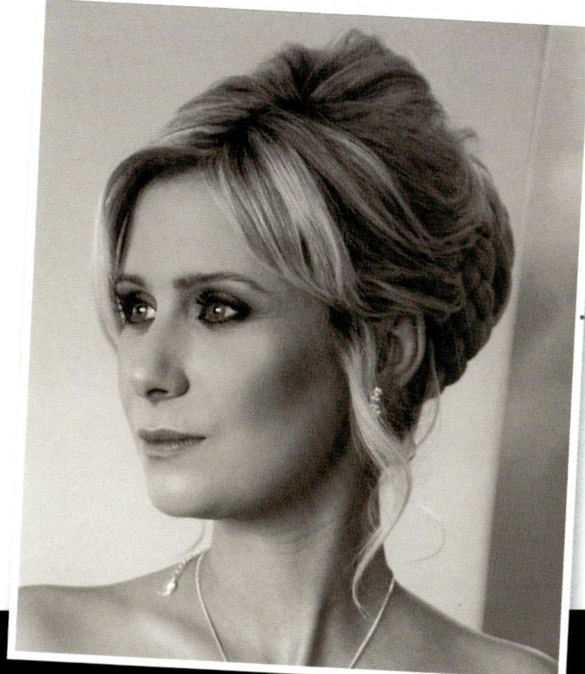

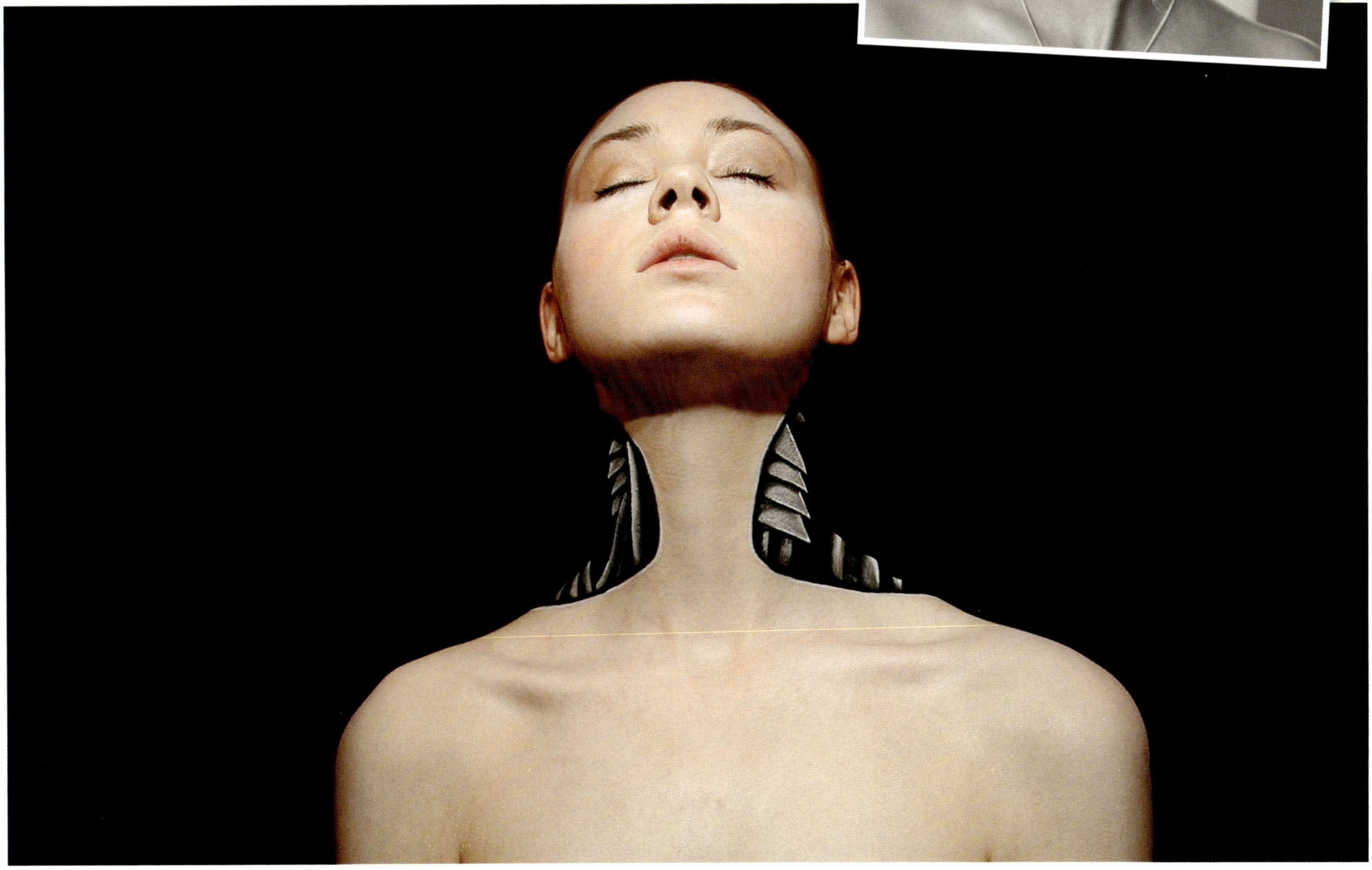

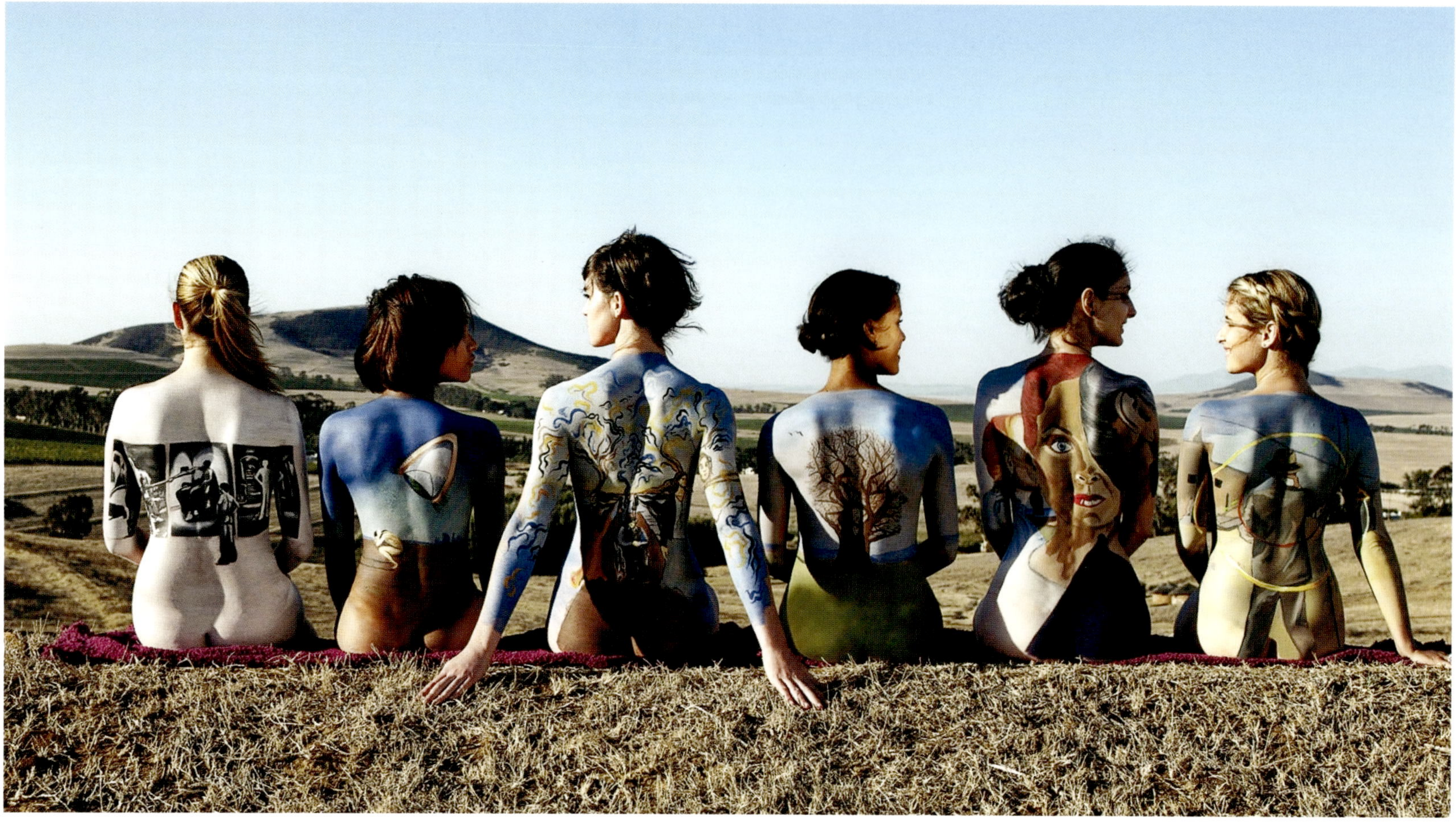

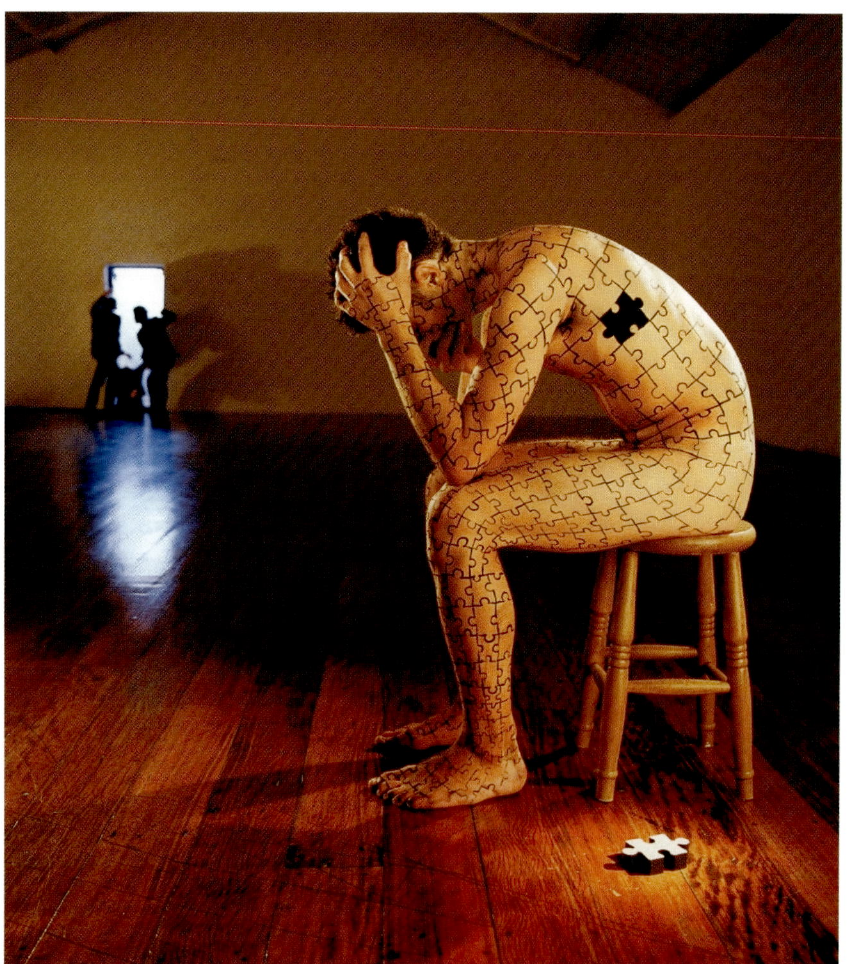

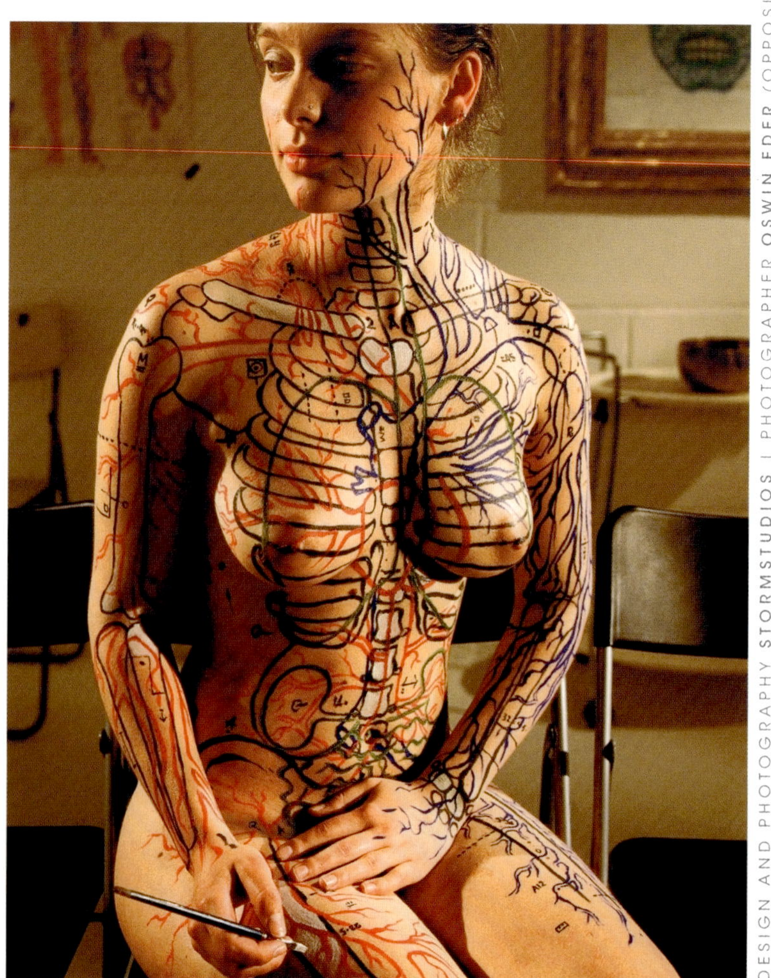

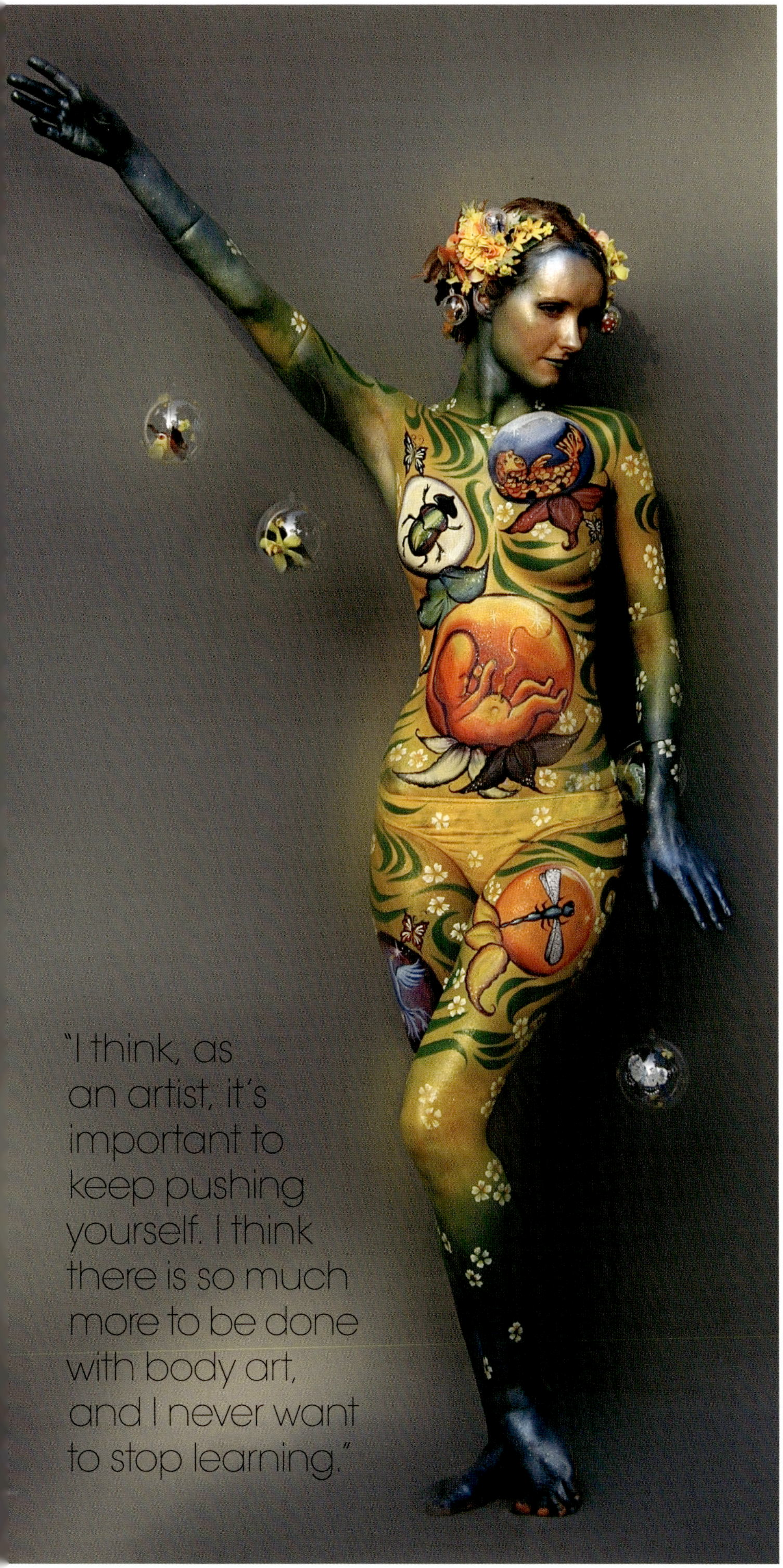

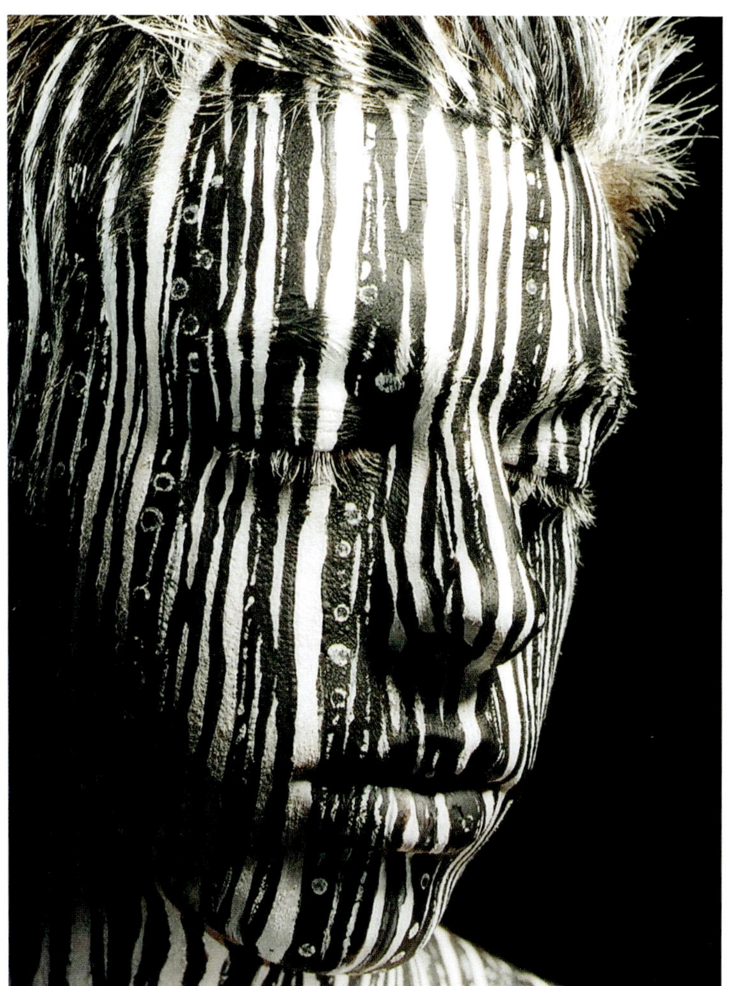

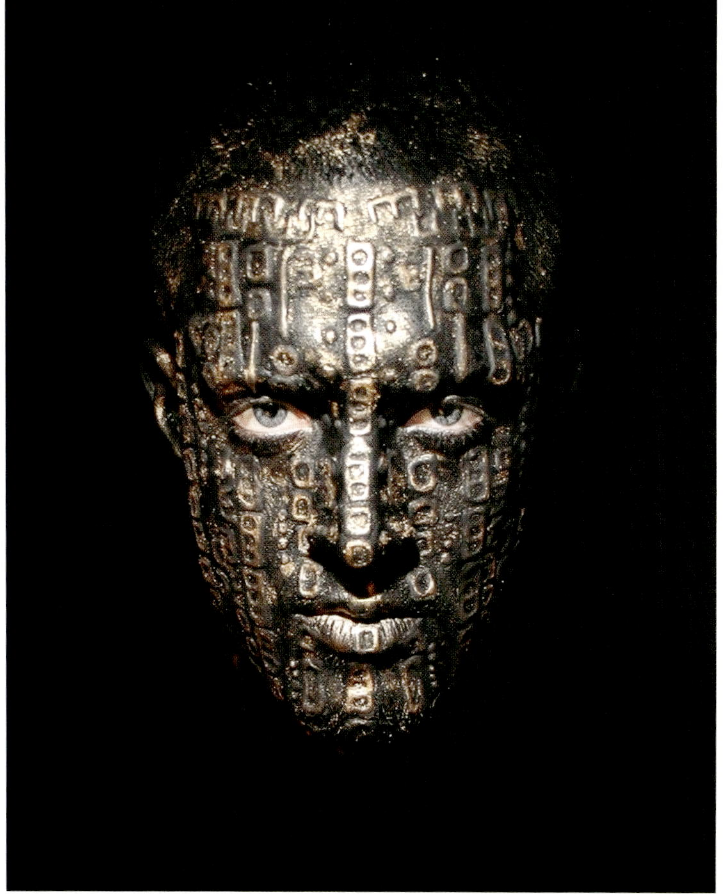

"I think, as an artist, it's important to keep pushing yourself. I think there is so much more to be done with body art, and I never want to stop learning."

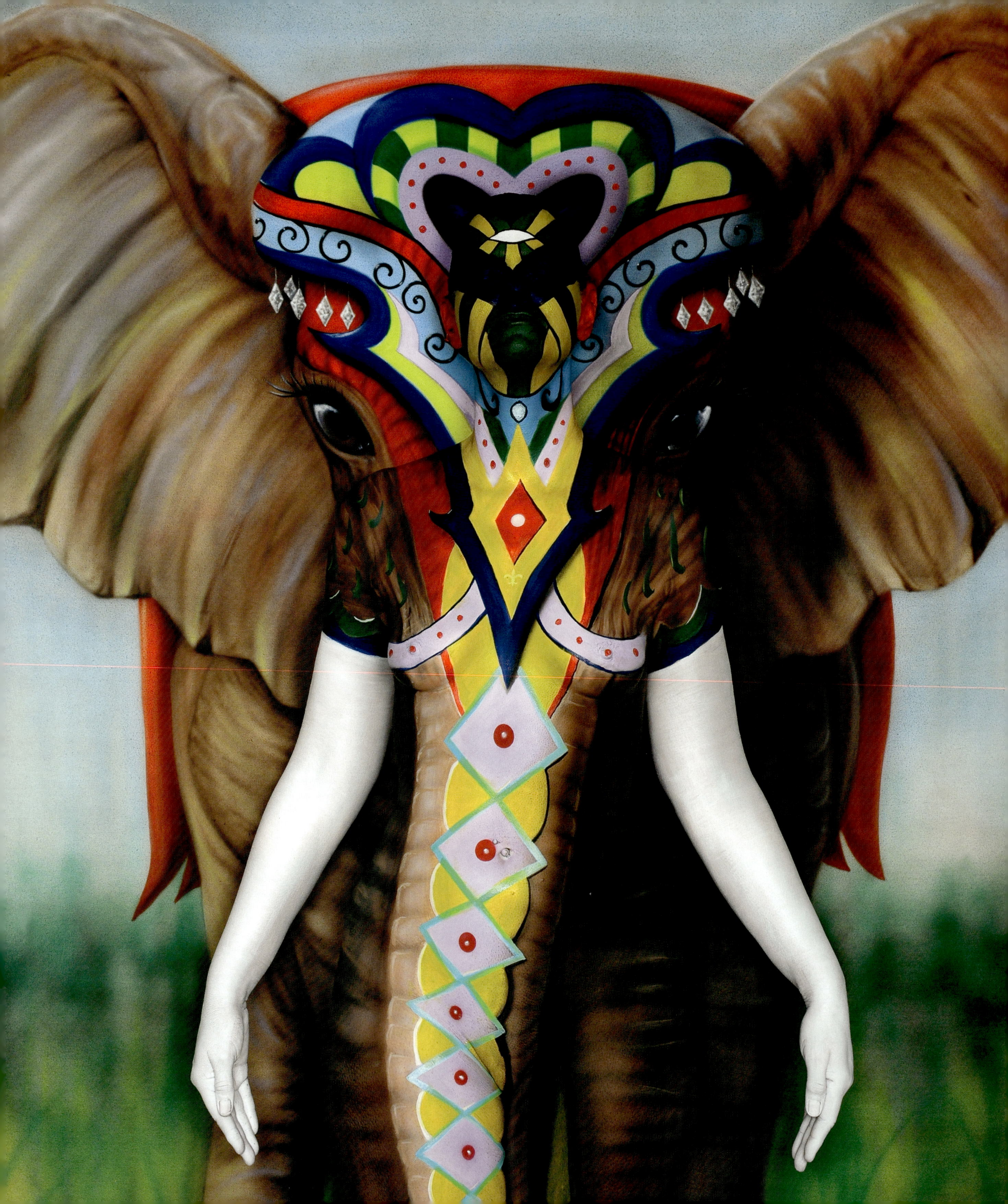

Craig Tracy

Craig Tracy is a master airbrush artist and painter. He combines his work with both the living form and traditional canvas art to create illusions in fine detail and abstract composition. Craig's compositions of the body harmonize natural shapes and reflect his appreciation for human beauty. One of his greatest achievements has been the creation of the Craig Tracy Gallery in New Orleans, the first gallery space dedicated purely to bodypainting.

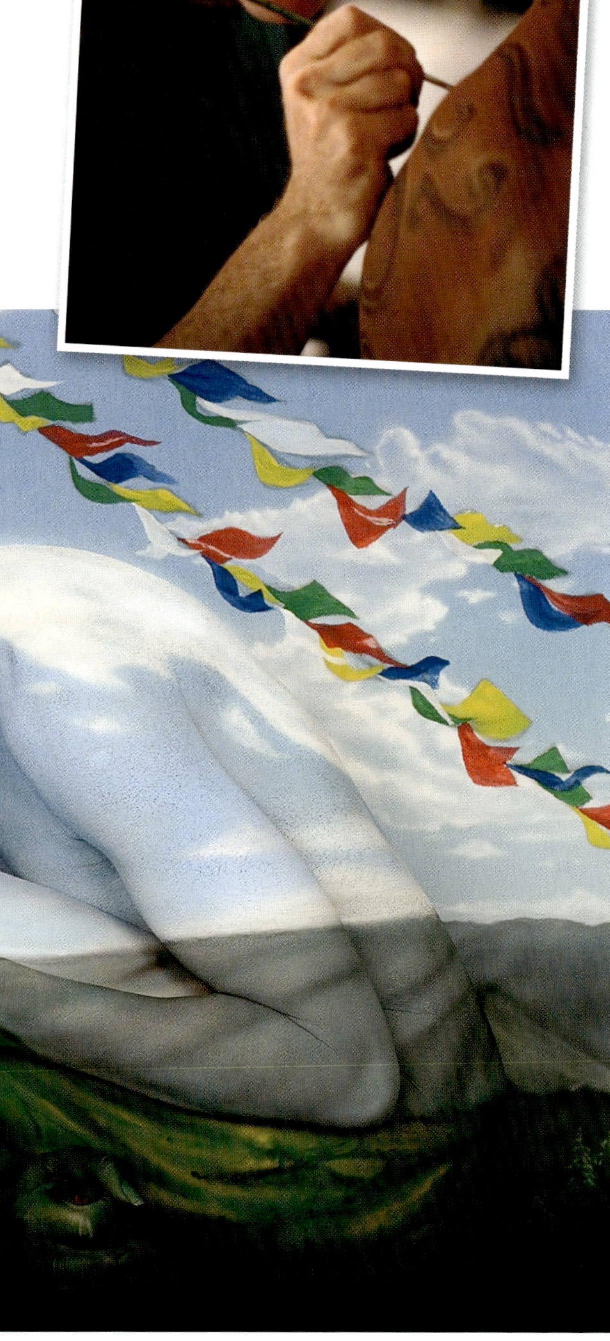

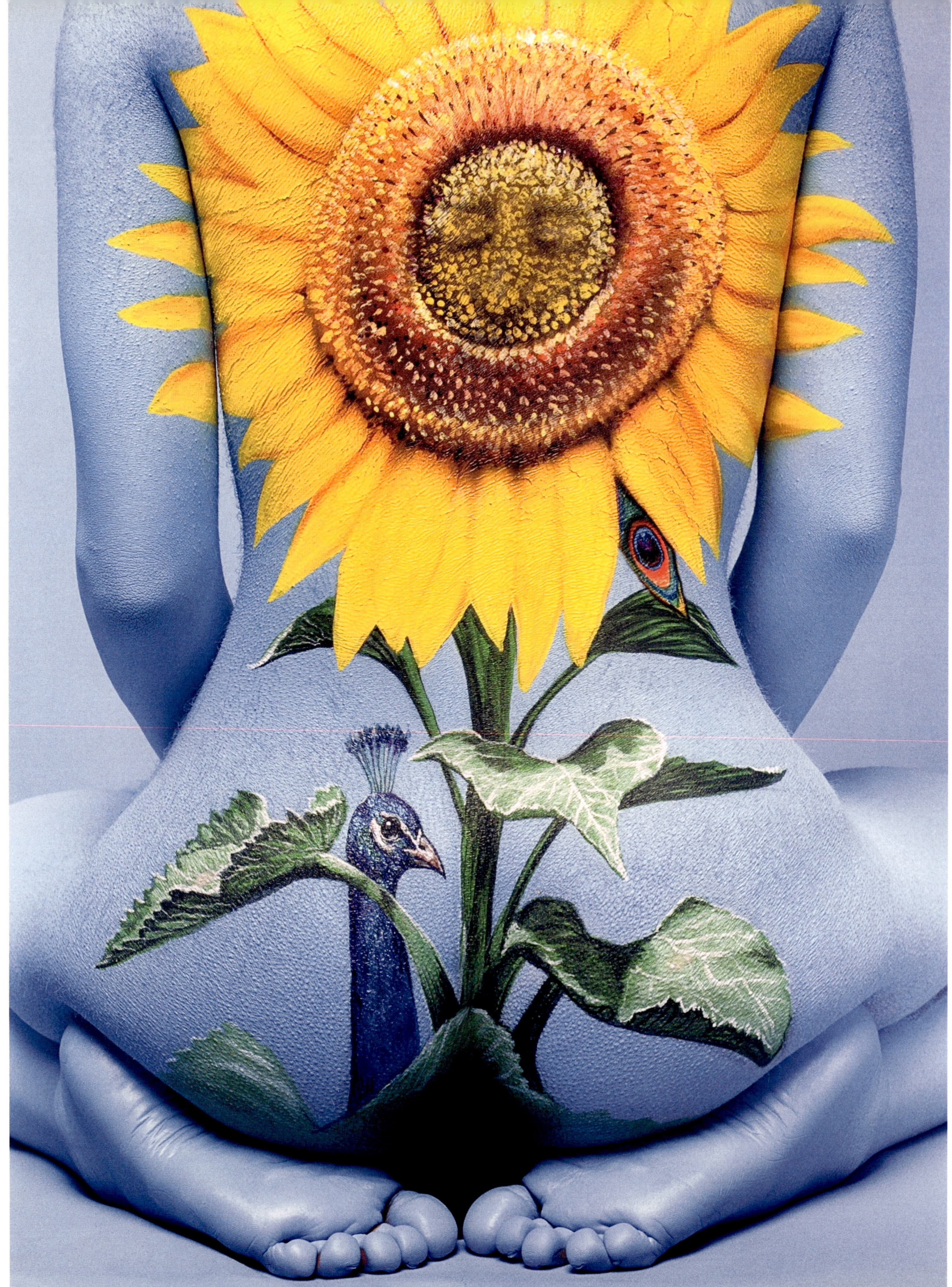

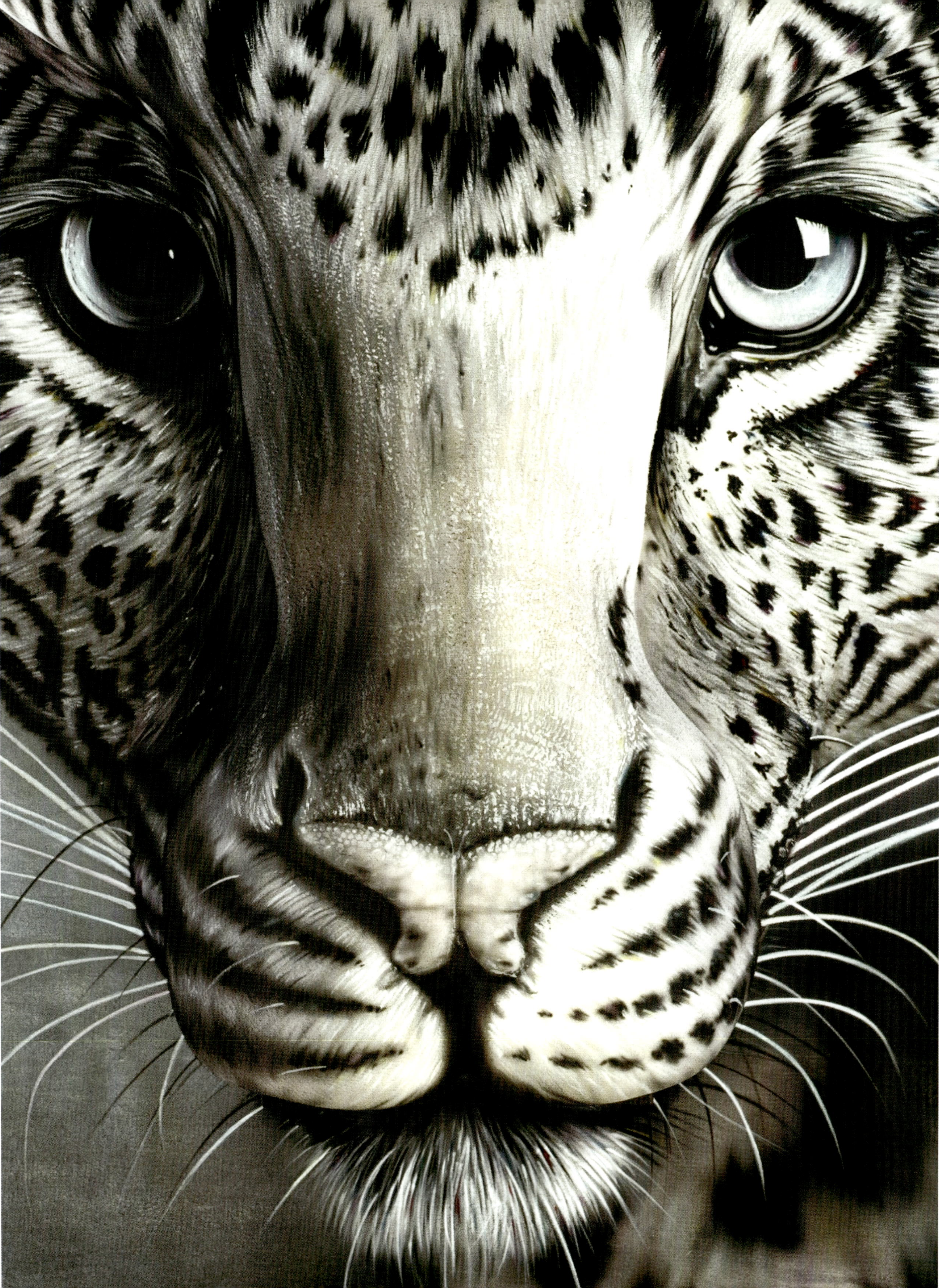

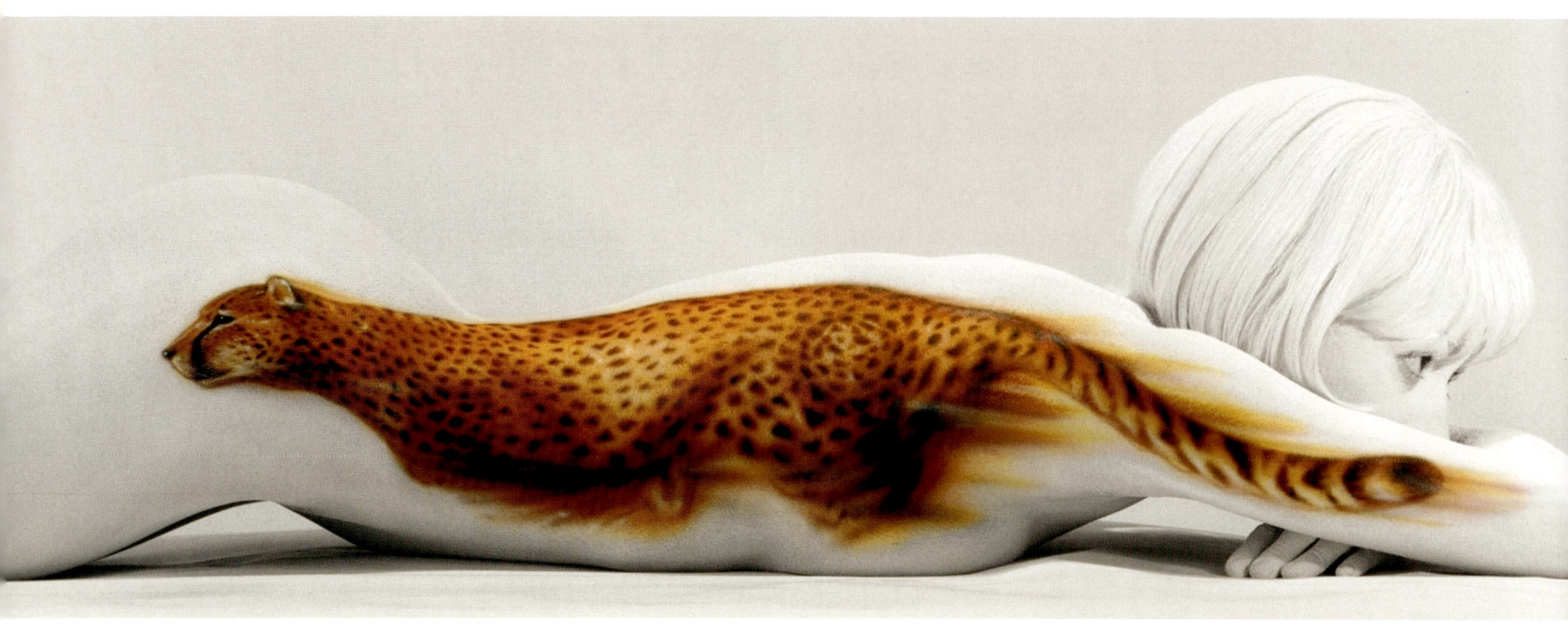

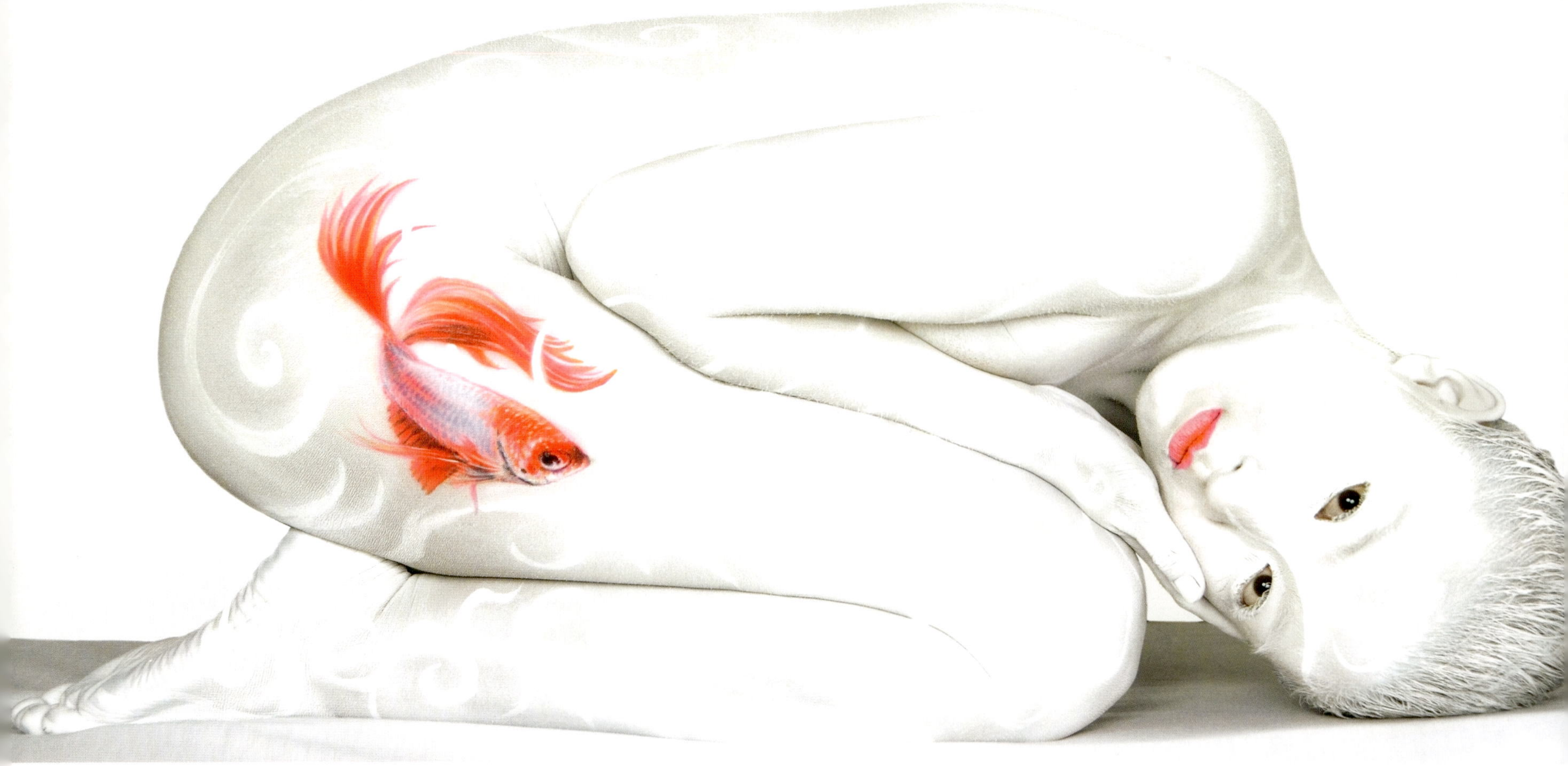

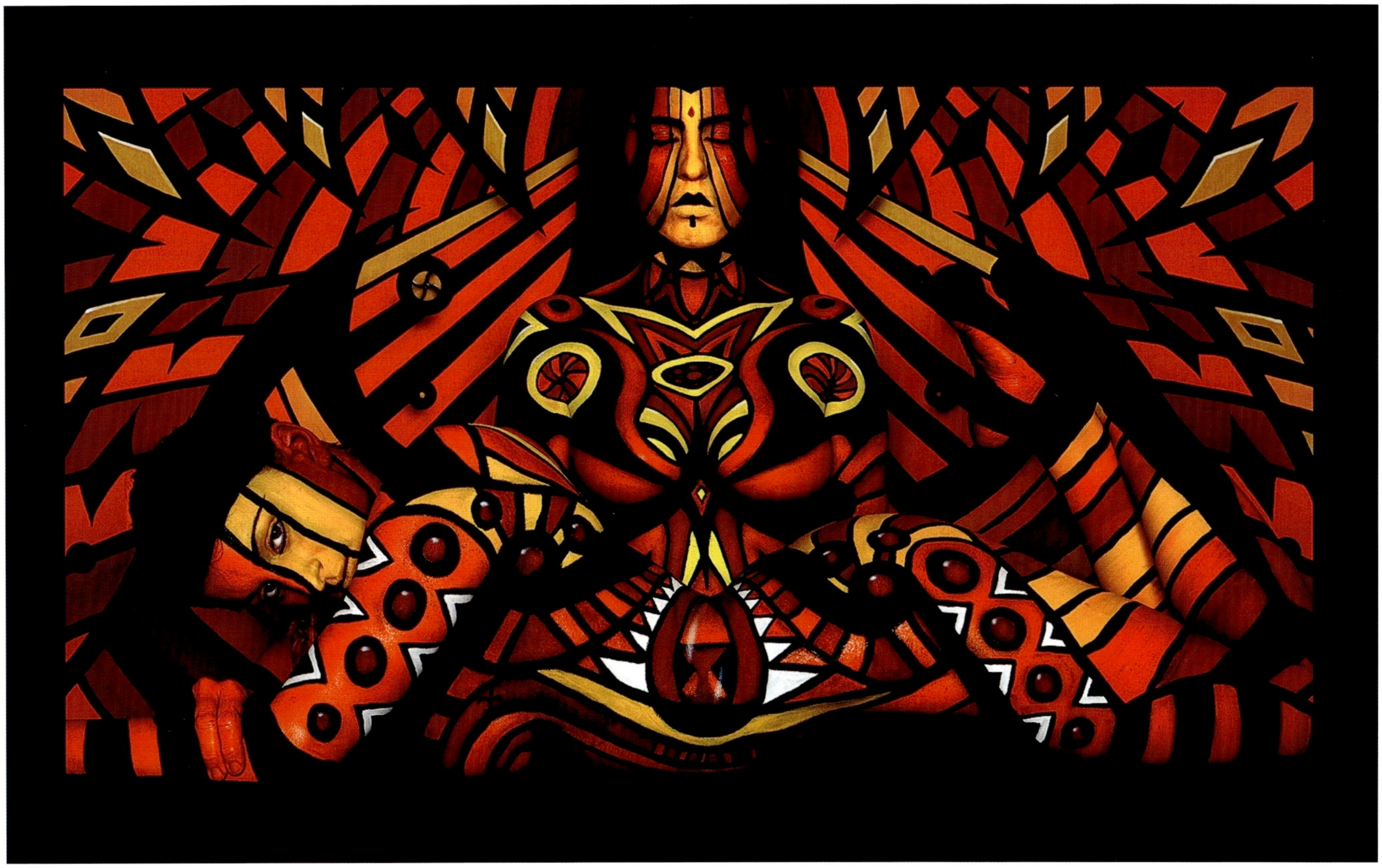

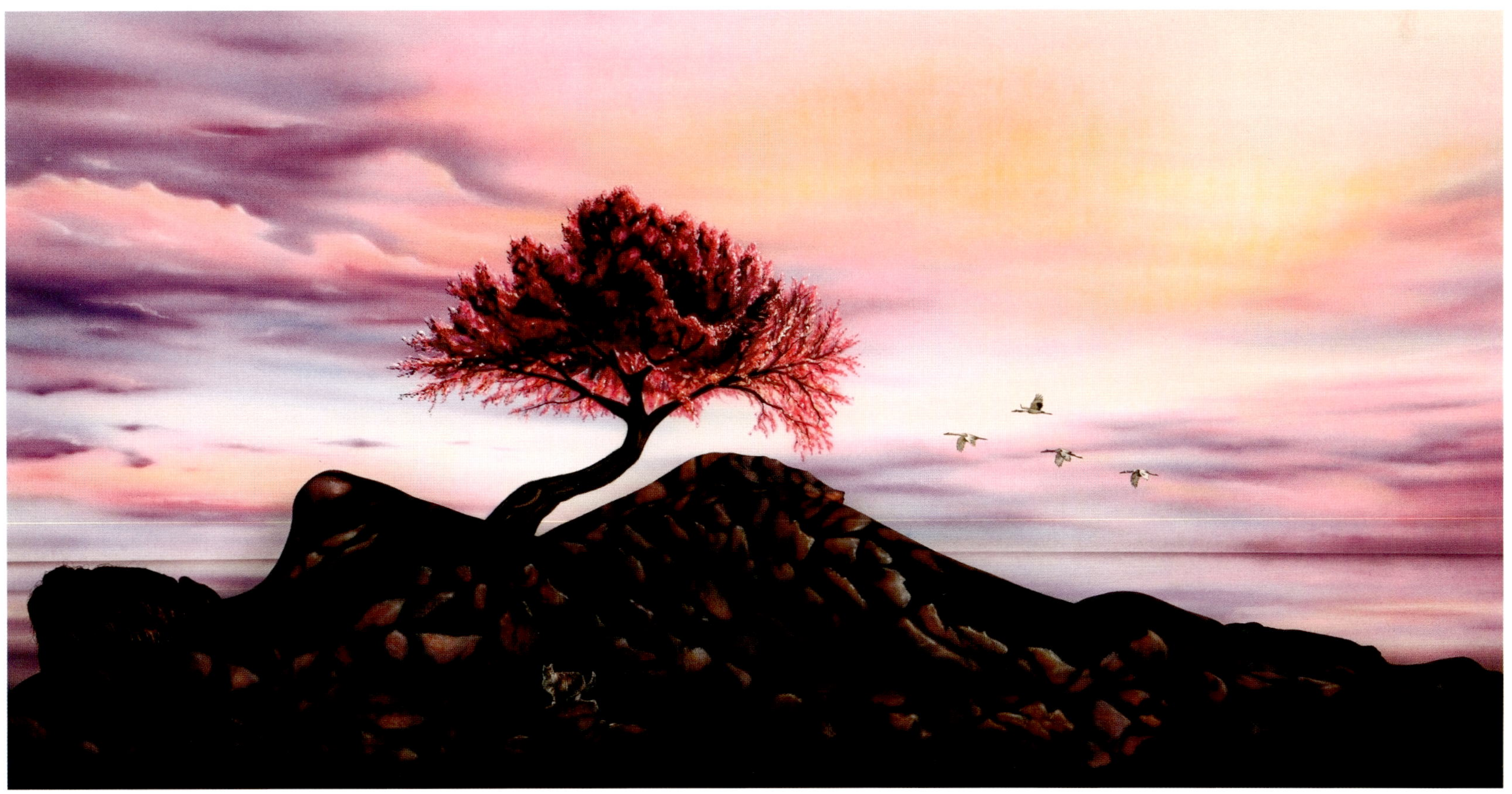

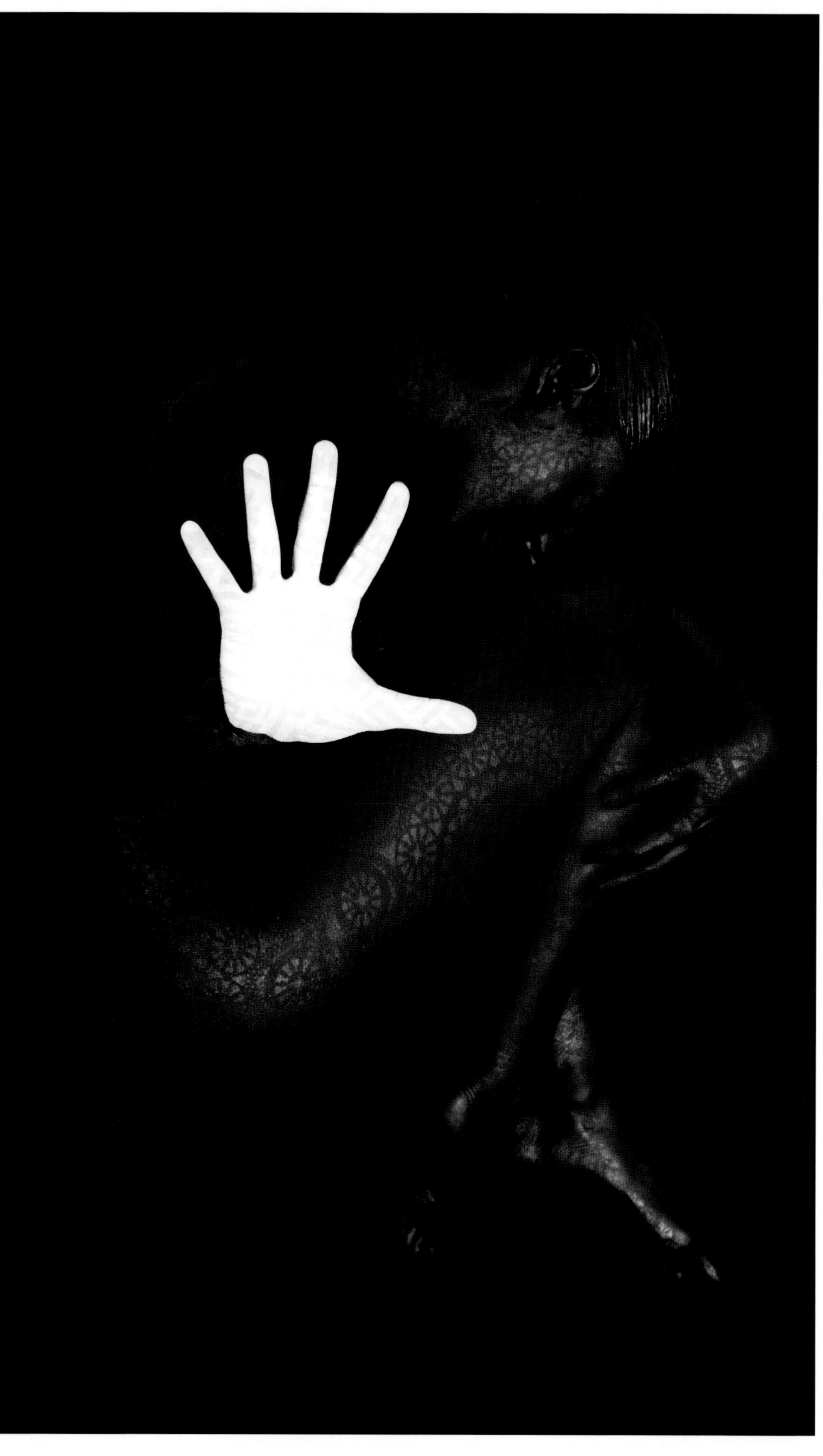

"I have been a professional artist since the age of sixteen. I have never had any other type of work since then. I lived and breathed art, and sadly enough I was never truly satisfied with the art I was seeing or creating. I felt like there must be something more interesting to create. The act of painting on traditional, conventional surfaces was utilitarian, and I needed more than the same old boring canvas, paper or wall to work with. I thought, 'What if I painted on us? What if I seriously painted on living, breathing human beings?' Now nothing even comes close to painting on people. People are my passion. Diamonds and gold are dull by comparison."

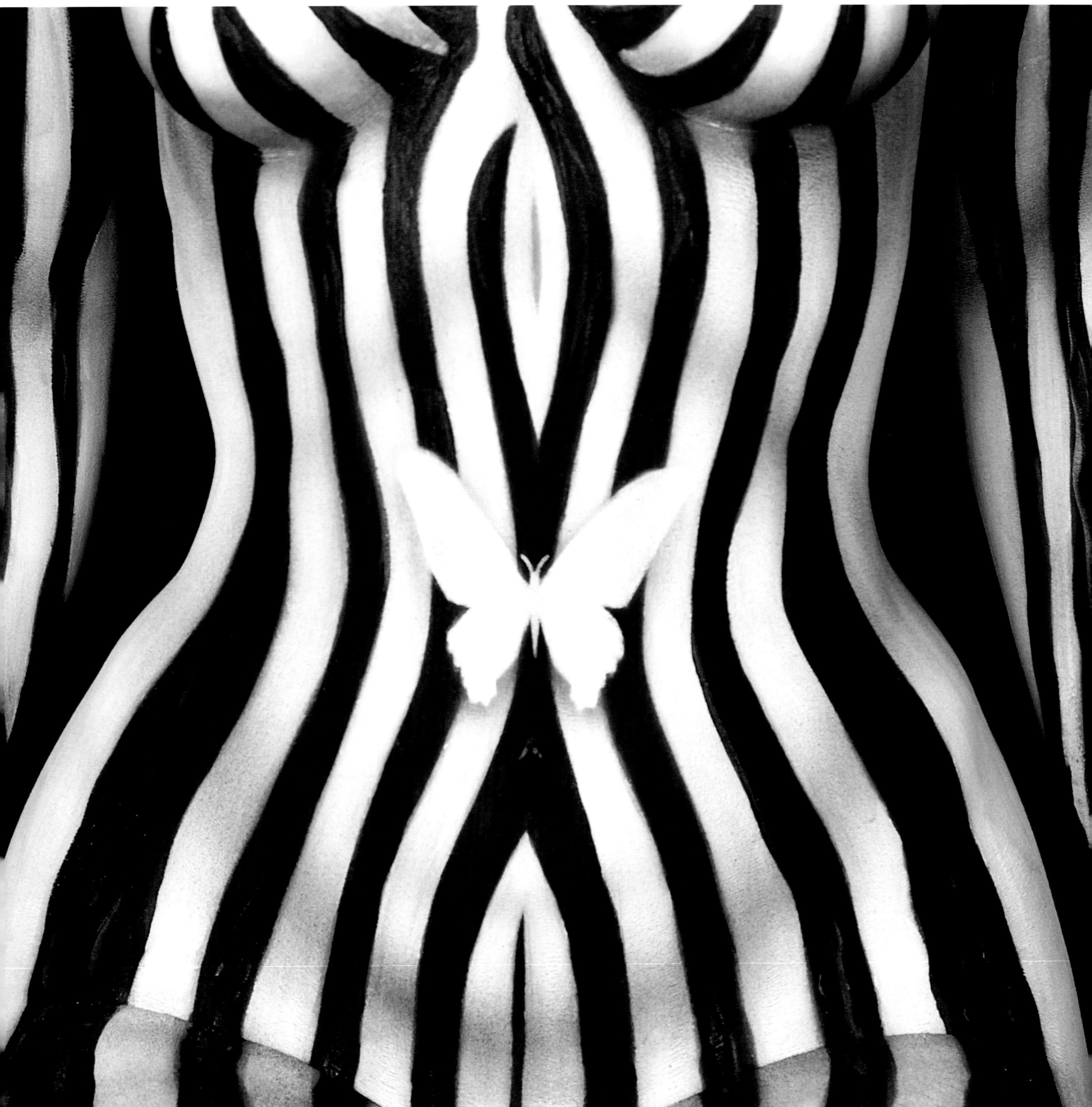

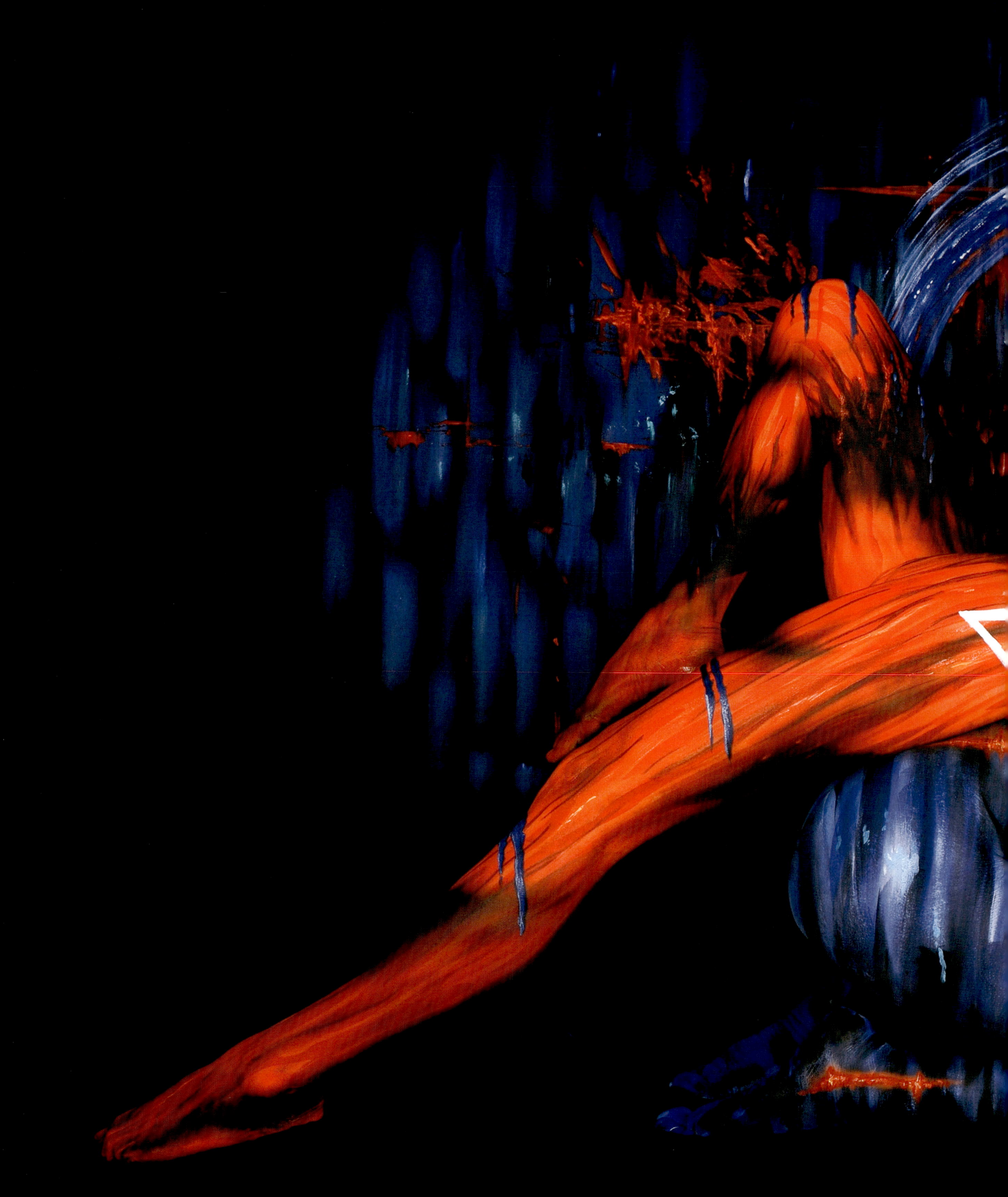

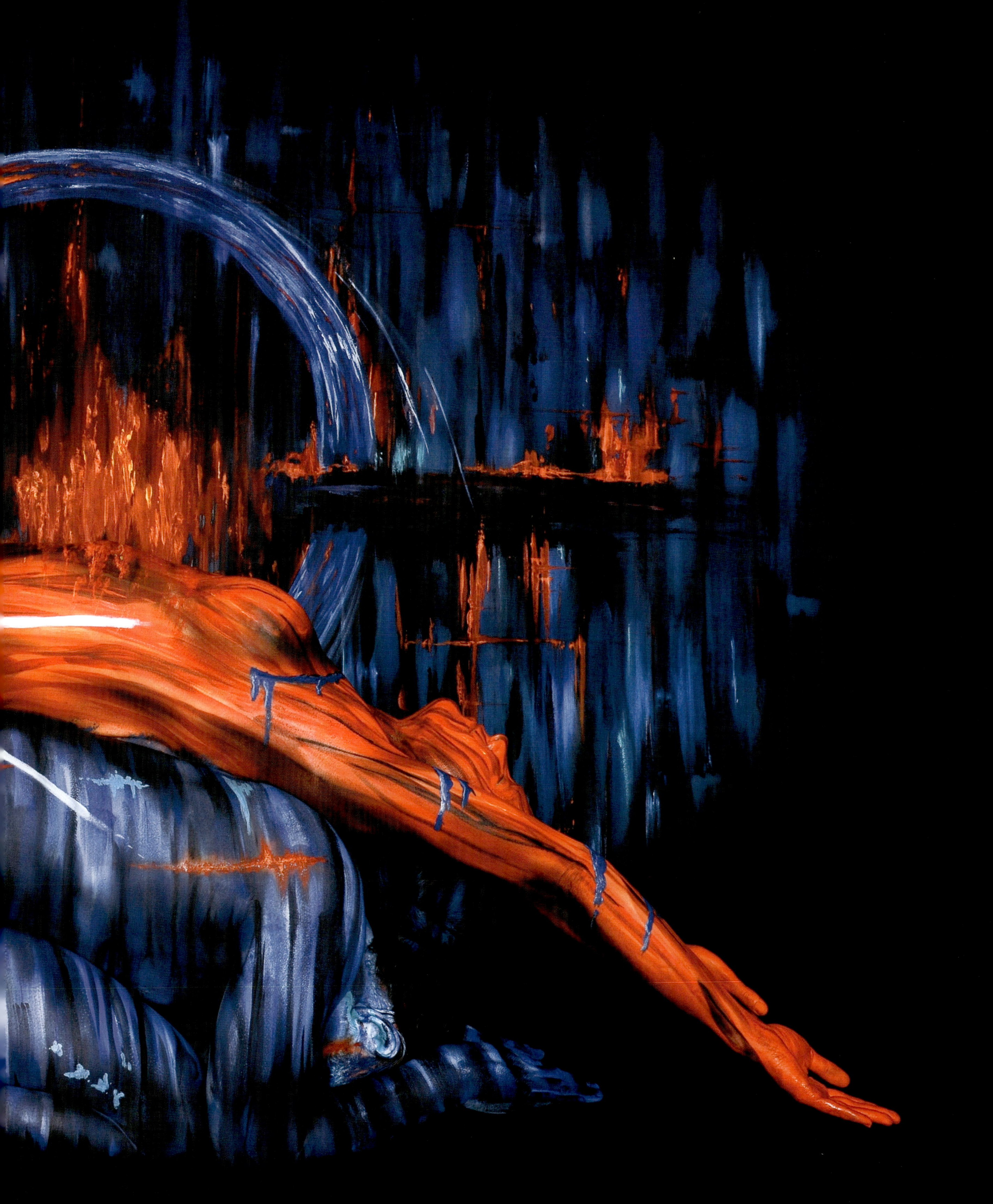

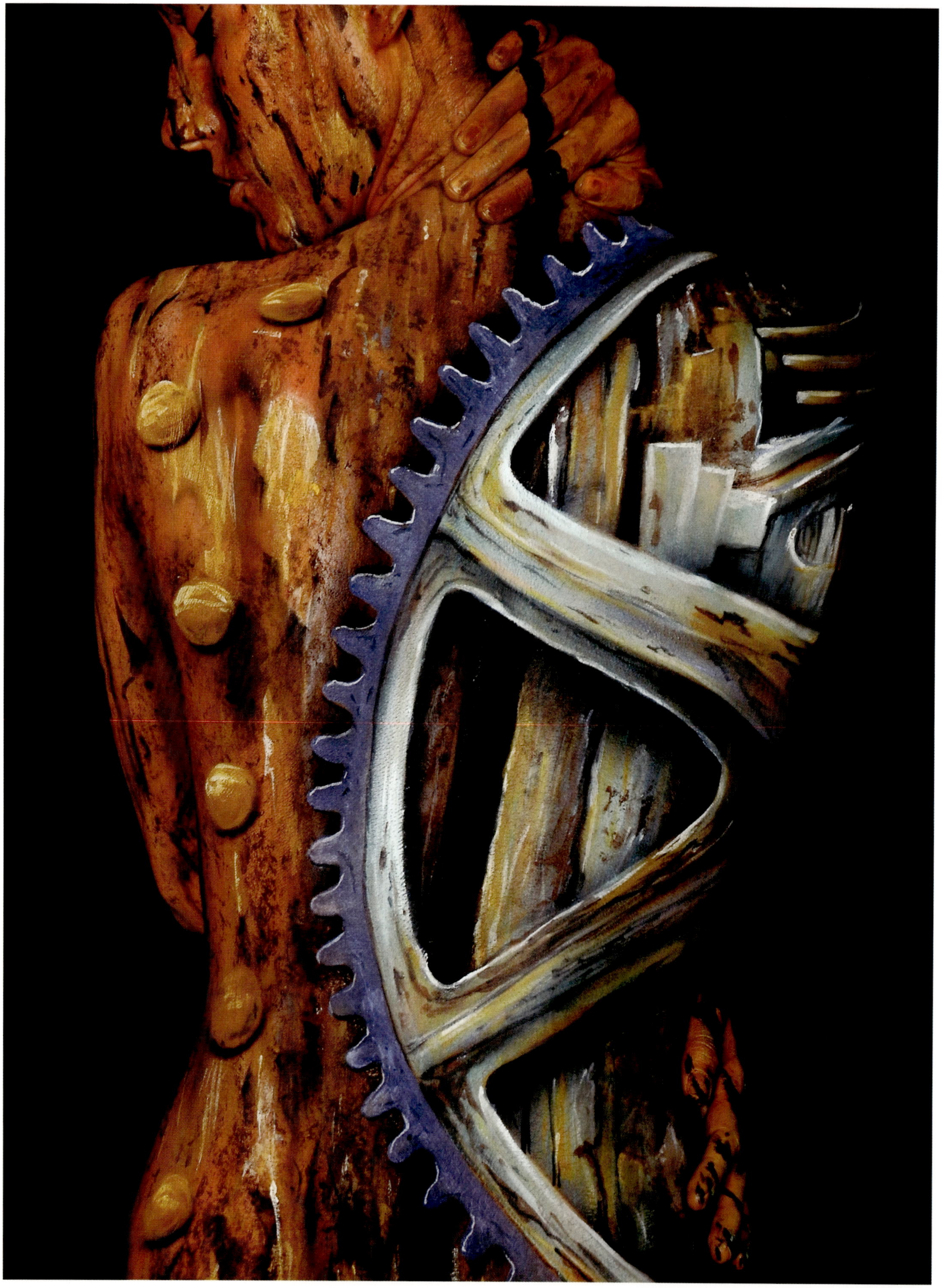

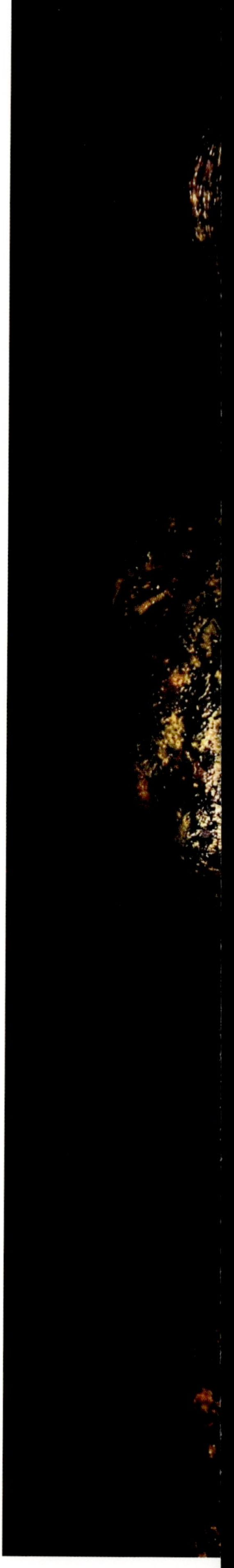

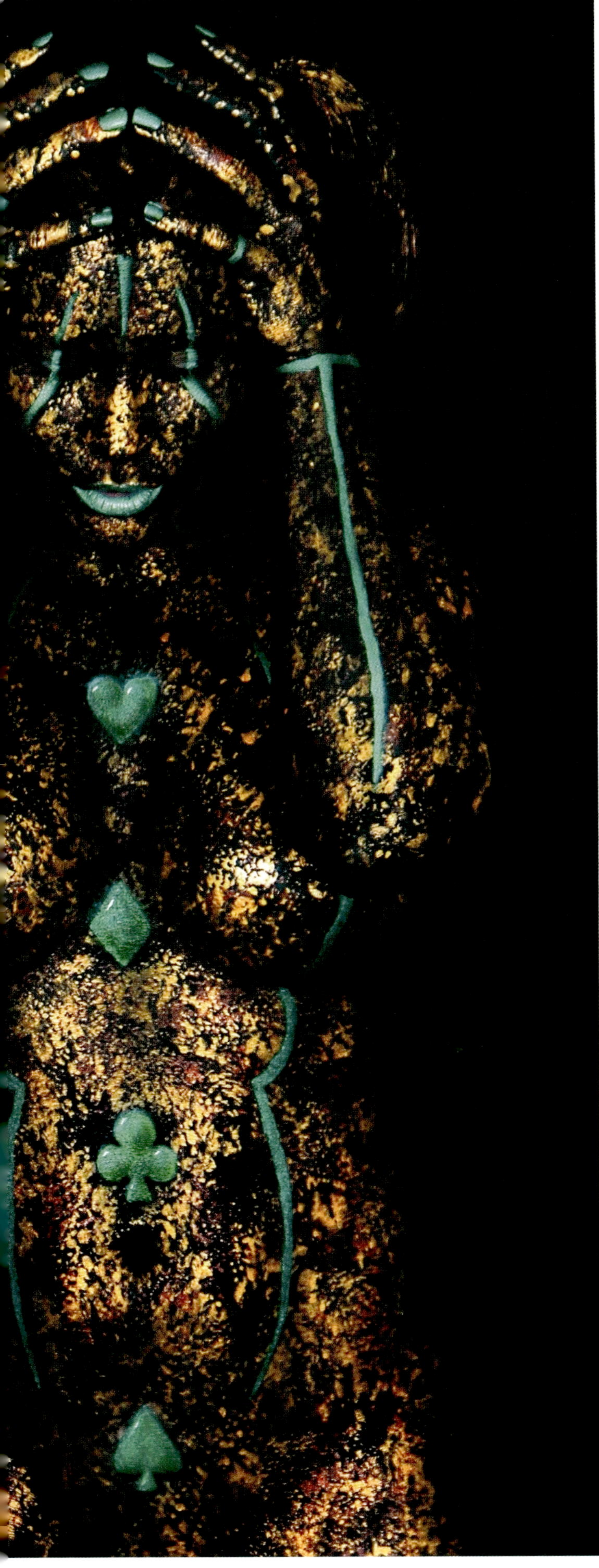

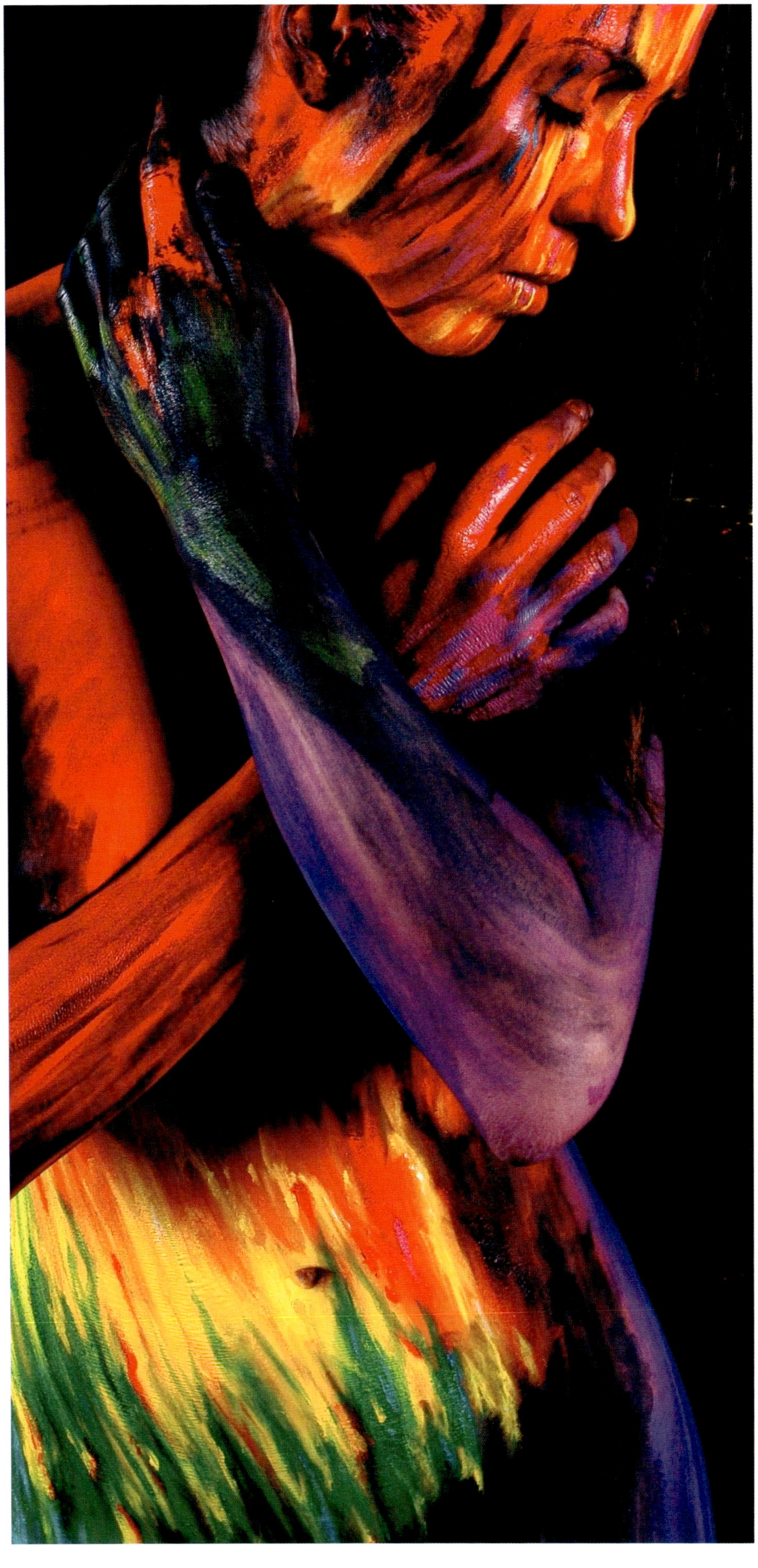

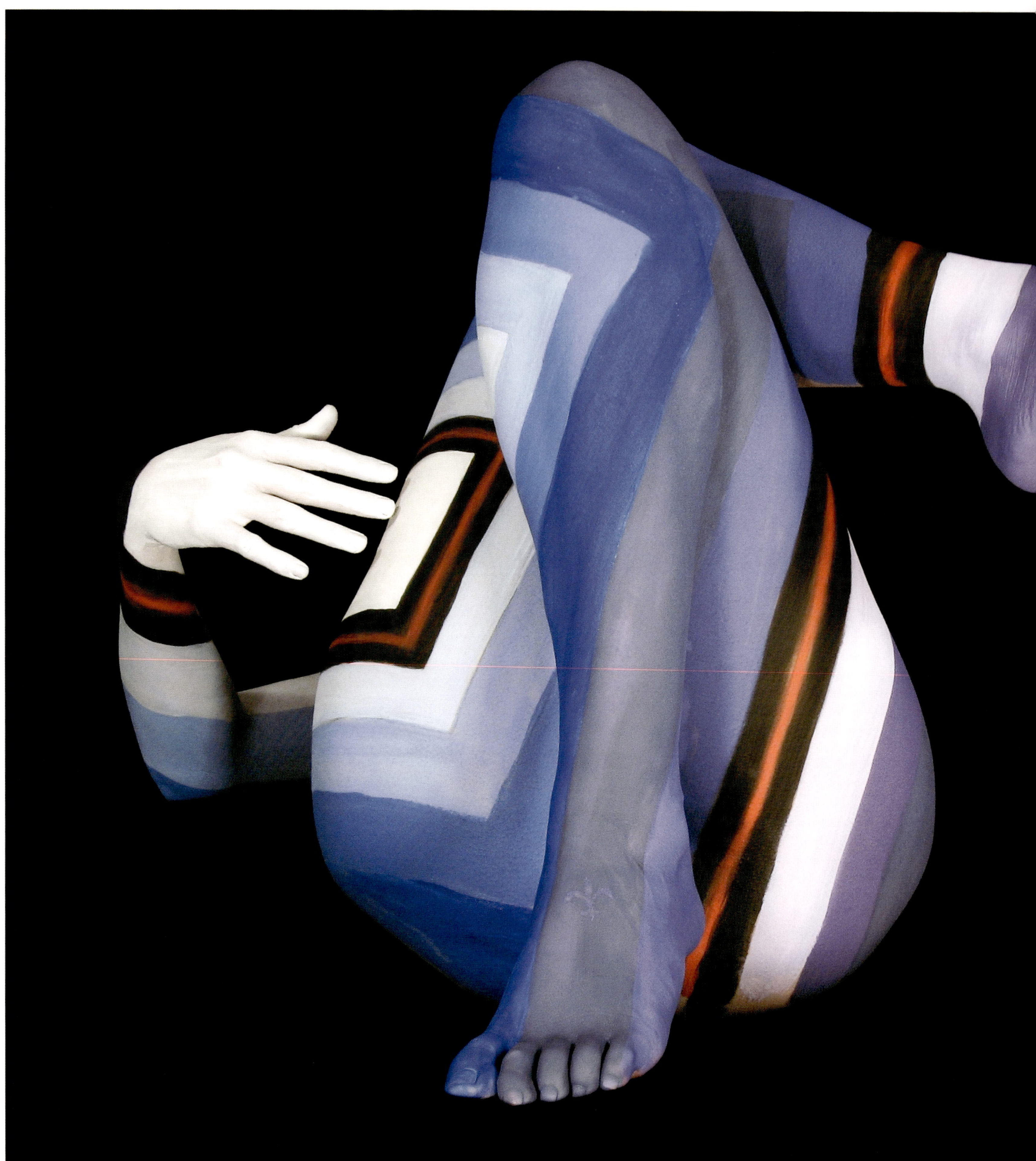

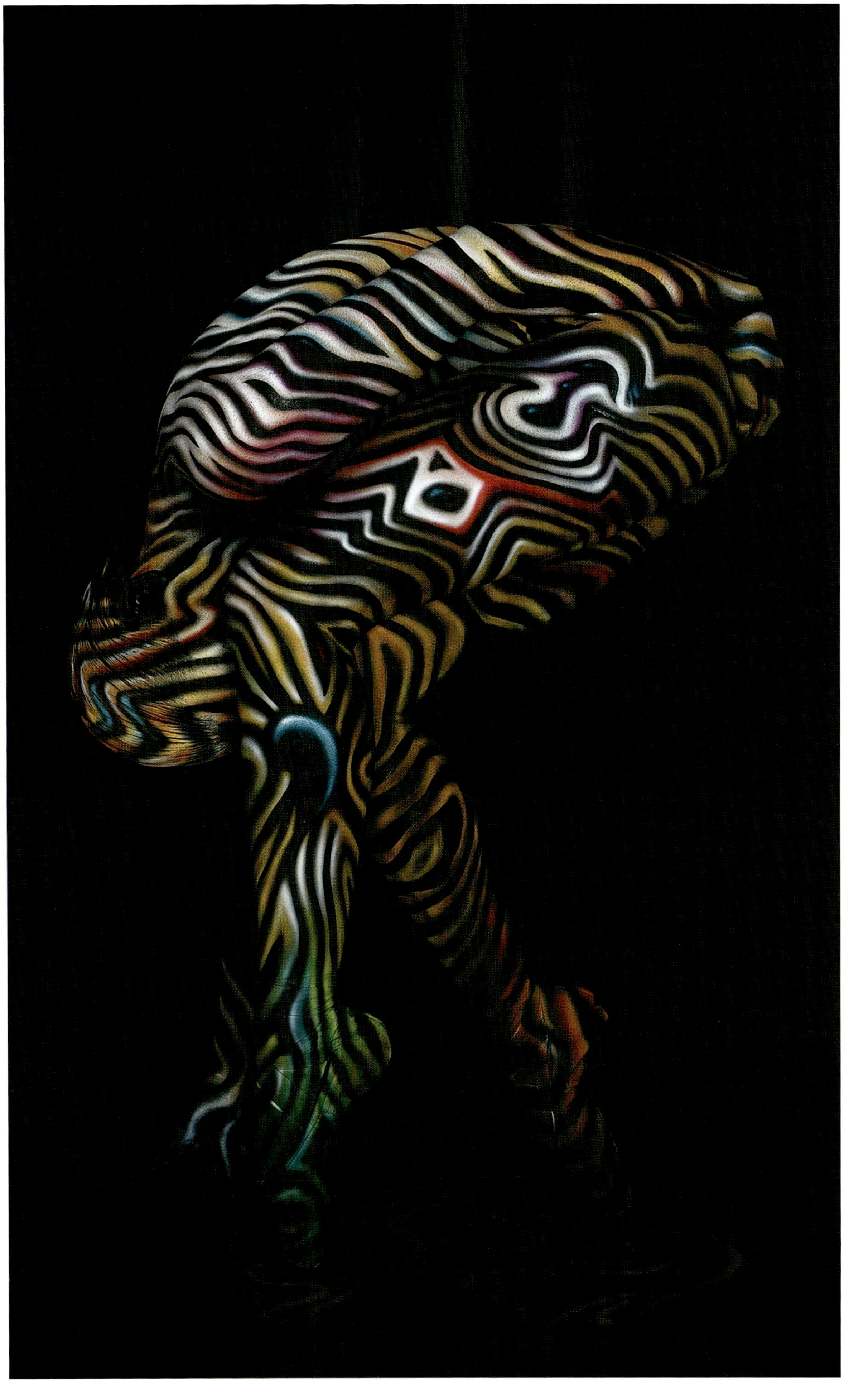

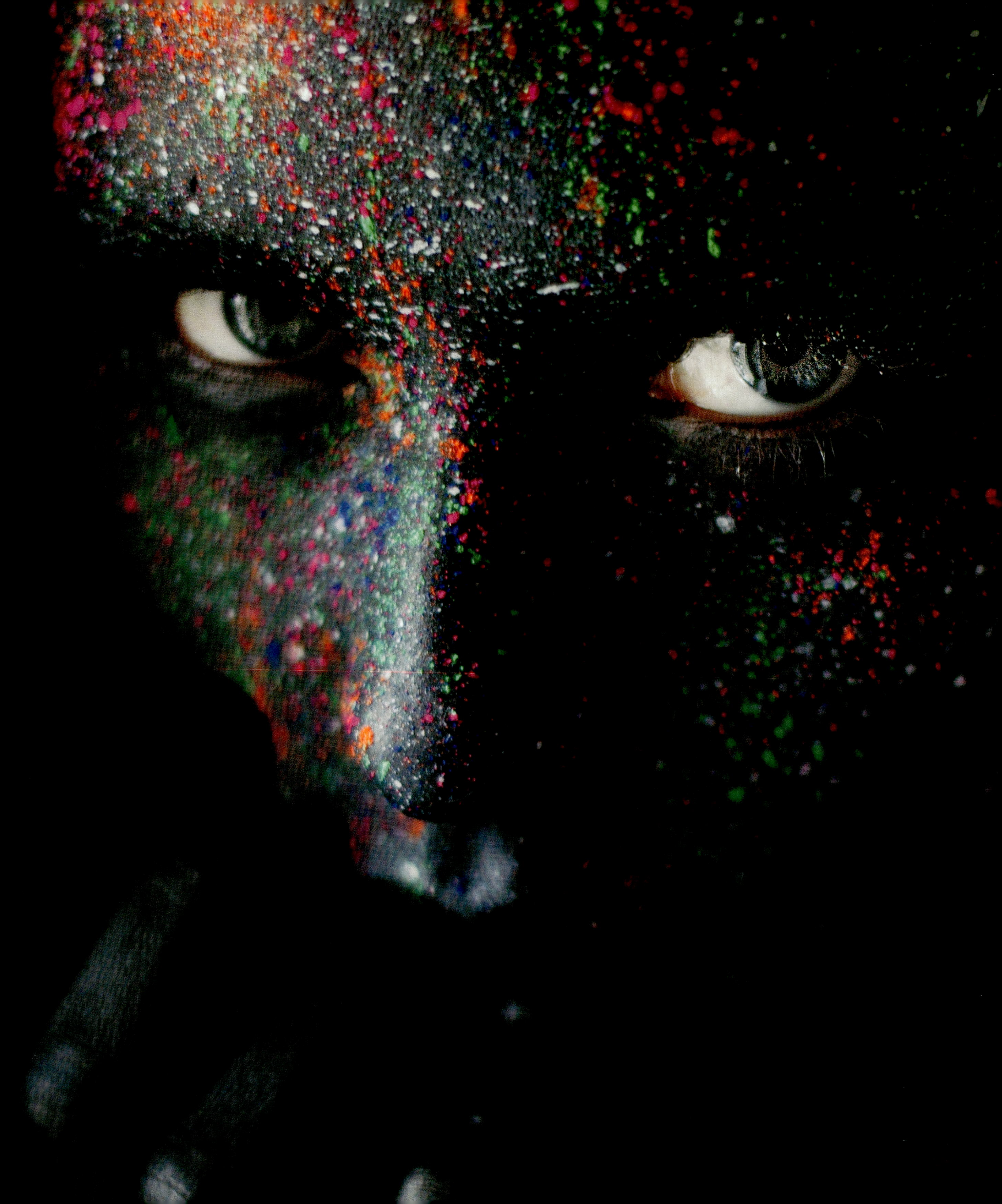

Einat Dan

WWW.EINATDAN.COM

Einat Dan is one of the leading bodypainters and makeup artists today. She has won countless titles at national and international competitions for body art in Europe and Asia. Einat founded her own line of bodypainting products and makeup brushes, and she teaches makeup and body art around the world. Einat has worked with many famous fashion labels and photographers, and her work can be seen on highly regarded magazine and book covers, and in campaigns and exhibitions.

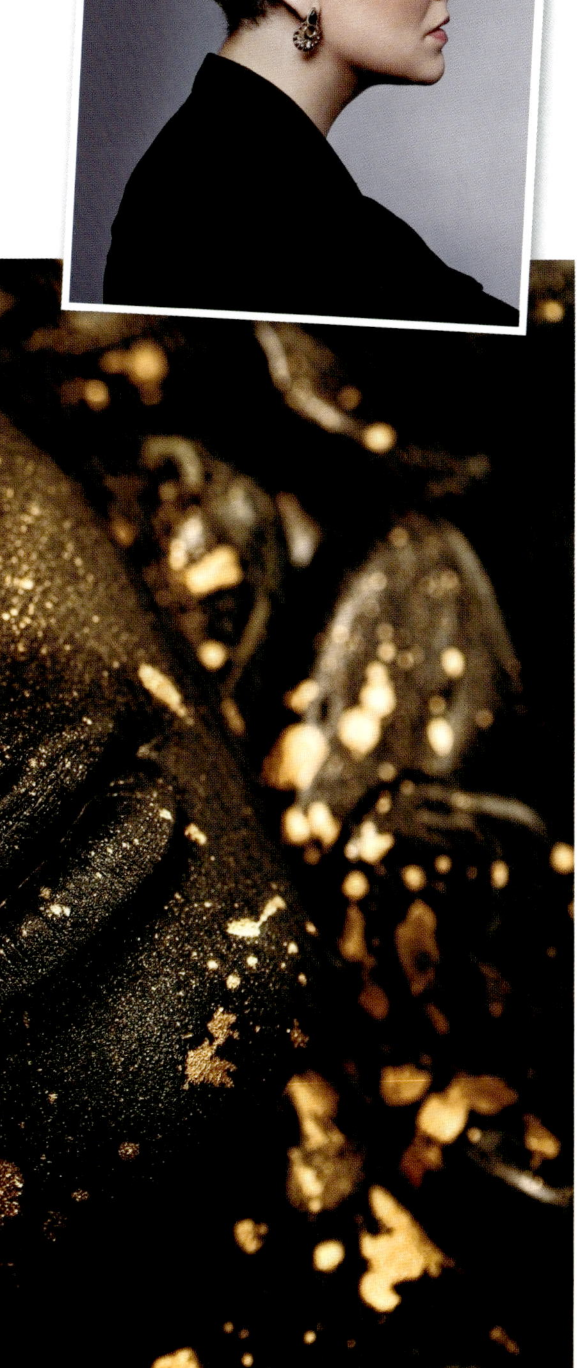

PHOTOGRAPHER JULIA NONI | PHOTOGRAPHER SUZANA HOLTGRAVE (OPPOSITE)

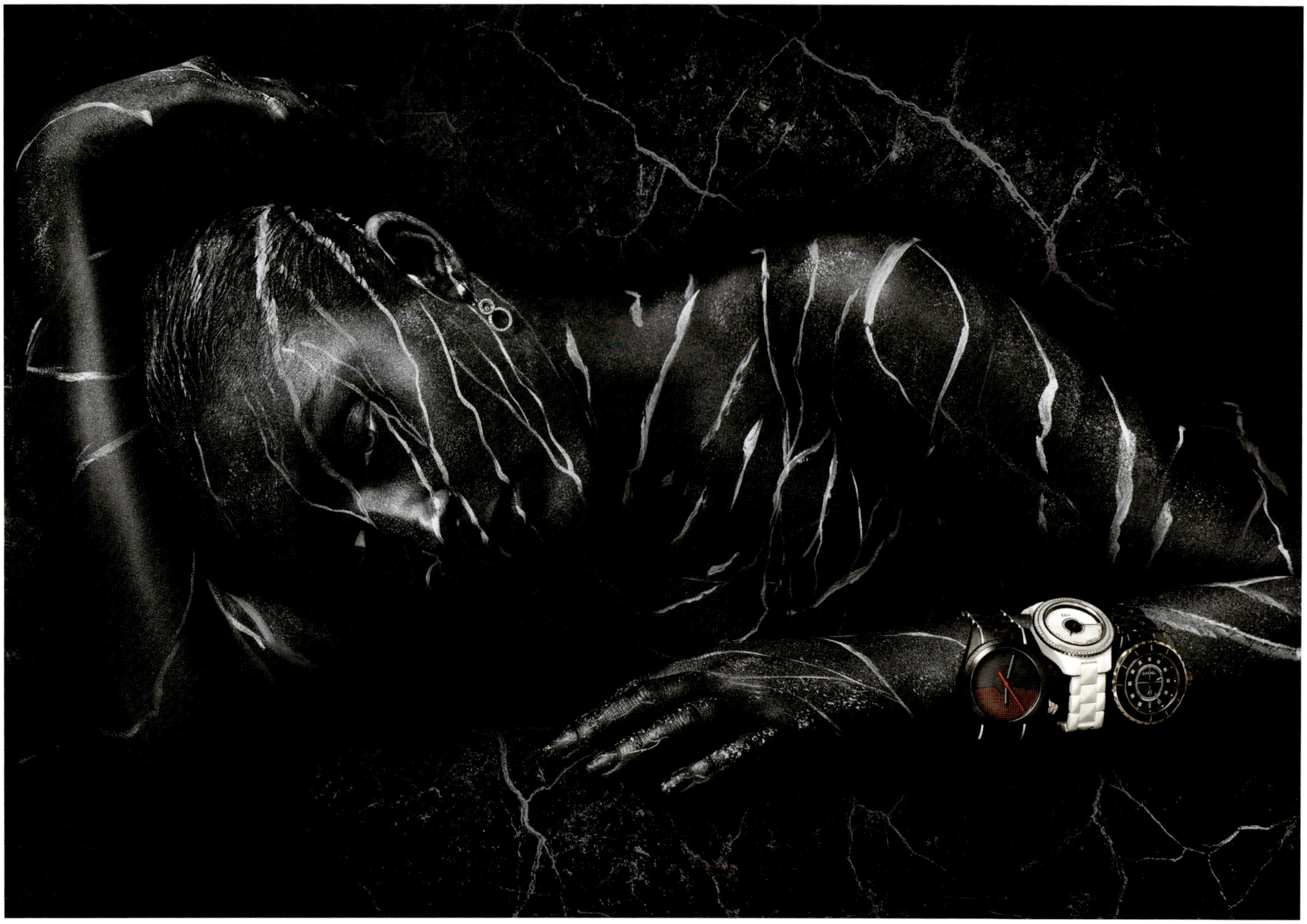

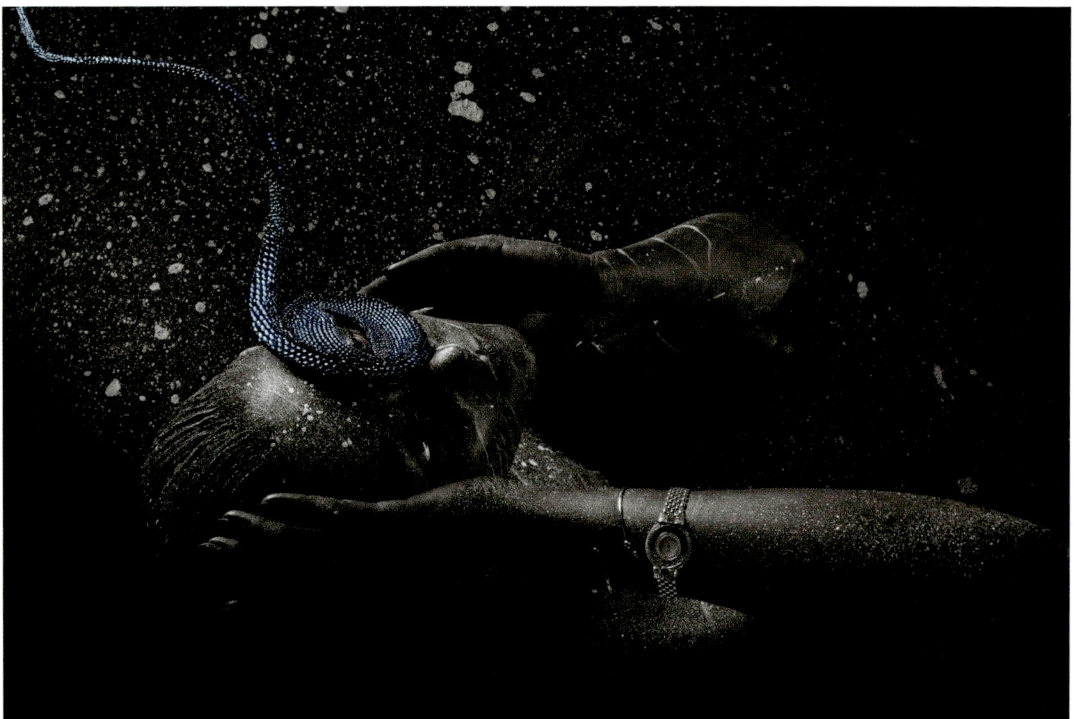
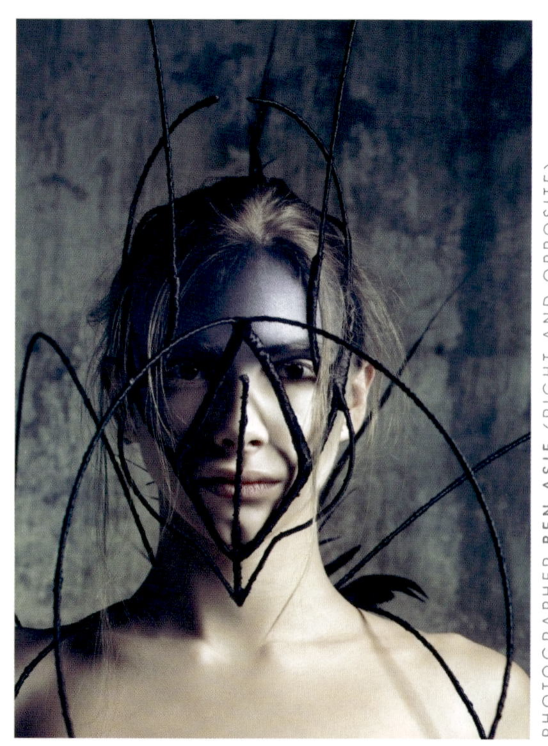

PHOTOGRAPHER CAMILLE SANSON (LEFT AND BOTTOM LEFT)

PHOTOGRAPHER BEN ASIF (RIGHT AND OPPOSITE)

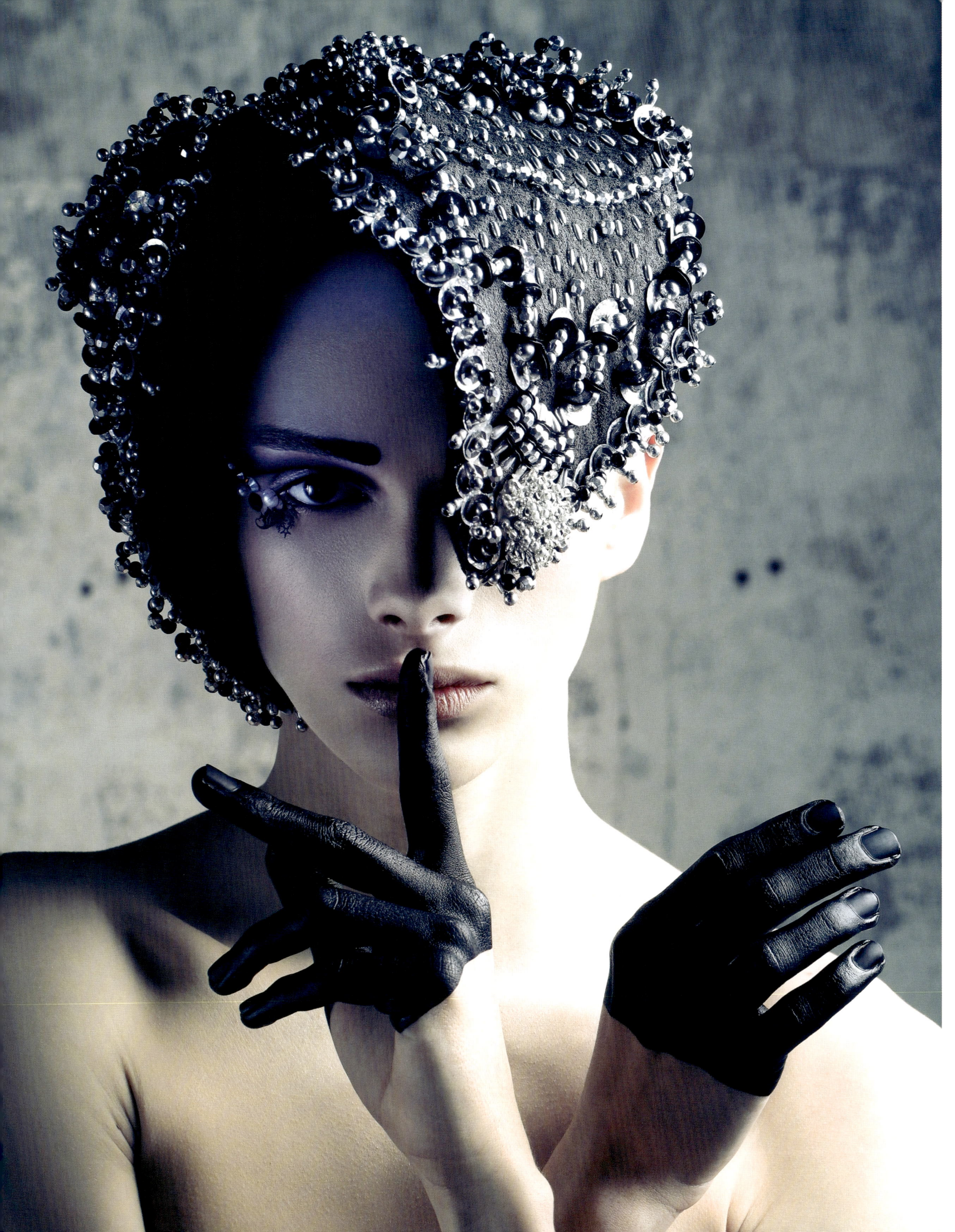

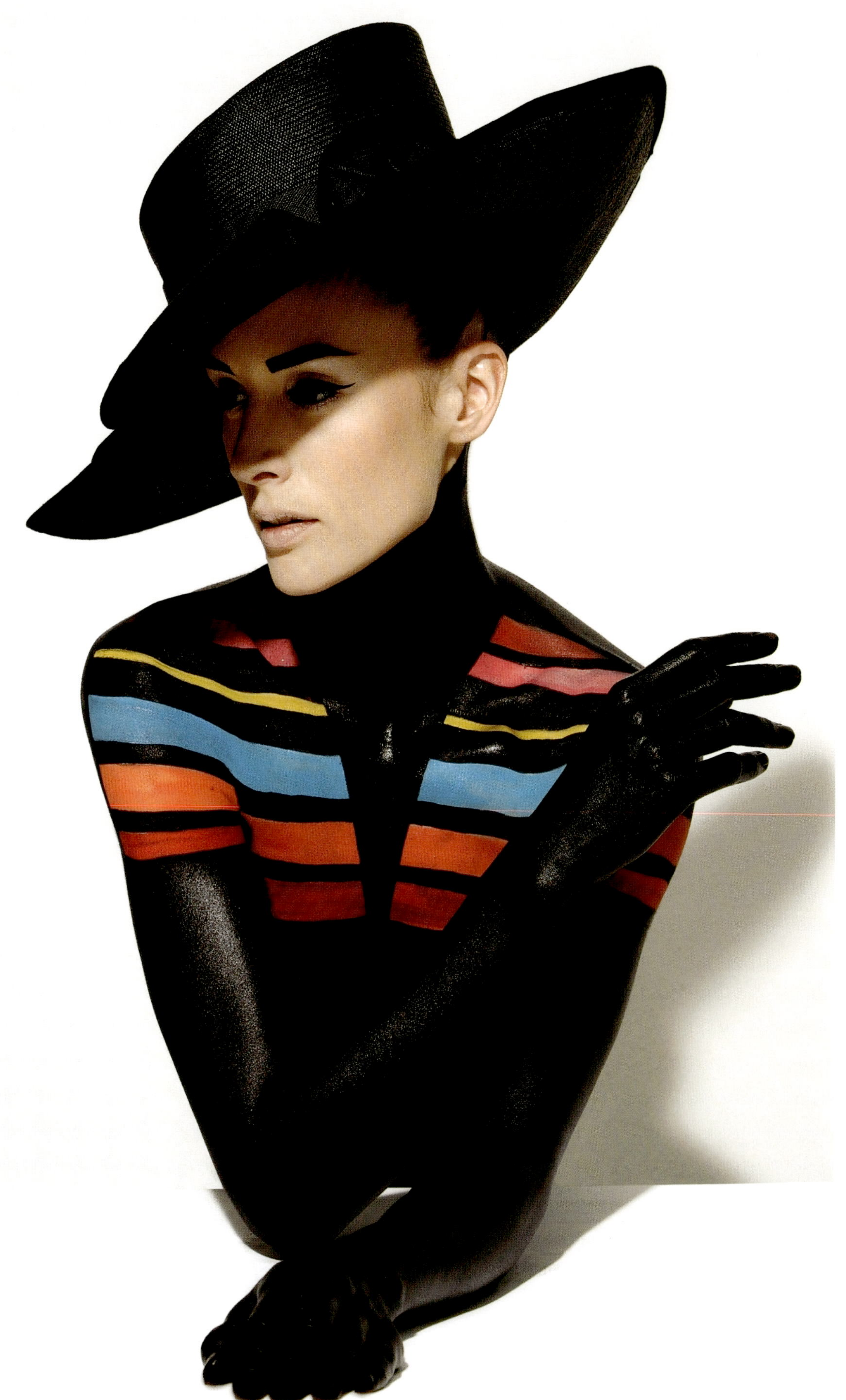

"I wish to create more and more. I wish to create every art story and every picture I have in my head with fashion makeup, fantasy and bodypainting. You control the brush; the brush does not control you."

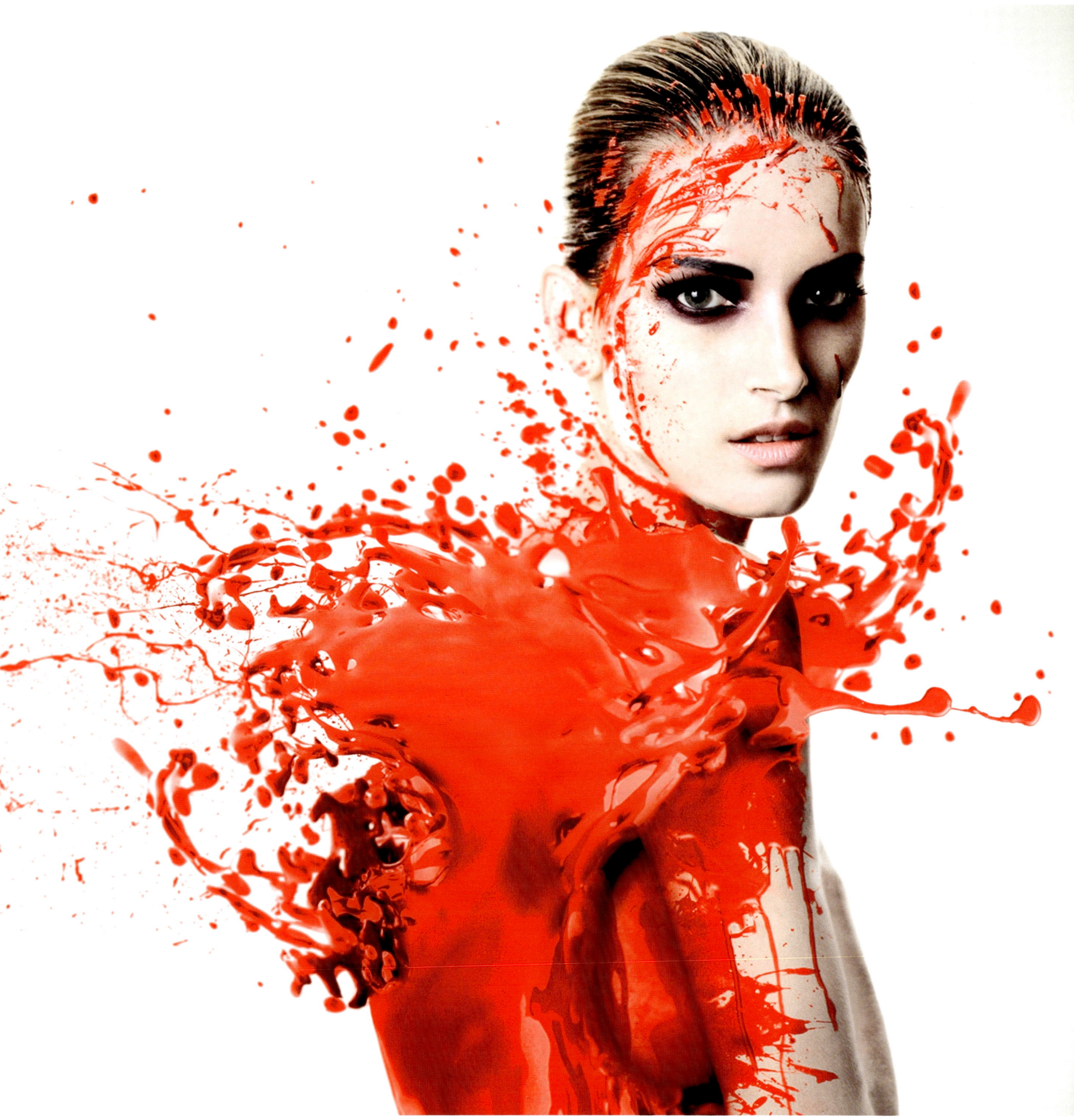

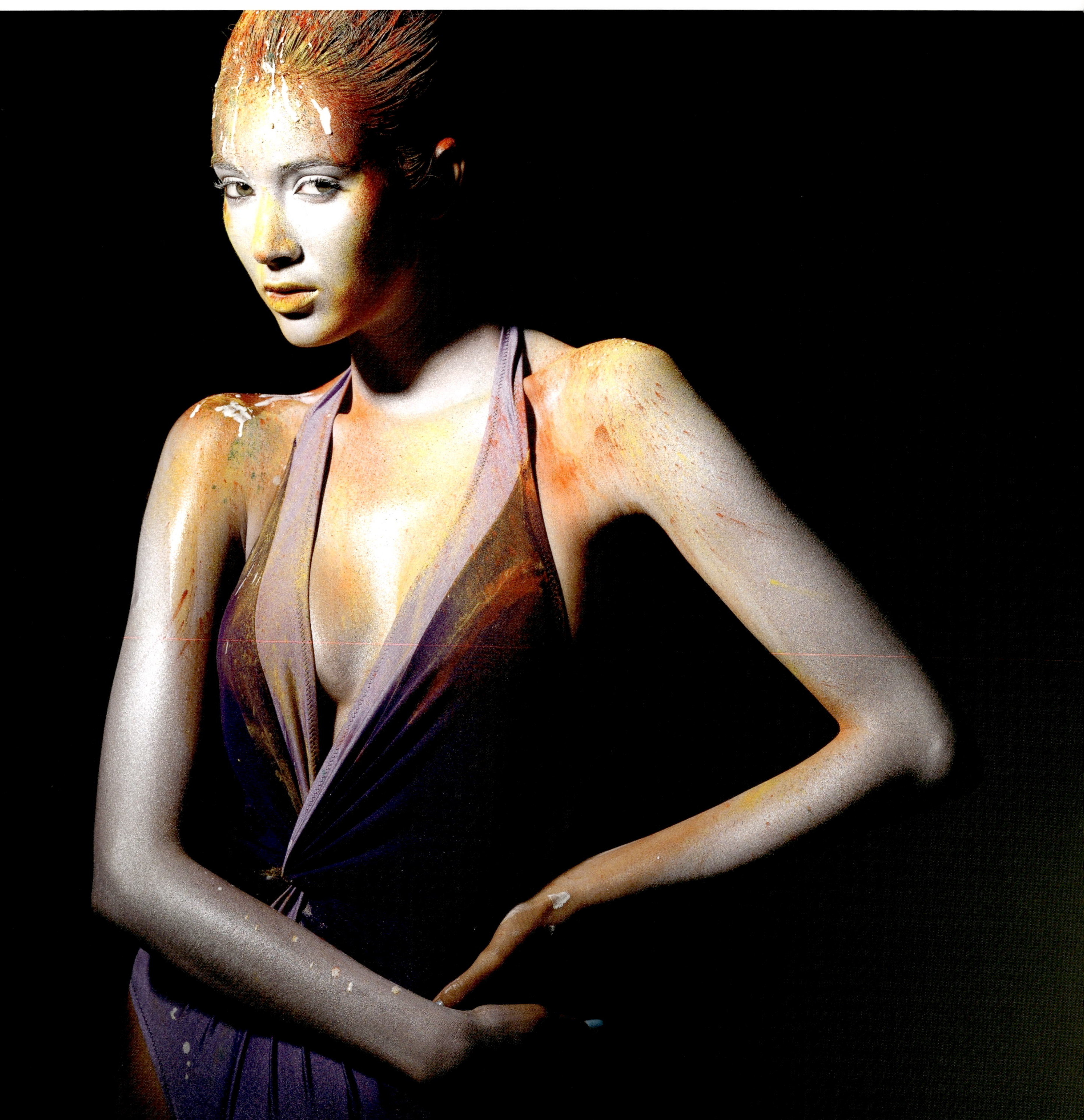

PHOTOGRAPHER MARGUERITE OELOFSE | PHOTOGRAPHER ALESSIO COCCHI (OPPOSITE)

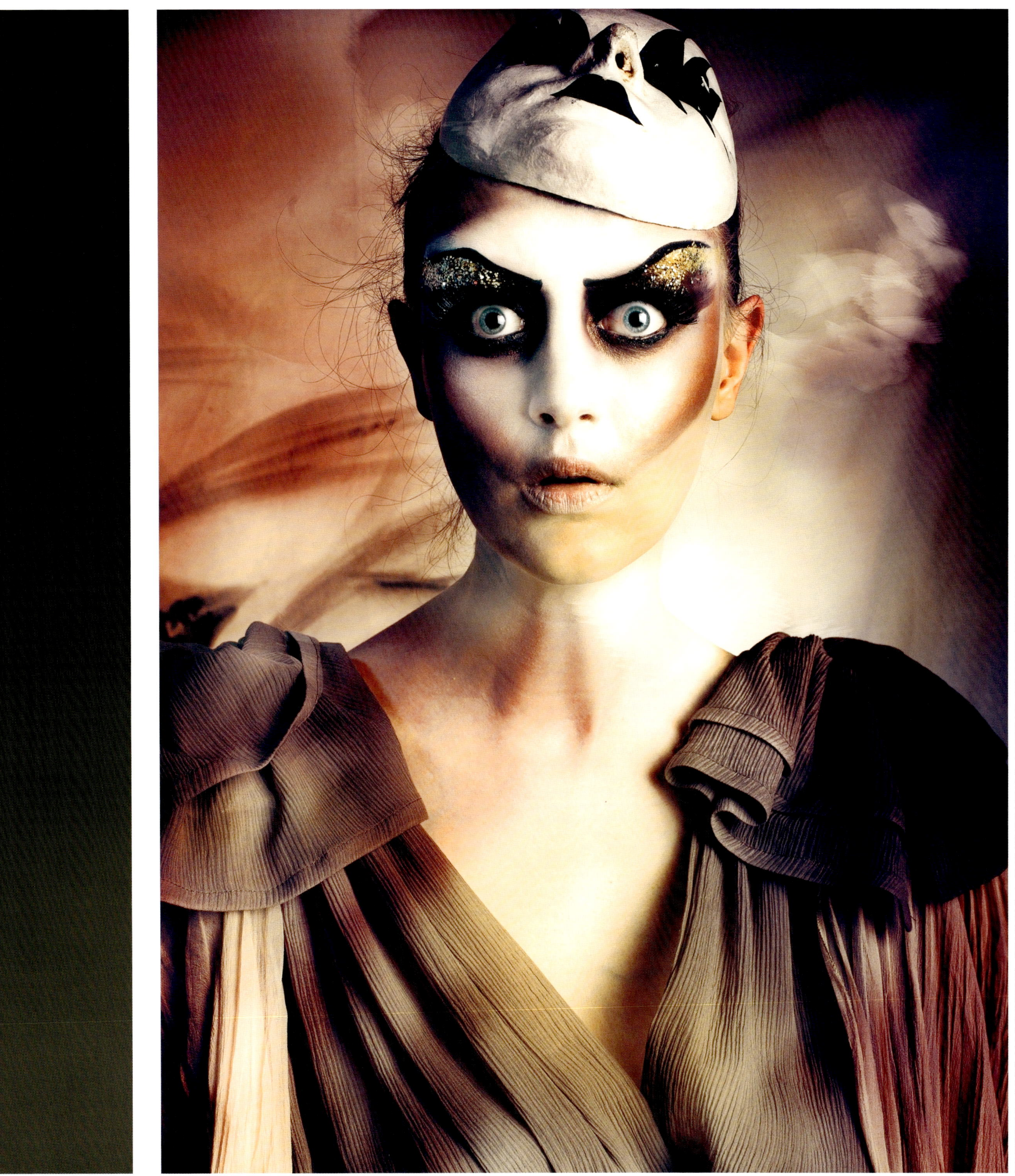

107

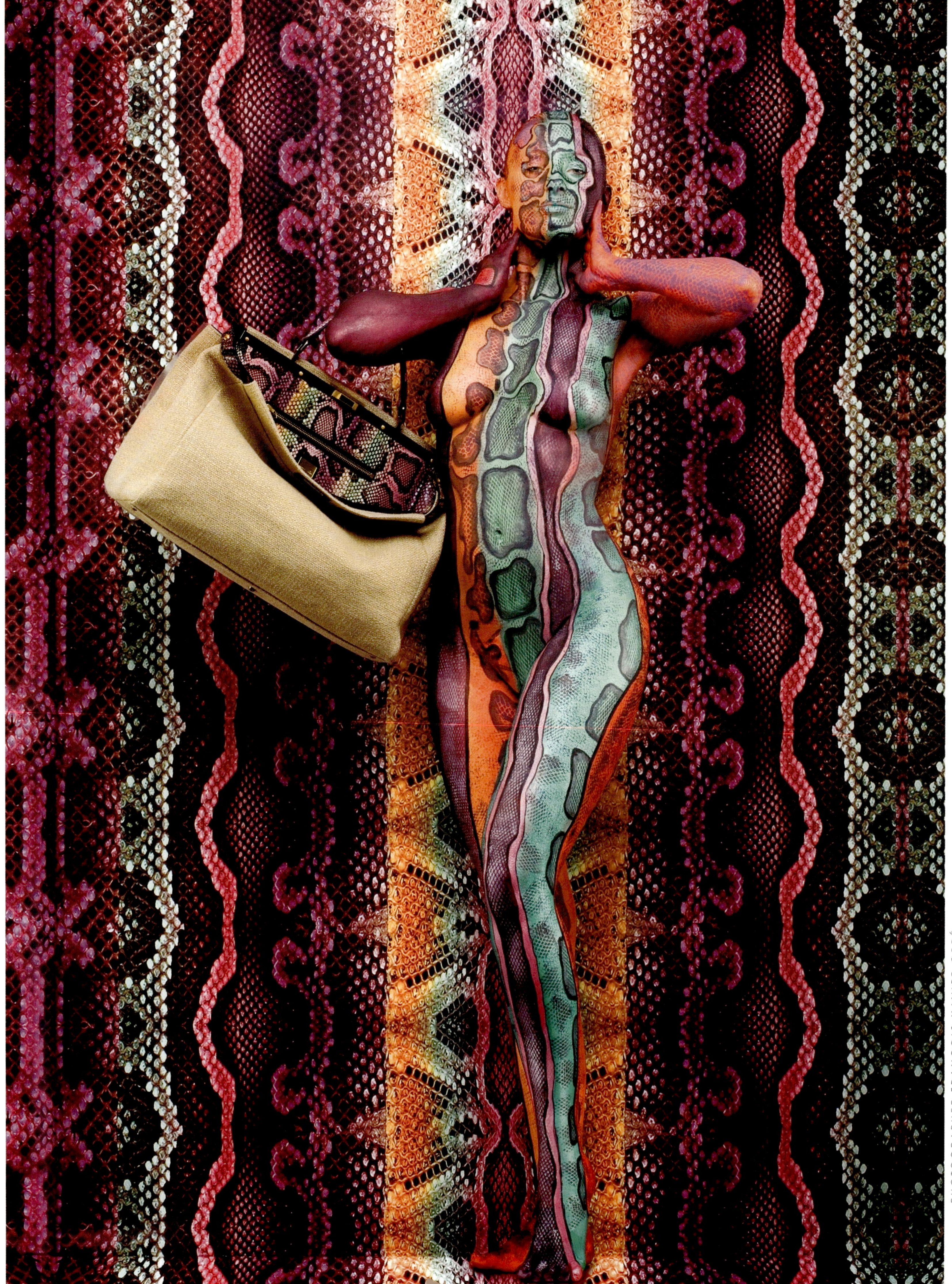

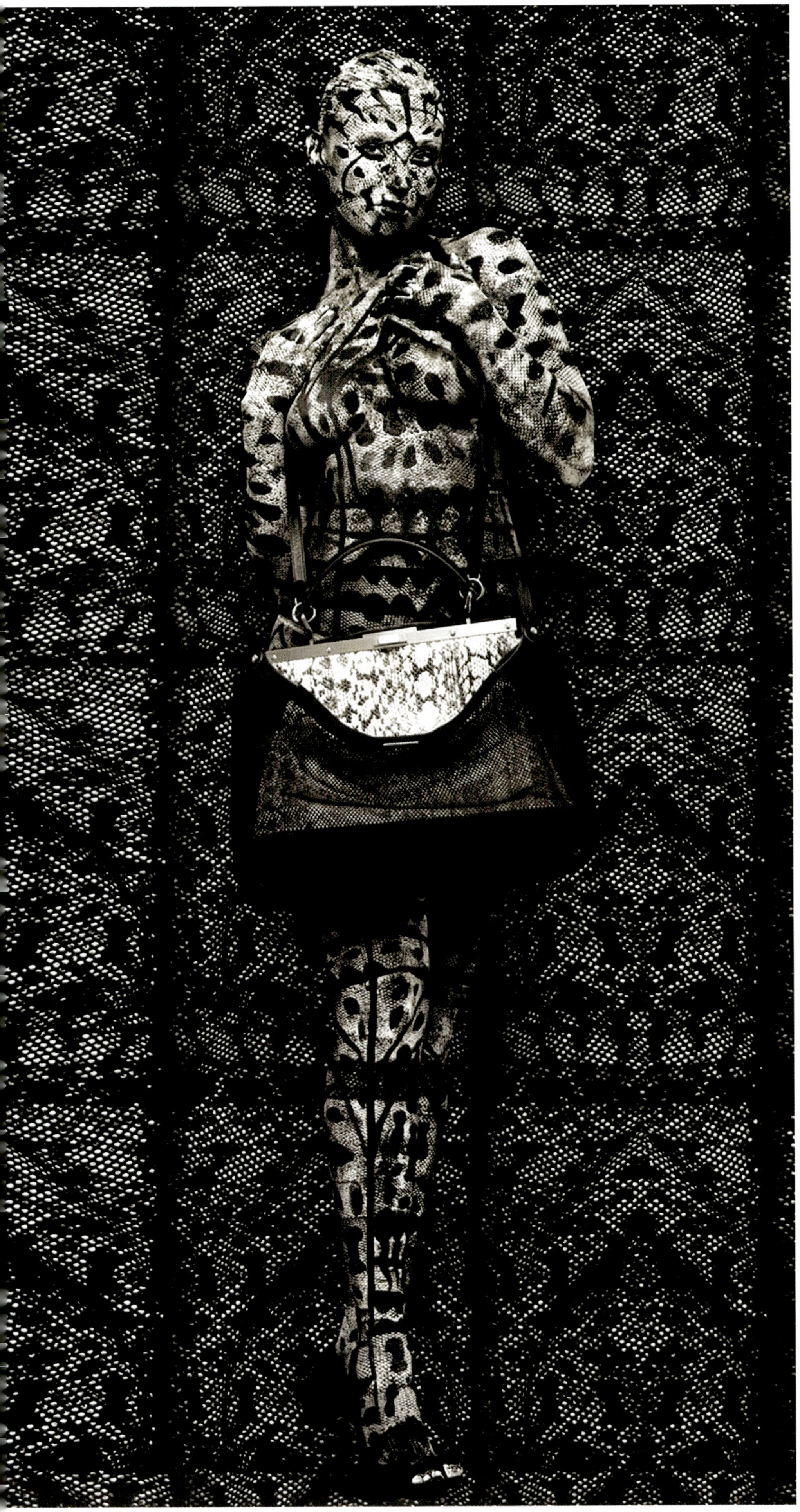

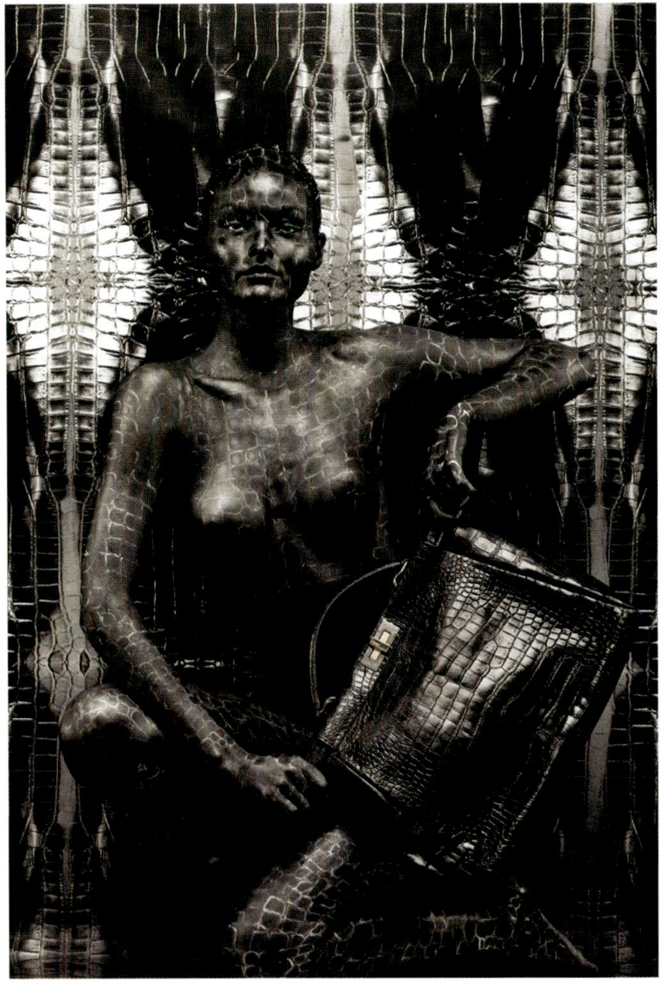

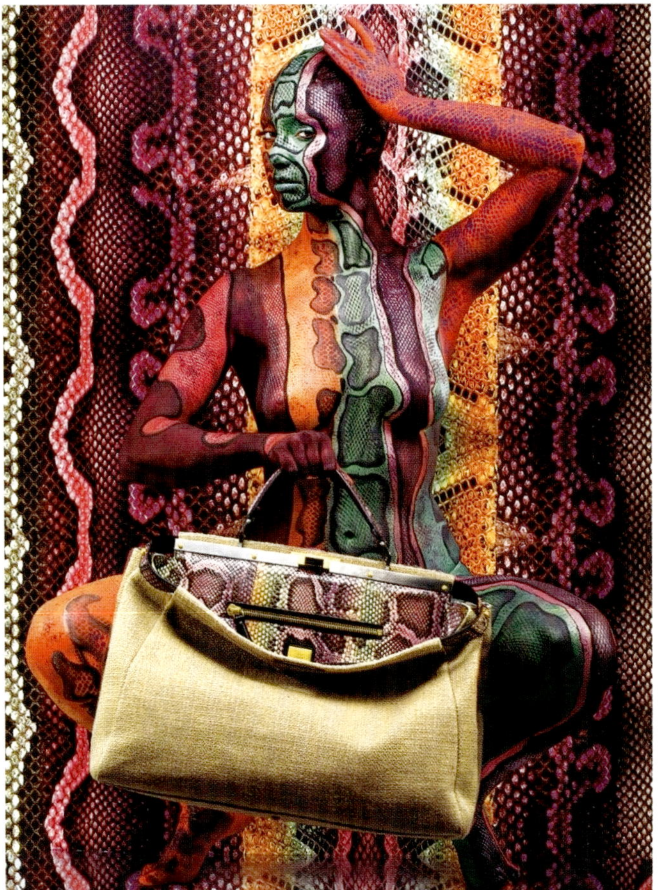

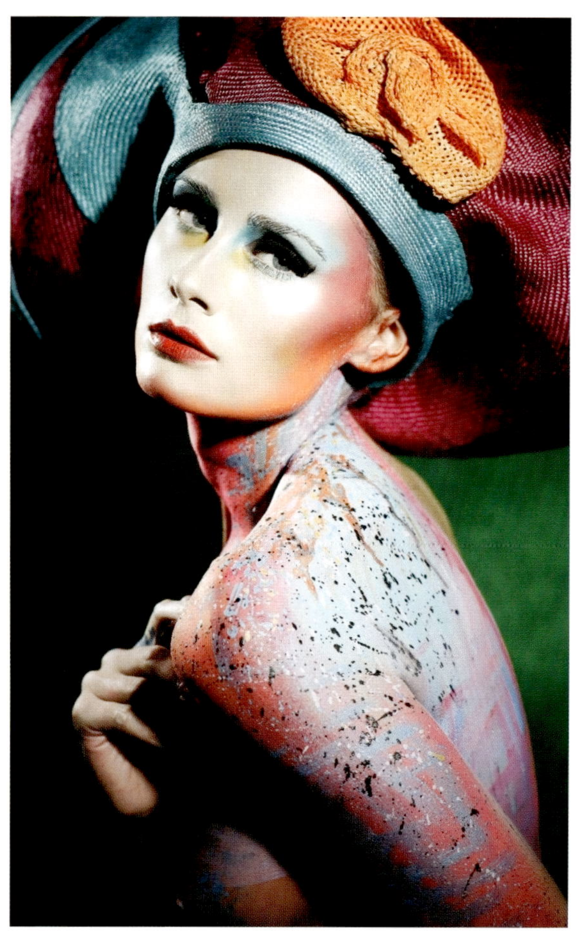

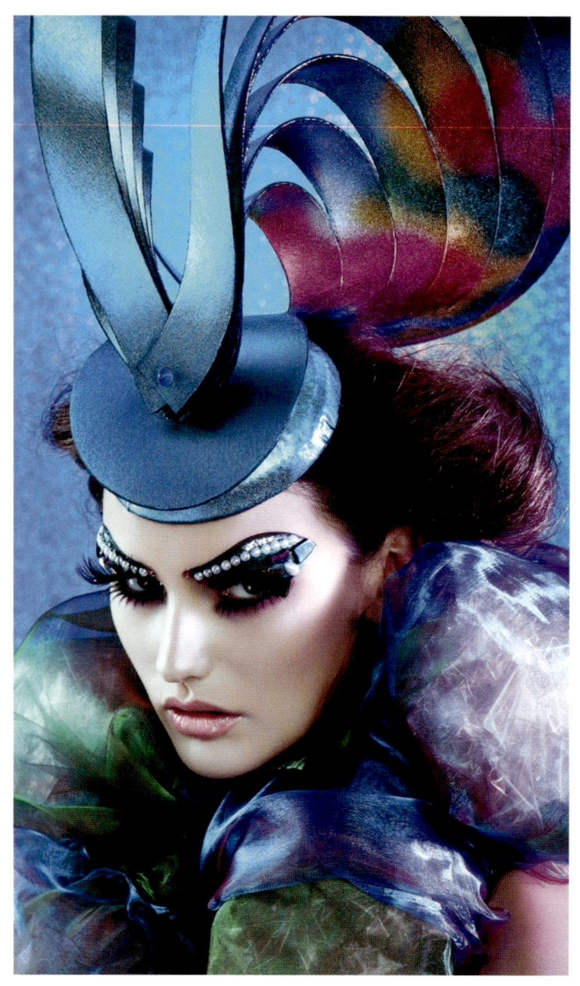

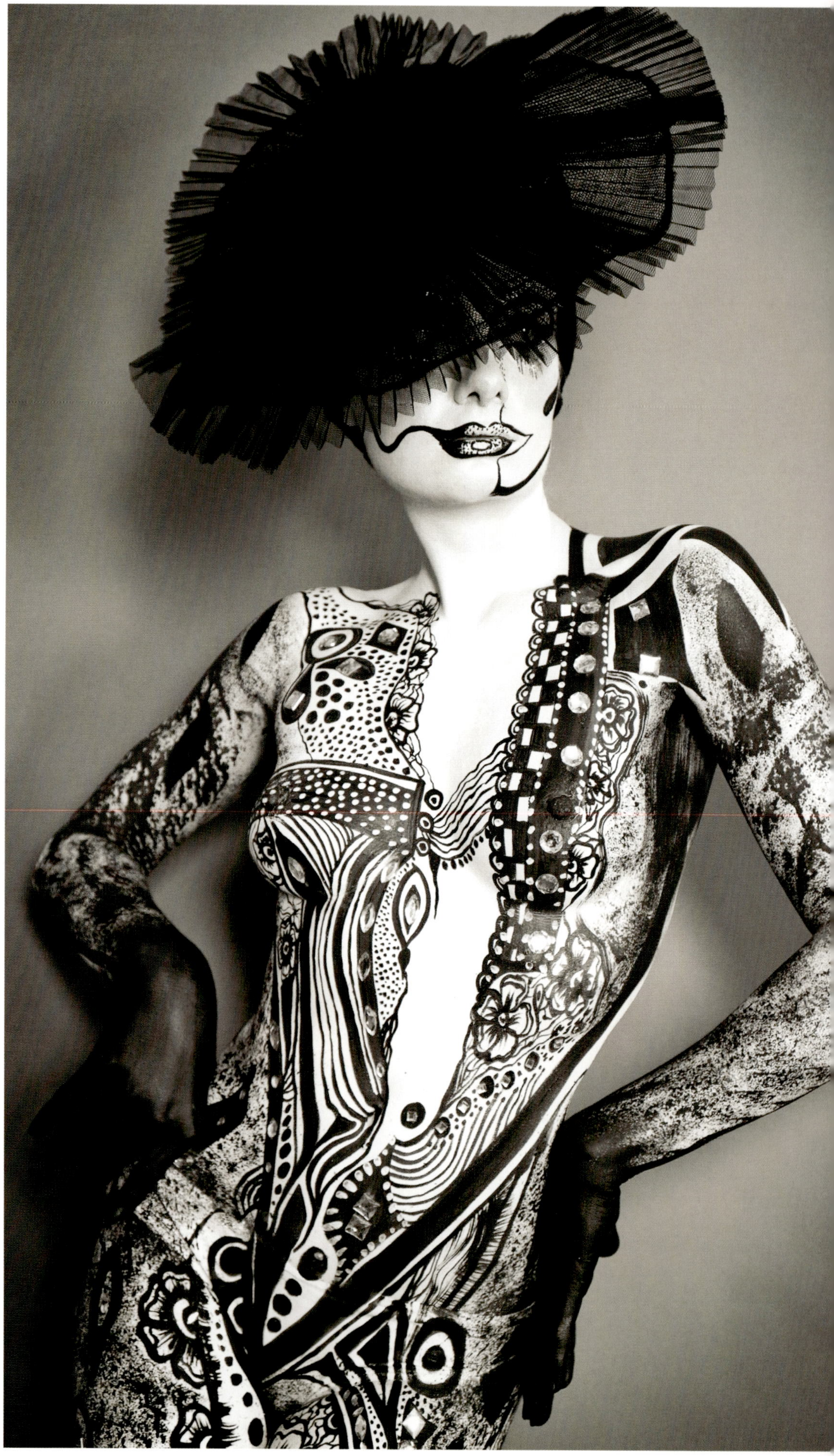

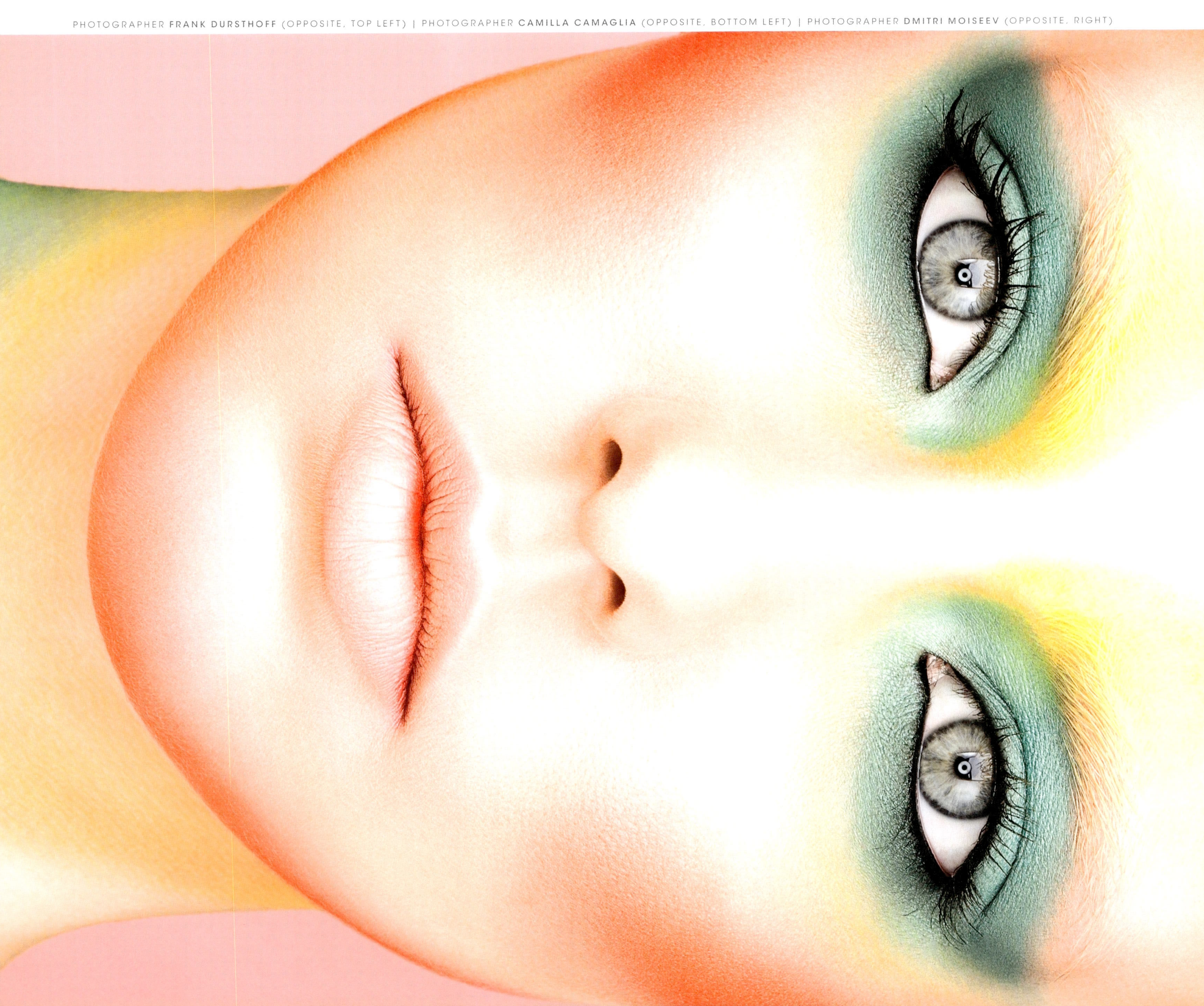
PHOTOGRAPHER FRANK DURSTHOFF (OPPOSITE, TOP LEFT) | PHOTOGRAPHER CAMILLA CAMAGLIA (OPPOSITE, BOTTOM LEFT) | PHOTOGRAPHER DMITRI MOISEEV (OPPOSITE, RIGHT)

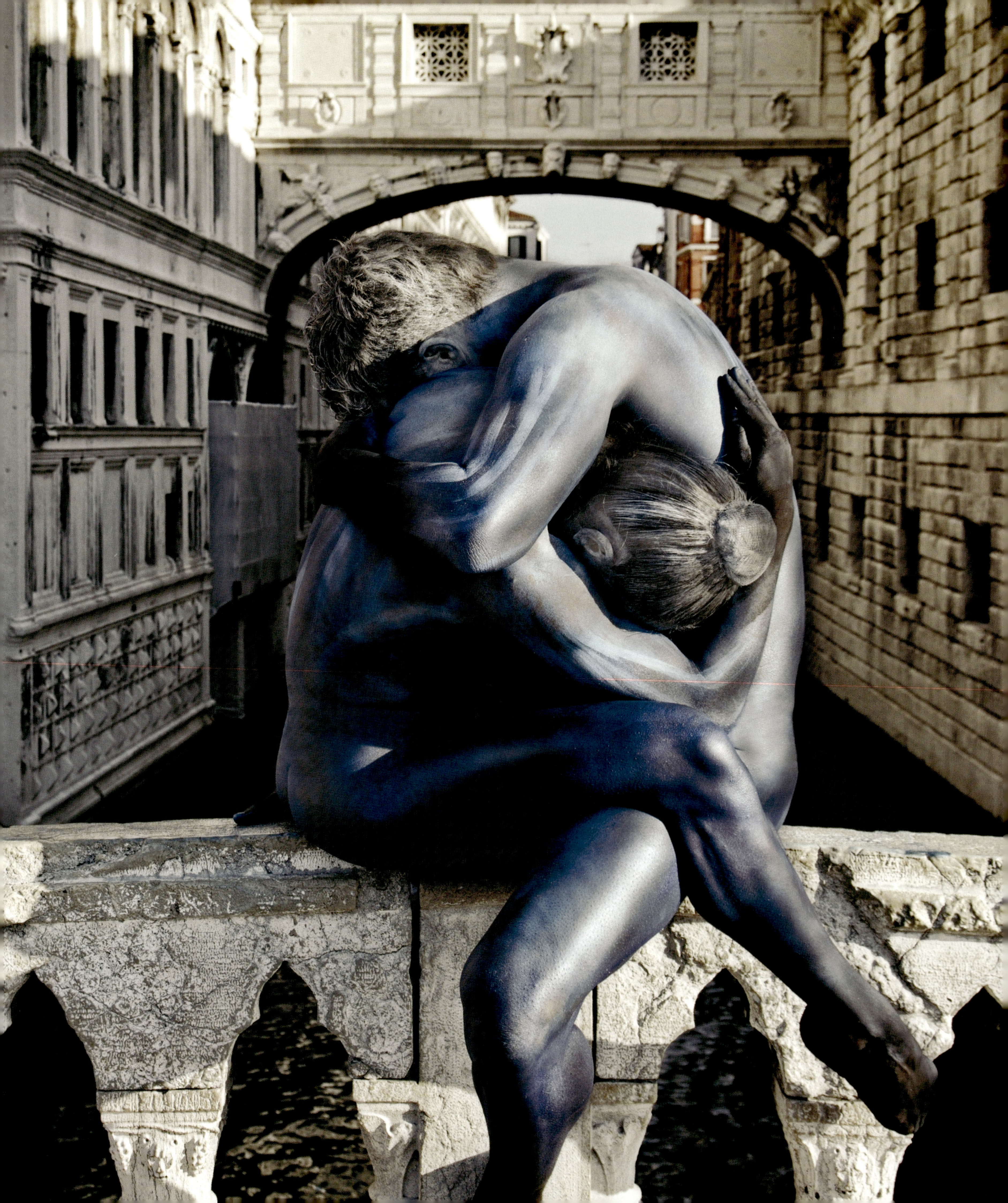

Elena Tagliapietra

WWW.MAKEUPANDBODYPAINTING.IT
WWW.ELENATAGLIAPIETRA.IT

Elena Tagliapietra is a Venetian artist. She is a protagonist in the Italian and international scene of bodypainting. Since 2004 Elena has worked in the fashion industry as a makeup artist and a bodypainter. She has become well-known internationally. Elena won the Italian title of bodypainting in 2007; she came in third at the World Bodypainting Festival in 2011 and participated in the Body Art Fashion Show in 2012 and 2013. In 2008 and 2009 she judged the Italian Bodypainting Festival and has been the artistic director since 2010. She is a member of the ColorSensation team, a group of three Italian bodypainters qualified by the highest industry awards.

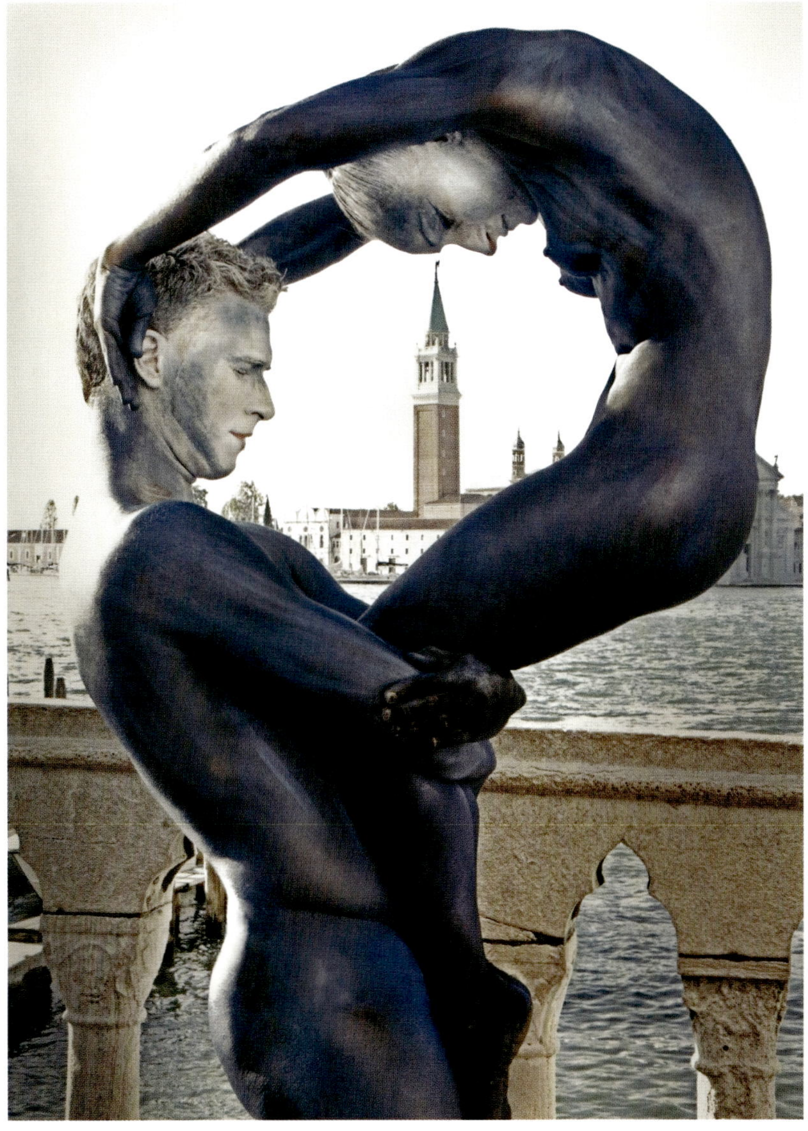

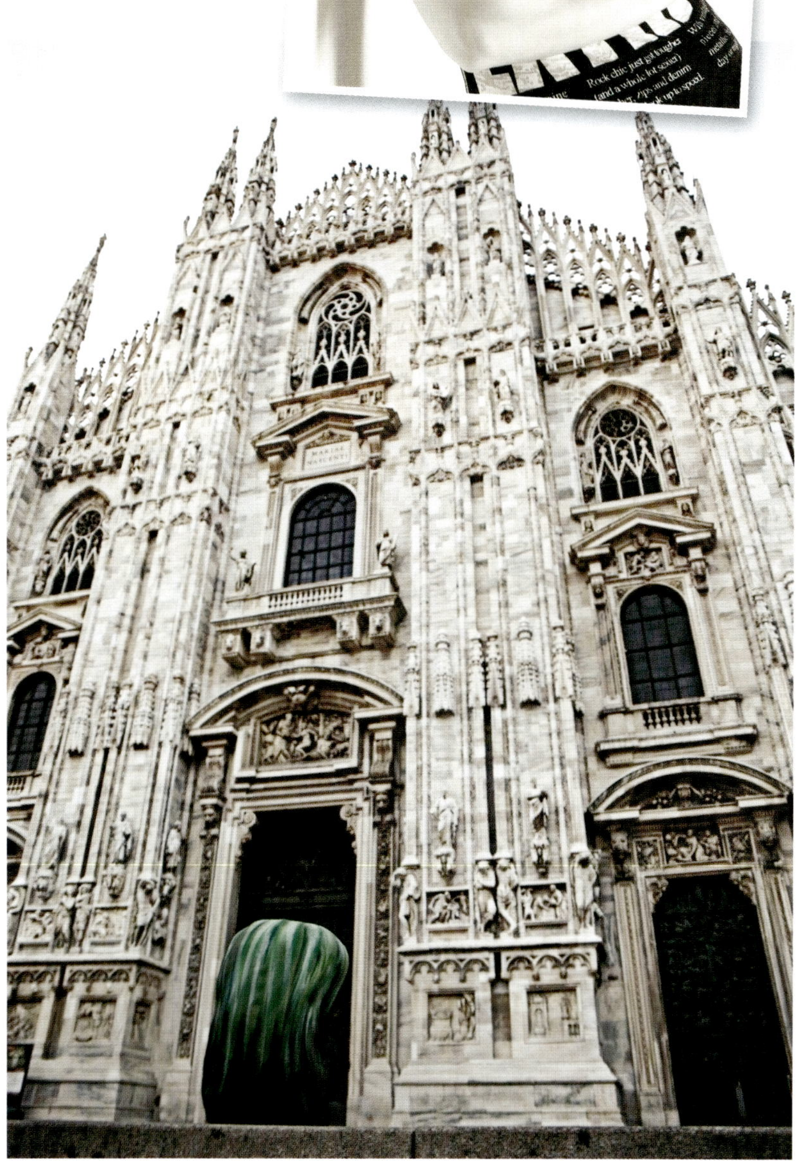

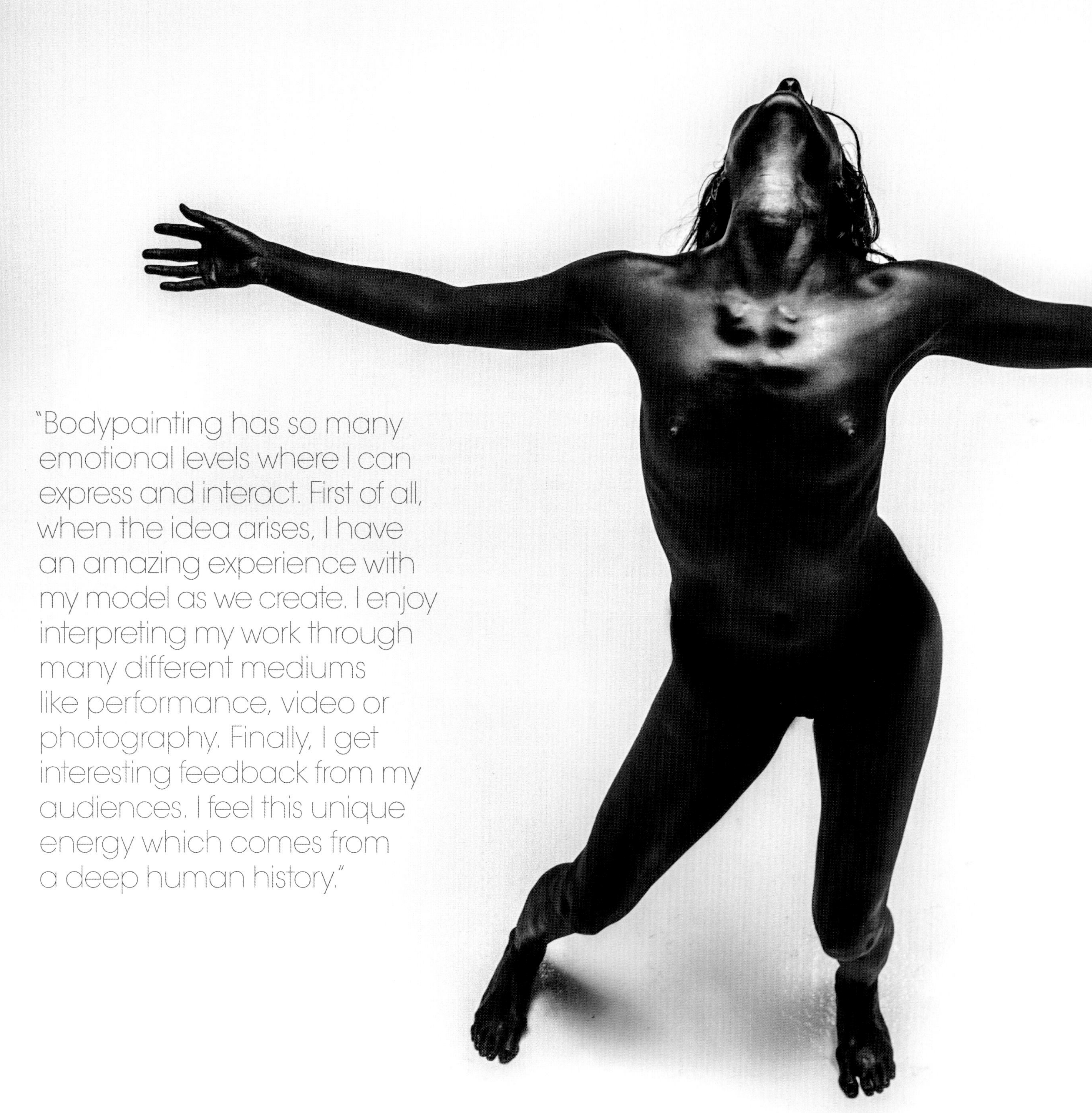

"Bodypainting has so many emotional levels where I can express and interact. First of all, when the idea arises, I have an amazing experience with my model as we create. I enjoy interpreting my work through many different mediums like performance, video or photography. Finally, I get interesting feedback from my audiences. I feel this unique energy which comes from a deep human history."

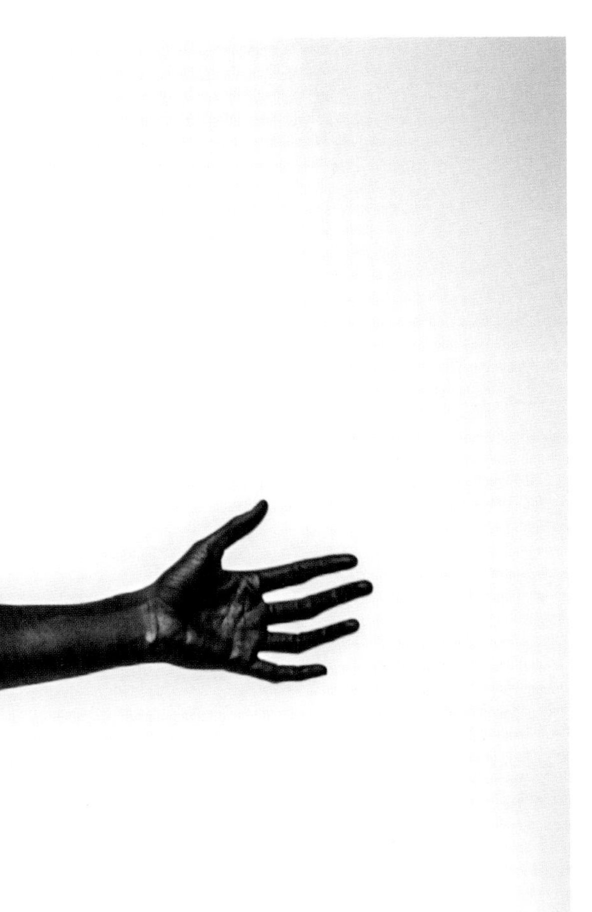

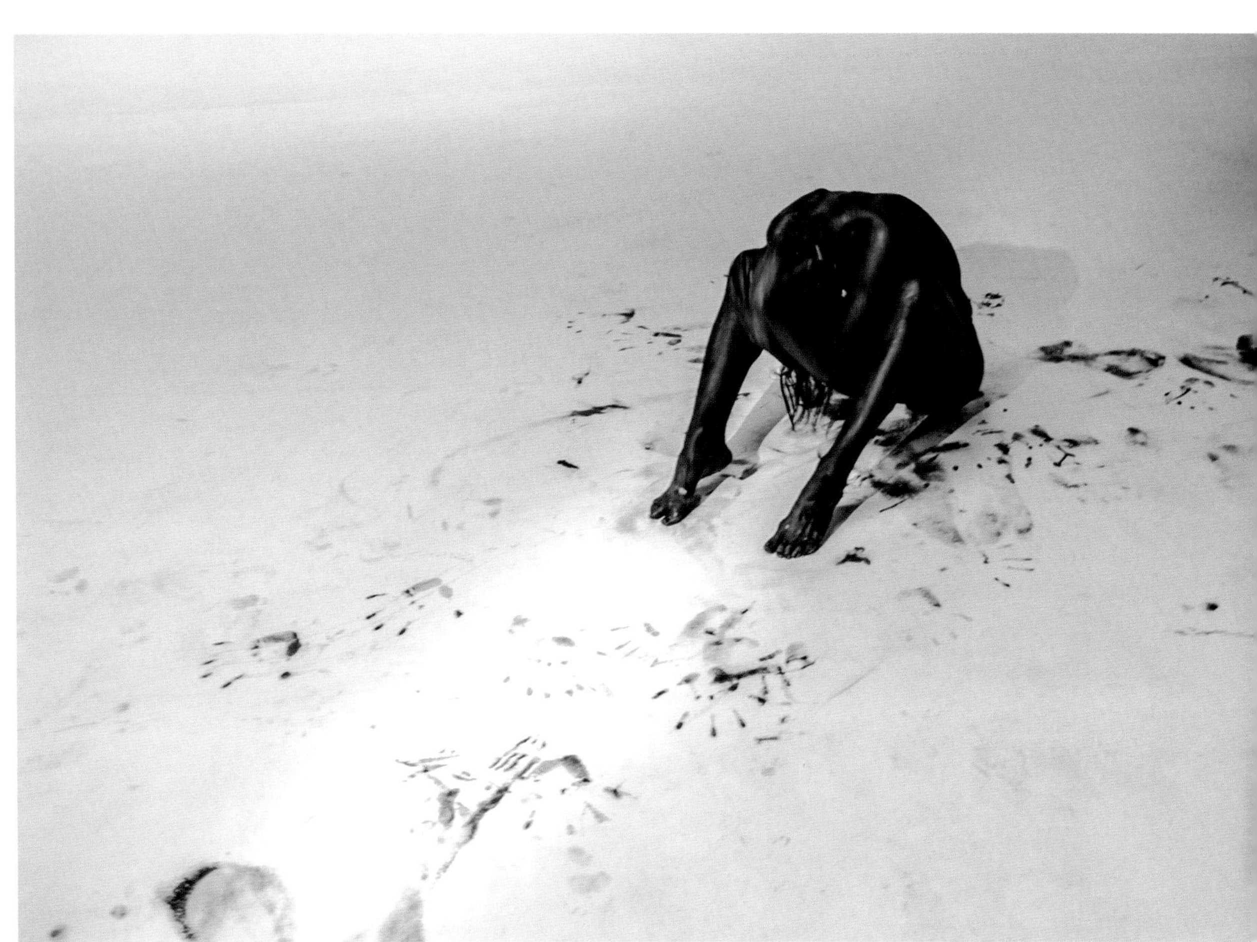

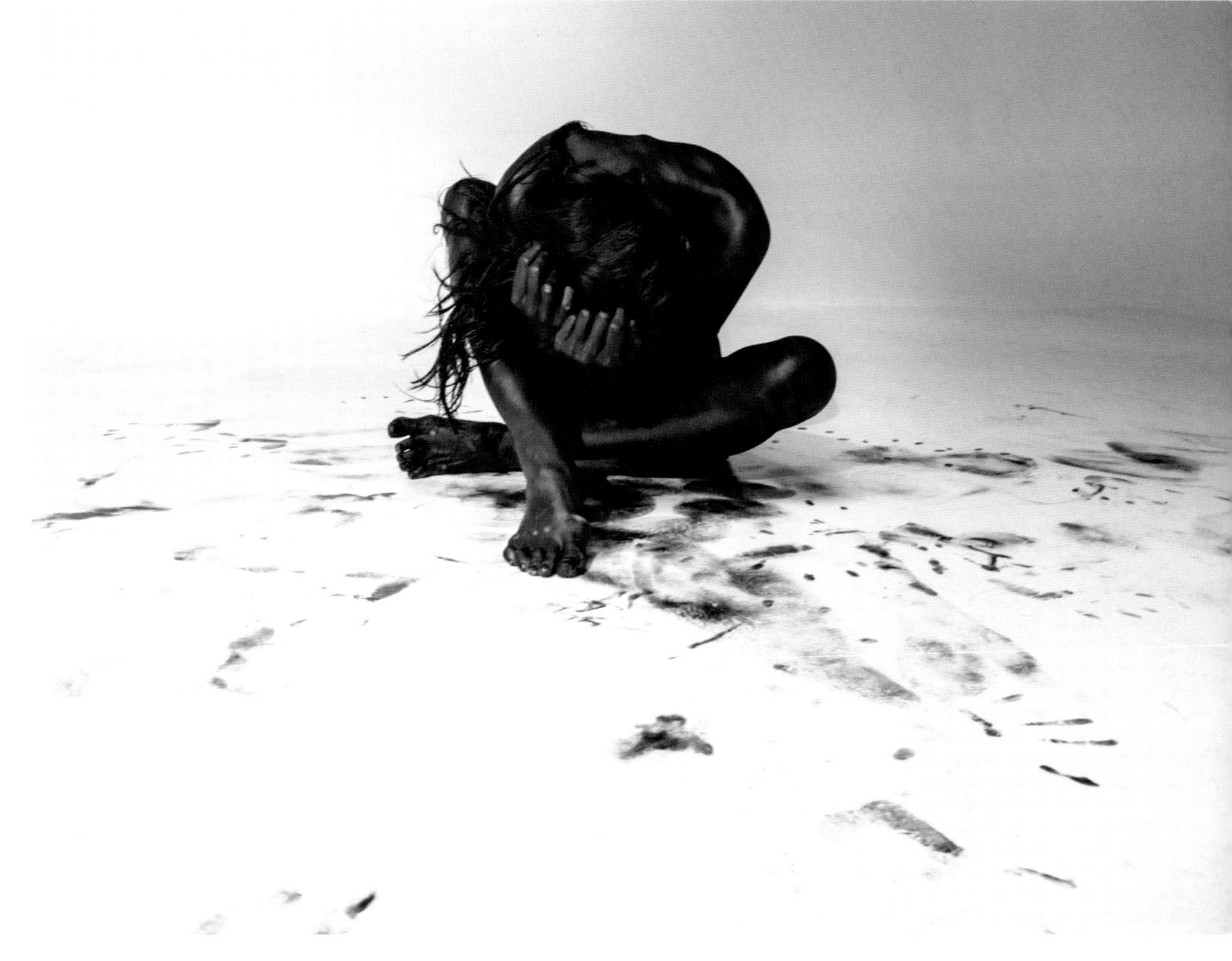

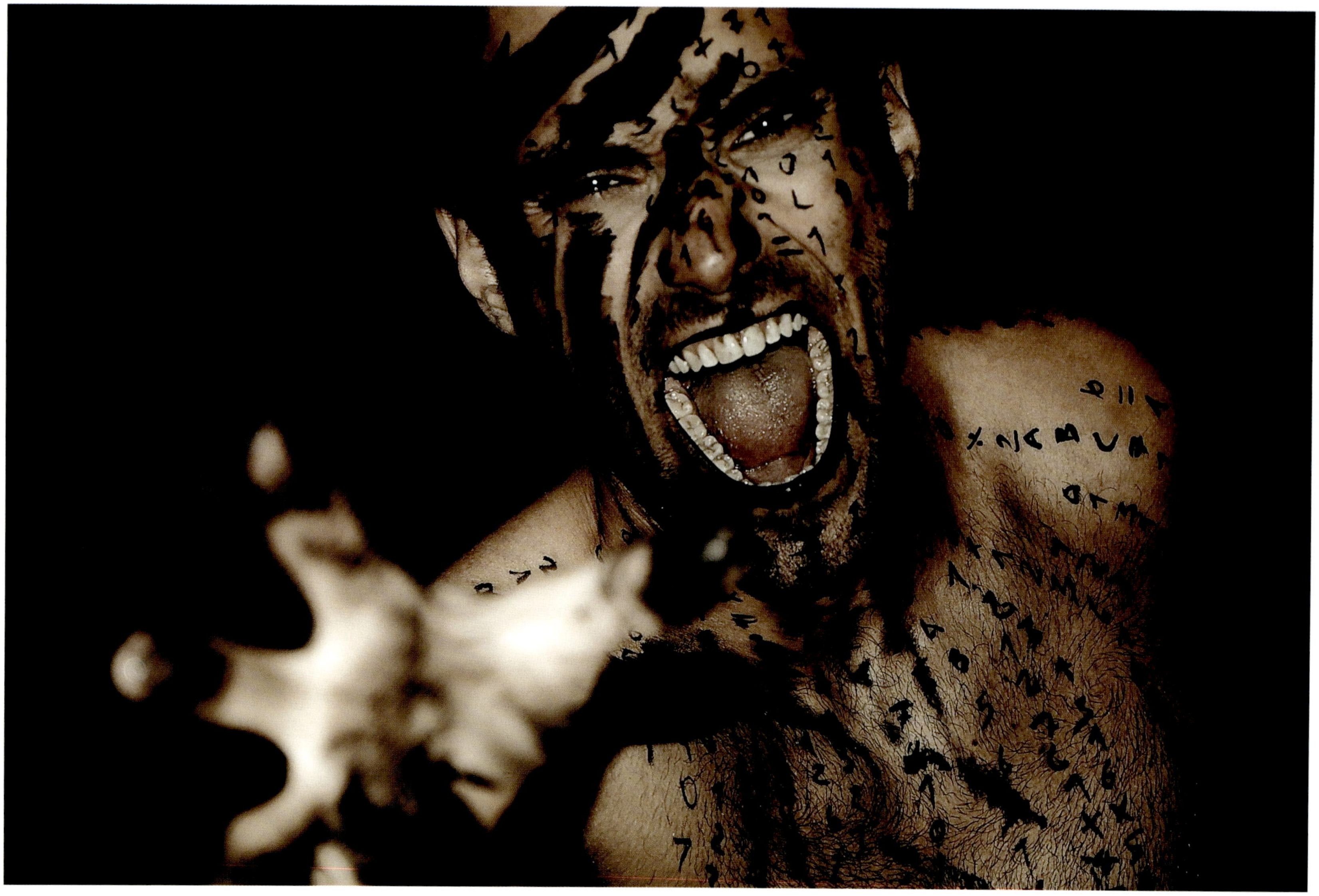

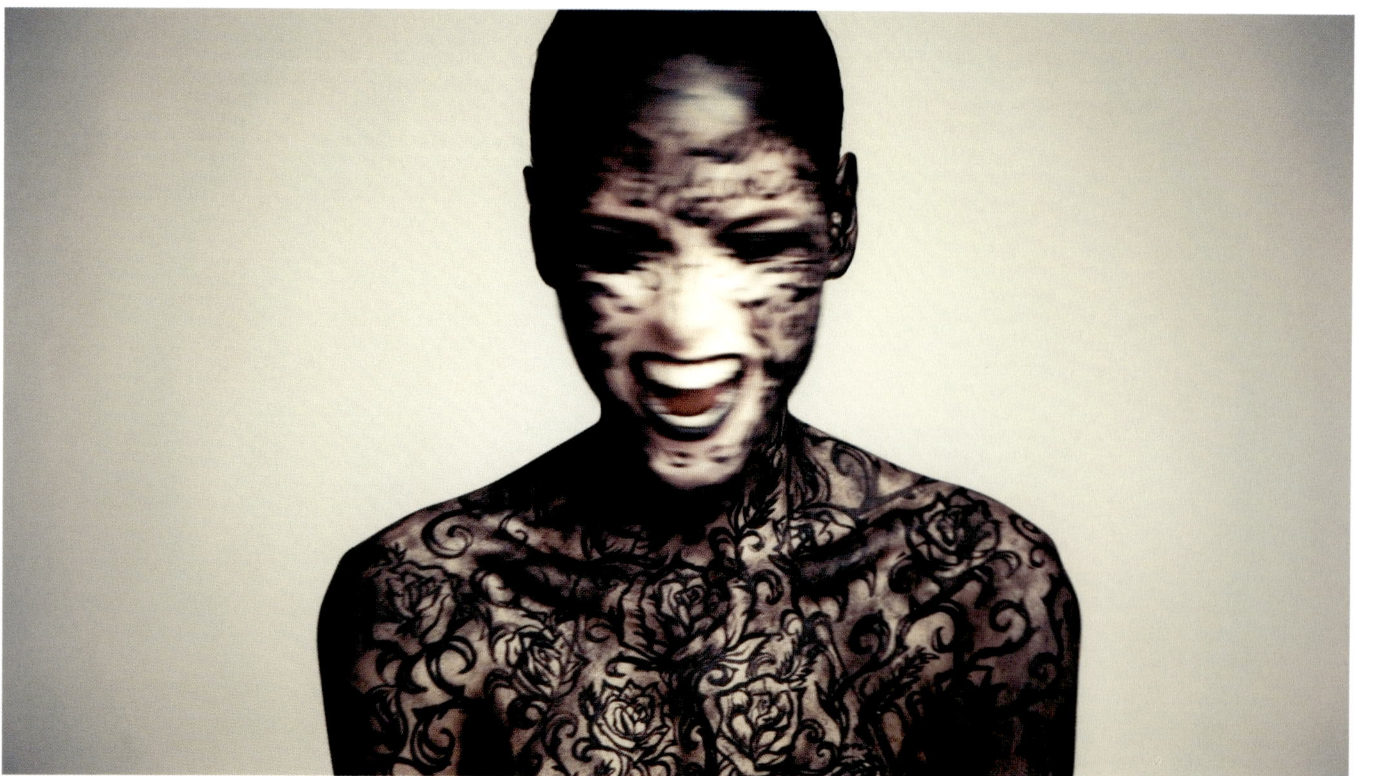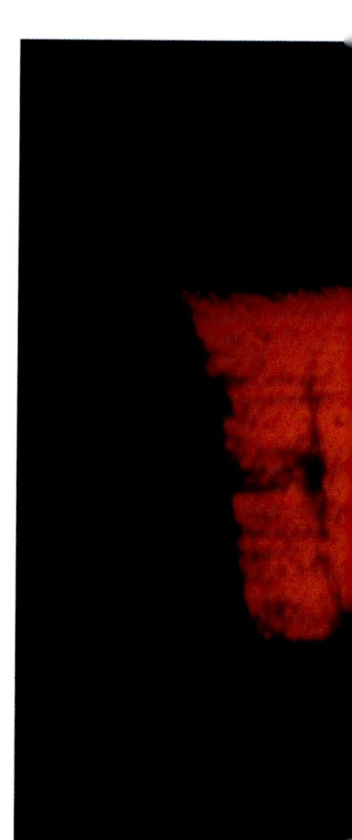

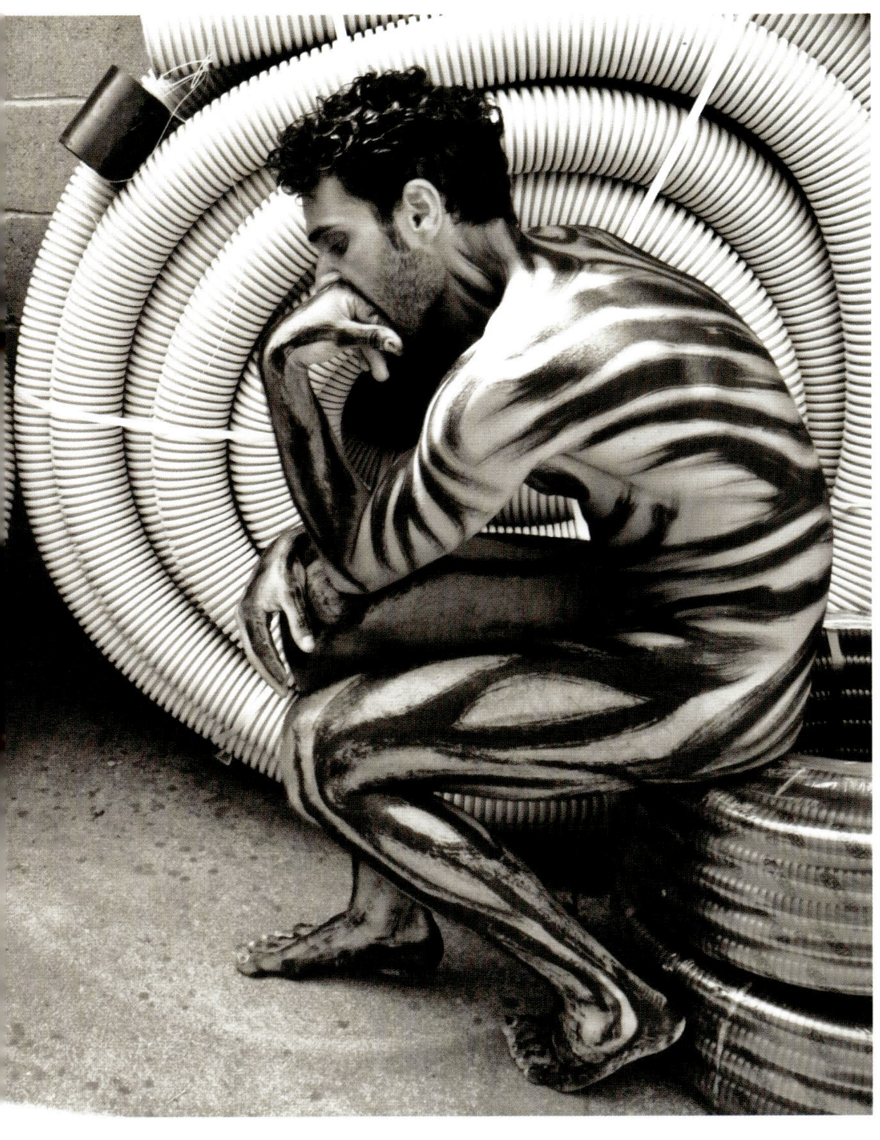
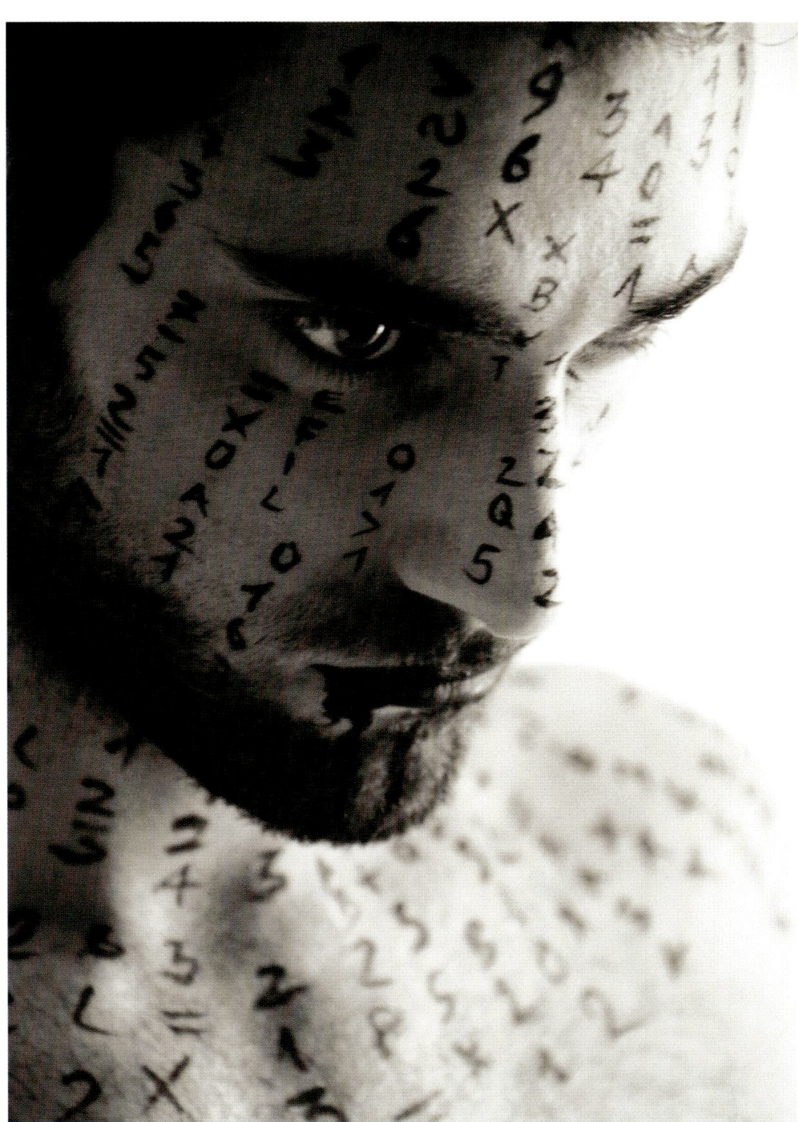
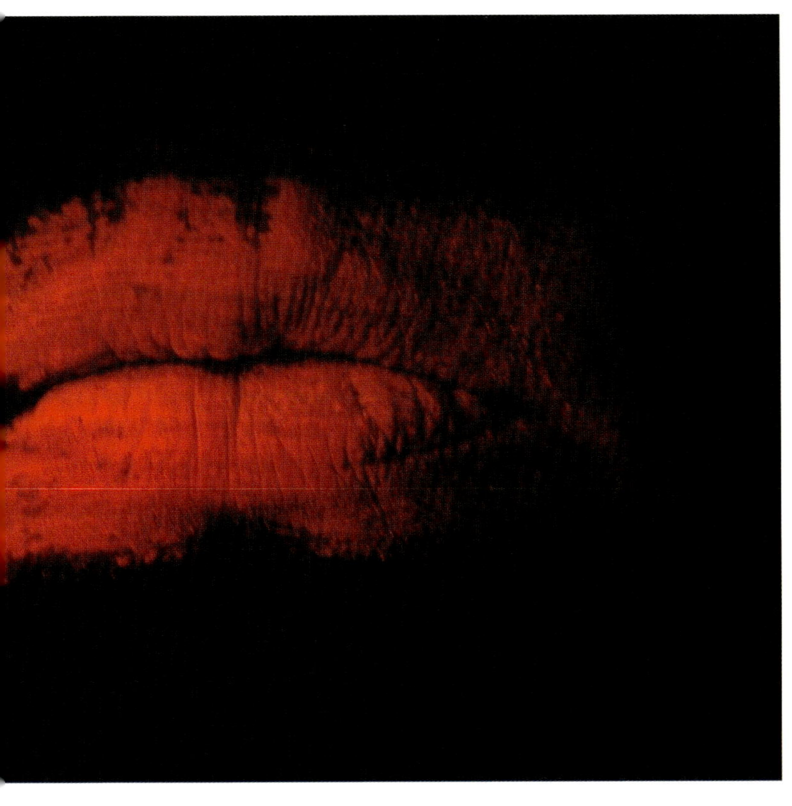
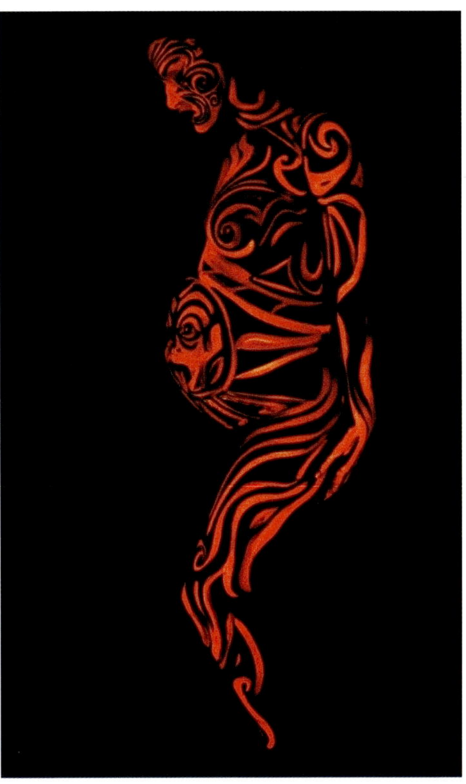
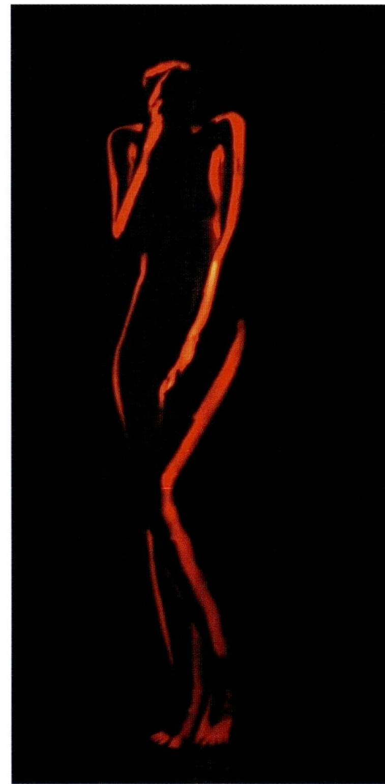

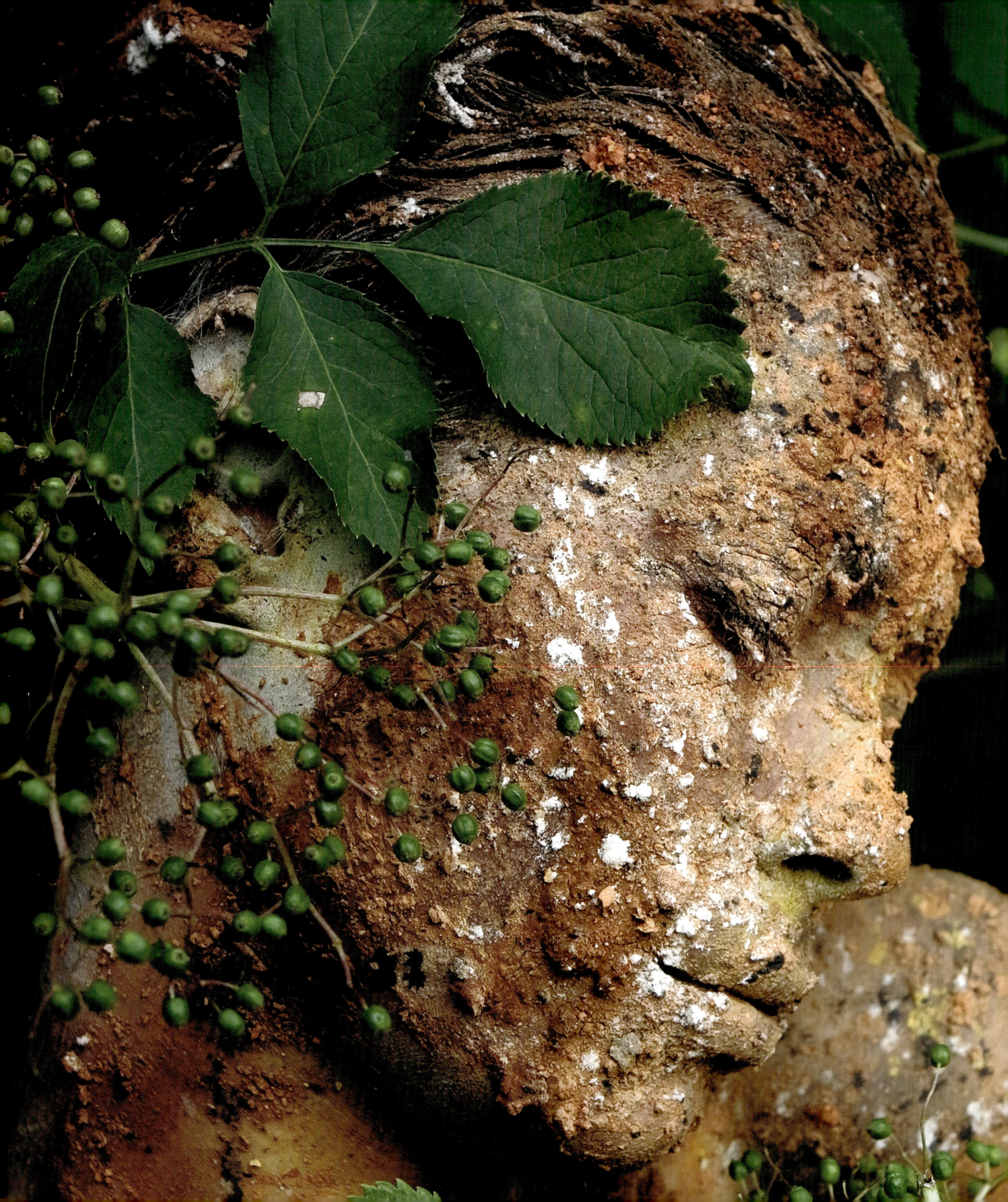

Filippo Ioco

WWW.IOCOBODYART.COM
WWW.FILIPPOIOCO.COM

Filippo Ioco is one of the most important and outstanding bodypainting artists of all time. The combination of experience, understanding, inspiration, innovation and courage has kept his work at the top for more than two decades. Filippo's advertising portfolio contains some of the most successful creations of body art for the media, and his art has been featured in music videos, on book covers and in television, commercials and print media—almost anywhere the eye can look. Filippo is comfortable working both with celebrities on live television with an audience of thousands and in a personal environment with an audience of two.

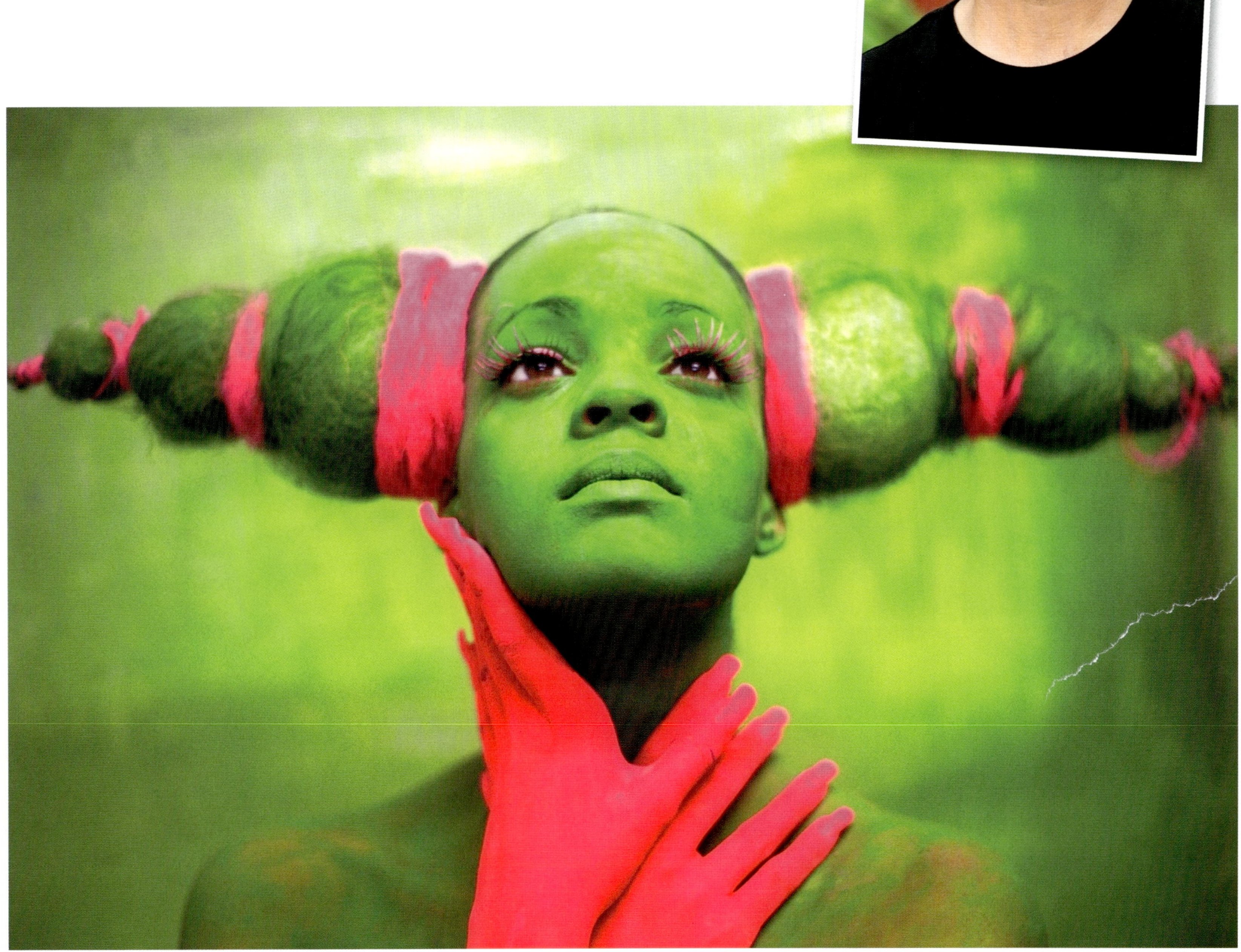

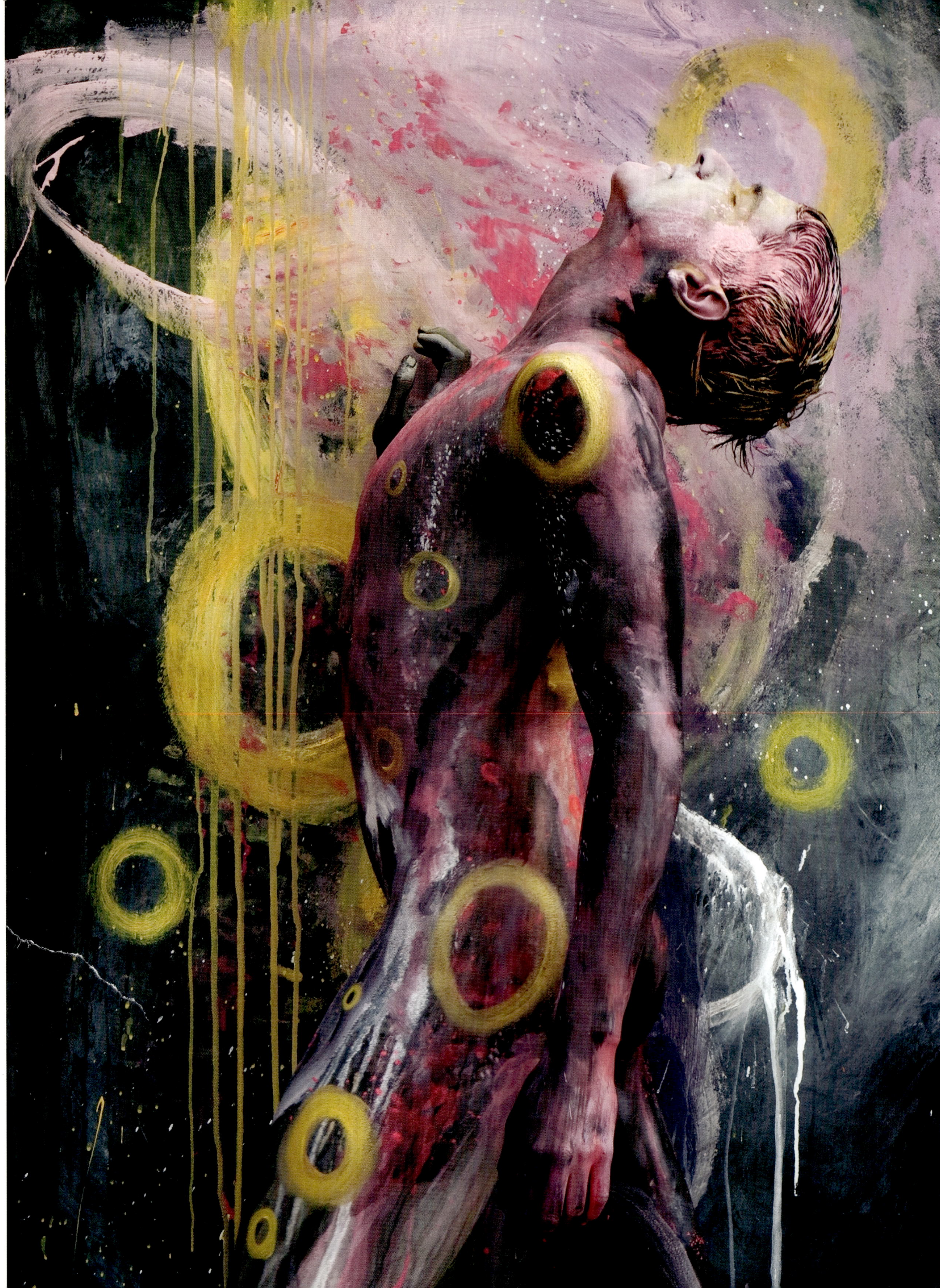

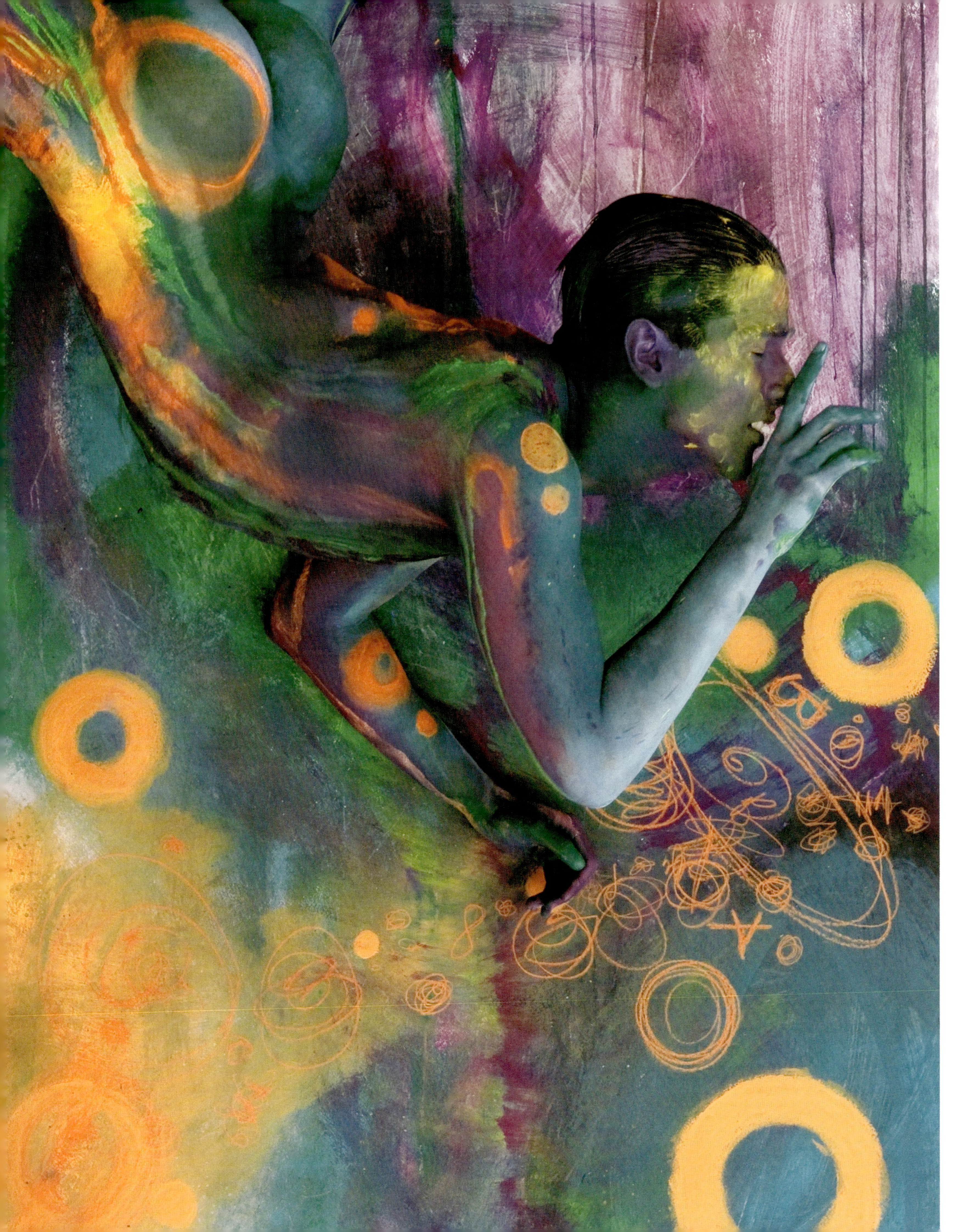

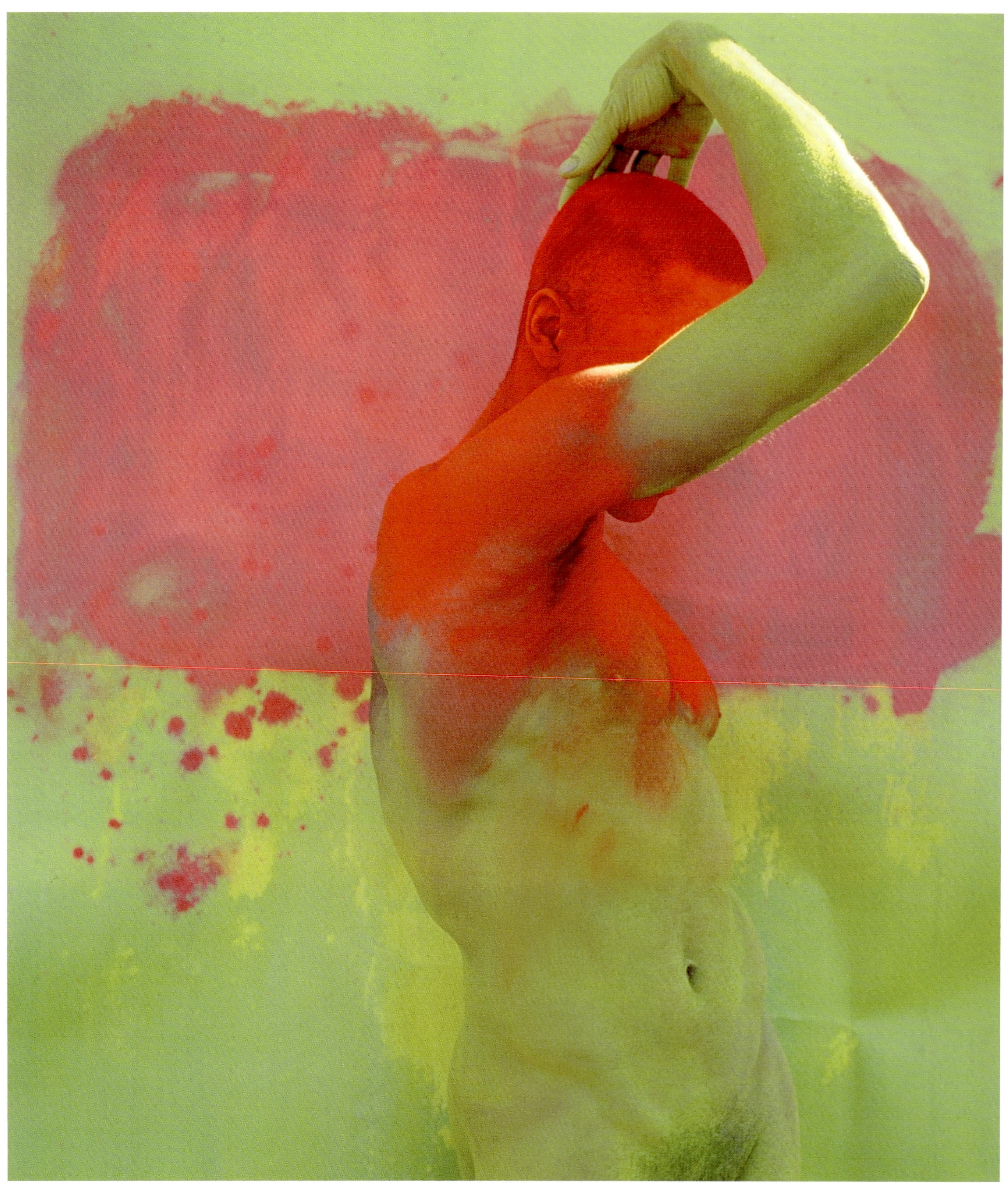

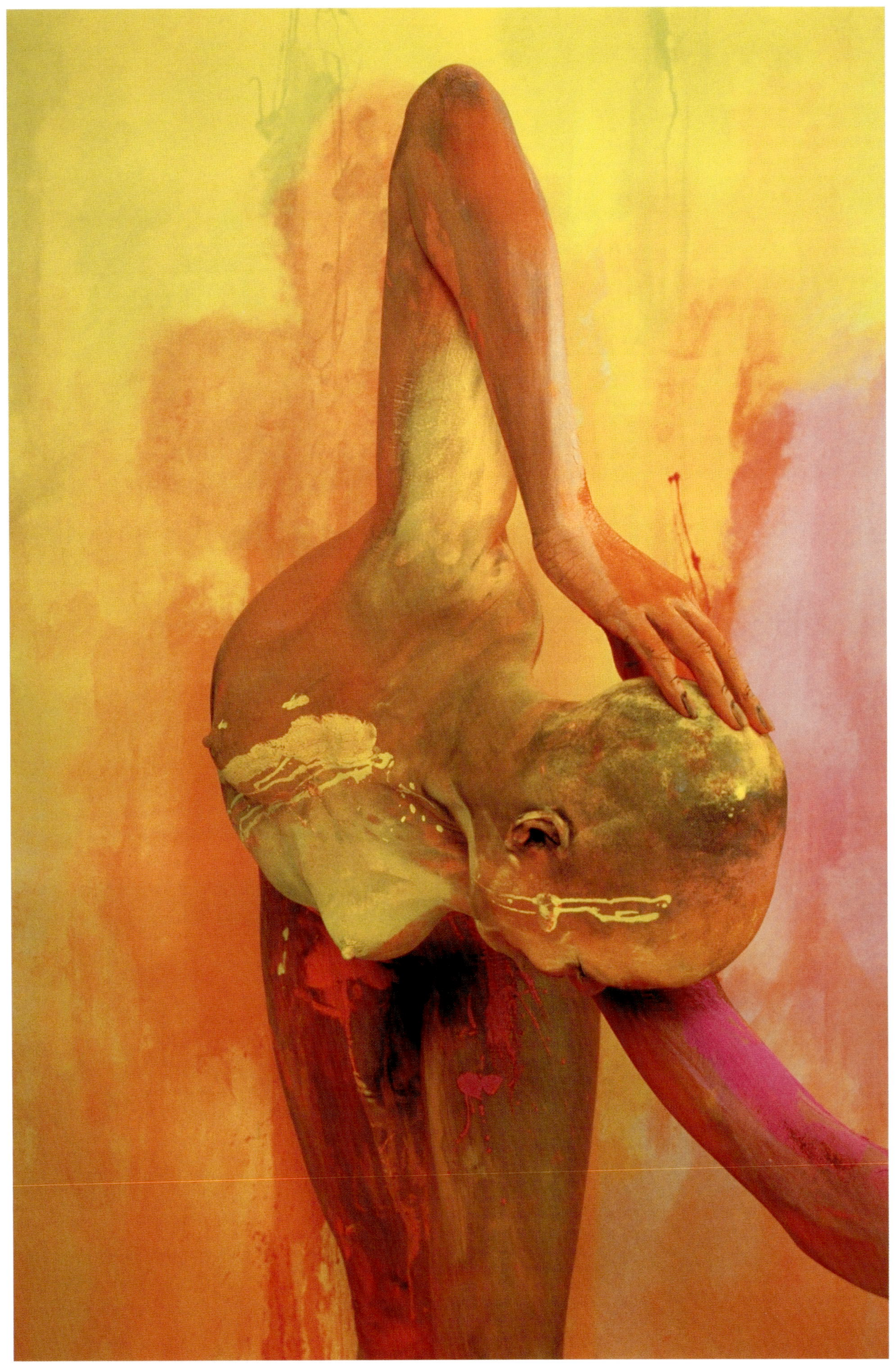

"My life is all
about art, color
and visual
stimulation.
If you were to
take away art,
I would be
gone as well."

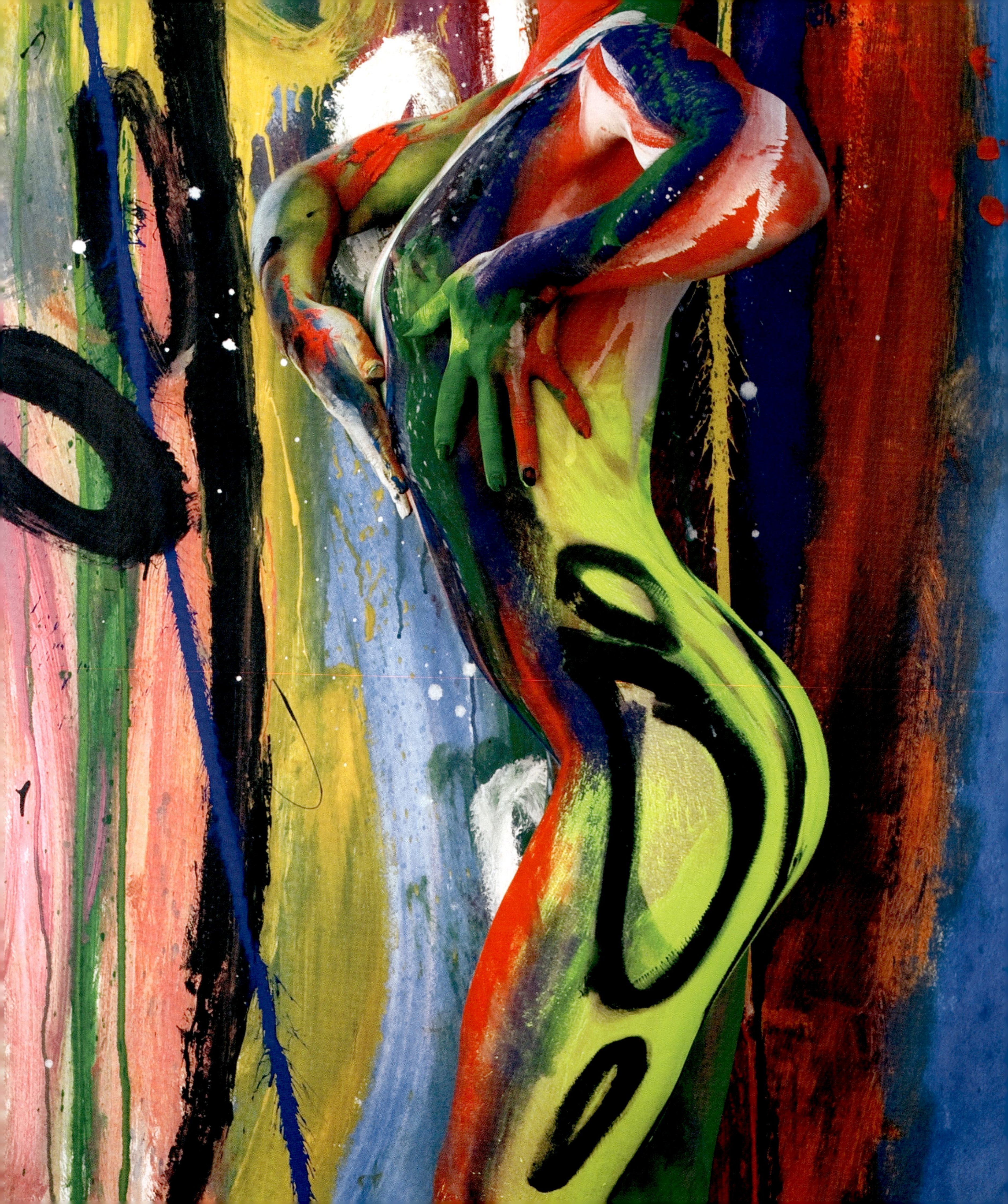

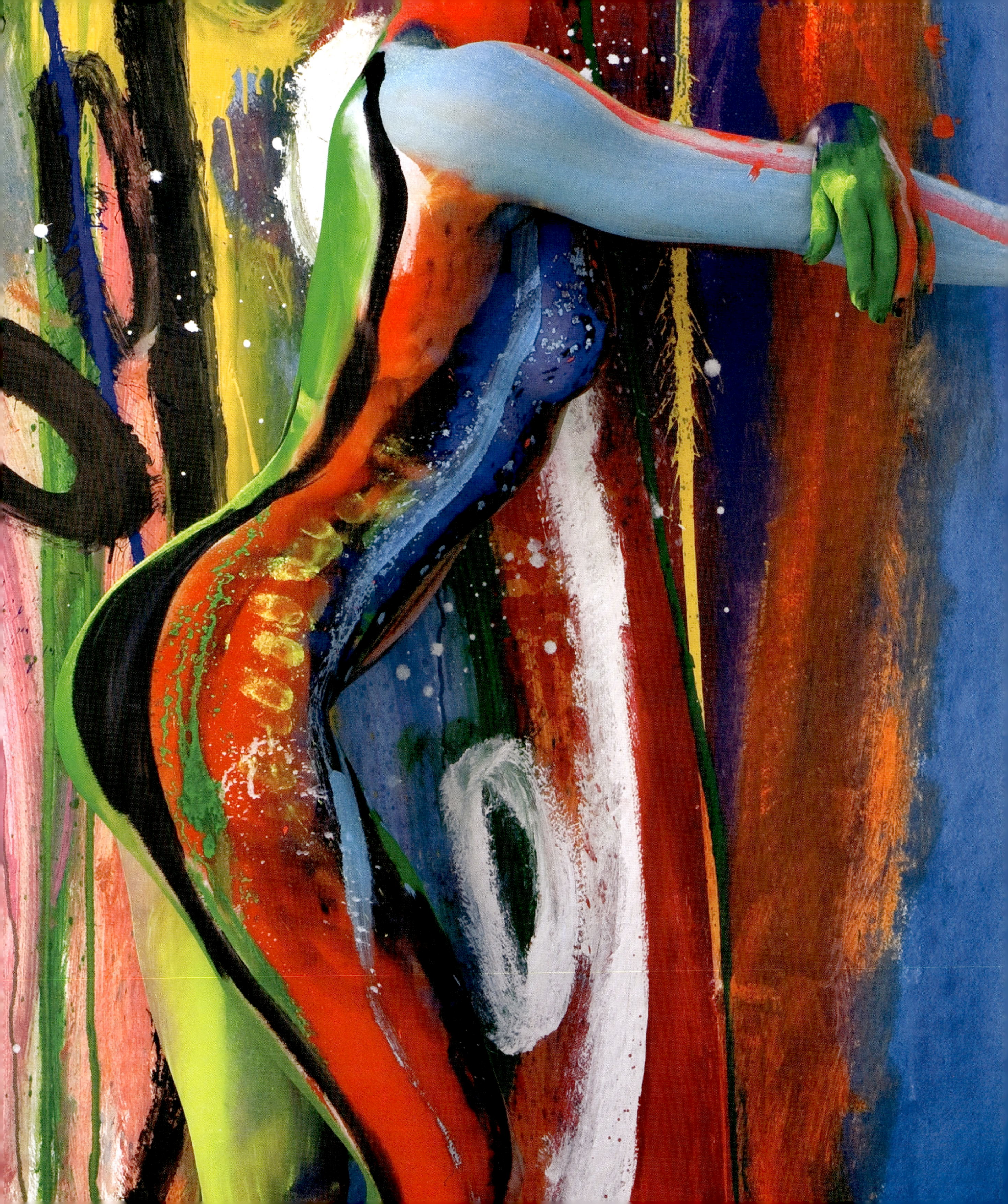

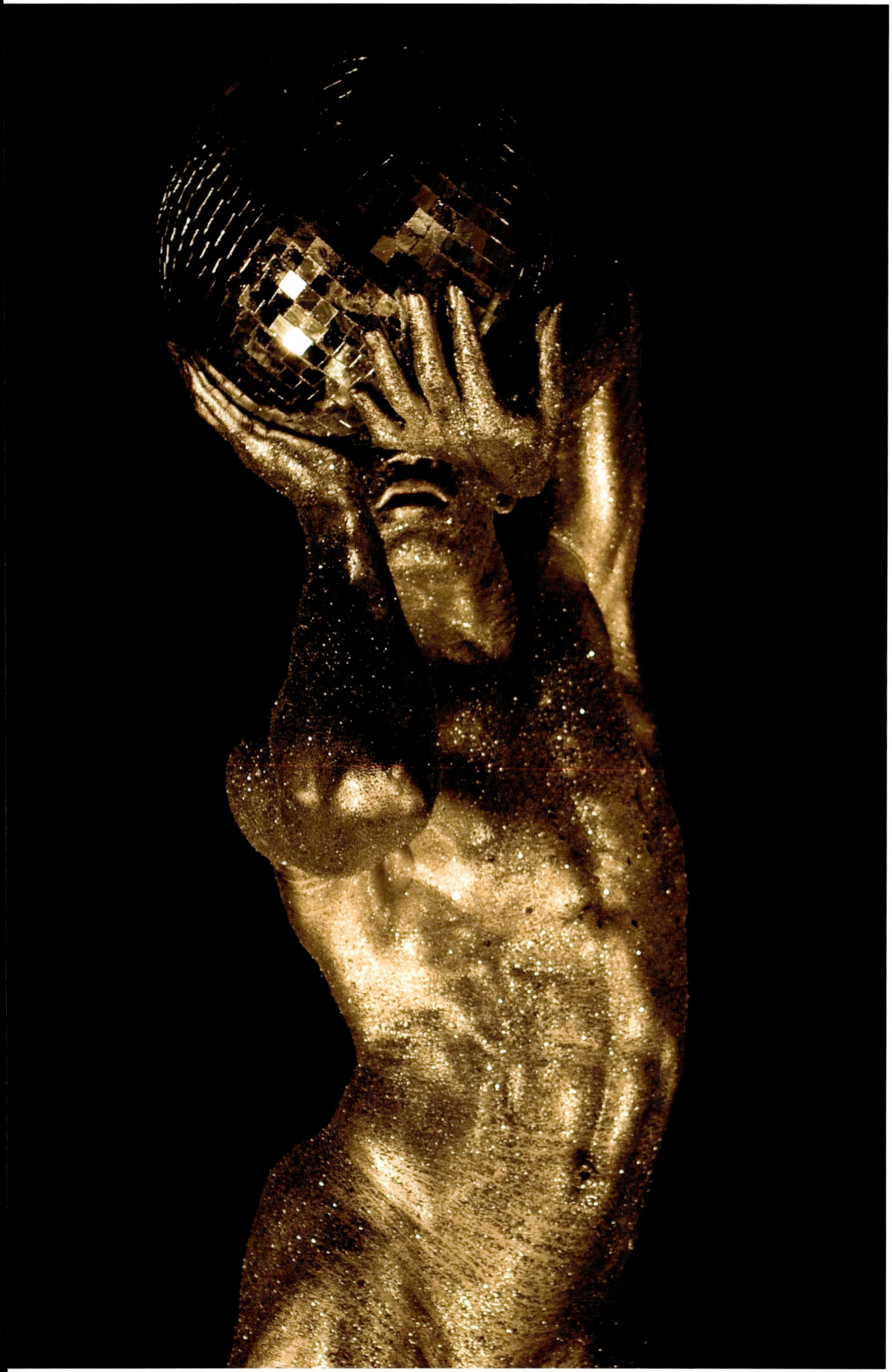

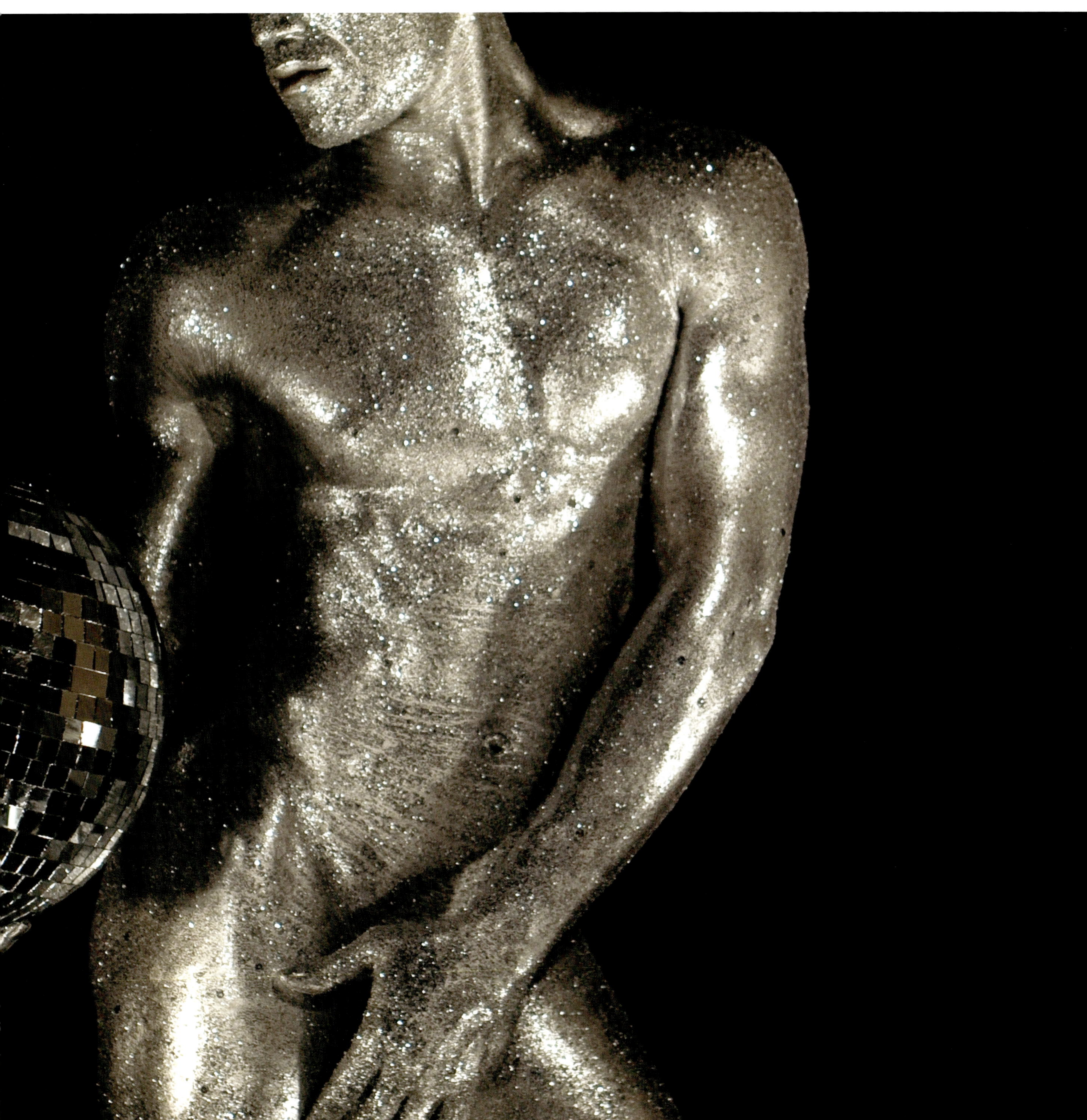

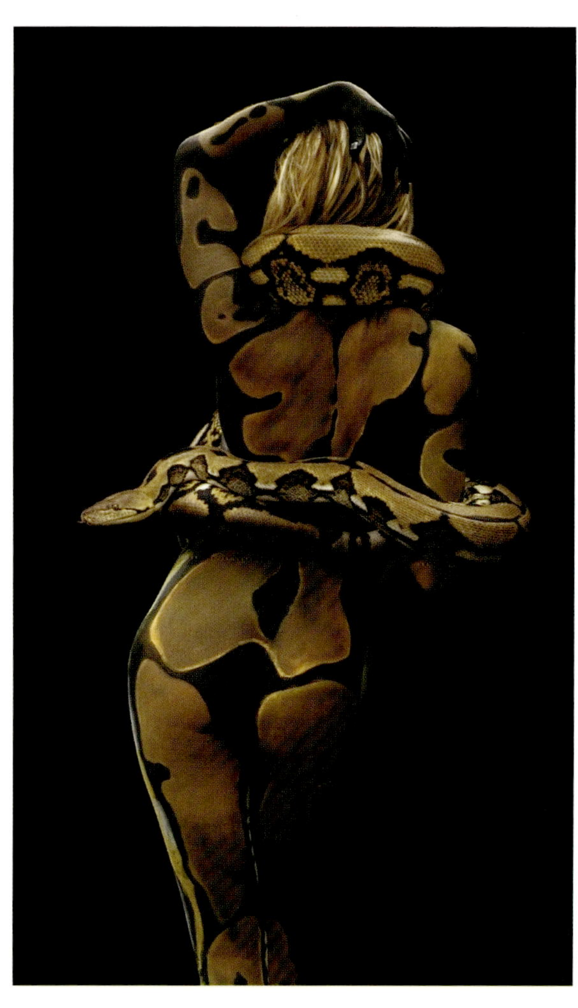
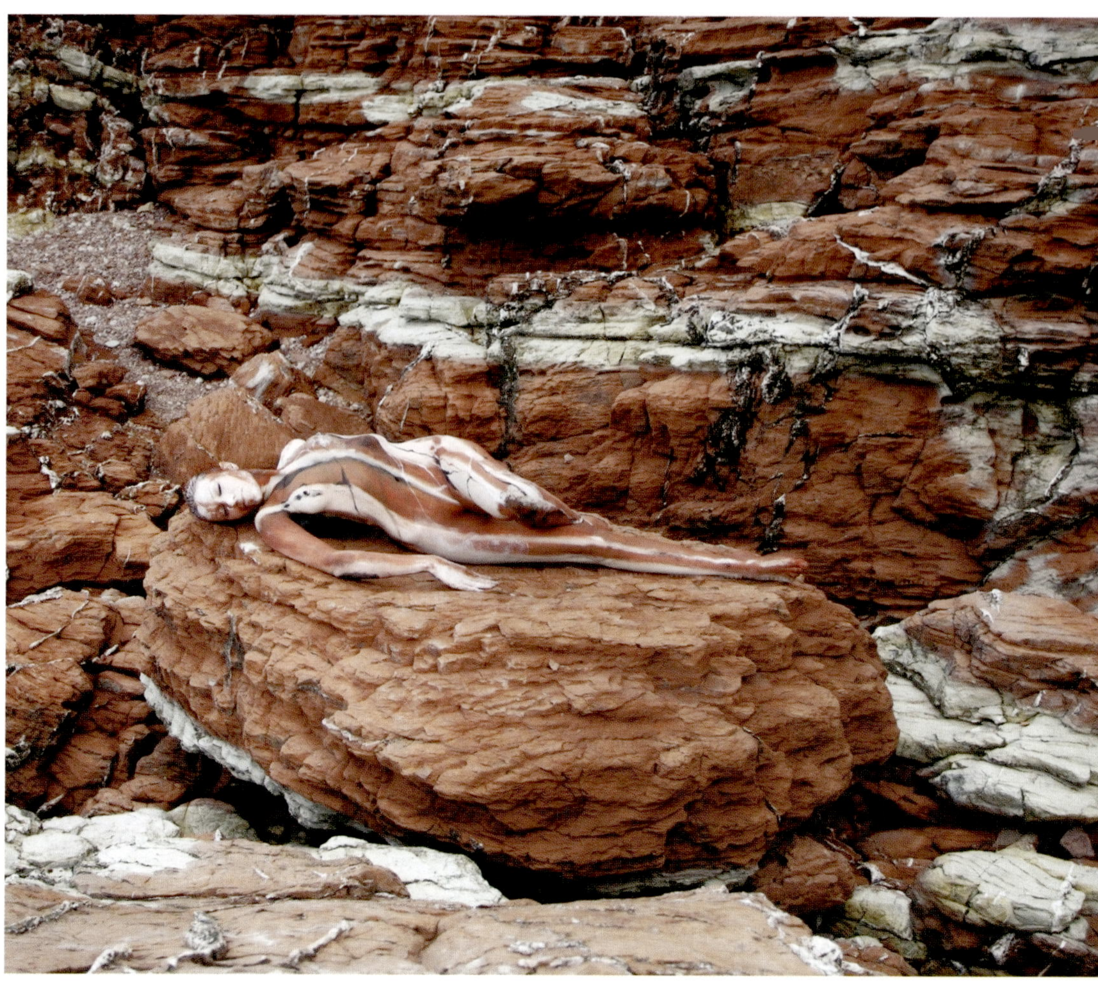
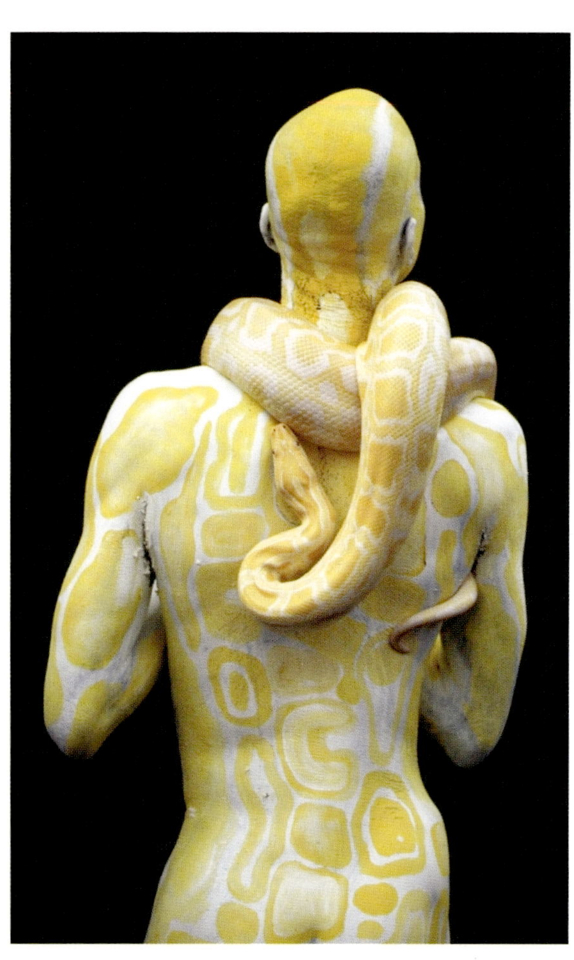
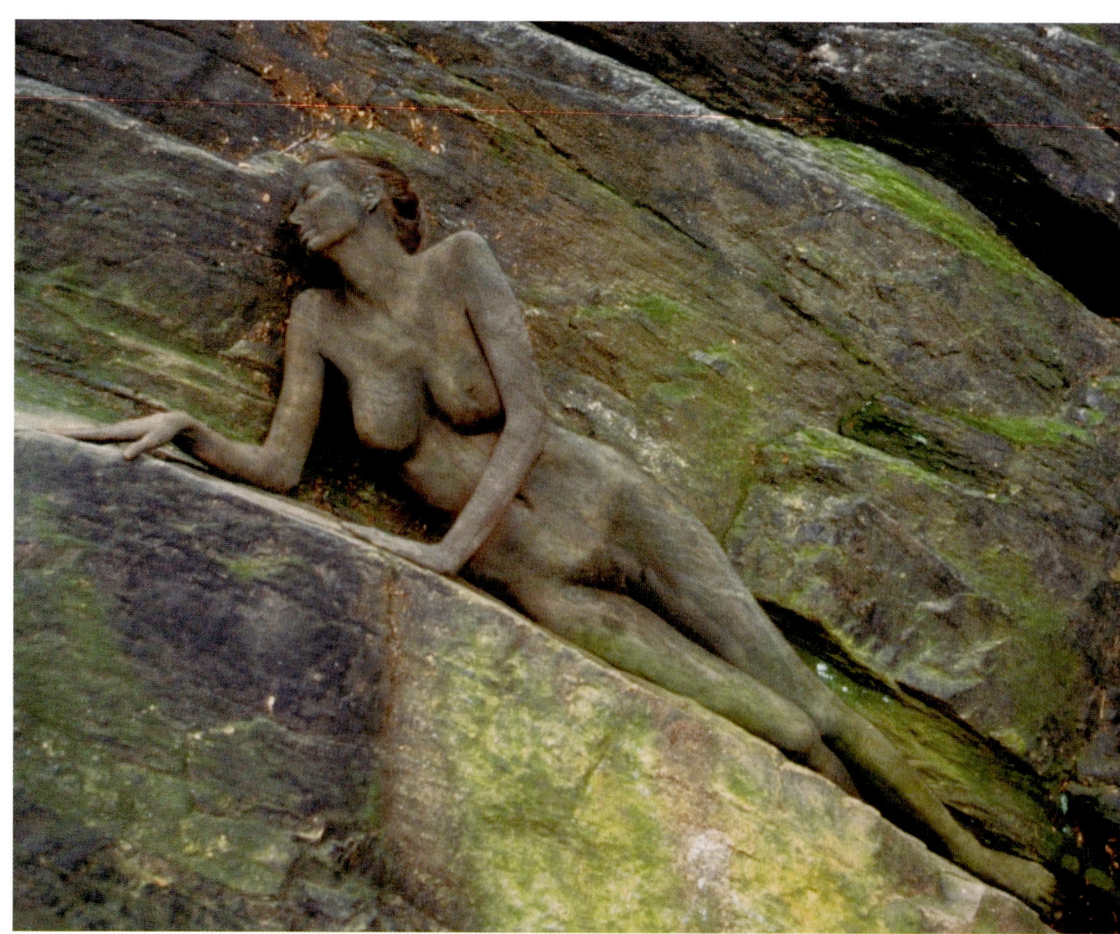

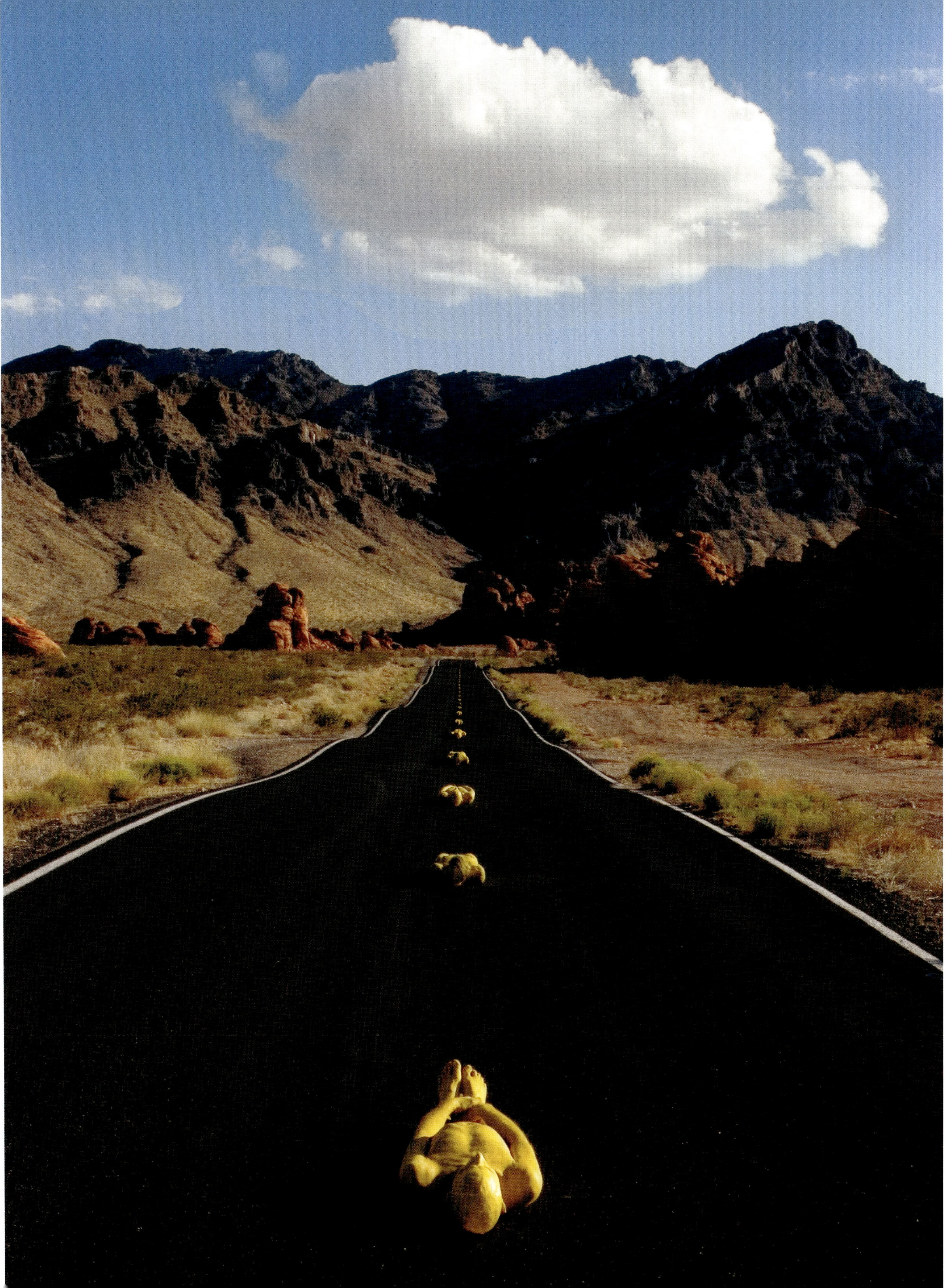

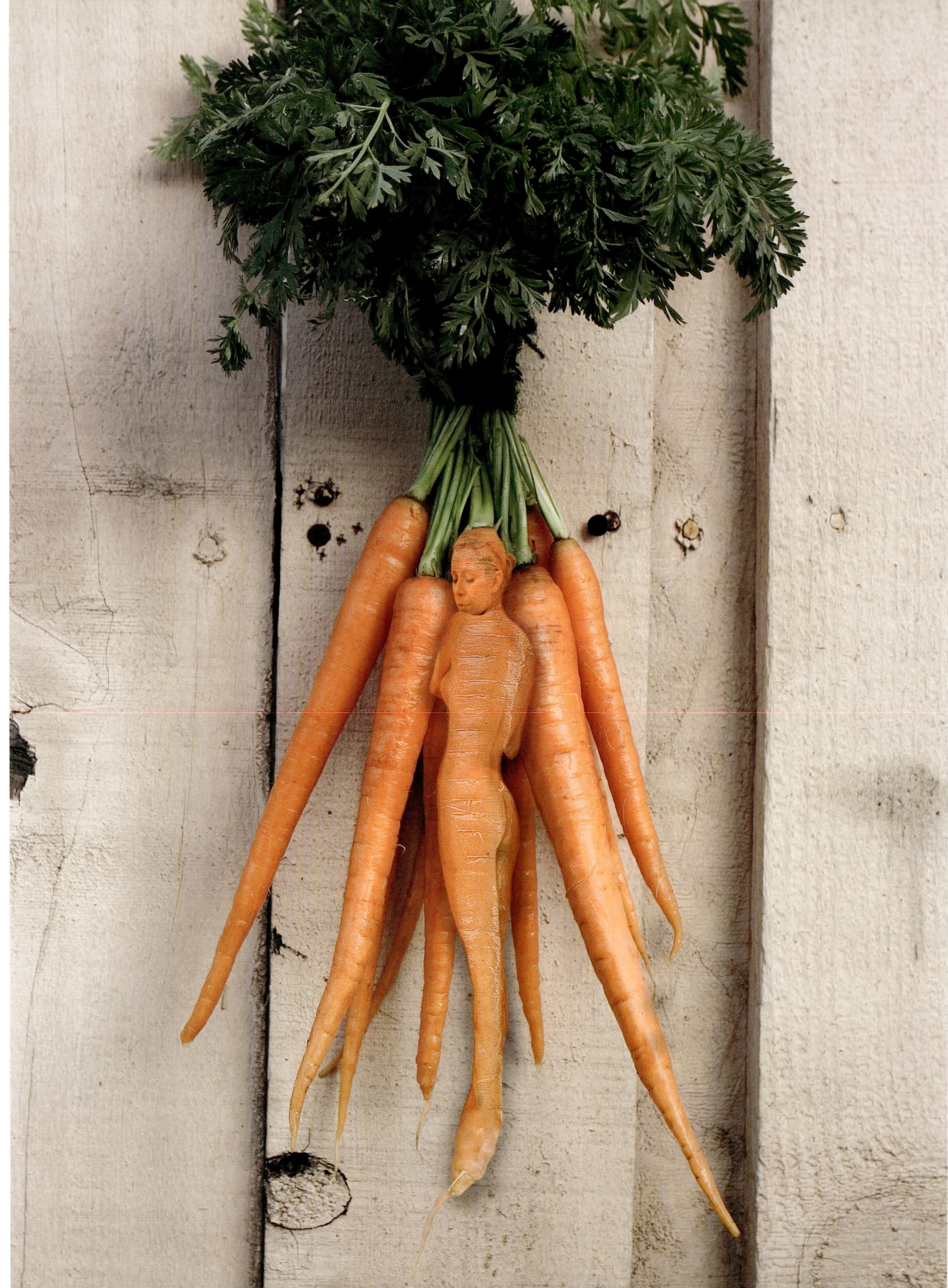

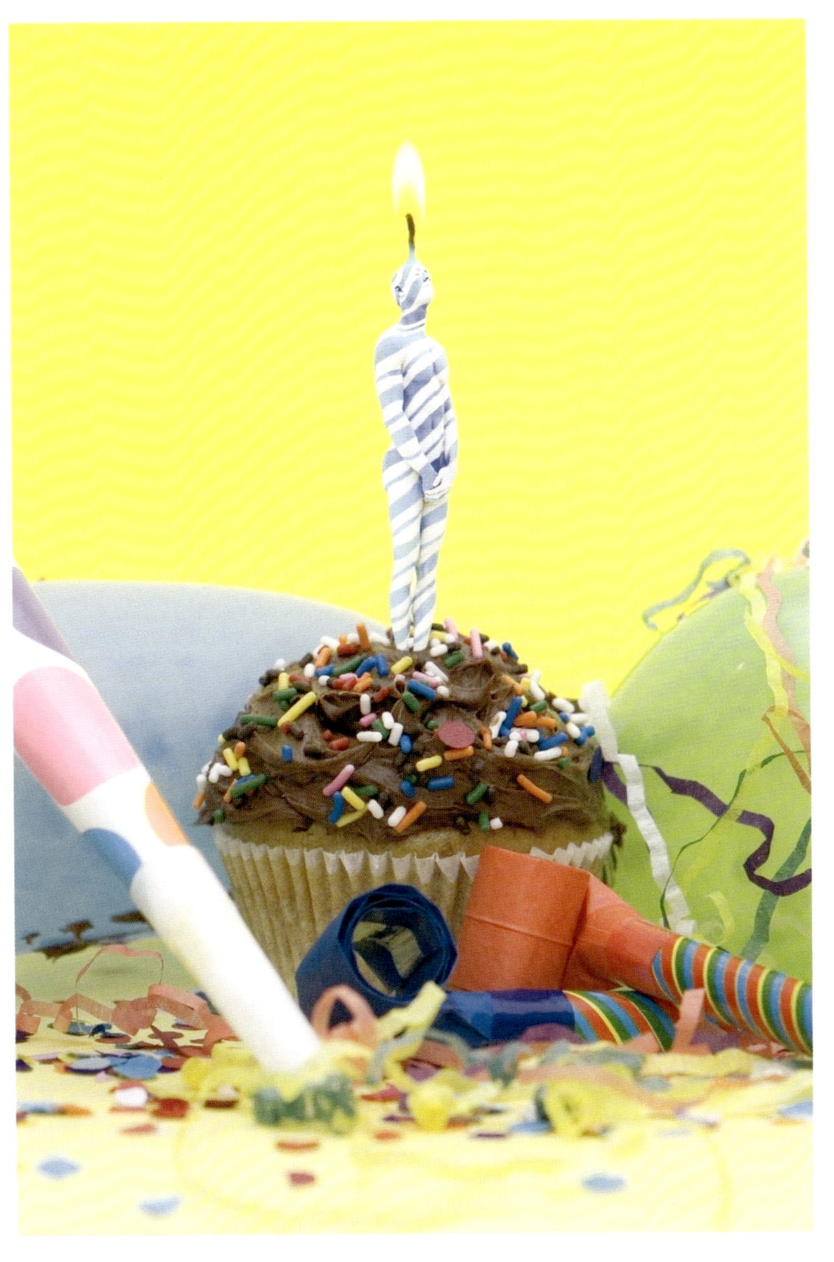

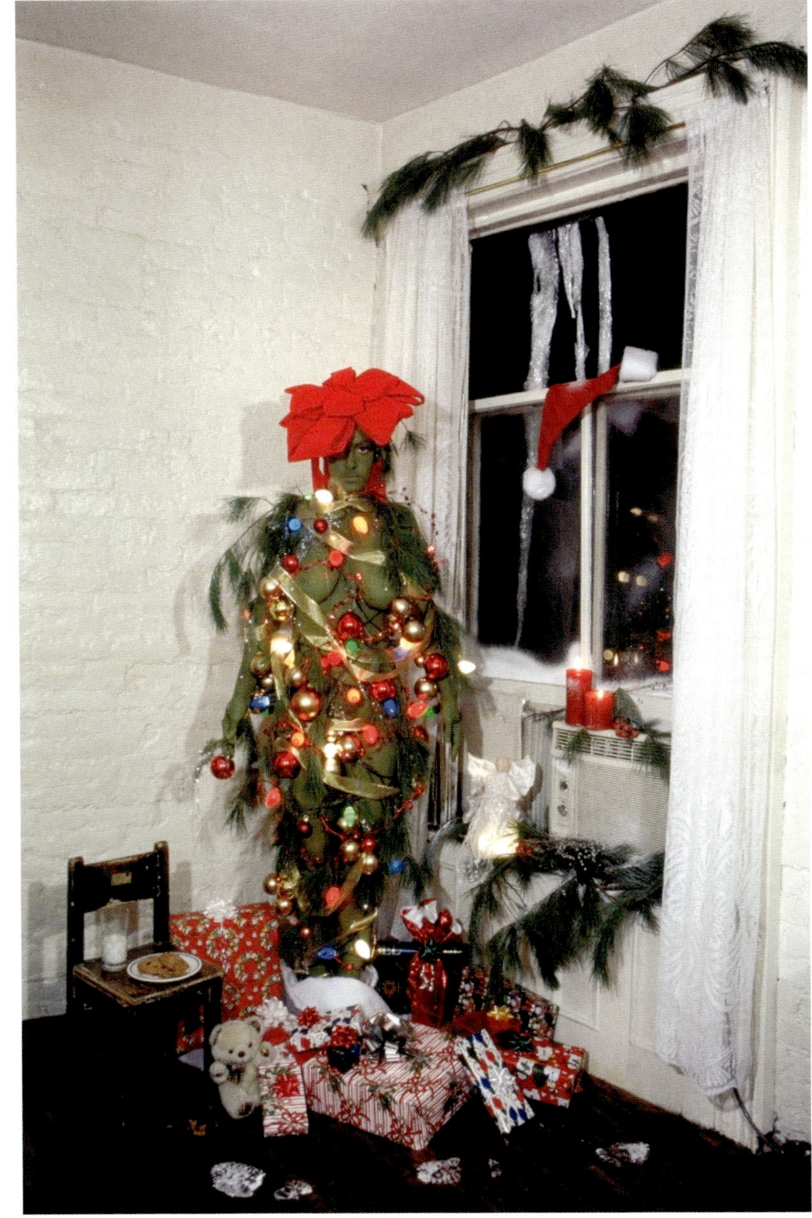

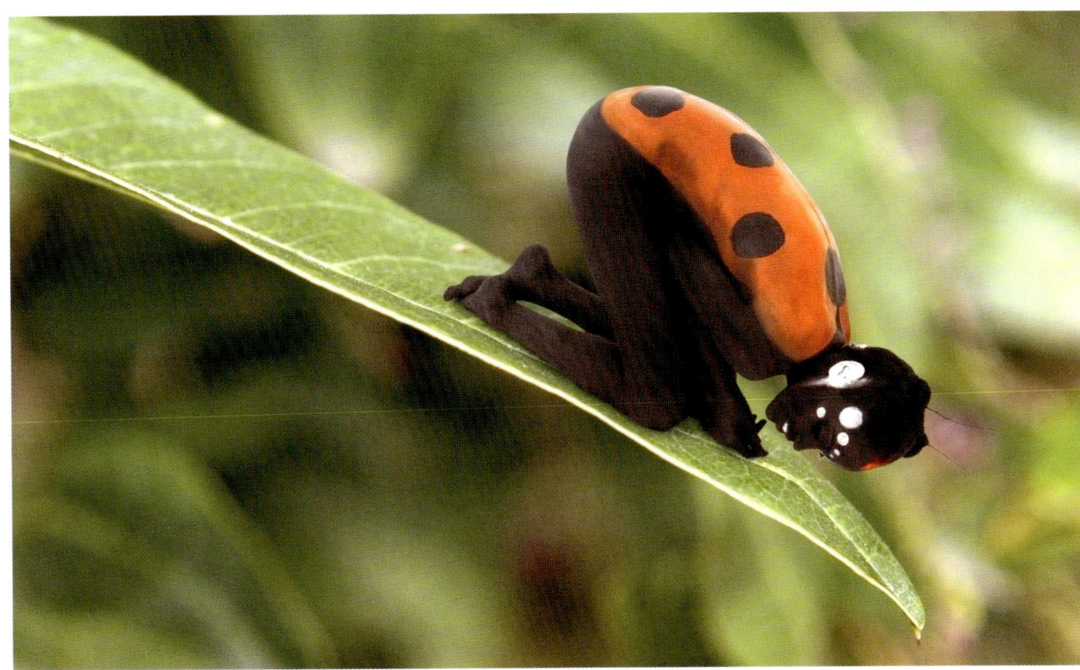

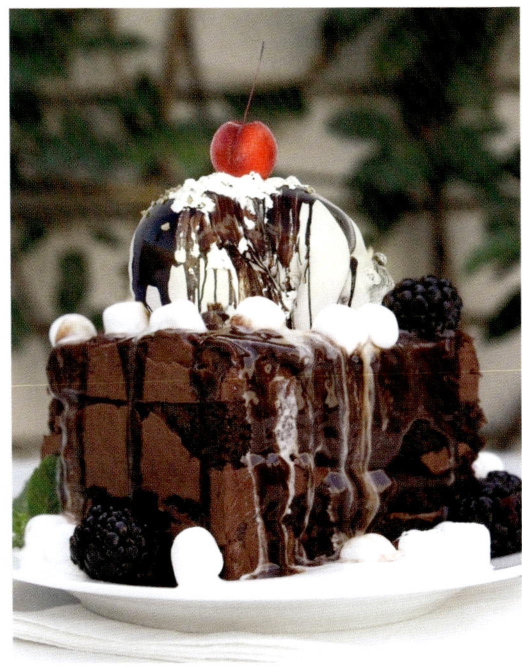

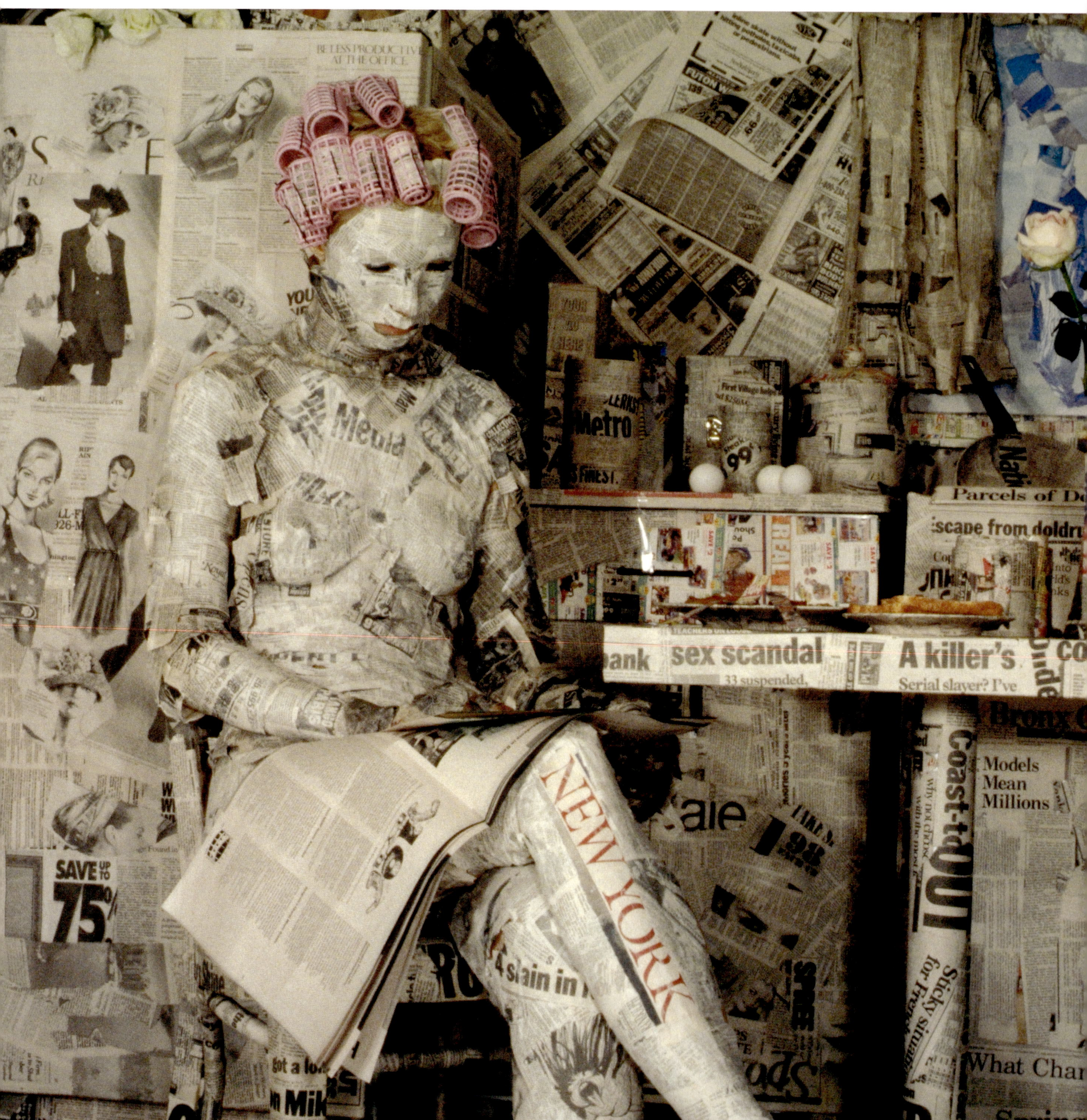

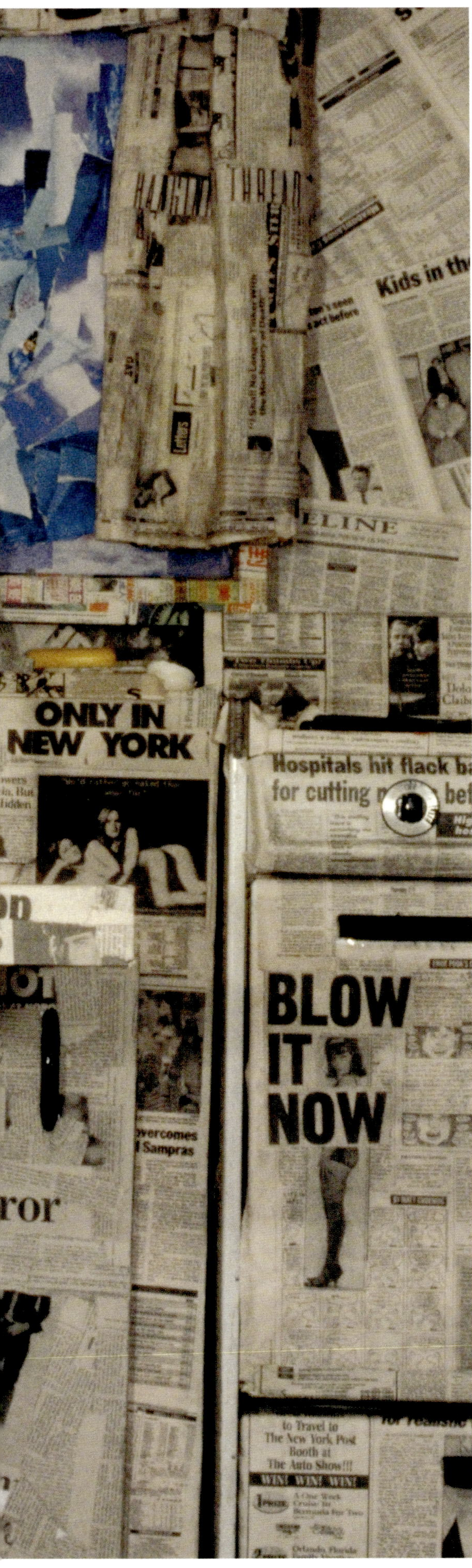
ONLY IN
NEW YORK
Hospitals hit flack ba
for cutting
BLOW
IT
NOW
Sampras

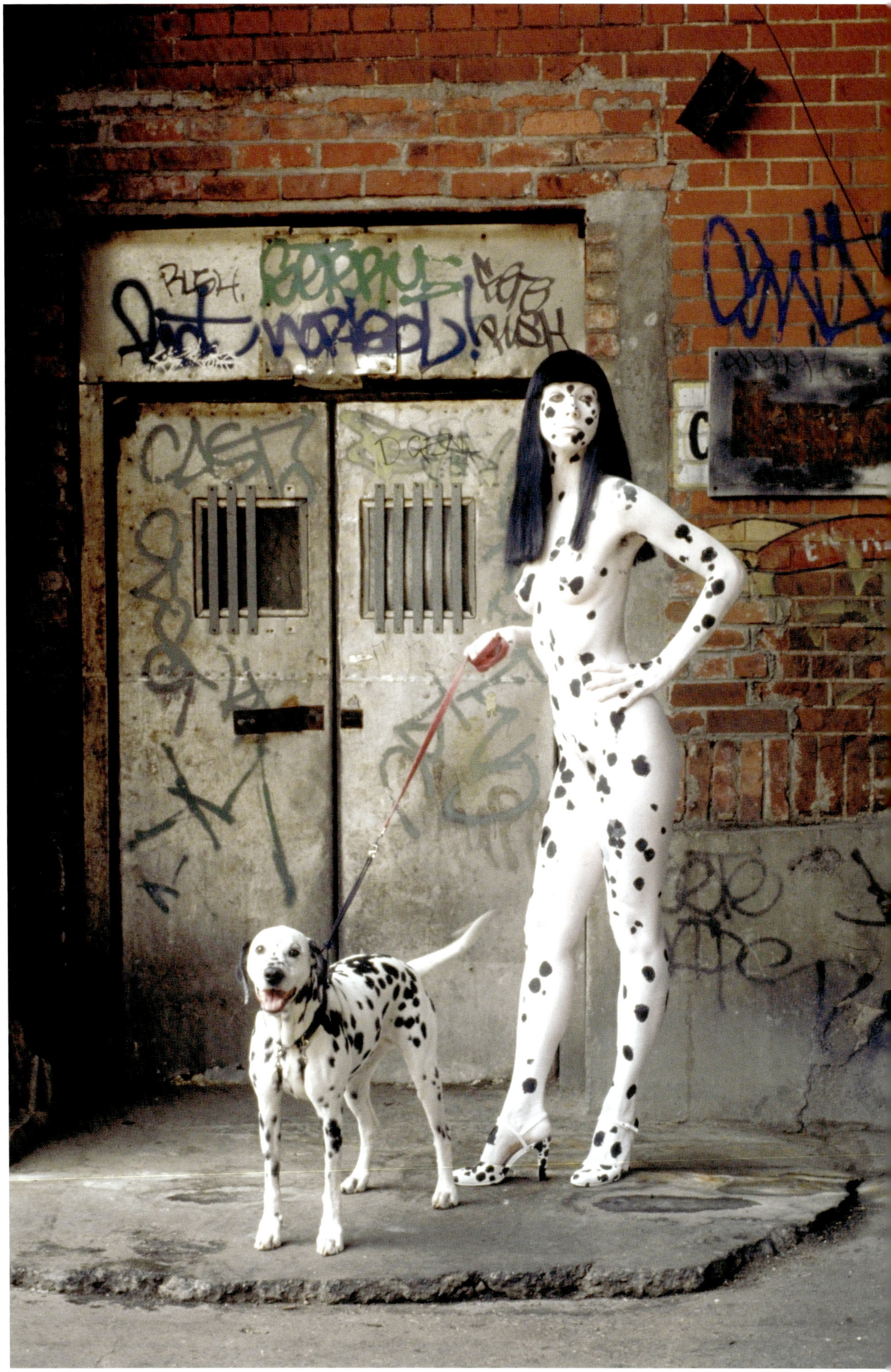

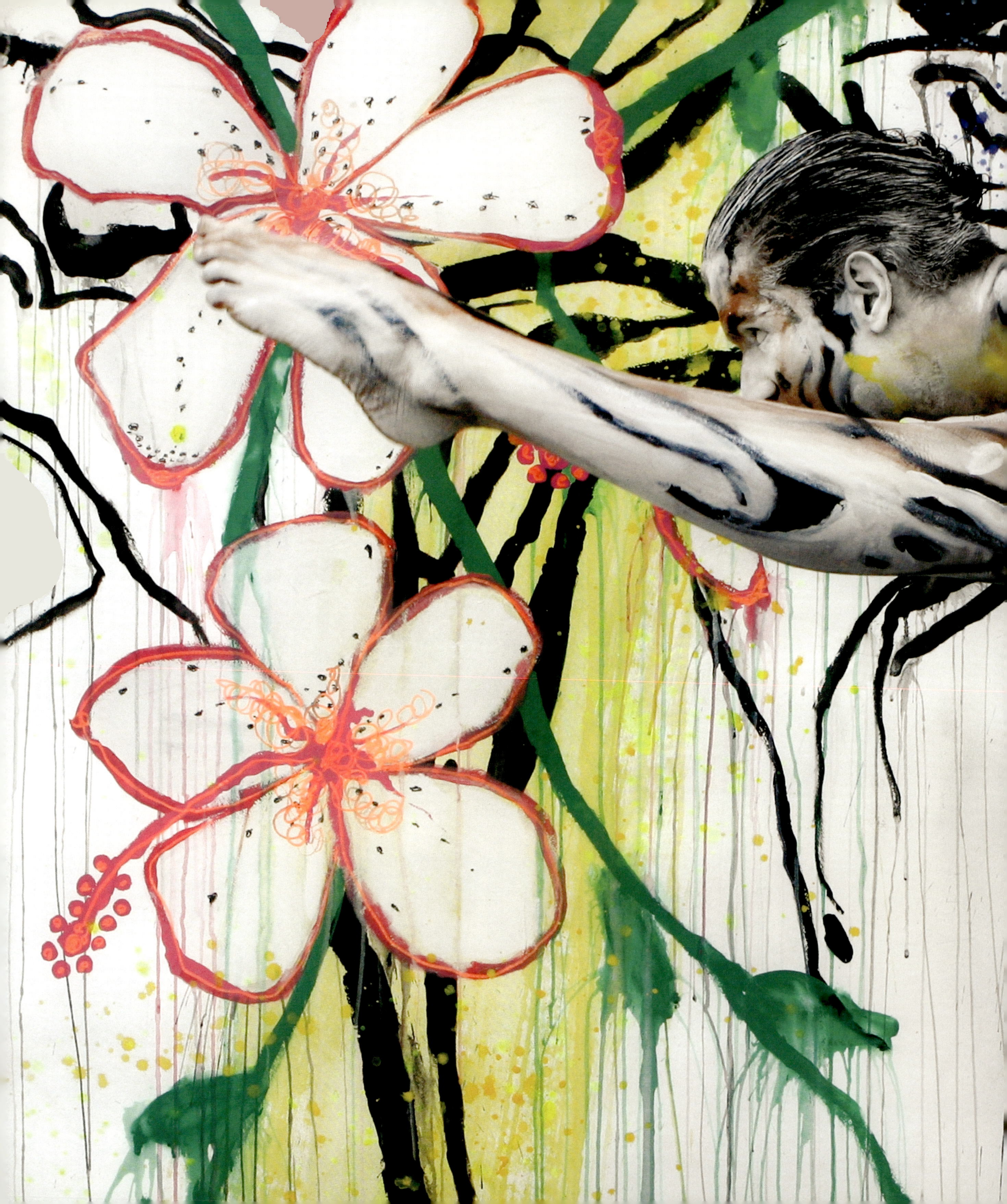

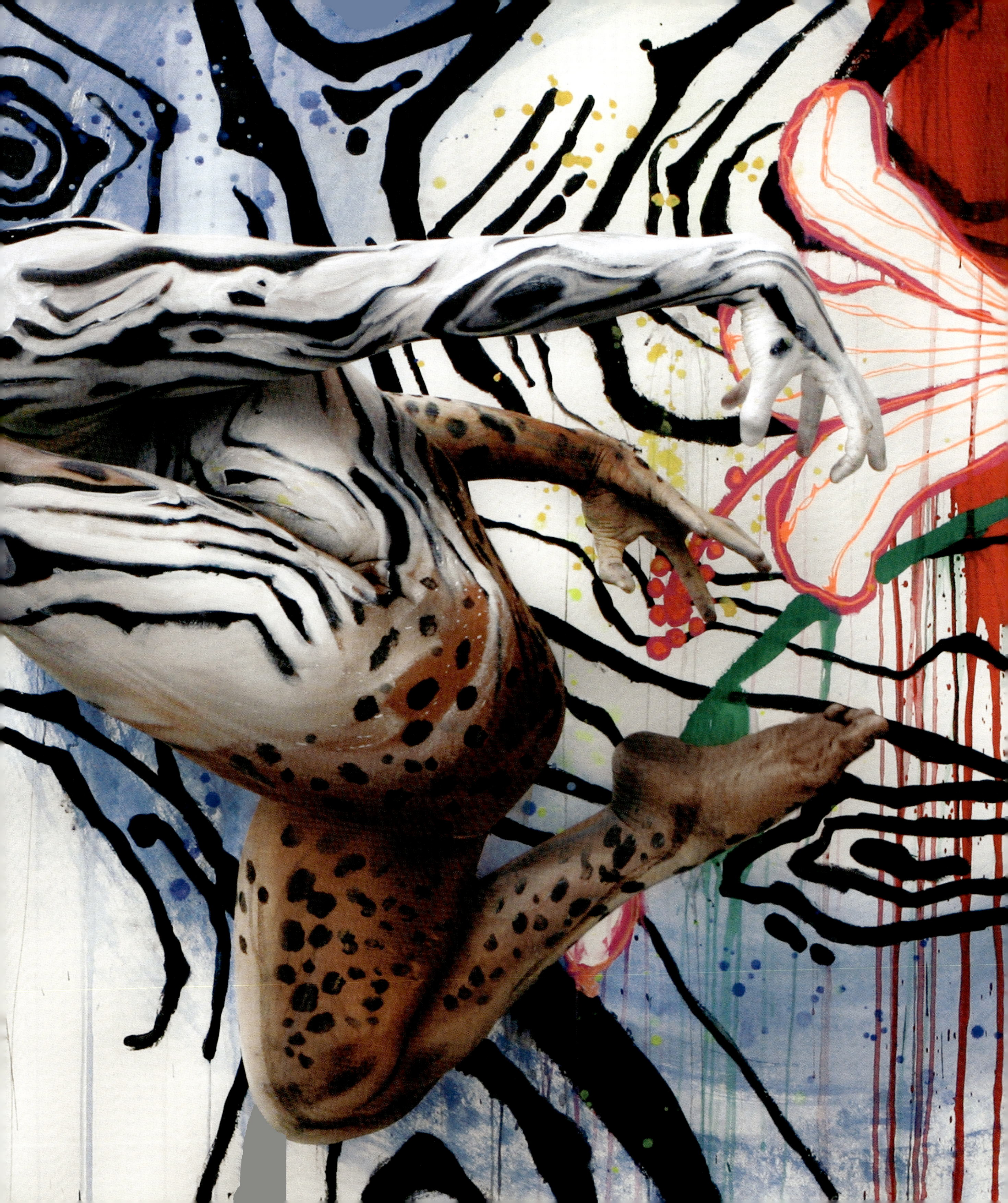

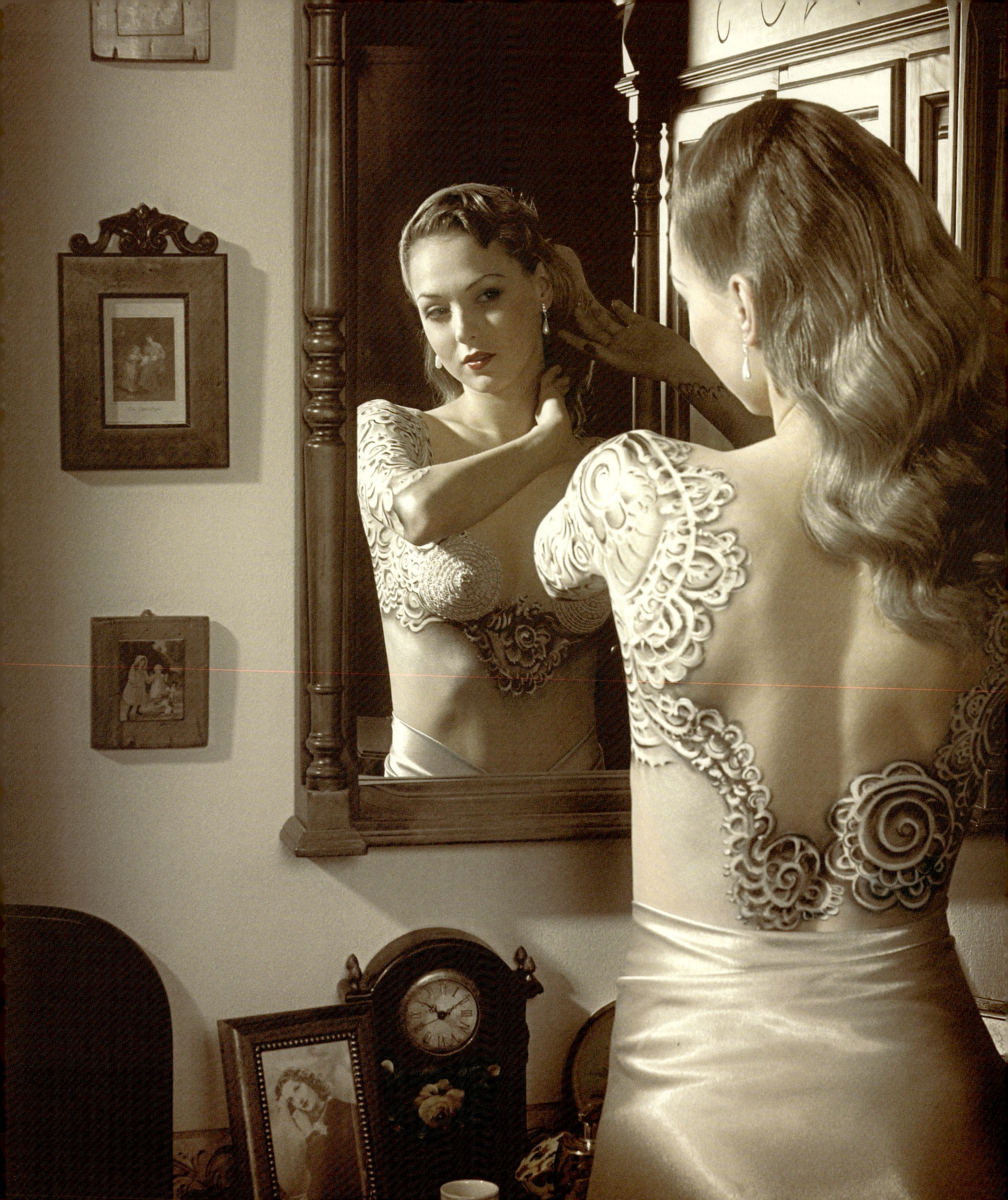

Helen Demi

WWW.STRANGEDREAMS.ORG
WWW.ART-DUO.COM

Helen Demi is a professional artist, teacher and performer from Moscow, Russia. Born into a family of artists and educators, she has been working in the art of bodypainting since 1998. Helen is the co-author of an anthology of Russian bodypainting, *People in the Paint*, together with Andrey Bartenev and Igor Isaev. She worked for the Stanislavski and Nemirovich-Danchenko Moscow Academic Music Theatre as a bodypainter with Deirdre Clancy for Frank Andersen (Napoli Ballet) and for *The Little Mermaid* ballet by John Neumeier. Helen is fond of conceptual bodypainting, which uses optical and meaningful illusions to reflect ideas through light, shadow and paint. This method helps viewers see the artist's worldview.

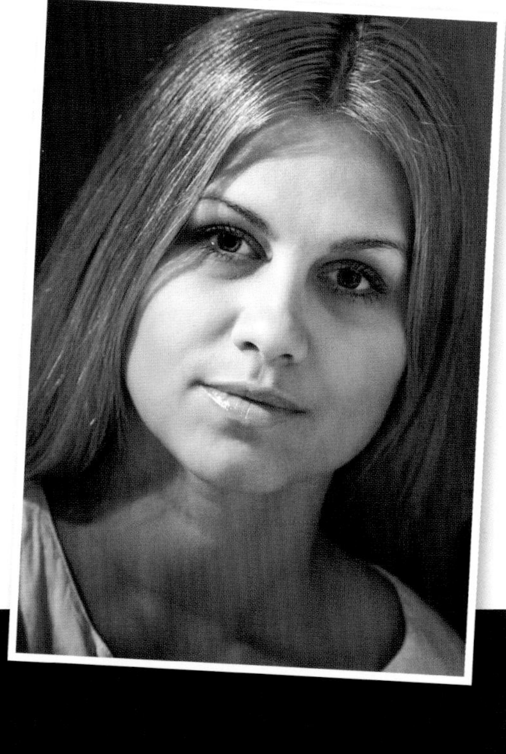

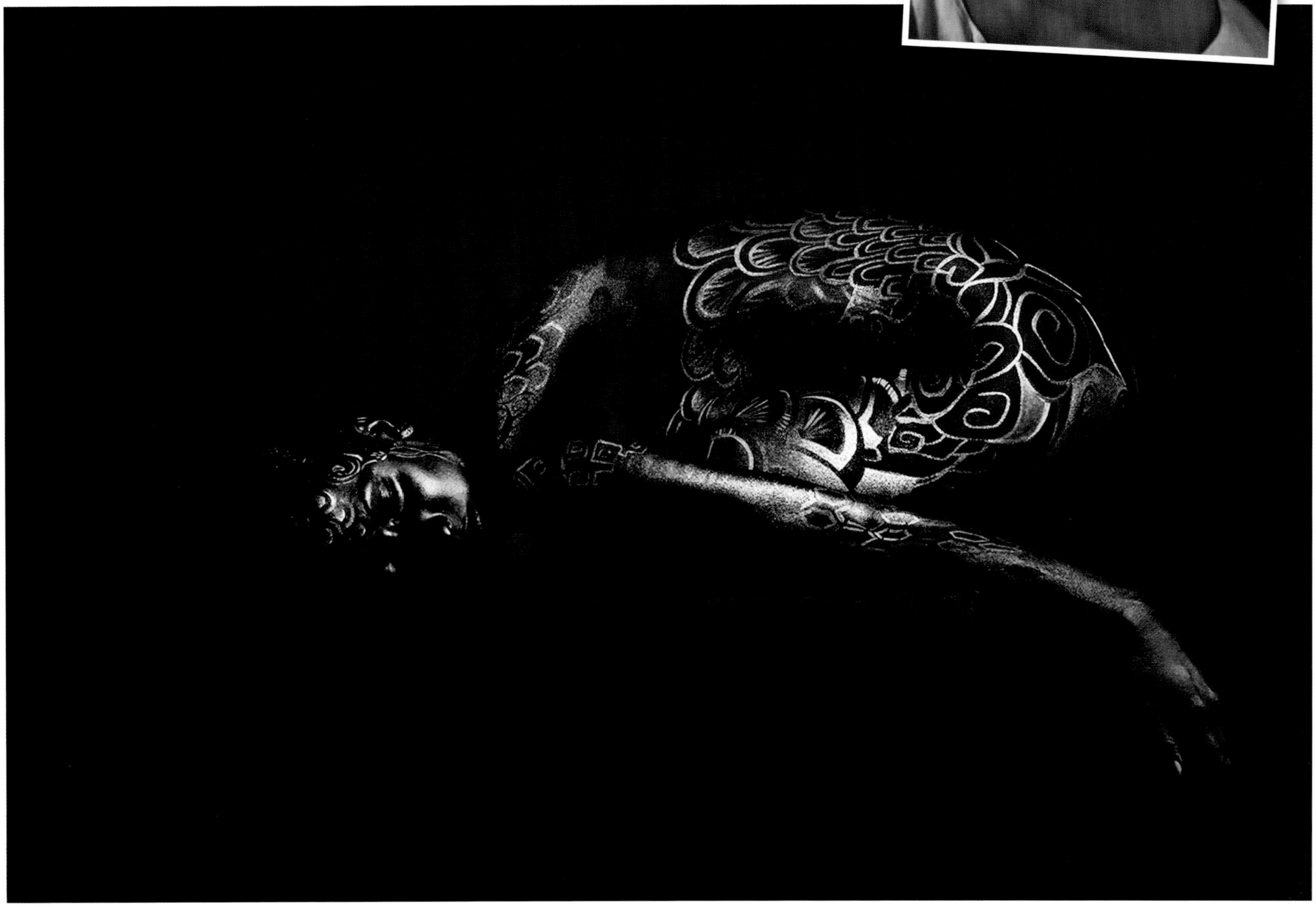

PHOTOGRAPHER MAX KALMYKOV (ALL PHOTOS)

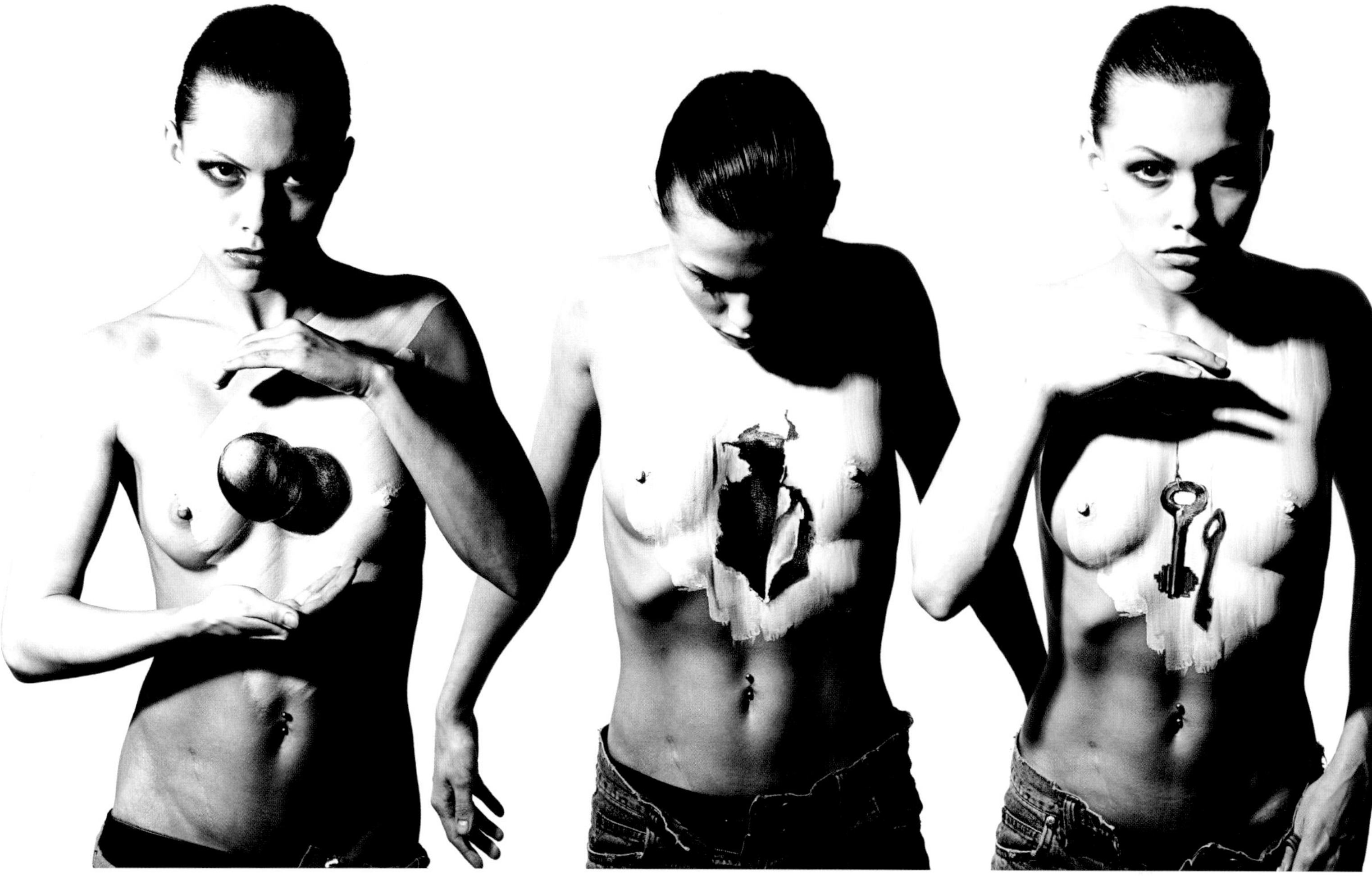

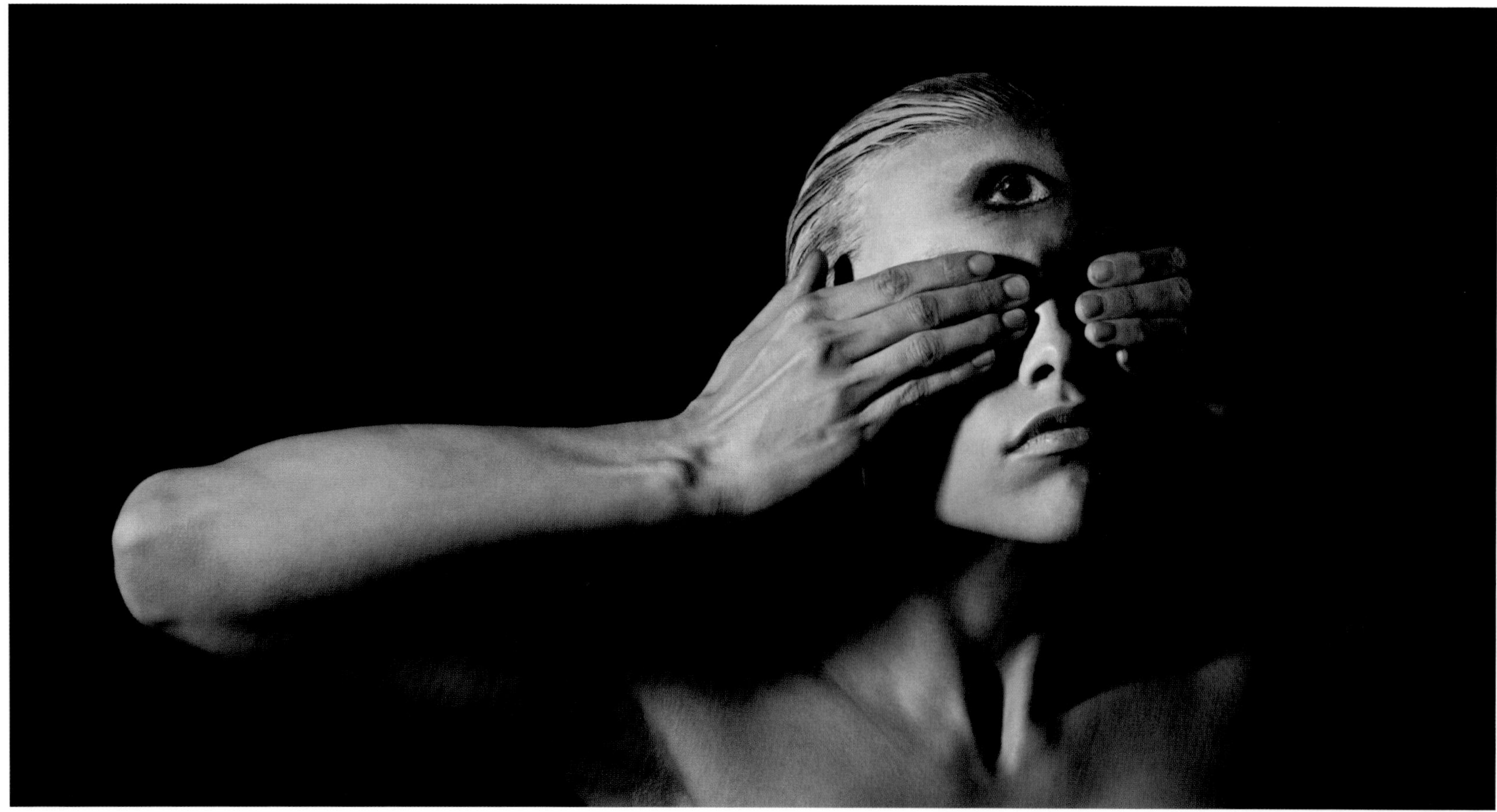

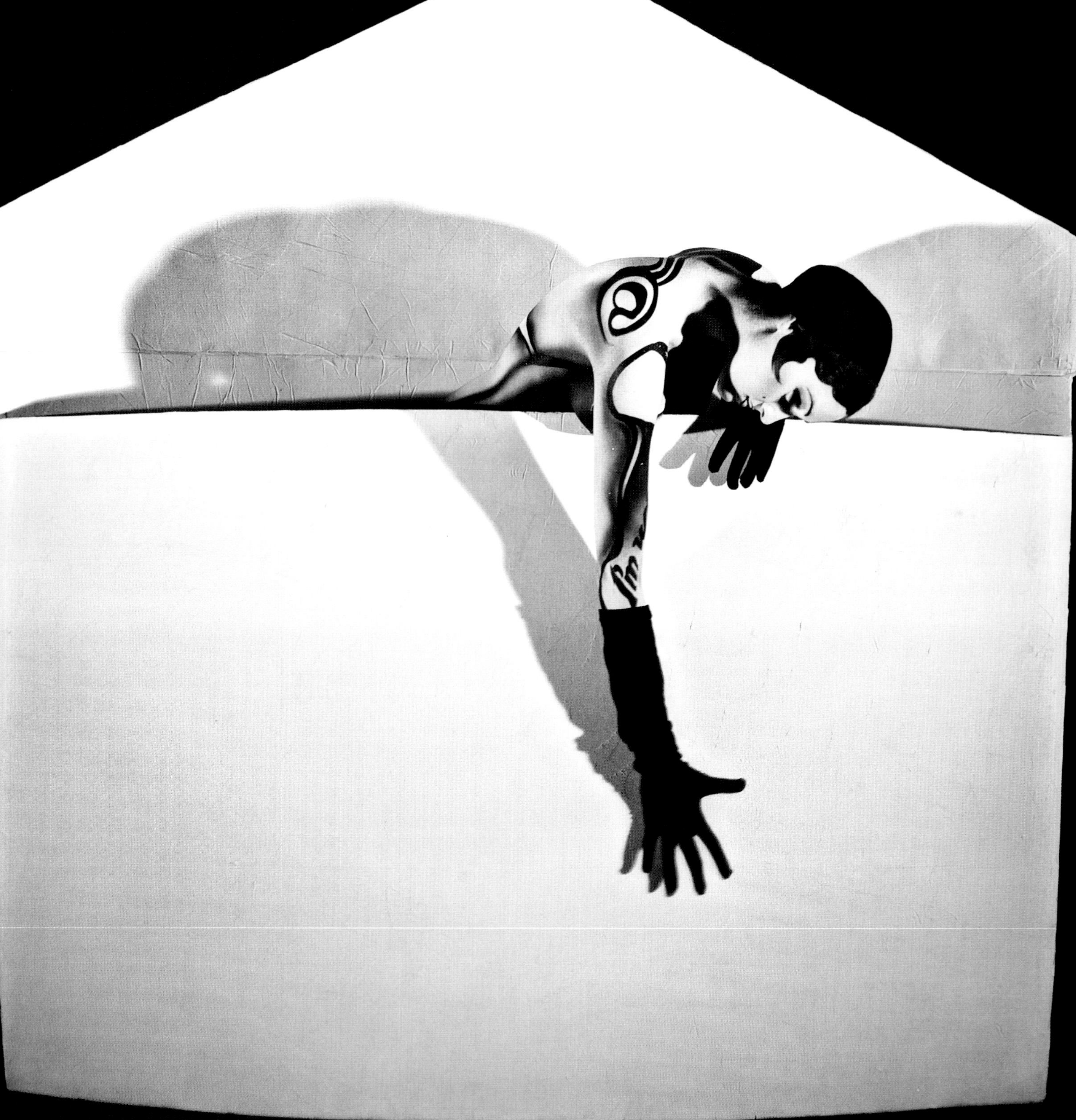

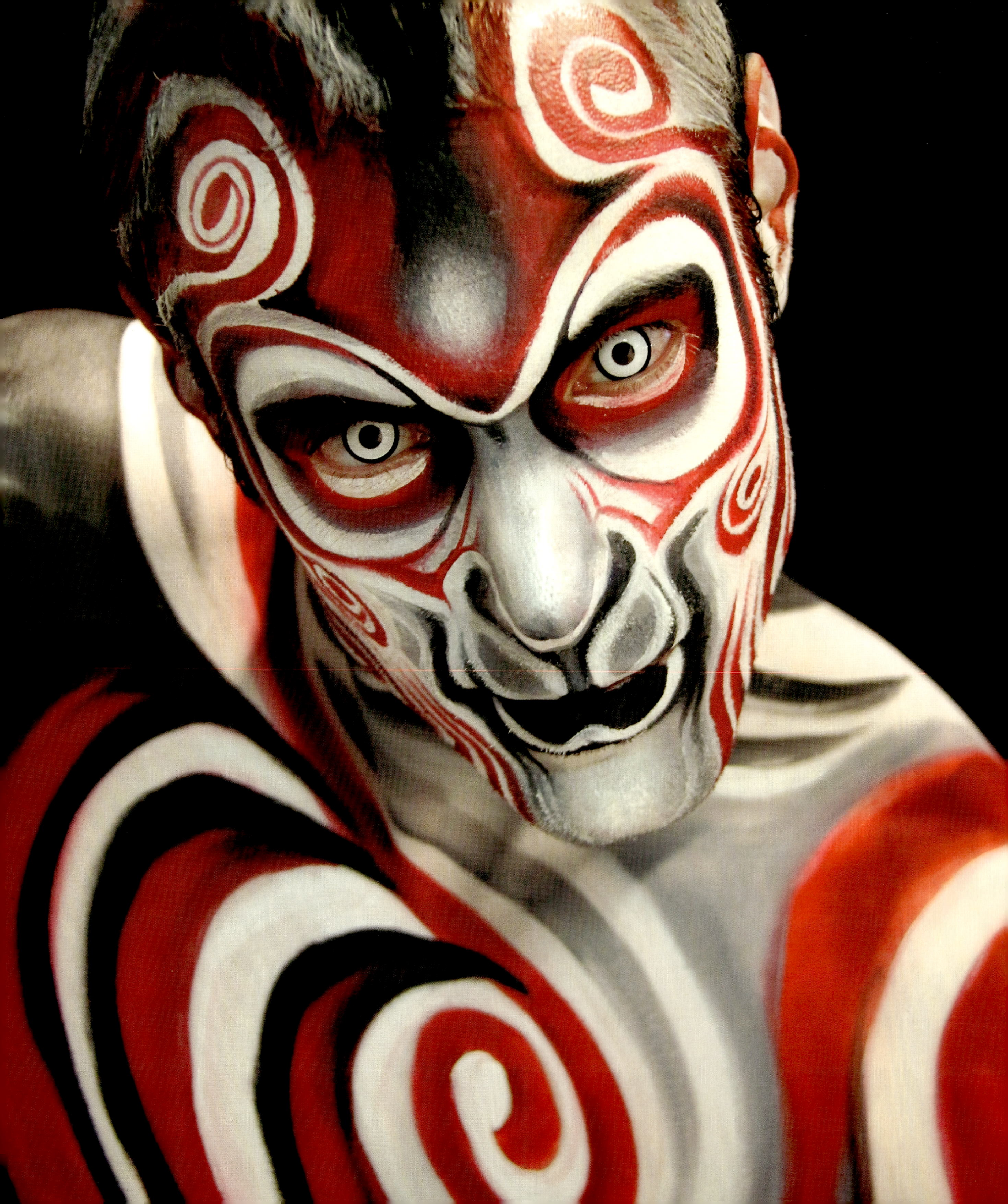

Jinny (Geneviève Houle)

Geneviève Houle, whom the world has come to know as Jinny, is a renowned face and bodypainting artist. Jinny continues to travel the world, sharing her passion with her fellow artists and students. Her vibrant abstract designs and clever use of color, combined with amazing brush control, make Jinny one of the most sought-after artists in her field. Jinny's creative and breathtaking work has been featured in international media, magazines and books, as well as TV, movies, commercials, conventions, shows and corporate events. Jinny has also put her name to a line of body art paints.

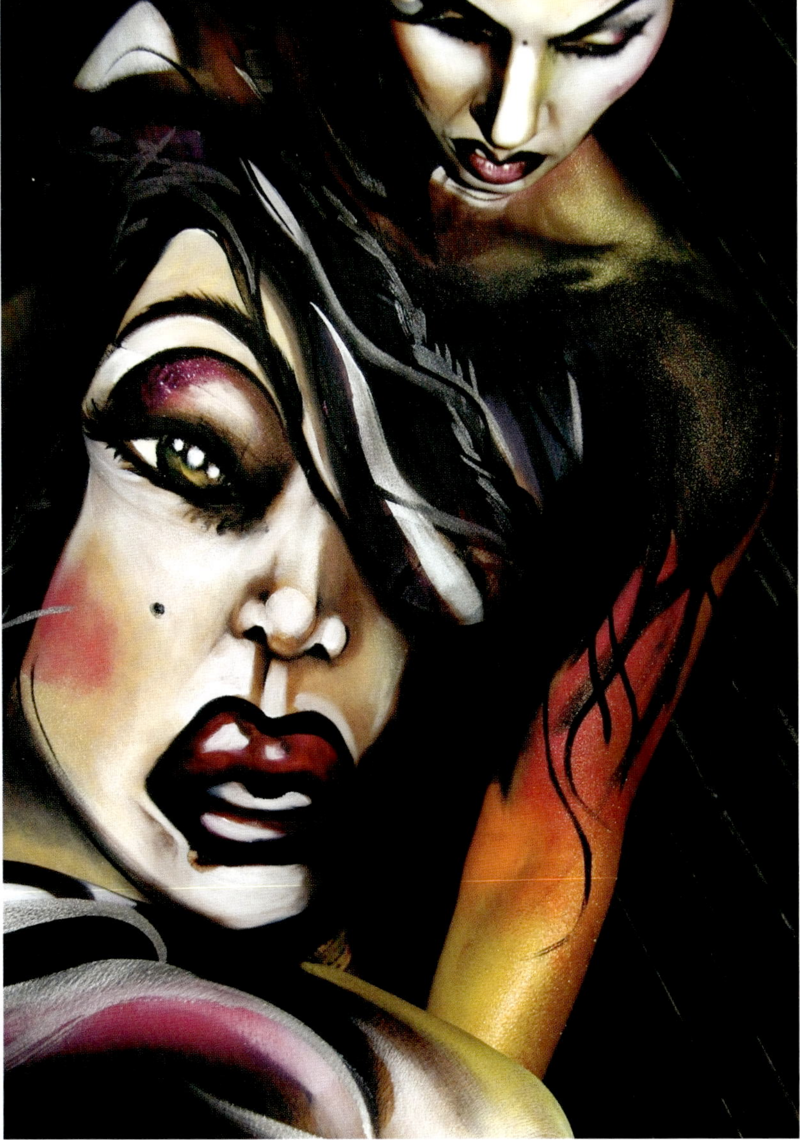

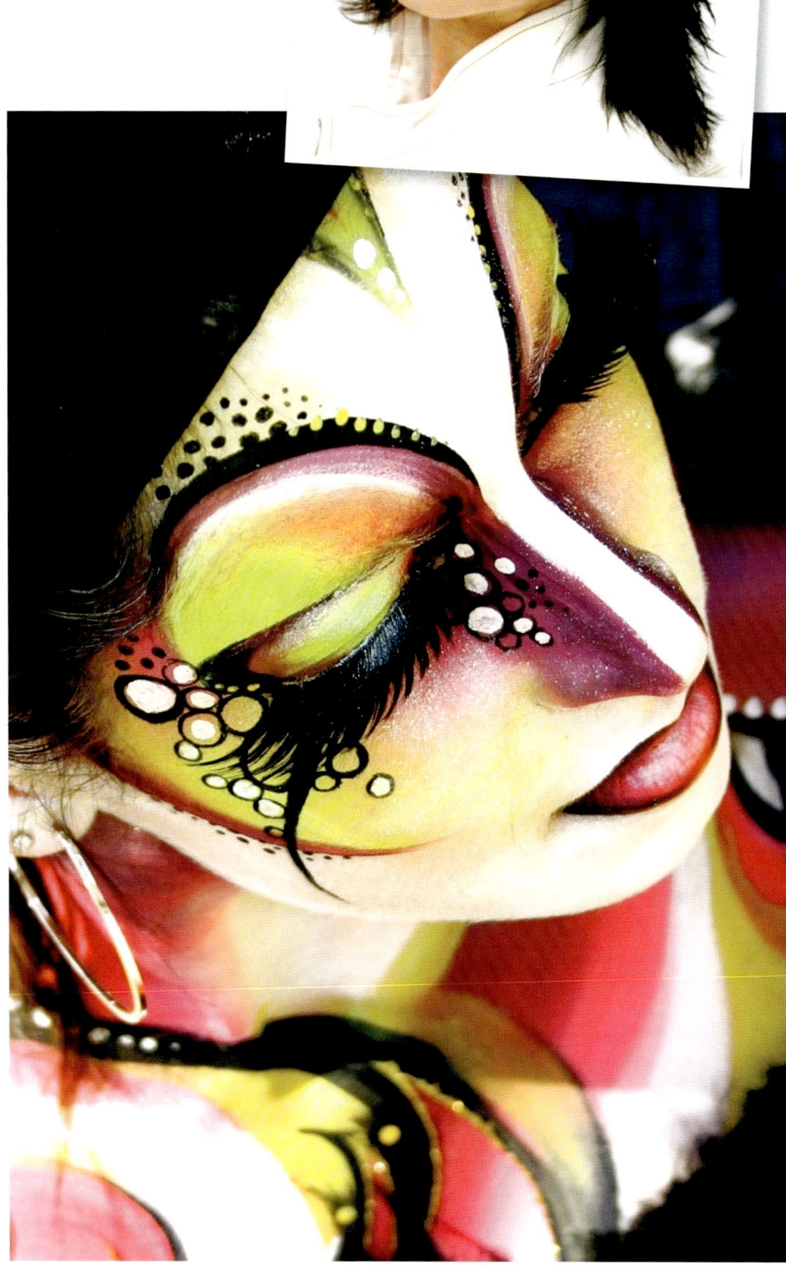

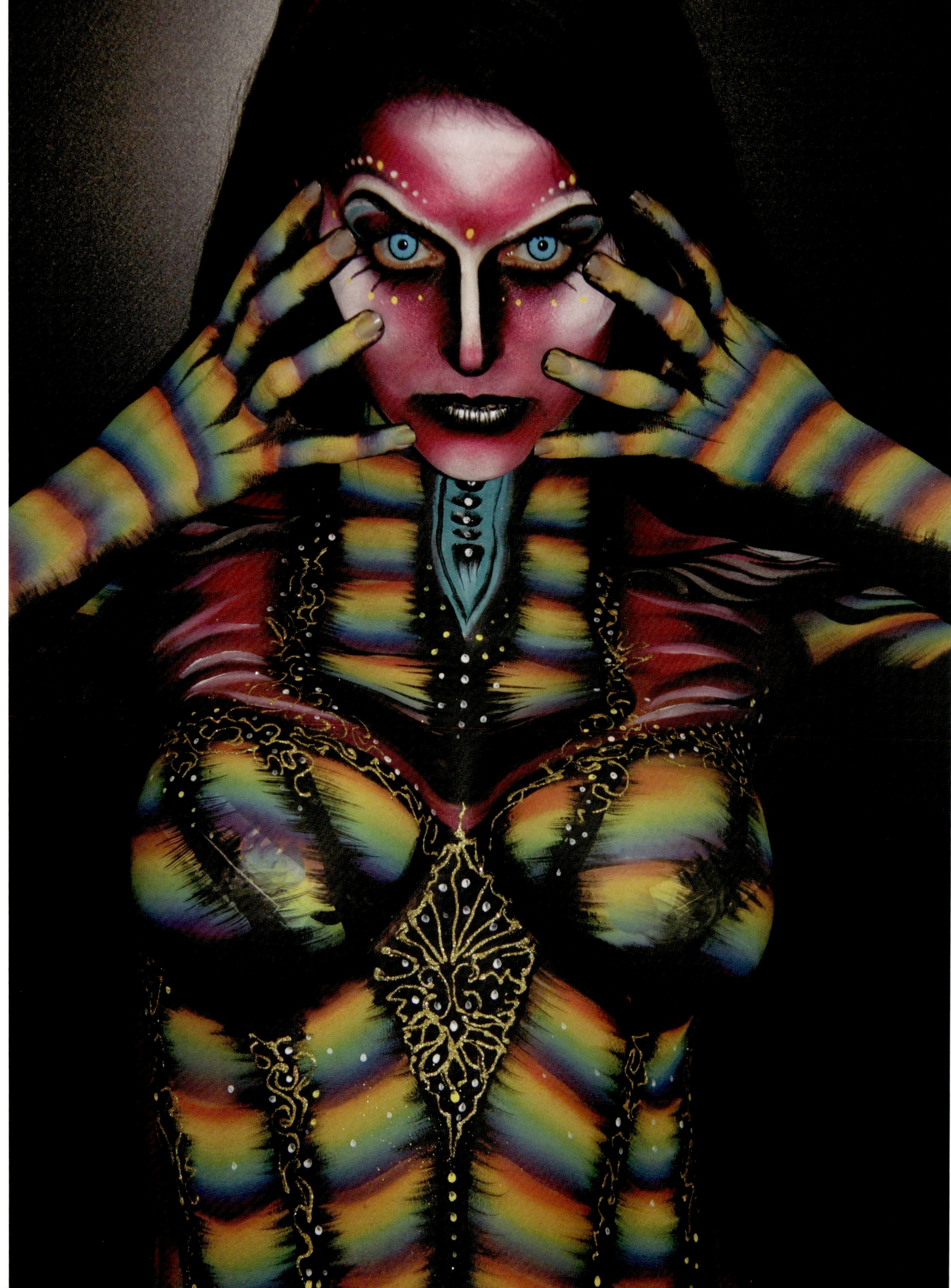

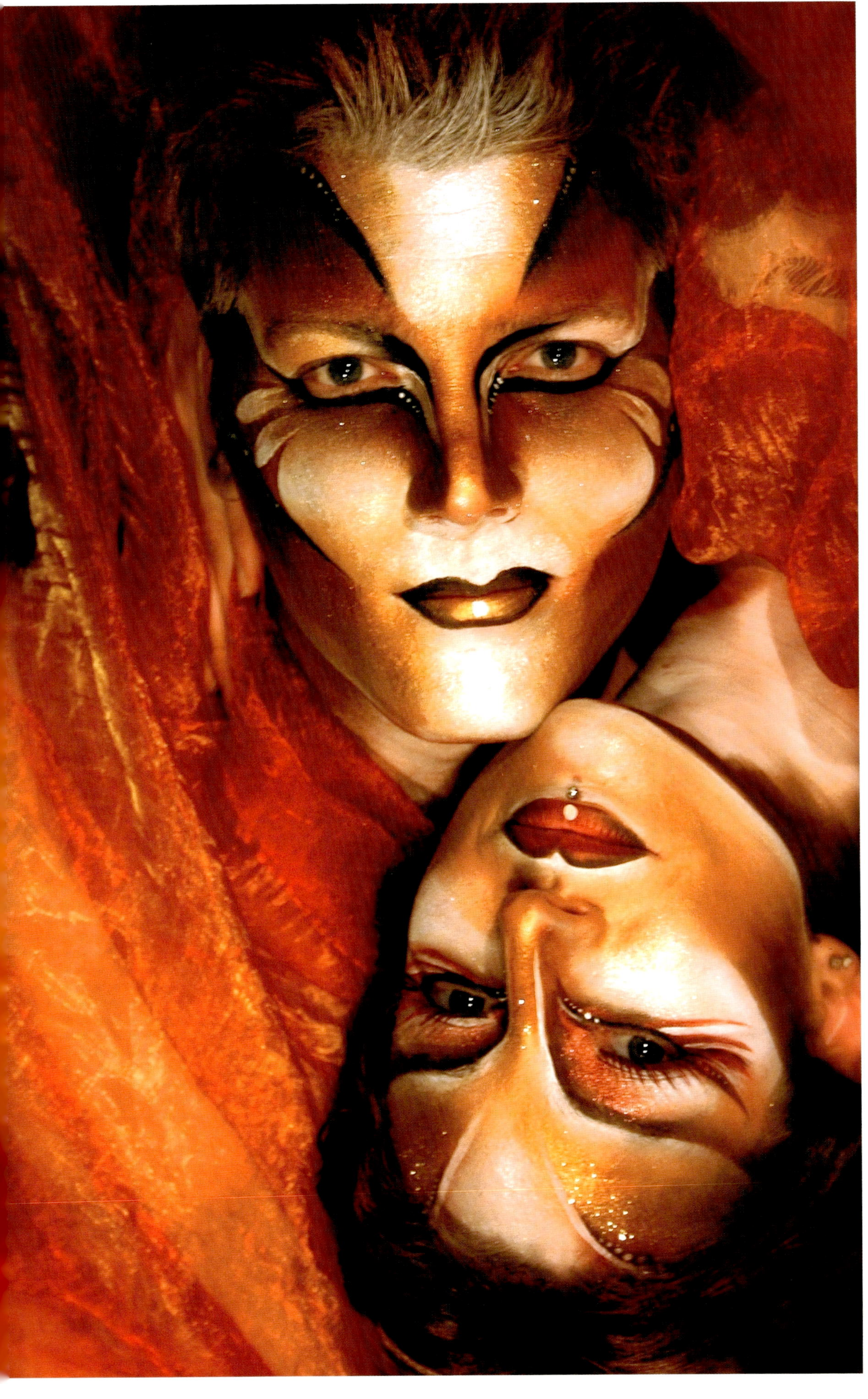

"Since I began doing bodypainting, I've always promoted its worth artistically. I want to make people forget about the nude body underneath. I want them to enjoy the whole creation. I not only judge others in competitions, I judge what I do each time. I want to improve every day. I want people to see my artwork and recognize my 'signature.'"

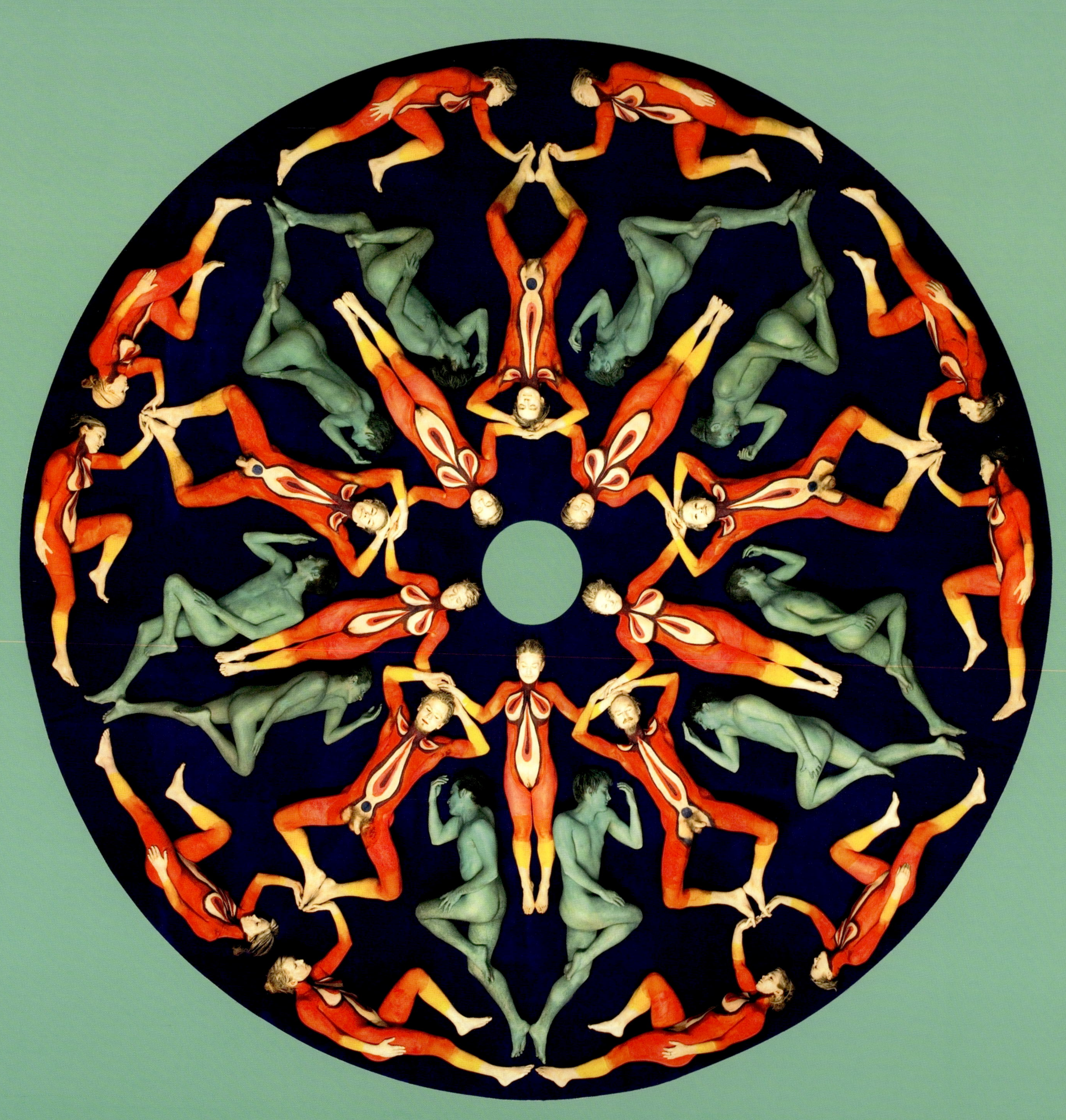

Johannes Stötter

Johannes Stötter is an artist, musician and fine-art bodypainter. He has won many awards around the world for his art, including being named a World Champion. Johannes has worked on teaching assignments in the medical industry to help students learn human anatomy through painting, and he has combined much of his spiritual understanding into his work. A master painter, Johannes can blend a human body into a landscape seamlessly, without the use of any projection or laser help. All of his work is hand painted with only his artistic eye as a guide.

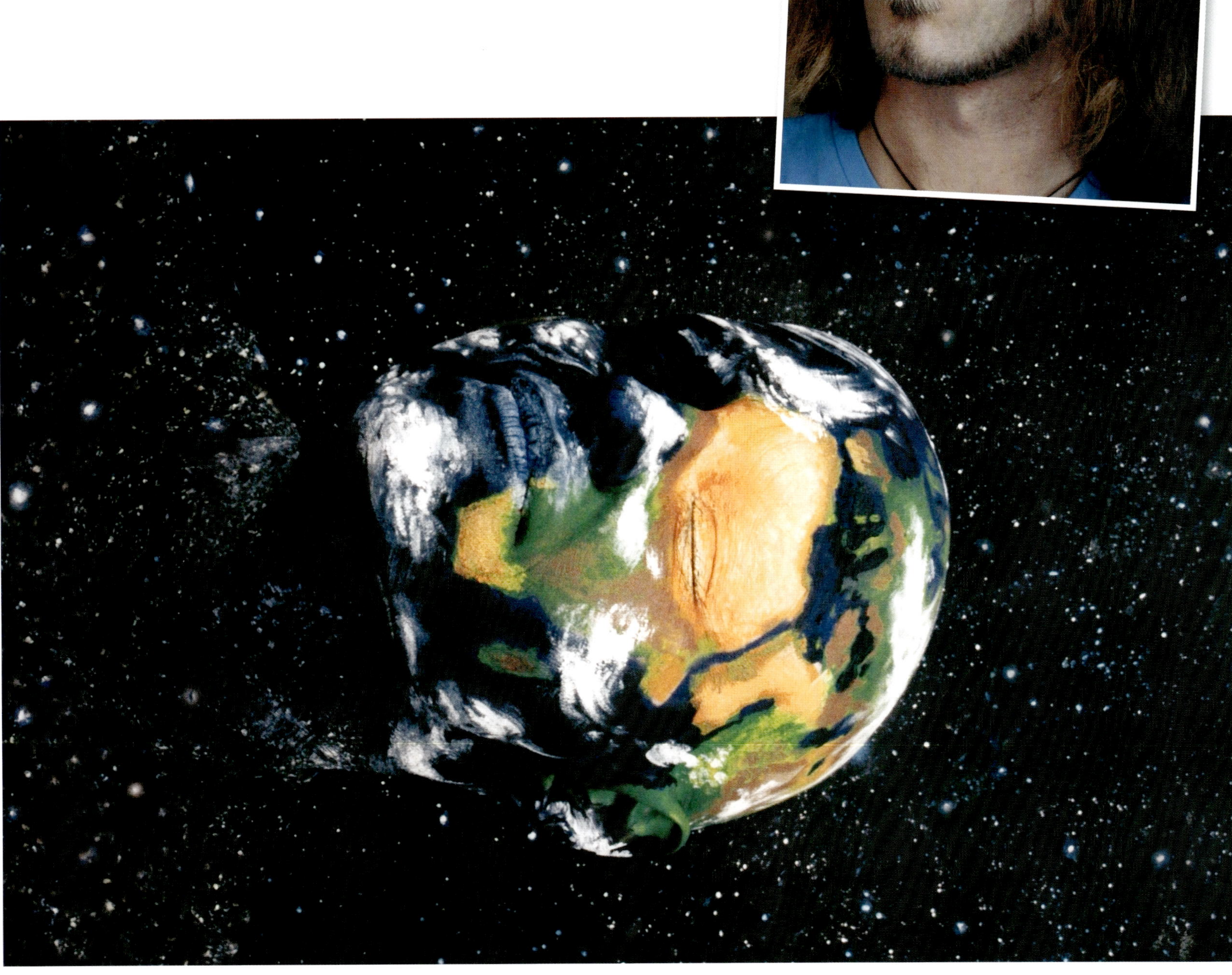

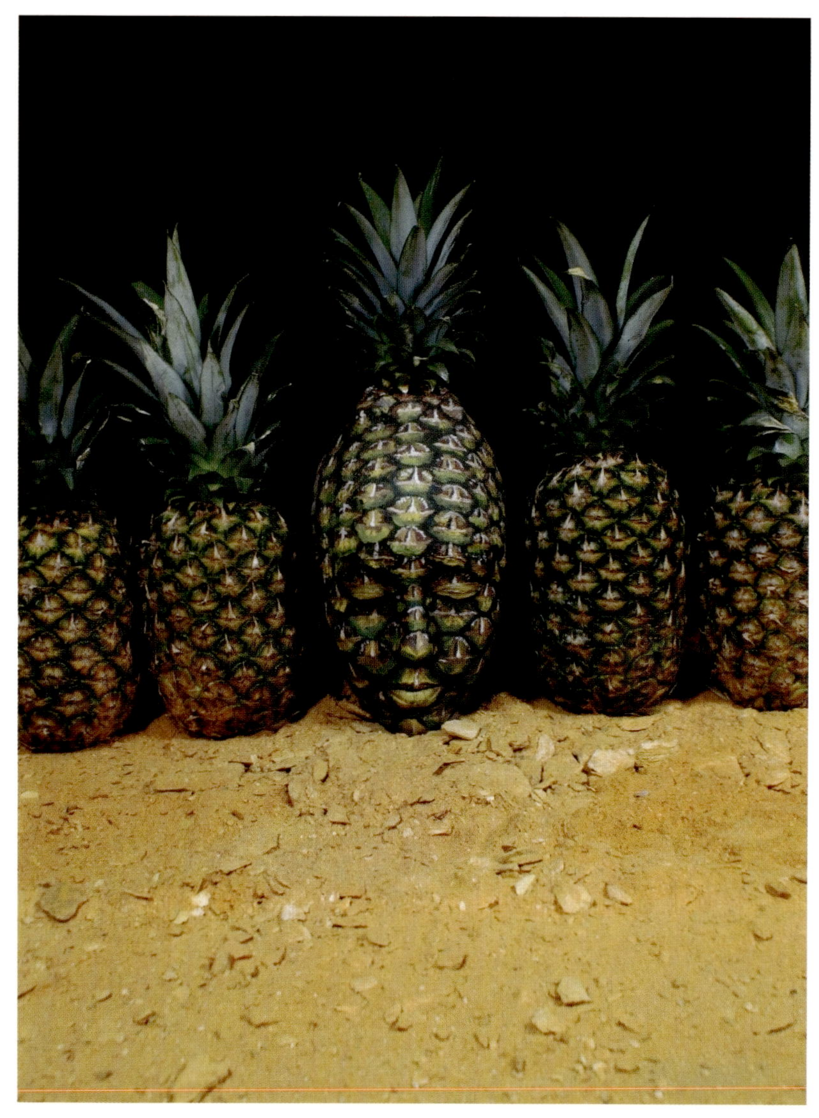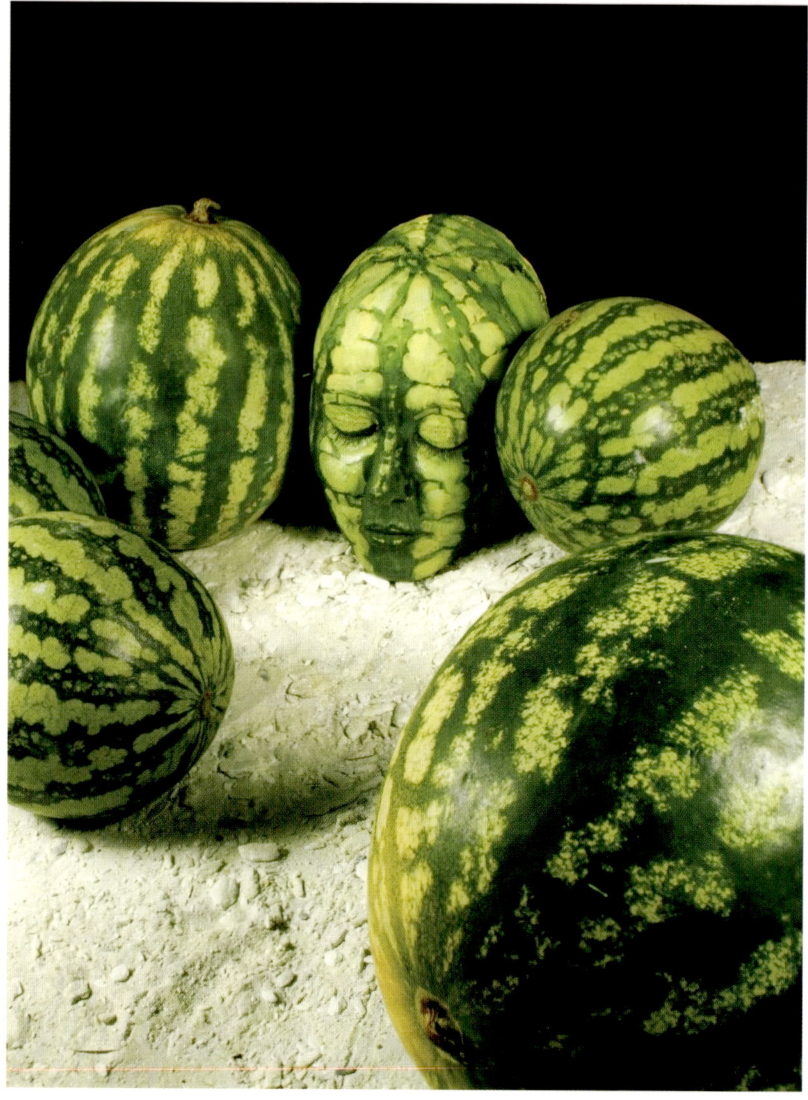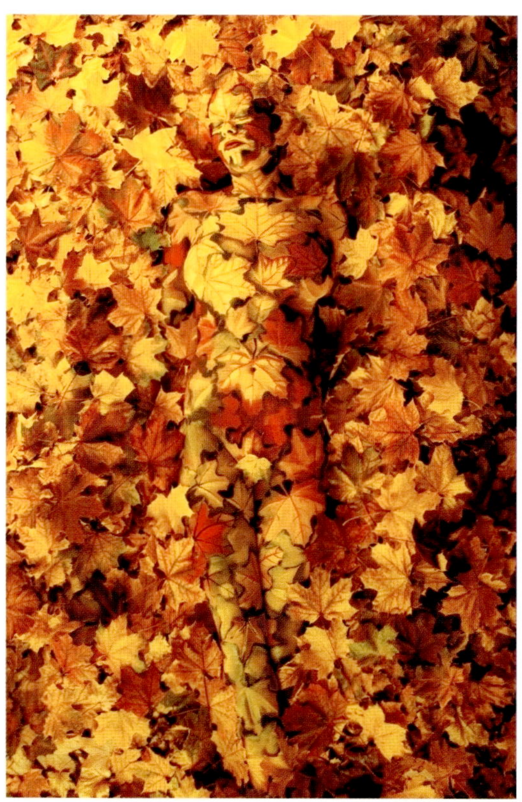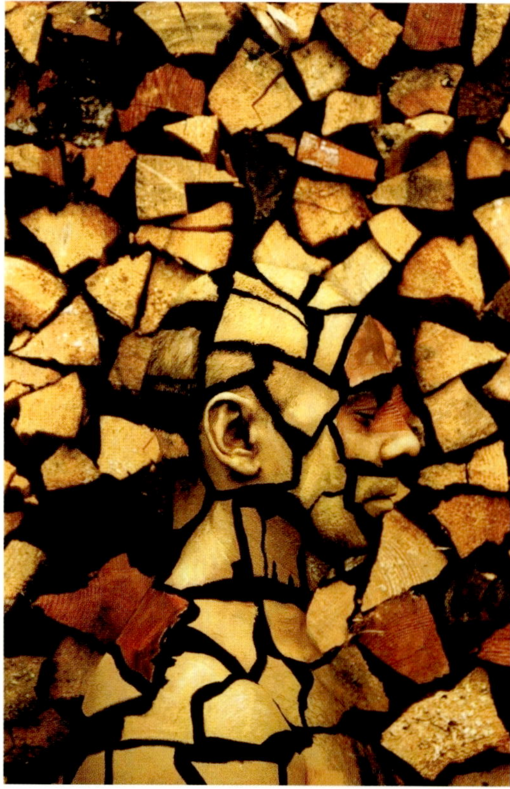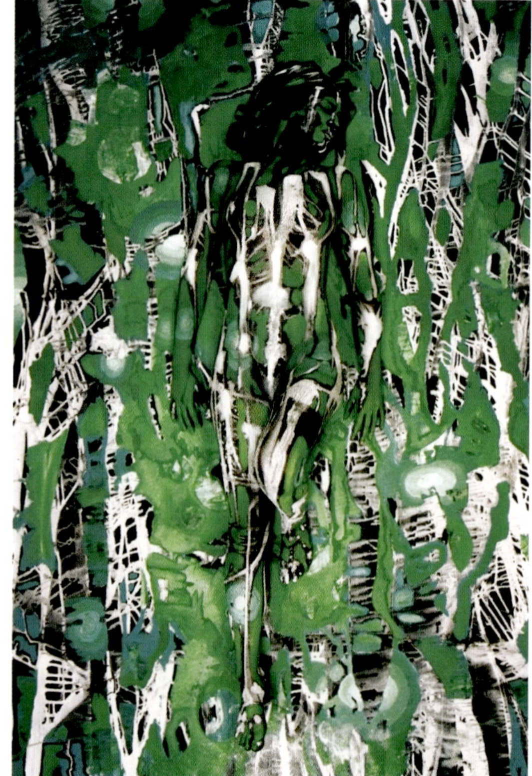

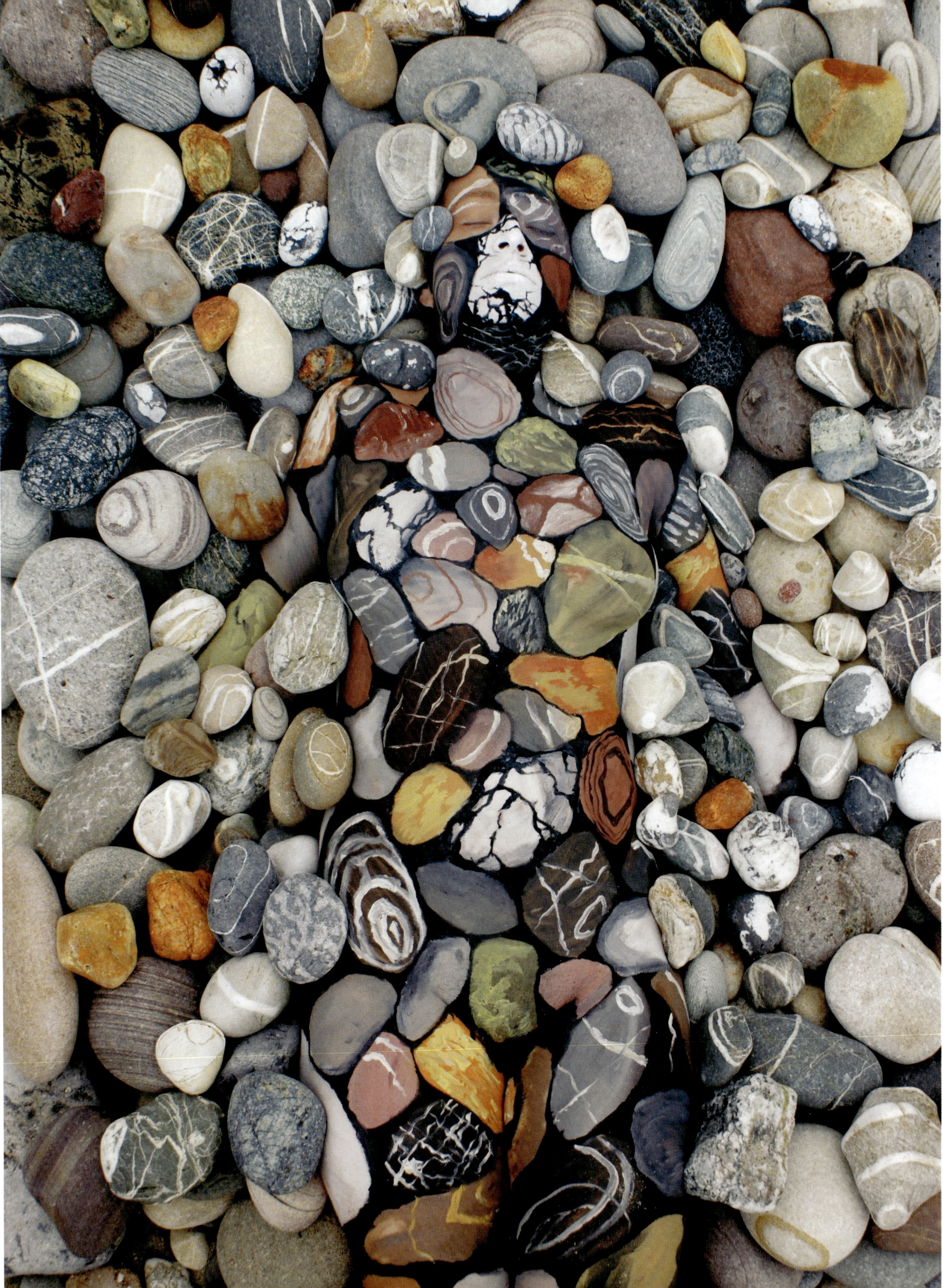

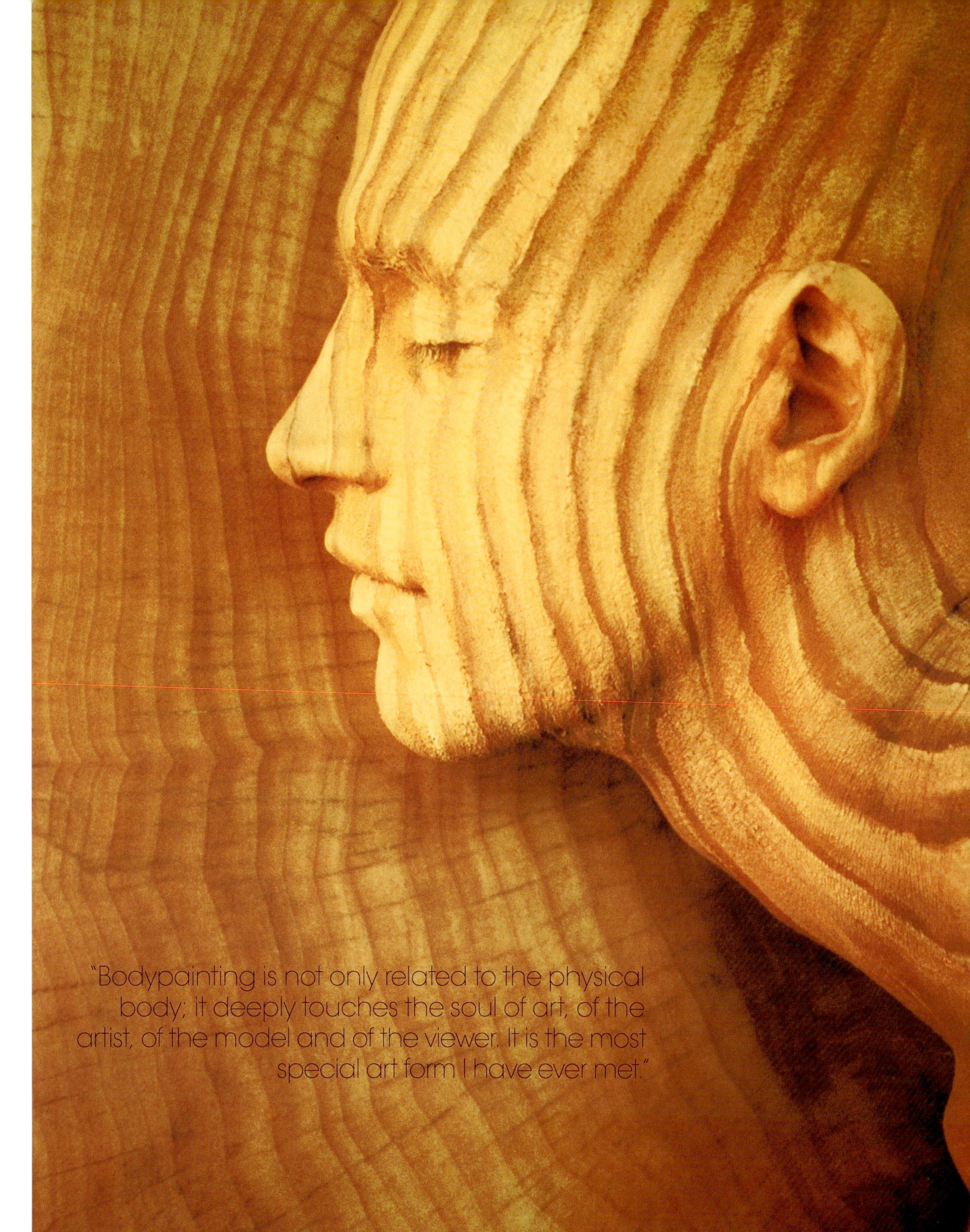
"Bodypainting is not only related to the physical
body; It deeply touches the soul of art, of the
artist, of the model and of the viewer. It is the most
special art form I have ever met."

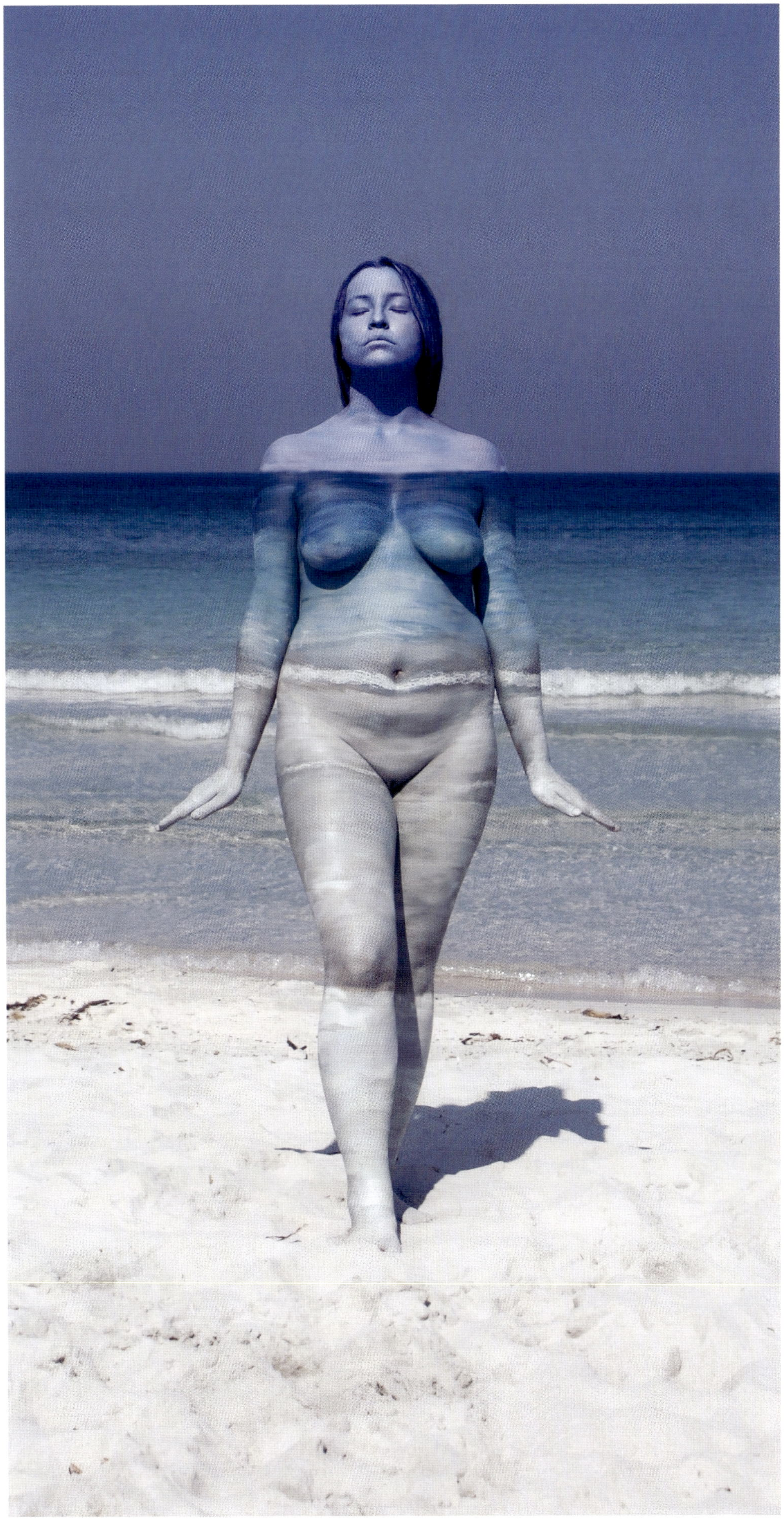

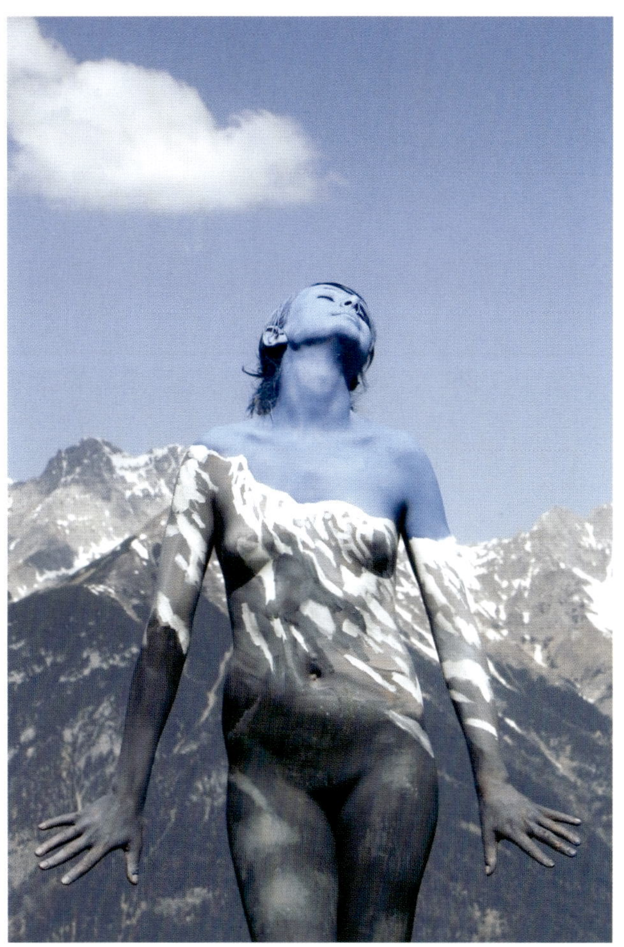

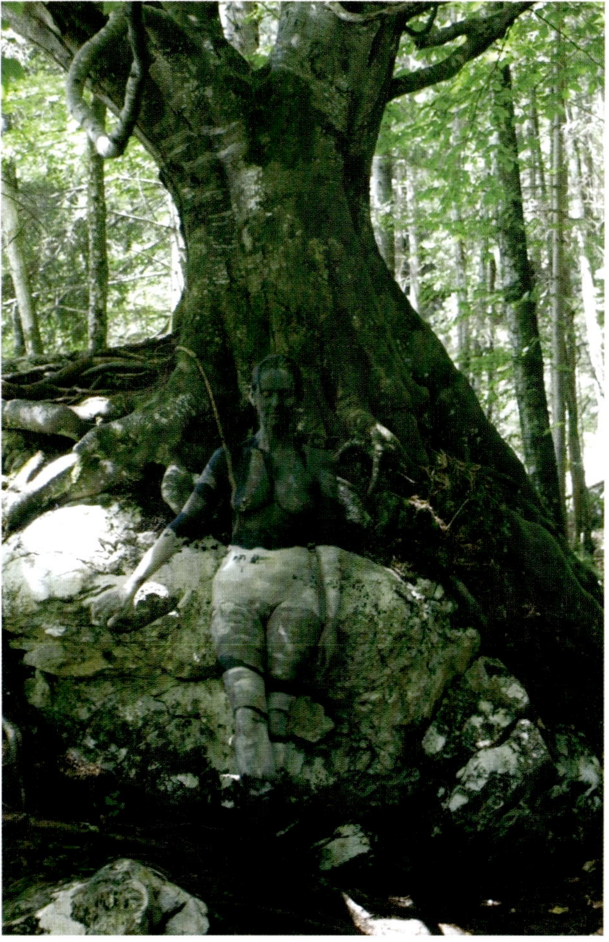

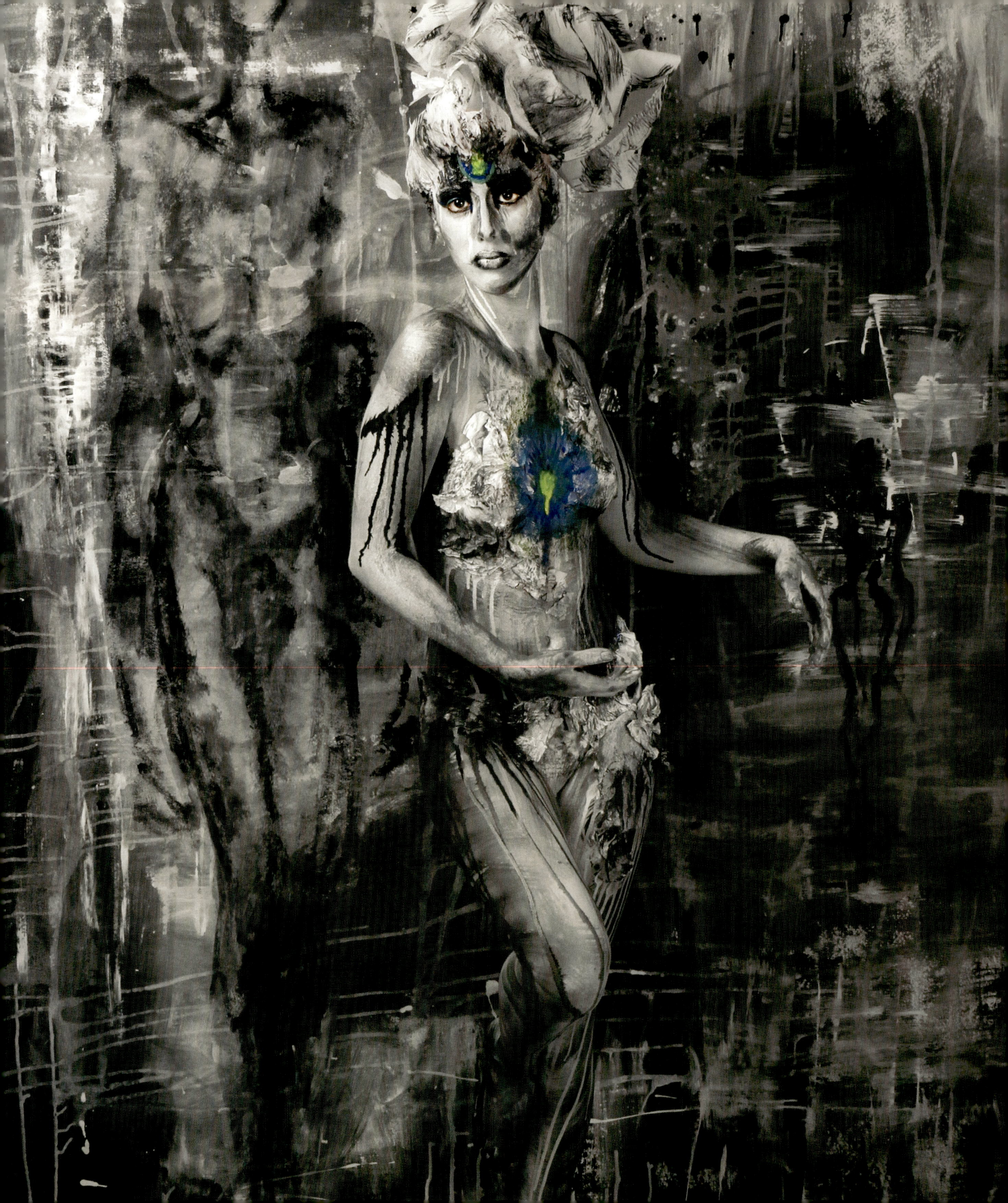

Karala B.

Karala B. is an author in the bodypainting industry with four body art books documenting the history and development of the industry. She designs and runs shows for the World Bodypainting Festival with up to fifteen artists and forty-five performers annually. Karala has personally experienced every aspect of body art as a presenter, painter, model, performer and photographer for more than fourteen years. She shares this insight with the world through writing and guest speaking.

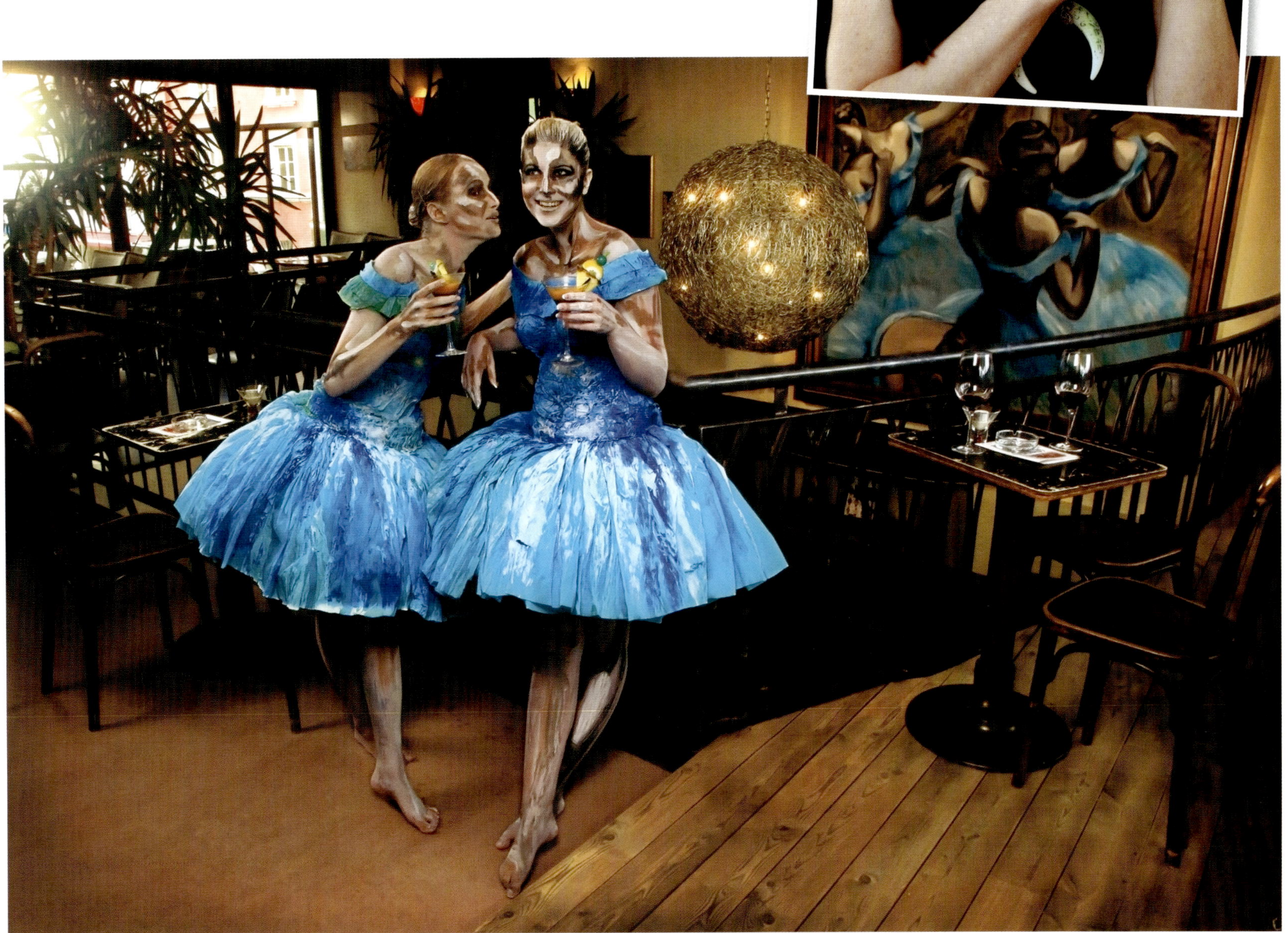

PHOTOGRAPHER JOSHUA DAVID LIM

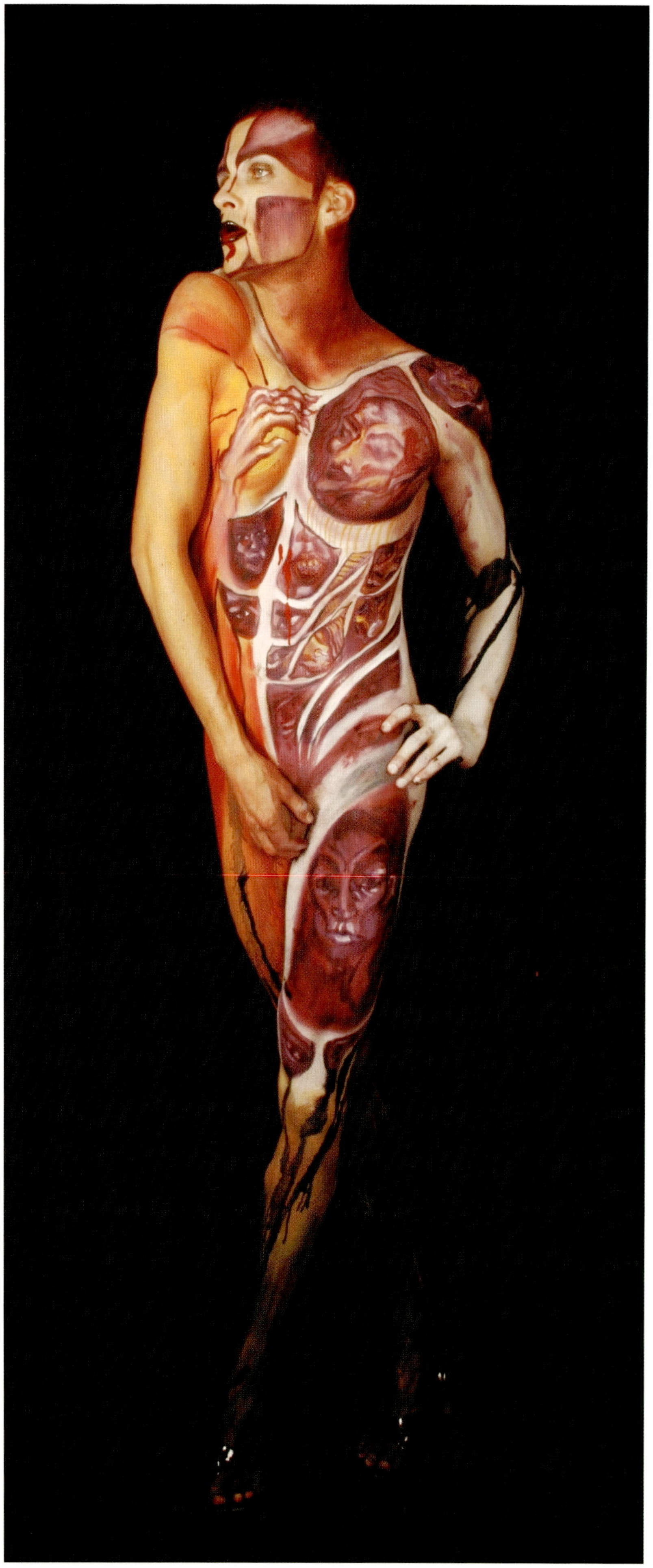

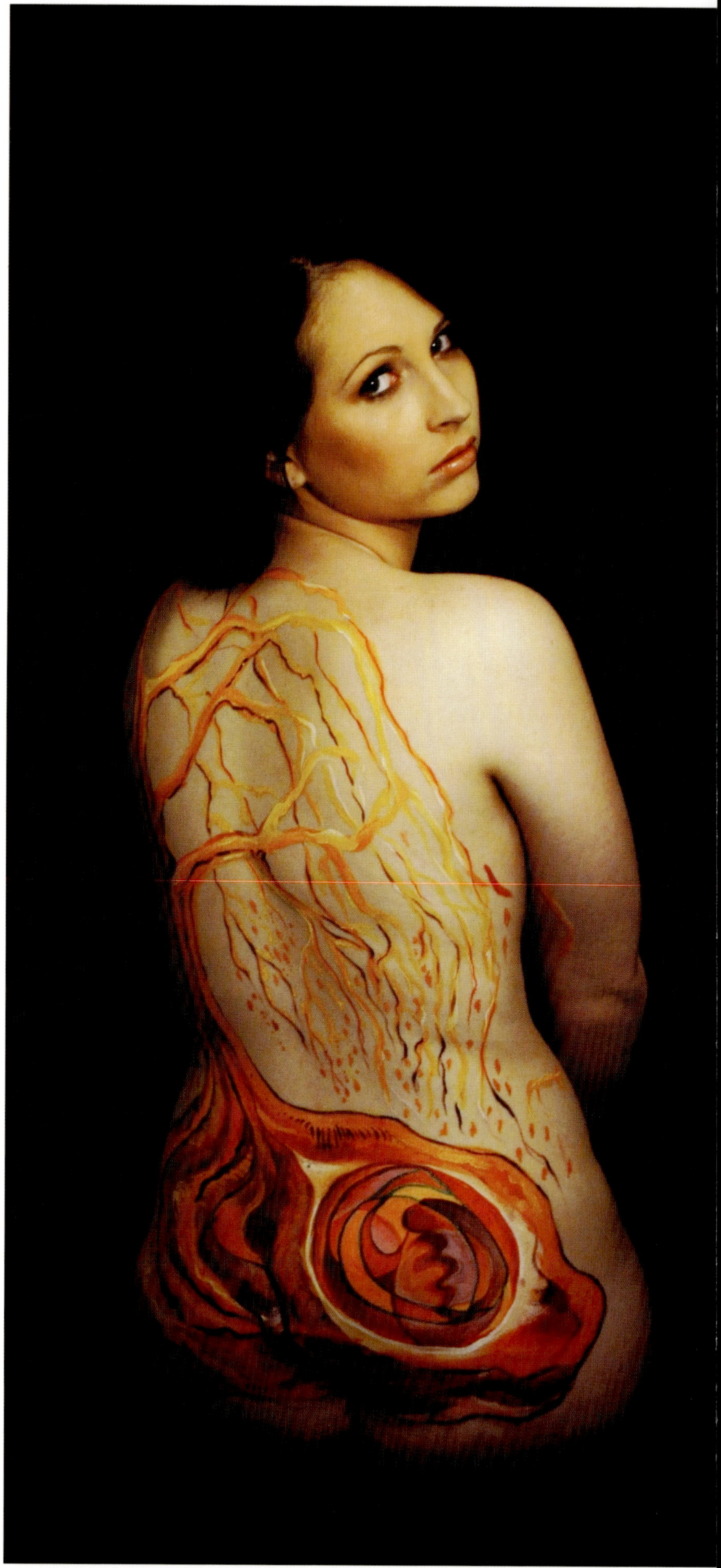

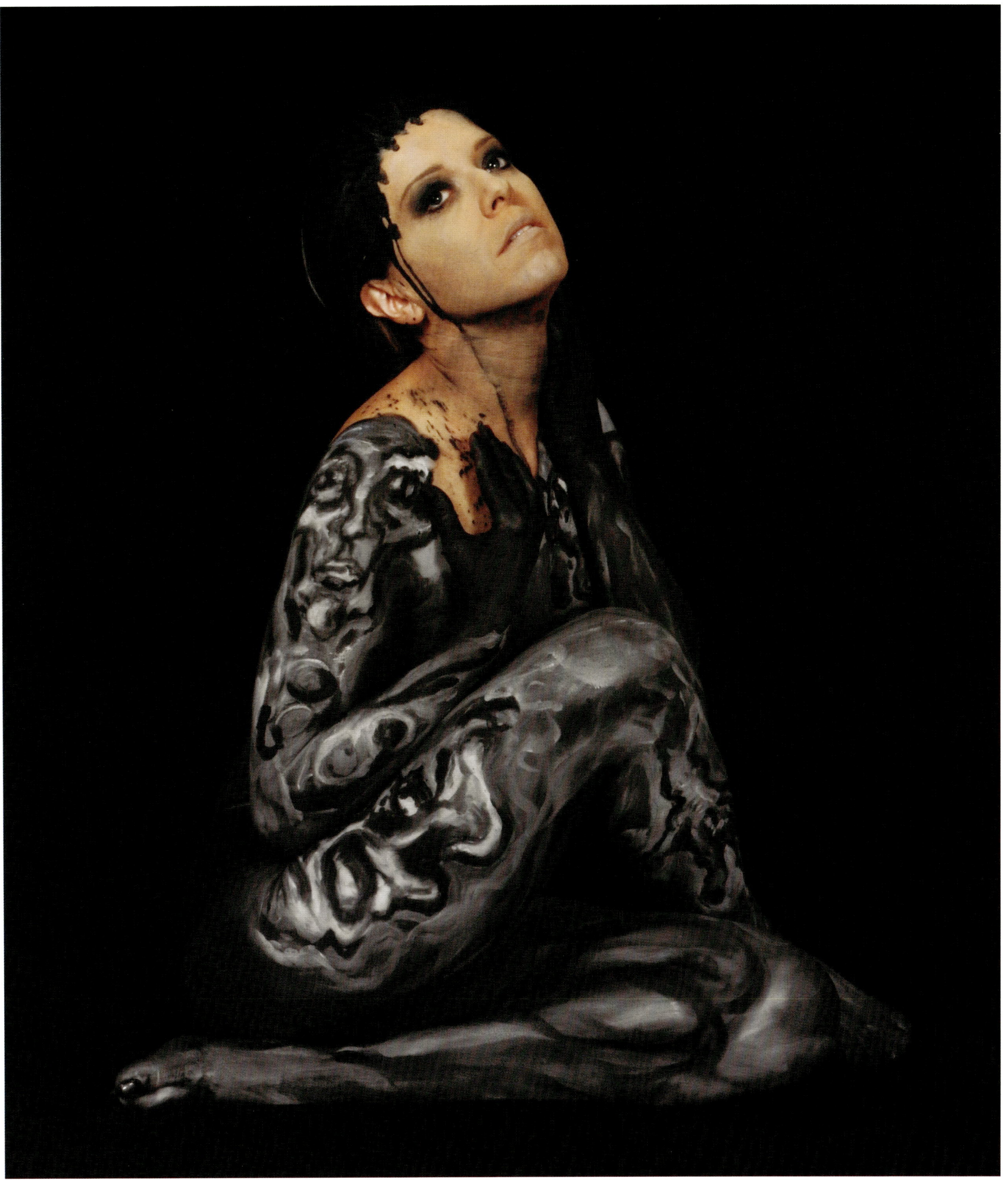

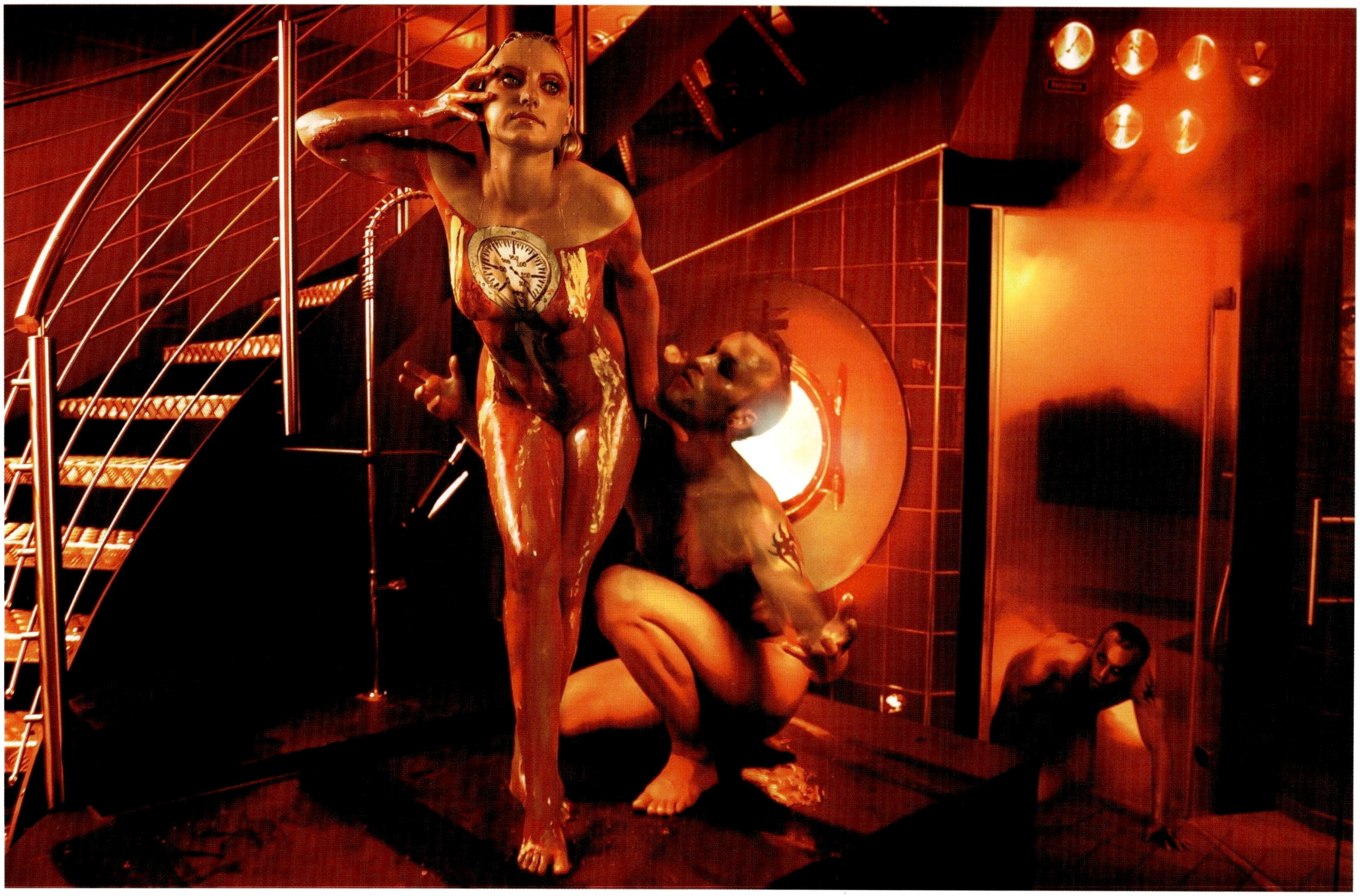

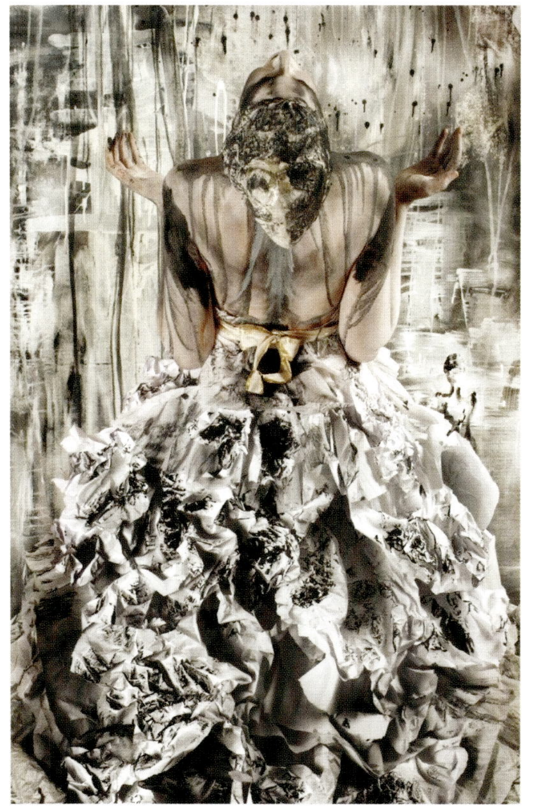

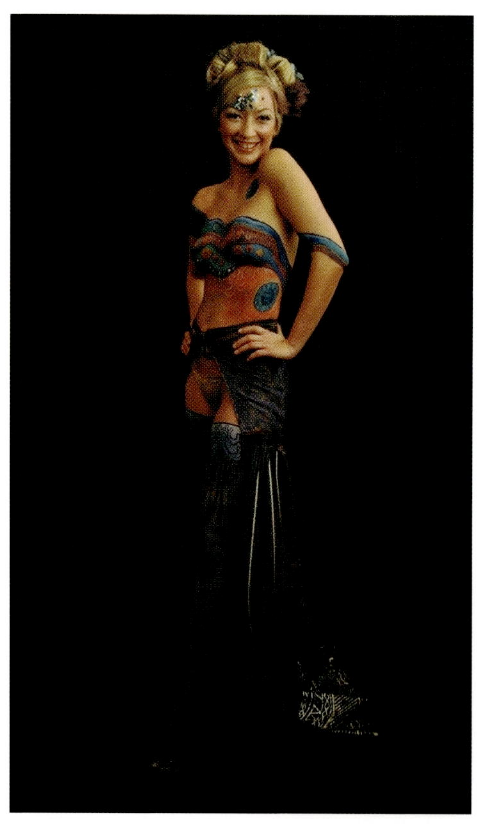

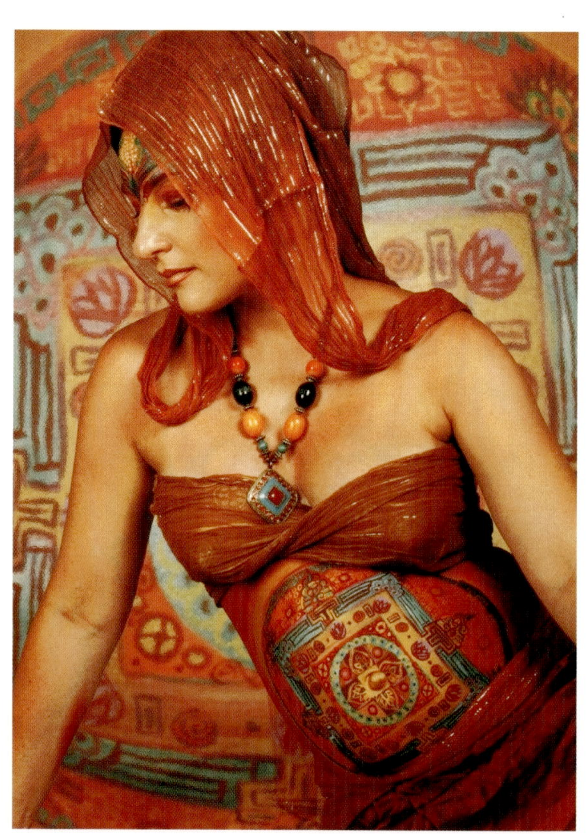

154

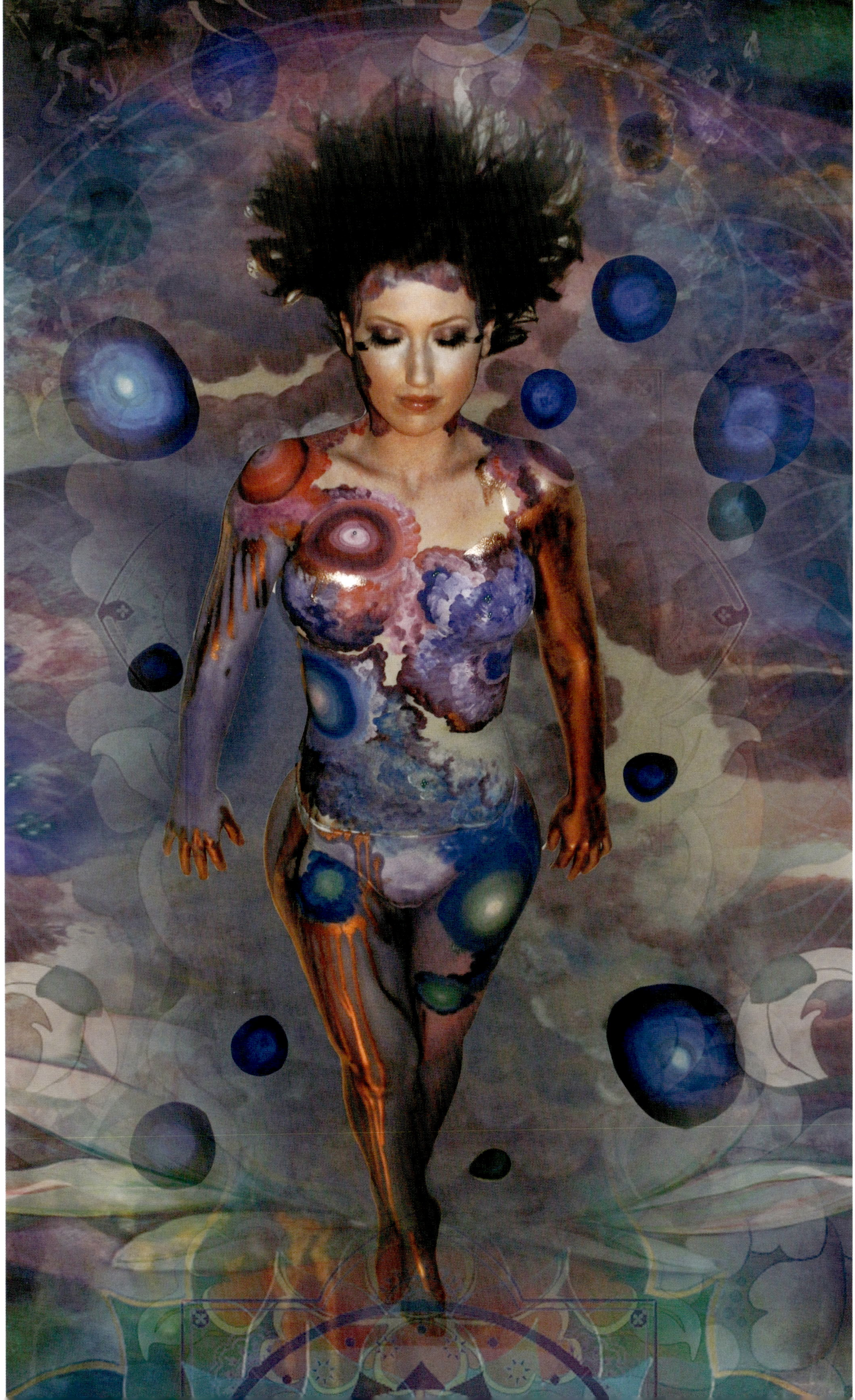

"Everything
you can
see is
made up
of shadow
and light.
Art is for
exploring
the spirit of
things."

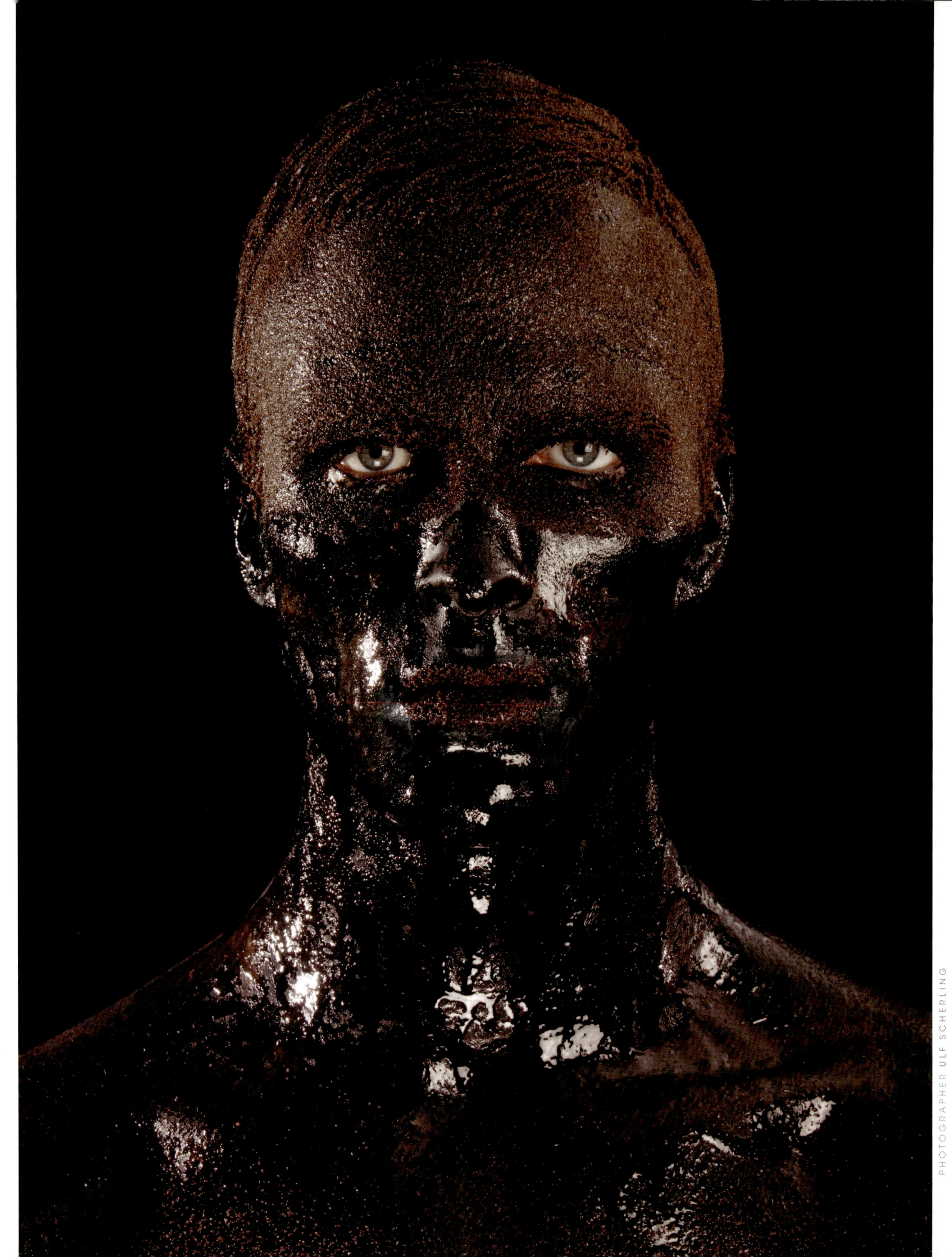

PHOTOGRAPHER ULF SCHERLING

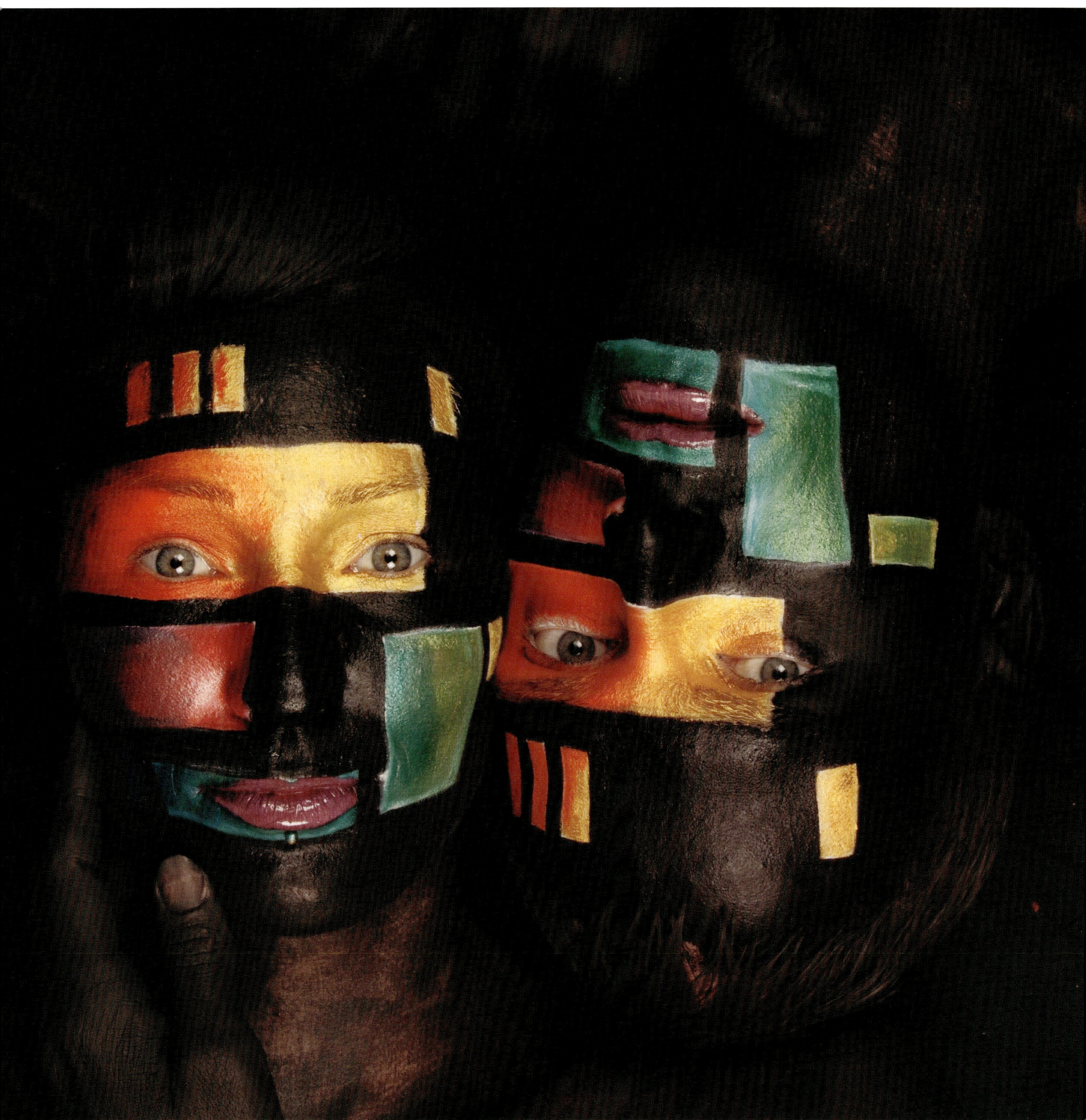

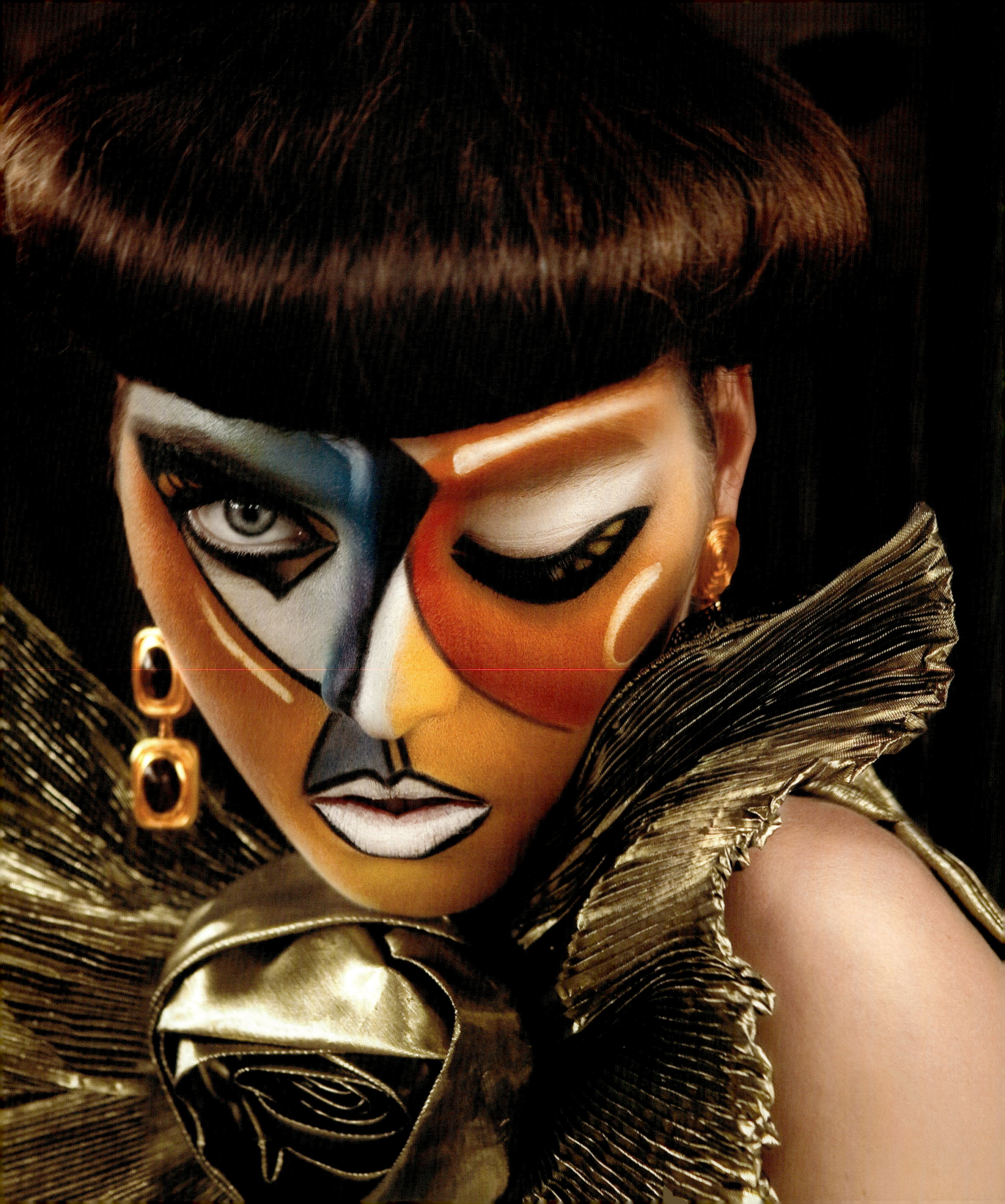

Karen Yiu

WWW.KARENYIU.COM

The art of Chinese-born Karen Yiu is rich, delicate and innovative. Karen's journey to becoming a bodypainting artist has crossed as much physical space as it has taken time and practice. Her journey began at the age of six, when she moved to Hong Kong and was exposed to the life and art of the city. Karen finished a degree in social work and on a whim took a makeup course with a Parisian tutor before moving to London and studying at the London College of Fashion, where she learned about body art for the first time. Karen has become the leading fashion body art specialist in Hong Kong.

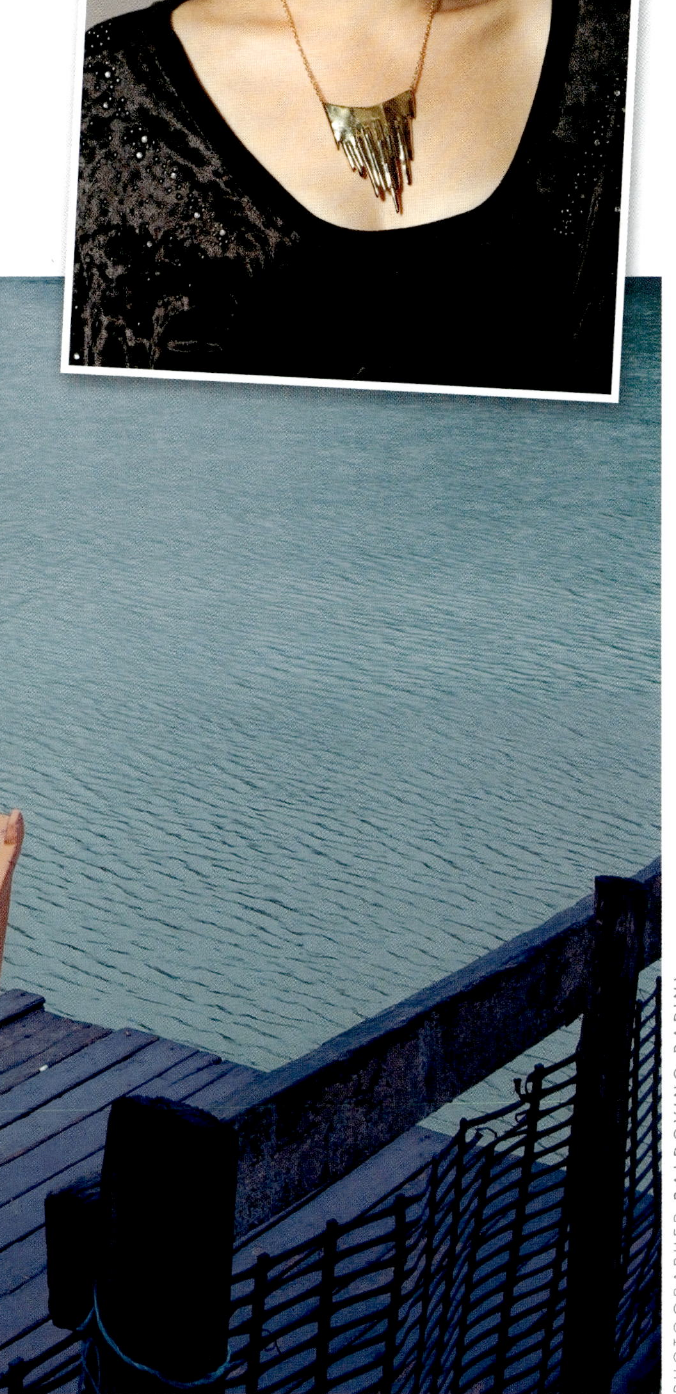

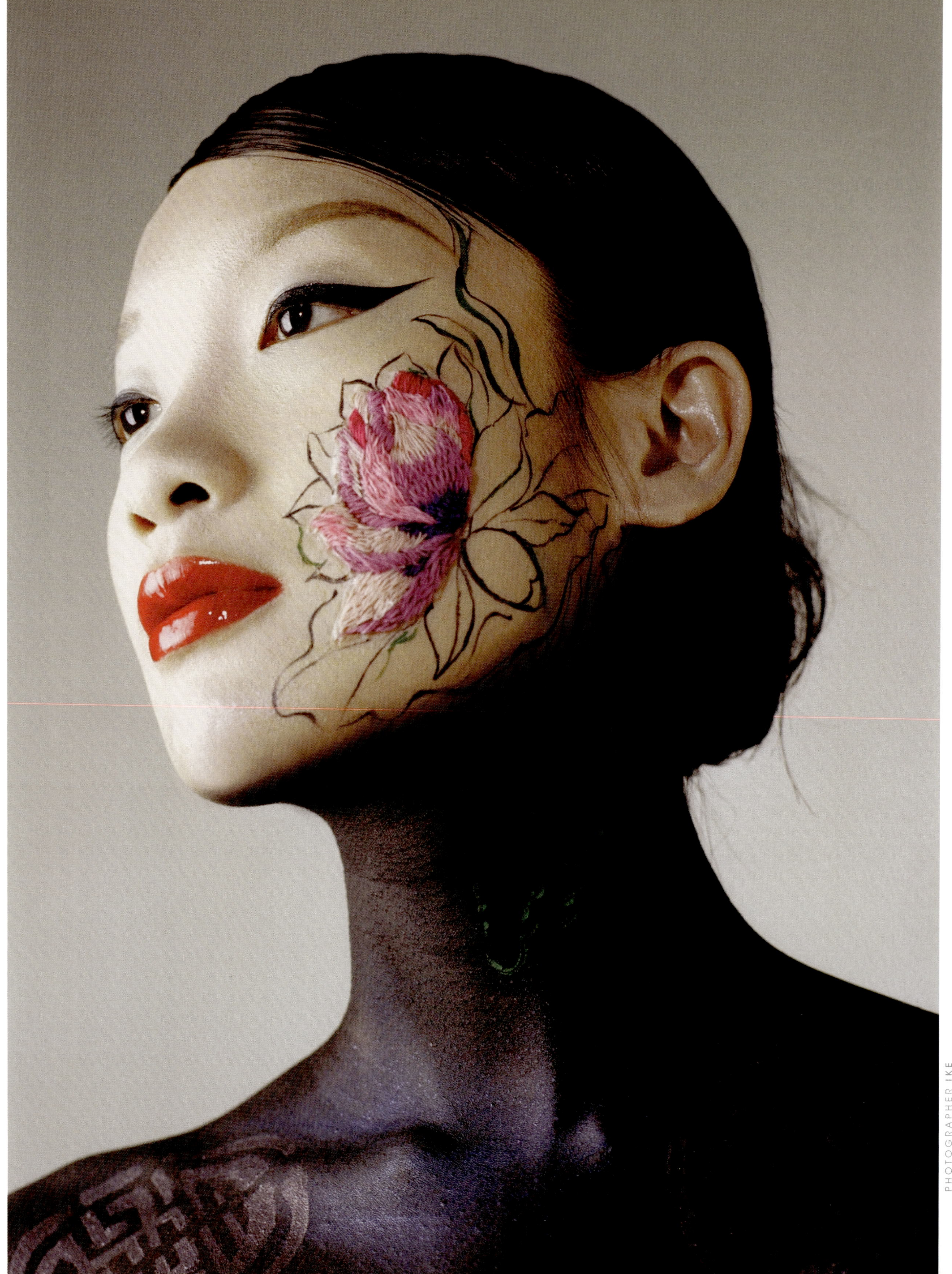
PHOTOGRAPHER IKE

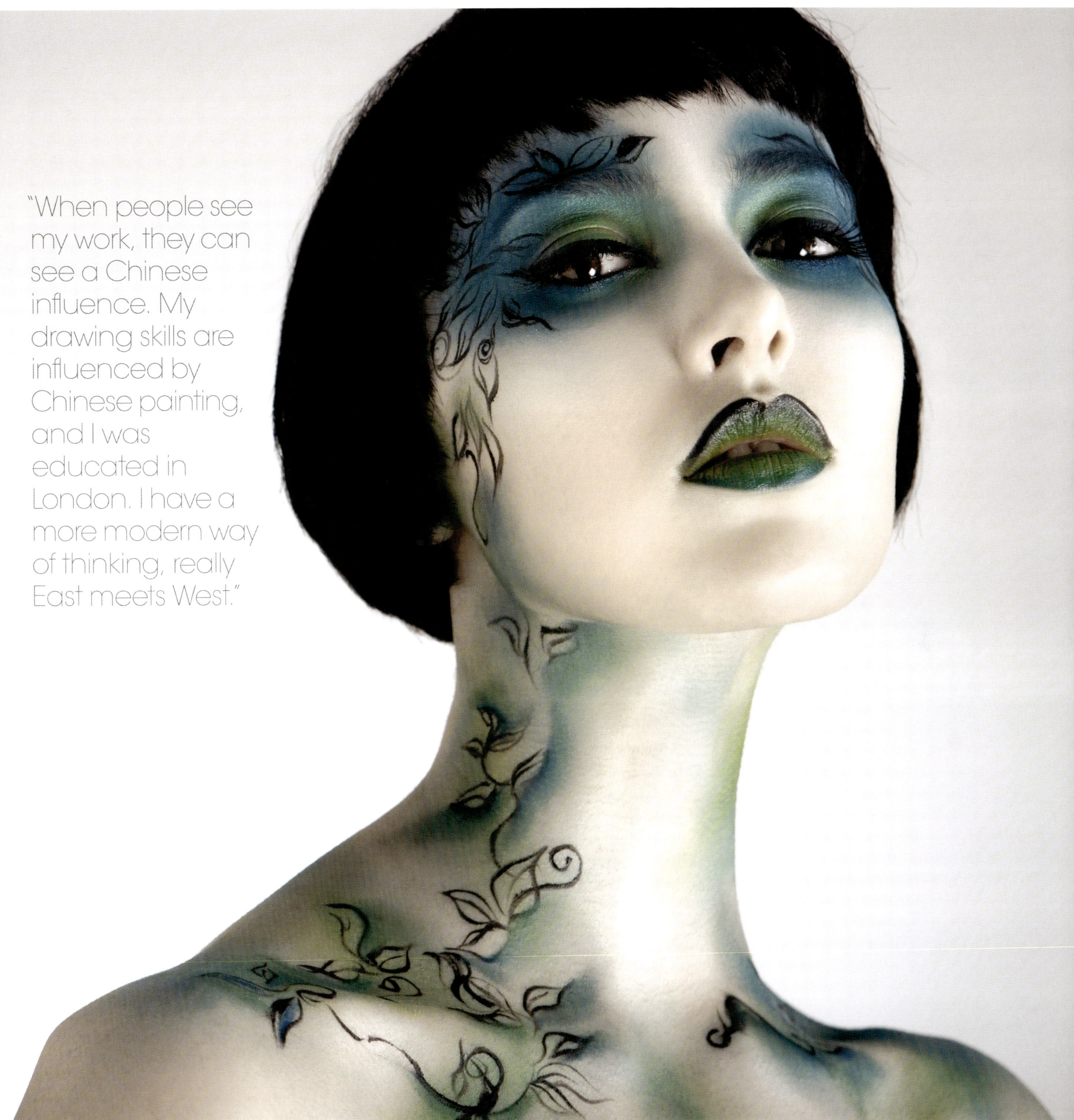

"When people see my work, they can see a Chinese influence. My drawing skills are influenced by Chinese painting, and I was educated in London. I have a more modern way of thinking, really East meets West."

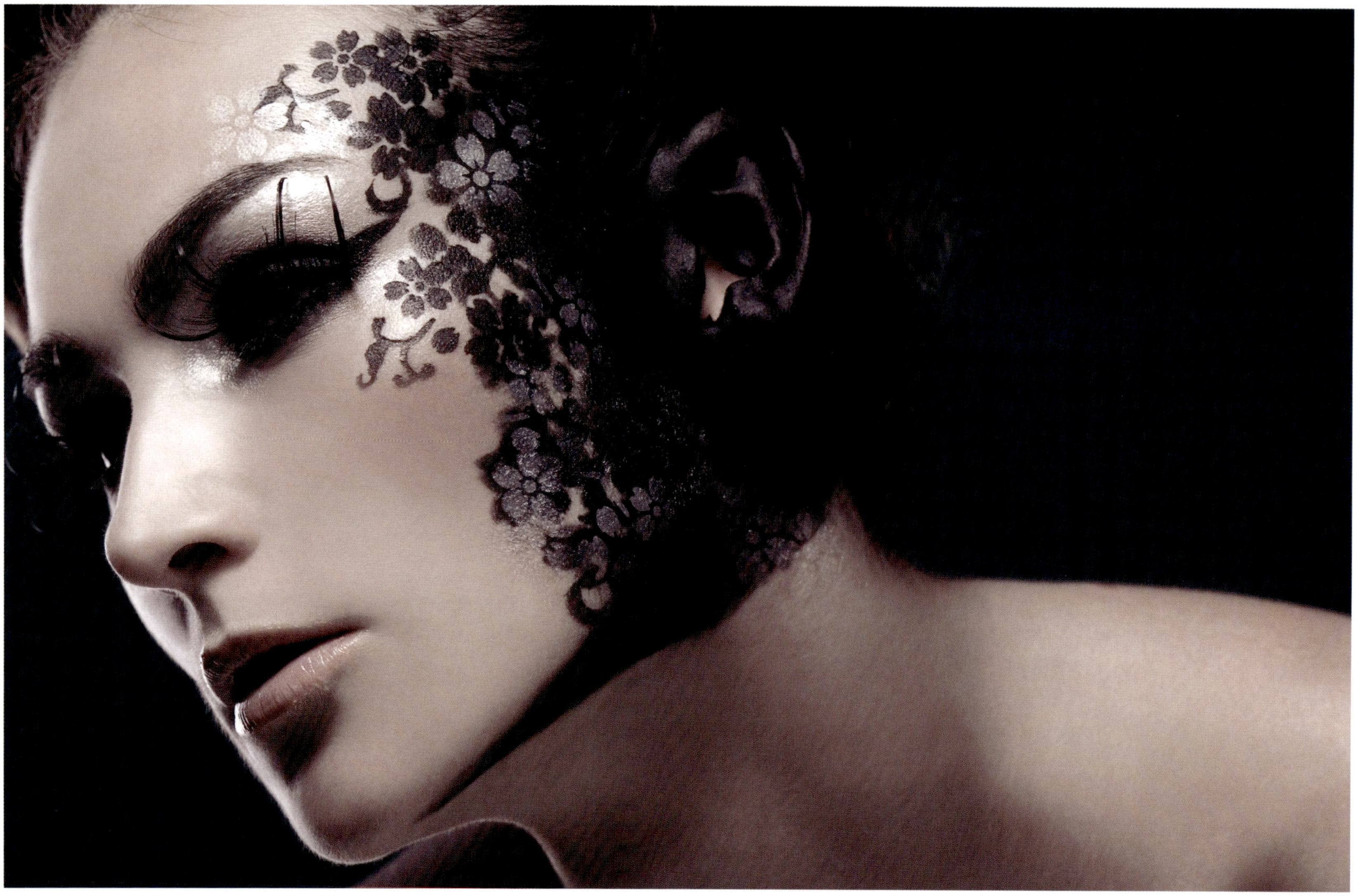

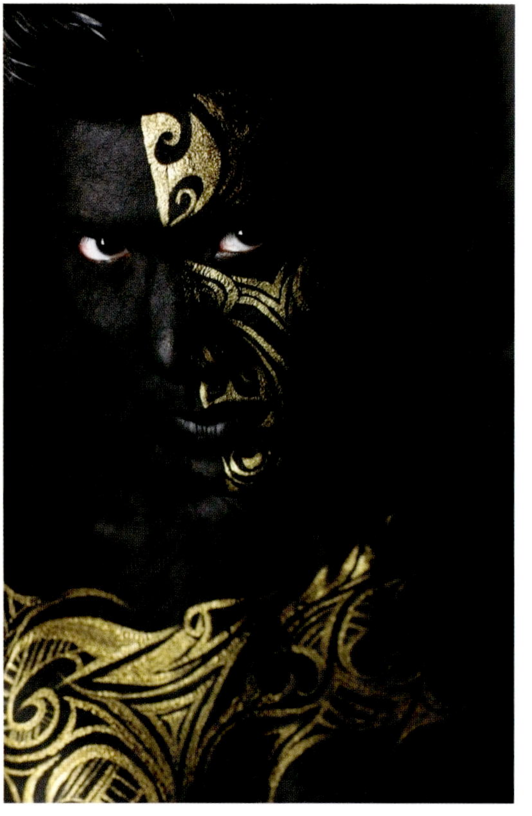

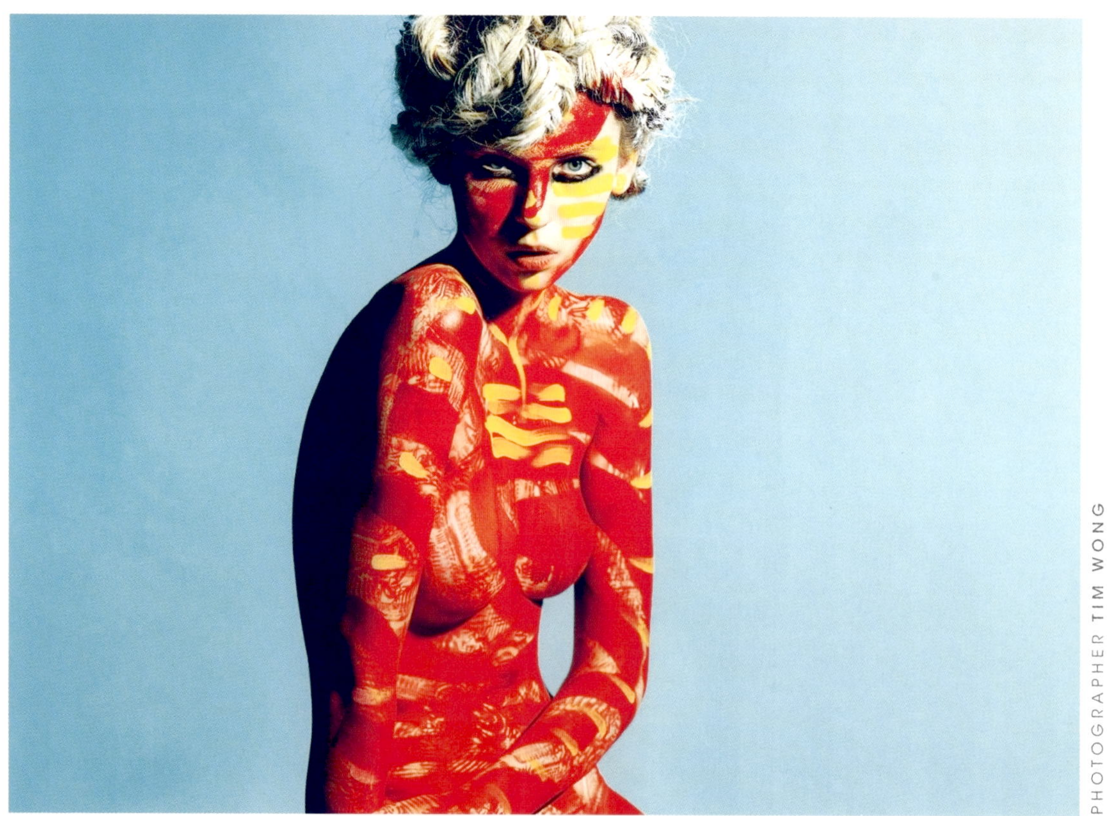

PHOTOGRAPHER IKE (LEFT, BOTTOM LEFT AND OPPOSITE)

PHOTOGRAPHER TIM WONG

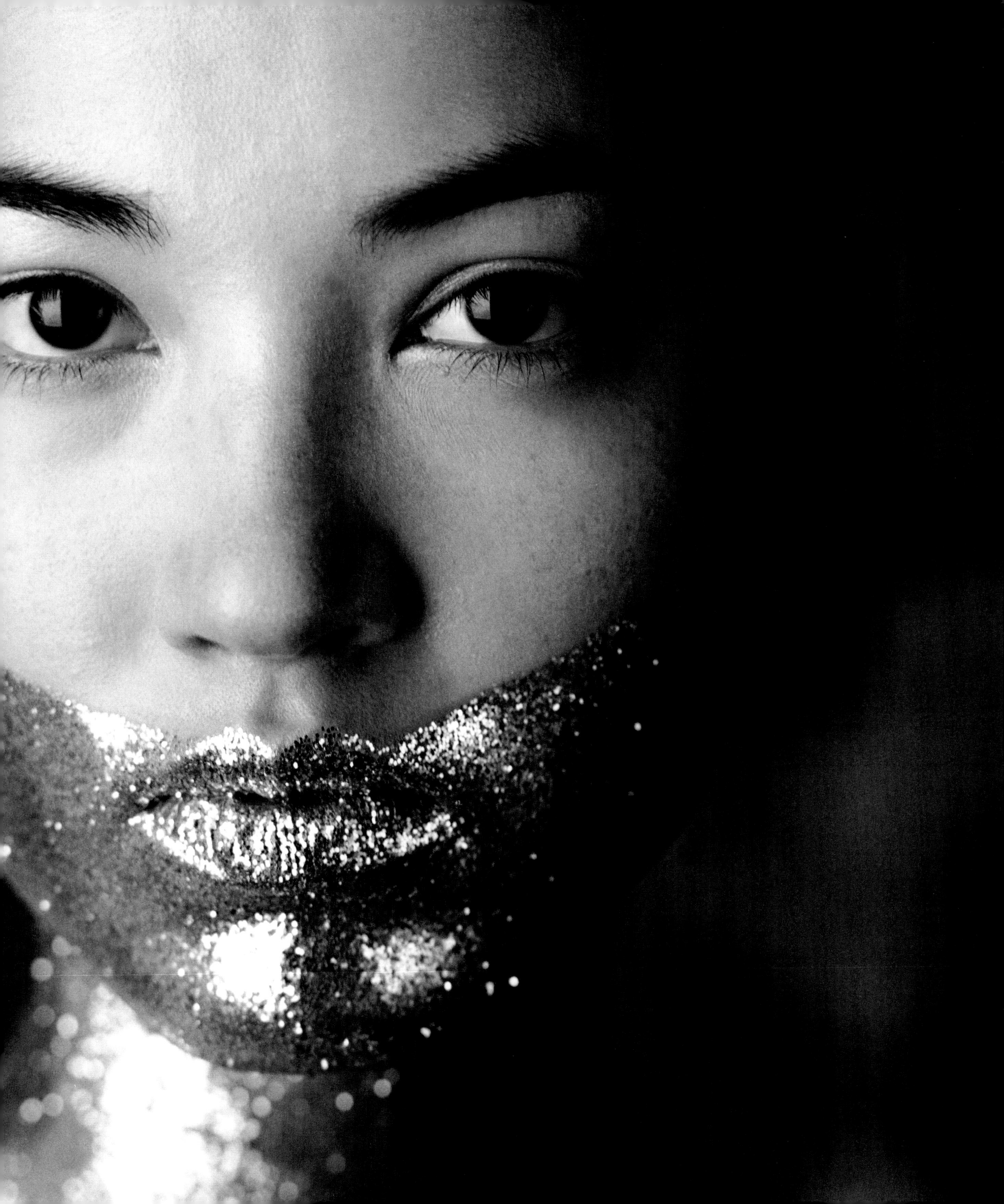

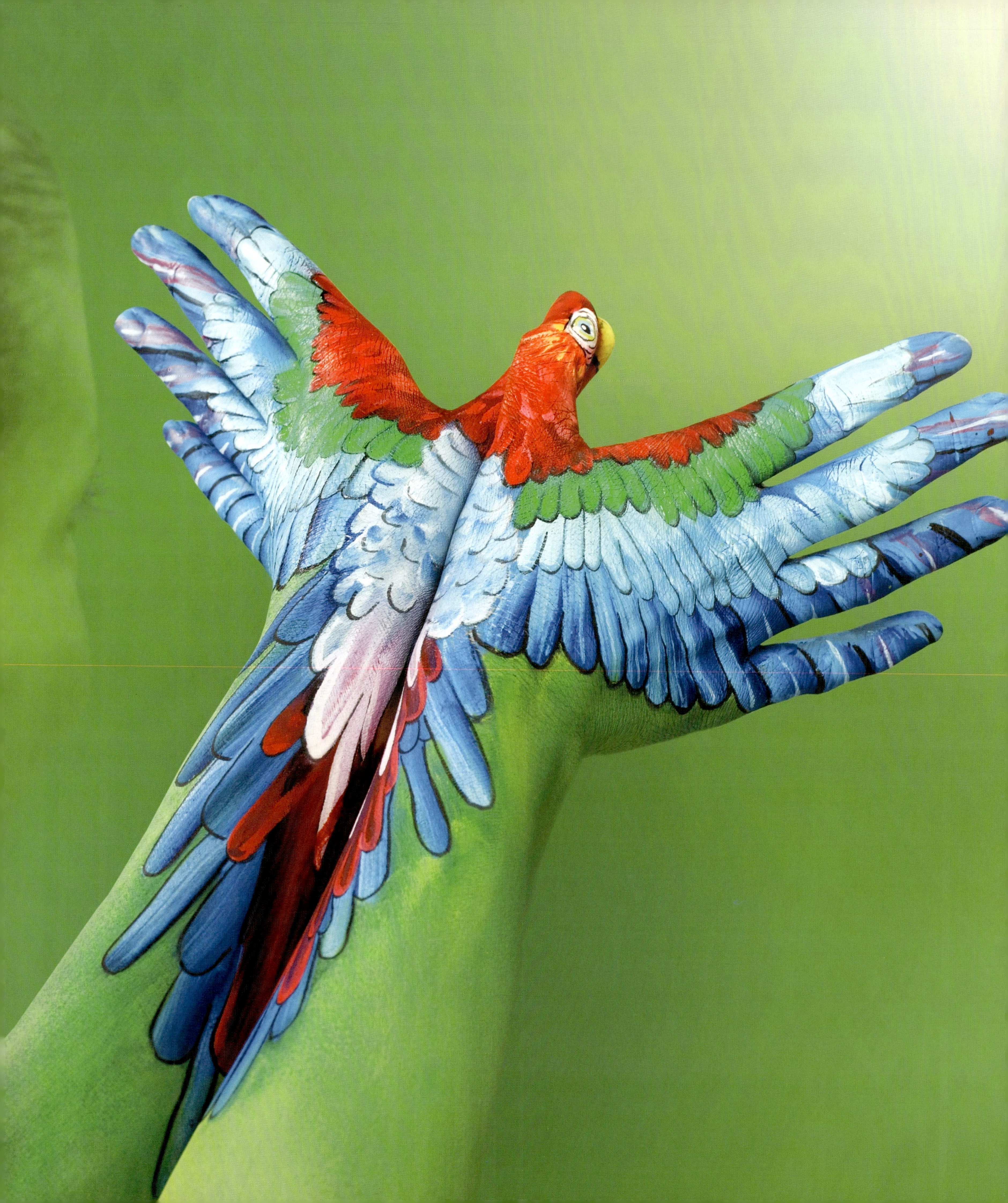

Kate Dean

Kate "Spinklesparks" Dean has been a professional face and bodypainter for more than twelve years. Based in Somerset, UK, Kate is a well-established and accomplished artist who prides herself on her high-quality paintings and professionalism. In 2009 she was crowned Freestyle Glitter Bodypainting Champion at the World Bodypainting Championships in Austria, and in 2010 she entered the Brush and Sponge World Awards.

In July 2010 Kate appeared as a featured artist in Issue 12 of *Illusion Magazine*, the magazine for face and bodypainters worldwide, and her work was included in *Body Art Fashion* by Karala B.

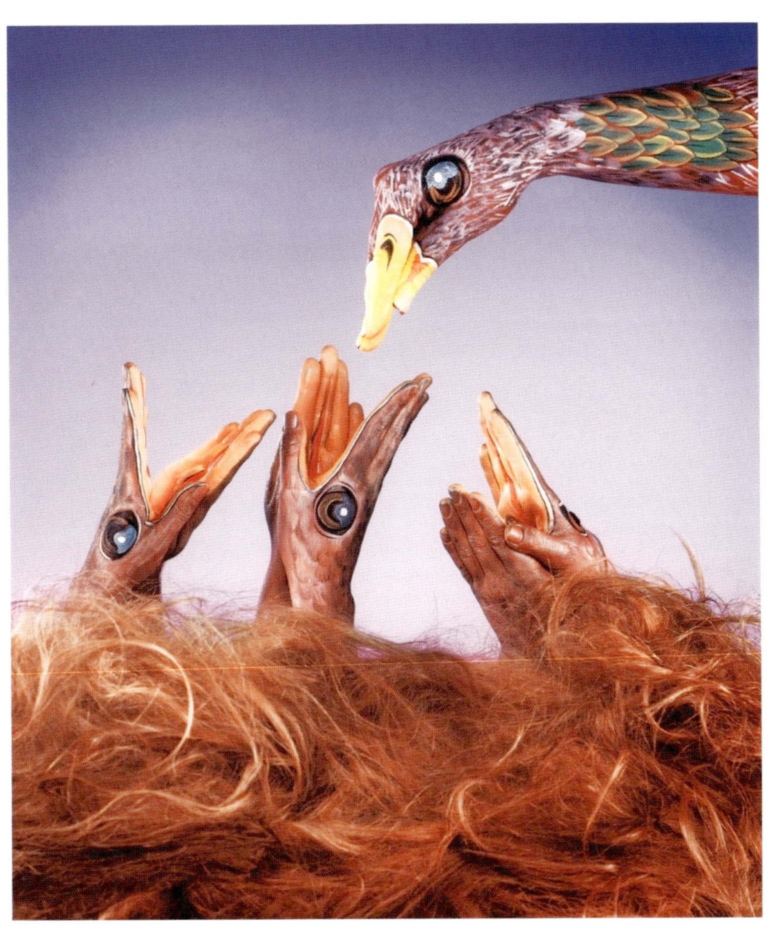

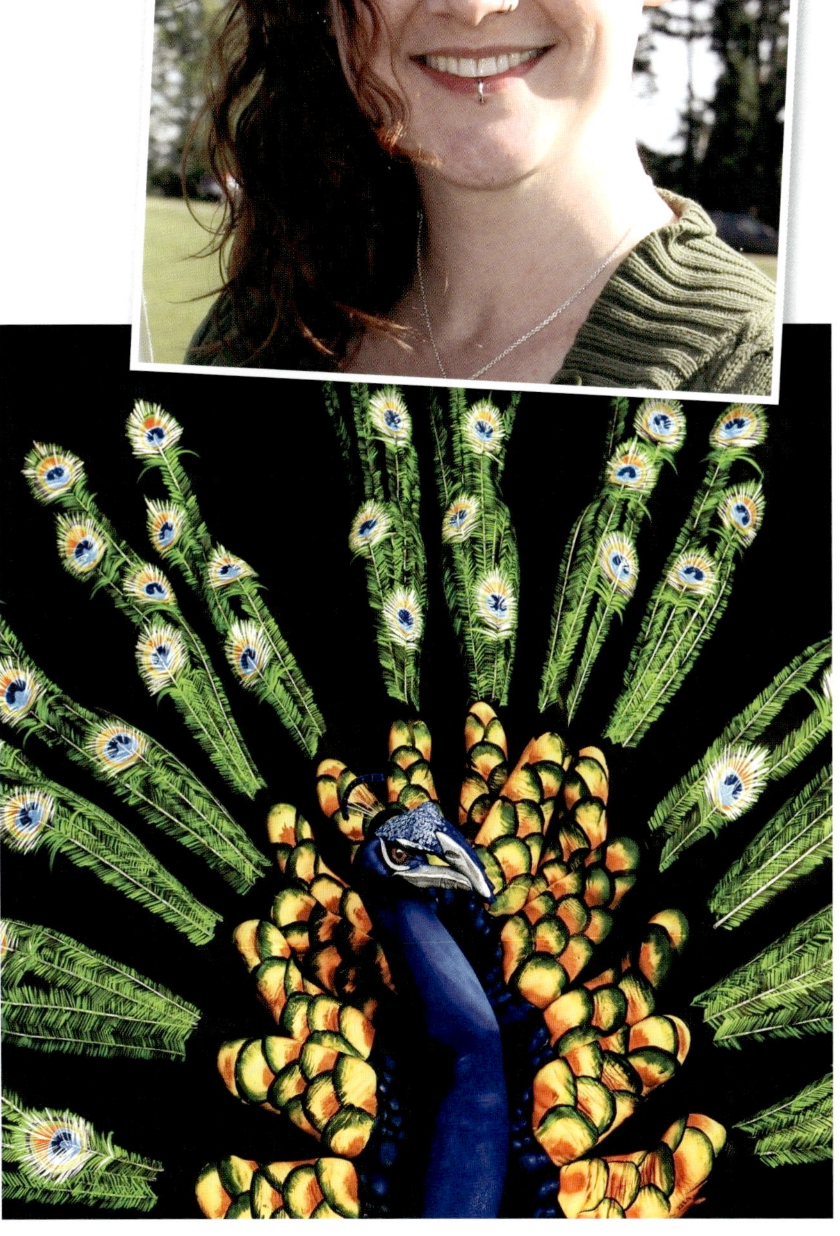

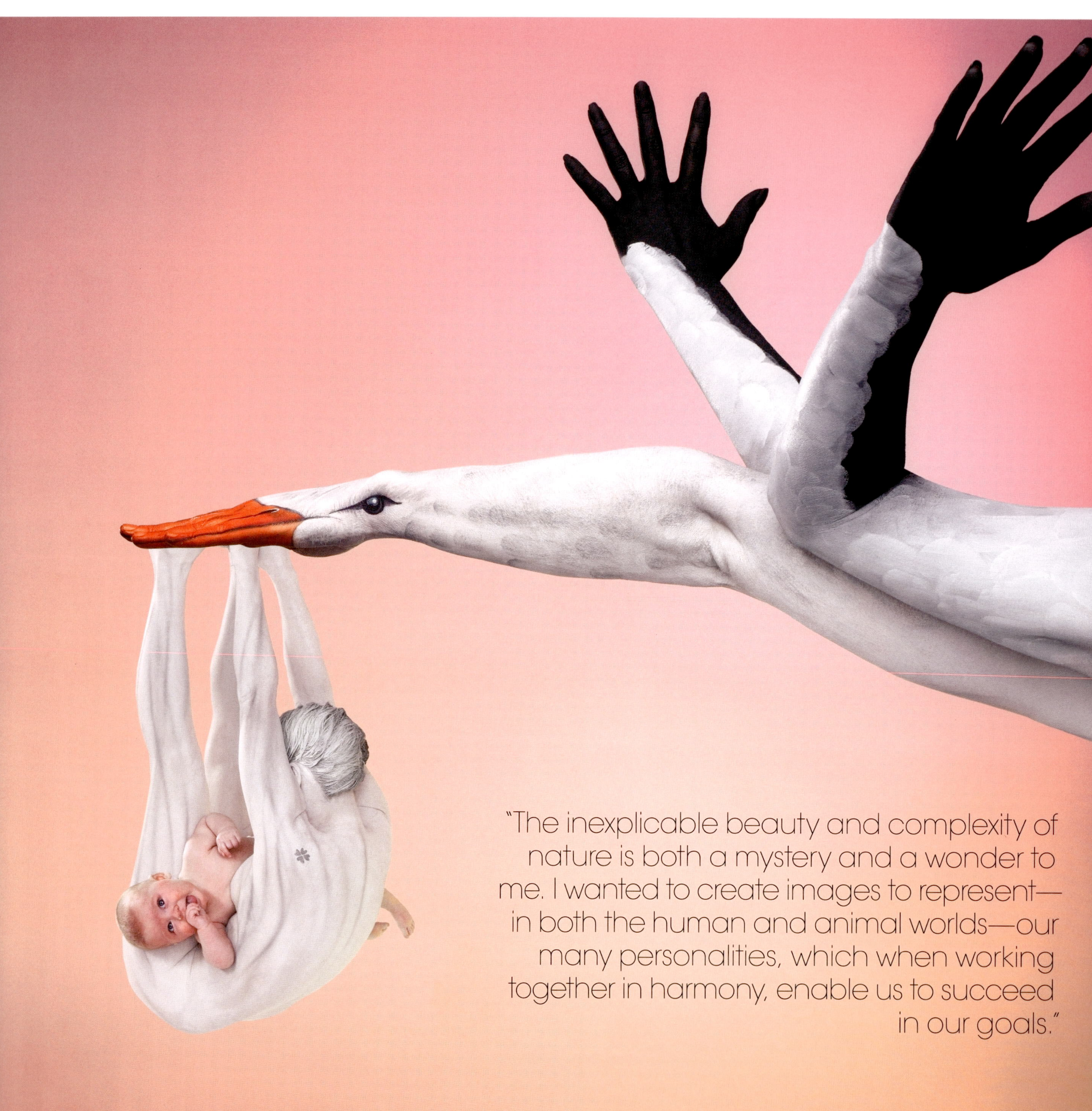

"The inexplicable beauty and complexity of nature is both a mystery and a wonder to me. I wanted to create images to represent— in both the human and animal worlds—our many personalities, which when working together in harmony, enable us to succeed in our goals."

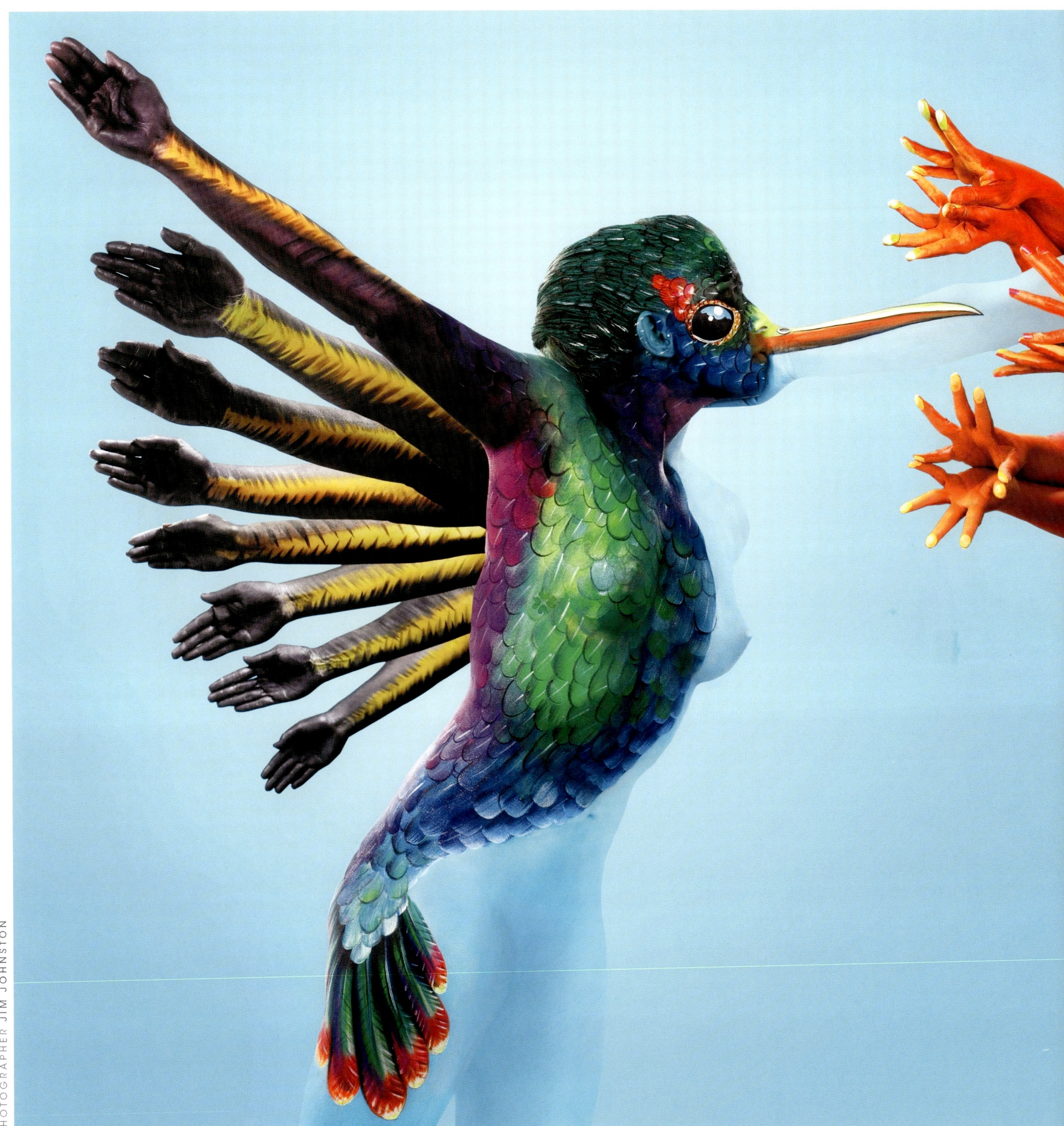

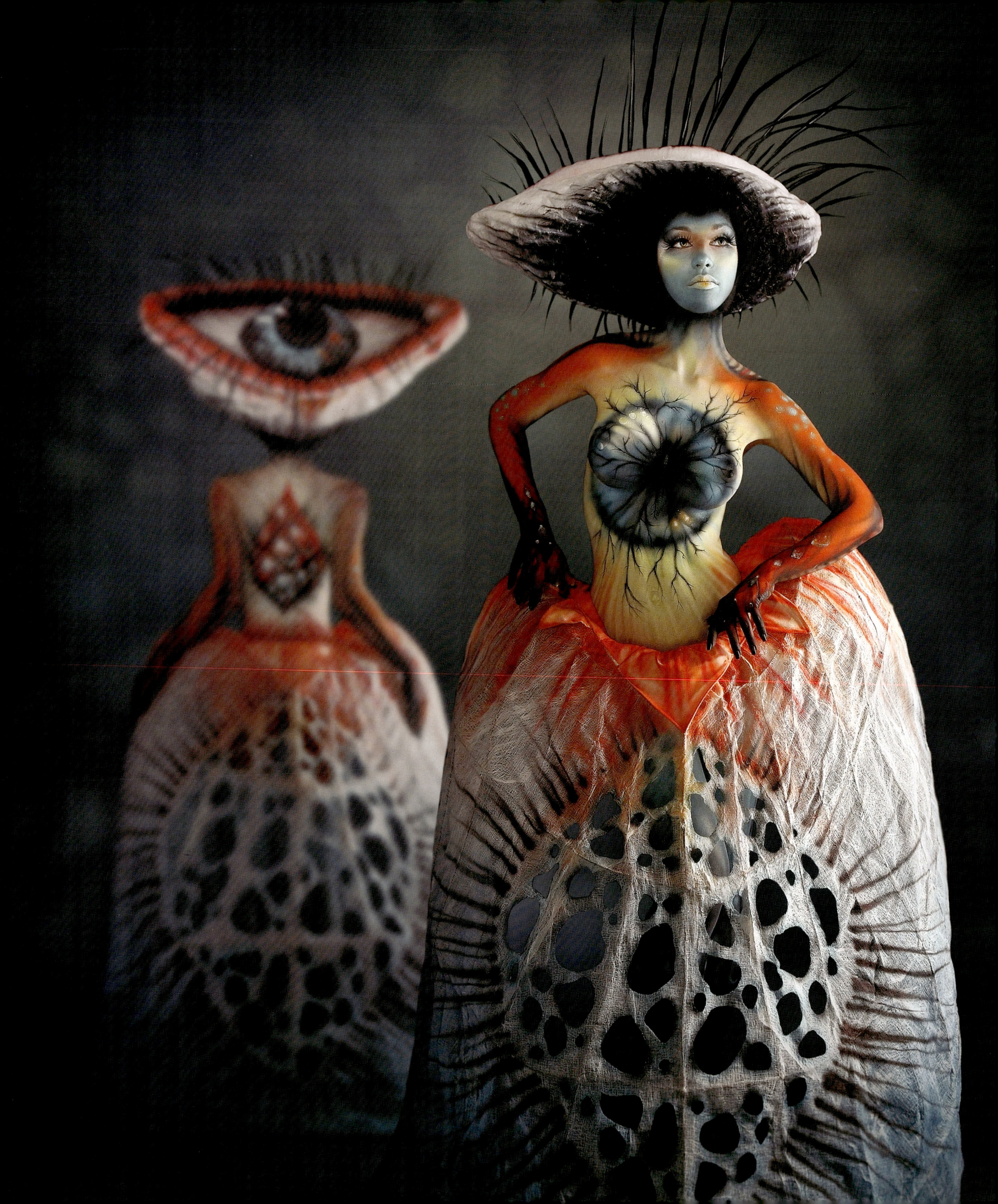

Kristina Elizarova

WWW.ELIZARTE.RU

When Kristina Elizarova began bodypainting with an airbrush in 2007, there was no school in her city where she could learn the technique. As a dedicated artist spending up to twenty hours on one drawing, it was a challenge to create fine art on a human body in only four hours. But the results have led Kristina on a trail of creation, and she quickly has become recognized as a newcomer to watch in the industry. While quietly creating in her own country, Russia, Kristina received worldwide respect as a bodypainter in a matter of days when her artwork was shared throughout the bodypainting community. Kristina now works and teaches internationally.

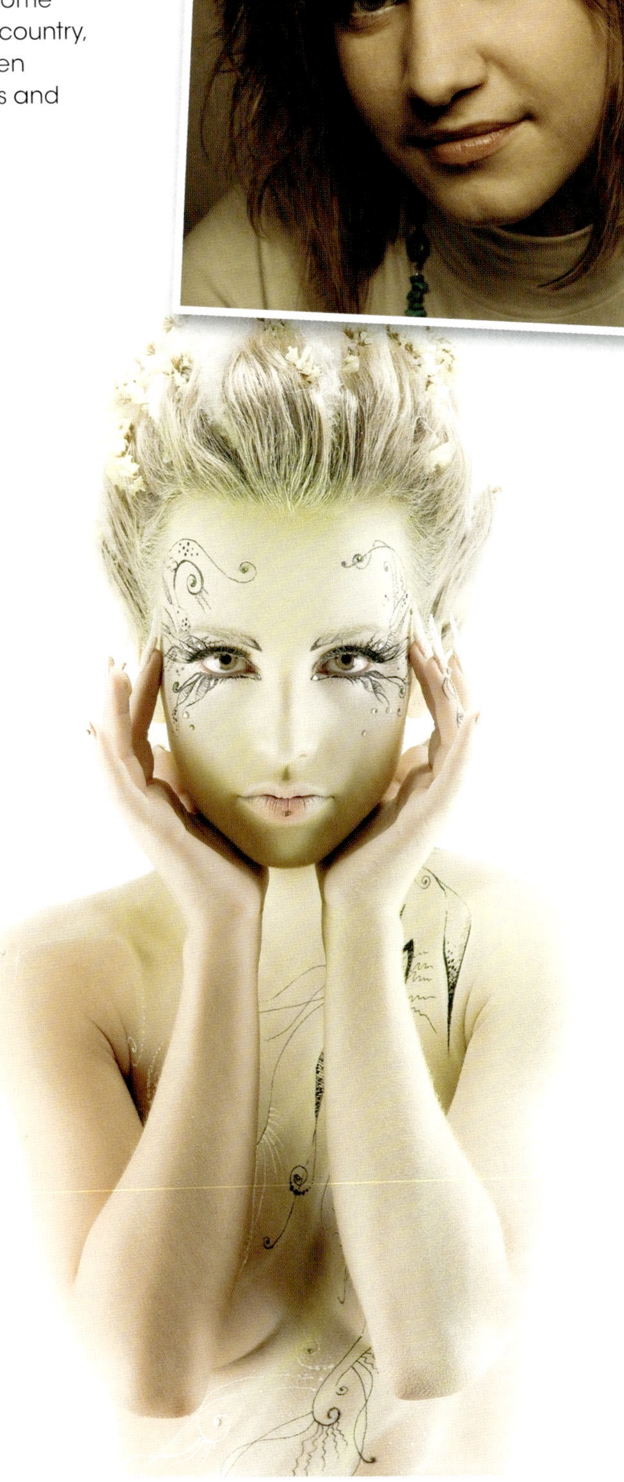

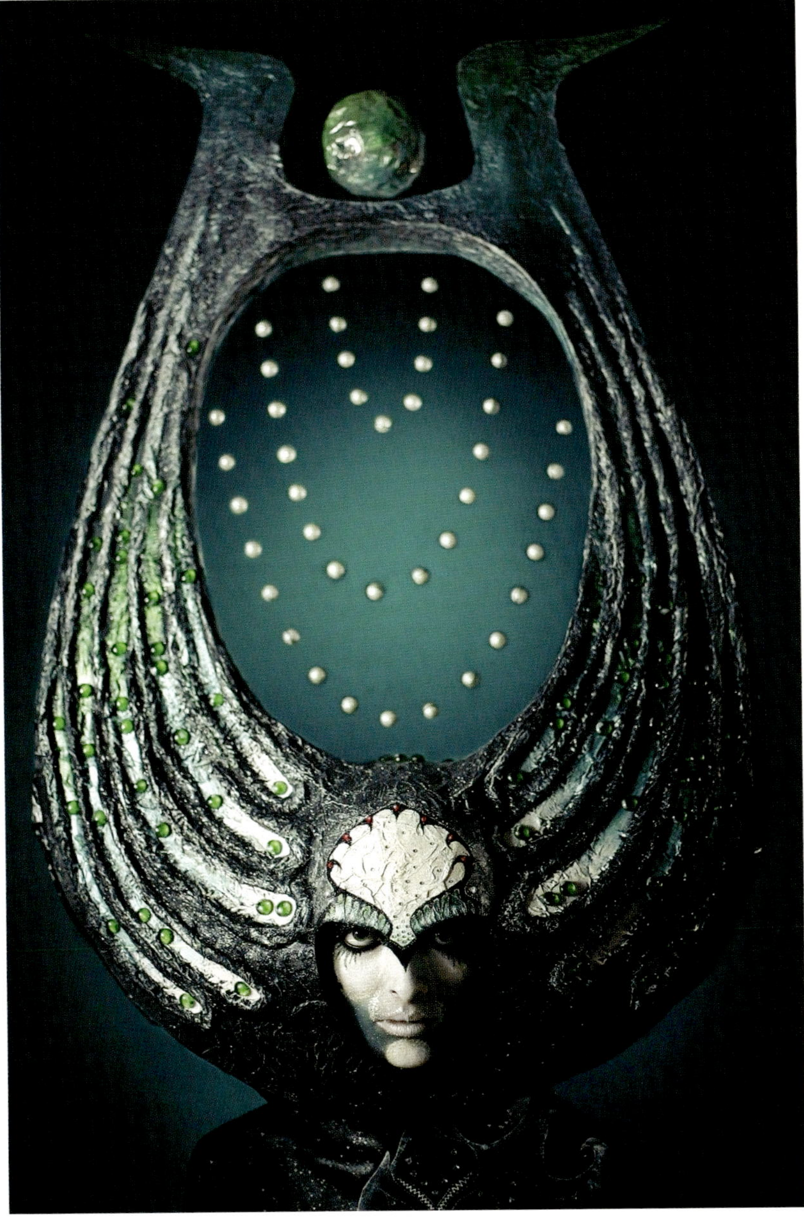

PHOTOGRAPHER MICKHAIL NEKRASOV | PHOTOGRAPHER ALEXANDR SENCHUK (LEFT)
PHOTOGRAPHER MICKHAIL SMIRNOV (OPPOSITE)

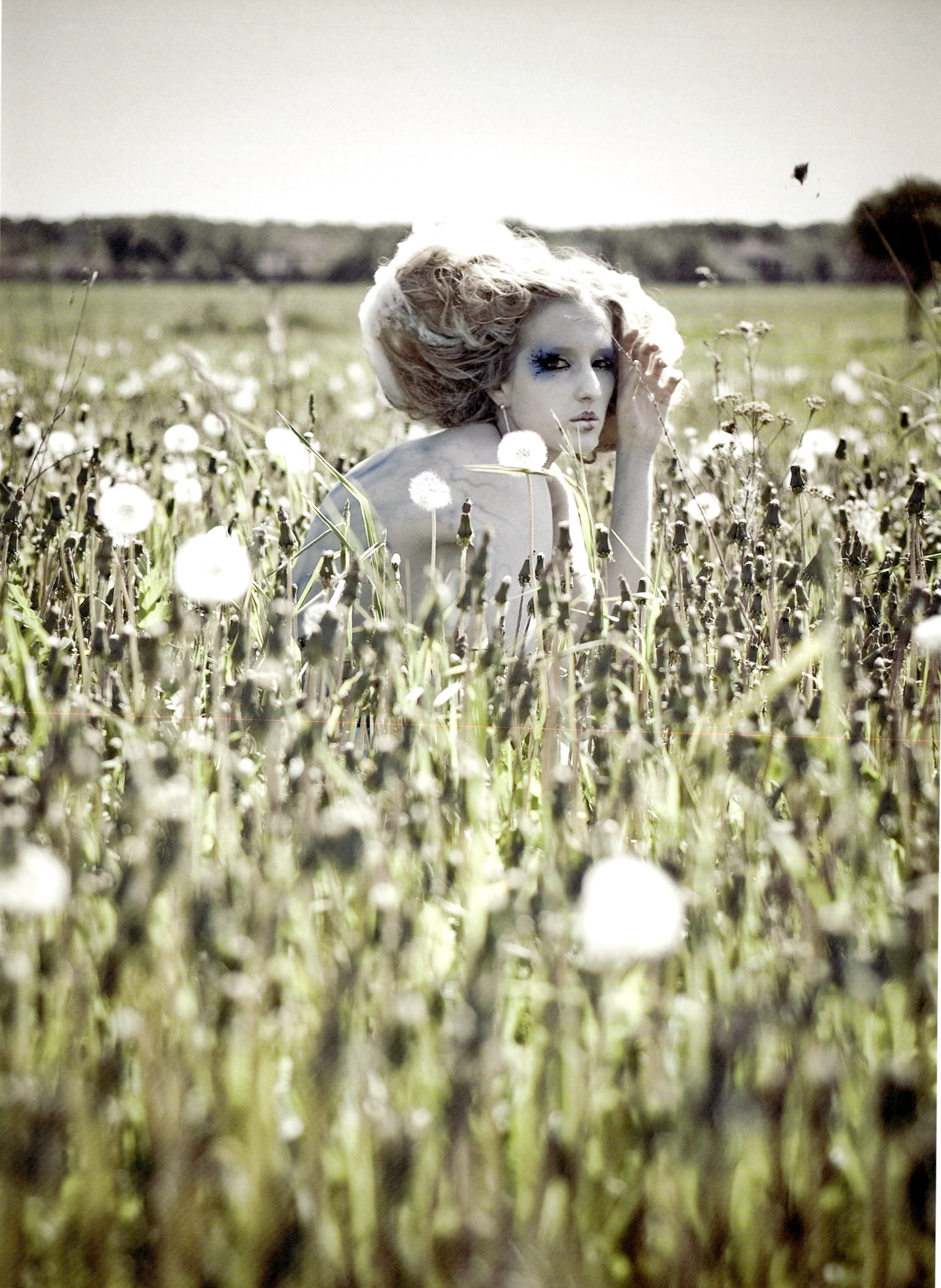

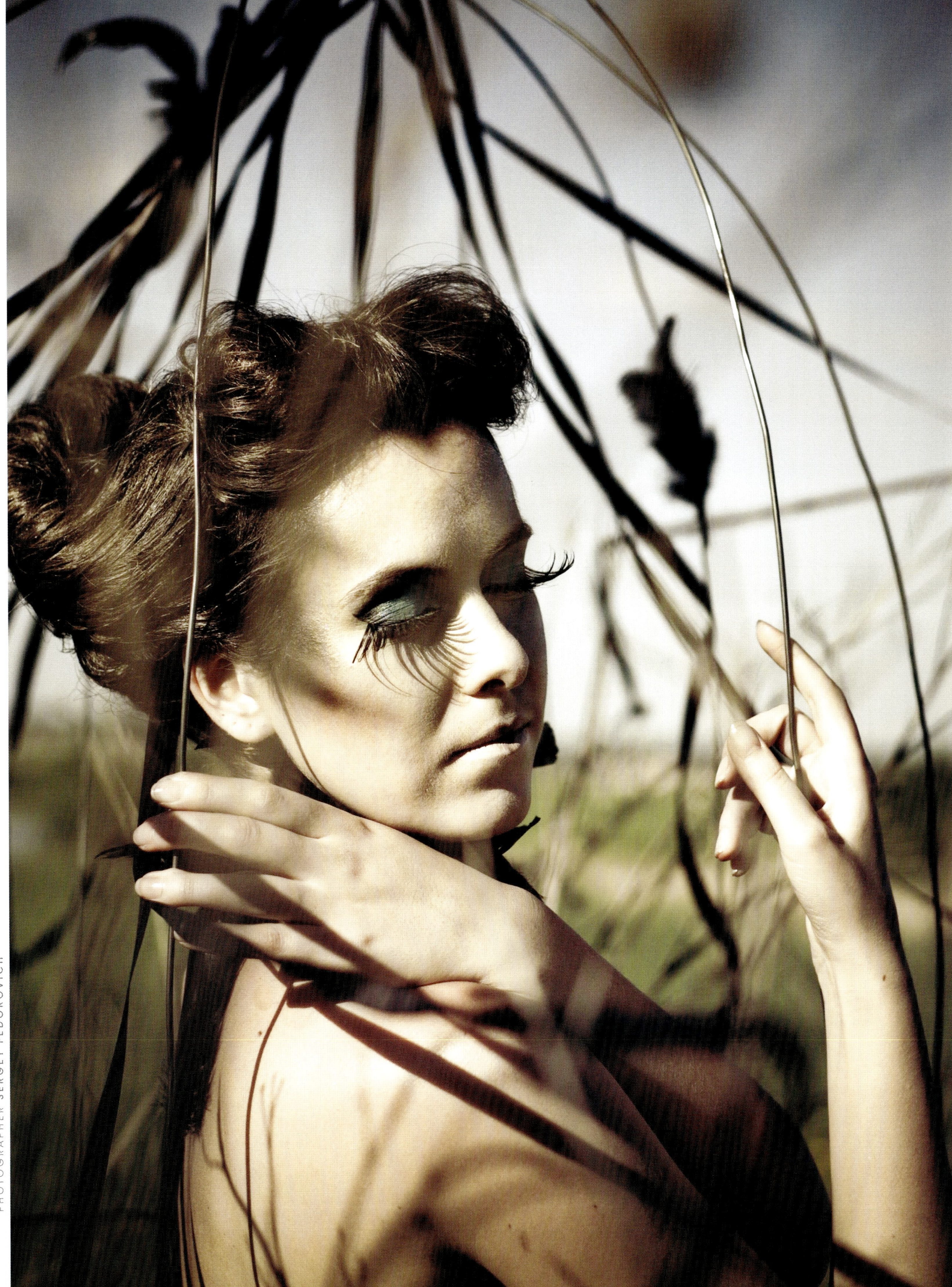
PHOTOGRAPHER SERGEY FEDOROVICH

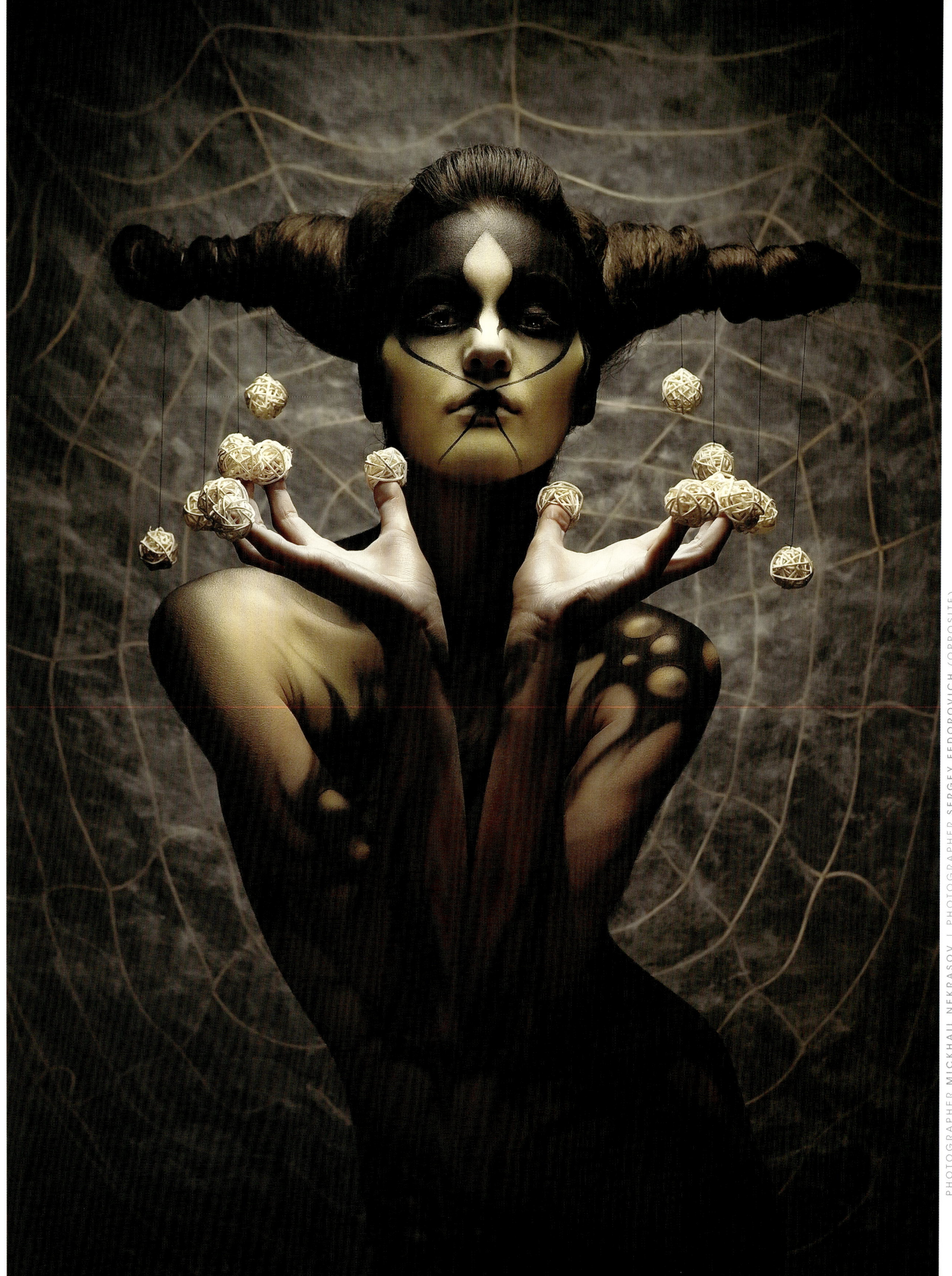

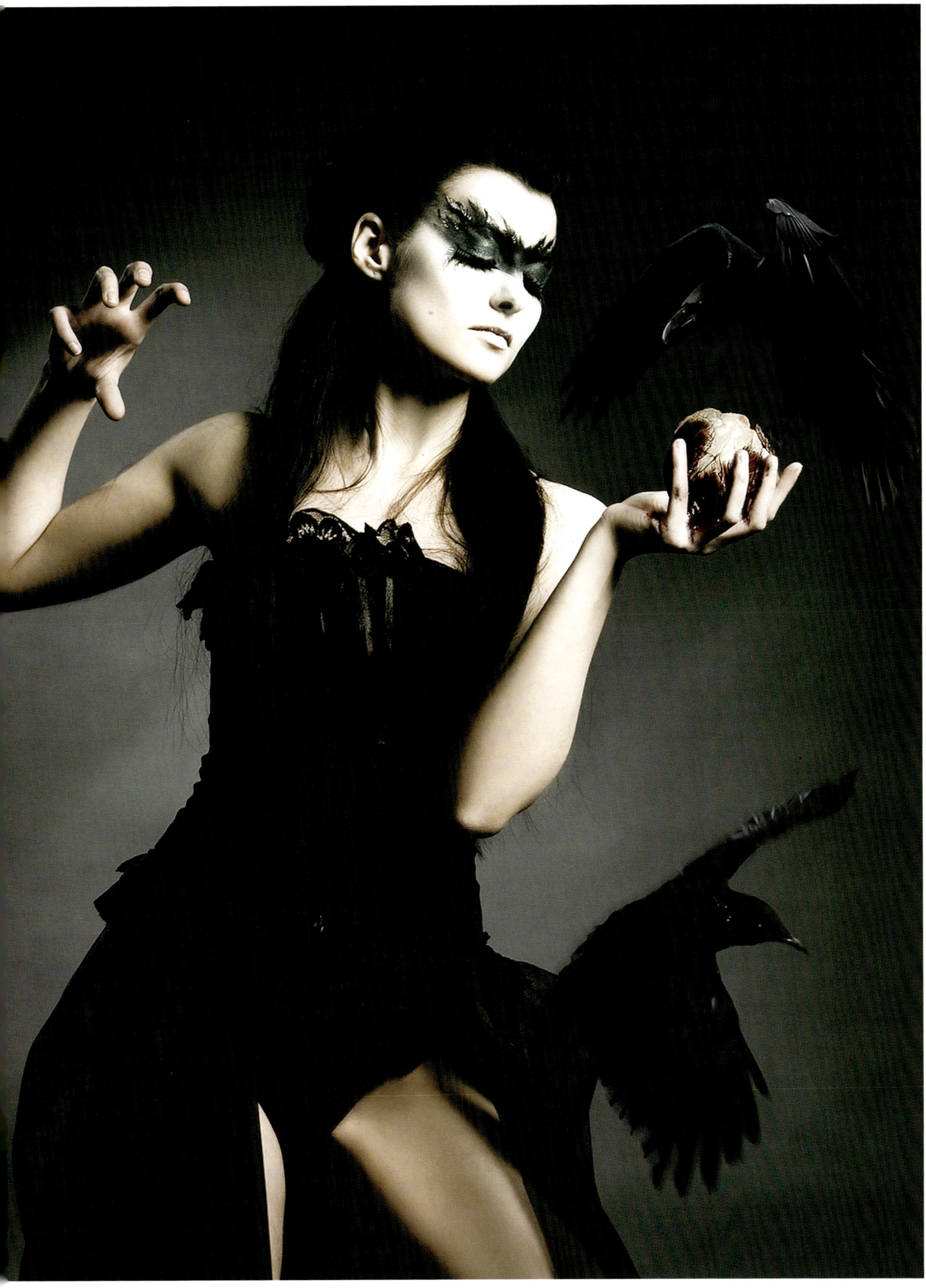

"Drawing on a body is a sign of the power of the person. It is displayed through the skin from within. The process of drawing and creating bewitches. When you observe from the outside, you see the art in the same way as the artist. You see that power."

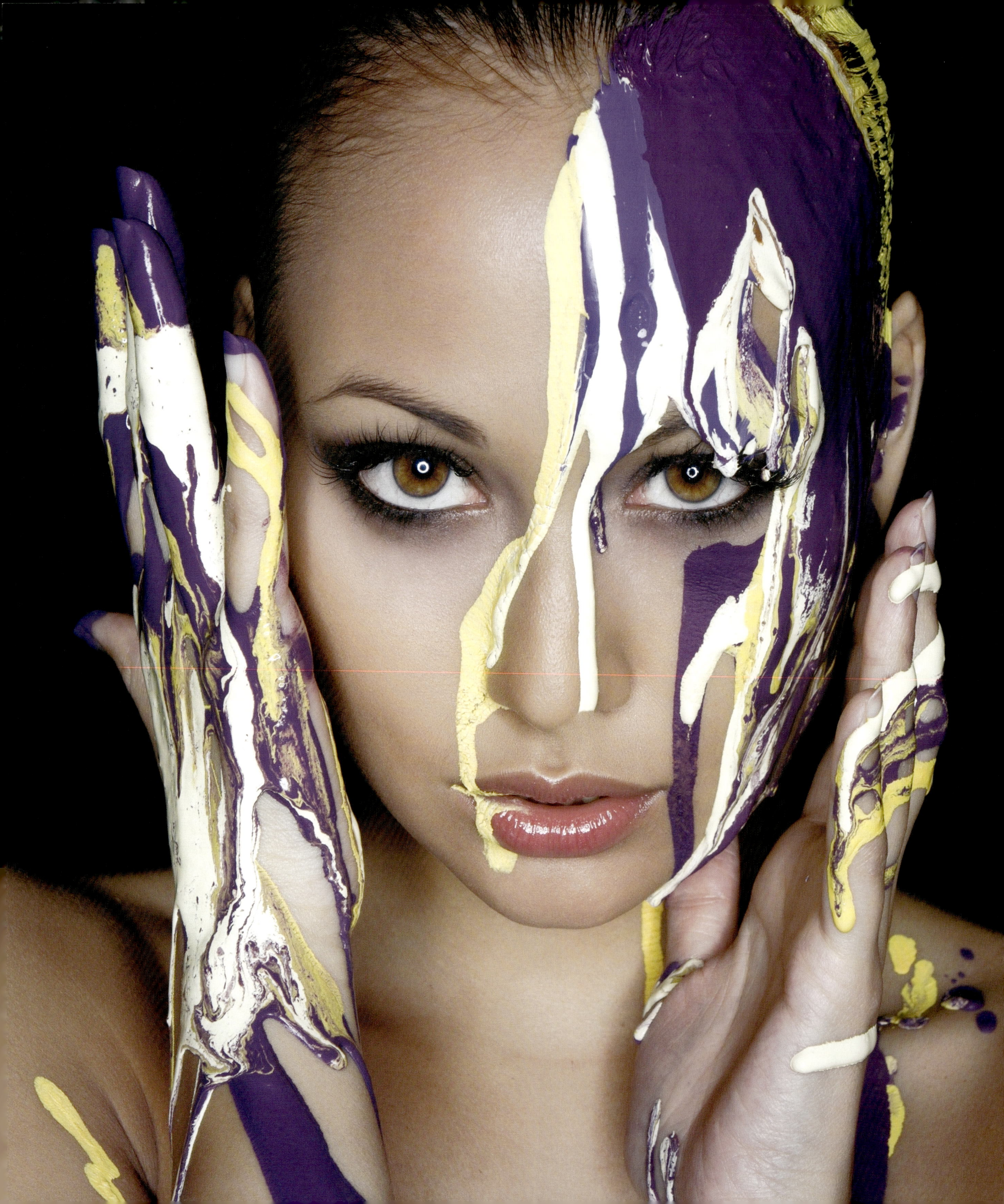

Mike Shane

Mike Shane's style of bodypainting is exhilarating and potent. Mike's creation of the action-painting style is an innovation and a breakthrough. The technique remains his alone, as he works in the now to color moments of space and time. Mike's work brings together all the necessary aspects of bodypainting—painter, performer and photographer—with such clarity of vision that his artwork is unforgettable.

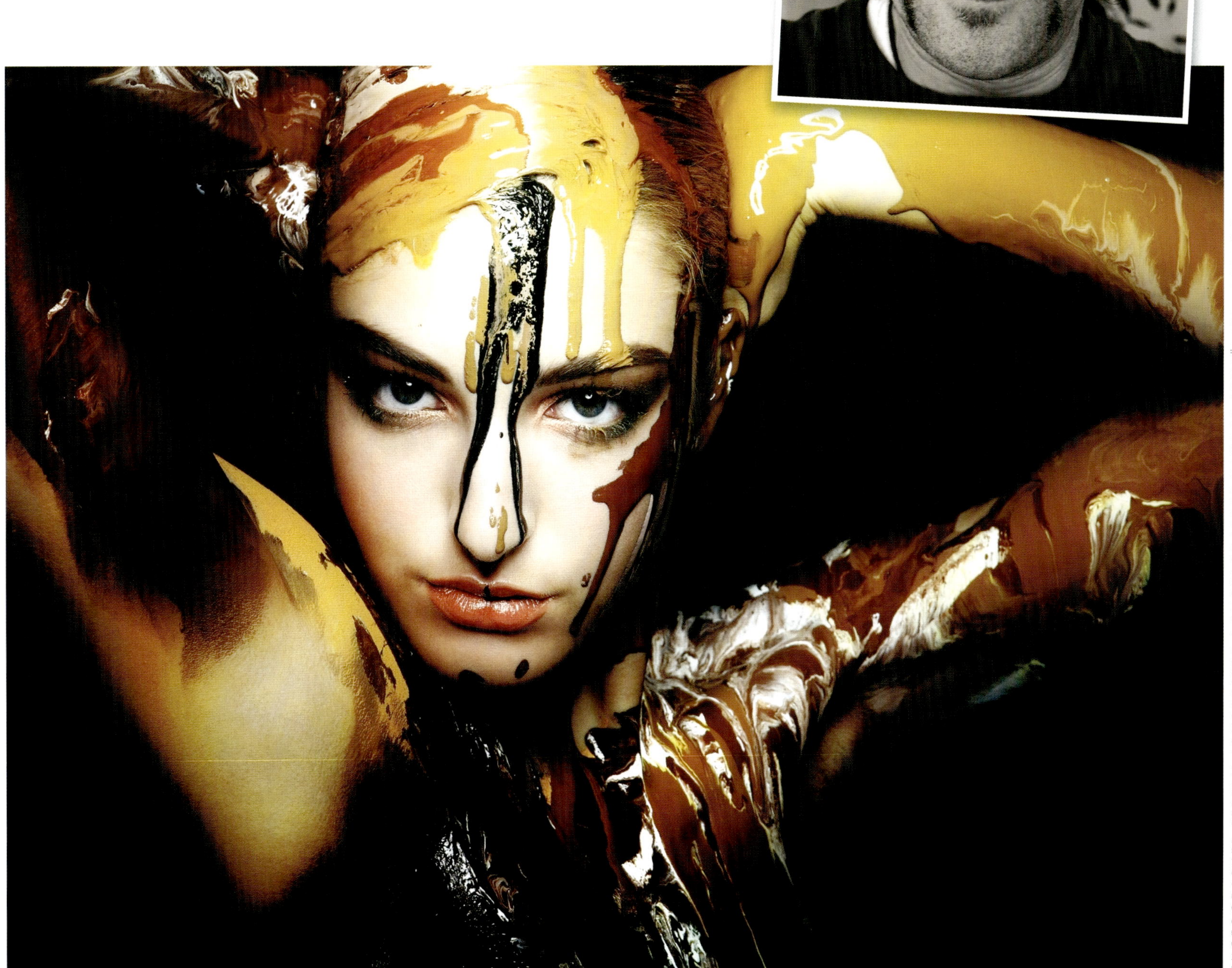

PHOTOGRAPHER STEFAN ARMBRUSTER | PHOTOGRAPHER HANNES ATZMÜLLER (OPPOSITE)

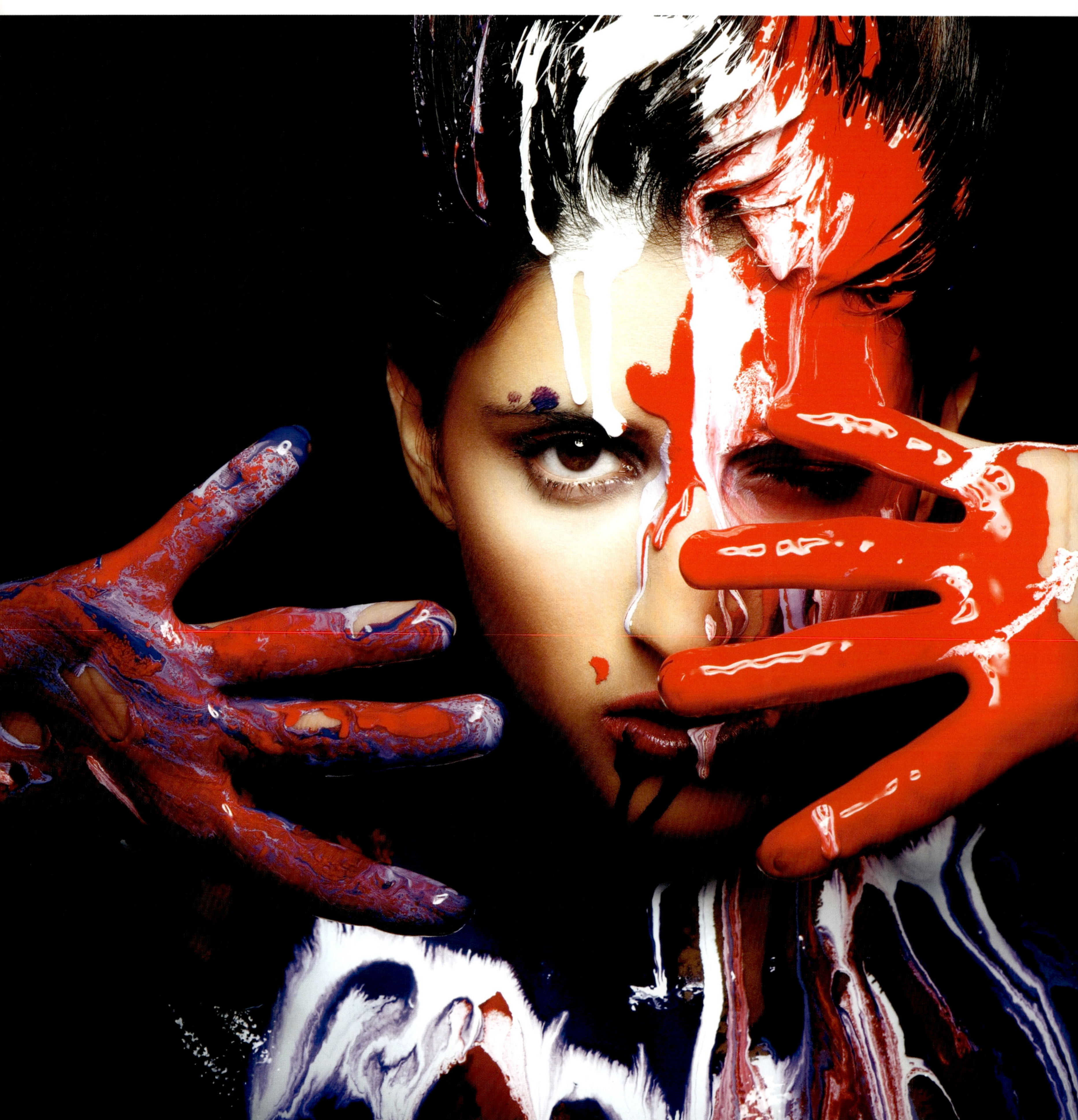

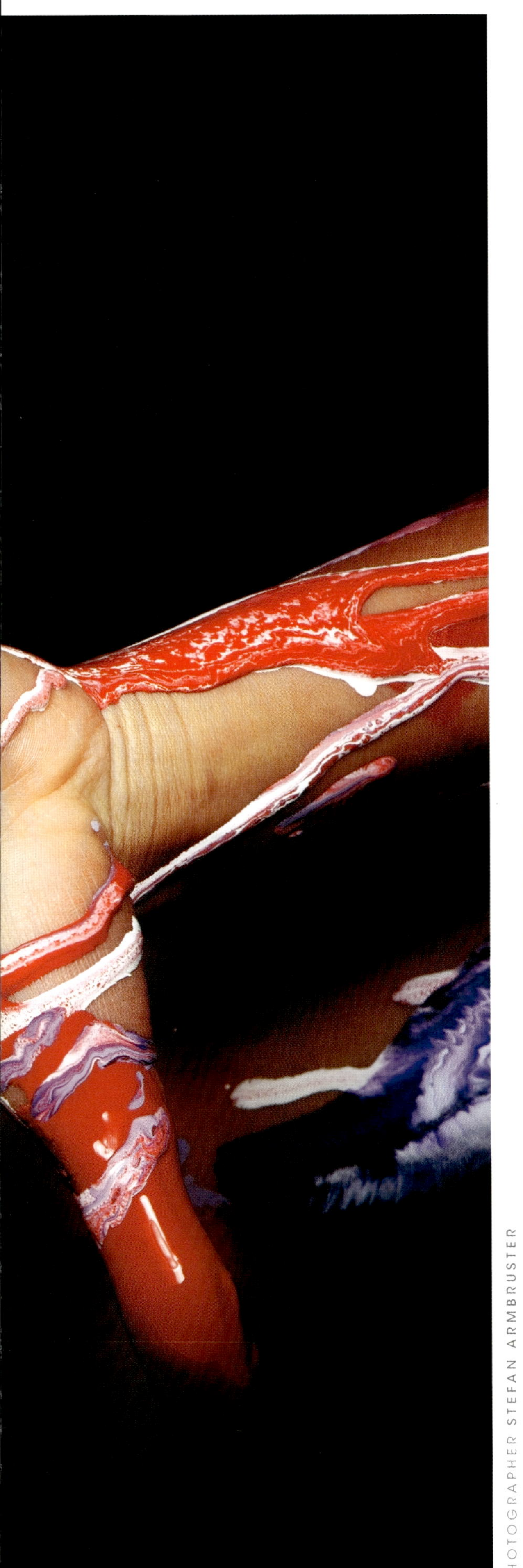

PHOTOGRAPHER STEFAN ARMBRUSTER

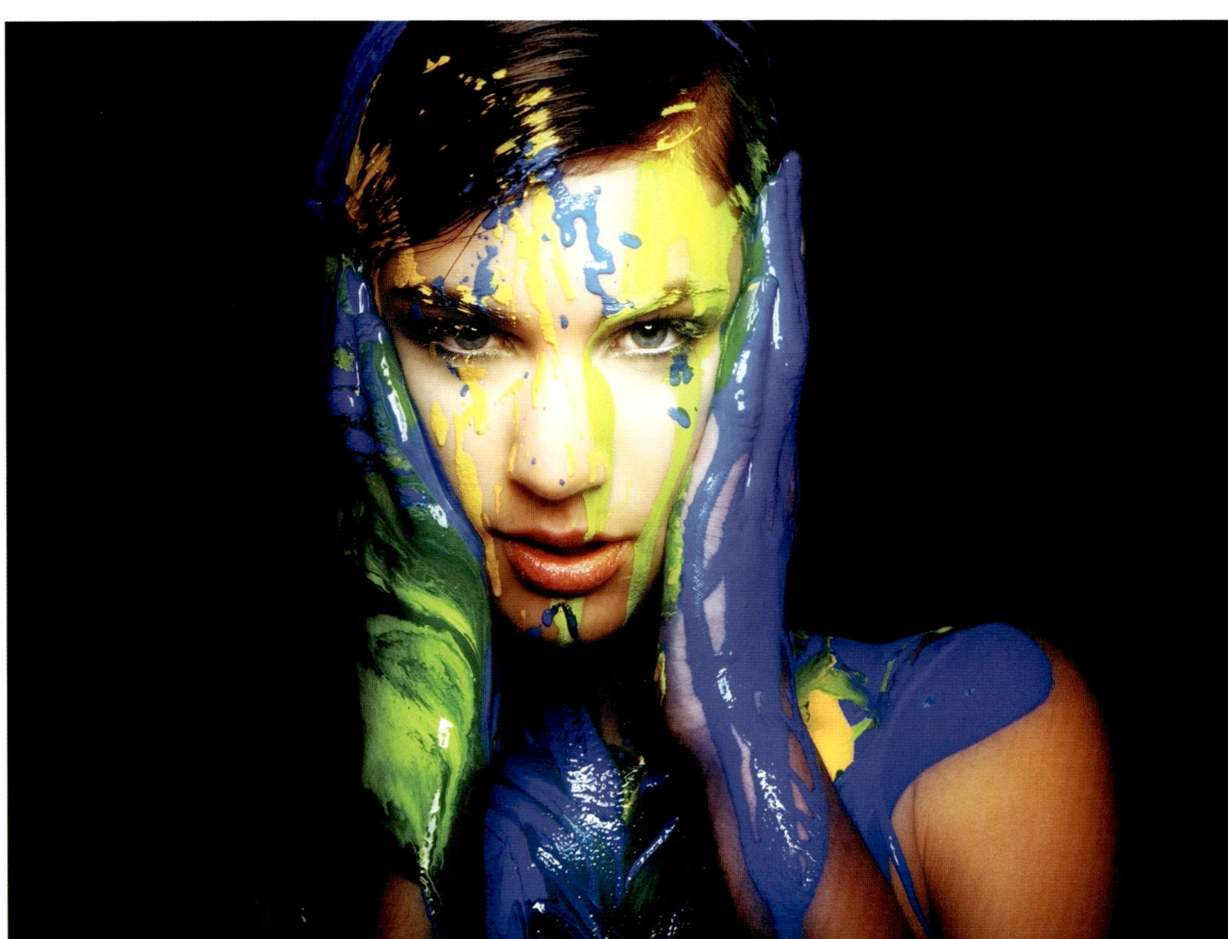

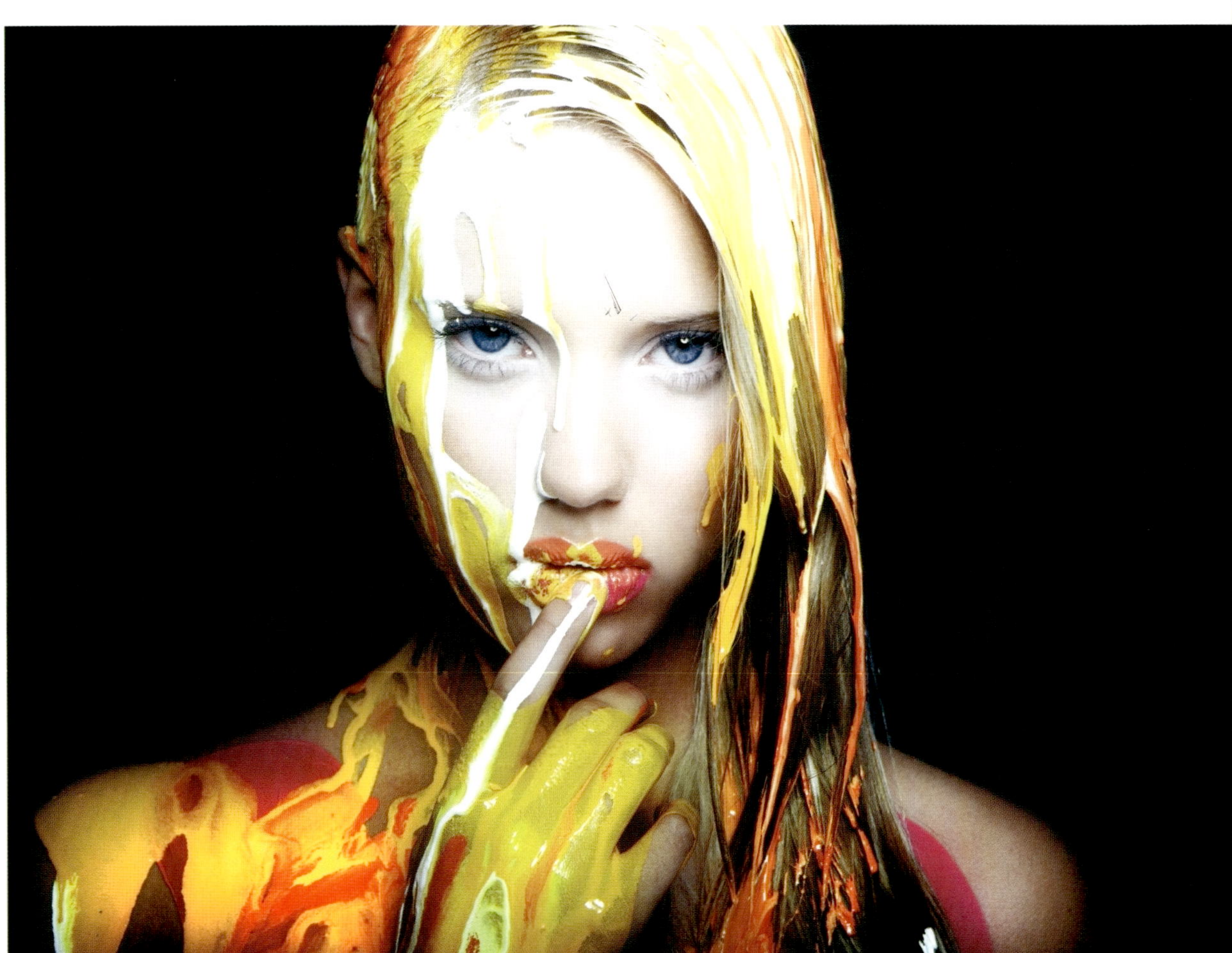

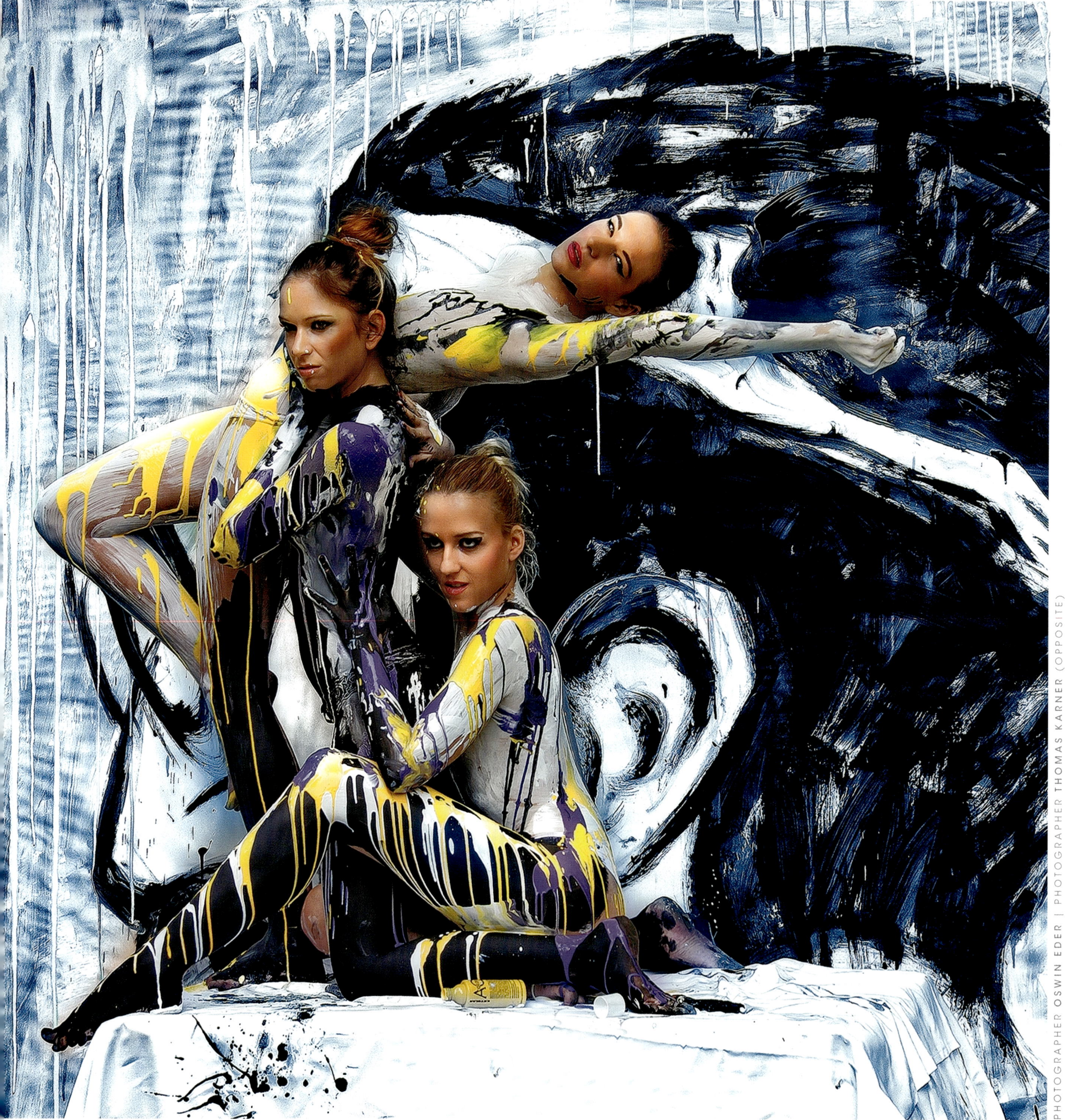

PHOTOGRAPHER OSWIN EDER | PHOTOGRAPHER THOMAS KARNER (OPPOSITE)

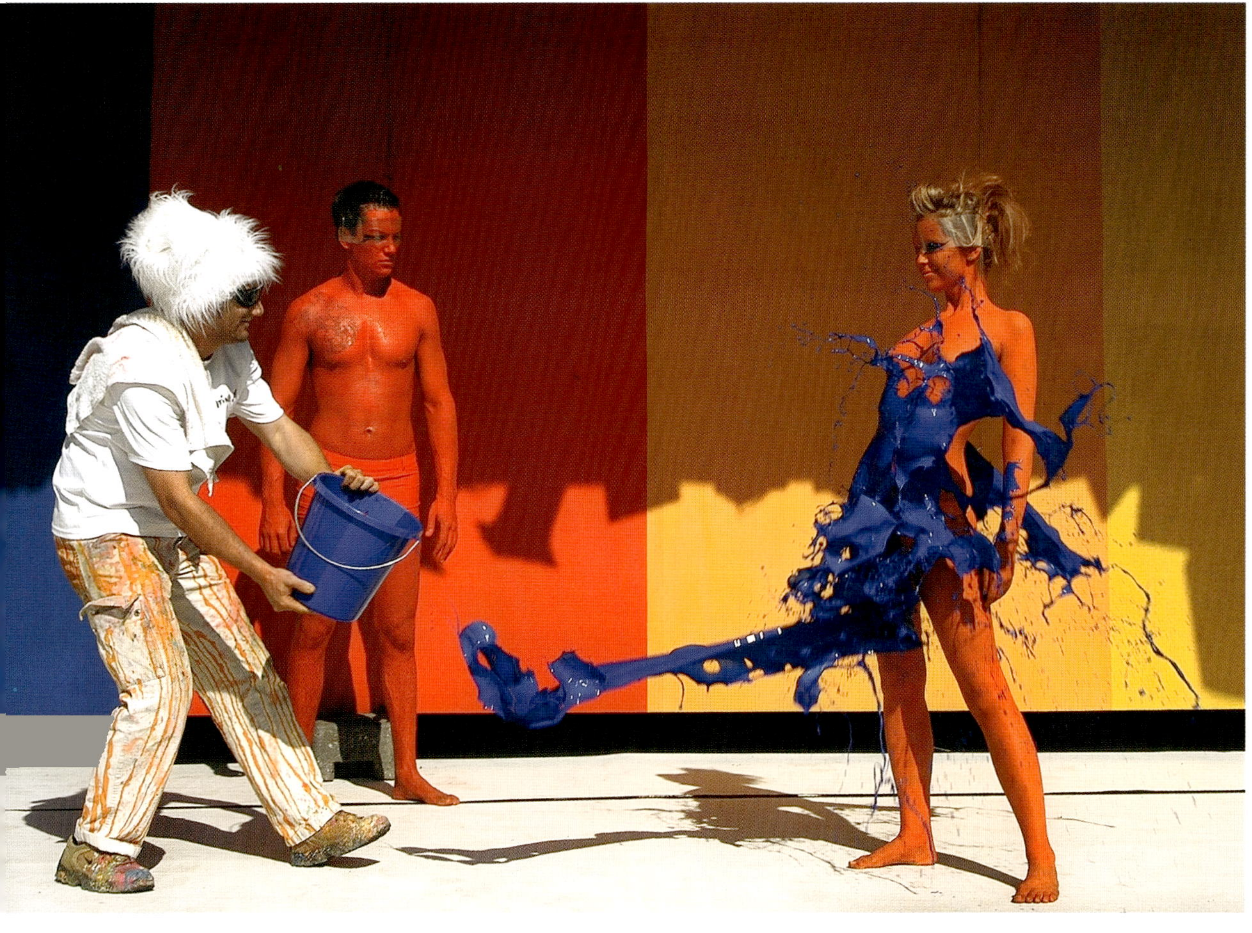

"When I started
my action-painting
bodypainting,
things really
changed in my life.
Everything shifted
and moved into
a different level.
I had recently
gotten to know
Tom Photo, a
brilliant Viennese
photographer.
After working with
him, I realized
that the topping
of a good
bodypainting
was a good
photograph
of it. This was
basically the start
of a new view
and new outputs
of my work."

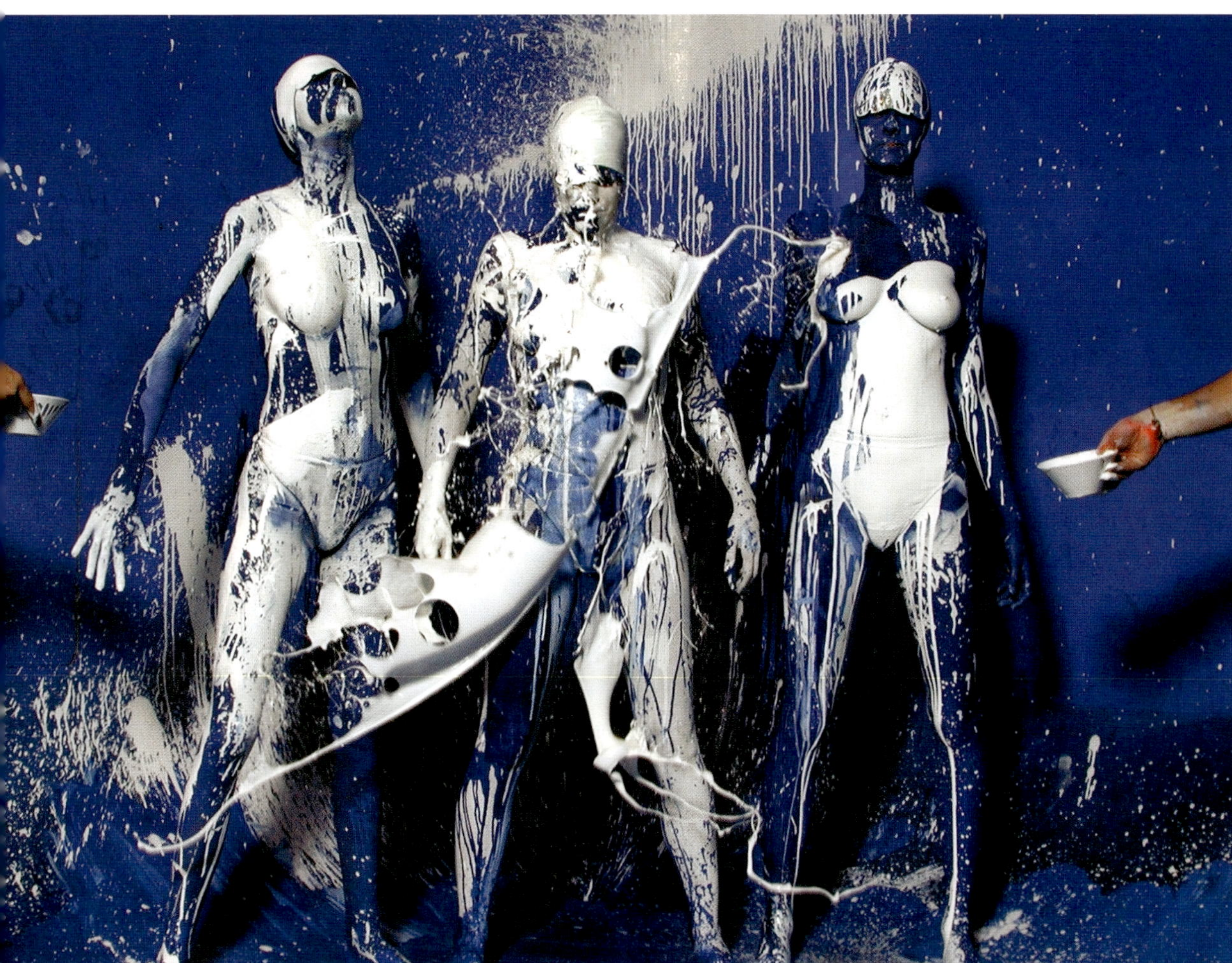

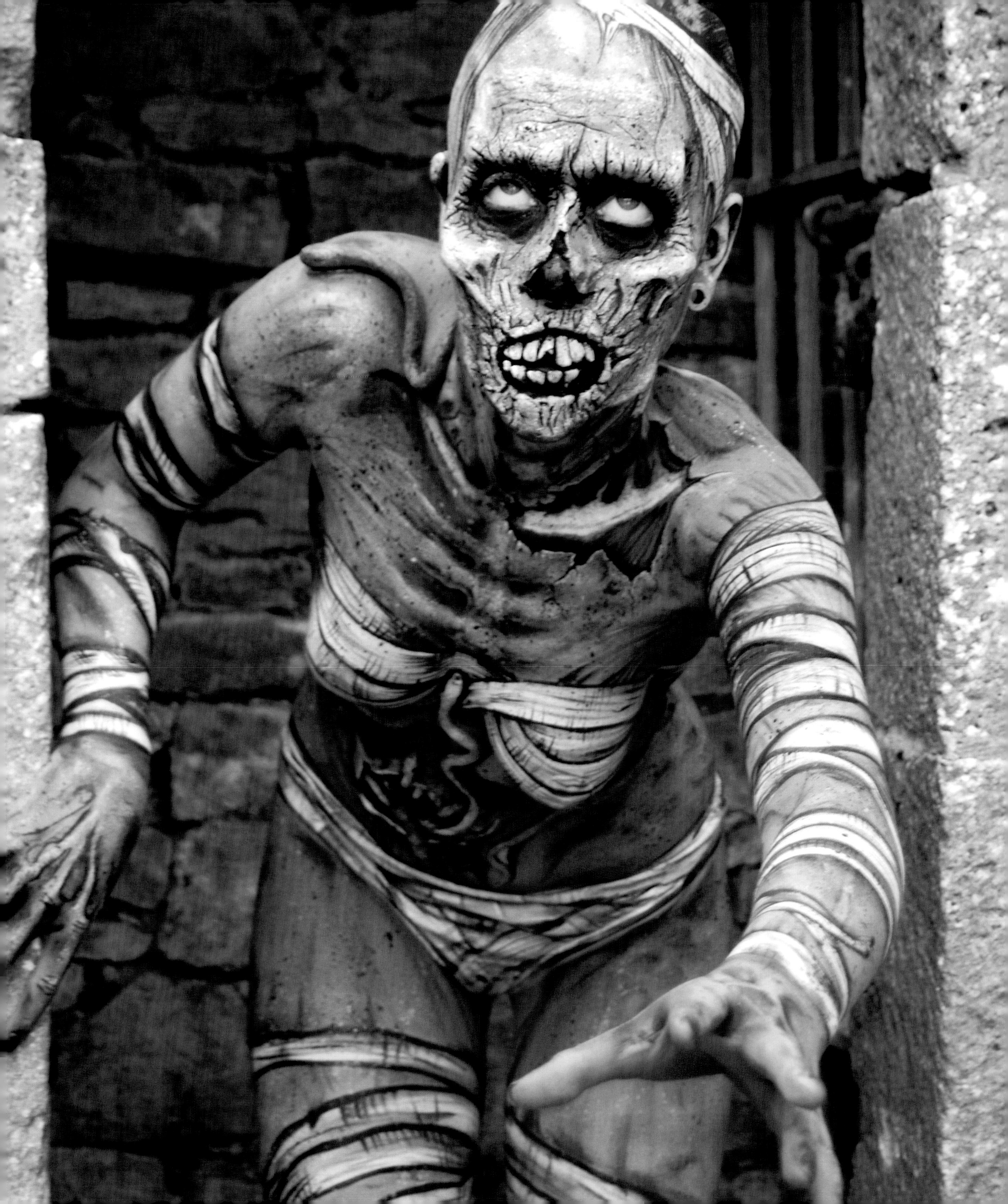

Nick & Brian Wolfe

The artist brothers Nick and Brian Wolfe have been at the forefront of bodypainting and have driven much of the development of the form in the United States. Just as in traditional forms of art, one of the first steps an artist takes is to study the anatomy of the human form. When drawing an arm, the artist must understand the bone structure: where the bones fit together and bend, where the muscles are attached to the bone and where fat can pad out the surrounding areas. Nick and Brian have taken this step in mixing anatomical knowledge with living art. Their anatomical understanding has been put to creative use in their dissections of human form and transformations of reality into the physically impossible. After Brian's passing in 2013, Nick has continued to push this style of art and teach their methods around the world.

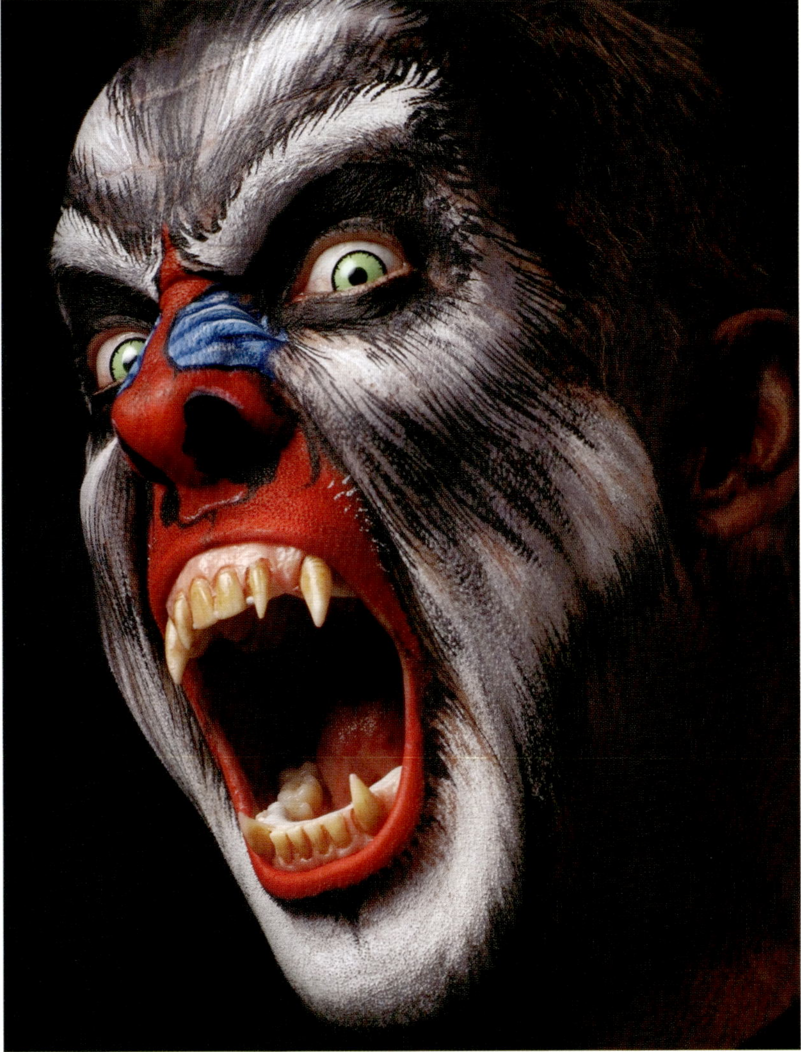

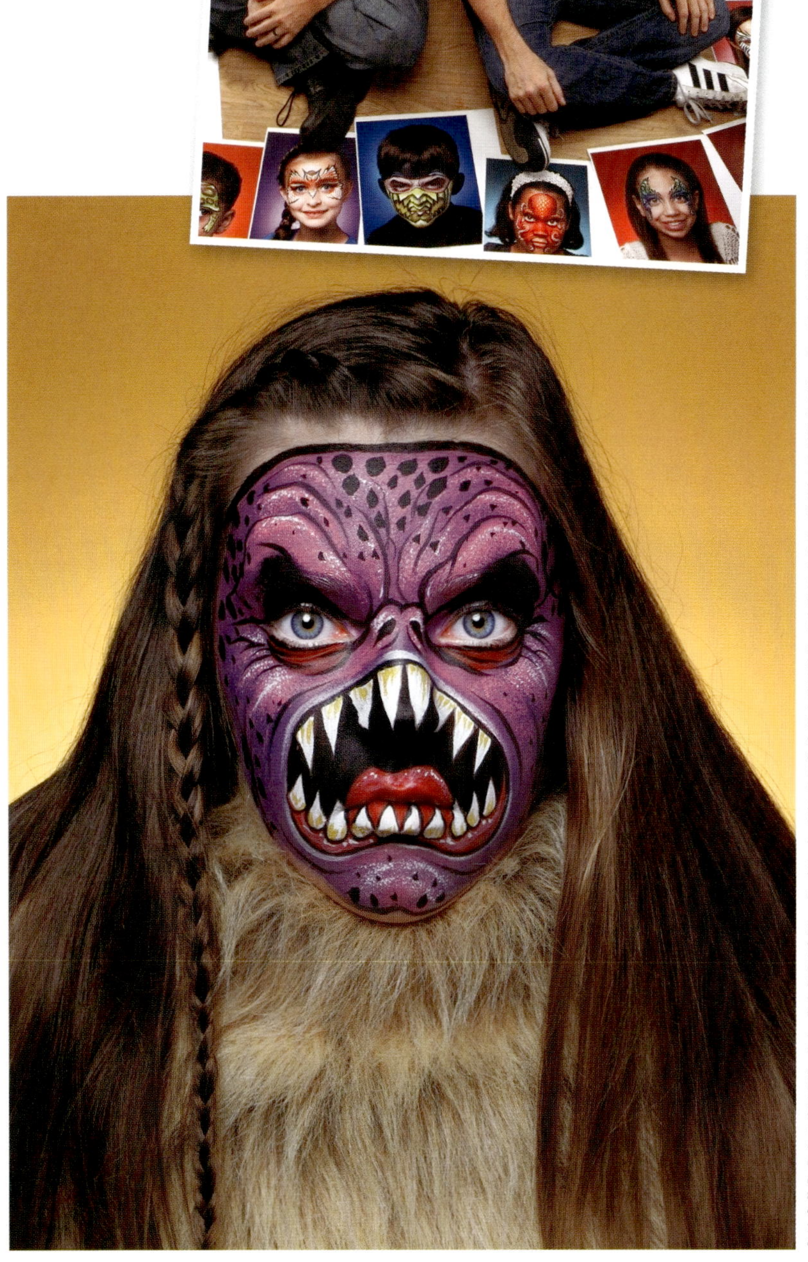

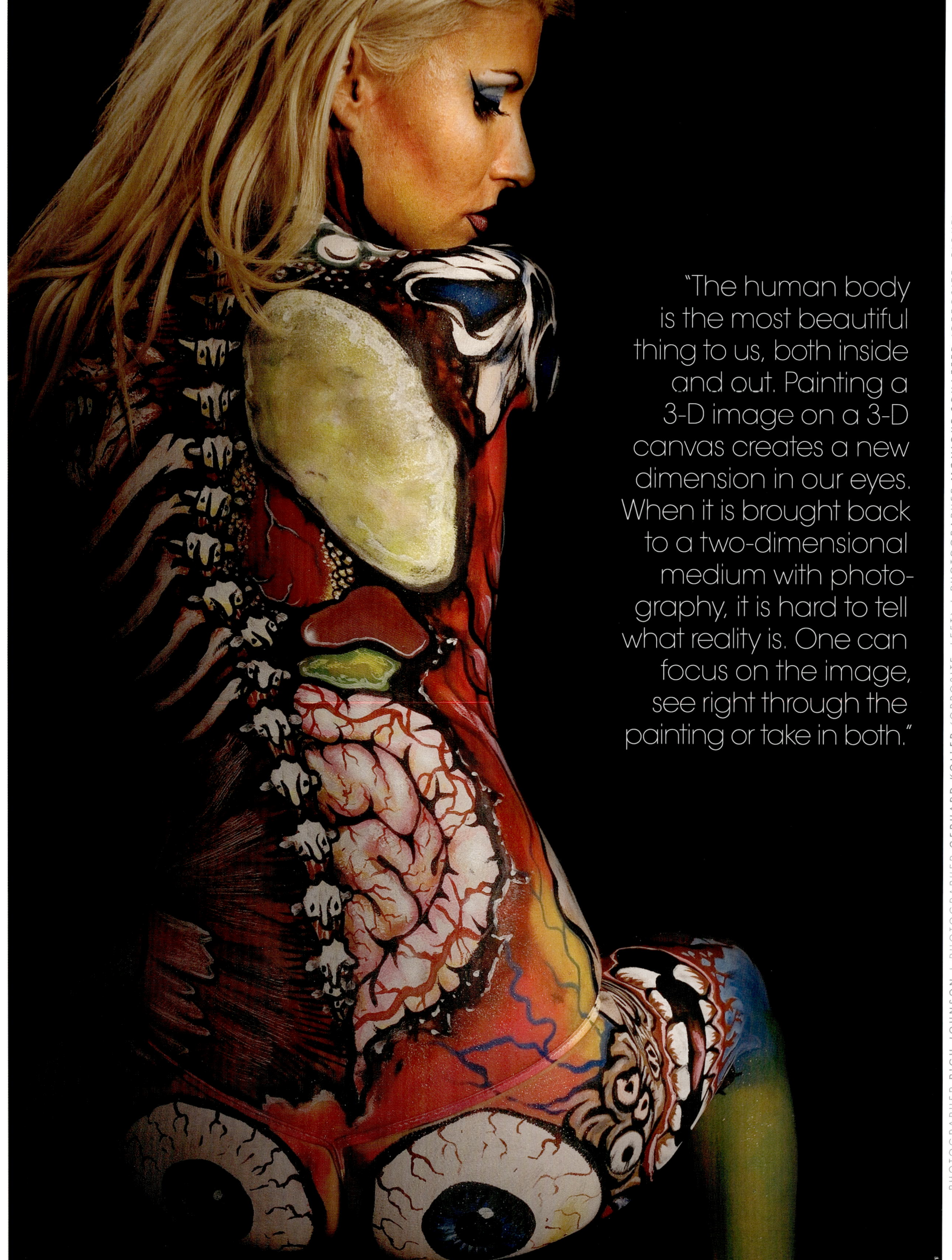

"The human body is the most beautiful thing to us, both inside and out. Painting a 3-D image on a 3-D canvas creates a new dimension in our eyes. When it is brought back to a two-dimensional medium with photography, it is hard to tell what reality is. One can focus on the image, see right through the painting or take in both."

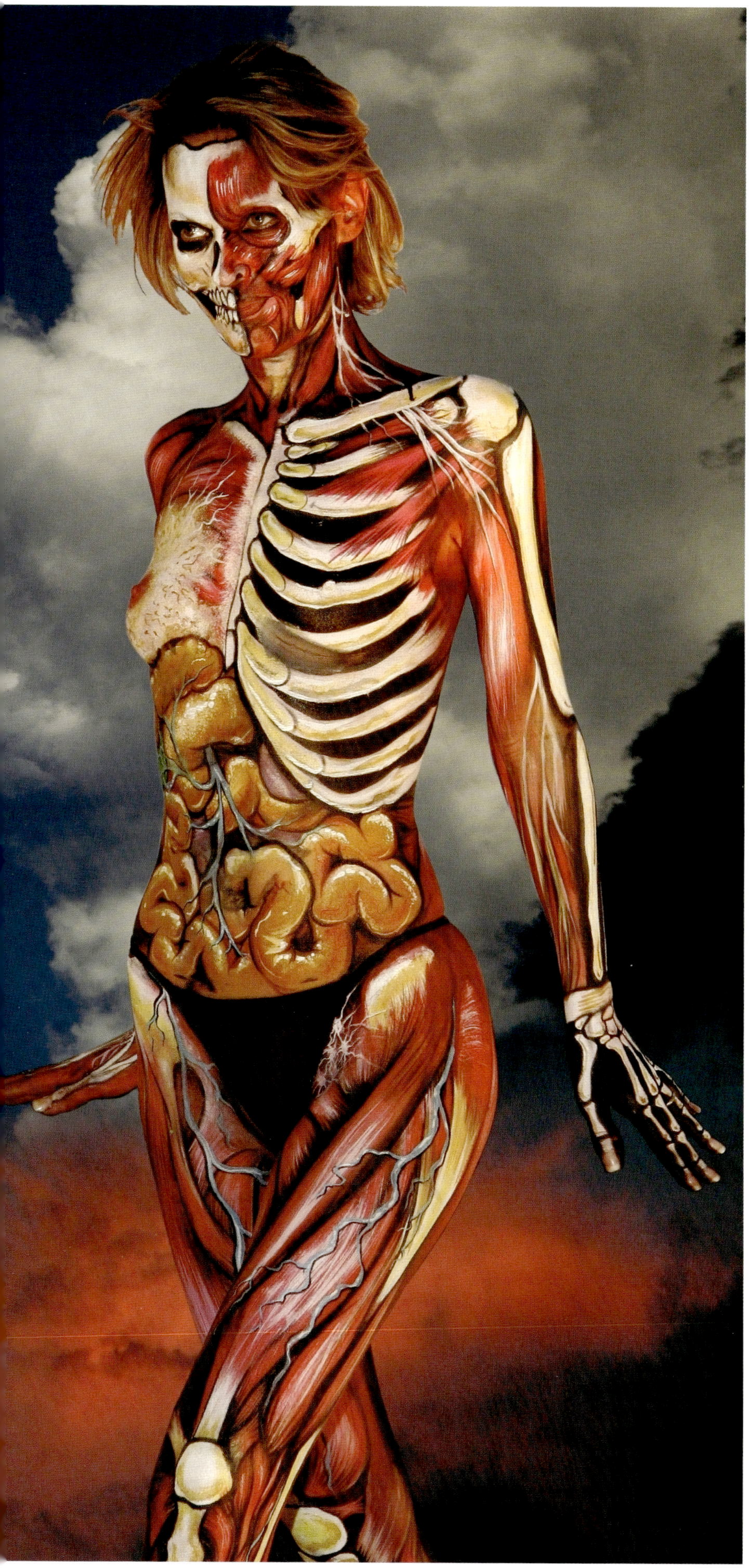

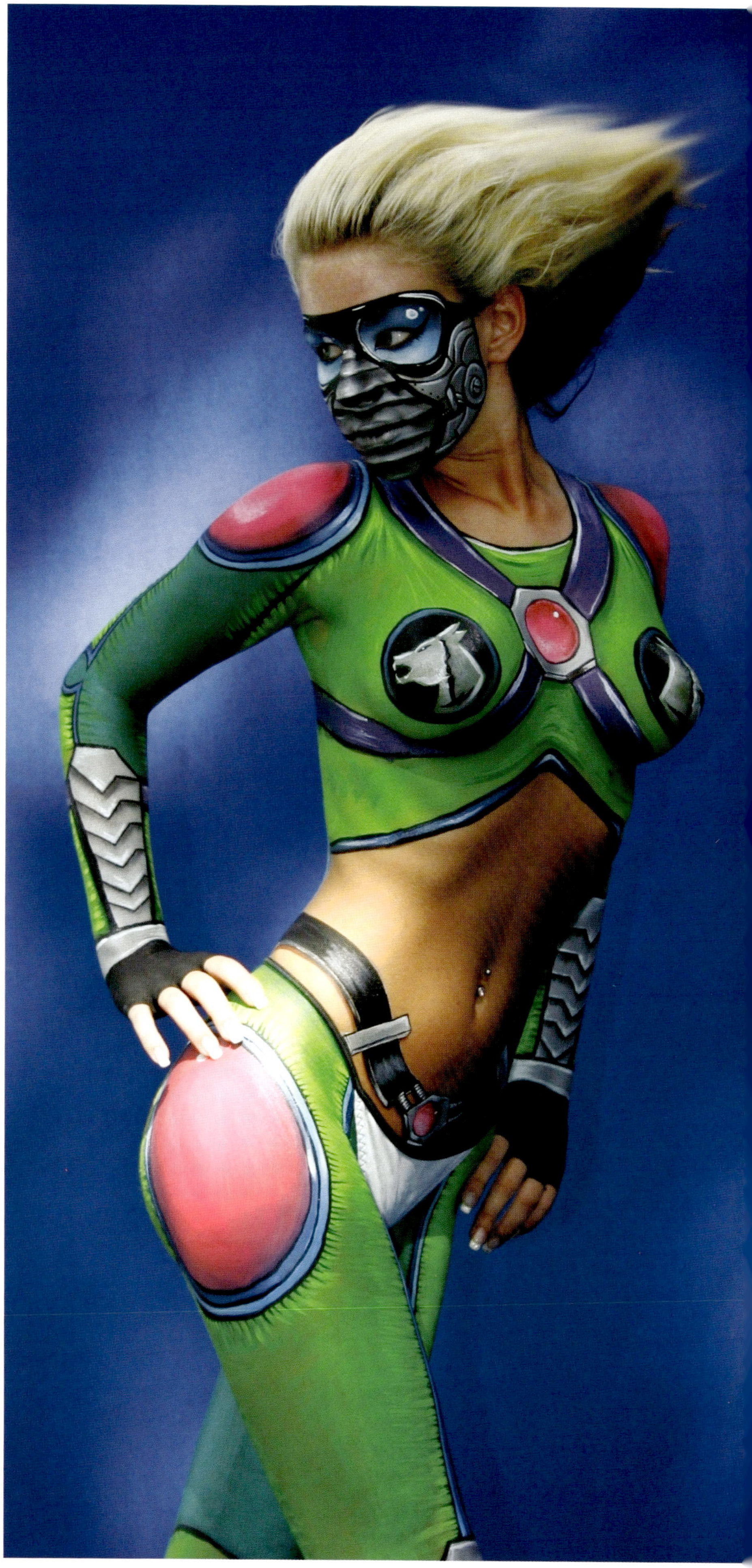

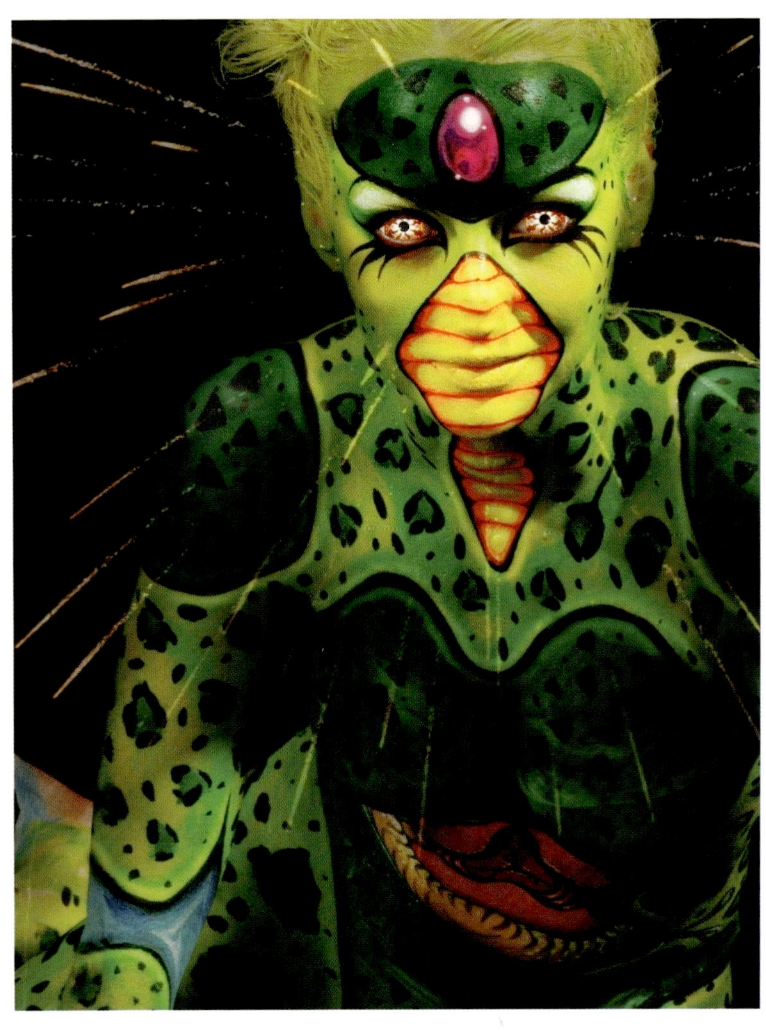

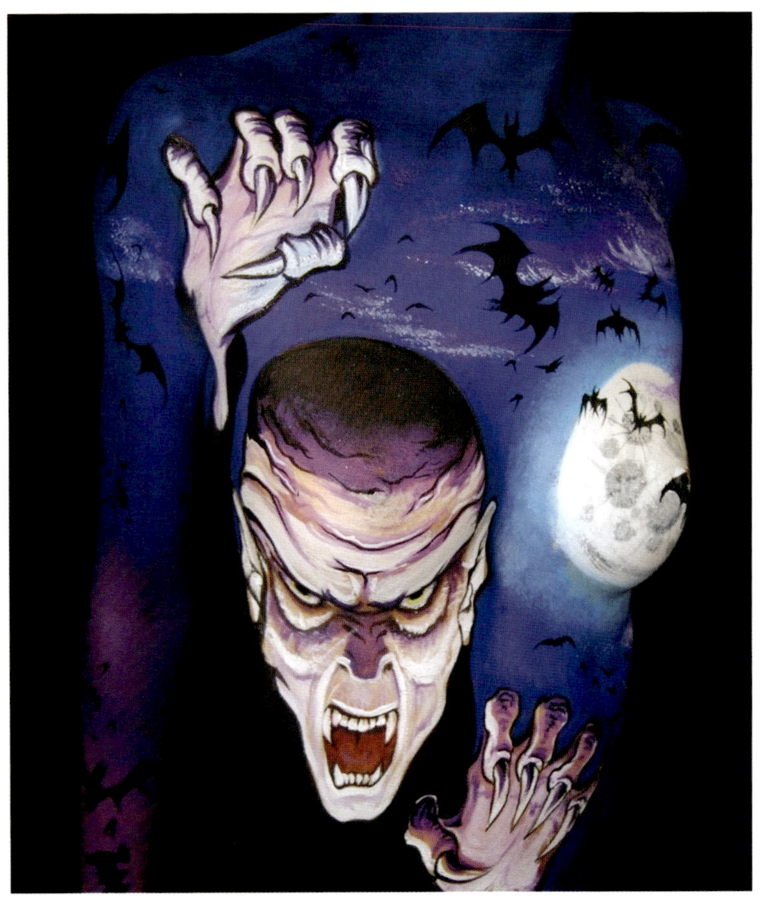

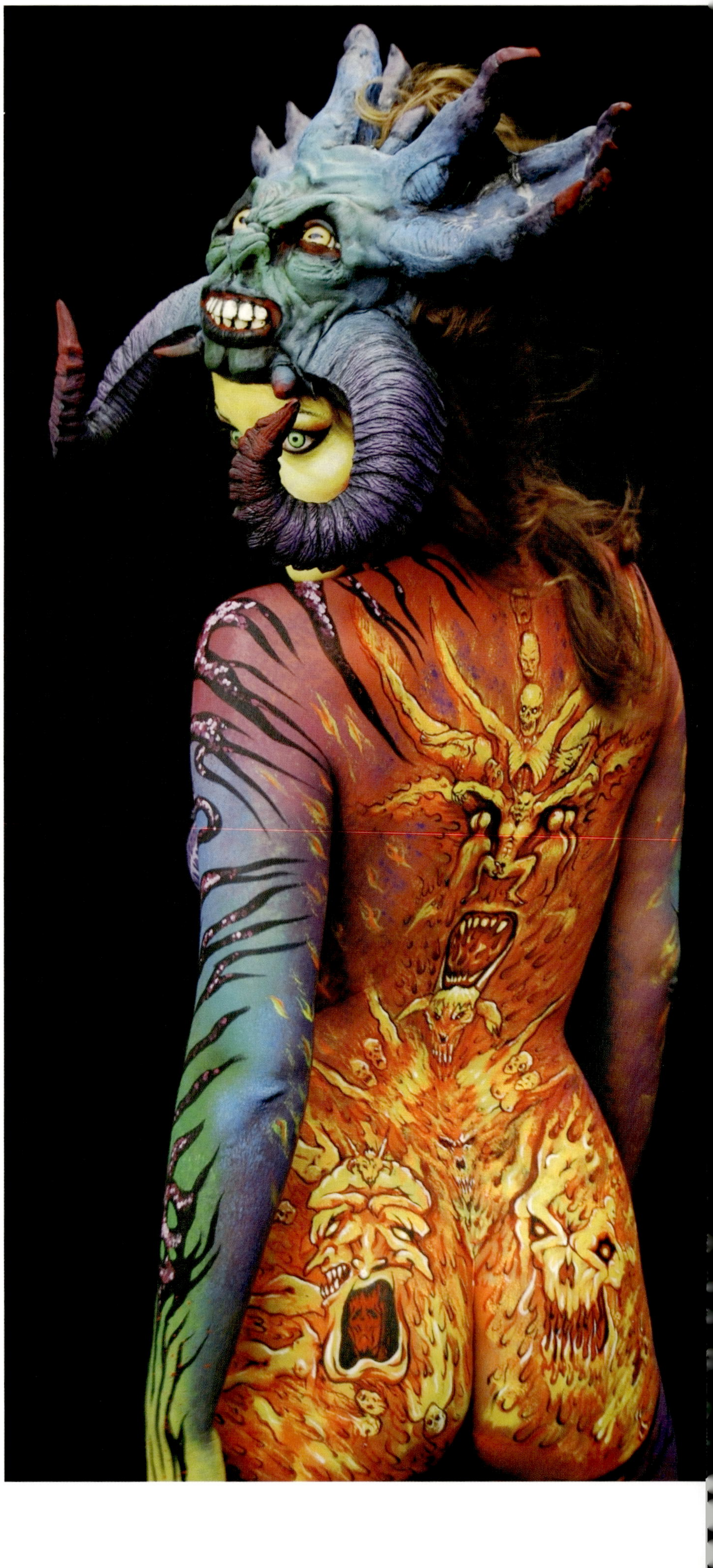

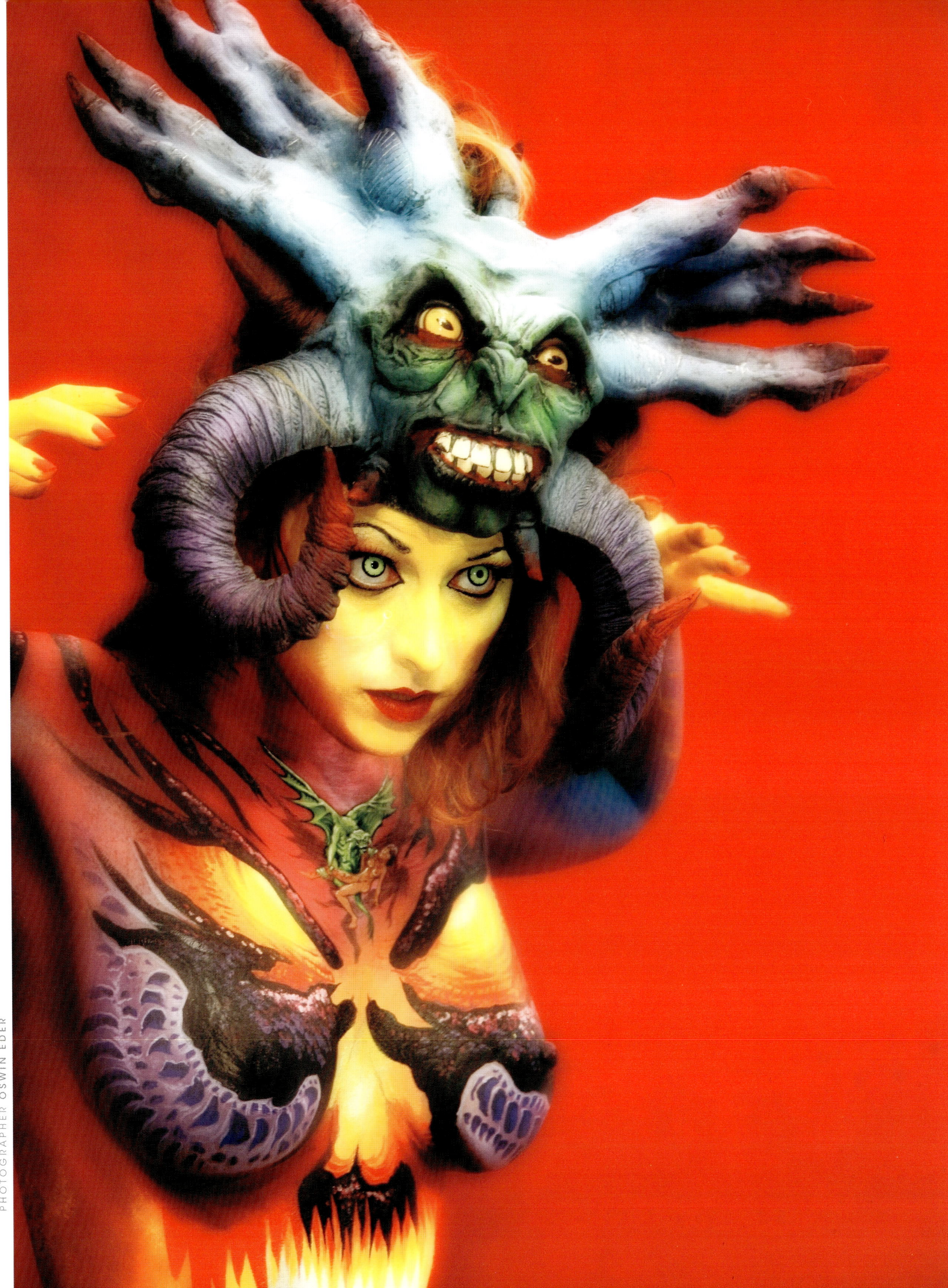

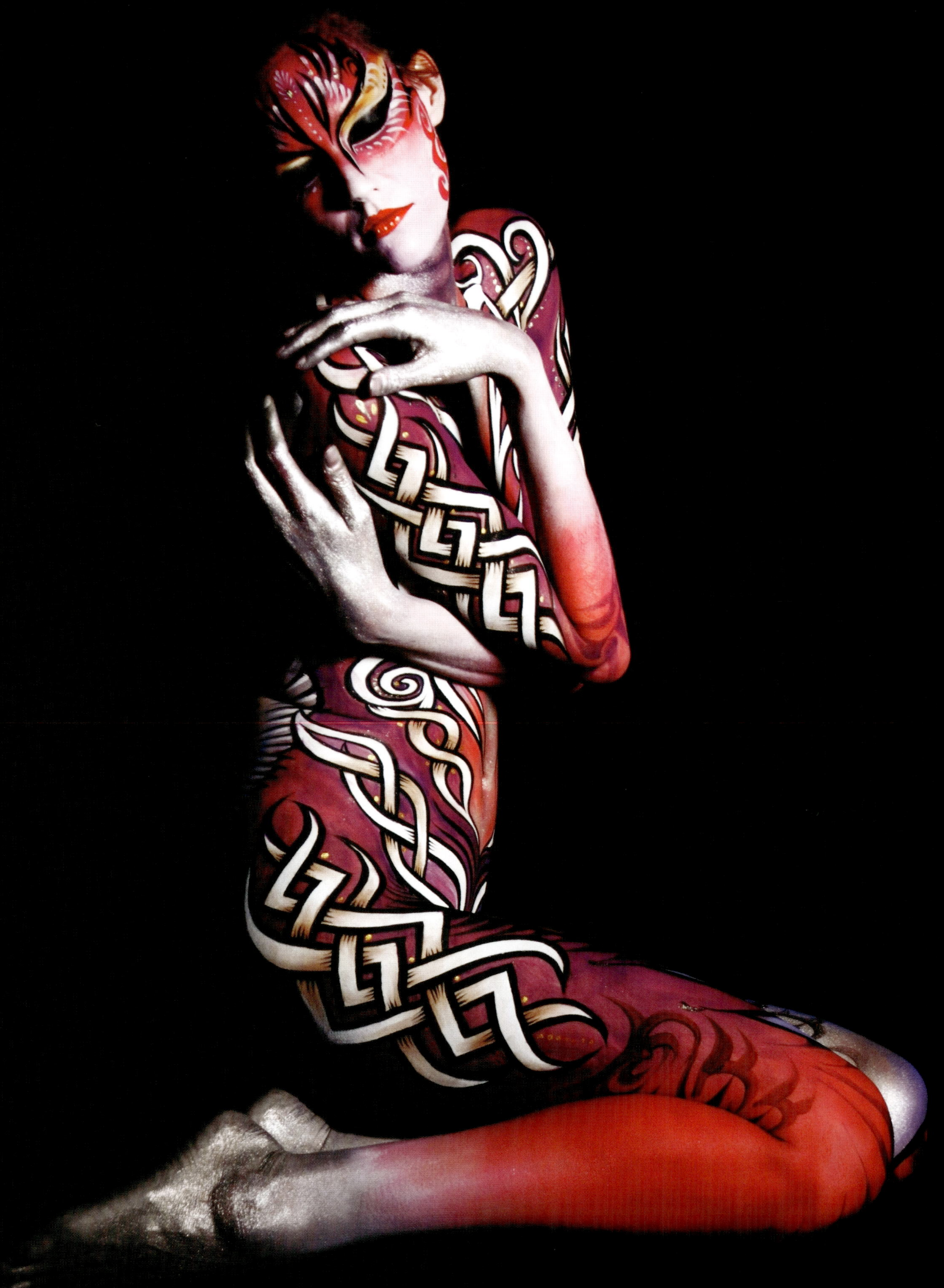

Scott Fray & Madelyn Greco

Scott Fray and Madelyn Greco are the only artists in history to have won World Championship titles in all three main body art categories at the World Bodypainting Festival. With a meteoric rise through the ranks to champion competitive status, the pair is currently focused on creating bodypainting images as a fine-art endeavor, with the goal of creating similar success in international galleries and museums. Scott and Madelyn also enjoy teaching and consulting at both university and professional levels.

Scott and Madelyn believe wholeheartedly in the transcendent nature of the work they create, coining the phrase, "soul-on-skin." They welcome the opportunity to view and translate into art some aspect of the deeper nature of their subject. They also count numerous experiences involving bodypaint sessions that seem to offer a subject healing or relief from old body-image and body-trauma issues.

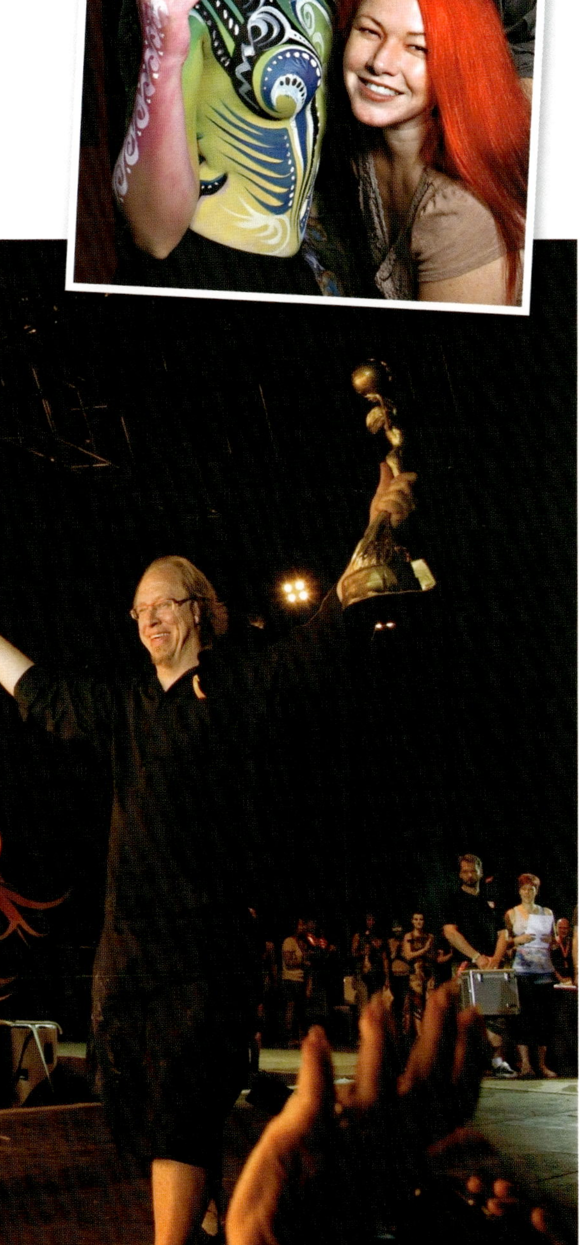

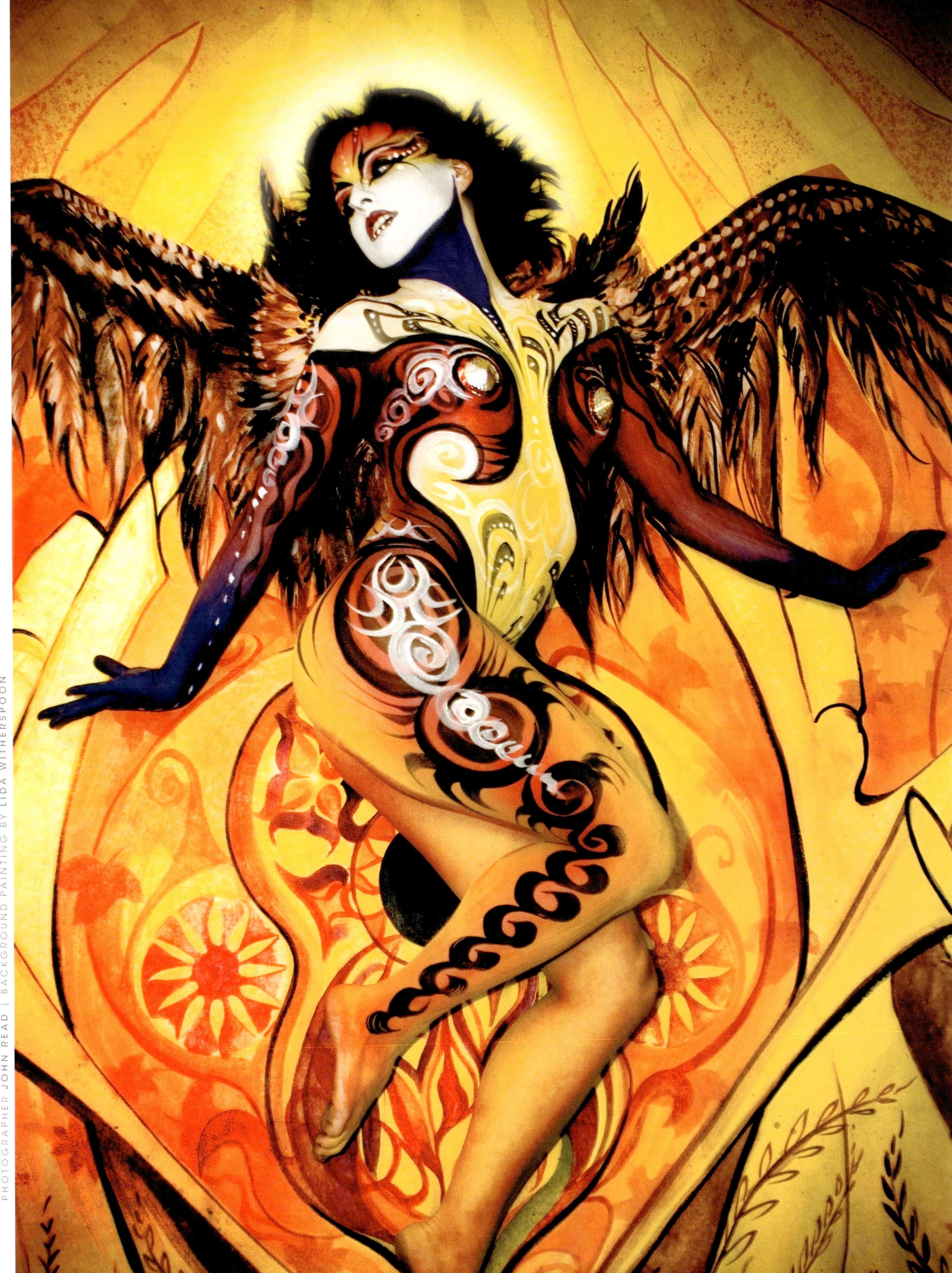

PHOTOGRAPHER JOHN READ | BACKGROUND PAINTING BY LIDA WITHERSPOON

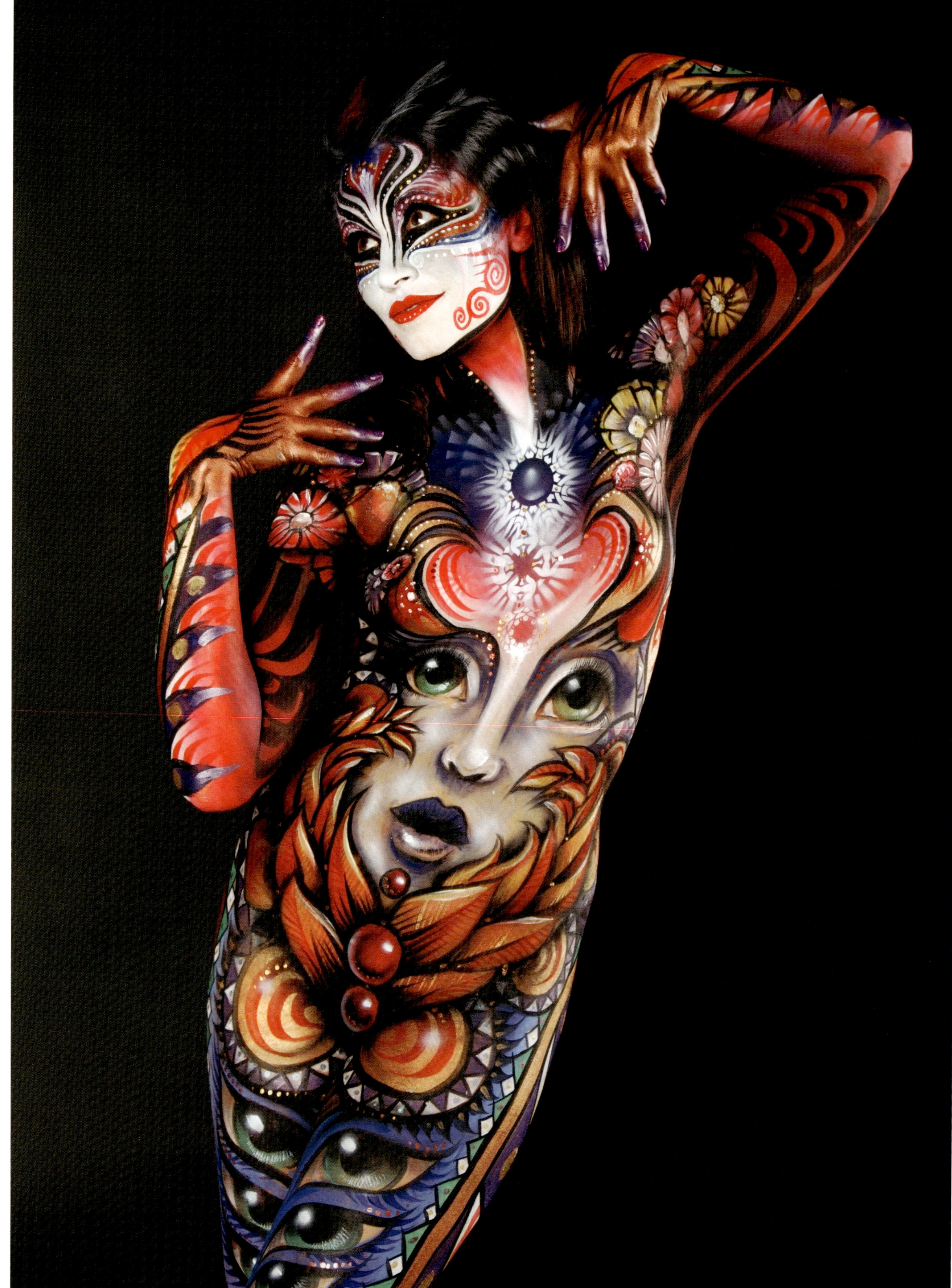

PHOTOGRAPHER DMITRI MOISEEV

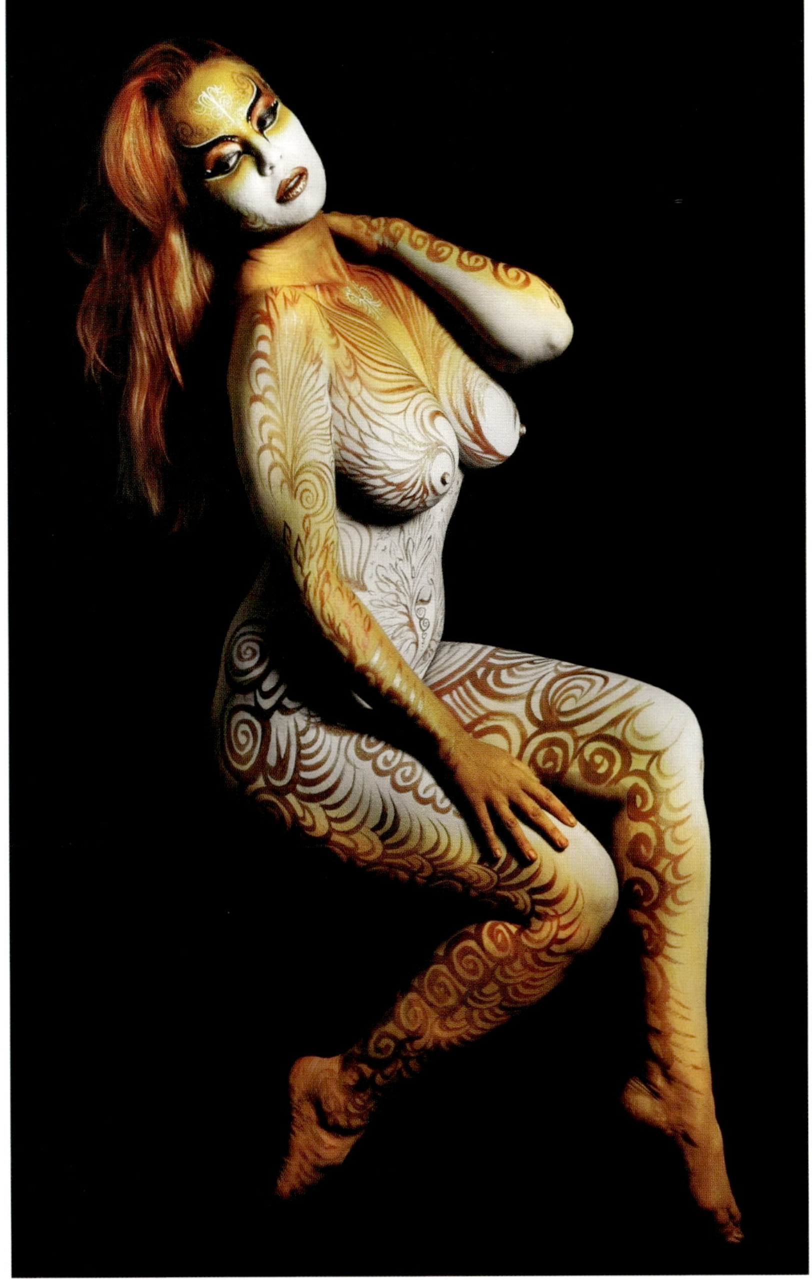

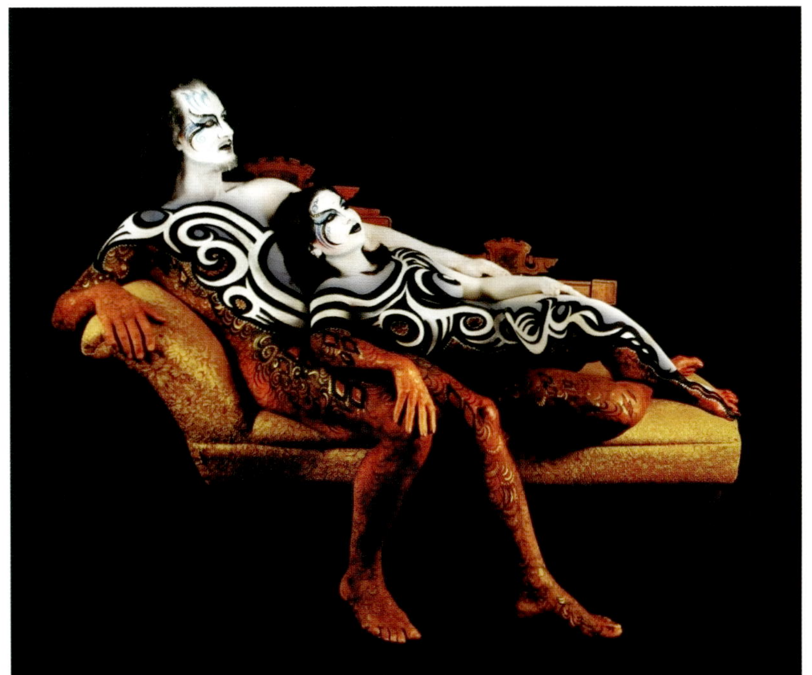

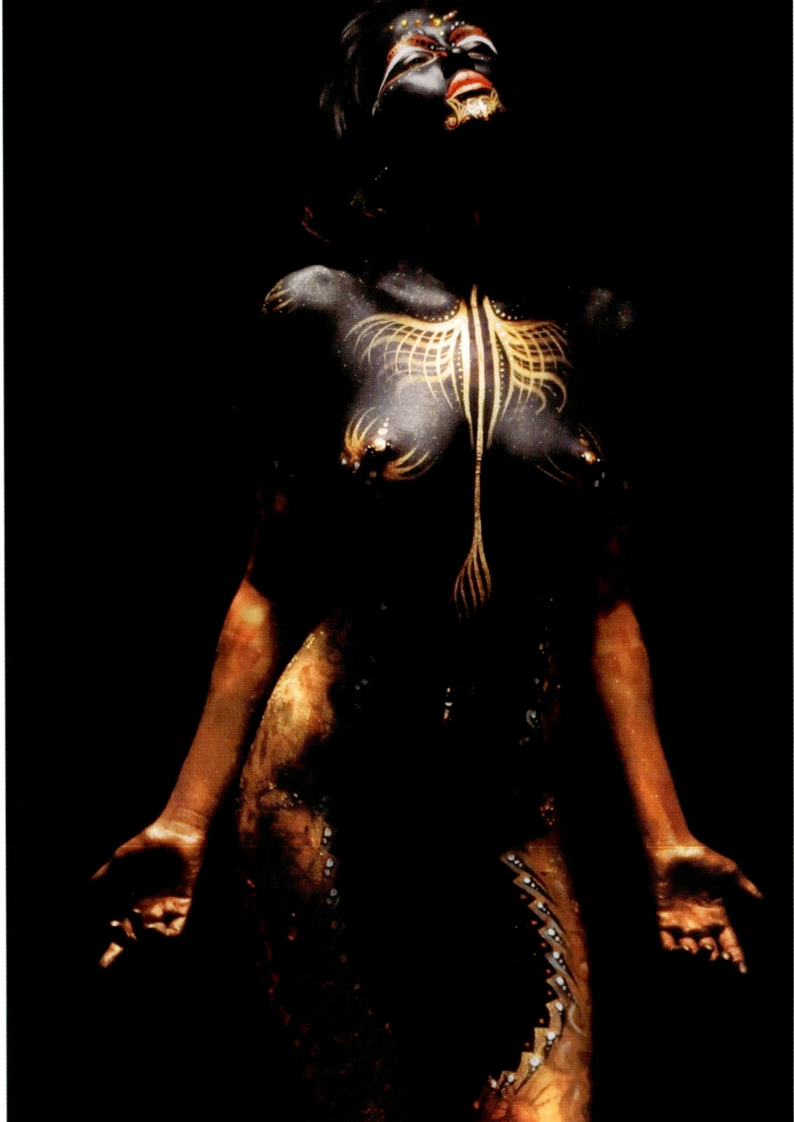

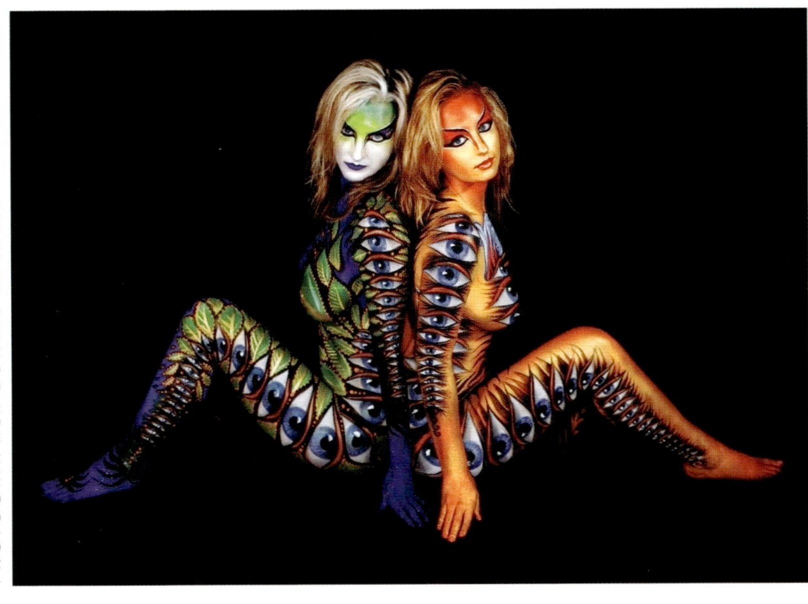

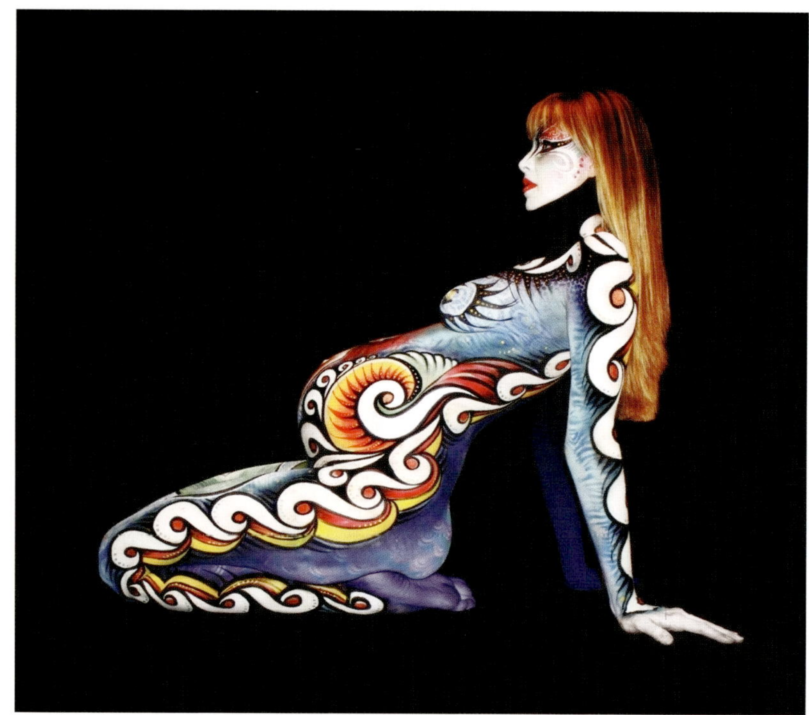

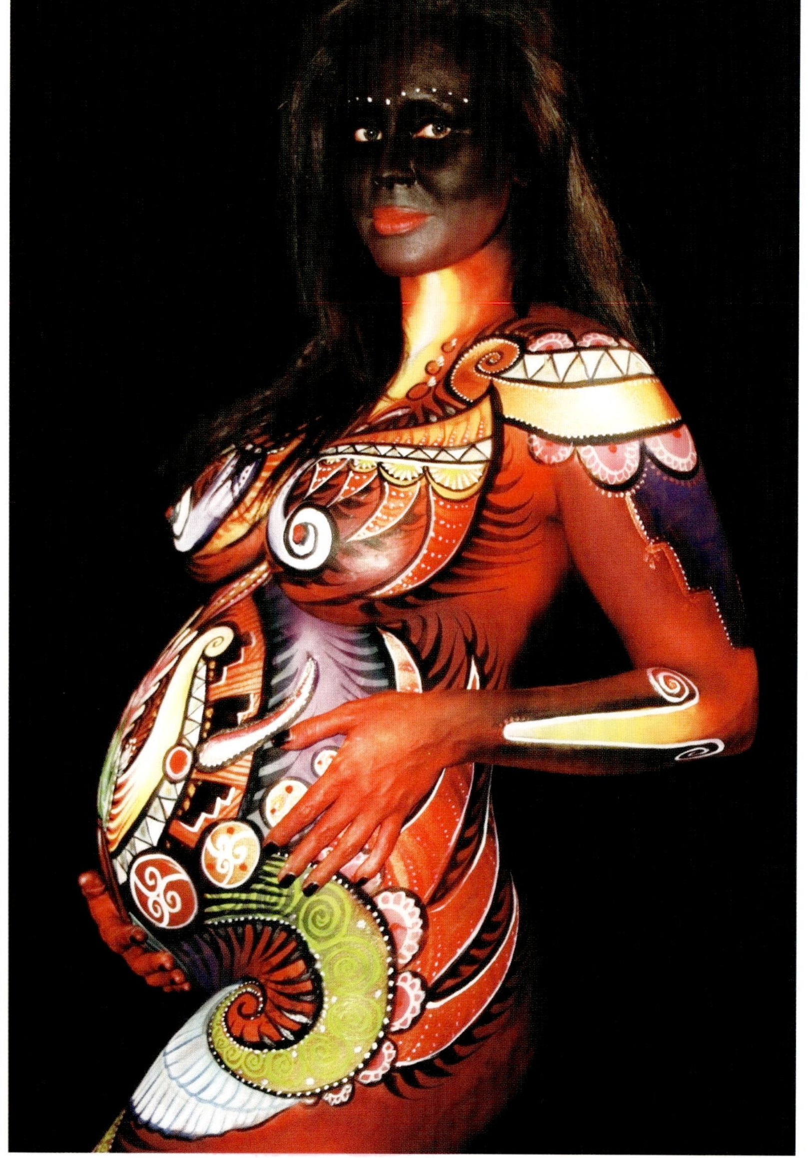

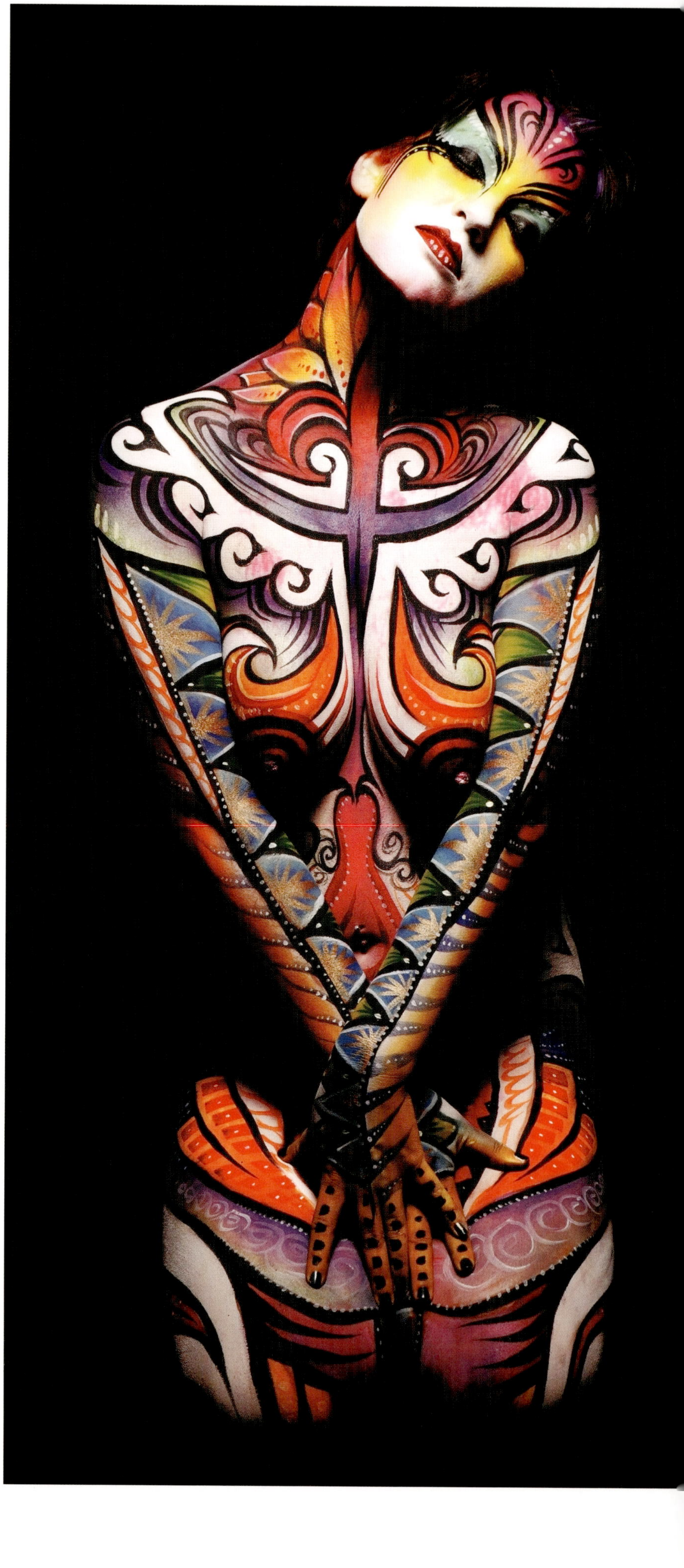

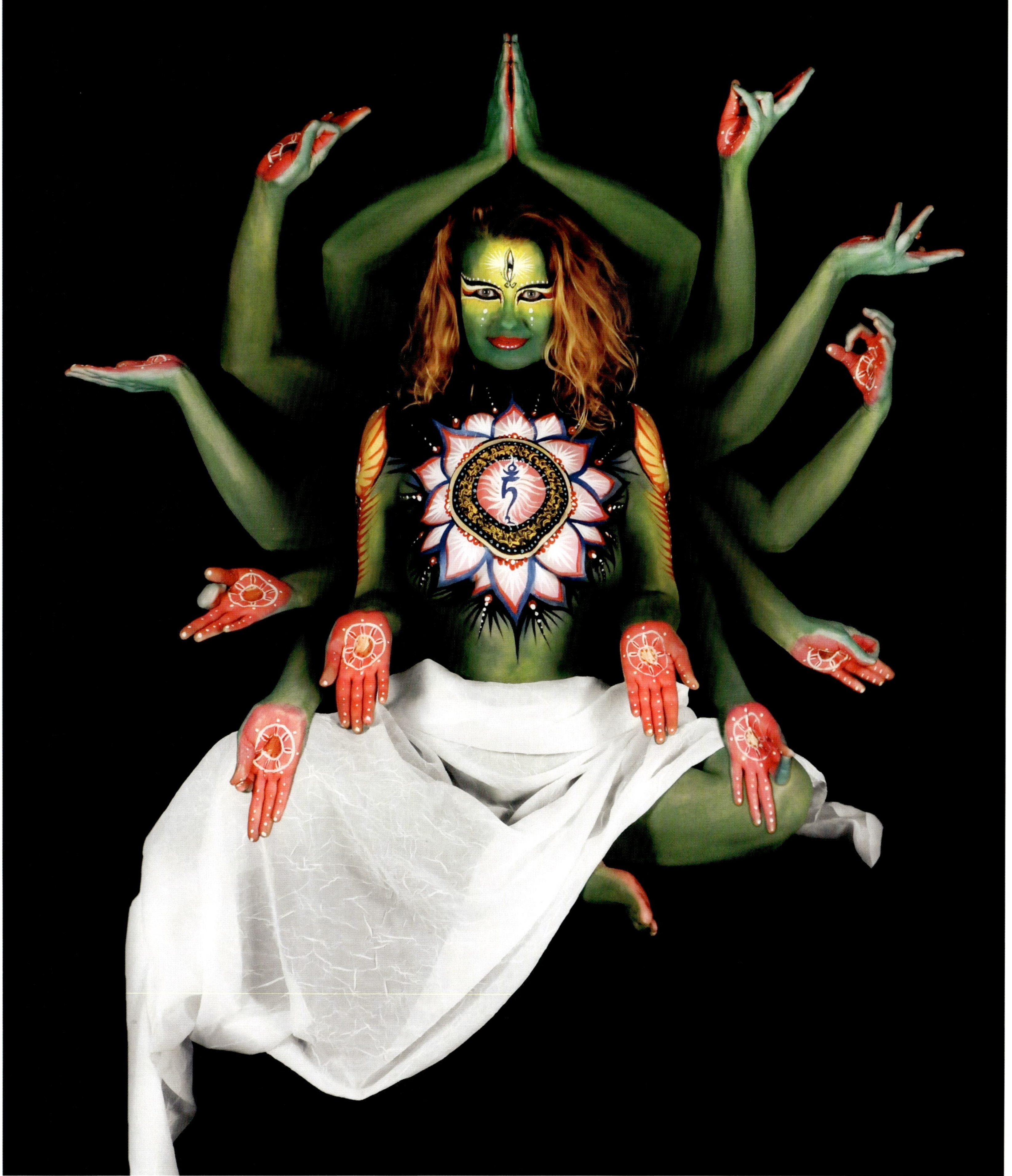

Gallery

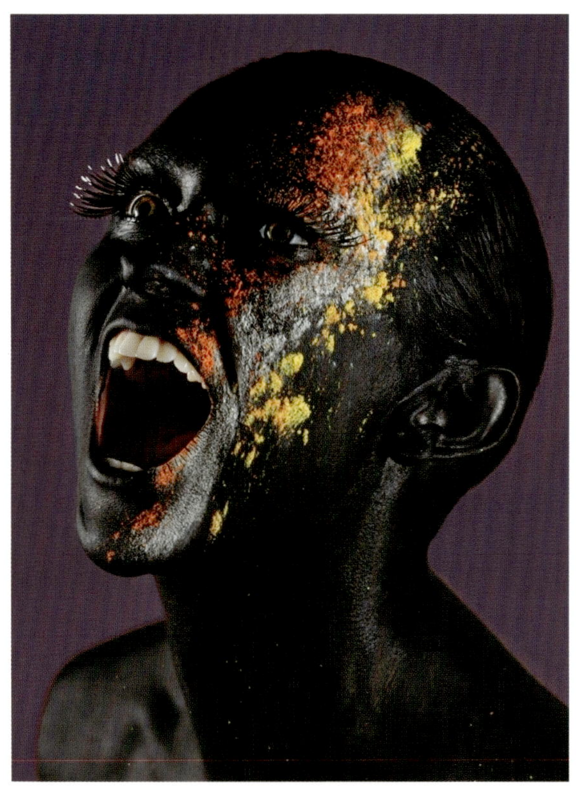

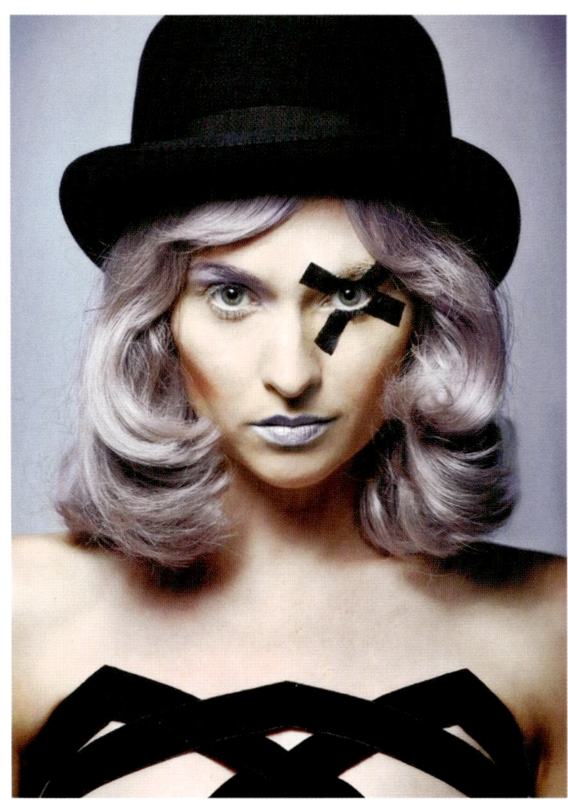

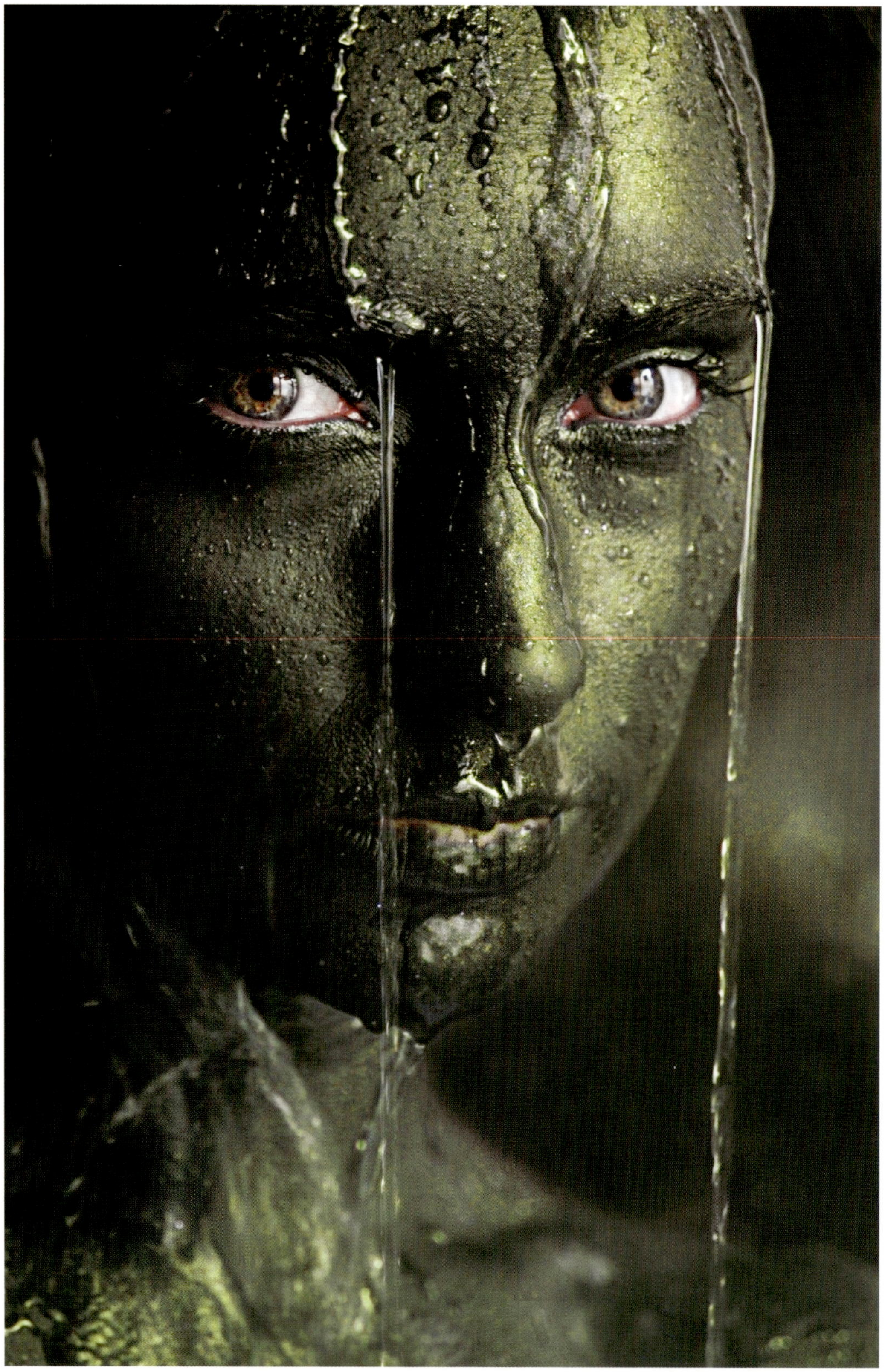

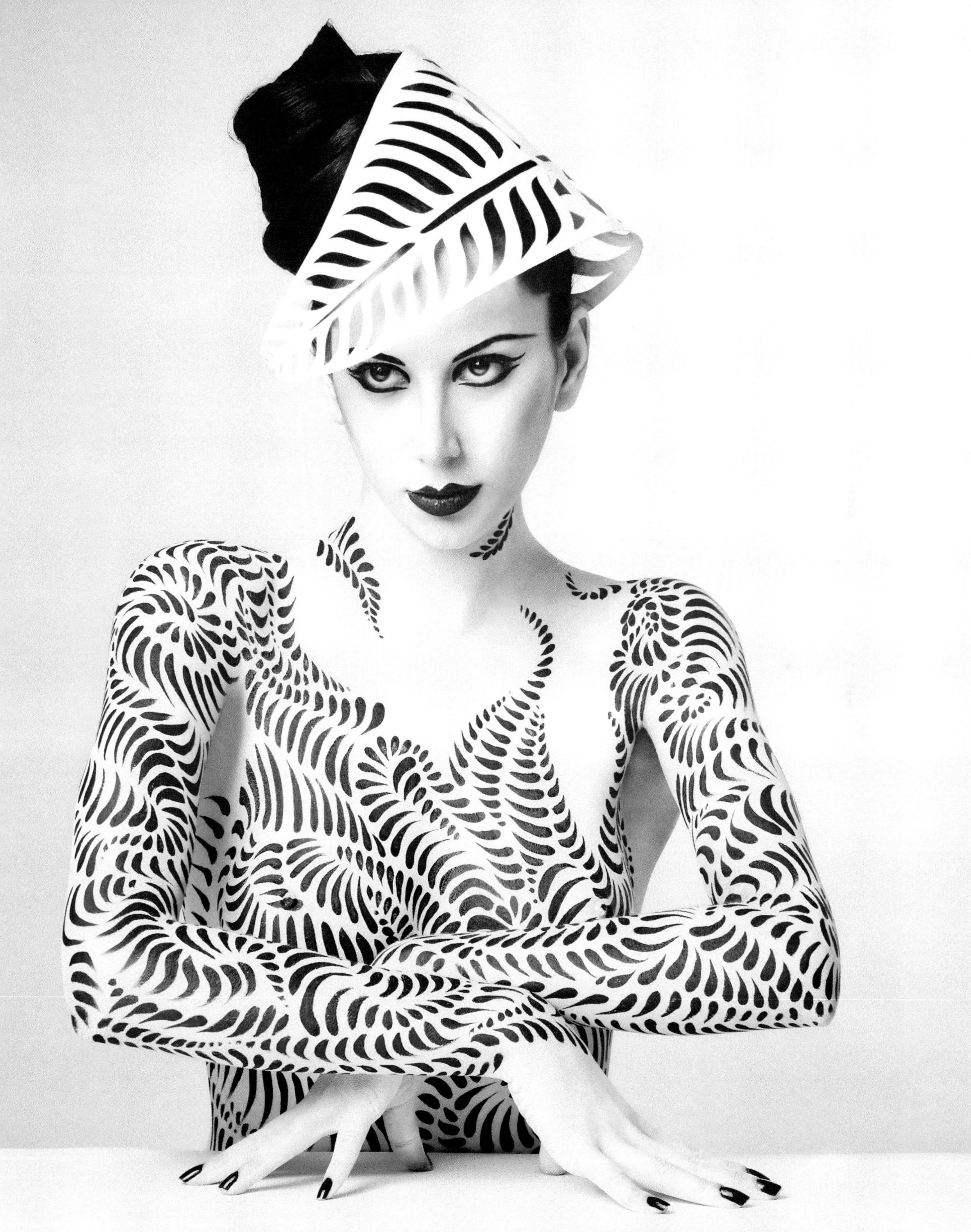

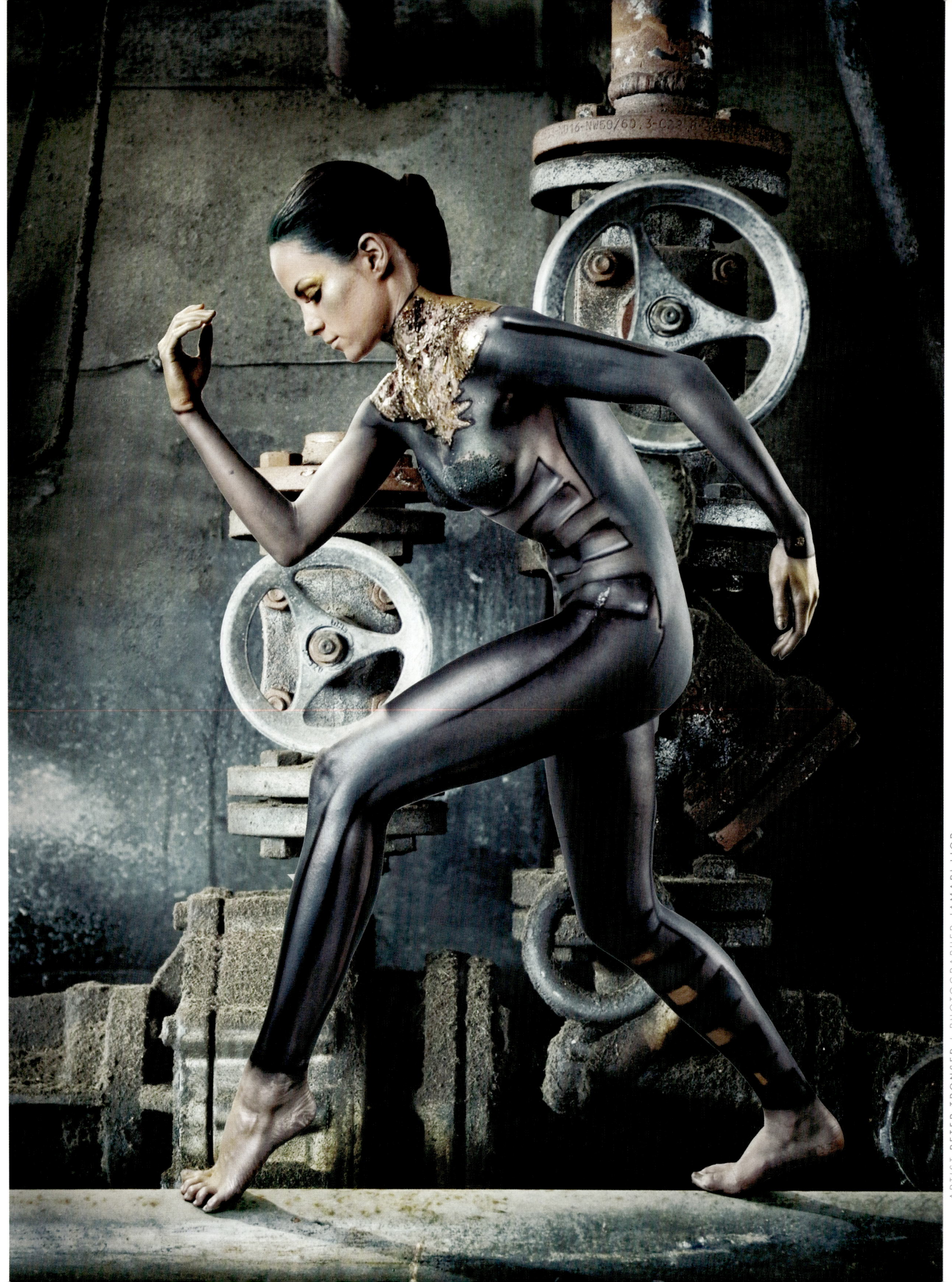

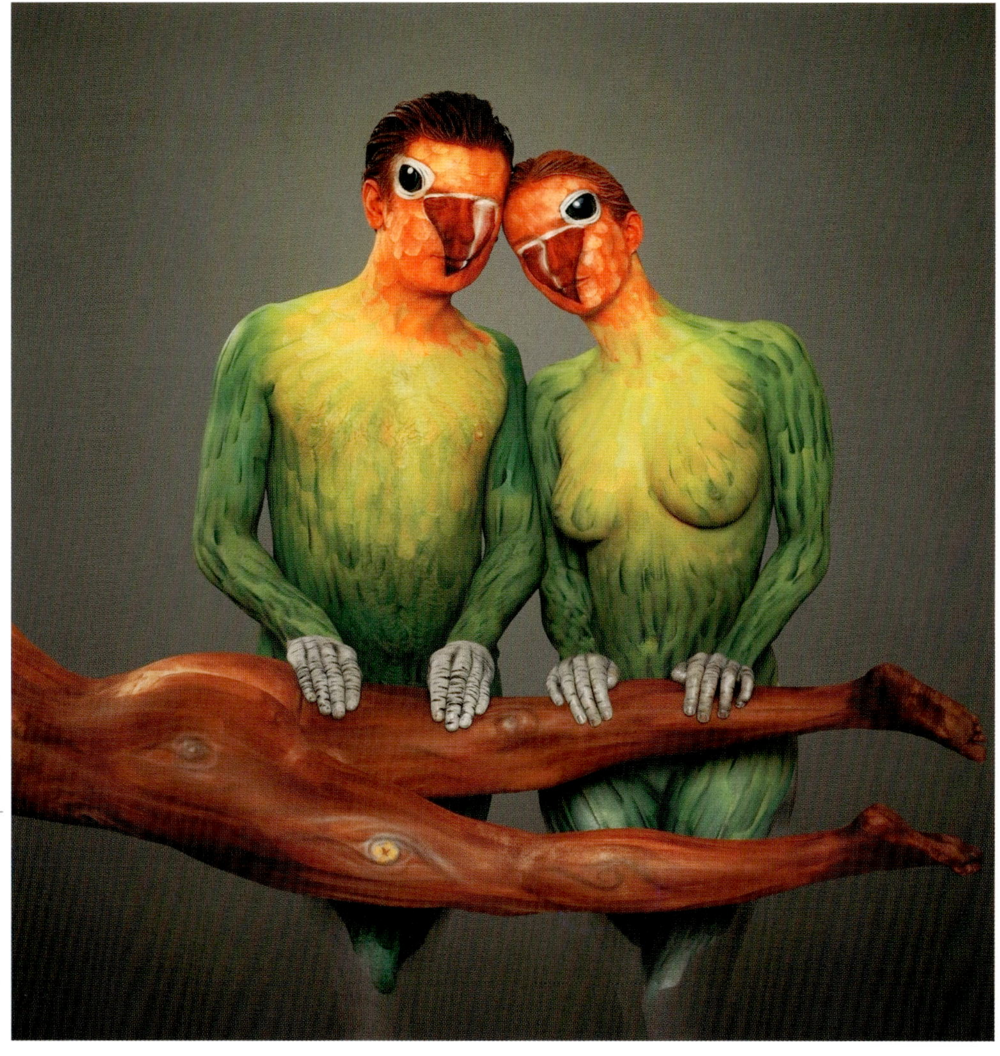

ARTIST KATE DEAN | PHOTOGRAPHER JIM JOHNSTON

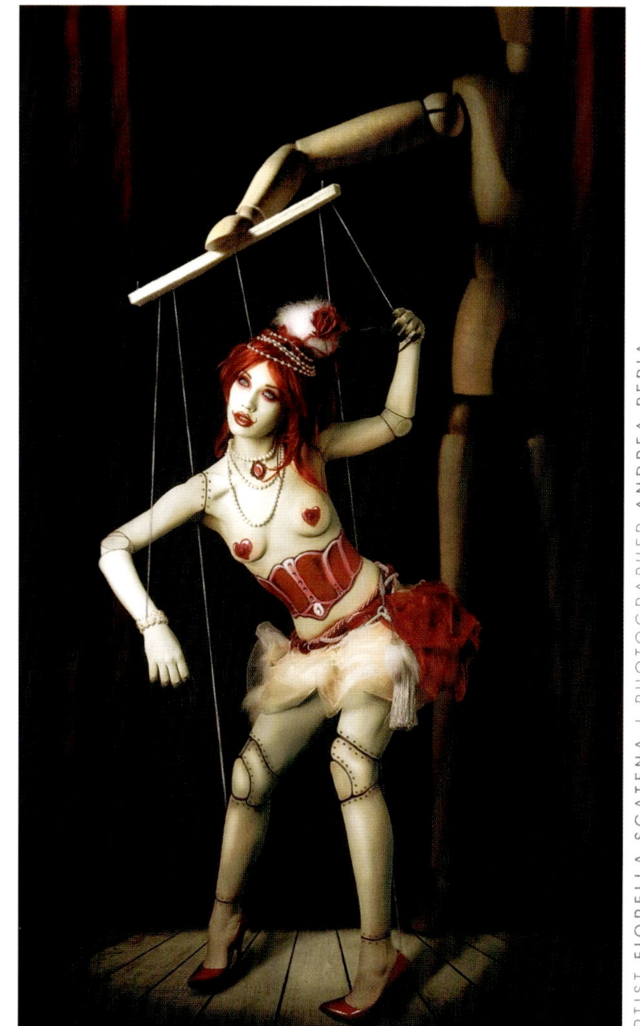

ARTIST FIORELLA SCATENA | PHOTOGRAPHER ANDREA PERIA

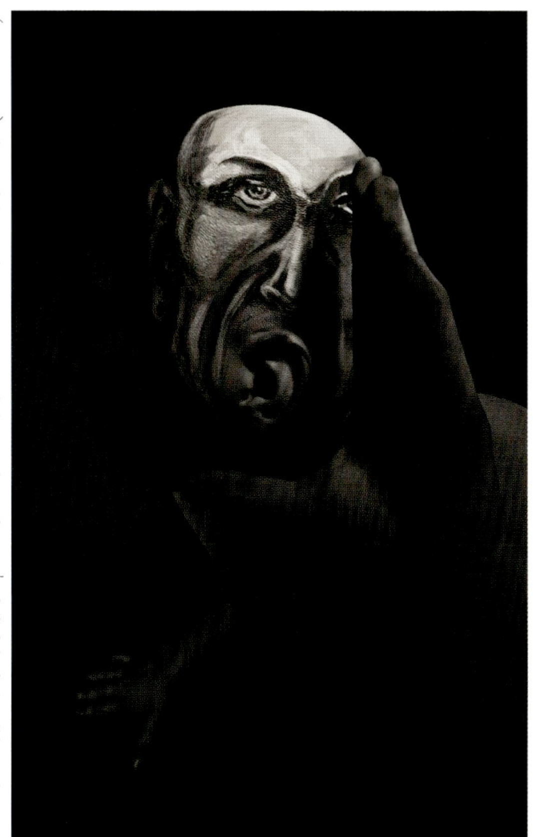

ARTIST HELEN DEMI | PHOTOGRAPHER MAX KALMYKOV
ARTIST FILIPPO LOCO | PHOTOGRAPHER FREDERICK ALGADO (CENTER)

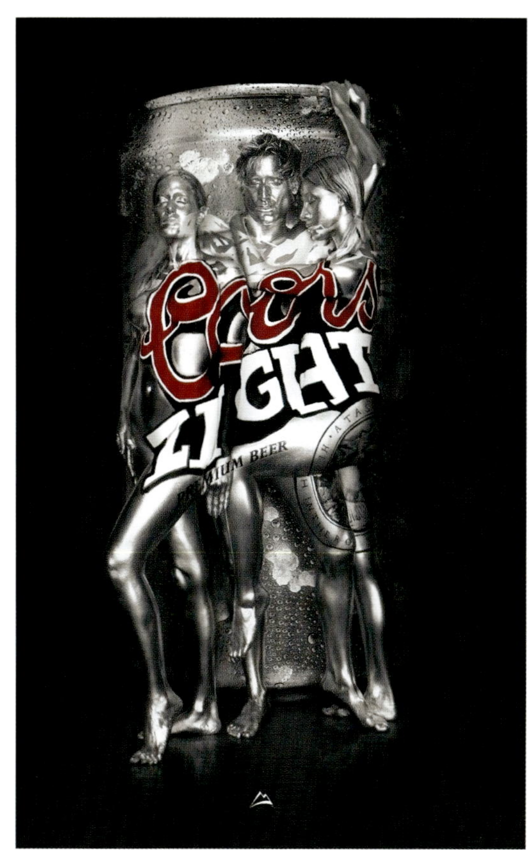

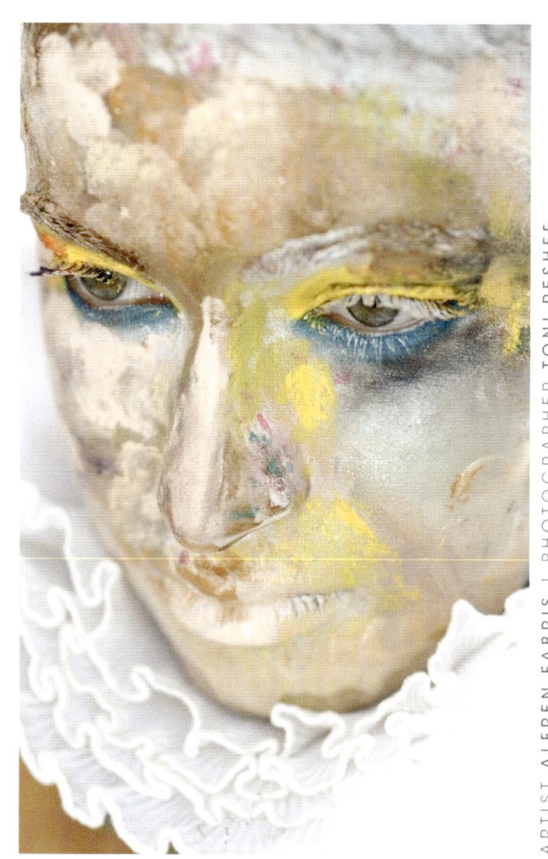

ARTIST ALFREN FABRIS | PHOTOGRAPHER TONI RESHEF

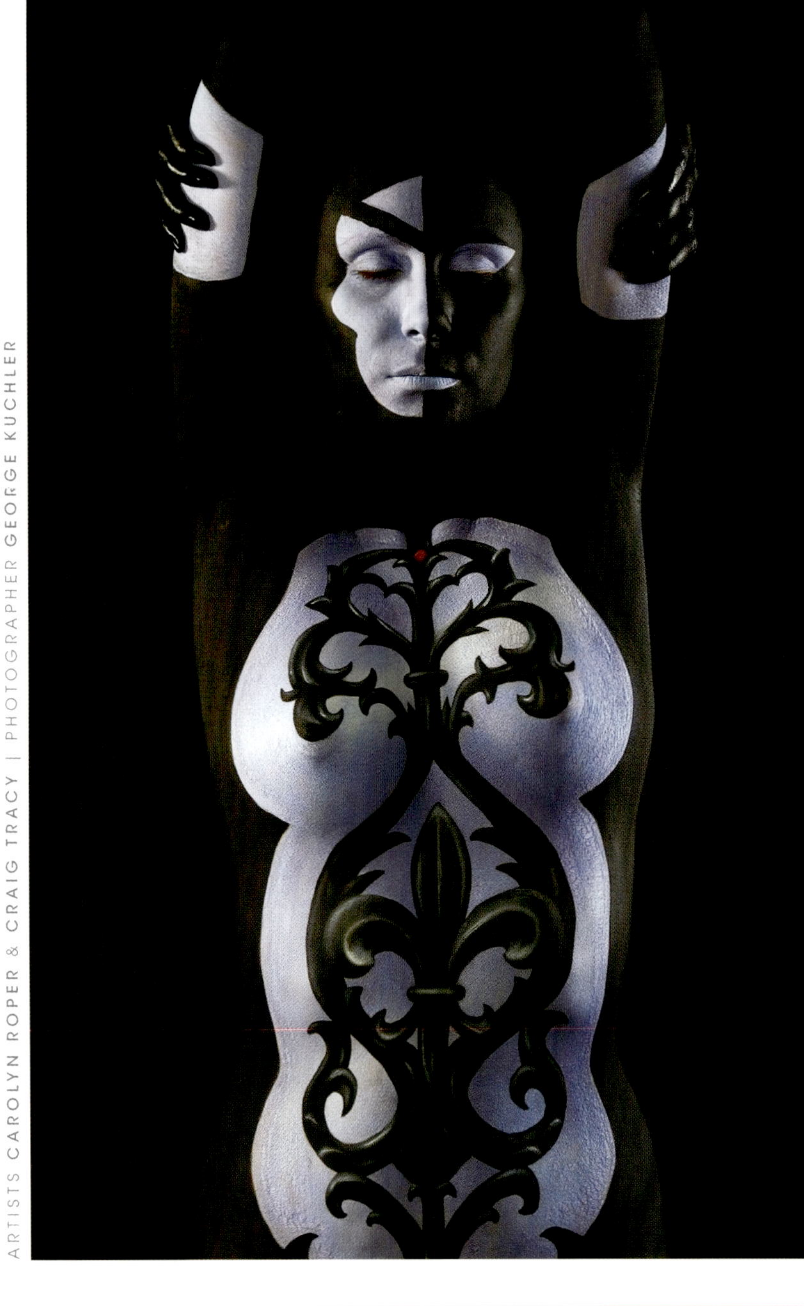
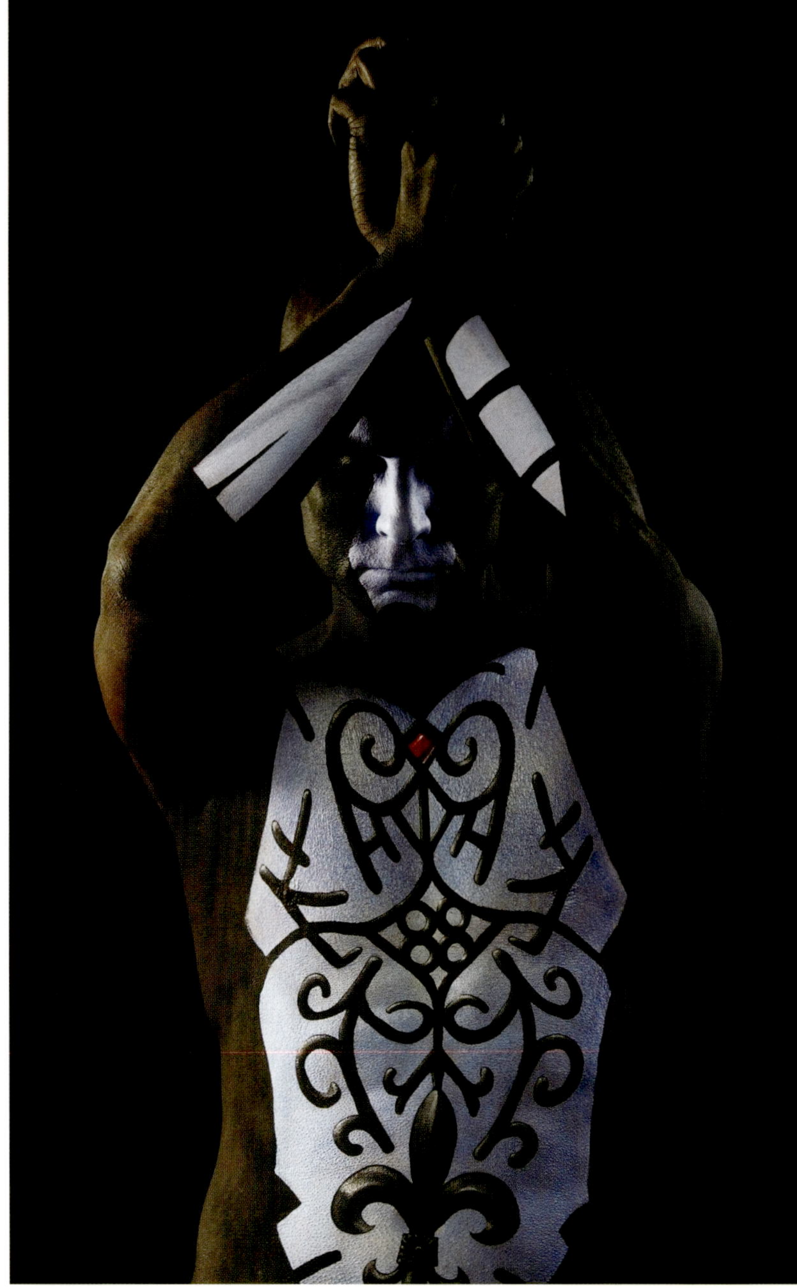

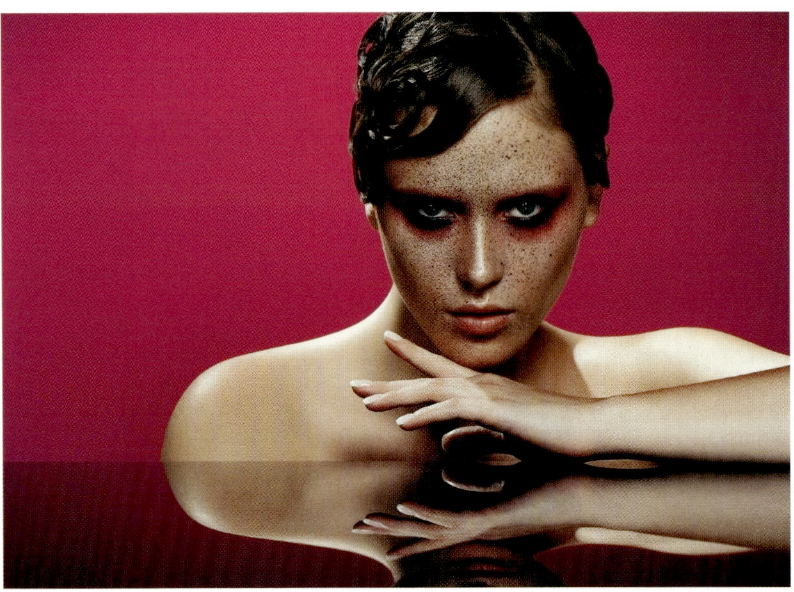
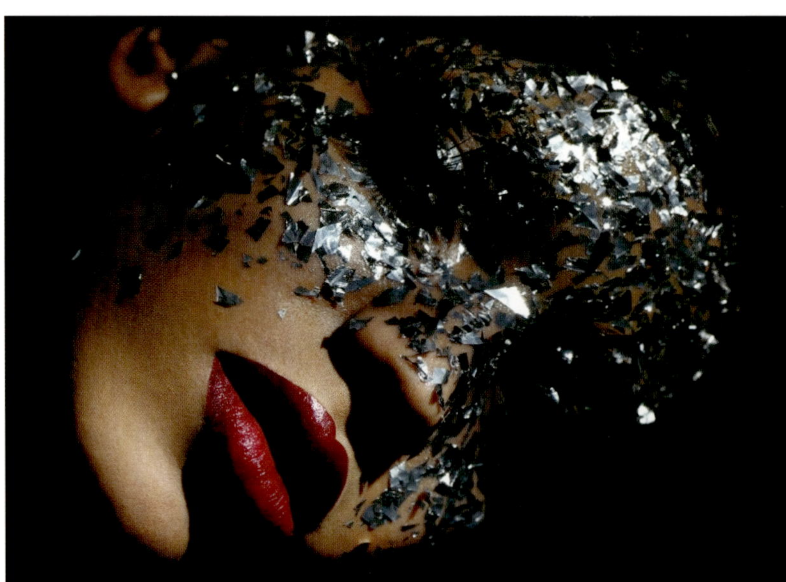

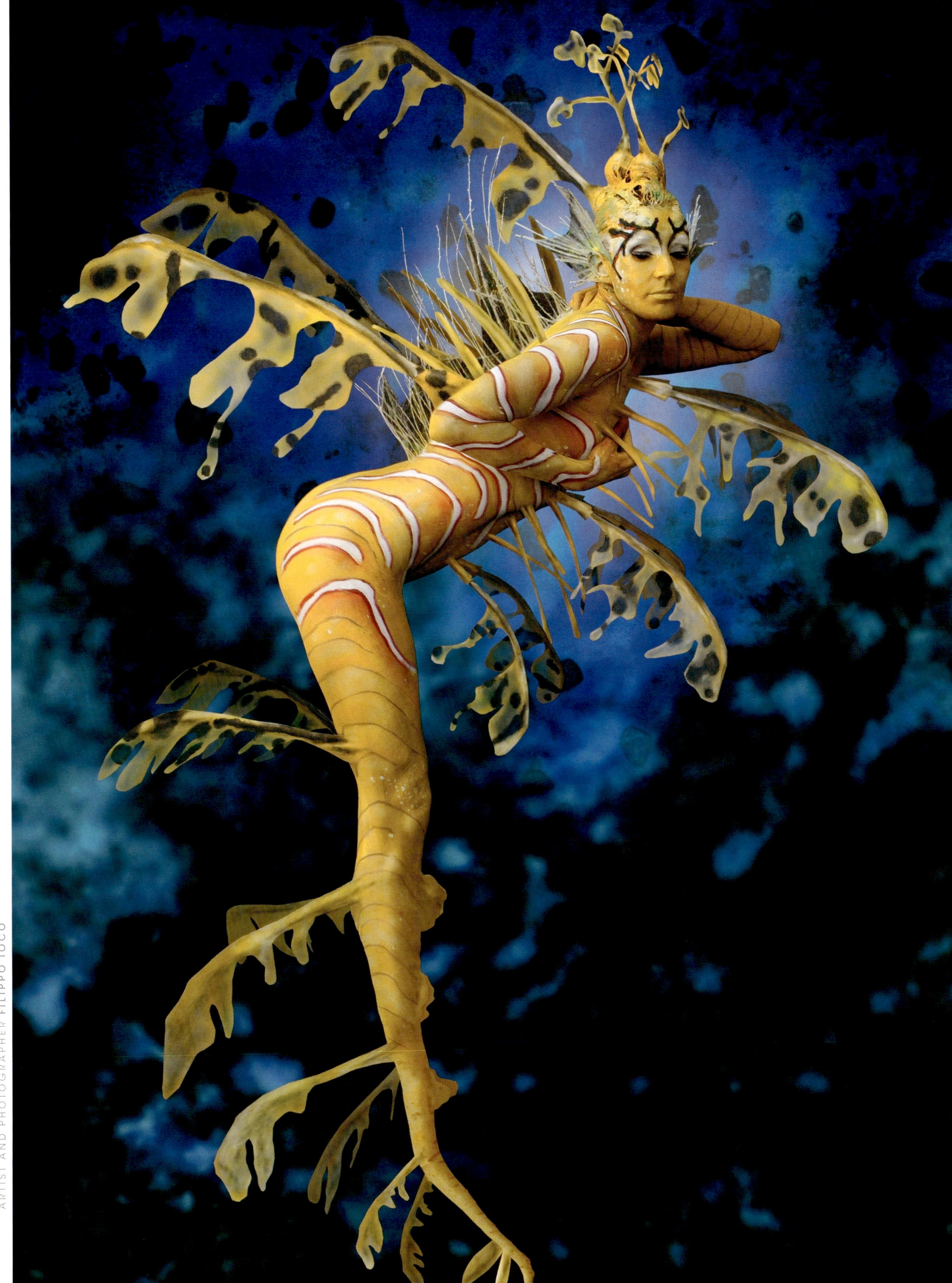

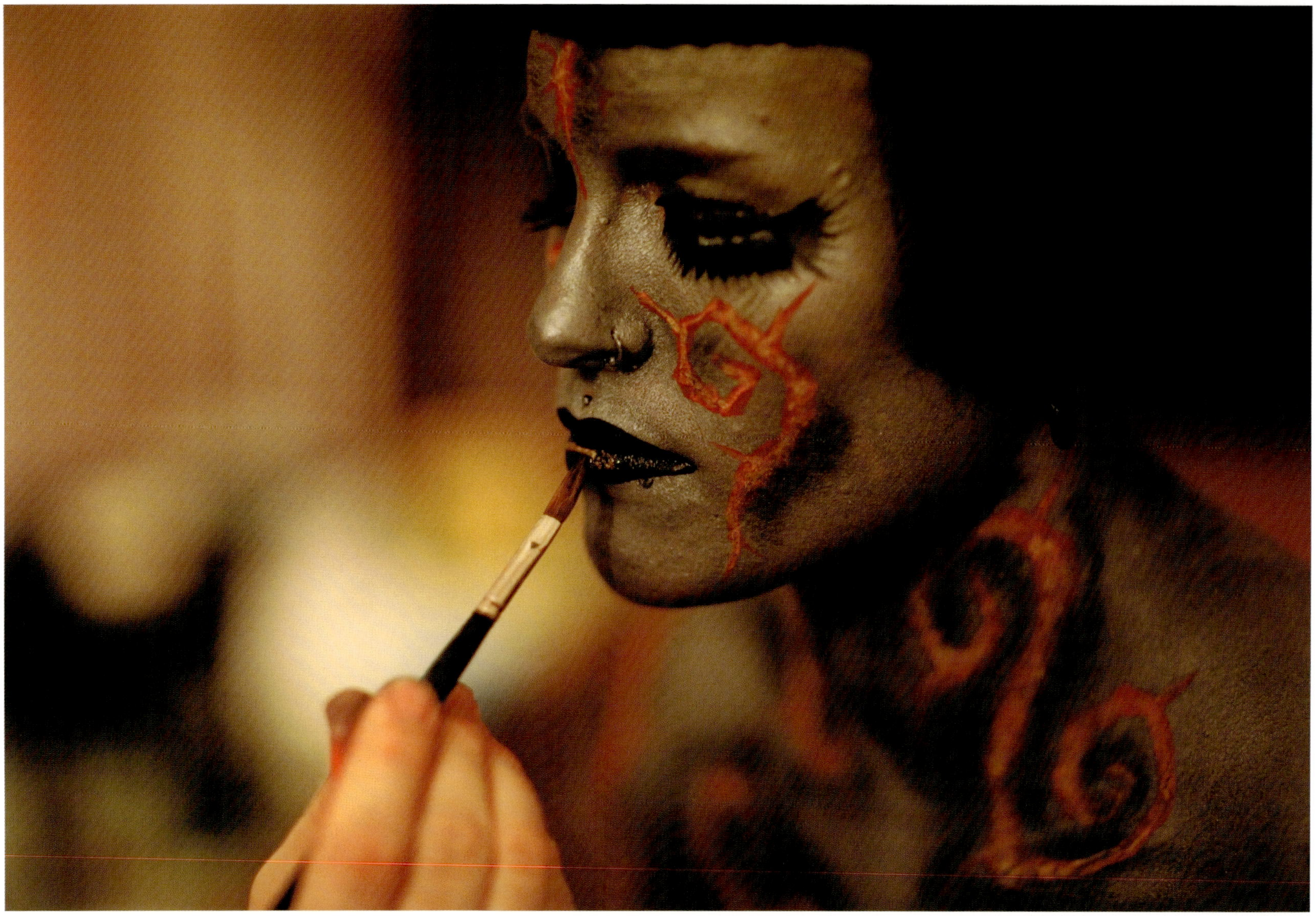

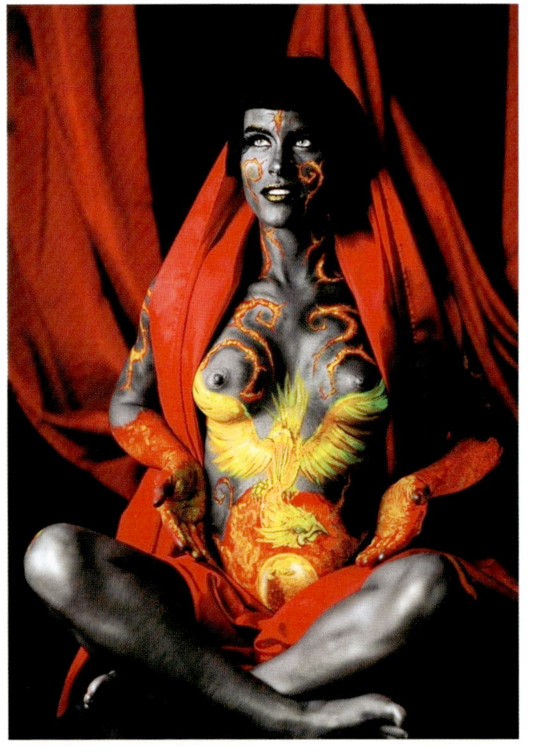
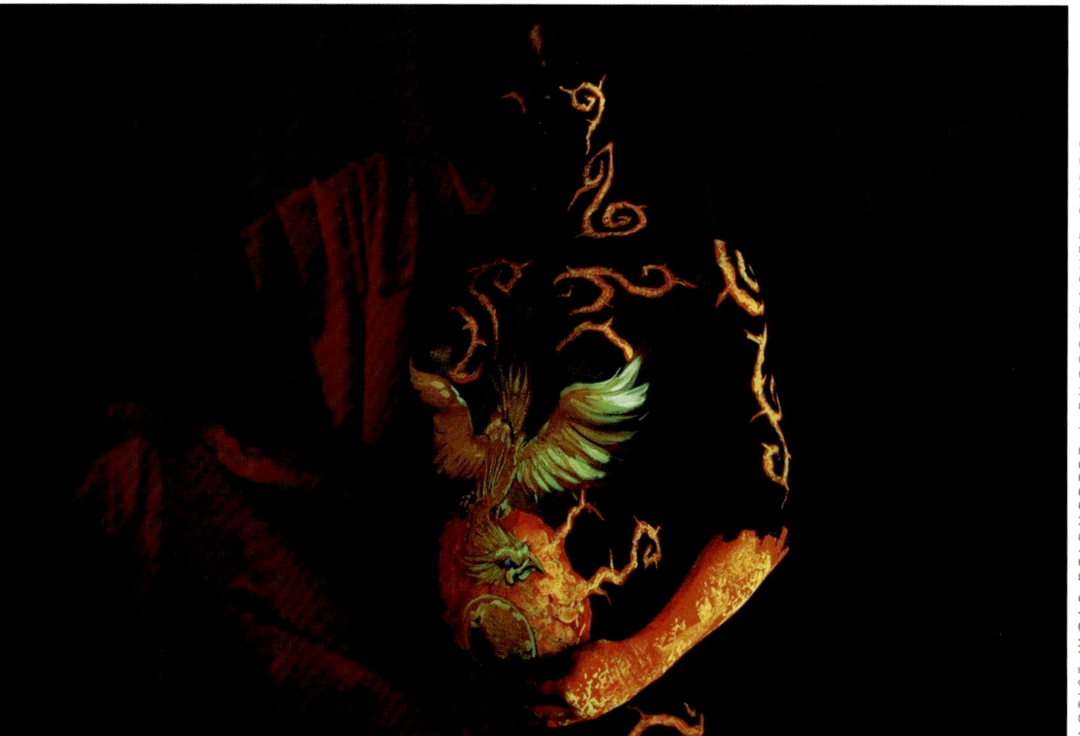

ARTIST WOLF REICHERTER | PHOTOGRAPHER ONDRO

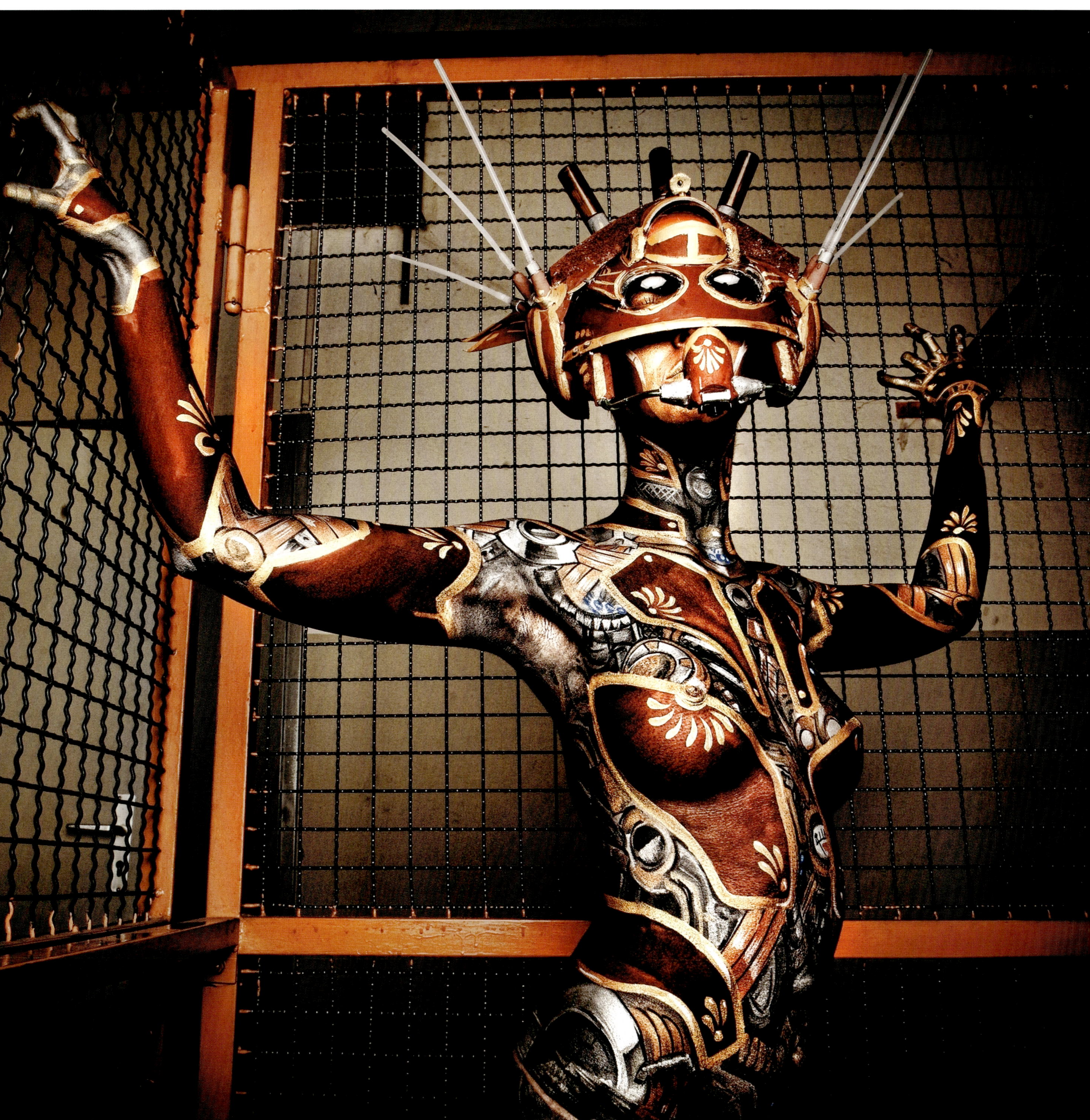

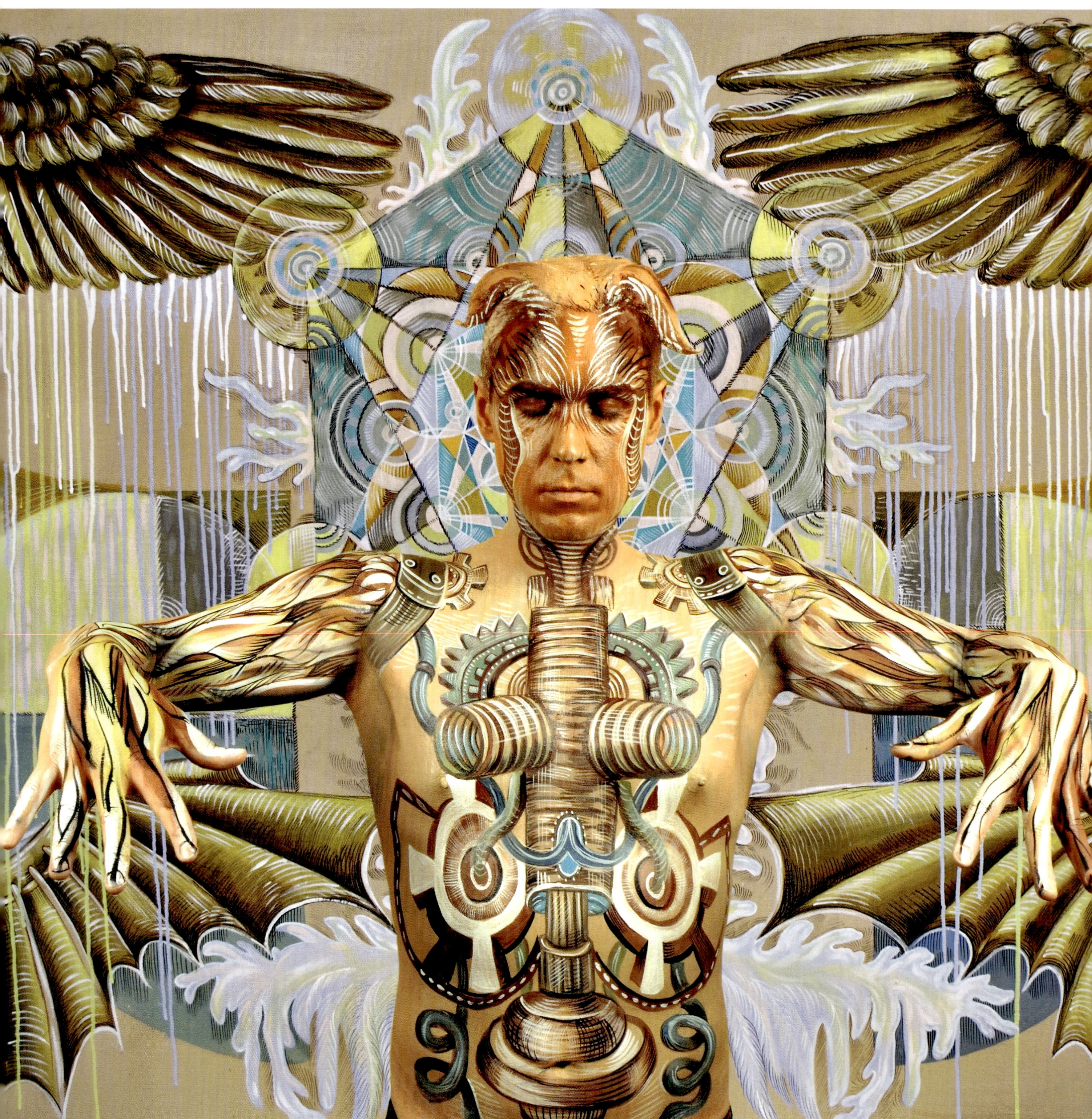

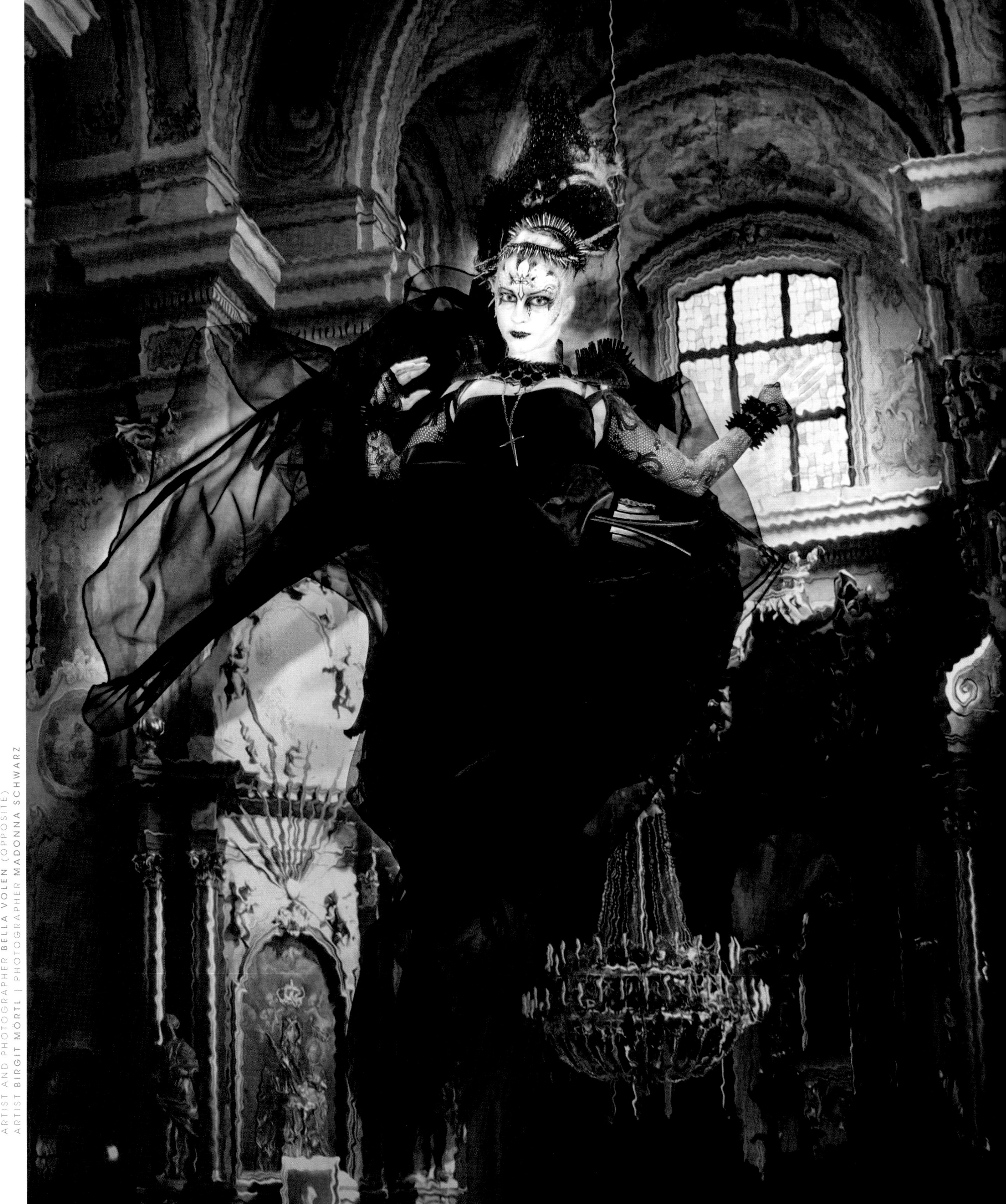

ARTIST AND PHOTOGRAPHER BELLA VOLEN (OPPOSITE)
ARTIST BIRGIT MÖRTL | PHOTOGRAPHER MADONNA SCHWARZ

Conclusion

Working with body art is a unique life experience. The very nature of the work enables the artist to be in contact with humans on an intimate level. When painting directly onto the skin of another person, the colors and symbols tend to awaken interesting emotional and cognitive states in both the artist and the model. The close proximity of bodies in concentration for long hours is like a combined meditation and conversation.

All bodypainting is art. Sometimes artists are working for a company or contractor, and sometimes they are working for themselves. There should be no change in the quality of the work, but there is often a difference in the spirit of the work. When bodypainters are able to create purely for the sake of art itself, they can channel their own muse and create a visual work of personal, political, social, racial, gender or spiritual significance. This is when bodypainting reaches into the world of fine art.

There are no boundaries or rules that specify exactly what a fine-art bodypainting is, but it can contain a message to the viewer. That message can be of personal importance to the artist and harmonize through color, composition and execution. A bodypainting artist can reach any height through purity of idea and expression.

These artists are spreading messages and sharing information through their thought, action and word. Some artists work with galleries to bring paintings into the houses of appreciators, and some travel the world, collaborating with other artists and performers to push themselves to even greater levels of creativity. The body art family is an international and often nomadic group of people who are broadening the experience of the art and what it means to be a bodypainter.

Every person has inner truths and greatness, love and vulnerability. Every individual experiences their own color of truth, and yet somehow, this billion-strong pallet of souls exchanging and experiencing their own truths paints an ever-changing, growing picture that is life.

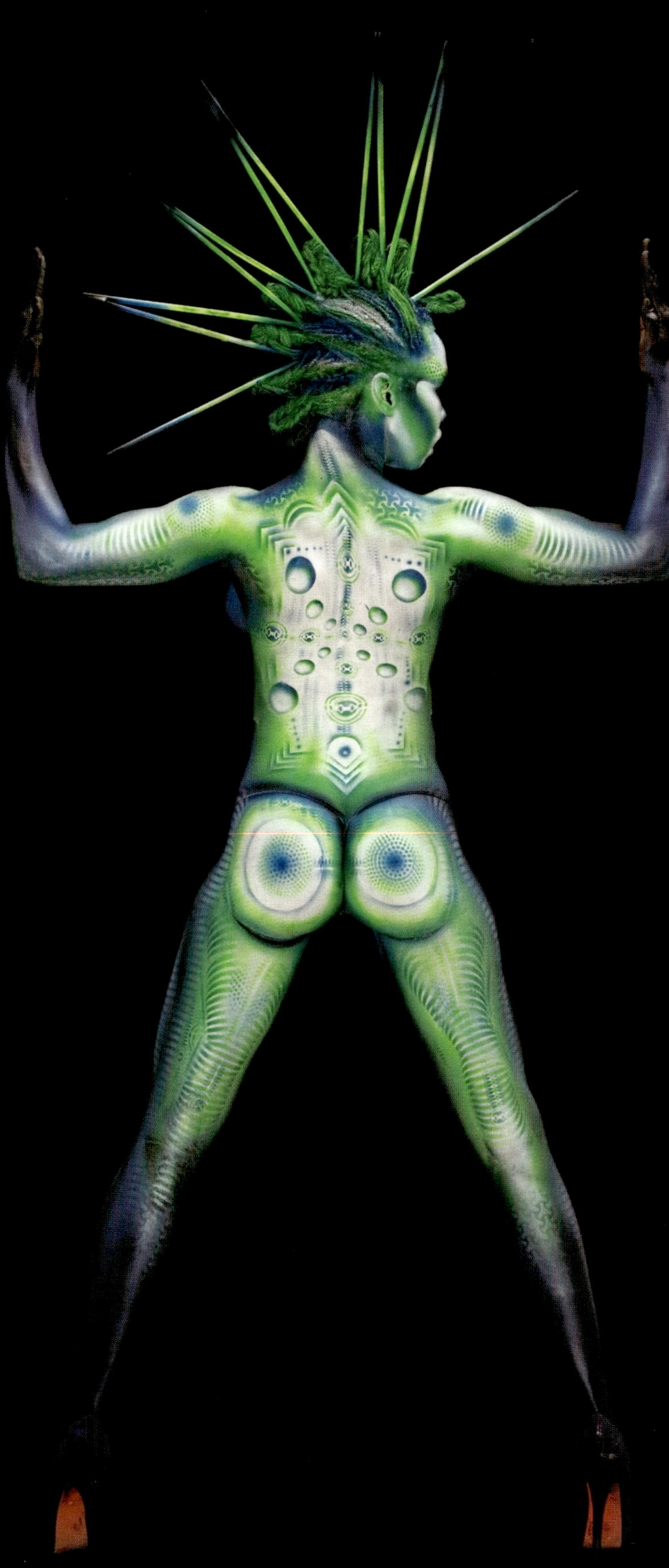

ABOUT THE AUTHOR

Karala B. Wallace is an artist and author from Sydney, Australia, living in the south of Austria. She is mostly known for her work in the body art industry, having written the first-ever combined work on body art, which included the history of the art form, its modern uses and profiles of iconic artists of the movement.

Karala began her work in the industry in 1999 and worked for the World Bodypainting Association from 2004 until 2010, researching the art form and its growth. She then dedicated her time to public speaking and writing books and articles to spread knowledge of the artists and their work in Europe, Australia and North America.

Her first three books were privately published through the World Bodypainting Association and Kryolan, including *Bringing Bodypainting to Life* (2008), *Body Art Fashion* (2011) and *Champion at Heart* (2013). These books sold internationally in more than fifteen countries and have become teaching guides in most makeup and body art institutes around the world.

Other projects from Karala B. Wallace have included a children's book series aimed at developing children's connections to the natural world; a series of five stage shows under the title "Body Art Fashion," which included up to fifteen of the world's best artists and around forty models and performers at the World Bodypainting Festival; English language communication work in Austria; and many performance-based and fashion-based art projects around the world.

ACKNOWLEDGMENTS

With every book I produce, the list of people I want to thank grows, which is beautiful.

First, thank you to all the artists, photographers and models who have taken part in creating this book. I am so happy to know you all and share these growing and mixing stories of our lives over the years.

Thank you to Brian Wolfe, whose idea it was to make this book in the first place. One of the last communications I had with you and such a special one.

Thank you to Mona and Beth from F+W Media for working on the project with me. It was a wonderful and unexpected surprise to be taken on by you.

Thank you to Alex Barendregt for creating the World Bodypainting Festival. Without your years of work and dedication, many of the artists in this book would never have met. Through your work, the level of ability in the bodypainting world has been challenged to grow to amazing heights.

Thank you to Joshua David Lim from Creative Confluence Media for your support as a photographer and collaborator in much of my work.

Thank you to Sebastian Langer, who just amazes me with his support and trust. You have shown me over and over again that Kryolan as a company has maintained a personal connection to the direction of the lives of bodypainting artists, no matter how large the company grows.

Of course my biggest thanks are again to Sammy B., the little man in my life who reminds me what it's all about and keeps it fun, and to Nitara, for waiting long enough to be born so we could get this book project finished!

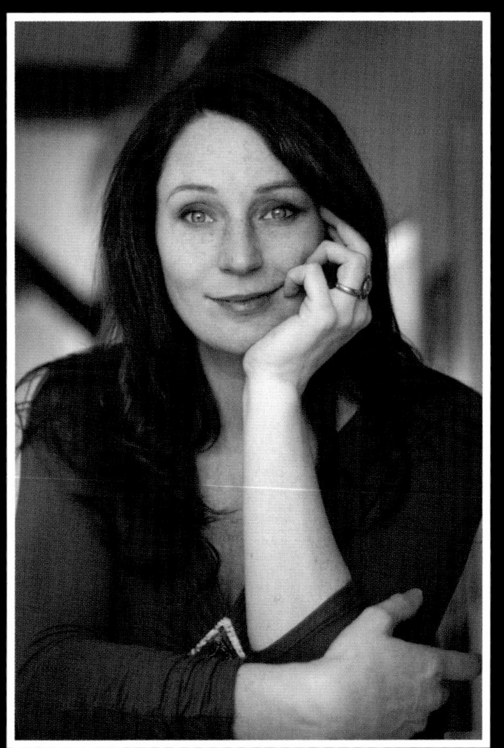

Index

A
action-painting style, 175
airbrush, 49, 169
Arfanotti, Matteo, 37
Art Color Ballet, 54–63

B
Barlini, Arianna, 27
Bartenev, Andrey, 137
Bartram, Julian, 31
Bartram, Yolanda, 28, 40, 195
Bastos, Joana, 13
Benomar, Sophia, 14, 38
bodypainting, 8, 204
  conceptual, 137
brush and sponge, 83
The Brushers, 29
Bull, Sahra, 35

C
canvas art, 87
Carugati, Benedetta, 26
Caze, Anne, 31
Choi, Hee-Kyung, 26
choreography, 55
Clancy, Deirdre, 137
ColorSensation, 113
costume design, 73
Craig Tracy Gallery, 87

D
Dan, Einat, 9, 16, 21, 38, 100–101, 102–111, 198
Dean, Kate, 164-165, 166-167, 196
Deksne, Inese, 15
Demi, Helen, 136–137, 138–139, 197

E
Elizarova, Kristina, 29, 37–38, 47,
  168–169, 170–173

F
Fabris, Alfren, 197
Fieldhouse, Raphaelle, 38
Fray, Scott, 10, 36, 186–187, 188–193
Fusilier, Julie, 41

G
Glinska, Agnieszka, 43–45, 54–55, 56–63
Greco, Madelyn, 186–187, 188–193

H
Hajek-Renner, Gabriela, 23
Hajlaoui, Houyam, 32
Hamel, Lorie, 24, 41
Hansen, Alex, 26, 33, 40, 48–49, 50–53
Herrera, Nick, 26, 33, 198
Houle, Geneviève (Jinny) 140–143

I
Ioco, Filippo, 118–119, 120–135, 197, 199
Isaev, Igor, 137

J
Jinny (Geneviève Houle), 140–143

K
Karala B. 150–151, 152–157
Kim, Min Ah, 37

L
Lein, Enrico, 17
Leis, Patrick, 38
Lockwood, Lara, 194

M
makeup art, 101, 113
Molnar, Eva, 34
Mörtl, Birgit, 25, 34–35, 72–73, 74-81, 203

P
paintloon, 65
Parhatskaja, Evgenia, 11, 39
Park, Ju Hee, 26
Pedersen, Sofia Bue, 18
performing art, 55
prosthetics, 49
Purvena, Lauma, 15

R
Reicherter, Wolf, 200–201
Roper, Carolyn, 20, 82–83, 84–85, 198
Rose, Francois, 13

S
Scatena, Fiorella, 30, 197
Schmid, Fredi, 20–21, 42
Schockmel, Lynn, 34
Shane, Mike, 174–175, 176–179
Sokolova, Olga, 29
Southern, Paula, 83
Stötter, Johannes, 33, 144–145, 146–149

T
Tagliapietra, Elena, 112–113, 114–117
Tracy, Craig, 86–87, 88–99
Tronser, Peter, 42, 196

U
Utting, Carly, 83

V
Vadócz, Edina, 33
van der Laan, Richard, 33
Vargas, Anabel, 198
Volen, Bella, 64–65, 66–71, 202
von der Linnepe, Gabi, 22

W
Wolfe, Brian, 4, 30, 46, 180–181, 182–185
Wolfe, Nick, 19, 30, 180–181, 182–185
World Bodypainting Festival, 11

Y
Yiu, Karen, 158–159, 160–163

Other fine IMPACT Books are available from your favorite bookstore, art supply store or online supplier. Visit our website at **fwmedia.com**.

18 17 16 15 14   5 4 3 2 1

Distributed in Canada by Fraser Direct
100 Armstrong Avenue
Georgetown, ON, Canada L7G 5S4
Tel: (905) 877-4411

Distributed in the U.K. and Europe
by F&W Media International LTD
Brunel House, Forde Close,
Newton Abbot, TQ12 4PU, UK
Tel: (+44) 1626 323200; Fax: (+44) 1626 323319
Email: enquiries@fwmedia.com

Distributed in Australia by Capricorn Link
P.O. Box 704, S. Windsor NSW, 2756 Australia
Tel: (02) 4560-1600; Fax: (02) 4577 5288
Email: books@capricornlink.com.au

ISBN 13: 978-1-4403-3700-0

Edited by **Beth Erikson**
Designed by **Jennifer Hoffman**
Production coordinated by **Mark Griffin**

COVER ART:
Agnieszka Glinska | Photographer Sylwia Boryczko
Johannes Stötter
Einat Dan | Photographer Suzana Holtgrave
Agnieszka Glinska | Photographer Darek Gutowski

ENDPAPER ART:
Filippo Ioco
Bella Volen
Kate Dean | Photographer Jim Johnston
Birgit Mörtl | Photographer Martin Aigner

TITLE PAGE ART:
Birgit Mörtl | Photographer Gerhard Merzeder

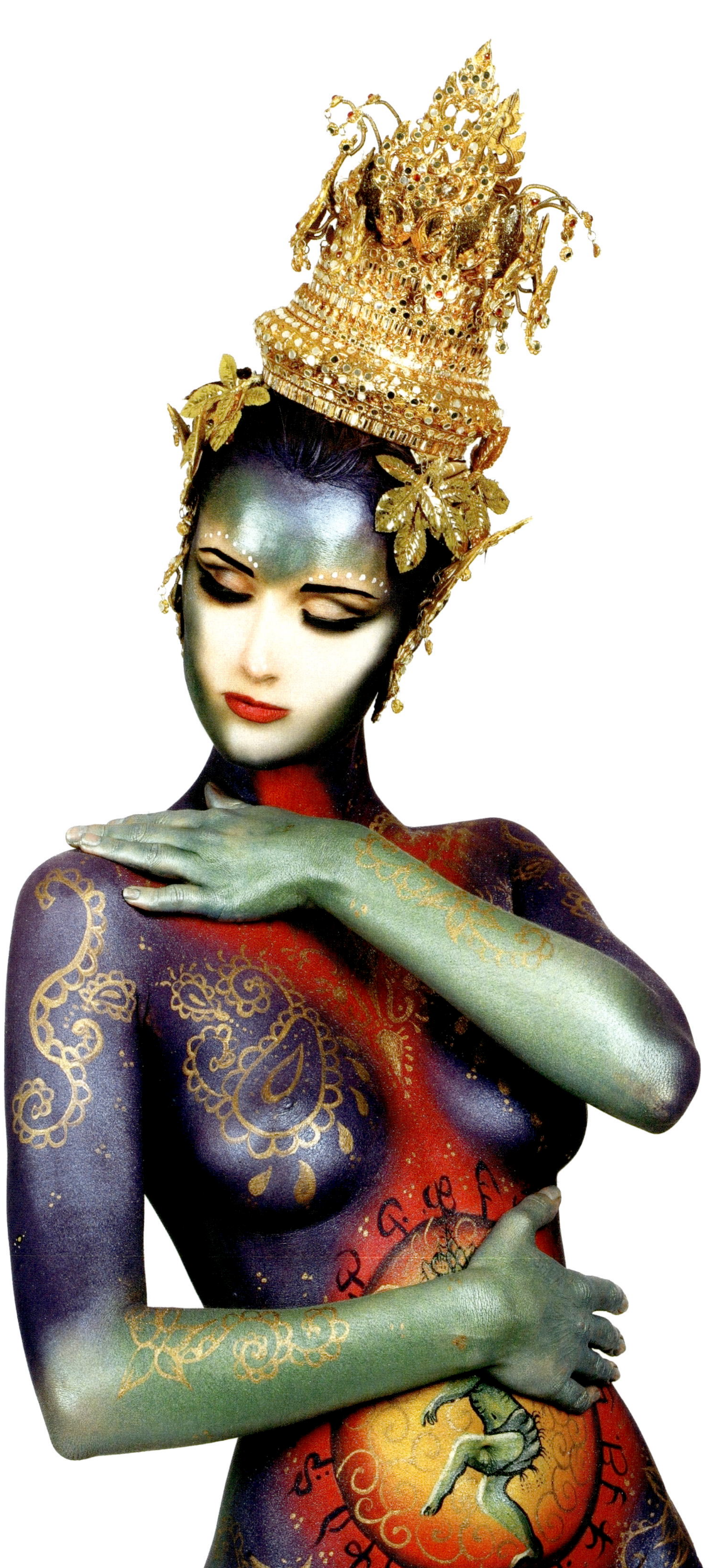

ARTIST CAROLYN ROPER | PHOTOGRAPHER JOACHIM BERGAUER

Ideas. Instruction. Inspiration.

DOWNLOAD FREE DESKTOP WALLPAPER AT IMPACT-BOOKS.COM/HUMANCANVAS.

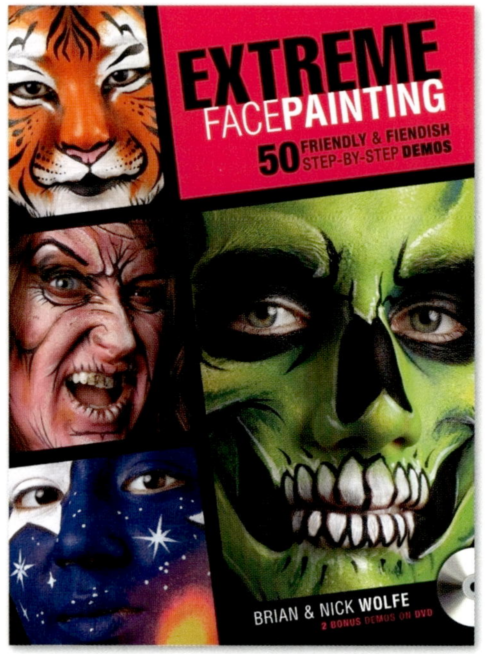

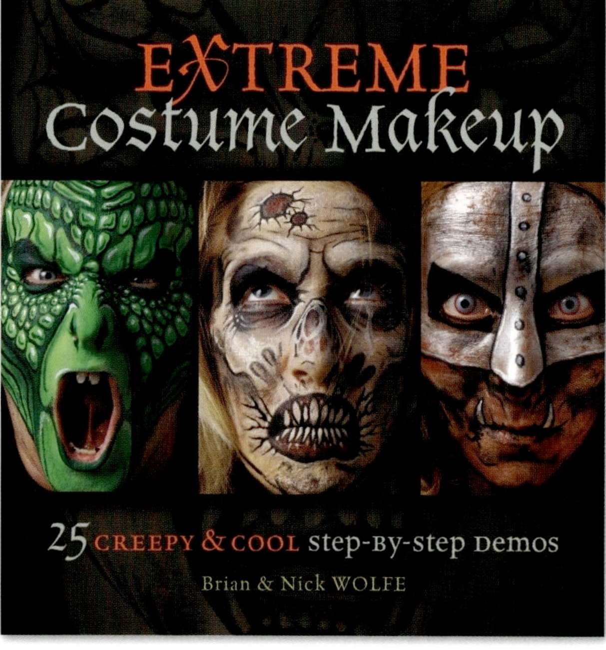

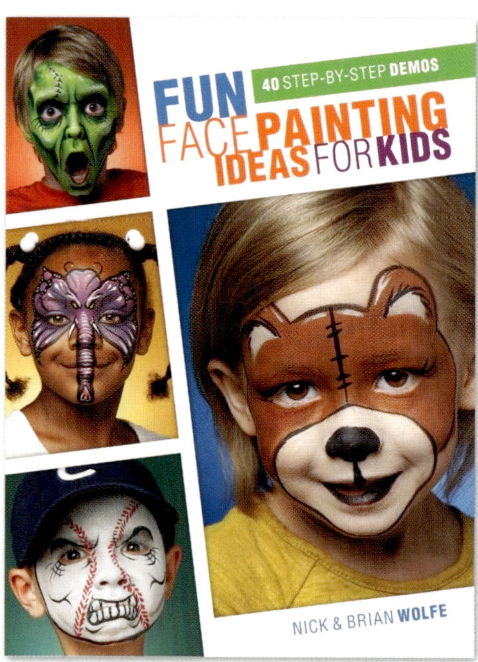

CHECK OUT THESE IMPACT TITLES FROM NICK & BRIAN WOLFE AT IMPACT-BOOKS.COM!

These and other fine **IMPACT** products are available at your local art & craft retailer, bookstore or online supplier. Visit our website at **impact-books.com**.

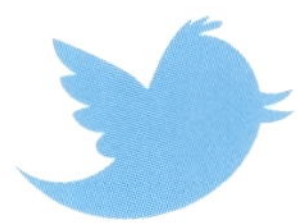
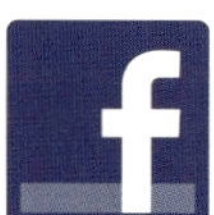

Follow **IMPACT** for the latest news, free wallpapers, free demos and chances to win free books!

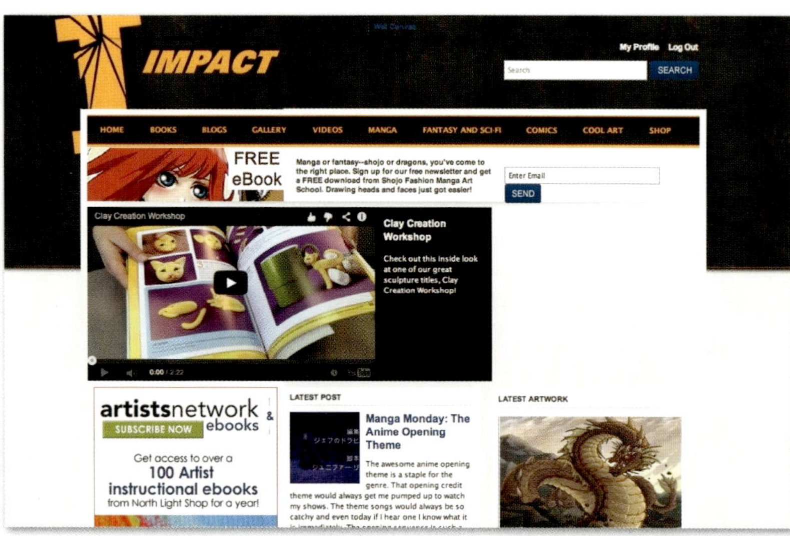

IMPACT-BOOKS.COM

- Connect with your favorite artists

- Get the latest in comic, fantasy and sci-fi art instruction, tips and techniques

- Be the first to get special deals on the products you need to improve your art

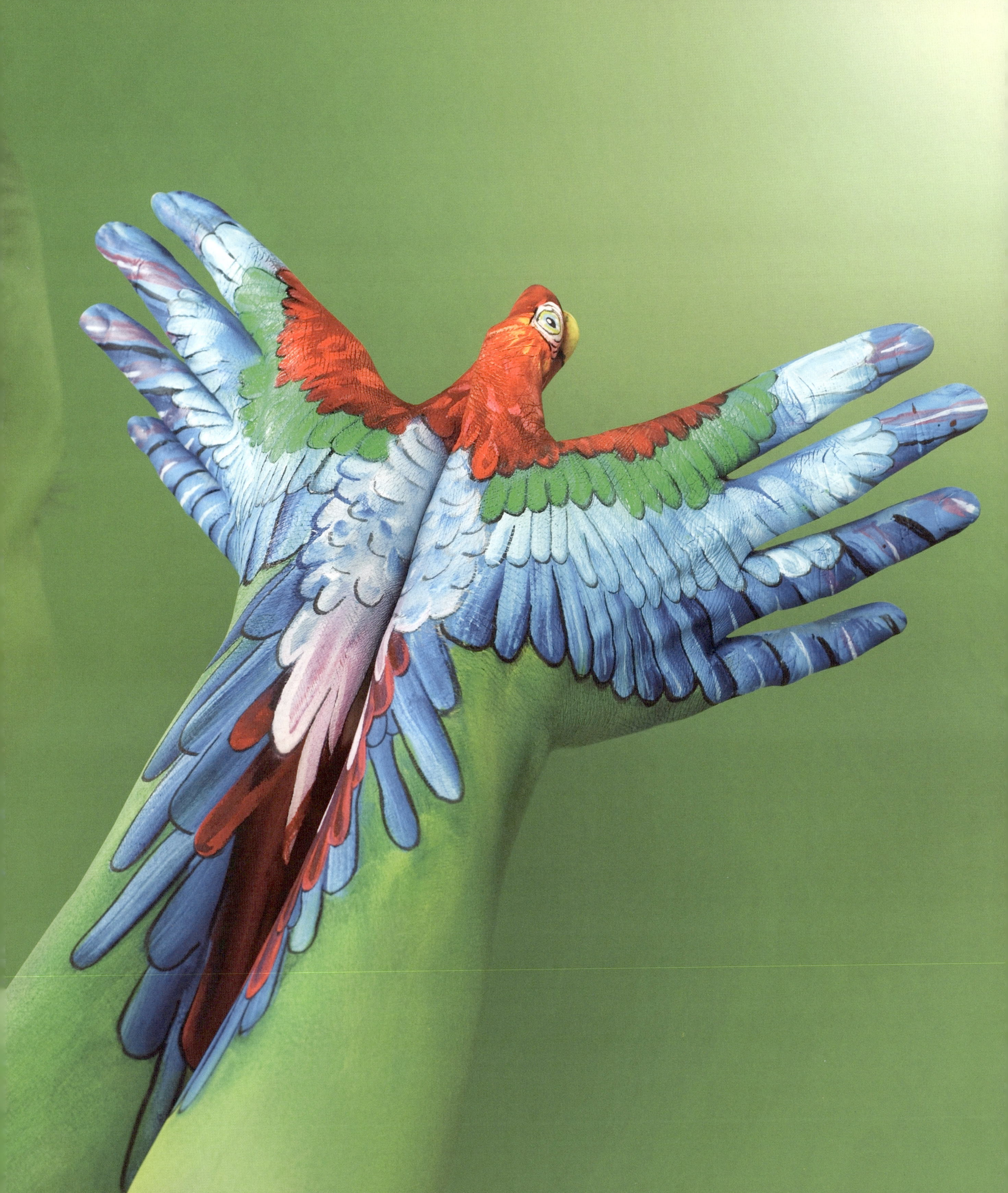

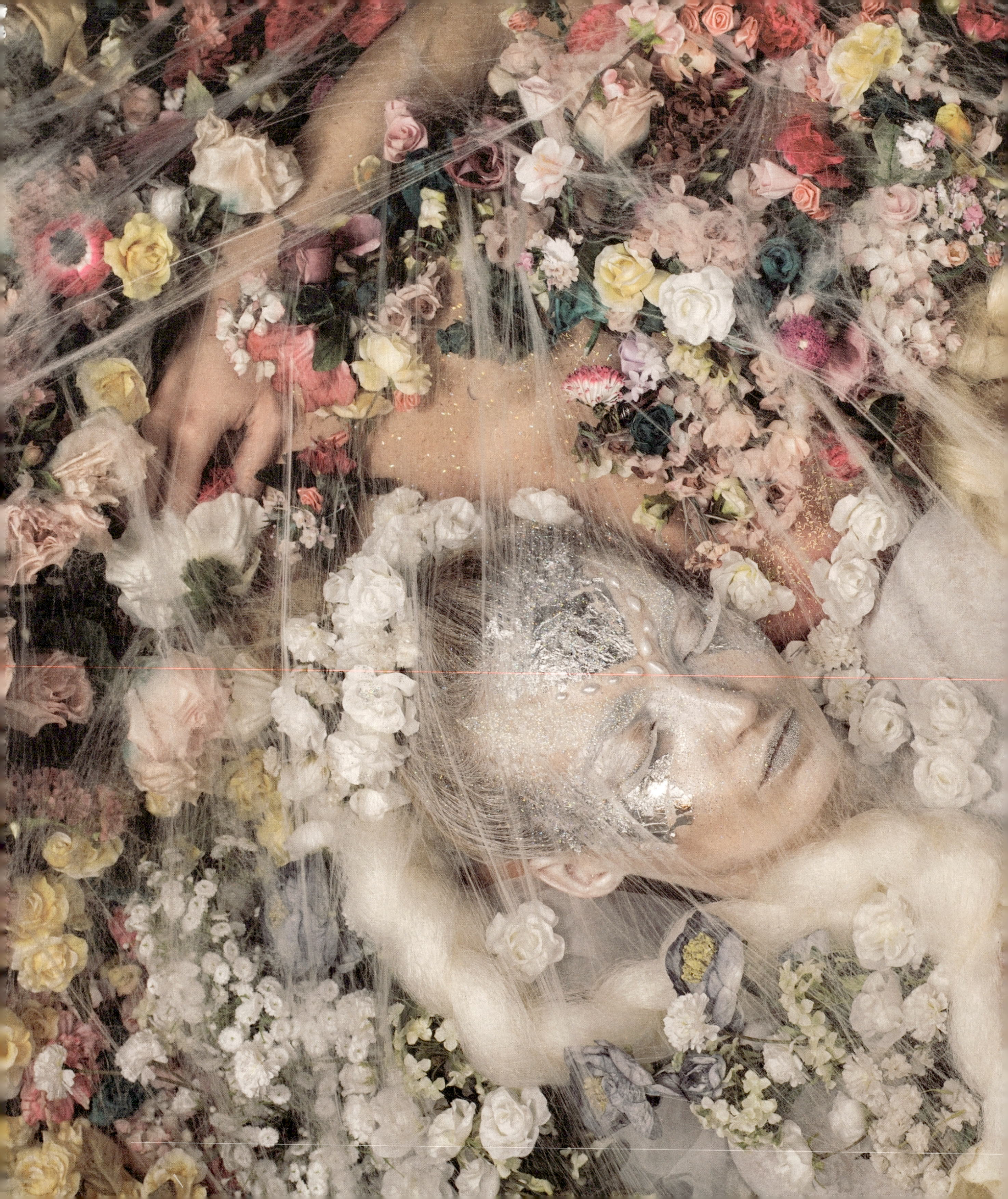